FAMILY MEDIATION

HOWARD H. IRVING
MICHAEL BENJAMIN

FAMILY
MEDIATION
CONTEMPORARY
ISSUES

SAGE Publications
International Educational and Professional Publisher
Thousand Oaks   London   New Delhi

For information address:

SAGE Publications, Inc.
2455 Teller Road
Thousand Oaks, California 91320
E-mail: order@sagepub.com

SAGE Publications Ltd.
6 Bonhill Street
London EC2A 4PU
United Kingdom

SAGE Publications India Pvt. Ltd.
M-32 Market
Greater Kailash I
New Delhi 110 048 India

Printed in the United States of America

Library of Congress Cataloging-in-Publication Data

Irving, Howard H.
    Family mediation: Contemporary issues / Howard H. Irving, Michael Benjamin.
        p. cm.
    Includes bibliographical references and index.
    ISBN 0-8039-7126-5 (cloth: acid-free paper). — ISBN 0-8039-7127-3 (pbk.: acid-free paper)
    1. Family mediation—North America.   I. Benjamin, Michael, 1950–
II. Title.
HQ10.5.N7I78   1995
306.85—dc20   95-8241

This book is printed on acid-free paper.

95 96 97 98 99 10 9 8 7 6 5 4 3 2 1

Sage Production Editor: Gillian Dickens   Typesetter: Christina M. Hill

Contents

Preface   ix
Hugh McIsaac

Acknowledgments   xiii

1. General Introduction   1

PART I: Background   9

2. Family Mediation Practice and the Knowledge Base:
   An Integrative Review of the Divorce Research Literature
   (Phases 1 Through 3)   11

   Introduction   11
   Divorce: Theoretical Conceptualization   14
   The Frequency of Divorce   16
   The Phases of Divorce   17

3. Family Mediation Practice and the Knowledge Base:
   An Integrative Review of the Divorce Research Literature
   (Phases 4 Through 5)   49

Phase 4: Short-Term Consequences   49
Phase 5: Long-Term Consequences   73
The Divorce Process and Family Mediation   89

PART II: Clinical Practice   **145**

4. Therapeutic Family Mediation:
  Practice Principles and Ecosystemic Processes   147

   Introduction   147
   The Clients   149
   General Therapeutic Concepts   149
   The Process of Intervention   153
   The Negotiation Process   164
   The Follow-Up Process   168
   Goals and Responsibilities   169
   Indications and Contraindications   172
   Casebook: Three Vignettes   174
   Discussion   195
   Conclusion   196

5. Toward a Feminist-Informed Model
  of Therapeutic Family Mediation   202

   Introduction   202
   The Feminist Critique   204
   Feminist-Informed Family Mediation   206
   Conclusion   221

PART III: Child Custody   **227**

6. Shared Parenting:
  Critical Review of the Research Literature   229

   Introduction   229
   Casebook: Shared Parenting   231
   Theory   233
   Methodology   237
   Analysis   241
   Results   243
   Global Evaluation   259
   Discussion   261

7. Shared Parenting and Sole Custody:
   A Complex Comparative Analysis   277

    Introduction   277
    Objectives and Methodology   279
    The Findings   281
    Discussion   292
    Implications: Policy and Practice   292

PART IV: Special Topics   **303**

8. Family Mediation and Ethnicity:
   A Critical but Neglected Dimension of Practice   306

    Introduction   306
    Core Dimensions   309
    Profiles of Four Ethnic Groups   313
    Discussion   352
    Final Word   365

9. Mediation in Child Protection Cases   377
   Allan E. Barsky

    Introduction   377
    The Context of Child Protection   378
    The Basics of Mediation in Child Protection Cases   381
    The Role of a Child Protection Mediator   387
    Value Dilemmas in Practice   394
    Conclusion   400

10. Research in Family Mediation: An Integrative Review   407

    Introduction   407
    Research in Family Mediation: A Review   408
    Summary   421
    Discussion   422
    Implications   424

PART V: Closing Thoughts   **435**

11. Thematic Issues and the Future of Family Mediation   437

    Introduction   437

Theme 1: Divorce   437

Theme 2: Mediation Practice   444

Theme 3: Child Custody   452

Theme 4: New Developments   458

Index   463

About the Authors   472

Preface

Twenty years ago, in several California courts and in the law offices of a Georgia lawyer who had undergone a very difficult divorce, the process of family mediation began. The California experiment was limited to custody and visitation issues, but O. J. Coogler's structured mediation applied to all issues.

It was in that context I first met Howard Irving, who visited our Los Angeles court in 1977 to see what we were doing. We did not have the advantage of any text. Indeed, we were flying by the seat of our pants. Yet the logic of parents resolving their own dispute over children and the importance of having both parents involved were obvious to us, if not to others. In fact, the philosophy of the day was more the one depicted in Saul Bellow's *Herzog*, in which father leaves the home, mother remarries, and the new stepfather takes over. The prevailing philosophy was contained in the Solnit, Goldstein, and Freud text *Beyond the Best Interest of the Child*, well named as it was.

The idea was that divorce was a reorganization of the family, not an end of the family. The concept of not being "divorced from" someone but being "divorced to" them was just being conceived. The idea parents might cooperate and the child could have two homes—Isa Ricci's *Mom's House; Dad's House*—was just being written. Ciji Ware was just beginning the personal journey that would lead to *Parents Sharing Custody* and the journey to produce such a wonderful and gifted son, who had the benefit of four loving adults.

An old African saying is, "It takes a village to raise a child." We were in the process of creating modern micro-villages, and Howard Irving was one of the first witnesses of this revolutionary process.

What we were witnessing was the birth of a new family system. This system was not better or worse than the old family system, the nuclear family, a relatively recent and perhaps transient family system. The nuclear family is a child of the Industrial Revolution. This new family system, labeled by Connie Ahrons as "the binuclear family" is a product of the postindustrial revolution and has emerged as a response to deep movements in the tectonic plates of our culture. Paradoxically, this new family system more closely resembles the old extended family.

Yet the labels and the processes to support this system had not been invented. Mediation and the notion of cooperative parenting were just beginning to emerge. That divorce occurs in the spousal role—not in the parental role—began to be recognized and honored.

In Los Angeles, we turned to a labor-negotiation model, recognizing the concepts from marital therapy did not apply. We were to help the parties reach their own solution and separate the parental issues from the spousal ones. We recognized the need to focus on underlying issues and needs—to focus on "what was wrong," not "who was wrong." We identified the need to find solutions benefiting all and to process differences like any policy decision through the testing of all possible options. We also recognized the difference between relationship issues in which there is not principle of "right or wrong" but rather the defining of roles to continue into the future. We recognized property and support were different from relationship concerns. Here principles of equity and fairness did apply: One does not divide a business or resell a house. Here the role of the attorney was paramount in representing the adverse interests of the parties. We recognized attorneys were critical in the successful use of the mediation process and began the slow evolution in the development of family law in which attorneys became more supportive of the mediation process and began to drop the adversarial trappings of their role while continuing to represent their clients' adverse interests.

Ury and Fisher published *Getting to Yes* from the Harvard Negotiation project and the witnessing of the forging of the Camp David Accord. In this text we witnessed the common thread between the disputes we were resolving and the resolution of large-scale international disputes. Robert Mnookin's seminal article from the April 1979 *Yale Law Journal*, "Bargaining in the Shadow of the Law: The Case of Divorce in the Courts," burst on the scene with blinding clarity. We felt like the prisoner in the Dostoyevsky's *Notes from the Underground;* here was someone who understood the importance of the parties bargaining in the shadow of the law tapping on our prison wall.

And so reading Professors Irving and Benjamin's book takes us back along this 20-year journey to the beginning of our work. This text captures the scope of the evolutionary process of family mediation and provides a scaffolding for those who will carry on the important work of reforming the way we help families transit the process of divorce through the insight and perspective of 20 years. We commend this book to you, the reader, and wish we might have had it when we began.

Although we did not write this book, we certainly have lived it.

Hugh McIsaac
Manzanita, Oregon

Acknowledgments

This book was undertaken to build on and reflect the changes of our earlier work in family mediation. Much is owed to the late Meyer Elkin, who was inspirational in the writing of this book. We also owe a debt to Hugh McIsaac, whose work in dispute resolution contributed to many of our ideas for this book.

Our colleagues at the University of Toronto Faculty of Social Work have been most helpful in sharing their insights, which I have tried to incorporate in this book. They include Ben Schlesinger, Heather Munroe-Blum, Nico Trocmé, and Duncan Lindsey, to mention a few.

A special thank to the teaching group of the Family Mediation Course, including Risa Eisen, Deborah Mecklinger, Sharon Bar David, and Phil Epstein.

Much is owed to our colleagues in Hong Kong and Israel who have given us a deeper appreciation of the true value of diversity in mediation.

The chapter on child protection mediation (Chapter 9) was written by Allan Barsky (Faculty of Social Work, University of Calgary), who has made an invaluable contribution to our work. Lilianne Davis shared with us her material on an interesting case situation. We are most grateful to her.

We are grateful to our editor, Jim Nageotte, for his belief in the book and ongoing encouragement. We want to extend our further gratitude to Gillian Dickens, our Production Editor, who guided the manuscript through to publication.

We would like to thank the many families who have given us so much of themselves and the students who have been involved in our research. We have learned a great deal from all of them.

Finally, this book is dedicated to the memory of the late Sylvia Irving. She lives and practiced mediation in her daily life, knowing the real value of caring and understanding. We hope this book does justice to her ideals.

Howard Irving
Michael Benjamin

1

General Introduction

Although mediation per se has a long history worldwide, the prominence of family mediation in North America is relatively recent, dating from the mid-1970s (Brown, 1982; Irving & Benjamin, 1987).[1] In the early 1980s, the texts (e.g., Folberg & Taylor, 1984; Saposnek, 1983) are simultaneously tentative and confident: They are tentative in the sense that family mediation was a fledgling technology whose survival was not assured. Legislators and jurists remained justifiably skeptical and perhaps somewhat threatened, whereas the general public was largely uninformed. They are confident because in advocating for the legitimacy of mediation, proponents often made exaggerated claims about its efficacy and application while distorting the role and effects of the adversarial system.

By the 1990s, the legal landscape had changed (Cox, 1993; Kronby, 1991), and with it the place and position of family mediation. Divorce rates had stabilized at close to the highest level in this century (see chapters 2 and 3 of this volume). With more than 1 million couples divorcing every year, what was once a trickle has become an avalanche, overwhelming available judicial resources. One obvious consequence has been a search for ways to reduce the crushing burden on the courts.

One approach, spurred by feminist demands for equality before the law (Fineman, 1988) has been legal reform. The shift to no-fault divorce statutes, although incomplete, has nevertheless been substantial (Jacobs, 1988). For couples seeking a divorce in which neither partner is interested or prepared to contest the action, the divorcing process has been reduced to an administrative routine, with no court appearances required. At the same time, however, it is important to see such reform in context, as one of a variety of legal initiatives—regarding employment equity, gender equality, and so on—whose thrust has been to accent individual rights and freedoms. This is a salient trend. More and more, people are unwilling to accommodate to existing institutions and their anonymous procedures. Rather, they increasingly demand a say in matters that touch their lives, with divorce an obvious case in point.

It is the confluence, we believe, of these trends—rising concern for individual rights and efforts at appropriate court diversion—that has caused the rise to prominence of a variety of measures whose collective purpose is *alternative dispute resolution* (ADR) (Astor, 1991) outside or more correctly, alongside, the formal judicial system (Mnookin & Kornhauser, 1979). Among them, family mediation has been the best known and most frequently used (Hauser-Dann, 1988; Myers, Gallas, Hanson, & Keilitz, 1988). Indeed, various indicators suggest that family mediation has entered the mainstream. For example, whereas the handful of first-generation practitioners acquired their expertise by the seat of their pants, training programs have since proliferated (Bartoletti, 1991; Steir & Hamilton, 1984). The population of second-generation practitioners is steadily increasing. ADR in general and family mediation in particular are now formally recognized and available in most jurisdictions (Emery, 1994),[2] and mandated in some states, notably California (Saposnek, Hamburg, Delano, & Michaelson, 1984). Similarly, local associations of family mediators are widespread, with national counterparts having recently come into being in Canada, such as Mediation Canada (Devlin & Ryan, 1986), and in the United States, such as the Academy of Family Mediators and the Association of Family and Conciliation Courts (Folberg & Milne, 1988). In turn, these associations continue to struggle with standards of practice and codes of ethics (Engram & Markowitz, 1985; Grebe, 1989), such that although some form of accreditation is still a way off, we now see it as inevitable (see chapter 11). In short, the professionalization of family mediation is well under way and continuing apace. The same is true of research (Kressel, Pruitt, & Associates, 1989). Not only has the annual number of studies increased steadily—witness the recent publication of several bibliographies[3]—but more important, so has their methodological rigor. Furthermore, their substantive focus has shifted, from a nearsighted but necessary concern with outcome to a more productive and creative concern with process (Donohue, 1989; Kelly, 1989; see chapter 10).

Taken together, these various developments speak of the maturation of family mediation, from toddler to adolescent. Like all adolescents, its focus, properly, is neither on the past nor the present but on the future. It is in that spirit—of adventure, progress, and prophesy—that this volume was prepared. To anticipate the future, one must understand the present. In that sense, this volume takes the form of a prediction, identifying five themes that we think are likely to chart the future of family mediation.

The first theme concerns the divorcing process itself. For many years, divorce was heavily stigmatized and thus not considered an appropriate topic for inquiry. So long as the numbers remained small, this stance could be sustained. However, as family mediation was being established, divorce rates shot up and old restrictions fell in their wake. At present, divorce is a hot topic, a development that is double-edged from the perspective of mediation. On the one hand, the increase in divorce rates has been a primary base for a corresponding increase in demand for mediation services. On the other hand, that same increase has fueled an explosive increase in the size of the available research literature. This trend has created a dilemma for practitioners, students, and others in the field: Developments in the research literature should provide feedback to shape practice, but the requirements of service delivery and the demands associated with acquiring and maintaining clinical expertise or both leaves little time for keeping up with the literature. Part II seeks to solve this dilemma by providing a thorough and up-to-date review of the divorce literature geared to family mediation. It also places in perspective many of the clinical issues dealt with in later chapters.

The second theme concerns the nature of mediation practice. At present, there is no one universally accepted model of family mediation. On the contrary, the field is fractured by a variety of competing models. Seen in overview, however, two divergent approaches can be distinguished. One is structural in orientation; that is, proponents see their job as creating a structure to assist spouses to resolve their differences, but otherwise leave them unchanged. Another is therapeutic in orientation. Although proponents seek to assist spouses in resolving their differences, they argue that it is frequently not possible to do so without inducing limited change, either in the spouses, their mutual relations, or both. Part III addresses one such model, *Therapeutic Family Mediation* (TFM). The section describes and discusses the practice principles and methods underpinning TFM, using original case history material to display how it is used with couples at different stages of readiness for mediation. In addition, this discussion highlights a key contextual issue. This concerns the feminist critique of family mediation, which has received limited attention in the mediation literature. Chapter 5 presents the first systematic overview of this debate and although critical of some of the arguments takes the position that a feminist-informed model of mediation is appropriate.

The third theme concerns the controversy surrounding the custody option known as joint custody or, as we prefer to call it, *shared parenting* (SP). Accrued discussion about SP is now voluminous, typified by much passion and little data and thus producing rather more heat than light. The chapters that make up Part III seek to get past the rhetoric in two ways: by providing a thoughtful, up-to-date, and systematic review of available empirical studies and by summarizing our comparative study on the topic. Both approaches suggest that a dogmatic position on best custody option is rendered untenable by the heterogeneity of divorcing families. Rather, we argue that children's best interests are served by parenting plans fitted to the needs of individual families that emphasize ongoing parental commitment and responsibility rather than parental custody or ownership.

The fourth theme addresses new developments in family mediation that are emerging into prominence, namely, ethnicity, child welfare mediation, and family mediation research. Psychiatry has long recognized the profound significance of ethnic identity in shaping how people construe problems, display symptoms, and elect or refuse to seek treatment. Recently, similar insights have begun to permeate the field of family therapy. In contrast, family mediation shows little awareness of this issue, continuing to speak about clients in generic terms. The first part of Part IV attempts to show by means of a substantive review of several literatures that such lack of sensitivity to ethnicity diversity is inconsistent with good practice and decreases the likelihood that efforts at intervention may inadvertently do harm.

As to child welfare, since the mid-1960s, charges of child abuse have necessarily pitted parents against state agencies. Typically, this conflict occurred in the adversarial context of the court, thus placing already vulnerable children at very real risk of institutional reabuse. A recent and still controversial change has been to apply the notion of mediation to child welfare cases. Accordingly, the second part of Part IV provides a systematic overview of this new area of mediation practice, with its advantages and its risks.

Turning to research, studies of mediation may strike many practitioners as remote from their day-to-day practice. We argue, on the contrary, that such work provides an important reality check and has become increasingly relevant as a source of ideas for practice. However, although the literature is expanding rapidly, reviews of that literature are in short supply. Accordingly, the final part of Part IV provides an integrative review of that literature, with an eye to its implications for research, policy making, and practice.

Finally, the fifth theme concerns the future of family mediation. Although in the past it was possible to discuss the future of mediation, such efforts represented acts of faith and bravado, because no one could be sure that mediation had a future. Confident that such a future is assured, a substantive discussion is now practical. Accordingly, in the closing chapter, we revisit each of the preceding themes with an eye to the future of family mediation. This review will highlight critical issues and their likely or desirable outcomes over the next decade.

This volume, then, provides an in-depth inquiry into specific topics and addresses a wide range of issues within contemporary family mediation. Scholarly yet accessible, it combines exploration of resonant themes and issues in mediation with practical concern for clinical methods periodically augmented with the use of case history material. We think that this volume will appeal to a wide audience. First and foremost, it speaks to mediation practitioners—including students, novice practitioners, and seasoned professionals—aware of the issues and seeking solutions to their day-to-day practice problems. In the same vein, it has much to offer those who are thinking of entering the field and those who regularly deal with mediators, including judicial personnel (lawyers, judges, probation officers, etc.), mental health professionals (social workers, psychologists, psychiatrists, family therapists, etc.), and other service professionals (doctors, guidance counselors, pastoral counselors, nurses, etc.). Finally, for those simply interested in the field and where it is heading in the near future, we intend this volume to be valuable and stimulating.

NOTES

1. In the United States, the Family and Conciliation Court in Los Angeles was created in the late 1930s. However, it remained relatively isolated until the late 1970s, when the conditions to support a family mediation movement were right.

2. See also Folberg and Milne (1988) and Marlow and Sauber (1990).

3. See Health and Welfare Canada (1985), Helm and Moore (1992), Helm and Wright (1992), Helm, Odom, and Wright (1991), and Stone (1991).

REFERENCES

Astor, H. (1991). Feminist issues in ADR. *Law Institute Journal, 65*, 69-71.

Bartoletti, M. D. (1991). Hands-on mediation training in a private-practice setting. *Mediation Quarterly, 8*, 239-247.

Brown, D. G. (1982). Divorce and family mediation: History, review, future directions. *Conciliation Courts Review, 20*(1), 1-20.

Cox, F. D. (1993). *Human intimacy: Marriage, the family and its meaning* (6th ed.). St Paul, MN: West.

Devlin, A., & Ryan, J. P. (1986). Family mediation in Canada: Past, present, and future developments. *Mediation Quarterly, 11*, 93-108.

Donohue, W. A. (1989). Mediator communicative competence: A research program review. In K. Kressel, D. G. Pruitt, & Associates (Eds.), *Mediation research: The process and effectiveness of third-party intervention*. San Francisco: Jossey-Bass.

Emery, R. E. (1994). *Renegotiating family relationships: Divorce, child custody, and mediation*. New York: Guilford.

Engram, P. S., & Markowitz, J. R. (1985). Ethical issues in mediation: Divorce and labor compared. *Mediation Quarterly, 8*, 19-32.

Fineman, M. (1988). Dominant discourse, professional language and legal change in . child custody decision-making. *Harvard Law Review, 101*(4), 727-774.

Folberg, J., & Milne, A. (Eds.). (1988). *Divorce mediation: Theory and practice*. New York: Guilford.

Folberg J., & Taylor, L. (1984). *Family mediation: theory and practice*. San Francisco: Jossey-Bass.

Grebe, S. C. (1989). Ethical issues in conflict resolution: Divorce mediation. *Negotiation Journal, 5*(2), 179-190.

Hauser-Dann, J. (1988). Divorce mediation: A growing field? *Arbitration Journal, 43*(2), 15-22.

Health and Welfare Canada. (1985). *Mediation and divorce: A bibliography* (Catalog No. H74-15/1985). Ottawa: Health & Welfare Canada, Program Information.

Helm, B., & Moore, A. M. (1992). Dispute resolution in the psychological abstracts in 1990 and 1991. *Mediation Quarterly, 10*(2), 213-223.

Helm, B., & Wright, J. K. (1992). Publication patterns in the growth years: Dispute resolution in the psychological abstracts, 1986-1989. *Mediation Quarterly, 9*(3), 275-294.

Helm, B., Odom, S., & Wright, J. K. (1991). Publication patterns in the early years: Dispute resolution in the psychological abstracts, 1980-1985. *Mediation Quarterly, 9*(1), 87-103.

Hinchcliff, C. L. (1990). *Dispute resolution: A selected bibliography, 1987-88.* Washington, DC: American Bar Association, Standing Committee on Dispute Resolution.

Irving, H. H., & Benjamin, M. (1987). *Family mediation: Theory and practice of dispute resolution.* Toronto: Carswell.

Jacobs, H. (1988). *Silent revolution: The transformation of divorce law in the United States.* Chicago: University of Chicago Press.

Kelly, J. B. (1989). Mediated and adversarial divorce: Respondents' perceptions of their processes and outcomes. *Mediation Quarterly, 24,* 71-88.

Kressel, K., Pruitt, D. G., & Associates (Eds.). (1989). *Mediation research: The process and effectiveness of third-party intervention.* San Francisco: Jossey-Bass.

Kronby, M. C. (1991). *Canadian family law* (5th ed.). Toronto: Stoddart.

Marlow, L., & Sauber, R. S. (1990). *The handbook of divorce mediation.* New York: Plenum.

Mnookin, R. H., & Kornhauser, L. (1979). Bargaining in the shadow of the law. *Yale Law Journal, 88,* 950-997.

Myers, S., Gallas, G., Hanson, R., & Keilitz, S. (1988). Divorce mediation in the States: Institutionalization, use, and assessment. *State Court Journal, 12*(4), 17-25.

Saposnek, D. T. (1983). *Mediating child custody disputes: A systematic guide for family therapists, court counselors, attorneys, and judges.* San Francisco: Jossey-Bass.

Saposnek, D. T., Hamburg, J., Delano, C. D., & Michaelson, H. (1984). How has mandatory mediation fared? Research findings of the first year's follow-up. *Conciliation Courts Review, 22,* 7-19.

Steir, S., & Hamilton, N. (1984). Teaching divorce mediation: Creating a better fit between family system and the legal system. *Albany Law Review, 48,* 693-718.

Stone, G. P. (1991). *Family and interpersonal mediation: A bibliography of the periodical literature, 1980-1989.* Guelph, Ontario: Family Mediation Canada.

PART I

Background

As a function of their background, practitioners view separation and divorce from one of two perspectives. Those with legal training tend to adopt a structural perspective in which divorce is seen as a legal event shaped by the contingencies associated with current statutes. Thus, mediation will revolve around the resolution of issues associated with custody and access, the distribution of chattel, and the size and nature of financial support. These issues are also relevant to those with therapeutic training. However, the latter will be more inclined to adopt a psychological perspective in which divorce is seen as a personal process. Thus for them mediation will focus, at least in part, on dealing with feelings, resolving lingering attachments, coping with stress, and the like.

With the increasing currency of systems theory among practitioners with therapeutic training, an alternative has recently come into prominence, namely, an ecological perspective. Proponents of this view, ourselves included, adopt a more holistic stance, viewing divorce as a process composed of the interaction of a variety of elements, including statutes and psychological states, but also patterns of interpersonal relating (both within the family and between the family and extended kin), child development and the risks to its normal progression, demographic factors (such as ethnicity and income), relations among peers, and community resources (such as the involvement of professionals and agencies). It

9

includes, too, sensitivity to divorce as a process that unfolds in time, such that the combination of relevant factors will change as couples move from one phase of the process to another.

These considerations frame the two chapters that constitute Part I, which provides one of the most up-to-date, complete, and systematic reviews of the divorce literature available. It makes clear that (a) this literature is increasing at an exponential rate; (b) the likelihood of divorce is much greater in the United States than in Canada; (c) there is increasing consensus about certain issues, for example, that when divorce is intensely conflictual, long-term harm can be expected among a substantial minority of children; (d) there are some issues about which debate continues to be very active, for example, the long-term financial consequences of divorce among different groups of women or the developmental consequences of different custody options; and, perhaps most obvious, (e) divorce is an extremely complex process, with knowledge of a given couple's position in that process critical to a thorough assessment of their clinical requirements. Throughout the section, data are linked to concerns relevant to mediation practitioners, with special emphasis on a handful of issues that become the focus of detailed concern in later sections.

2

Family Mediation Practice and the Knowledge Base

An Integrative Review of the Divorce Research Literature (Phases 1 Through 3)

INTRODUCTION

The past 40 years have seen a radical change in the way clinical practitioners, researchers, theorists, and society at large have come to think about divorce (Masheter, 1990). Before 1960, divorce was a relatively rare event in North America and heavily stigmatized (Bloom, Asher, & White, 1978; McKie, Prentice, & Reed, 1983). Even the research literature gave it very little attention (Goode, 1949, 1956; Locke, 1951). Equally important, it was seen as a one-time event so that when research did finally begin, the researchers of the day tended to be concerned almost entirely with the negative consequences of divorce and its statistical correlates (Kitson, Babri, & Roach, 1985). The experiences

AUTHORS' NOTE: We wish to express our appreciation to Brian Pettigrew, MSW, and Peggy Patterson, PhD, of the University of Guelph, for their helpful comments and suggestions on an earlier draft of this chapter.

of families undergoing separation and divorce were largely ignored and the possibility of anything other than a negative outcome was discounted (Ahrons & Rodgers, 1987; Kitson & Raschke, 1981).

As separation and divorce became more common, they came to receive increasing research attention.[1] This research showed that although separation and divorce were typically experienced as traumatic and intensely painful for those directly involved (Albrecht, 1980),[2] for most people the pain eventually abated and they got on with their lives (Emery, 1988); only a minority suffered serious pathological consequences over the short term (Bloom et al., 1978; Johnston & Campbell, 1988) or the long term (Hetherington, 1989; Wallerstein & Blakeslee, 1989); indeed, for a minority, divorce was experienced as a crisis promoting growth and development (Ambert, 1989; Veevers, 1991).[3]

In addition, it became increasingly obvious that although divorce may be a discrete legal event (Perlman, 1982), in the lives of those directly involved, divorce was more fruitfully seen as a complex process that unfolds through time (Bohannon, 1985; Kaslow & Schwartz, 1987), involves a degree of mutual influence among a wide range of actors (Johnston & Campbell, 1988), and typically begins several years before divorce proceedings are formally initiated (Ahrons, 1983a, 1983b; Ahrons & Wallisch, 1987).[4]

In effect, separated, divorcing, and divorced couples are distributed along a temporal and relational continuum. At any given point in time, some couples may have barely begun, having just reached the decision to divorce. Others may be nearly finished, having weathered the divorce per se and begun the process of reorganizing their lives as unmarried persons. Of these, some couples will never meet again; others, especially those with children, will still be linked and thus will continue to interact. Others still may have moved past the divorce, having remarried and perhaps begun new families, thus giving rise to "binuclear" family systems (Ahrons & Wallisch, 1987), that is, two distinct kinship systems connected through the children. Of these, some will divorce more than once, producing increasingly complex divorce "chains" (Bohannan, 1971) or "networks" (Ambert, 1989).

All of these variations are represented among the separated, divorcing, or divorced families who enter family mediation, which makes the provision of quality service to such clients extremely challenging. To meet that challenge requires that mediation practitioners have considerable clinical expertise and current legal knowledge, but also knowledge about the divorcing process, especially in regard to the psychological states and relational processes likely to accompany it. This demand places the busy professional on the horns of a dilemma. On the one hand, with little spare time to keep up with the large and complex research literature on divorce, the temptation is to make clinical decisions solely on the basis of what has worked in the past. On the other hand, this decision places the practitioner at risk of providing less than the best available service, because decisions are not informed by the most recent research findings. This chapter and the next seek to fill that gap by providing the practitioner with an integrative review of research findings across all phases of the divorcing process. The objectives of these chapters then are threefold: to summarize the range of our current knowledge about divorcing family systems; to highlight those areas of research likely to be especially pertinent to mediation practitioners, including areas in which debate is ongoing; and to identify a handful of issues likely to be of major concern in the next decade. In turn, these issues will be the focus of much of the balance of this text, as we explore contemporary issues in family mediation. In an effort to minimize redundancy, all references cited in chapters 2 and 3 will be listed at the end of chapter 3. Note as well that much material of interest to readers with specialized interests has been placed in the notes.

We divide the review that follows into four sections. First, we briefly discuss the current state of theory in the area of divorce. This issue is important, for how we conceptualize divorce directly affects how practitioners interpret what they see and, in turn, how and to what ends they intervene. Second, we describe the frequency of divorce in North America, that is, in the United States and Canada. This description places divorce in a comparative context, especially how the data relate to the majority of couples who have not divorced. Next, we somewhat arbitrarily distinguish among five phases of the divorcing process, using them as a framework within which to organize and review the data about divorce. Phases 1 through 3 will be discussed in this chapter; discussion of phases 4 through 5 will be deferred to chapter 3.

Finally, in chapter 3, we derive from this review six issues that we see as salient to family mediation practice, now and in the future.

DIVORCE:
THEORETICAL CONCEPTUALIZATION

In all areas of research, theory is used to indicate what findings mean and how otherwise disparate findings tie together and to make predictions about possible connections between findings. In this light, it is significant that observers agree that divorce research is characterized by a dearth of theory (Guttman, 1993; White, 1990; Whiteside, 1989). This statement, however, is deceptively simple, for it is subject to multiple interpretations.

In one sense, it points to the fact that over the last decade, of the thousands of studies published the majority were atheoretical, that is, they were empirical studies uninformed by theory. This is not to say that theory has not been used to guide some divorce research. Indeed, the choice of theory appears to split on disciplinary grounds, with clinical researchers preferring one set of theories[5] and academic researchers preferring another.[6] Most recently, Gately and Schwebel (1991, 1992) have advanced the "challenge" model to account for favorable postdivorce outcomes in children.

This proliferation of theories, however, does not change the fact that none of these theories has been widely used, and none to our knowledge has ever been systematically tested against available data. Our reading of the literature suggests that the field appears to be evolving toward a more comprehensive model. We predict that such a model is likely to involve integration of at least the following five theoretical concerns, each of which is necessary but not sufficient to an adequate appreciation of available data.

Family Development. Ahrons and Rodgers (1987) have perhaps been most persuasive in arguing that the manner in which families cope with separation and divorce is, among other things, importantly influenced by their position in the life cycle.[7] This stage has salient implications for the subsequent development of individual members

(Breunlin, 1989). It also suggests the need for variation in mediation practice according to the developmental needs of client families.

Patterns of Relating. A second factor is the patterns of relating that characterize the family system *before* divorce. In this regard, divorce experience appears to vary systematically by family type (Ahrons & Rodgers, 1987; Ahrons & Wallisch, 1986). These various models point to a high degree of continuity in the ways spouses relate to each other before and after divorce. They also suggest that some family types are likely to be considerably more amenable to mediation than others.

Sociocultural Variation. A key limitation of available developmental models is their tendency to use white, middle-class families as their normative standard. There is, however, ample evidence of systematic differences in family developmental processes based on sociocultural variation (Devore & Schlesinger, 1987; Everett, 1988). This difference extends to divorce, with salient implications for mediation practice (see chapter 8).

Ecological Context. Divorce extends beyond the immediate family system to encompass a much larger ecological field, including extended kin, other members of the family's social network, and others in the areas of law and social services who are involved with one or several phases of the divorcing process (Johnston & Campbell, 1988; see also chapter 4). The ecological context thus directly affects the divorcing process and in turn who might need to be included in or excluded from mediation.

Consequences Over Time. Finally, a great deal of interest in the consequences of divorce has concerned short-term outcomes, with efforts to track divorcing families through time still uncommon (Hetherington, 1989; Wallerstein & Blakeslee, 1989). The results show that divorce involves multiple outcomes. Wallerstein and Blakeslee (1989, p. xx) perhaps capture best the dynamic character of the divorcing process when they say that

> The families in our study have followed many different paths over the years, and their experience makes up a broad network of possibilities. . . . Most

important, we know that roads can widen and fork at different places, opening up new vistas, new opportunities, and ways to head off trouble ahead.

THE FREQUENCY OF DIVORCE

In 1991 there were just under 1.2 million divorces in the United States (Cox, 1993)[8] and 77,031 in Canada (Statistics Canada, 1991).[9] In both countries, 40% to 50% of those divorcing had one or more dependent children (Ambert, 1990; Cox, 1993),[10, 11] so that each year in North America not less than 4 million people are directly affected by divorce. This estimate is extremely conservative because it necessarily excludes an unknown number of couples who have separated informally and have not filed for divorce (Furstenberg, 1990) as well as a large number of adults and children who will become directly involved in these families through the remarriage of one or both spouses (Ambert, 1989). Furthermore, it fails to take account of those indirectly but significantly affected by these divorces, including grandparents, relatives, friends, and even neighbors (Ahrons, 1983b; Goldsmith, 1982). Thus it is not unreasonable to speculate that each year perhaps 10 million people are directly or indirectly affected by divorce.

These figures are alarming both because they are large and because they represent significant increases from past years.[12] However, they are also misleading, because they are unrelated to either the size or the composition of the population. Accordingly, alternate means of describing the frequency of divorce have been developed.

One of these means expresses the number of divorces as a proportion of the total population. Cox (1993), using 1992 data, estimated that in any given year in the United States, 2% to 3% of all marriages end in divorce and an additional 3% are involved in legal separation. In Canada, the 1991 census (cited in the *Toronto Star*, September 27, 1992, p. A10) showed that of all married females 15 years of age or older, 5.1% were divorced (3.3%) or separated (1.8%).[13]

The other method converts the number of divorces into a rate per unit population.[14] This showed, first, that the crude divorce rate in 1989 in the United States and Canada was 4.8 and 3.1, respectively (Dickinson & Leming, 1990; Statistics Canada, 1991),[15] and second, that the divorce rate peaked in the United States in 1979 and 1981 when the crude divorce rate was 5.3, from which it has declined and stabilized (Fisher, 1992; Furstenberg & Cherlin, 1991).[16, 17]

In the United States, these data have been interpreted to mean an overall lifetime probability of divorce of between 49% (Furstenberg, 1990; Glick, 1984a) and 65% (Martin & Bumpass, 1989).[18] It also means that an estimated 41% of all children born to ever-married women will experience family disruption before the age of 16, mostly because of divorce (Reiss & Lee, 1988).[19, 20, 21] This prediction compares to a 33% lifetime probability of divorce in Canada (Adams & Nagnur, 1989; McKie et al., 1983).

However, these figures, too, must be put in context. Among couples who do not divorce, their marriages will last an average of 48 years in the United States (Dickinson & Leming, 1990) and 35 years in Canada (Vanier Institute of the Family, 1991). This means that 90% of ever-married adults will indeed realize the traditional ideal of one marital partner for life (Vanier Institute of the Family, 1991).[22] Furthermore, because the majority of divorced spouses remarry (Fisher, 1992; Moore, 1988), the time that most divorced adults spend without a partner is relatively short, an average of 2 years among divorced men and 5 years among divorced women (Adams & Nagnur, 1989). Taken in conjunction with a steadily increasing life span, what these various figures mean is that "women will spend more years alone with their spouses than in the company of children: the opposite of what most married women have experienced . . . perhaps for most of human history" (Jones, Marsden, & Tepperman, 1990, p. 14).[23]

For our purposes, it will suffice to conclude that divorce shows regularities at the population level that presumably translate into regularities of individual experience. Any adequate appreciation of the divorcing process will need to take both objective and subjective realms into account.

THE PHASES OF DIVORCE

As noted above, one way to think about the divorce process is to divide it into a series of stages or phases. A number of process schemes are available.[24] The five phases described below and in chapter 3 reflect our integration of these schemes with our clinical experience.[25]

Phase 1: The Decision to Divorce

The divorce process typically begins as much as 3 years before the divorce is formally initiated, as the couple's relationship comes to be experienced by one or both as initially problematic and then increasingly intolerable (Kitson, Babri, & Roach, 1985). This typically takes some combination of four forms: the problems spouses complain about; the level of marital conflict and interpersonal cohesion they experience; the state of each partner's feelings for the other; and the diverse consequences of personal distress.

Marital Problems. Four classes of behavior (as distinct from legal grounds for divorce) on the part of one spouse are typically perceived by the other as a problem related to their decision to end their marital relationship (Gigy & Kelly, 1992). These behaviors include adultery (Kurdek & Blisk, 1983),[26] alcohol or drug abuse or both (Albrecht, Bahr, & Goodman, 1983),[28] spousal violence (Isaacs, Montalvo, & Abelson, 1986; Johnston & Campbell, 1988),[29] and the perceived nonfulfillment of spousal role obligations and responsibilities (Ahrons & Rodgers, 1987; Thurnher, Fenn, Melichar, & Chiriboga, 1983). Additional areas of difficulty include poor communication, perceived discrepancy in core values, failure to derive personal satisfaction from the relationship (Kurdek & Blisk, 1983), sexual problems, and difficulties associated with obligations to the extended family (Kitson & Sussman, 1982).[30, 31]

Marital Cohesion. These problems are typically associated with increasing interpersonal conflict and a correspondingly low level of marital cohesion (Ahrons & Rodgers, 1987; Ambert, 1990), especially among those undergoing a "difficult" divorce (Isaacs et al., 1986). In effect, physical separation is typically preceded by a process of gradual emotional separation. So aversive may this process become for one or both spouses (Kurdek & Blisk, 1983) and so destructive of the children (Lamb, 1977a; Wallerstein & Blakeslee, 1989) that it may lead to one or more marital separations (Kitson et al., 1985), each typically of short duration (Bumpass, Martin, & Sweet, 1991).[32] The return of the departed spouse is explained on a variety of grounds (Arnold, Wheeler, & Pendrith, 1980), including a renewed desire to make the marriage work, continued feelings of love and affection, concern for the welfare of the children, discovery that separation was a distasteful experience, and the realization that few alternatives obtain because of pregnancy or lack of financial resources.

Personal Feelings. Finally, such conflict is usually associated with a range of negative feelings, including rage, anger, blame, hurt, depression, denial, and low self-esteem (Ahrons & Rodgers, 1987).[33] This response is especially so among women, who tend to report being angrier than their spouses (Hetherington, 1989; Wallerstein & Blakeslee, 1989).[34] In this period, one or both spouses reports being very unhappy and under intense stress (Gove & Sin, 1989).[35] For example, as Pleck and Manocherian (1988) emphasize, throughout this and all subsequent phases, one or both spouses will be subject to abrupt mood swings, from high to low, with the intensity of each swing only slowly diminishing through time until these swings cease altogether.[36] Publicly, however, as Vaughan (1986) notes, to-be-divorced couples typically behave as if nothing were wrong, hence the typical shock and surprise of family and friends when one or both spouses finally publicly declare their intention to divorce.

In fact, in retrospect many divorced couples report that the period leading up to the decision to separate permanently is the most difficult and distressing aspect of this phase (Robinson, 1993; Wallerstein & Blakeslee, 1989).[37] Indeed, Thurnher et al. (1983) argue that the decision to divorce is often more an attempt to escape from such distress rather than a movement *toward* personal satisfaction. Ambert (1989) provides a case in point, reporting that in 30% of her sample the decision to separate was made for the "wrong" reasons, that is, impulsively, and for reasons unrelated to the quality of the marital relationship. These spouses indicated that with the exception of the previous 2 years, their relationship had been "above average" in happiness, and that their decision to divorce had typically been prompted by an impulsive affair their spouse had had but did not intend to pursue. Indeed, having initiated the divorcing process, both spouses were often shocked at how quickly events proceeded, in turn bringing initial satisfaction followed by depression and despair.

Consequences. More important, it should be emphasized that the presence of conflict and distress by no means ensures either separation or divorce (Ambert & Baker, 1984; Vaughan, 1986). Rather, couples may cope with their marital problems in a number of ways, although at the potential cost of emotional "divorce" (Ahrons, 1983a; Committee on the Family, 1981). For example, some couples seem able to withstand a great deal of conflict without distress (Cuber & Haroff, 1977). Some may seek to avoid it by "inducting" or drawing a child into the marital relationship (Minuchin, 1974; Vogel & Bell, 1968). Others may knowingly choose to remain together for a variety of reasons (Ambert, 1990; Vaughan, 1986), including religious conviction, fear of social censure, scare economic resources, concern for the children, habituation to the marital relationship, and the absence of more attractive alternatives. Still others may seek to avoid family dissolution by becoming involved in marital therapy (Ambert, 1989),[38] often with success (Gurman & Kniskern, 1981; Lazarus, 1981; Thomlison, 1984).

From the perspective of the mediation practitioner, three aspects of this phase stand out. First, it is during this phase of the divorcing process that the patterns are set down that will likely carry on in mediation, which highlights the importance of careful initial assessment because some patterns will be more amenable to mediation than others. Second, the intense emotionality of this phase, augmented by processes in Phase 2, is salient for mediation in two senses: It undermines the capacity of such clients to think clearly and rationally and it places them under intense stress. The mediator can play a critical role in providing divorcing spouses with emotional support not only to get through this period, but also to help them think through the sorts of issues central to the future well-being of themselves and their children. Finally, however certain clients may first appear regarding their desire to divorce, these data suggest that it is important for mediators to help clients explore the reconciliation option.

Phase 2: Marital Separation

In the course of married life, most couples encounter problems in response to which the majority of husbands and wives consider the possibility of divorce (Huber & Spitze, 1980). Of those couples who encounter serious marital problems, a minority decide that permanent separation appears to be the only recourse. Available information about couples in this phase of the divorcing process concerns couple characteristics and marital relations.

Couple Characteristics. A substantial proportion of the literature attends to the association between separation and at least six demographic attributes of divorcing couples.

1. *Social Class.* Poor or working-class couples are at substantially greater risk of separation than their middle- and upper-class counterparts (Hum & Choudry, 1992; Zinn & Eitzen, 1990).[39] This likelihood is reflected in the fact that few divorcing couples have accumulated much in the way of financial assets (Weitzman, 1992b). In the United States, for example, Teachman and Polonko (1990) found that only one third of all divorcing couples had more than $5,000 in assets, although Holden and Smock (1991) reported that the median value of the assets of 1,800 separated Wisconsin couples was $7,800.

Further, Tzeng (1992) shows that separation is related to "socio-economic heterogamy," that is, significant differences between the spouses in occupational status, income, and education: the greater the differences, the greater the risk of separation (see Bumpass et al., 1991).[40] Often overlooked in this regard, Tzeng notes, are changes in the relative status of spouses through time; spouses who are relatively equal at marriage but become progressively more unequal with experience simultaneously increase their risk of separation.[41]

Finally, features of family life that are related to separation similarly vary by social class. Thus Kennedy and Dutton (1989), for example, found that spousal abuse was inversely related to class, and Gifford (1985) reports that separated spouses with a history of violence were much more likely than those without such a history to contest their divorce in court (see Phase 3, p. 29).

2. *Age at Marriage.* In North America, couples in the 20 to 29 age range are more likely to marry than couples at any other age (McKie et al., 1983; Sev'er, 1992). It is hardly surprising then that age at marriage and separation are inversely related; the younger the couple at marriage, the greater the risk of their subsequent divorce (Thornton & Rodgers, 1987).[42] Similarly, a large difference in age between the

spouses (10 or more years) exposes them to a heightened risk of later divorce (Bumpass & Sweet, 1972; McKie et al., 1983).

3. *Children.* As noted, of all couples who divorce, about 50% in the United States (Cox, 1993)[43] and about 40% (in 1989, cited in *Lawyers Weekly,* January 15, 1993, p. 8) in Canada (McKie et al., 1983; Nett, 1993) have one or more dependent children.[44] To the extent that children represent a commitment, both emotional and financial, they reduce the risk of separation (Levitan, Belous, & Gallo, 1988). Thus, couples with preschool children are less likely to separate than couples with no children (Koo, Suchindran, & Griffith, 1984).[45] However, the inhibiting effect of children is much reduced under certain conditions: if there are four or more children (Smith & Meitz, 1983); if the children are the product of a premarital pregnancy (O'Connel & Rodgers, 1984; Teachman, 1982), if the interval between births is very short (Fergusson, Horwood, & Shannon, 1984), if the parents are teenagers (Smith & Meitz, 1983), or if the children are school aged or older, or both (Waite, Haggstrom, & Kanouse, 1985).

4. *Residential Mobility.* Separation is almost always associated with the creation of two different households. As such, residential mobility among separated couples is commonplace (Arnold et al., 1980; McLanahan & Booth, 1989), with McLanahan (1983), for example, noting that within the first year of separation, 38% of women changed residences. Moreover, given the link between separation and class, such moves are often to higher cost, poorer quality housing (Oberlander, 1988; Webber, 1991). As for separated men, 7% to 50% of those leaving the matrimonial home (typically husbands) travel from one state or province to another (Cherlin, 1981; McKie et al., 1983).

5. *Marital Status.* Given the historically high divorce rate, an increasing proportion of couples try to preempt that outcome by first living together (Cox, 1993),[46, 47] with 60% of these subsequently marrying (Newcomb, 1986). To date, however, it is unclear whether this strategy is likely to be successful, because data on the topic are mixed (see Stone, 1990; Trussel & Rao, 1989; White, 1987).[48] As noted, evidence is much more consistent about the increased risk of separation among remarried couples (Norton & Moorman, 1987)[49] (see chapter 3, Phase 5).

6. *Ethnicity.* There is consensus in the literature that blacks have a higher risk of separation than do whites or Hispanics (Cox, 1993; Kitson et al., 1985; White, 1990). In part, this finding is probably related to social class, because blacks and Hispanics are more likely than whites to be poor (Cherlin, 1981). However, as Griffiths et al. (1984) show, this association may also be related to blacks' lesser tendency to marry when pregnant or to remarry following divorce.[50] Hines and Boyd-Franklin (1982), following Minuchin, Montalvo, Guerney, Rosman, and Schumer (1967), explain these findings:

> Solutions to [marital] disharmony, when sought, tend to be informal. Extended family members or ministers may be consulted, and there may be long periods of separation without either partner moving to dissolve the relationship legally. Traditionally, separation has been viewed as more socially acceptable than divorce. . . . The high tolerance for suffering and the expectation that "troubles" are inevitable has been influenced undoubtedly by the strong religious orientation and upbringing of most blacks and their history of oppression.

Thus, American blacks have a different attitude toward separation than whites, Hispanics, or other blacks, for example, from the Caribbean (see Brice, 1982).

What emerges is a composite picture of the "typical" couple whose marriage ends in divorce. They will likely be in their mid-30s, have been married about 8 years, and have two dependent children. The separation will result in the husband leaving the matrimonial home to form a new household. For both spouses, the future will be uncertain because neither can usually claim an advanced education, high-level job skills, or rich income. In addition, their separation will confront them with the need to support two households on an income that previously barely supported one.

Marital Relations. These facts, although important, tell us little about the experience of families confronted with permanent marital separation. Here, the data are less straightforward and far from complete.

This phase of the divorcing process begins when the tension and conflict of the preceding phase become intolerable for one or both partners. One partner then leaves the matrimonial home with no intention of returning.[51] In 60% to 70% of cases, the "final" separation is initiated by the wife against her husband's opposition (Adams & Nagnur, 1989; Ahrons & Rodgers, 1987),[52] especially if she is less than 30 years old and has dependent children (Wallerstein & Blakeslee, 1989). Indeed, because the decision to end the relationship has typically been brewing for some time (from months to years), by the time she makes it explicit the partners are at very different places in their relationship. As Vaughan (1986) notes, "By the time the still-loving partner realizes the relationship is in serious trouble, the other person is already gone in a number of ways" (p. 6).[53]

However, the notion that the wife typically initiates the divorce can also be misleading. Several researchers (Federico, 1979; Hill, Rubin, & Peplau, 1976) have noted that wives more than husbands tend to be more willing to confront marital problems and be more articulate in their expression. By contrast, husbands may be unaware of the problems or at least unwilling to discuss them openly. Consequently, those husbands who subconsciously wish to leave the relationship but are unwilling to initiate it themselves may encourage their wives to do so. As Goode (1956, pp. 136-137) explains, husbands may even go further than that by

> engag[ing] in behaviour whose function, if not intent, whose result, if not aim, is to force the other spouse to ask for the divorce first. . . . Thereby the husband frees himself to some extent from the guilt burden, since he did not ask for the divorce.[54, 55]

Moreover, even the "final" separation itself may be uncertain, for a substantial minority of couples subsequently discuss the possibility of reconciliation and a smaller group actually return to their marital relationship (Kitson et al., 1985; White, 1990). Alternative outcomes may be involved in special cases.

One case in point concerns couples in which one spouse "suddenly" deserts the other (Sprenkle & Cyrus, 1983; Todres, 1978). Whether in fact it is all that sudden is often unclear, with the departing spouse often reporting having left clues as to their intentions for some time before actually leaving, clues the deserted spouse did not recognize or only attended to subconsciously (Hart, 1976, 1978). In either event, for the deserted spouse such "emotional abandonment" (Sprenkle & Cyrus, 1983) is typically experienced as devastating and may significantly slow subsequently efforts to reorganize his or her life (Hart, 1978).

Another special case involves couples characterized by marital violence. In such instances, the attachment of the male batterer to his spouse may be so intense that any attempt on her part to leave the relationship may result in an escalation of violence (Jaffe, Wolfe, & Wilson, 1990; Sonkin & Durphy, 1982), up to and including murder (Bean, 1992; Sonkin, Martin, & Walker, 1985).

Among couples for whom separation does signal the end of their marital relationship, the final step is seldom undertaken on the spur of the moment. Cases of desertion excepted, separation and its consequences are typically first discussed between the spouses (Flavell, 1979). Others, including friends and relatives, may also be consulted, with the spouse who is thinking of ending the marriage finding support for his or her intentions (Arnold et al., 1980; Hetherington, 1987, 1989). The process itself further redefines the couple's relationship. In Vaughan's (1986) words,

> Getting out of a relationship entails a redefinition of self at several levels: in the private thoughts of the individual, between partners, and in the larger social context in which the relationship exists. As these changing definitions become public—first between the two, then to family and friends, and finally to acquaintances and strangers—the response of others perpetuates the separate paths the partners have begun. (p. 6)

Finally, as a function of their age, the children may also be consulted (Toomin, 1974; Young, 1983), although Wallerstein and Blakeslee (1989) found that that applied to fewer than 10% of the children in their sample. Failure to do so or to correct children's tendency to blame themselves for the impending separation may have at least short-term negative consequences for the children's subsequent adjustment (Grynch & Fincham, 1990; Jacobson, 1987; Wallerstein & Kelly, 1980).

More generally, Sprenkle and Cyrus (1983) argue that the way in which the separation is handled can importantly influence subsequent coping and adaptation. The pain and upset are typically lessened when both partners know that a separation is impending and have sufficient time to prepare emotionally for it. The upshot of these discussions varies as a function of family type.

Among the majority of couples whose relations are functional, such discussions typically confirm the decision to separate permanently, although in many cases, as noted above, the decision is a unilateral one made against opposition (Wallerstein & Blakeslee, 1989).[56] Moreover, the spouse who initiated the separation may have already begun the process of adjustment and reorganization some time before the separation takes place (Golan, 1981; Hart, 1978). Indeed, recent evidence indicates that women may engage in a variety of anticipatory behaviors in preparation for the separation (Kitson, 1992),[57] including building a secret nest egg, getting a job, opening a joint bank account, and gaining or supplementing their education and marketable job skills.[58] They may also seek assistance in moving out of the marital relationship by linking up with a transitional person (Vaughan, 1986), including a divorce therapist (Sprenkle & Storm, 1983; Ulrich, 1986).

In contrast, among couples whose relations are dysfunctional, such discussions may lead to what has variously been described as a "divorce-transition impasse" (Johnston & Campbell, 1988) or a "deadlock" (Isaacs et al., 1986; see Lochkar, 1992). In effect, such couples get "stuck" at the separation phase and are unable to move forward. Johnston and Campbell (1988) suggest that this situation results from a confluence of external, interactional, and intrapsychic processes. Kin, new partners, and various legal and mental health professionals take sides, thus escalating the conflict. Conflict is additionally sustained by a long history of destructive marital relations (often including violence), a traumatic separation (e.g., involving humiliation of one spouse by the other spouse's lover), or by an ambivalent separation (involving conflict between an idealized image of the other spouse and a negatively polarized one). Finally, the impact of the first two processes is heightened by the spouses' psychological vulnerability to what the authors call "narcissistic hurt" (based on a longstanding personality disorder or the reactivation of an earlier traumatic loss).

Whatever the bases of their "impasse," events both before and after the separation have three consequences: an increased frequency of "crazy" behavior, a real possibility of serious violence, and a much increased likelihood of "parenting abdication" (Isaacs et al., 1986).

Given that 64% of the spouses in Johnston and Campbell's (1988) sample were assessed as personality disordered, "crazy" behavior was hardly surprising, including breaking into and damaging the other's apartment, trying to run the spouse over with a car, or spreading vicious rumors about the spouse to ruin his or her reputation. More important for its implications for the larger divorcing population was the fact that 74% exhibited moderate to superior adaptive functioning before the separation. On this basis, the authors argue that in psychologically vulnerable spouses, extreme levels of stress may temporarily provoke behavior that seems to involve personality disorders.

Next, the likelihood of violence is important in two respects. First, such behavior may represent intensification of a pattern of behavior that predates and indeed may be the primary basis for the separation (see Wallerstein & Blakeslee, 1989) or may reflect a transitory response to stress. Second, such data underline the likelihood that patterns of interaction that predate the separation are likely to continue despite it. Consequently, postseparation marital violence is far from rare (see Lupri, 1989; Smith, 1987).

Third, in their preoccupation with the deteriorating marital relationship, the majority of spouses involved in "difficult" divorces appear to forget about their children. A later section discusses what this means in detail. Here, it suffices to say that spouses temporarily become less adequate parents or they abandon their parenting role (Isaacs et al., 1986). Such behavior is not limited to "difficult" divorces, but extends to nonclinical divorcing families as well (Wallerstein & Blakeslee, 1989). In our view, what is important about these data is that such behavior is *not* a consequence of the separation, but rather reflects a pattern of interaction that predates the separation by months or even years. Consequently, our later discussion of the consequences of divorce for children will be framed by the view that they are likely the cumulative product of years of unintentional neglect.

Finally, although we reserve detailed discussion of the consequences of separation to a later section, one additional variable warrants brief discussion here: attachment. Although a number of factors determines each spouse's adjustment to the marital separation, Weiss (1975, 1979a) argues that the extent to which separation is experienced as traumatic is directly related to the depth of commitment each spouse feels for their marital partner. When the level of commmitment is low, the level of perceived trauma will also be low. This may be because the relationship has never achieved a deep level of commitment for one or both partners (Kressel & Deutsch, 1977) or because of a gradual erosion of commitment as the relationship comes to be experienced as increasingly intolerable. In either event, Weiss argues that the impact of the divorcing process will be relatively mild.

Conversely, Weiss argues, when the level of commitment is high, irrespective of the duration of the relationship, the level of perceived trauma is also likely to be high, which is the norm for the majority of separated spouses (Hetherington, 1987, 1989).[59] Although we believe Weiss's thesis has merit, we also regard it as problematic in light of evidence about family type. In the process of getting on with one's life following separation, the relationship between most former spouses, even those who still like each other, undergoes a process of gradual but apparently inexorable decline, as spouses drift apart (Ambert, 1989). For spouses undergoing a "difficult" divorce and an "ambivalent separation" (Johnston & Campbell, 1988), lingering attachment may prevent the reorganization necessary to moving on to a new life. However, as Masheter (1990) argues, among spouses who remain relatively cordial, such attachment, especially in the period immediately following the separation, may provide a positive, indeed an invaluable, source of support.[60]

From the perspective of the mediation practitioner, six aspects of this phase stand out. The first concerns flexibility or the lack of it. Many divorcing spouses have limited financial resources and are under extreme stress, with much happening at once. For the mediation practitioner, this situation implies providing service to clients who may be confronted with a very narrow range of options. Second, these data suggest that spouses enter the divorcing processes with different levels of readiness, the spouse who initiates the process ahead of the other. In our experience, such differences have the potential to turn into blockages in mediation. Third, these data begin to establish a pattern that becomes clear in later phases, namely, that the divorcing process places many children at considerable risk, either because they believe themselves at fault or because of parental abdication. The spouses are not the only clients for whom service is being sought; mediators have a responsibility to the children, too, and thus need to assess their level of need. Fourth, these data highlight another pattern that will become clearer in later phases, namely, the critical importance of building certain safeguards into the mediation process. The possibility of violence or other "crazy" behavior cannot be taken lightly. Rather, service delivery must be so structured to prevent the occurrence of such conduct or to terminate service should it occur anyway. Fifth, data in this phase make clear that although clients may seek service on their own, their conduct may be concurrently shaped by a variety of others, kin and friends, but also professionals. Practitioners need to be aware of the identity and ongoing impact of these others to decide whether they might need to be included in sessions. Finally, this review raises the issue of ethnicity and the extent to which variation in ethnicity might imply variation in clinical practice. For more discussion see chapter 8.

Phase 3: Litigation and the Family Court

Separation refers to relations between marital partners; divorce is a legal term and points to official recognition of the termination of a marital relationship as required by law. At present, statutory regimes governing divorce vary between the United States and Canada (Pask, 1993a; Payne, 1988; Peters, 1989; Walker & Elrod, 1993). In the United States, divorce law comes under the jurisdiction of the states, although federal laws govern related matters such as taxation, child support, and welfare (McLanahan & Garfinkel, 1993).[61] In Canada it is split, with a federal statute (Divorce Act [1985]) governing divorce itself, whereas provincial statutes govern matters concerning property and child custody.

Despite such variation, in all jurisdictions spouses who wish to divorce must petition the court, thus setting in motion a process that may involve up to six steps (Erickson, 1988; Kronby, 1991): (a) one spouse files a petition to divorce with the court; (b) the other spouse is served notice of this petition; (c) in special cases a temporary hearing may be called (e.g., to discuss temporary custody of the children or interim spousal or child support or both); (d) discovery of the facts, including formal testimony by the spouses and (where applicable) expert witnesses as well as the submission of written depositions;[62] (e) filing of settlement documents indicating an agreement between the spouses (arrived at through negotiation between the lawyers repre-

senting the spouses) and stipulating the terms of their agreement; and
(f) failing (e) above, a contested hearing in court before a judge of the
family court.

In most jurisdictions across North America, when the action is
uncontested, there is a waiting period before the divorce decree is
finalized.[63] Furthermore, in light of recent changes to divorce statutes
across North America,[64] all jurisdictions in the United States and
Canada now involve "no fault" divorce (Kay, 1987, 1990)[65] in which it
is sufficient simply to declare that the marriage has broken down
irreparably; it is no longer necessary to present evidence that one or
the other spouse is at fault.

However, fault grounds have not been entirely removed. Rather, it
varies across jurisdiction, with 15 states having pure no fault, 21 having
primarily no fault but recognizing fault, and 14 states and Washington,
D.C., with primarily fault but recognizing no fault (Kay, 1987, 1990;
note 18). Similarly, Freed and Walker (1989) note variation in the
application of fault: In regard to property and child support, 22 states
and Washington, D.C., retain fault, whereas 17 states exclude it; in
regard to spousal support, 11 states and Washington, D.C., retain fault,
whereas 29 states exclude it; and, in another 8 states, evidence of
marital misconduct blocks an award of alimony. In Canada, both
federal and provincial statutes are primarily no fault but recognize
fault grounds (Kronby, 1991; Payne, 1988).

Across North America, about 95% of all petitions for divorce are
uncontested (Bishop, 1987)[66, 67] and a *decree nisi* temporarily terminating the relationship readily handed down (Cherlin, 1981; McKie et al.,
1983). As for the balance, petitions for divorce may be contested,
dismissed by the court, or withdrawn by the petitioner spouse (see
Kitson & Langlie, 1984). In most cases, petitions for divorce are handled through negotiation between the lawyers representing the two
spouses, with or without the involvement of a judge (Kressel, 1985). A
small but increasing proportion are dealt with by the parties themselves with the assistance of a family mediator (Emery & Wyer, 1987).[68, 69]
Presumably, mediated cases in which the parties reach a full agreement
would be formally counted as "uncontested." Finally, in many jurisdictions, a temporary decree is followed by a 90-day appeal period
after which a *decree absolute* is handed down, permanently terminating
the marital relationship and freeing the spouses to remarry.

To understand the events of this phase of the divorcing process, we again distinguish between couple characteristics and marital relations.

Couple Characteristics. The litigation phase of the divorcing process involves at least four aspects.

1. *Grounds for Divorce.* Grounds for divorce vary across jurisdictions. Historically, across North American jurisdictions, some 45 grounds for divorce have been used (Jacobs, 1988; Kephart, 1972, chap. 20), although until recently only 10 to 15 were in common use (see Nye & Berardo, 1973, chap. 18). Of these, four predominate: marital break-down (irreconcilable differences), noncohabitation (including separation and desertion for a specified minimal duration), adultery, and mental or physical cruelty or both. So long as the grounds for divorce involved the idea of fault, there was a poor fit between "official" and "real" or subjective grounds (White, 1990). For example, the most commonly reported "official" grounds are noncohabitation, adultery, and cruelty, in that order. By contrast, their most common "subjective" counterparts are adultery,[70] alcohol abuse (see Braid, 1972), violence, and lack of communication (see Kitson et al., 1985). As McKie et al. (1983) comment, the structure of the law and the family court force petitioners to take the path of least resistance.

2. *Contested Proceedings.* However mundane, the processing of documents in uncontested cases remains relatively expensive, especially given the meager resources of most applicants. For example, between 1968 and 1979, McKie et al. (1983) estimated that the total cost of divorce in Canada was in excess of $500 million, assuming a modest $500 per case. However, this cost per case pales by comparison to the costs associated with contesting a divorce application (Kressel, 1985). These costs are usually directly related to the presence of children, with nearly twice as many contested cases among spouses with children compared to those without (Kitson et al., 1985). It can also be extremely expensive, with the lawyer for each spouse typically requesting an initial retainer of $10,000 or more in anticipation of a contested case (Erickson, 1988). Moreover, although such cases account for only a small proportion of all divorce cases (see above), their numbers are anything but small and account for the majority of cases in family courts across North America.

3. *Duration.* Despite the relatively simple nature of most divorce actions, the path through the court is often a slow one. Only about 65% of petitioners will have received a *decree nisi* within 6 months and about 90% within 12 months. At the end of that year, only about 75% of Canadian petitioners will have totally completed their divorce proceedings (McKie et al., 1983).

This torturous course through the court appears to be related to three variables: the presence of children, the willingness of spouses to fight out their marital battles in court, and the choice of grounds for the petition. The symbolic significance of children can hardly be overstated, such that litigation around child custody can be bitter and protracted (Wallerstein & Blakeslee, 1989).[71] Indeed, Grief and Hegar (1992) see such litigation as the primary cause of up to 350,000 children a year being abducted by divorcing parents in the United States.[72] Furthermore, as we have seen above, "difficult" divorces are typically characterized by intense conflict, often involving multiple returns to court. In the study by Johnston and Campbell (1988), for example, whereas 50% of the sample had been separated for 2 years, only 29% had received a final divorce decree. On average, these couples spent 17 months struggling (from 1 month to 8 years) over the custody of their children. As for grounds, claims of adultery are processed much faster than those of mental and physical cruelty (Fersh & Verling, 1976; McKie et al., 1983).

4. *Outcome.* Of those who petition for a divorce, most get it eventually; only a small fraction (6%) do not, either because the petitioner discontinued the action or the case was dismissed by the judge (Kitson et al., 1985; McKie et al., 1983). The immediate outcome involves four matters: (a) the distribution of matrimonial property and assets, (b) spousal support, (c) child support, and (d) child custody (along with the related matter of child access and visitation).

Matrimonial Property. As to matrimonial property, legal regimes vary across jurisdictions, some favoring the common-law approach, others preferring the community property approach. In the common-law approach, spouses retain individual ownership of the assets they brought into the relationship as well as those they acquired while married. In the community property approach, everything acquired by the spouses after marriage is shared equally. In the United States, both Kay (1990) and Weitzman (1992a) note that 42 states use a common-law approach whereas eight states use a community property approach, although recent changes in rules and procedures have blurred the division between regimes. In Canada, most provinces favor a community property approach (Kronby, 1991). Furthermore, recent statutory changes in the United States and Canada have begun to recognize nontangible "career assets" as property (Kronby, 1991; Weitzman, 1992a),[73] although the issue remains controversial, with commentary (Perlman, 1982) and research (Weitzman, 1985; Welch & Price-Bonham, 1983) suggesting that women continue to be dealt with unfairly. Conversely, Seltzer and Garfinkel (1990) found that in the United States wives were typically awarded just over half of all the family assets.

Spousal Support. Turning to spousal support ("alimony"), although current statutes regard the spouses as "equal," spousal support is awarded in only 15% of divorce cases in the United States (Bahr, 1983; Weitzman, 1985, 1992b) and in only 6% of cases (in 1988) in Canada (cited in *Lawyers Weekly*, January 15, 1993, p. 8). Furthermore, such support is awarded only for as long as is deemed necessary for the spouse in need, typically the wife, to acquire such additional education, training, or both as to render her self-supporting.

This approach to spousal support seems to be changing. In the United States, Weitzman (1992b) notes that recent statutory changes appear to recognize the inequality between men and women after divorce, whereas Cox (1993) reports that several states[74] have amended their statutes to allow for long-term or permanent spousal support in cases of special need. In Canada, in a recent case (*Moge v. Moge*, SCC 1235-021, December 17, 1992), the Supreme Court of Canada struck down the "self-sufficiency model" of spousal support, recognizing instead that the financial harm done to women by divorce may be longstanding. Consequently, it denied a husband's application to discontinue spousal support after 19 years. However, we agree with Weitzman (1992b) that it is still too soon to tell if such changes will significantly alter the pattern of spousal support awards.

Child Support. Next, child support applies when there are minor children of the marriage and custody is awarded to one spouse, thus forcing that spouse to incur additional expenses (Kahn & Kamerman, 1987). In the United States (Furstenberg, 1990; United States Department of Education, 1988) and Canada (Economic Council, 1992), of divorcing spouses with children, 61% (in 1985) and 68% (in 1989), respectively, were awarded child support. However, American (Buehler, 1989; Kahn & Kamerman, 1987)[75] and Canadian (Bala, 1991)[76] observers have repeatedly noted that neither judges nor legislators appear to have much sense of how much it costs to raise children.[77] Consequently, such awards are often small, averaging between $1,500 and $3,000 per year per spouse and representing between 15% (or less) (Boyd, 1989)[78] and 30% of the paying spouse's annual income (Holden & Smock, 1991).[79, 80] Such awards are understandable when the spouse's income is low; they are less comprehensible when that income is sizable, as seen in Wallerstein and Blakeslee's (1989) study.

Moreover, in addition to large disparities in the average income of husbands and wives and complementary differences in rates of poverty (Department of Justice, 1990; McLanahan & Garfinkel, 1993)[81] are added other inequalities. In Canada, these include the "glass ceiling" on awards applied by judges to protect husbands (Grassby, 1991), tax policy favoring those who pay support (fathers) over those to whom it has been awarded (mothers; Zweibel, 1993), and payment levels that are not indexed to the cost of living, so that the real value of multiyear awards declines through time (Kitchen, 1992).

Child Custody. Finally, custody is generically defined as "care and control" of the children. In practice, it is useful to distinguish between legal and physical child custody. The former refers to control over decisions relating to child care, both on a day-to-day basis as well as about major matters such as health, education, and religious instruction. The latter, physical custody, refers to where the child resides on a day-to-day basis. In the most common case, "sole custody," wherein custody is given to one or the other parent,[82] legal and physical custody overlap; the child(ren) live with the parent to whom custody has been given and it is he or she who is responsible for providing daily care and for making all major decisions about their welfare. In the case of joint custody or shared parenting, the same may be true (legal and physical shared parenting) or not, with legal custody given to both parents, but physical custody given to one or the other.

Because both case law and judicial opinion have recently favored sole maternal custody (Boyd, 1989; Derdeyn, 1976; Emery, 1988), it is hardly surprising that in 88% of the American cases examined by Teachman and Polonko (1990)[83] and in 83% of all cases (in 1989) in Canada (cited in *Lawyers Weekly*, January 15, 1993, p. 8), mothers were awarded custody by default, because their spouses did not petition for custody (Department of Justice, 1993, p. 13).[84, 85] This outcome has not changed over at least the last decade (Allen, 1991).[86] Furthermore, in such cases fathers are nearly always granted access to their children.[87] In contrast, fathers who petition for custody are successful roughly half the time (McKie et al., 1983; Taylor, 1993; Turner, 1984).[88]

This clear preference for maternal sole custody is paradoxical. On the one hand, concern for the "best interests" of the child has come to be universally accepted as a general principle (Derdeyn, 1976). This would make two expectations reasonable, that (a) the adjudication of custody cases be based on the best and most recent information available and (b) the recent preference for maternal sole custody has changed, with more joint custody and paternal sole custody awards rendered. The facts contradict both statements.

Study of judicial behavior in custody cases indicates that the basis for such decision making is typically vague, discretionary, speculative, and laden with common sense and personal values (Cox & Cease, 1978; Kressel, 1985; Lawrence, 1968). One study of child custody adjudication, for example, identified 299 decision-making criteria (Pearson, Munson, & Thoennes, 1982). Fineberg (1979) explains why he finds this state of affairs remarkable:

> If the best interests of the child are the goal of custody adjudication, then the law should ideally act in accordance, not in conflict with the current scientific knowledge about child development. When the central issue is the emotional and psychological health of the child, it seems incredulous that the "common sense approach" or the "practical experiences" of the Court have, until now, provided almost the sole basis on which custody decisions have been reached. (p. 437)

Much the same applies to judicial preference for maternal sole custody. As the North American data presented above demonstrates, that preference remains very much in force. As for joint custody, in the

United States in 1991 in 44 states joint custody was optional (25 [50%]), presumed (12 [24%]), or mandated (7 [14%]); it is not favored or is precluded in only six (12%) states (Folberg, 1991, Appendix A). Similarly, Furstenberg, Peterson, Nord, and Zill (1983), in a cross-national study of divorced parents, found that 3% of their sample were involved in a shared parenting arrangement. They noted too that the relative novelty of this option at that time implied that the 3% figure probably represented a low estimate. This assessment was confirmed by Weitzman (1985), who reported data from her own and several unpublished studies showing that the proportion of parents who select a shared parenting custody arrangement has increased in recent years. For example, recent studies report rates of joint physical custody ranging from 7% to 33%,[89] whereas Kelly (1993, p. 42) observes that joint legal custody is "now the norm in California" (see Selleck, Draughn, Waddle, & Buco, 1989).[90]

The situation is more ambiguous in Canada. Although both federal and provincial statutes recognize that child custody may involve more than one person, no official statistics are maintained about joint custody awards. However, the Department of Justice (1993, p. 13), using Statistics Canada data, has estimated that of the divorce cases involving custody awards in 1990, 14% involved a joint custody award. Moreover, our experience suggests that joint custody (also known as shared parenting) is relatively common and becoming more so. This opinion is suggested by the fact that during about 6 months in 1984, we contacted 201 parents involved in such an arrangement in metropolitan Toronto alone (see chapter 6). Similarly, recent case law suggests increasing judicial acceptance of this custody option in Canada.[91]

The thrust of this portrayal of divorce litigation is that even though the vast majority of cases are uncontested, divorce remains a slow, painful, and expensive process. For those who contest, it can mean much more of all three: much slower, much more painful, and several orders of magnitude more expensive. Moreover, as Kressel (1985) points out, the fact that petitions for divorce are not contested does not ensure that the spouses are not still in conflict, an issue the next section addresses.

Taking all of these factors into account, King (1993, p. 10) reached the following conclusion about the way in which divorce cases are handled by the California family court system but which, in our view, is generally applicable across North America, that

> the adversary system is a monster with a life and a momentum of its own that too often places the case beyond the control of the parties, their attorneys, and the judges. The system creates an accusatory atmosphere that destroys communication and cooperation. The adversary system works well for litigants who will never see each other again, but it is too slow, too expensive, and too impersonal and does not help divorcing spouses who will have to remain in contact with each other for years because of children or support obligations.

Marital Relations. Information about marital relations adds substance to the portrait presented above. As will become evident, much of what we know about the effects of this phase of the divorcing process on family members is anecdotal, based on the observations of clinical actors who have had extensive dealings with divorce in the court system. In contrast, systematic data reported in scientific studies are far and few between.

Thus, there is general agreement that when marital conflict is carried into court, especially when it centers on the issue of child custody, the results can yield the most acrimonious, bitter, and protracted cases ever heard (Committee on the Family, 1981). In part, this conflict may reflect the state of the marital relationship. Clinical observers suggest that such conflict can be significantly escalated when it encounters the adversarial structure of the court (Coogler, 1977; Kressel, 1985; McKie et al., 1983), which, in practice (if not intent), operates to exacerbate rather than diffuse intense negative feelings between spouses in opposition (Kressel, 1985).[92] The court structure tends to deemphasize shared feelings, goals, and values (Scheslinger, 1977), reinforce spouses' desire to inflict hurt on each other (Watson, 1969), and intensifies negative affect by encouraging opposition and confrontation (Noble & Noble, 1975; Perlman, 1982; Weiss, 1975, 1979a).

In this context, the lawyer is one of two critical judicial actors (Kronby, 1991; Wolfson, 1992).[93] The aging clinical literature is problematic because it is at considerable variance with contemporary experience.

Although the former is relentlessly negative (Conway, 1970; Doane & Cohen, 1981; Felner, Primavera, Farber, & Bishop, 1982; Irving, Benjamin, Bohm, & Macdonald, 1981; Smith, 1981), our experience suggests that family lawyers are an invaluable resource to divorcing spouses. Their knowledge of the law provides divorcing spouses with a basis for making informed and fateful choices. Their objectivity helps spouses to think coherently and rationally at a time when much else in their life is chaotic. And their support for spouses in distress may come at a time when it may be perceived by spouses as essential to their continued sanity. On the one hand, such efforts are consistent with the cooperative style of many lawyers (Williams, 1983, 1984). This is especially true given the recent influx of women into the profession with the general support of feminist principles. On the other hand, these same efforts may be importantly constrained, both by the competitive demands of the adversarial system (see above) and by their clients, whose desire to fight in order to punish their errant spouses may push lawyers into unnecessarily conflictual positions (Kressel, 1985).[94]

Irrespective of one's view of lawyers and the courts, differences in the readiness of the spouses to separate may leave one of them especially vulnerable to additional trauma associated with the process of litigation (Irving, 1979; Kressel, 1985; Schlesinger, 1979). One manifestation of this dilemma may involve irrational agreement on the part of the more vulnerable spouse to any terms so long as they offer the slightest hope of reconciliation (Irving, 1980). Another is the willingness of parents to make trade-offs in an effort to reach settlement, including such matters as custody, child visitation, child support, and matrimonial property (Teachman & Polonko, 1990). Even so, there is surprisingly little empirical data about the relationship between involvement in adversarial proceeding and spousal adjustment. What evidence there is suggests that there is no direct relationship between the two (Spanier & Anderson, 1979).

As for the children, they are often caught in the middle of this battle (Hetherington, 1987; Sheffner & Suarez, 1975; Wallerstein & Blakeslee, 1989). However inadvertently, children often end up becoming both the weapon and the prize in such disputes (Goldstein, Freud, & Solnit, 1973; Wallerstein & Kelly, 1980). The clinical evidence suggests that children suffer bitterly for their involvement in adversarial proceedings (Elkin, 1977; Irving & Bohm, 1981). However, more systematic evidence of a direct link between child involvement in adversarial proceedings and their subsequent adjustment is rare. Three studies by Wolman and Taylor (1991), Saayman and Saayman (1989), and Kruk (1991, 1992, 1993, 1994) provide revealing examples.

The work of Saayman and Saayman (1989) is one of only two studies we know of that directly examines the effect of court proceedings on later child adjustment. Although all the children examined were in the normal range, just under half were judged neurotic or antisocial. The two best predictors of child adjustment, each operating independently, were coparental conflict and involvement in adversarial proceedings. On this basis, the authors concluded (p. 341) that "it is the *very structure of the adversarial system* which is potentially damaging to the children of divorce." Wolman and Taylor (1991) compared the responses of children whose parents had or had not contested custody in the court. In contrast to Saayman and Saayman (1989), they found that children in the contested group reported less anger and guilt than their noncontested counterparts.

The work of Kruk (1991, 1992, 1993, 1994) addresses the same topic indirectly, by inquiring into the bases for paternal disengagement and especially the ways in which lawyers inadvertently contribute to this outcome. In this context, Furstenberg and Cherlin (1991) suggest that many men regard marriage and child care as an inseparable role set. Consequently, when men divorce they sever ties not only with their spouses but also with their children (see Atkin & Rubin, 1976; Furstenberg, 1990).[95] Such framing places the onus of this process on the fathers.[96] Kruk's work offers a more complex explanation for father disengagement. This explanation has two parts: Fathers who were close to their children in marriage were much more likely than fathers who were distant to experience intense distress at becoming "weekend fathers" (Silver & Silver, 1981);[97] and efforts by fathers to maintain contact with their children were impeded by conflict with their former spouses which, in turn, was significantly exacerbated by the behavior of the father's lawyer. Thus, in seeking to protect and defend their client's rights, lawyers inadvertently promoted father disengagement by forcing the parties to take extreme positions; prohibiting direct communication between the spouses; undercutting previous parenting plans; supporting and insisting that fathers support maternal sole

custody despite considerable variation in the previous parenting
involvement of fathers (see Bartz & Witcher, 1978); engaging in protracted and competitive negotiation; and generally engendering in
fathers feelings of powerlessness to affect the future course of their
relationship with their children.

None of this is to suggest that the legal phase of the divorcing process
must necessarily be destructive. As mentioned above, Williams (1983,
1984) found that the behavior of many lawyers exemplified a cooperative approach to negotiation, although Kelly and Duryee (1992) found
that women were more likely than men to be satisfied with their
experience of litigation in court. Nevertheless, our reading of this
material suggests that the adversarial system, although essential, is
rather ill suited to the full range of issues typical of contested cases of
divorce (see Emery, 1988). Consequently, it places an extraordinary
burden on divorcing families when they are already under great stress
and vulnerable to the potential for additional harm. That said, for those
undergoing a "difficult" divorce there appear to be few alternatives,
for they themselves typically demand their day in court; only family
mediation may offer some an acceptable alternative (Johnston &
Campbell, 1988).

From the perspective of the mediation practitioner, four aspects of
this phase stand out. The first speaks to the rationale that underpins
mediation, namely, offering divorcing couples in conflict an alternative
to litigation. Indeed, for couples deadlocked in mediation, the potential consequences, both psychological and financial, of court involvement are a useful reminder of what may happen should they be unable
to reach agreement. The second concerns fairness and the local legal
regime. In a sense, this aspect refers to the practitioner's legal education, for it is imperative that he or she know in advance what is
possible, likely, or required in the jurisdiction. In another sense, it refers
to trends in judicial behavior which, historically at least, have consistently disadvantaged women. Such trends represent one basis on
which to assess the fairness of clients' self-generated agreements.
Third, fairness arises again in these data, this time concerning the
tendency for some spouses, under intense stress, to agree to almost
anything if it offers any hope of ending the process and stopping the
pain. This situation creates an ethical dilemma for mediation practi-

tioners dedicated to the principle of neutrality. The issue remains contentious, with some mediators willing to accept any agreement so long as it is arrived at voluntarily, whereas others prefer to intervene to ensure an agreement that is fair to both former partners (see chapter 4). Finally, the data point to the importance of children. For mediators, cases involving children are likely to be more difficult, complex, and emotionally intense than those in which children are not involved.

NOTES

1. For a slightly dated bibliography on divorce, see Schlesinger (1985).

2. See also Hetherington (1979), Holmes and Rahe (1967), Spanier and Casto (1979), and Weiss (1975).

3. See also Kaslow and Hyatt (1981), Krause (1979), and Longfellow (1979).

4. See also Brown (1976), Ferguson (1978), Kressel and Deutsch (1977), McCubbin and Patterson (1983), and Salts (1979).

5. Examples include stress (Golan, 1981; Hetherington, 1989; Rodgers, 1986), object relations (Kernberg, 1967; Mahler, 1971; Masterson, 1981), family development (Ahrons & Rodgers, 1987; Kaslow & Schwartz, 1987), and ecosystems (Emery, Joyce, & Fincham, 1987; Johnston & Campbell, 1988; Rodgers & Conrad, 1986) theories.

6. Examples include social control (Berger, 1988), coalition (Gamson, 1969), attribution (Heider, 1958; Jones & Davis, 1965; Kelley, 1973), exchange (Levinger, 1965, 1979a, 1979b), symbolic interaction (Ebaugh, 1988; Vaughn, 1986), and expectation-states (Berger, Rosenholtz, & Zelditch, 1980; Johnston, 1985) theories (see also Sev'er, 1992).

7. See also Kaslow and Schwartz (1987) and Pleck and Manocherian (1988).

8. In 1992 the figure had risen to 1,210,000 (Cox, 1993). See also Dickinson and Leming (1990), United States Department of Education (1988), and Zinn and Eitzen (1990).

9. The comparable figure for the United Kingdom (in 1987) was 151,000 (Stone, 1990).

10. See also Cherlin (1981), Furstenberg and Cherlin (1991), Sev'er (1992), and Zinn and Eitzen (1990).

11. For example, in 1984, 1.1 million children under 18 years old (representing 1.7% of all children in that year) were involved in their parents' divorce (United States Department of Education, 1988). In Canada, of all divorce cases in 1990, 27,367 included custody orders involving 47,631 children (Department of Justice, 1993, p. 13).

12. For example, Phillips (1988) notes that in 1910 there were 83,000 divorces in the United States, whereas Pleck and Manocherian (1988) observe that the number of divorces had risen to 413,000 by 1962.

13. Similarly, using 1985 data Ahrons and Rodgers (1987) show that of 81 million adult men and 90 million adult women, 6.5% and 8.7%, respectively, were divorced. In Canada, of all families with children under 15 years old (in 1990), 4.8% were separated or divorced (McKie, 1993). Of the balance, 78.6% involved intact marriages, 15.9% involved never-married single parents, and 0.7% involved widowed single parents.

14. The crude rate is the number of divorces in a given year expressed as a rate per 1,000 total population. The refined rate is the number of divorces in a given year expressed as a rate per 1,000 married women aged 15 or greater.

15. In the same years, the refined divorce rate in the United States and Canada was 21.5 (Zinn & Eitzen, 1990) and 13.0 (Nett, 1993), respectively. In 1992, the crude divorce rate in the United States had marginally declined to 4.7 (Cox, 1993). In 1991, the crude divorce rate in Canada was 2.82, down from 2.95 in 1990. Across Canada's 10 provinces, crude divorce rates varied from 3.30 (in Alberta) to 1.60 (in Newfoundland), with Ontario, Canada's most populous province, recording a divorce rate of 2.75.

16. This trend is consistent with the projections of Masnick and Bane (1980).

17. Two additional trends are noteworthy. First, compared to other industrialized western nations, the United States has the highest divorce rate in the world (Ambert, 1990; Cox, 1993; Goode, 1992; Riley, 1991). However, Fisher (1992), based on United Nations data from 62 countries, notes comparable rates in traditional societies (see Friedl, 1975). Second, since national recordkeeping began in the United States in 1867 (Emery, 1988), the divorce rate has, with few exceptions, risen steadily, with a comparable pattern but much lower rates elsewhere in the industrialized world (Phillips, 1988). For example, in 1990 the average crude divorce rate in European Economic Community countries was 1.7 (Statistics Canada, 1991). Various observers have argued that the rise in the divorce rates worldwide is related to the increase in industrialization and urbanization (Fisher, 1992; Kitson et al., 1985; Phillips, 1988). Related explanations include: (a) patterns of immigration (Statistics Canada, 1991); (b) the ability of women to acquire financial resources independent of their spouses, typically through employment (Fisher, 1992; see Duffy & Pupo, 1992); and (c) the inverse relationship between the divorce rate and the birth rate (when the latter is low, the former is likely to be high; Cox, 1993).

18. Uhlenberg, Cooney, and Boyd (1990) predict that of all white women who marry in 1990, only 37% will *not* have been divorced at least once by the year 2025.

19. However, this probability varies by race (whites, 38%; blacks, 75%; Bumpass, 1984; Cox, 1993) and age (the likelihood of divorce decreases with age; Zinn & Eitzen, 1990).

20. These figures vary by race: 33% among white children, 65% among black children (Zinn & Eitzen, 1990).

21. Single-parent families can be created by any of five means: "(1) through the death of a married parent, (2) through separation or divorce of a married parent, (3) through union dissolution of a parent living common-law, (4) through birth to an unmarried woman . . . or (5) through adoption of a child to a single parent" (Eichler, 1993, p. 140). In recent years, divorce has became the major reason for the rapid rise in the population of single-parent families in North America (Wojtkiewicz, McLanahan, & Garfinkel, 1990), most of them headed by women.

22. In the United States and Canada (Robinson & McVey, 1985) and in the United Kingdom (Stone, 1990), the average rate of family dissolution (about 30%) was until very recently about the same for the cohort married in 1824 as for the cohort married in 1984, except that divorce rather than death has become the leading cause. These figures apply to most industrialized countries and only slightly less so to the United States.

23. Three additional regularities referring to the timing of divorce are noteworthy. Thus, Fisher (1992) observes that worldwide divorce is most frequent after 4 years of marriage, whereas the median duration of marriages that end in divorce is 7 years (see United States Department of Education, 1988). In the United States, divorce frequency

peaks between years 2 and 3, with a median duration of 6.5 years (Dickinson & Leming, 1990). Specifically, Eshleman (1985) reports that in the United States, 34% of divorces occur after 1 to 4 years of marriage, 28% occur after 5 to 9 years, and 33% occur after 10 or more years. In Canada, divorce frequency peaks at year 3, with an average duration of 12.4 years (Statistics Canada, 1991). Moreover, in the United States divorce frequency peaks among men aged 20 to 24 and among women aged 20 to 29 (Fisher, 1992). In Canada, the comparable age for both sexes is 25 to 34 (Adams & Nagnur, 1989), although the average age of divorced spouses is 39 years for men and 36 years for women (Beaujot, 1990).

These data are subject to multiple complementary interpretations. For example, they lead Pleck and Manocherian (1988) to conclude that marriages are most at risk of divorce during the first phase of the family life cycle, before or soon after children arrive. Fisher (1992), following Tenov's (1979) theory of love and infatuation ("limerance"), notes that the divorce frequency peak corresponds perfectly with the normal duration of infatuation, that is, between 2 and 3 years. Finally, Nett (1993) argues that marriages that end after only a short duration are marriage "mistakes," whereas those that end after many years are marriage "failures."

24. Bohannan (1971) distinguishes among six "stations" of divorce (emotional, legal, economic, coparental, community, psychic). Wiseman (1975) discusses five stages of divorce (denial, loss, anger, reorientation, acceptance), Chiancola (1978) three (emotional distance, reacting to separation, refocusing on self), Golan (1981) three (estrangement, formalization, new life), Wallerstein and Blakeslee (1989) three (acute, transitional, renewed stability), and Ahrons and Rodgers (1987) five (individual cognition, family metacognition, systemic separation, systemic reorganization, and family redefinition) (see also Everett, 1987; Froiland & Hozman, 1977; Guttman, 1993; Kaslow, 1984, 1988; Kessler, 1975; Trafford, 1982). By far the most elaborate is that of Vaughan (1986, p. 201) who distinguishes between 120 categories and subcategories of what she calls "uncoupling" (see Vaughan, 1985).

25. The substantive discussion that follows is hardly comprehensive; that would require a book-length treatment. For more information, see reviews by Ambert (1990); Atkeson, Forehand, and Rickard, (1982); Dickinson and Leming (1990); Emery (1988); Everett (1987); Fersh and Verling (1976); Furstenberg and Cherlin (1991); Jacobs (1982); Kanoy and Cunningham (1984); Kitson and Raschke (1981); Kitson et al. (1985); Lowery and Settle (1985); Nelson (1985); Nett (1993); Philips (1988); Pleck and Manocherian (1988); Reiss and Lee (1988); Riley (1991); Stone (1990); Wallerstein (1991); White and Mika (1983); and Zinn and Eitzen (1990).

26. See also Hetherington (1987, 1989), Kelly (1982), Kitson and Sussman (1982), and Nock (1987).

27. In recent years, the literature on adultery has expanded greatly. For a nonexhaustive list of sources, see Atwater (1987), Botwin (1988), Brown (1987, 1991), Corey (1989), Fisher (1992), Hill et al. (1976), Hunt (1969), Lampe (1987), Lawson (1988), Moultrup (1990), Neubeck (1969), Pagels (1988), Pittman (1989), Prestrack, Martin, and Martin (1985), Smith (1991), Tavris and Sadd (1977), Thompson (1983, 1984), and Vaughan (1990).

28. See also Albrecht and Kunz (1980) and Arnold et al. (1980).

29. See also Jaffe et al. (1990), O'Brien (1971), Kennedy and Dutton (1989), and McLeer (1981).

30. In a survey of 160 societies, Betzig (1989) lists a similar array of marital complaints, as does Stone (1990) for the United Kingdom, whereas Emery (1988) notes that

in the United States the frequency of such complaints has changed over the past century. For example, complaints about desertion and drunkenness have gone down, whereas those about violence have gone up.

31. Smith (1991) argues that learning disability may also contribute to divorce (p. 162). Having a learning disabled child, for example, may be so stressful as to convince one parent to leave the marital relationship. Conversely, one of the spouses may not be aware that they themselves are learning disabled. Associated with a range of difficulties in social relations, learning disability includes "tactile defensiveness" (p. 163), a disorder of the sensory system in which sufferers "cannot tell the difference between a hard touch and a soft, gentle touching," and so withdraw from all touching. The extent to which having a child with other forms of disability might contribute to parental divorce is not known.

32. Bumpass et al. (1991) found that 40% of their sample had had at least one separation, 18% two or more. Of those who had separated, 45% of these episodes had lasted one month or less and 95% lasted less than 12 months.

33. See also Weiss (1976, 1977, 1979a) and Wiseman (1975).

34. There is increasing recognition that men and women respond to and cope with the divorcing process differently (see Pleck & Manocherian, 1988; Volgy, 1991).

35. See also Hodges and Bloom (1986), Menaghan (1983), and White and Booth (1991).

36. Indeed, recent evidence indicates that such stress is reflected in changes in brain chemistry (Sabelli, Carlson-Sabelli, & Javaid, 1990). Furthermore, Sabelli et al. (1990) report that spouses going through divorce show low levels of a brain neurotransmitter (phenylethylamine [PEA]), which is associated with feelings of elation, exhilaration, and euphoria. The authors speculate that this decline in PEA is probably the result of depression, although PEA subsequently rises sharply during court proceedings (Sabelli, 1991).

37. See also Albrecht (1980), Bloom et al. (1978), and Chiriboga and Cutler (1977).

38. See also Ard and Ard (1976); Brannen and Collard (1982); Gurman (1982); and Nadelson, Polansky, and Mathews (1981). Here, Ambert (1989) found that the likelihood of seeking marital therapy was greater among those who had been divorced more than once compared to those who had been divorced only once (79% versus 29%).

39. See also Ambert (1990), Bernard (1966), Carter and Glick (1970), Cutright (1971), Dickinson and Leming (1990), Gibson (1974), Kitson et al. (1985), Levinger (1965), and Reiss and Lee (1988).

40. Related differences in religion and ethnicity similarly increase the risk of separation (Bohannan, 1985; London & Wilson, 1988; see Glenn & Supancic, 1984).

41. However, this thesis remains controversial. For example, several authors (Fisher, 1992; Spitze & South, 1985; Whyte, 1990) point to evidence that the risk of separation increases as each partner contributes equally to the family's financial resources; that is, women with good jobs and good pay are more likely to separate than their stay-at-home counterparts who are financially dependent on their spouses. Similarly, there is evidence that the relationship between education and the risk of separation is far from uniform. Known as the "Glick effect" (Glick, 1957), this shows that in some cases the risk of separation increases as education increases (Greenstein, 1985). Consequently, Reiss and Lee (1988) and Greenstein (1990) have argued that the relationship between social class and the risk of separation may involve a conditional effect based on the degree to which (a) wives' employment involves traditional work (in terms of type and

hours of employment) and low pay (see Hiller & Philliber, 1982; Philliber & Hiller, 1983), and (b) their husbands approve of the work that they do (Spitze & South, 1985).

42. See also Ambert (1990), Arnold et al. (1980), Bloom et al. (1978), Bumpass et al. (1991), Burchinal and Chancellor (1963), Fisher (1992), Levitan et al. (1988), Norton and Glick (1976), Reiss and Lee (1988), and Ross and Sawhill (1975).

43. See also Cherlin (1981), Furstenberg and Cherlin (1991), and Levitan et al. (1988); Zinn and Eitzen (1990).

44. Fisher's (1992) examination of United Nations data for divorce in 45 nations indicated that 39% of couples had no children, 26% had one child, 19% had two children, and 11% had three or more children.

45. The inhibiting effect of children appears greatest for the first child, especially if it is male (Morgan, Lye, & Condran, 1988).

46. See also Bower and Christopherson (1977) and Macklin (1980).

47. In 1990, there were 2.9 million common-law or cohabiting couples in the United States, representing 3% of all households (Cox, 1993). The comparable Canadian figures for the same year are 1.6 million and 12% (Stout, 1991).

48. Moreover, the experience of separation among former cohabitors is strikingly similar to that among the formerly married (Mika & Bloom, 1980).

49. However, Castro-Martin and Bumpass (1989) caution that first marriers and remarriers constitute different "risk pools," making it unwise to directly compare their respective likelihood of separation.

50. Some, however, take issue with the general consensus and argue on methodological grounds that the association between divorce and ethnicity may be significantly exaggerated. Kitson with Holmes (1992), for example, in a study in suburban Cleveland, found that when various sociodemographic variables were held constant, blacks were *less* likely than whites to divorce.

51. In a small but unknown proportion of cases, spouses "separate" but continue to live together, perhaps on different floors (in homes as opposed to apartments). In our experience, this situation typically occurs when husbands wish to seek custody of their children and are advised by their lawyer to remain in the home to avoid the later charge that they "abandoned" their children when they moved out (see Cochrane, 1991).

52. See also Ambert (1990), Goldsmith (1980, 1982), and McKie et al. (1983).

53. Furthermore, Vaughan (1986, p. 127) argues that the advantage gained by the initiator carries over to shape postseparation adjustment: "I find, however, that the role taken in the leavetaking is the primary determinant of how separation will be borne. . . . The initiator is better prepared than the partner. Regardless of sex, age, occupation, or income—regardless of social class, duration of the relationship, social networks, or other factors known to be related to the disruptiveness of this experience—the initiator . . . has had the advantage of time, having begun uncoupling earlier. And the time has been spent preparing for the physical break."

54. However, Vaughan (1986, p. 221, note 34) argues that such an explanation, based on sex-role socialization, both oversimplifies and distorts and that "power" has greater explanatory value. Accordingly, she argues that available statistical evidence about who initiates the separation process may be distorted by the following: (a) women initiate because they have been manipulated into doing so by the more powerful male initiator; (b) women in this situation recognize it and report it to researchers as manipulation because men use overt rule violation strategies to achieve their end; (c) men initiate because they have been manipulated into doing so by their more powerful female initiator; (d) men in this situation are *not* likely to recognize it because women use subtle,

indirect strategies when they perceive their partner as more powerful; and (e) if men do recognize that they have been manipulated, they may be unwilling to admit it.

55. Moreover, as Vaughan (1986, p. 6) notes, "Over the course of a long relationship, these roles [of initiator and other partner] may be passed back and forth, with one person assuming the role of initiator at one time and the other acting to end the relationship at another. How the roles get passed back and forth is, in fact, one of the more intriguing aspects of the process."

56. See also Ambert (1980, 1990), Bloom et al. (1978), Goldsmith (1982), and Peters (1983).

57. See also Peterson (1989), Potuchek (1992), and Roach and Kitson (1989).

58. However, Gorlick (1992) notes that in Canada the structure of student aid programs acts as a barrier to educational achievement among separated mothers.

59. See also Bloom et al. (1978), Price-Bonham and Balswick (1980), Raschke (1987), and Wallerstein and Blakeslee (1989).

60. In accord with a typological approach, McCall (1982) distinguishes between fives sorts of postseparation relationships between the former spouses: attachment; social structural; commitment; benefit-dependability; and investment.

61. For a history of American divorce law, see Jacobs (1988).

62. Divorce statutes assume complete disclosure whereas under the rules of ethics a lawyer for one side is not required to volunteer anything unless and until requested by the other side (Erickson, 1988).

63. Across United States jurisdictions this waiting period ranges between 30 days and 12 months. In Canada, changes to the law (Divorce Act [1985]) shortened the waiting period from 3 years to 12 months. For information about the British approach, see Stone (1990).

64. See Foote (1988), Freed and Walker (1989, 1990), Jacobs (1988), and Walker and Elrod (1993).

65. See Phillips (1988), Survey of American Family Law (1985), Weitzman (1985), and Wheeler (1974).

66. See also Emery (1988), King (1993), McKie et al. (1983), Nett (1993), and Wallerstein and Blakeslee (1989).

67. A study of 908 divorce cases in California found that only 1.4% were contested (Mnookin et al., 1990). Similarly, a study of all divorce cases in four Canadian cities in 1988 showed that only 3% went to trial (Department of Justice, 1993, p. 18).

68. See also Kaslow (1988), Kelly (1991, in press), Landau (1988), Mnookin et al. (1990), and Schwebel, Gately, and Milburn (in press).

69. In some American states (such as California), mediation is mandatory; couples who still cannot agree are then free to contest their case in court. In Canada, mediation can only be entered into voluntarily.

70. In this context, Vaughan (1986, p. 23) observes that, "unlike a healthy relationship in which partners grow in new directions but maintain bonds of interdependence between their separate interests, uncoupling is characterized by the pursuit of alternatives in ways that sever ties instead of strengthen them." Infidelity is a case in point by creating "multiple nonshareable secrets" (Vaughan, 1986, p. 24).

71. For a history of child custody law in the United States, see Mason (1993).

72. There is disagreement about the total number of parental abductions per year in the United States. Finkelhor, Hotaling, and Sedlak (1991), for example, estimated that there were 163,000 parental abductions in 1988. In contrast, the problem is much less prominent in Canada. There, in 1990 of 61,000 missing children, 45,000 (74%) were runaways compared to 432 parental abductions (0.7%; McDonald, 1992). Of the latter,

"77% of them were located within the same year" (Department of Justice, 1993, p. 151). Wherever they occur, such abductions, say Wallerstein and Blakeslee (1989), are typically motivated more by a desire to hurt the other spouse than out of parental love, and often leave the children worse off than before.

73. In the United States, these include future earning capacity as well as benefits and entitlements associated with employment, such as pensions and other retirement benefits, medical insurance, Social Security, and educational and professional degrees (Weitzman, 1992a).

74. These include California, Florida, Minnesota, New York, and South Carolina (Cox, 1993).

75. See also Garfinkel (1992), McLanahan and Garfinkel (1991, 1993), and Seltzer (1991).

76. See also Department of Justice (1987, 1990); Economic Council (1992); Kitchen (1992); McCall and Pask (1990); McCall, Hornick, and Wallace (1988); Pask and McCall (1989); Rogerson (1991a, 1991b); and Steward and Steel (1990).

77. The U.S. Department of Agriculture has estimated that the total cost of raising a child (from birth to 18) in a midwestern city is $92,000 (in constant 1986 dollars) or $184,000 for two children (United States Department of Education, 1988). A recent Canadian study found that average annual child care costs for a single child in Winnipeg, Manitoba, varied from $9,000 (for preschool children) to $6,000 (for adolescents). For two children (a boy and a girl), these annual costs accumulate to a total of $271,000 by the time the children reach the end of the 18th year. The most recent update of these data to 1993 (reported in the *Financial Post*, April 2, 1994, p. 18) show that these costs have risen to a combined total of $305,000.

78. See also Holden and Smock (1991) and Pleck and Manocherian (1988).

79. See also Kitchen (1992), Pask (1993b), and Weitzman (1985).

80. In 10% of such cases, wives are ordered to pay child support to their husbands (Hanson, 1980), typically at a lower level than comparable awards from husbands to wives (Christensen, Dahl, & Rettig, 1990).

81. In the United States, McLanahan and Garfinkel (1993) note that 45% of custodial mothers are poor (see McLanahan & Garfinkel, 1991), whereas in Canada the Department of Justice (1990) reports that after child support was paid, 65% of custodial mothers were poor compared to 16% of noncustodial fathers (see also Eastman, 1992; Goldberg & Kremen, 1987; Harman, 1992).

82. In rare instances, split custody involves awarding custody of one or more children to one parent, and one or more children to the other parent. Custody may also be split between a parent and other relatives such as grandparents.

83. See also Maccoby and Mnookin (1992) and Pearson et al. (1983).

84. For fathers seeking custody, several researchers (Gasser & Taylor, 1976; Hanson, 1980; Mendes, 1976a, 1976b, 1979) have distinguished between "seekers" and "assenters," that is, between those who want custody and those who accept it if it is thrust on them. Ambert (1989) argues on the basis of Canadian data that the high proportion of women who are awarded custody conceals a sizable proportion of "assenters," women who accept custody though they do not really want it but are afraid of the social consequences were they to refuse. In a similar vein, Mnookin et al. (1990), using American data, found that 20% of the fathers in their sample initially preferred sole maternal custody despite asking for physical joint custody in their divorce petitions, probably, the authors speculate, as a bargaining tactic to persuade their spouses to accept a less generous financial settlement.

85. Cramer (1986) reports that gay parents face special constraints, fearing losing custody of their children should they disclose their sexual orientation. More generally, confronted by judges who take a traditional view of the family, divorcing gay or lesbian partners face a variety of obstacles before the law (Casey, 1994). Consequently, they have recently begun to look with favor on family mediation (Bryant, 1992).

86. See also Bernard, Ward, and Knoppers (1992), Freed and Walker (1990), Hodges (1991), McKie et al. (1983), Warshak (1992), and Weitzman (1985).

87. In only 2.4% of all divorce cases in four Canadian cities in 1988 was paternal access denied (Department of Justice, 1993, p. 9).

88. A minority of custodial fathers confront the problem of coping with child care responsibilities never before encountered (George & Wilding, 1972; Gersick, 1979; Kurdek, 1981; Orthner, Brown, & Ferguson, 1976). For a slightly dated review of this literature see Hanson (1985).

89. See, for example, Johnston and Campbell (1988), Kelly (in press), Kline, Tschann, Johnston, and Wallerstein (1989); Maccoby, Depner, and Mnookin (1988); Maccoby and Mnookin (1992); Mnookin, Maccoby, Albiston, and Depner (1990); and Teachman and Polonko (1990).

90. The typical award involves joint legal custody in which the children (typically) live with their mother (Shrier, Simring, Grief, Shapiro, & Lindenthal, 1989; Shrier, Simring, Shapiro, Grief, & Lindenthal, 1991). An alternative arrangement involves the "bird's nest" (Woolley, 1978, 1980) in which the children remain in the matrimonial home while the parents take turns living there with them.

91. Recent examples include *Parsons v. Parsons* (1985) R.F.L. (2d) 83 (Nfld. S.C.); *Abbott v. Taylor* (1986) 2 R.F.L. (3d) 163 (Man. CA); *Nurmi v. Nurmi* (1988) 16 R.F.L. (3d) 201 (Ont. UFC); *Doucette v. Doucette* (1986) 73 N.B.R. (2d) 407 (NBQB); Droit de Famille— 361 (1987) 8 R.F.L. (3d) 272 (Que. SpC).

92. See also Elkin (1977); Golan (1981); Kressel and Deutsch (1977); Wallerstein and Kelly (1980); and Westman, Cline, Swift, and Kramer (1970).

93. See also Kronby (1991), Shover (1973), and Wheeler (1974).

94. In consequence, lawyers often have a difficult time with clients undergoing divorce (Felner et al., 1982).

95. As of roughly 1980, available data indicated that about half of all children in maternal sole custody seldom or never see their fathers (Ambert, 1990; Furstenberg & Spanier, 1984). For example, Furstenberg et al. (1983) compared the visitation frequency of noncustodial mothers and fathers. Although 31% of the mothers visited their children one or more times weekly, this was true of only 16% of the fathers. Further, these proportions diminish through time (Dudley, 1991; Furstenberg & Nord, 1985; Seltzer & Bianchi, 1988; cf. Ambert, 1989), especially for father-daughter pairs (Hess & Camara, 1979). However, the past decade has seen a steady increase in the level of noncustodial paternal involvement (Braver, Wolchik, Sandler, Forgas, & Zvetina, 1991; Kelly, in press; Seltzer, Schaeffer, & Charng, 1989). Healy, Malley, and Stewart (1990), for example, found that 65% of fathers visit their children at least every other week, whereas Kelly (in press) reports that on average children spend about 30% of their time with their father. Seltzer et al. (1989) report similar findings, noting, however, that visitation frequency is inversely related to child age and elapsed time since the separation (see Arditti, 1992; Teachman, in press).

96. Although voluntary paternal disengagement may be the norm, there are cases in which fathers have been pushed or forced to part from their children (Boss, 1977; Farber, 1964; Hill, 1949).

97. See also Dreyfus (1979), Goldsmith (1980), Grief (1979), Hetherington, Cox, and Cox (1976), Keshet and Rosenthal (1978), Stinson (1991), and Teachman (in press).

3

Family Mediation Practice
and the Knowledge Base

An Integrative Review of the
Divorce Research Literature
(Phases 4 Through 5)

PHASE 4: SHORT-TERM CONSEQUENCES

Of the five phases of the divorcing process, the consequences that accrue within 3 years of separation or divorce have received the most detailed research attention (Kitson, Babri, & Roach, 1985; Nelson, 1985). This information consistently distinguishes between consequences for the spouses and the children. Before proceeding, however, two qualifications are in order. First, from an ecosystemic perspective (Ambert, 1992; Benjamin, 1983), treating spouses and children as separate and apart is epistemologically problematic, because parents and children are necessarily linked; what affects one will almost certainly affect the others. Thus it makes more sense to speak about changes in the organization of spousal and parent-child relationships (Ahrons & Rodgers, 1987). Conversely, Wallerstein and Blakeslee (1989) argue that what is good for the parents may not necessarily be good for the

49

children, because the things that are likely to enhance adult life may make the parents less available to the children, adversely affecting the latter's adjustment to divorce. The fact is, however, that the bulk of the literature treats adult and child effects separately, with this conceptualization reflected throughout much of the research. Accordingly, in this and the next section, we will continue to distinguish between adults and children, both in the interests of clarity and mindful of the relative absence of systemic data.[1]

Second, as the literature on Phases 4 and 5 is voluminous, so our coverage of it is extensive, which, in our judgment, was necessary for two reasons. First, real life obscures the neat divisions between phases, with one phase overlapping another. Thus although Phase 4 is said below to begin after the divorce is complete, in practice consequences accrue to the family member starting in Phase 1. In turn, the mediation process is importantly shaped by ongoing consequences: the level of distress and dislocation; the financial, social, and psychological consequences of the divorcing process; and the demands of the children whose lives may have been seriously disrupted. Second, it is important that mediators understand just what the consequences of divorce can be, for their interventions have the potential to mitigate or exacerbate at least some of those consequences.

The Adult Partners

The entire adjustment and reorganization process occasioned by divorce takes between 2 and 4 years (Weiss, 1975), typically closer to 4 than 2 (Everett, 1991; Fisher, 1992).[2] Of that interval, most divorcing spouses indicate that the first 12 to 18 months after separation are the most stressful and upsetting (Melichor & Chiriboga, 1988).[3] In consequence, a range and variety of problems are much more common among divorcing than intact couples (Stack, 1980, 1990),[4] including substantially increased rates of health and physical disorders, emotional difficulties, mental disorders, accidents, suicide,[5] alcohol and substance abuse, death, and a generally reduced sense of subjective well-being (Gove & Sin, 1989). Separated and divorcing spouses are likely to report difficulty working effectively, poor health, weight changes, insomnia, sexual dysfunction, increased use of alcohol and/or tobacco together with lingering psychological effects, including feelings of grief (Crosby, Gage, & Raymond, 1983), helplessness, low self-esteem (Shook & Jurish, 1992), lack of control over events, loneliness, anger, loss, frustration, identity problems, and dissatisfaction about forced lifestyle changes (Pleck & Manocherian, 1988).

This said, several qualifications are in order related primarily to social class, gender, children, and age. Although distress related to divorce is nearly universal, working- and lower-class couples with few resources are still likely to suffer more than their middle- and upper-class counterparts (Amato & Partridge, 1987; Ambert, 1989). Women are more likely to report acute distress during the first few months whereas men can retreat into work, only feeling the full emotional effects of the divorcing process after a year or more (Melichor & Chiriboga, 1988).[6] Spouses with children are especially vulnerable to distress (Emberson & Gove, 1989; Hughes, 1989) because custodial parents must now contend with all child-rearing demands alone (Statistics Canada, 1994; Thompson & Ensinger, 1989). Finally, middle-aged and older women have an especially difficult time coping with divorce (Weitzman, 1985) having been forced into an "unplanned career" (Shaw, 1983) when divorced unexpectedly "displaces" them as homemakers (Morgan, 1991).

Thus, over the short term there are multiple consequences of separation and divorce. In what follows, data about these consequences will be grouped into four categories: psychological, interactional (coparental), social, and financial.

Psychological Consequences. Ending a long, intimate relationship typically has devastating psychological consequences for both spouses. The feelings involved include trauma, anxiety, depression, and lowered self-esteem (Hetherington, 1989).[7] It may also involve obsessive thoughts about the past and the future (Vaughan, 1986; Weiss, 1975, 1979b), psychosomatic disorders (Bloom, Asher, & White, 1978), loneliness, anger, bitterness, and sexual frustration (Hetherington, 1987).[8] Despite these feelings, as many as 25% of divorcing spouses also report powerful feelings of continued attachment to their former partner (Brown, Felton, Munela, & Whitman, 1980; Brown, Felton, Whitman, & Munela, 1980).[9] Generally, wives tend to experience greater distress as well as greater relief following divorce than husbands (Spanier & Thompson, 1984).[10] The combination of these various psychological states yields a stress profile not unlike that associated with bereavement (Kitson, Babri, Roach, & Placidi, 1989).[11] And as with other forms of grief, the effects tend to pass with time (McLanahan, 1983).[12]

These feelings, however, do not all dissipate at the same rate (Ambert, 1990).[13] Typically, the initial sense of trauma disappears first, within 5 to 8 weeks. The anxiety and identity changes go next, declining gradually over a year or more. Feelings of depression endure the longest, fading away rapidly over the first 5 to 8 months and then more slowly for the next year.[14] Although in the minority, among some spouses such feelings can be associated with psychiatric or medical symptoms, significantly prolonging their process of adjustment (Kitson & Sussman, 1982; Morrison, 1974).

Interactional Consequences (Coparental Relationship). Relations between former spouses are rarely friendly, often conflictual for years, and tend to decline gradually through time (Ambert, 1988a, 1988b).[15] Nevertheless, it would be incorrect to characterize all such relationships in negative terms. Rather, coparental relations tend to vary widely. Maccoby, Depner, and Mnookin (1990), for example, found that the couples in their (U.S.) sample were distributed as follows: cooperative (25%), conflictual (33%), disengaged (33%), and mixed (9%). Similarly, Ambert (1989) found that in her (Canadian) sample, couples were friendly (20%), unfriendly (20%), mixed (33%), or indifferent (because they were no longer in contact, 27%).

The level and quality of contact appears related to four variables: social class, communication quality, gender, and the presence of children. Children link former spouses together; their absence dramatically increases the likelihood that former spouses will be indifferent to each other (Ambert, 1989). Sharp differences in available resources following separation (wives typically downward, husbands typically stable, [see Financial Consequences below]) similarly reduce the likelihood of continued contact but increase the likelihood that such contact, when it occurs, will be conflictual (Ambert, 1989). In turn, this feeds back to increase the likelihood that spouses will see things differently (spousal congruence) and inaccurately (perceptual accuracy), thus additionally reducing residual feelings of friendliness (Ahrons, 1983a; Ambert, 1989). Coparental relations are also related to the quality of communication, with poor communication (typically predating the separation) associated with conflictual relations (Maccoby et al., 1990). Finally, gender plays a role, with women more than men negatively affected by the residual hostility of the prior marriage (thus prolonging the adjustment process [Kitson & Sussman, 1982; Weiss, 1975]), but less likely to have the hurt of the divorce undone by involvement in a new romantic relationship (Coysh, Johnston, Tschann, Wallerstein, & Klein, 1989).

Social Consequences. Each spouse stands at the center of a network of relationships, first with the children and the former partner, then with parents and in-laws, extended kin, and finally with friends, coworkers, and others. Each of these social relationships is in some way affected by the separation and divorcing process.

Having dealt above with former spouses and children, we turn first to relations between former spouses and other kin. Here the findings are mixed. Although some observers point to the social isolation of divorced spouses from married friends and in-laws (Colletta, 1979b),[16] others point to the continuity of relations with kin (Anspach, 1976)[17] and note the vital importance of social support to postdivorce adjustment (Chiriboga, Coho, Stein, & Roberts, 1979; Goldsmith, 1982).[18]

The key to such variation appears to be the interaction between gender, financial resources, and postdivorce adjustment (Milardo, 1987; Veevers, 1988). Financial resources sustain two trends: the ability to remain financially independent of kin and the opportunity to meet people and make new friends, including new romantic partners (Ambert, 1983; Arendell, 1986; Gerstel, 1988). As a function of both their respective financial circumstances (see below) and their gender-based preferences, divorcing men tend to interact more than women with a wider array of divorced and single friends and less with kin (Ambert, 1988b; Milardo, 1987; Myers, 1989). For example, as a function of their age, it is not uncommon for divorced men to begin dating again within 3 to 6 months (Hetherington, 1989)[19] in search of a new romantic partner (Cherlin, 1981; Hajal & Rosenberg, 1978). In many cases, such renewed intimacy will have been achieved within 2 years. This ability to relate in an intimate way to another person is directly related to opportunity, but also to their postdivorce adjustment success (Hetherington, Cox, & Cox, 1977, 1978; Raschke, 1977a). Men are thus freer to meet others and more rapidly connect with a new partner, but until then are less likely to have received adequate social support.[20]

In contrast, divorced women, because of their greater financial dependence, have fewer opportunities to meet new people and so tend to interact within a smaller network of others, including female friends and especially kin (McKenry & Price, 1991).[21] For example, Ambert (1989) found that when asked who they would turn to first for help, female former spouses were far more likely to select kin (new spouse, 63%; parents, 39%; sister, 37%) as opposed to their former spouse (16%).[22]

In a similar vein, although relations with male in-laws tend to decline through time, not infrequently women turn to and receive help from their female in-laws. The big losers in this regard tend to be the paternal grandparents, for whom divorce followed by maternal sole custody often means loss or disruption of their involvement with their grandchildren (Wilcoxon, 1987).[23, 24]

Finally, in this context another type of intimate relationship deserves mention, that between a divorced spouse in distress and a counselor of some sort (e.g., physician, psychiatrist, psychologist, social worker). About a third of divorcing spouses seek such aid, with most reporting that it was useful in helping them cope with a highly stressful period in their lives (Brannen & Collard, 1982).[25]

Financial Consequences. As noted above, the sources of income available to divorced spouses vary by gender: Divorced men continue to depend on their employment income whereas divorced women, especially those with children, may derive income from employment, spousal support (alimony), child support, and welfare (or other forms of state support; McLanahan & Garfinkel, 1993).

Irrespective of the income's source, all evidence suggests that women's income is both lower and less reliable than their male counterparts' (Finnie, 1993).[26] Women's financial picture starts with the fact that women with custody of their children must now fulfill alone child care and other household responsibilities that were previously split between both spouses, which commonly produces "role overload" (Colletta, 1979a, 1983).[27] The result is lifestyle changes frequently described as "chaotic" (Hetherington, Cox, & Cox, 1979) or "complex" (Sanick & Maudlin, 1986). Furthermore, within 12 months of separation, the majority of women will have entered the workforce, from which they derive both social support (Riley, 1991) and about 60% of their income (Peterson, 1989).[28] However, the distribution of income in the labor market remains inequitable (Eastman, 1992). Women receive lower wages for the same work and tend to be segregated to the service sector, where wages are low and the likelihood of advancement limited (Bielby & Baron, 1986; Duffy & Pupo, 1992; Wilson, 1991).[29] In particular, middle-aged and senior women have very few options for increasing their income, leaving them dependent on a meager Social Security pension (Iams & Ycas, 1988).

Of the small proportion of women awarded spousal support in the United States, the majority (73%) receive the full amount (Kitson with Holmes, 1992). However, this trend belies the sharp contrast in the financial situations of the divorced women who receive spousal support and the divorced husbands who pay it. In Canada, for example, in 1988 the average annual income of those paying spousal support was $25,000; the comparable figure for those receiving support was $10,500 (Department of Justice, 1990). The same study revealed two related trends: first, whereas 66% of divorced women with children had total annual incomes below the Statistics Canada poverty line (74% when spousal support was excluded), the same was true of only 10% of their former husbands after paying support. Second, the amount of support was inversely related to time on social assistance: Those receiving no spousal support (nearly 50%) remained on welfare an average of 4 years compared to those receiving more than $200 per month (6%), who remained on welfare an average of less than 2 years.

As for child support, the likelihood of receiving the full amount awarded is low across North America: Of the women with such an award, only about one quarter receives the full amount and about one third receives virtually nothing (Furstenberg, 1990; Kahn & Kamerman, 1987).[30, 31, 32] In response, recent statutory changes in the United States (Cox, 1993) and Canada (Kitchen, 1992) have made it much more difficult for husbands to avoid paying support awards.[33]

Finally, Cooper (1994) and McLanahan and Garfinkel (1993) document the ambivalent attitude that policymakers have shown sole support parents in the United States. On the one hand, Aid to Families with Dependent Children (AFDC) is not indexed to the cost of living, such that the real value of state subsidies has declined by 30% in recent years. On the other hand, the Family Support Act (1988) increased federal funding to states' programs, offering sole support mothers job training and alternate child care. Similarly, the Child Support Enforcement Amendment (1984) had by 1991 ensured that all states had accepted guidelines for the amount of child support awarded. Both Cooper (1994) and McLanahan and Garfinkel (1993) argue that to date the impact of such legislation has been slight. Eichler (1993) and Sev'er (1992) argue that similar inequalities apply in Canada.

On average, then, divorced women in the United States and Canada can expect a 30% decline in their predivorce annual income (Finnie, 1993; Hoffman & Duncan, 1988),[34,35] with about one third likely to drop below the poverty line in consequence (Furstenberg, 1990; Kneisser, McElroy, & Wilcox, 1988).

These data support two conclusions about which there is general agreement in the literature, namely, that the immediate consequence of divorce is that women experience a sharp decline in income compared to income stability or increase among men (Duncan & Hoffman, 1985)[36] and the resulting stress may be the single most important source of postdivorce adjustment difficulty among women (Ambert, 1985).[37] Indeed, such data led Pearce (1979) to coin the phrase that has since become virtually synonymous with women's financial experience of divorce: "the feminization of poverty."[38]

Although compelling, these conclusions nevertheless require careful qualification in light of recent data, especially the work of Morgan (1989, 1991), who compared the experience of intact, separated, divorced, and widowed middle-aged women over a period of 15 years. Among other things, her results indicated that

- Divorce and separation are responsible for a financial loss from which women never recover.
- Divorce and separation place about 14% of women at risk of intermittent poverty, although this phenomenon varied by social class at the point of separation or divorce. Those with the highest annual income remained relatively high but suffered the highest relative loss of income following separation or divorce. Those with the lowest income slipped into poverty, though 10% actually showed an increase in income (because of decreased need). The least poor were employed white women with the highest income at divorce or separation (see Furstenberg, 1990).[39]

- Over time, the proportion of divorced and separated women who entered the labor market increased to 80%, most working full time. At the same time, however, working reduced spousal and child support payments, which served as a serious disincentive to work among women with the lowest employment-related income.

These findings make clear that although separation and divorce are commonly associated with an enduring net financial loss for women, this relationship involves a *conditional probability* based on social class, ethnicity, and employment status. Holden and Smock (1991) go further, arguing that divorced women's financial status is only superficially related to divorce and, more important, a function of various structural features of North American society, including the inequitable marital division of labor (especially child care), gender inequality in the labor market, and lack of adequate postdivorce financial transfers.

More generally, then, nearly all spouses experience the divorcing process as intensely painful and very stressful. Although these consequences are unavoidable, they can at least be mitigated under certain conditions: *if* resources (financial, social) are in plentiful supply; *if* steady and enjoyable employment is available for those who want and/or need it; *if* opportunities are available to met new people, including potential new partners; *if* lifestyle, residential, and related changes can be minimized; and *if* relations with former spouses are cordial or at least only mildly conflictual (see Thiriot & Buckner, 1991). For many divorcing spouses, one, several, or all of these conditions are absent, thus substantially prolonging their adjustment to and reorganization following divorce. Even so, most spouses at least survive the experience; only a minority do not, dying through divorce-related illness, accident, or suicide.

From the perspective of the mediation practitioner, three aspects of this phase stand out. The first and most obvious concerns stress. Short of the death of a spouse or child, divorce is the most stressful life event for both former partners. For the practitioner, this is significant in two respects. First, it suggests that the level of stress and the client's coping strategies be the focus of assessment. As we have seen, divorcing spouses are distributed on a continuum. Before initiating service, it is important to know where on that continuum an individual client stands, to know what he or she needs and can or cannot be expected to do. Second, such stress speaks to clients' need for support. The second respect highlights the web of social relationships of which divorcing spouses are typically a part. Here too assessment is critical, to determine how that network may have changed, the extent to which it is providing the client with adequate support, and whether any of these network members are likely to have a significant effect on the course of mediation and thus need to be part of one or more service sessions. Finally, client finances should also be included in the assessment process, not just as another indicator of stress, but, as important, as the basis for assessing the flexibility they are likely to have when the negotiation process begins. Generally, the fewer the clients' financial resources, the fewer their negotiation options. In addition, financial inequality between the former partners should raise serious questions about the fairness of a negotiated agreement.

The Children

Although we may sympathize with the plight of divorcing partners, at least they enter the process voluntarily, as adults. Neither is true of their children. They are typically swept up in the process involuntarily (Everett, 1987, 1989, 1993; Wallerstein & Blakeslee, 1989) and seldom consulted in the bargain. It is reasonable to assume that, necessarily immature, they, more than their parents, may be especially vulnerable to psychological harm. As a result, research into the effects of divorce on children has produced a voluminous literature. In reviewing these data,[40] we will follow Emery (1988) in distinguishing between consequences and family process correlates.

Consequences. Children distribute on a continuum in terms of their response to their parent's divorce. A minority exhibit no consequences whatsoever or at least show only minor effects (Kurdek & Siesky, 1980a, 1980b).[41] Others may show positive effects (Warshak & Santrock, 1983),[42] especially if one or both of their parents were immature, irresponsible, abusive, or exhibited signs of mental disorder (Guidubaldi & Cleminshaw, 1985).[43] However, the majority give clear indications of distress and disruption (Hetherington, 1987, 1989).[44]

Following Emery (1988), more specific consideration of this range of consequences may be divided into six categories (see Hodges, 1986);

exploration of a seventh category (adult functioning) will be deferred to the next section.

1. *External Problems.* There is considerable evidence that compared to children in intact families, children experiencing the divorcing process are more likely to display a range of behavioral problems, including delinquency, aggression, and especially disobedience or noncompliance (Dawson, 1991).[45] In addition, Hodges and Bloom (1986) note increased problems with friends.

2. *Internal Problems.* Just as the divorcing process is intensely stressful for adults, so it is for children, with a range of psychological signs and symptoms commonplace, including fear, bewilderment, blame, anger, depression, insecurity, rejection, helplessness, frustration, shame, and lowered self-esteem (Wallerstein & Kelly, 1974, 1975, 1976, 1980).[46, 47] This response is not restricted to young children, but includes adolescents attending college or university (Farber, Felner, & Primavera, 1985).[48, 49] However, the evidence is not entirely consistent. Smith (1990) found that lowered self-esteem applied to children only when the divorce had occurred since the children had entered grade three, that is, was relatively recent (see Raschke & Raschke, 1979).

3. *Intellectual and Academic Functioning.* Compared to their intact counterparts, children experiencing divorce do less well at school (Bisnaire, Fireston, & Rynard, 1990),[50] display lower academic self-concept (Long, Forehand, Fauber, & Brody, 1987), and higher absenteeism (Nastasi, 1988, cited in Kelly, 1993), although the magnitude of these differences is not great (Guildubaldi, Perry, & Cleminshaw, 1984). However, available data are not consistent. Researchers working with adolescents found that divorce was associated not only with lowered academic performance but also reduced academic aspirations (Ambert & Saucier, 1983, 1984; Keith & Finlay, 1988; Wallerstein & Kelly, 1976). In contrast, Smith (1990), working with preadolescent children, found that divorce appears to affect negatively academic self-concept but *not* performance, whereas Tuzlat and Hillock (1986) report no change in academic performance. Finally, McLanahan (1985) confirmed a decline in academic performance, but argues that at least half of that decline is related to low family income.

4. *Gender Roles, Heterosexual Behavior.* There is some evidence that young boys undergoing the divorcing process are more likely than their intact counterparts to behave in ways suggesting confusion regarding their gender identity (Hetherington, Cox, & Cox, 1982). Conversely, young and late adolescent girls in divorcing families are more likely to be sexually active than their intact counterparts (Booth, Brinkerhoff, & White, 1984).[51] In addition, there is some evidence that college students whose parents have divorced report more problems than their nondivorced counterparts with intimacy, dating, and the like (Everett, 1993; Gabardi & Rosen, 1991, 1992; Nelson, Allison, & Sundre, 1992). One consequence is that students from divorced families, especially girls, are less likely to expect to enter traditional marriages (Marlar & Jacobs, 1992).

5. *Prosocial Skills.* Weiss (1979c) has argued that the demands of the divorcing process force children to "grow up" faster than they would otherwise do, especially as regards prosocial skills, that is, skills associated with interpersonal interaction (e.g., communication, empathy, social competence). Some support for this thesis comes from the longitudinal research of Block, Block, and Morrison (1981) and Hetherington (1989), but only for girls.

6. *Use of Mental Health Services.* Finally, there is some evidence that children from divorcing as opposed to intact homes are more likely to make use of psychiatric and other mental health services (Dawson, 1991).[52] On the basis of their review, Bloom et al. (1978) suggest that between 10% and 20% of children experiencing their parents' divorce show such severe disturbance as to require psychiatric care. Others have noted related declines in children's health-related behaviors (Saucier & Ambert, 1983).

Thus, a high proportion of children experiencing their parents' divorce display a range of consequences, some positive, most negative, although even over the short term children displaying negative effects show steady improvement (Emery, 1988).[53] Note, however, that these data are not always consistent and furthermore that variations appear to apply in regard to the age and gender of the children in question. For example, Emery (1988) stresses that although serious problems are overrepresented among children of divorce, children of divorce are *not* overrepresented among children with serious problems. Lowery and Settle (1985), based on their review, argue that children of divorce may experience fewer problems than children in intact but unhappy and conflictual families (see Kinard & Reinherz, 1984). Abelsohn and Saayman (1991) note the contradictory character of the research regarding adolescents. These and related considerations led Emery (1988) to conclude that family process mechanisms are likely to be more reliable predictors of child consequences than (divorced) family status per se. We concur and so turn next to data concerning these mechanisms.

Family Process Mechanisms. Our reading of these data suggest that the consequences for children of divorce are likely conditional, based on covariation among at least four factors: child gender, child age, parent-child relations, and social class.

Child Gender. Over the short term there are striking differences in the typical responses of boys and girls to their parents' divorce. As noted above, although children of divorce are likely to show evidence of distress, it is more acute for preadolescent boys than girls (Plunkett, Schaefer, Kalter, Okla, & Schreier, 1986),[54] especially with regard to "undercontrolled" or aggressive behavior (Emery, Hetherington, & DiLalla, 1984; Wallerstein & Blakeslee, 1989). However, when divorce occurs in adolescence, girls tend to be more acutely affected than boys (Frost & Pakiz, 1990). Although some contradictory evidence has been reported,[55] even more important is the lack of consensus as to why these gender differences exist at all. Whitehead (1979), for example, speculates that it relates to the way boys and girls are socialized in Western society, with boys tending to "act out" and girls tending to withdraw. Others (Santrock & Warshak, 1979; Wallerstein & Blakeslee, 1989) argue that it may relate to variation in gender-based developmental needs, with boys in maternal sole custody homes deprived of a critical role model (their fathers) in ways that girls are not and thus understandably more acutely distressed. Still others argue in favor of particular family dynamics (see Abelsohn & Saayman, 1991). Block et al. (1986), for example, using longitudinal data, compared the "undercontrolled" behavior of boys in intact and to-be-divorced families. The results indicated that compared to boys in intact homes, those in to-be-divorced families displayed higher rates of "undercontrolled" behavior. That is, in these divorced families, dysfunction manifested in a child acting out predated the divorcing process.[56] Finally, other possibilities include gender-based differences in social competence, locus of control (Ankenbrandt, 1986; Krantz, Clark, Pruyn, & Usher, 1985; Kurdek & Berg, 1983), and temperament (Hetherington, 1989).

Child Age. As for child age, it too has been associated with variations in child behavior. Much of the available data indicates that younger children are more vulnerable to adverse consequences than their older counterparts (Kalter, Kloner, Schreiser, & Okla, 1989; Kalter, Reimer, Brickman, & Chen, 1985).[57] As Emery (1988) notes, however, these findings are based on local samples using research designs that confound age at divorce, current age, and duration since the divorce. Taking such objections into account, Allison and Furstenberg (1989) used national data to confirm the inverse relationship between age and consequences, but only as a function of duration since the divorce: Immediately following the separation differences between younger and older children were marked, but lessened through time (see also Zaslow, 1988, 1989). They also argue that the evidence that young children are necessarily the most adversely affected by their parents' divorce is neither "strong nor consistent."

Again, the basis for the relationship between age and consequences is not altogether clear. Hetherington, Cox, and Cox (1985) discuss the relationship between age, vulnerability, and change-related stress, because divorcing as opposed to intact families experience significantly more major life changes over a comparatively short time (see also Stolberg, Complair, Currier, & Wells, 1987). Kurdek (1981) speculates and Grynch and Fincham (1990) demonstrate that it may be because young children are more likely than their adolescent counterparts to explain their parents' divorce in terms of their own conduct (i.e., their "badness"); those who blame other family members for the events they are being forced to experience may, in consequence, be less vulnerable to harm (Young, 1983). Weiss (1979b) notes that older children are typically able to withstand higher levels of parental deprivation without becoming distressed, whereas Wallerstein and Kelly (1976) observe that older children are not only less dependent on parental nurturance and protection, but more able to avoid becoming caught up in parental problems. Finkel (1974, 1975), speaking about college students, argues that older children are more able to use cognitive reevaluation to convert traumatic events (such as might accompany divorce) into growth potentiating experiences. Still other explanations might be invoked: a constellation of personality attributes (such as autonomy, intelligence, flexibility, and high self-esteem) appears to allow some children to be especially resilient in the face of serious stress associated with a range of life events and circumstances, including divorce (Garmezy, 1981)[58]; alternately, recent evidence that the relationship between each child and each parent is unique (Dunn & Plomin, 1991) suggests that different outcomes reflect differences in parent-child relations.

Parent-Child Relationships. Turning next to parent-child relationships, for young children these relations constitute the primary influence that shapes who they are and who they think themselves to be; even with older children, with their widening experience of the world, parental influence diminishes only gradually (Newson & Newson, 1976). Available evidence affirms this conclusion in families undergoing separation and divorce. In reviewing these data, however, it is useful to distinguish between (a) direct, (b) indirect, and (c) timing effects on children's adjustment.

1. *Direct Effects.* Direct effects refer to the consequences of the face-to-face relationships between parents and children. With respect to divorcing families, the traditional interpretation has been that child adjustment is tied to his or her relationship with *both* parents (Kelly, 1982; Kurdek & Blisk, 1983; Rosen, 1977, 1979). Recently, Furstenberg and Cherlin (1991) have argued that the child's relationship with the custodial parent (typically the mother) is paramount; the relationship with the noncustodial parent (typically the father) is less important. We suspect that these apparently contradictory views are probably complementary, child adjustment being conditional on a range of interacting processes, four in particular: (a) the reciprocal adjustment of the custodial parent and the child(ren) living with her or him, (b) the quality of the relationship between the custodial parent and the children, (c) gender congruence between the custodial parent and the children, and (d) the degree of involvement of the noncustodial parent.

As to reciprocal adjustment, the evidence indicates that the better the mother has adjusted to the divorcing process (Kurdek & Blisk, 1983)[59], the better the relationship between her and her child(ren) (Berman & Turk, 1981)[60] and the better the latter's adjustment (Copeland, 1985).[61] In part, the latter may relate to the fact that mother's adjustment models for her children how to cope with life crises and troubled interpersonal relationships (Kaslow & Hyatt, 1981). In addition, maternal adjustment may differentially affect child adjustment as a function of child gender. Kalter et al. (1989), for example, found that mother's *social* adjustment was positively related to the adjustment of sons whereas mother's *psychological* adjustment was positively related to the adjustment of daughters.

However, whereas it was once thought that the direction of influence is necessarily from parent to child, it is now recognized that the relationship is a reciprocal one, with children influencing parents (Ambert, 1992). In that light, it is hardly surprising that positive child adjustment also enhances and supports maternal adjustment (Hetherington et al., 1978).[62] This said, the single best predictor of short-term maternal adjustment remains her baseline adjustment at the point of separation or divorce (Coysh et al., 1989).

Although this reciprocal association between parent and child adjustment is an important one, it obviously begs the question of the basis or bases of either parent or child adjustment per se; the adjustment of the other in the relationship can only be part of the story. Variables affecting the adjustment of custodial parents have been examined above. One of the missing variables with regard to child adjustment is the quality of the relationship between custodial parent and children, which appears to turn on several dimensions.

One of these, noted previously, is the degree of "parental abdication" (Isaacs, Montalvo, & Abelson, 1986) or "diminished parenting" (Wallerstein, 1988b; Wallerstein & Kelly, 1980; see Teleki, 1983).[63] Under the intense stress of the divorcing process, a substantial proportion of previously adequate parents become increasingly insensitive to the children's needs (Appel, 1985) or completely abandon their parenting responsibilities (Isaacs et al., 1986), with devastating consequences for child adjustment. For example, such parents may become blind to child misconduct, fail to keep regular hours for bedtime or meals, ignore previous standards of cleanliness or dress, become oblivious to holidays or other family rituals, no longer be available to help with school-work, and so forth.

Less blatant but equally consequential for child adjustment is the evolution of dysfunctional patterns of parent-child interaction,[64] either directly related to the divorcing process (Wallerstein & Blakeslee, 1989) or predating that process but significantly exacerbated by it (Isaacs et al., 1986; Johnston & Campbell, 1988). For example, parents may become dependent on their children for support, ask their opinion in romantic and sexual matters, provide wildly oscillating levels of emotional support, compete for attention and affection with their former spouse, encourage the children to "spy" on their former spouse, consistently belittle the former spouse to the children, encourage them to say bad things about the former spouse in court, and so on. Conversely, an "authoritative" parenting style—one characterized by warmth, clear rules of conduct, and extensive verbal exchanges—is associated with enhanced child social competence and maturity (Santrock & Warshak, 1979; Stolberg et al., 1987). Similarly, to the extent that the absence of the noncustodial parent creates vacant role positions in the family (Schwebel, Fine, Morcland, & Prindle, 1988), the number, gender, and age of the children affect the likelihood that a given child will have the opportunity to fill those roles (McPhee, 1985; Peterson, Leigh, & Day, 1984; Vess, Moreland, & Schwebel, 1985) and, in doing so, gain feelings of mastery and privilege (see Vess, Schwebel, & Moreland, 1983).

Recently, Abelsohn and Saayman (1991) have presented evidence that shows that in divorcing families with adolescents, both abdication and interactional dysfunction are significantly more common among divorcing families who seek clinical help as opposed to those who do not. They find these data consistent with an ecosystemic perspective that conceptualizes individual adjustment as a function of family organization. In passing, they also note a positive effect of divorce, namely, that adolescent exposure to parental distress appears associated with increased adolescent social competence.

As to the latter finding, this response may vary by gender, a matter to which these authors do not refer. Other researchers, however, have consistently reported a strong association between child adjustment and parent-child gender congruence. Same-sexed pairs (i.e., mothers and daughters, fathers and sons) fare better than their opposite-sex counterparts (i.e., mothers and sons, fathers and daughters; Camara &

Resnick, 1987).[65,66] The basis of this association remains open to debate. It may, for example, be reactive, as mothers try to cope with the extreme distress of sons (noted above). It may predate the divorcing process, reflecting ongoing family dysfunction. It may reflect a mismatch between developmental needs (of sons for male role models) and custodial arrangements (maternal sole custody) and so on.[67]

Finally, evidence about the relations between noncustodial fathers and their children is mixed. We have alluded to the fact that a large proportion of noncustodial parents (most of them fathers) abandon their children. The ensuing debate turns on the issue of visitation frequency versus relationship quality.

On the one hand, most authorities suggest that child adjustment is directly related to visitation frequency: More frequent contact is associated with improved child adjustment (Hess & Camara, 1979; Hetherington, 1979).[68] For example, Bisnaire et al. (1990) found that high paternal contact was positively associated with child behavioral adjustment, peer relations, and school performance, especially among boys. Others report a positive association but qualified by child age and gender as well as degree of father-child closeness and level of coparental conflict (Healy, Malley, & Stewart, 1990; Thomas & Forehand, 1993). However, these correlations between paternal visitation and child adjustment tend to be low and only somewhat higher when such visits receive maternal support and approval (Guidubaldi & Perry, 1985).[69] Others disagree (Furstenberg & Cherlin, 1991; Furstenberg, Morgan, & Allison, 1987), arguing that evidence of an association between child adjustment and the closeness of the noncustodial parent is weak and inconsistent. For example, several studies report no relationship between paternal visitation frequency and child adjustment (Furstenberg et al., 1987; Furstenberg & Nord, 1985; Kalter et al., 1989; Kline et al., 1989).

On the other hand, children's response to parental disengagement appears to turn on the quality of the preseparation father-child relationship. If the relationship was previously poor, loss of contact may be greeted with relief (Hetherington et al., 1979). If it was good, its loss may produce intense distress (Wallerstein & Kelly, 1980). Similarly, among fathers who maintain contact with their children, Thomas and Forehand (1993) found that poor quality relations increased the likelihood of child conduct problems whereas good quality relations were associated with reduced child anxiety and withdrawal problems. Moreover, Hetherington, Cox, and Cox (1982) caution that the separation process may produce an increased interest in parenting among fathers who were previously uninvolved. Furthermore, relations between fathers and their children may vary with child age. Evidence shows that adolescents are especially vulnerable to loyalty conflicts, with the relationship between fathers and daughters especially at risk (Cooney, Smyer, Hagestad, & Klock, 1986): Daughters are especially likely to be angry with their fathers for abandoning them, even if their fathers did not initiate the separation (Ahrons & Rodgers, 1987). The argument cannot be resolved without additional data, some of which will be reviewed in later subsections.

2. *Indirect Effects.* We turn next to indirect effects, primarily the effect of coparental interaction on parent-child relations, but also to the effect of other people who have a relationship with the children. The thrust of these data is consistent with an ecosystemic perspective, that is, to understand the effect of the divorcing process on children requires attention to all the persons and relationships that touch on them directly or indirectly.

A case in point concerns the effect of coparental relations on child adjustment. Much evidence indicates an inverse relationship between coparental conflict and child adjustment: The more intense, bitter, and prolonged the conflict between former spouses, the more adverse the consequences for child adjustment (Booth et al., 1984; Christopoulos, Cohn, Shaw, Joyce, Kraft, & Emery, 1987).[70, 71]

However, these data are problematic in two ways. First, the correlations between conflict and child adjustment are low, suggesting to Kelly (1993) that conflict does not produce a consistent outcome in children. Kalter et al. (1989), for example, found that maternal adjustment was a better predictor of child adjustment than conflict. Conversely, Camara and Resnick (1989) found that the impact of conflict varied as a function of the conflict resolution strategy in use, with "verbal attack" versus "compromise" having different effects on young children. Moreover, these data are complicated by temporal effects as coparental conflict tends in general to diminish gradually through time (Kelly, 1991; Maccoby, Depner, & Mnookin, 1990).

Second, data linking conflict with child adjustment leave unclear the basis or bases of the effect, that is, why should coparental conflict affect children as it does. Kelly (1993), following Buchanan, Maccoby, and Dornbusch (1991), suggests that the effect may vary as a function of the extent to which conflict is directly expressed with and through the children. Thus, adverse adjustment is far more likely in high-conflict divorcing families among children who feel caught in the middle as opposed to those who do not feel caught in this way. Why in a given family one sibling is likely to get "caught" but another is not is far from clear, although speculative explanations abound (as seen above for child gender and age differences). In a similar vein, high coparental conflict may undermine or completely disrupt the relationship between the noncustodial parent (typically the father) and the children (Hodges, in press).[72] In cases where paternal involvement in child rearing was high before the divorce, such disruption may have important negative consequences for the adjustment of both fathers (Kruk, 1992) and children (Braver, Wolchik, Sandler, Forgas, & Zvetina, 1991).[73]

Moreover, related data speak to the compensatory effect of positive relationship(s) in the lives of children to offset other negative influences. For example, a friendly coparental relationship, by providing an important source of maternal support, acts to positively influence child adjustment and self-esteem (Ambert, 1988a).[74] Similarly, a supportive relationship between one parent and the children will help buffer them from the effects of a negative relationship between the children and the other parent (Hetherington et al., 1979). Recent evidence, however, suggests that mothers and fathers may be unequal in this regard. Although a good relationship between the children and their noncustodial mother will protect them from the effects of a poor relationship with their custodial father, a good relationship with their noncustodial father will only provide partial protection from a poor relationship with their custodial mother (Camara & Resnick, 1988).

Furthermore, a positive relationship between the children and other familial or nonfamilial adults appears able to exert this compensatory effect (Isaacs & Leon, 1986).[75] Children evolve a hierarchy of attachment figures (Ainsworth, 1979; Lamb, 1977a, 1977b) such that relations with other relatives (uncles, aunts, grandparents) and nonrelated adults (teachers, neighbors) may stand in the place of the children's absent or inadequate parents, thus enhancing the children's post-divorce adjustment and social competence (Guidubaldi, Cleminshaw, Perry, & McLaughlin, 1983).[76]

3. *Timing Effects.* The preponderance of cross-sectional studies in this literature make it easy to forget that the divorcing process unfolds through time and even 2 or 3 years is a long time in the life of children. In this context, the evidence for timing effects varies as a function of the divorcing family's clinical status.

Ambert (1984), for example, followed up samples of upper-, middle-, and lower-class custodial mothers and fathers 2 years after initial testing. She found that parental satisfaction had risen significantly over time, especially among lower-class custodial mothers, which in some cases reflected the fact that the most troublesome child had gone to live with the other parent.

Hetherington (1987, 1989) tracked a sample of nonclinical families over 6 years. Evidence that custodial mothers dealt more harshly with their sons than their daughters was marked by the end of postseparation year 1. By the end of year 2, the magnitude of these differences had diminished considerably and had vanished completely by the end of year 6.

In contrast, Isaacs et al. (1986) compared clinical and nonclinical divorcing families over 3 years. They addressed the timing effects issue in several ways, reporting evidence that the way in which the first 12 months was handled was critical for child adjustment by the end of year 3. For example, in regard to visiting by the noncustodial parent, their data show that visitation consistency or scheduling was more salient than visitation frequency. But this was only so over time: Only minor differences in child adjustment by the end of year 1 turned into very large differences by the end of year 3. Related data speak to the adverse impact of coparental conflict on child adjustment. For their sample of children, this association was conditional on shifting from scheduled to unscheduled visiting by the noncustodial parent. Scheduled visiting buffered the children against coparental hostility, with adverse effects by the end of year 1 having disappeared entirely by the end of year 3. Indeed, scheduled visiting by noncustodial fathers was the single best predictor of child social competence by the end of year

3. Finally, although children in nonclinical families were much better adjusted than their clinical counterparts at the end of year 1, these differences had virtually disappeared by the end of year 3. However, this phenomenon was not uniformly true: Children who were seriously disturbed at the end of year 1 were likely to continue to be disturbed at the end of year 3. Thus, across several dimensions, tracking divorcing families through time suggests that what appear as sharp differences in cross-section turn into complex, conditional relationships when viewed longitudinally. Coping strategies that appeared to have little effect in year 1 turned out to be highly consequential by year 3, with fathers whose involvement with their children remained consistent especially noteworthy in this regard. And clinical status in year 1 appeared salient in some respects but not others.

Social Class. Voluminous evidence shows that socioeconomic status (SES), or social class, profoundly shapes family life (Chalfant, 1985). Compared to their middle- and upper-class counterparts, working- and lower-class parents are more likely to rely on punitive and instrumental disciplinary methods (Colon, 1980; Gecas, 1979), whereas for children, working- and lower-class life involves a significantly increased risk of poor health, psychiatric disorders, and death (Blum, Boyle, & Offord, 1988; Offord & Boyle, 1987; Williams & Kornblum, 1985).

That being so, it seems reasonable to expect that variation in social class would be implicated in the consequences of the divorcing process, especially for children. As seen above, various researchers have duly noted social class as a demographic correlate of divorce. Curiously, however, the same researchers have only rarely used social class as an explanatory or design variable, or both (Ambert, 1984, 1989), despite early suggestions that such usage would be fruitful (Herzog & Sudia, 1973). Accordingly, Ambert (1985, p. 22) has argued that, "studies on divorce which present findings based on one SES group, or even without considering SES, may be seriously limited."

The result is that evidence of the relationship between social class and child adjustment following marital separation is both limited and inconsistent. For example, Ambert (1984, 1985), using longitudinal data, compared the behavior of children in mother- versus father-custody families. Like other studies cited above, this showed that mothers had substantially more difficulty than fathers dealing with their children, especially boys. On further analysis, however, Ambert concluded that " 'net' longitudinal improvements of children's behavior and of parental satisfaction . . . occurred strictly in families that enjoyed a decent standard of living."[77] In contrast, Desimone-Luis, O'Mahoney, and Hunt (1979) found that income decline was more closely related to child adjustment than income level per se. Similar findings have been noted by others.[78] In either case, given that inadequate income is an obvious source of stress, evidence of a direct relationship between stress and child adjustment is relevant here. These data show that overwhelming stress adversely effects child adjustment (Hetherington et al., 1985; Raphe & Arthur, 1978; Stolberg et al., 1987), whereas moderate stress promotes growth and mastery (Hetherington, 1989), especially if stressful experiences are spread over time as opposed to being bunched together (Hetherington, 1989).

These data, scant as they are, nevertheless support two conclusions: first, that the hardship associated with working- and lower-class status (whether it involves a change in class standing or not) can only make a painful transition more difficult, with adverse consequences for child adjustment highly likely; second, that various inconsistencies noted in previous sections may at least in part be artifacts of the failure of researchers to attend to systematic variations on the basis of social class.

More generally then, most children, like most adults, respond to the divorcing process with acute distress and disruption. Over the following 2 or 3 years, most children, like most adults, will have adjusted successfully; that is, their distress will have dissipated or disappeared and their daily lives will have resumed their routine form. However, what is true of most children is not true for some. What determines the short-term consequences, then, is conditional on a range of factors: *if* marital and parent-child relations before the separation were not manifestly dysfunctional; *if* the parent with whom they live is not manifestly dysfunctional; *if* that parent adjusts well and *if* he or she continues to provide consistent supportive care; *if* material resources continue to be available adequately and *if* unavoidable lifestyle changes are not too drastic; *if* coparental relations are cordial or at least not unduly conflictual; *if* coparental conflict is not exacerbated by a court battle; *if* the noncustodial parent is not manifestly dysfunctional;

if that parent is consistent in contributing to the children's financial support and maintains involvement with the children on a consistent and predictable basis, even if this means less frequent visits; and *if* the children have access to relations with supportive adults other than their parents. As with adults, for many children all of these conditions will not be met, either immediately following the separation, for some months, or throughout the next 2 or 3 years. As a result, for a minority of children (whose proportion is unknown or variable across a range of problems) the short-term consequences of the divorcing process leave them vulnerable to long-term harm. It is to this final phase of the divorcing process that we turn.

From the perspective of the mediation practitioner, five aspects of this phase stand out. The first and most pressing concerns harm. One of the critical bases for any mediated agreement is that the terms be designed to ensure the least possible harm to the children. The data reviewed above make absolutely clear that the potential for the divorcing process to be destructive of children is high. Mediation practitioners already know this, in short, what is at stake in helping conflicted couples reach agreement. These data suggest that it is equally important that divorcing couples also be fully aware of the potential consequences of their action or inaction.

Second, we have repeatedly seen evidence of gender differences in children's responses to the divorcing process. This assessment issue is important and suggests the need to inquire in some detail into the identity of members of the family and the quality of the relations among them. In turn, the quality of those relations raises a third issue, namely, that the terms of any agreement made will continue to affect family relations for some years to come. As we have seen, temporal effects can be important, with even apparently minor effects in the present having very significant effects 2 or 3 years later. That temporal perspective should be one of the considerations in fashioning a mediated agreement, both in the mind of the practitioner and in the minds of the spouses in conflict.

A fourth issue concerns the potential importance of the regular (if not necessarily frequent) involvement with the children of the noncustodial parent, typically, the father. This issue is as contentious in the literature as it is for many custodial parents. Some of the latter will object that fathers who have shown little interest in parenting before the divorce have a weak case when claiming such an interest after divorce. Such emotional and political jockeying aside, the preponderance of the evidence reviewed above suggests that paternal involvement, providing it is genuine and consistent, can positively affect later child adjustment and development. This information should be available to clients and should bias mediators in favor of liberal access or shared parenting (see chapters 6 and 7).

Finally, these data call attention to the complexity of the ecological field and thus the various people who contribute directly or indirectly to the postdivorce adjustment of children. We have noted how this complexity bears on who should participate in practice sessions. However, it also speaks to the options available in deriving a mediated agreement. Alone, an inadequate parent may represent a danger to children. The help of another family member, a friend, or a friendly neighbor may significantly mitigate that negative effect and so may need to be acknowledged in a mediated agreement.

PHASE 5: LONG-TERM CONSEQUENCES

In contrast to "disaster" models of the divorcing process, recent efforts conceptualize it as a "normative transition" (Ahrons, 1983a), much like marriage, parenthood, or paid employment. As such, it is seen as a stressful but commonplace event which, although it necessarily changes the life course of those involved, nevertheless represents an experience that is relatively quickly transformed into faded memory.

Although appealing, such a view is predicated more on a series of assumptions than on empirical data. Researchers have sought to close this gap in the divorce literature using several different methods.[79, 80] The thrust of these studies is that for a varying but substantial proportion of former spouses and their children, divorce continues to have significant consequences for a much longer duration than was previously thought. Furthermore, such consequences distribute on a continuum of life chances, with four groups or positions distinguished. For one group, divorce is nothing less than a transformational experience; it induces significant growth and opens up a range of positive possibilities that would otherwise not have been available. For another group, divorce is the basis for improved subjective well-being by providing the possibility of moving from an unsatisfactory marriage to a new, stable, and rewarding relationship. In other respects, however, for this group, not much else has changed and dramatic changes in life chances do *not* occur. For a third group, on balance divorce leaves them slightly worse off than before, with an increased likelihood of repeating the divorcing process in a subsequent marriage. For this group, divorce somewhat restricts life chances, and thus may be tinged with regret and perhaps nostalgia for what might have been had the divorce never occurred. For the last group, divorce is an unmitigated disaster from which they appear not to recover, even decades later. Bitter and resentful, this group associates divorce with significantly reduced life chances but with an increased likelihood of multiple divorces and thus of potential unrealized or seriously distorted.

In reviewing the data that depicts this continuum of divorce effects, we again distinguish between adults and children, although as is apparent, the lives of both are inevitably intertwined.

Adults

For the formerly married, the long-term consequences of divorce turn on two issues: (a) whether they have remarried, and, if they have, (b) whether that relationship remains intact or ends in divorce.

Remarriage. The increasing acceptability of cohabitation (Cox, 1993; Stout, 1991) has meant that over the past 20 years the rate of remarriage among divorced spouses has been slowly but steadily declining (Uhlenberg, Cooney, & Boyd, 1990). Nevertheless, the majority of divorced spouses (about 75%) eventually remarry, typically within 5 years (Fisher, 1992).[81] However, although true, this statement is more obfuscating than enlightening, for the likelihood of remarriage is critically related to at least four variables: age, social class, family type (Glick & Lin, 1987), and gender.[82, 83]

First, remarriage is inversely related to age. For example, census data show that of all divorced women in the United States in 1985, 48% remarried in their 20s, 33% in their 30s, 11% in their 40s, and only 3% in their 50s (Wallerstein & Blakeslee, 1989). Similarly, of the middle-aged women in Morgan's (1991) sample, only 29% remarried during the course of her 15-year study.

Here age appears as a surrogate or stand-in for the operational variables of motivation and opportunity. Women (and men) whose first marriage lasted only a short time, who are therefore young and who may want more children,[84] may look forward eagerly to a second intimate relationship. For many young women, then, divorce offers freedom and new opportunity. Such is frequently not the case among women whose divorce signals the end of a long-standing marriage. For these women (and men), whose children are grown and gone, and who had expected a quiet retirement only to be forced into the labor market, marriage is now regarded with bitterness. Indeed, Wallerstein and Blakeslee (1989, p. 138) note that many such women say they feel "dead inside." Thus divorced partners vary in their desire to remarry.

Even among those who want to remarry, however, age is also related to differential opportunity (Veevers, 1991). Ours is a youth-oriented society that often equates age with attractiveness and desirability. Consequently, women (and men) who divorce while still in their 20s have access to a broad range of eligible others as potential spouses. Thus, young divorced spouses who are motivated to remarry have ample opportunity to do so. However, this situation becomes increasingly less so with age, additionally complicated by gender inequality, both in status and life span. Older men can substitute status for youth and thus remain attractive to younger women. Not so for older women, whose age denotes a loss of attractiveness. They are thus unable to attract younger men, although they are at an age when the number of men older than themselves is dwindling rapidly. Older divorced spouses, then, have fewer opportunities to meet eligible others, although less so for men than women.

This linkage between age, attractiveness, and opportunity is not just driven by age. It is also related to social class, both in regard to access and mobility (Ambert, 1983; Gerstel, 1988). Material and other resources (such as education, occupational skills, and material assets)[85] are directly related both to attractiveness and access to eligible others. To get out of the house and meet the eligible others whom one desires requires resources (for child care, transportation, clothes, etc.) which, in turn, help determine attractiveness in social intercourse (Bumpass, Sweet, & Castro-Martin, 1990). Women's typical loss of financial resources following divorce, discussed above, thus operates differentially. Women who, despite a relatively major loss in income, retain their upper- or middle-class status have a clear advantage in meeting eligible others over their working- and lower-class counterparts whose financial losses, although relatively modest, drive them down in class standing, perhaps even into poverty.

Indeed, social mobility, the desire to move up in class standing, is another reason to seek remarriage. Here the data are unclear, with some researchers indicating that remarriage typically accomplishes this end (Fethke, 1989)[86] and others indicating that it typically does not (Morgan, 1991). Following Morgan (1991), the solution to this apparent contradiction may be whether divorce results in a loss of class standing. Marriage overwhelmingly occurs between persons within the same social class (Adams, 1979). Divorced spouses able to retain their class standing are thus likely to interact with eligible others within that class. For them, remarriage is likely to restore income lost through divorce. This same marital dynamic, however, also applies to those for whom divorce means a gain or loss in class standing. An increase in standing, more typical of men than women, will operate such that remarriage is likely to stabilize or even increase upward mobility. A loss in standing, more typical of women than men, will operate such that remarriage is likely to stabilize or even increase downward mobility.

To complicate matters, there is good reason to think that the likelihood of remarriage is related to family type. Following Ambert (1989), recall that relations between former spouses vary from friendly to angry to indifferent. To our knowledge, the relationship between such variation and remarriage has not been explored empirically. Nevertheless, given what we know of the significant effect of such relations (see above), it seems reasonable to expect that such a relationship should exist. For example, compared to those with children, divorced couples who were childless were much more likely to be indifferent to each other. Couples in this category will thus have no effect whatever on the likelihood that either spouse will remarry. In contrast, couples who relate as friends accelerate the postdivorce adjustment of both spouses and thus should increase the likelihood of remarriage, at least as regards spousal motivation. Couples who relate on the basis of anger slow their mutual adjustment, while sustaining spousal preoccupation with the previous relationship. Recall too that women seem less able than men to shrug off the damaging effects of hostile relations, whereas Wallerstein and Blakeslee (1989) note being surprised by the much greater psychological continuity (i.e., the lack of change) before and after divorce among men compared to women. In turn, we would expect these various processes to diminish both motivation and opportunity to remarry.

Finally, it will now be apparent that all of these processes—motivation, attractiveness, opportunity, access, status, mobility, and coparental relations—vary systematically by gender, typically favoring men over women. In the United States, of all divorced spouses, 80% of the men and less than 70% of the women eventually remarry (Levitan, Belous, & Gallo, 1988; Norton & Moorman, 1987). In Canada, the same applies to 76% of the men and 64% of the women (Adams & Nagnur, 1989).[87] The long-term results are twofold.

First, for many of those who permanently eschew marriage or who want to remarry but are unable to find a suitable partner, divorce yields either a restriction of life chances or a full-fledged disaster. Among women, it typically means a permanent loss of income compared to their intact counterparts (Duncan & Hoffman, 1985; National Institute for Child Support Enforcement, 1986). For both men and women, typically older, it results in feelings of bitterness, futility, injustice, and loneliness (Wallerstein & Blakeslee, 1989). Loneliness is especially prominent among older men who, in parting from their wives, have also lost the social circle of others that she alone sustained (see Rubin, 1985).

Finally, for those who find a suitable partner and remarry, gender differences remain. Compared to men, women are less likely to remarry and, among those who do, will typically involve a longer elapsed time between divorce and remarriage.

Remarriage Stability. For divorced spouses, remarriage simultaneously represents getting past the pain of the divorce and a second chance at a new and better life (Hetherington, 1989). However, such hopes are often dashed; remarriages are even less stable than first marriages, with 55% ending in divorce (Furstenberg & Spanier, 1984).[88, 89] This instability appears to be a function of three variables: structural complexity, marital history, and gender.[90]

Remarriage creates what have variously been called "binuclear" (Ahrons & Rodgers, 1987) or "linked" (Jacobson, 1987) family systems (see Whiteside, 1989) or marital "chains" and "networks" (Ambert, 1989). In Ambert's terminology, a network involves at least one relationship apart from the formerly married pair (say, between a former spouse and her former spouse's new spouse) and a chain involves no such relationship. In her study of 49 chains, 71% constituted a network, with 40% of these characterized as "positive." In nearly all cases (95%), networks arose out of interaction pertaining to one or more children of the previous marital relationship. Related data have recently been reported by Hobart (1988, 1991; Hobart & Brown, 1989). Thus divorce tends to give rise to family systems that are both structurally and relationally more complex than the nuclear systems from which they arose and less stable in consequence (see Visher & Visher, 1987).

If structural complexity is one reason for the instability of such systems, another appears to be the marital history of the respective partners. Remarriage typically involves spouses who have both been previously divorced (Leslie & Korman, 1985). However, the risk of divorce increases when remarriage involves pairing a divorced husband with a never-married wife (Aquirre & Parr, 1982).

That risk increases still more when one or both of the remarried partners has been multiply divorced (Dickinson & Leming, 1990). For example, Ambert (1989) compared spouses who had been divorced once or two or more times. She found that compared to the former, the latter had a less stable family background, a less stable life course, and fewer close social ties; were less likely to fulfill a parental role following divorce; and had a more erratic employment history.

Finally, men and women respond to remarriage differently. Coysh et al. (1989), for example, found that, compared to men, women were less likely to have the hurt of the divorce undone by involvement in a new romantic relationship. Similarly, gender differences emerge in regard to life satisfaction, although the findings are mixed. Furstenberg and Spanier (1985), for example, noted that 3 or 4 years after their divorce most spouses reported an improved sense of well-being, whether or not they had remarried. Jacobs (1982) found that 10 years after a divorce women were more likely than men to report improved life satisfaction coupled with a sense of growth. Wallerstein and Blakeslee (1989, pp. 30, 40), to their surprise, found that 15 years after divorce the dominant pattern involved "winners and losers," in which one spouse was typically much happier than the former partner, the satisfied spouse having entered into a stable remarriage while the dissatisfied spouse had never remarried or had impulsively remarried and then redivorced, in some cases several times.

Should these data prove representative of nonclinical families, they suggest that 10 to 15 years after divorce spouses will be distributed on a continuum, with roughly half no better and no worse off than before their divorce, 25% much worse off than before, and 25% much better off. On balance, divorce appears to favor men over women, although there are clearly winners and losers among both.

In contrast, among clinical families, the long-term consequences of divorce appear less optimistic. Johnston and Campbell (1988, pp. 254-255), for example, found that almost 5 years after divorce, relations among 80% of the couples in their sample remained dysfunctional to some extent and "almost two-fifths of the families showed no obvious improvement. In fact, 15 percent of the total sample had actually deteriorated over the follow-up period," with "ominous" implications for long-term child development, to which we turn next.

For the mediation practitioner, these data raise two issues worthy of note. The first is simply a warning that what they help conflicted couples craft as an agreement may have long-term consequences. It is the responsibility of the mediator to do his or her utmost to ensure that those consequences are more likely to be positive than negative. Second, these data once again call our attention to the fact that women are more likely than men to be disadvantaged by the divorcing process. Clearly, this will not be true in every case. Nevertheless, it highlights the importance of approaching practice vigilant for signs of inequality between the former partners (see chapter 4).

Children

Over the long term, the "children" in question vary widely in age, from the late teens and early 20s (some attending college or university) up to the early 40s. In reviewing data about these "children" of divorce, we again distinguish between consequences and family process mechanisms. Before proceeding, however, we should note that researchers' estimates of the incidence of particular deficits vary.

Rather than get caught up in the numbers, our use of the phrases "a minority" and "a substantial minority" refer to 15% to 25% and 26% to 40%, respectively.

Consequences. To organize the data regarding the long-term consequences of divorce among the "children," we will again rely on Emery's (1988) six-variable taxonomy.

1. *External Problems.* Data indicate that compared to their intact counterparts, children of divorce exhibit more behavior problems, especially undercontrolled behaviors (such as aggression, hostility, and noncompliance) among males (Allison & Furstenberg, 1989).[91] In addition, Wallerstein and Blakeslee (1989) found that a substantial minority of the boys and a minority of the girls (all 19 to 23 years of age) developed a history of delinquent behavior, whereas a minority of both sexes abused alcohol, behavior that they had not witnessed among their parents.

2. *Internal Problems.* Data about internal problems are consistent in direction but inconsistent in detail (see Ganong & Coleman, 1984). For example, several researchers report that children of divorce tend to be less well adjusted than their intact counterparts (Amato & Keith, 1991; Southward & Schwarz, 1987). This includes evidence of increased depression, anxiety, hostility, suicidal ideation, and self-blame (Adams, Lohrenz, & Harper, 1973; Buchanan, Maccoby, & Dornbusch, 1991, 1992)[92] coupled with reduced self-esteem and ego identification (Allison & Furstenberg, 1989; Grossman, Shea, & Adams, 1980).

However, other researchers either report no such differences or replicate the findings but in a qualified way. Amato (1989), for example, found no difference between children from intact as opposed to divorced families in regard to self-esteem, but the latter did exhibit a much lower sense of power and control, a function, the author suggests, of their lower educational attainment (see #3 below). In contrast, Wallerstein and Blakeslee (1989) suggest that the psychological consequences of the divorcing process vary by age (at the time of the divorce) and gender. For example, over the long term, older as opposed to younger children were more likely to adjust poorly (35% versus 68%), including having a variety of psychological problems. A minority of children (especially girls) were preoccupied by a fear of abandonment and were characterized by low self-esteem and inhibition of anger. In particular, such girls showed a delayed reaction to the divorcing process in the form of deep depression, whereas a substantial minority of boys was emotionally inhibited and tended to deny their feelings. In addition, recent evidence indicates that compared to their intact counterparts, children of divorce are much more likely to see divorce as an acceptable solution to marital problems (Amato & Booth, 1991).

3. *Intellectual and Academic Functioning.* There is good agreement in the literature that the educational attainment of children of divorce is typically lower than that of their intact counterparts (Guidubaldi, 1988).[93] In Wallerstein and Blakeslee's (1989) sample, for example, this was especially true of boys, only 50% of whom attended college, compared to 85% of their friends. A substantial minority of these boys were also underachievers, that is, they showed no ambition, such that there was a major discrepancy between their capacity and life goals. Furthermore, because education attainment is highly correlated with occupational achievement and social mobility, reduced educational achievement means that children of divorce are more likely than their intact counterparts to end up poor, especially among males (Gee, 1993; McLanahan, 1992; Parsons, 1990).[94]

4. *Gender Role, Heterosexual Behavior.* Gender roles have been given little attention in the divorce literature. An exception is the work of Vess et al. (1983). In general, this work showed no difference in the sex-role development of male and female college students from intact or divorced families. However, such differences did appear under one circumstance: when divorce occurred before age 5. In these cases, compared to their intact counterparts, the males were more masculine and the females more feminine.

As regards heterosexual behavior, the children of divorce are more likely than those from intact families to be involved in romantic relationships that are both dysfunctional and unstable. For example, compared to their intact counterparts, the behavior of college students from divorced families (especially women) is more likely characterized by sexual permissiveness leading to multiple partners but few stable relationships (Fine et al., 1983; Southward & Schwarz, 1987); cohabitation as opposed to marriage (Booth et al., 1984); marriage at an early age (Keith & Finlay, 1988); marital violence (Christopoulos et al., 1987; Kalmuss, 1984); and divorce (Glenn & Kramer, 1985).[95, 96] These observations come together in the work of Wallerstein and Blakeslee (1989), who also emphasize gender differences. For example, among their findings are the following:

- Although a minority of both the women and the men married impulsively at an early age, within 10 years all the women were divorced, but most of the men remained married.
- A minority of the children witnessed marital violence. Of these, a majority had been or were still involved in a violent heterosexual relationship, either as the abuser (among men) or the victim (among women). In either case, violence was always associated with low self-esteem and intense feelings of parental rejection.
- A minority of the women were sexually attracted to much older men, trading sex for parentlike care. Most of these relationships were fleeting, the women moving from one short-term relationship to another.
- A substantial minority of the men were socially withdrawn, celibate, and lonely. The few heterosexual relationships they entered into were nearly always of short duration.
- A minority of the women had multiple sexual partners, their response to feeling "empty inside" combined with high impulsivity.

5. *Prosocial Skills.* This issue has received scant attention in the literature. However, as we will see in the next section, there is considerable evidence of children (especially women) caring for their divorced parents (see Johnston & Campbell, 1988; Wallerstein & Blakeslee, 1989).

6. *Use of Mental Health Services.* A fair amount of evidence indicates that children of divorce are more likely to be consumers of mental health services than their intact counterparts. However, these data are not entirely consistent. For example, Wallerstein and Blakeslee (1989) found that a substantial minority of the children in their sample had been in therapy in an effort to cope with problems related to their parents' divorce. Similarly, Adams et al. (1973) and Guidubaldi (1988) report that college students from divorced families made more use of the mental health services available on campus. Although Gregory (1965) makes the identical observation about the use of psychiatric

services, there was no difference in the use of the counseling center between college students from intact as opposed to divorced families.

Based on their reviews of these data, Furstenberg and Cherlin (1991), Wallerstein (1991), and Kelly (1988) conclude, and we concur, that a substantial minority of children (exact proportion unknown) suffer long-term harm as a direct consequence of their parents' divorce. Hetherington (1987, 1989) agrees, but qualifies her response, arguing that such children distribute on a continuum of functioning, from maladaptive (typically male), to opportunistic but competent (involving both sexes), to caring and competent (typically female).[97]

Family Process Mechanisms. Of course, the fact that some children suffer harm whereas others do not begs the question of why this should be so.[98] At present, there is no definitive answer, because that would require a theory of divorce that does not yet exist. However, our review of available data suggests that either outcome is a conditional function of four factors: (a) the severity of the child's acute response to the divorcing process, (b) the degree of congruence between parental functioning and the child's gender-based developmental requirements, (c) the duration of that congruence, and (d) the structural demands of binuclear family systems.

1. With regard to divorce severity, recall that Wallerstein and Blakeslee (1989) found that whereas younger children were more acutely affected by the divorcing process compared to their older siblings, it was the former who did better in terms of long-term adjustment. This, they suggest, was because the younger children were buffered as the older children absorbed the brunt of their parent's distress. In short, irrespective of their immediate response, the divorcing process appears to have been more traumatic or severe for the older children compared to their younger siblings. This formulation is consistent with Johnston and Campbell (1988), who found that older children were much more likely than their younger siblings to become embroiled in their parent's disputes and to ally with one parent against the other. In effect, these older children had accepted the burden of trying to prevent their parents from destroying each other or the children, so that for them the divorcing process was experienced as extremely painful.

However, this cannot be the whole story. There is considerable evidence that the relationship between past experience and current behavior is typically indirect (Benjamin, 1980). For most individuals most of the time, the trauma of any given event dissipates through time; the longer the interval between then and now, the less likely that event will influence current behavior. However, there are two exceptions: if the event in question is only one of a string of similar events, perhaps ongoing, or the past event matches a similar event or events in the present. In either case, the past event will influence current behavior by increasing the individual's sensitivity to future events of a similar kind.

With respect to divorce, the evidence discussed under Short-Term Consequences suggests a population of children distributed on a continuum from unaffected to severely affected. In the context of long-term consequences, it suggests a population of children differentially sensitive to future experience and thus calls our attention to the character of their ongoing experience as the basis for the outcomes discussed above.

2. Another sensitizing factor appears to be the congruence between children's age- and gender-related developmental requirements and available patterns of parent-child interaction. Wallerstein and Blakeslee (1989), on the basis of evidence to be cited in the next subsection, advance a two-part argument: First, they suggest that in all children, a "normal" developmental trajectory requires that they believe that their parents are committed to them and give them priority; and that, second, in this regard fathers play a special role as a function of child age and gender. Males, they suggest, have a critical need for paternal involvement twice, once during the latency years (ages 6 to 9) and again in late adolescence. In contrast, females need such involvement in early adolescence and, in addition, have a greater need than males for family structure.

In either case, paternal role failure is likely to have predictable consequences for male and female children. In males, the mismatch between child need and paternal behavior helps explain boys' acute distress at the time of the separation and later underachievement and heterosexual instability. In females, the same mismatch in early adolescence helps explain their delayed depression. Conversely, an appropriate match between need and behavior helps explain the *lack* of long-term consequences for the majority of children of divorced parents.

In short, whereas severity focuses our attention on ongoing processes, developmental congruence does the same with respect to the character of parent-child relations, both nuclear and binuclear. It also cautions that we examine separately the experiences of male and female children.

3. This logic suggests the following two inferences: (a) There is a strong association between negative consequences of parental divorce and ongoing dysfunction in the relations between these children and their biological parents, stepparents, or both; and (b) there is a strong association between positive consequences of parental divorce and ongoing functional relations between these children and their biological parents, stepparents, or both. To our knowledge, the second inference has never been subjected to empirical investigation, although its logic is implicit in Masheter (1990). By contrast, the first inference finds consistent support in the data reviewed in this and the next subsection, in both of which we distinguish between male and female experience.

In general, divorced parents provide significantly less support (social, instrumental, financial) for their adult children than do their intact counterparts (White, 1992). This phenomenon is based not on any difference in available resources, but rather on a poorer quality parent-child relationship. It is less obvious between mothers and daughters than between mothers and sons. However, even when mothers and daughters relate well, more than a third of these relationships deteriorate over time (Wallerstein & Blakeslee, 1989). Still worse, in a minority of cases, such relations are characterized by maternal parenting abdication or inadequacy (Hetherington, 1989), which typically predates the divorcing process (Block et al., 1988) and only normalizes slowly, with improvements in maternal adjustment (Hetherington, 1987). Thus in nonclinical families, it was not uncommon for maternal parenting neglect to extend over a decade or more. In a minority of clinical families, such dysfunction may become chronic, with child parentification the common result (Johnston & Campbell, 1988), that is, the process whereby children care for their parents rather than the other way around. The long-term consequence, suggest Johnston and

Campbell (1988), is a significant reduction in children's capacity to develop a consistent sense of self, whereas Wallerstein and Blakeslee (1989) speak about psychological depletion and the stunting of children's emotional growth.

As for relations between adult daughters and their fathers, the major risk was of paternal disengagement—either physical or psychological—producing deep feelings of rejection and worthlessness (Wallerstein & Blakeslee, 1989). Over the long term, most fathers found it very hard to maintain a viable relationship with their children as a visiting parent. However, what was most striking about this account was the stark contrast between paternal and child perceptions. Whereas most fathers thought they were doing reasonably well by their children and perceived them to be satisfied, in fact 75% of the children in question felt abandoned; the fathers had no idea their children felt that way, despite paternal behavior that often appeared indifferent or uncaring.

It is important to note, however, that not all father-daughter relations in Wallerstein and Blakeslee's (1989) sample were so characterized. Many involved consistent and genuine support and affection. This was *not* associated with visitation frequency, but rather with these fathers' ability to make their daughters feel valued and important. Even so, such relations were extremely difficult to maintain over the long term. In more than half, good father-daughter relations at divorce subsequently deteriorated over time.

Turning to adult male children, they too sought relations with both their biological parents in which they felt valued and special. Sadly, they were less likely than their sisters to succeed in this effort. Relations between mothers and their sons, for example, were often characterized by conflict and hostility, which dissipated only slowly (Hetherington, 1989). Moreover, it was complicated by the results of persistent coparental anger and conflict (Wallerstein & Blakeslee, 1989). Here, parents (often mothers), seeking revenge on their former spouses, tried to destroy the relationship between the children and their fathers, severely damaging the children in the process.

Although such damage affects children irrespective of their gender, its effects were especially pernicious for the boys, given the salience of their relationship with their fathers. Indeed, Wallerstein and Blakeslee (1989) show that even a good relationship between mothers and sons provided only partial compensation for a poor relationship between fathers and sons. Sadly, that was often the case, the result of paternal parenting disengagement or abdication. Perhaps the most striking illustration of the former was the typical refusal of fathers to provide financial support for their children's education (especially their sons) past age 18, despite the fact that a quarter of these fathers had advanced university degrees.

Again, it must be emphasized that such conduct did not characterize all fathers (Hetherington, 1987; Wallerstein & Blakeslee, 1989), many of whom remained genuinely involved in their sons' lives. For these sons, postdivorce adjustment was typically unproblematic, as they came to see their parent's divorce as a closed chapter in their lives. For the rest, however, continued difficulty in their relations with one or both of their biological parents kept their parents' divorce forever alive in their present thinking, with negative consequences (Wallerstein & Blakeslee, 1989).

4. Finally, because the majority of divorced parents remarry, their biological parents were not the only sources of parental influence in the lives of adult children. They also had to contend with their stepparents, with variable consequences based on age and gender (Clingempeel & Segal, 1986; Santrock, Warshak, & Elliott, 1982).[99]

For the spouses in question, remarriage necessarily signifies the creation of a new and special bond. However, it may or may not extend to the children of previous relationships. Wallerstein and Blakeslee (1989), for example, report that half of the children whose mothers remarried did *not* feel welcome in their new family, and in another 25%, one child felt excluded although the others felt included.

In part, this situation appeared to be a function of age and gender. Typically, younger children had an easier time adjusting to life in their new binuclear family, which, in turn, enhanced their subsequent development. This was significantly less true for older children for whom life in their new family was associated with intense loyalty conflicts and consequently had a net negative effect on their subsequent development. There was also some variation by gender, with girls on the whole more accepting of this new arrangement whereas boys were typically more resistant.

In part, such effects also reflect the character of the various relationships that arise out of the formation of this new family. Wallerstein and Blakeslee (1989)[100] found that stepfathers were the focus of the most conflict, because as live-in parents they represented a serious threat to the relationship between the children and their visiting biological fathers. In contrast, stepmothers were less problematic because few of the children had lived with them while they were growing up. Thus stepmothers were never serious rivals for their mothers' affection. However, remarriage also represented a major change for biological mothers, involving a transfer of allegiance and confidence from their daughters to their new husbands. Consequently, remarriage reveals another "sleeper effect" of divorce, as daughters, having weathered the divorce by identifying with their mothers, now find themselves pushed aside in favor of mother's new husband and consequently in intense distress (Zaslow, 1988). Further, in remarrying, fathers' feelings for their children (especially sons), already blunted by the divorcing process, may be completely extinguished, as their commitment to the new marriage replaces all old attachments (Wallerstein & Blakeslee, 1989). The elapsed time between divorce and remarriage may also be consequential; Hodges and Bloom (1984) note that early remarriage prevented the development in children of enhanced competencies and self-esteem associated with learning to cope with various exigencies common in divorce (see Hodges, 1986, 1991).

All of these difficulties notwithstanding, evidence suggests that long-term child adjustment is likely to be better in remarried binuclear families compared to maternal single-parent families (Touliatos & Lindholm, 1980),[101] especially for male children (Hetherington et al., 1985; Peterson & Zill, 1986; Santrock et al., 1982).

Thus, for some children of divorce remarriage truly represents a "second chance" (Wallerstein & Blakeslee, 1989) at a new and better life. For others (especially males), it merely represents the continuation of longstanding processes of loss, rejection, and abandonment. For still others (especially females), it involves both the old and the new: reaffirmation of paternal rejection and the novel experience of maternal disengagement. In short, for some, remarriage is simply a visible symbol of a substantive reality, of an old life now fading into history, and a new and brighter future awaiting. For a substantial minority of others, it renders futile the one remaining hope of the end of their distress and dislocation, which predates the end of their parents' marriage and continues to the present.

For the mediation practitioner, these data highlight two issues noted as important. The first concerns the role of fathers and the potential for their involvement (or lack of it) in the lives of their children to enhance or undermine the children's long-term development. The onus is placed first on the parents and second on the mediator to create an agreement that will not only endure through time, but also have the greatest possible likelihood of yielding positive rather than negative outcomes. In short, these data confront practitioners with the need to think about agreements using a much longer time frame than they are accustomed to using. The second issue again calls our attention to the likelihood that through time the ecological field of divorced families will become increasingly complex. Although this possibility is not of concern to practitioners dealing with families divorcing for the first time, it will be critical in cases where clients are divorcing a second or later time.

THE DIVORCE PROCESS AND FAMILY MEDIATION

Family mediation is a complex undertaking that makes considerable demands on the practitioner, including mastering both skills and knowledge. The former include clinical skills related to assessment, intervention, and negotiation. The latter include knowledge about the law and legal procedures as well as related financial matters such as current tax and pension provisions. We suggest that insight into the divorcing process constitutes yet another facet fundamental to a practitioner's knowledge base.

In this context, it will now be apparent that knowledge of divorce is both extensive and voluminous, though hardly complete (consider social class and ethnicity). Furthermore, our review makes plain that divorce, far from being a discrete event, is a complex process that involves relations among a wide range of individuals and takes a variable course that may be complete in a year or two or continue to influence the life course decades later. In turn, the relevance of this information to mediation practice extends to two areas around which the following discussion is organized: dimensions and practice issues.

Dimensions

Our review suggests that the population of divorcing couples, and hence the potential clientele of mediation, is extraordinarily heterogeneous. In turn, intervention will greatly benefit from intake assessment that locates a given client couple across a range of central dimensions. What follows is a review of nine such dimensions with consideration of their relative clinical importance.

1. *Marital Interaction Pattern.* Of particular clinical salience is a sense of the couple's location on the continuum of family interaction patterns. For example, those who come close to Little's (1982) "fragile bonded" family will benefit, for example, from the opportunity to express their feelings and should be encouraged to do so by the mediator. In contrast, those who show evidence of Kressel, Jaffe, Tuchman, Watson, and Deutsch's (1980) "autistic" pattern would likely not benefit from ventilation; such efforts should be blocked by the mediator.

More generally, we suggest that thinking about a couple in terms of their position on a *functional continuum* will be of considerable clinical importance. Couples at the functional end of the continuum, for example, may require minimal intervention, merely supportive guidance as they grapple in negotiation with the problematic issues. Conversely, those at the dysfunctional end of the continuum may require highly specialized intervention if mediation is to be useful (see Johnston & Campbell, 1988). In the same vein, dysfunction may involve several dimensions, including cognitive or affective, personal or interpersonal, and endogenous versus situational. In the absence of such knowledge, there is the very real risk of doing unintended harm.

Of particular relevance in assessing a couple's position on the continuum are processes associated with conflict and attachment. Couples engaged in mild to moderate conflict will likely be more amenable to mediation than those whose conflict is intense and long-standing. Similarly, evidence of attachment on the part of one spouse but not the other speaks of spouses quite different in their readiness to engage in mediation. Unless both spouses can be brought into roughly equal levels of readiness, there is grave danger either that mediation will fail, as the spouses strive to achieve widely disparate objectives, or that any agreement will be less than equitable, as one spouse "gives away the store" in a futile effort at reconciliation.

2. *Violence.* Violence is an indicator of dysfunction of special importance, because it necessarily suggests inequality between the spouses in power, control, and decision making. The form of violence that has received the most attention in the mediation literature is wife abuse. Another that has received attention in the divorce literature is suicide. Both are forms of behavior whose indicators should routinely be part of intake assessment. Not only does the presence of either form of behavior have significant implications for practice (see Issues, p. 98), but failure to consider them may render the practitioner vulnerable to civil liability.

More generally, violence is relevant to the larger issue of *gender.* The above review makes clear that men and women respond differently to the demands of the divorcing process and that psychologically and financially women are more vulnerable to harm. Gender-based variation in response speaks to the issue of congruence between client need and mediator style. Specifically, these data suggest that one style or approach is *unlikely* to suit male and female clients equally well, so that considerable flexibility is required of mediators.

3. *Social Class.* Our knowledge of how the divorcing process varies by social class and ethnicity is admittedly limited. Nevertheless, what we know counsels caution on the part of mediators. Standards of evaluation and intervention are implicitly grounded in middle-class norms. When dealing with upper- or lower-class client couples, the automatic use of "standard" procedures may inadvertently do more harm than good.

More generally, in this context class calls attention to the critical importance of resources, especially financial and nonfinancial assets. Simply put, the more assets available for division between the spouses, the greater the range of options that can be considered in mediation. Thus, couples with no or very few assets are constrained to select among a very limited range of options, in turn imposing corresponding limits on the mediator. Furthermore, spouses are typically unequal in terms of the assets under their control. At separation husbands are usually better off than wives, which often becomes steadily more unequal through time. Thus, the phase of divorce is important to the degree of inequality between the spouses and the efforts the mediator needs to make to ensure that an agreement is fair and equitable.

As for nonfinancial resources, we have seen that here too the spouses are dissimilar, with husbands more likely dependent for support on friends whereas wives are more likely dependent on kin. Coupled with their greater resources, this difference means that husbands are freer than wives to find new romantic partners, whereas wives generally benefit from greater support. For the mediator, the impact of nonfinancial resources is double-edged. On the one hand, the more clients have sources of support, the less likely they are to depend on the mediator. On the other hand, the involvement of others is likely to complicate the mediator's task, for a variety of hidden agendas may be at play.

4. *Ethnicity.* The "standard" model that practitioners often follow assumes that client couples are not only middle class, but also white. The changing demographic shape of North America makes that assumption less and less reasonable. Indeed, in some states, "minority" groups will shortly represent more than half of the total population. In turn, as we have seen, there is considerable variation across ethnic groups, including the rate of divorce, the extent to which divorce is an acceptable way of resolving marital discord, the willingness to become involved with court processes, and the like. Consequently, in the absence of considerable substantive knowledge about a client couple's ethnicity—their origin, the extent to which they share group norms, and so forth—there is grave danger that the mediator will do more harm than good. These demographics suggest that ethnicity should be part of mediators' intake routine.

5. *Children.* As noted above, children are (typically) unwilling victims of the multiple hazards endemic to the divorcing process. Accordingly, they warrant special care and consideration to avoid harm or minimize it. Recent knowledge of the long-term consequences of the divorcing process helps place the acute responses of children in context. Although young children may show the most adverse effects over the short term, it may in fact be their older siblings who are at long-term developmental risk. Similarly, the developmental needs of boys

and girls appear to vary, especially at critical periods, and particularly with regard to the level and consistency of paternal involvement.

These considerations are relevant to mediation in two senses. First, one of the primary purposes of custody mediation is to ensure that the terms of any agreement are consistent with the "best interests" of the child(ren), both short and long term. Here the fact that boys and girls have rather different needs should be seen by mediators as critical in their assessment of the workability of any agreement. Second, children, especially older children, will necessarily be participants in the mediation process, whether or not they actually attend. In turn, they can complicate the mediator's task because they too are likely to have hidden agendas. Their effectiveness in imposing these agendas on the mediator speaks to the issue of whether they should be invited to participate in one or more sessions.

6. *Parenting*. Parent-child relations is another important area for inquiry and action. The above review indicates that couples vary in their parenting adequacy. In particular, several aspects of parenting deserve careful scrutiny: information, disengagement, and functioning.

As the divorcing process unfolds, it is common that parents have told their children virtually nothing about the impending separation. Parents are largely unaware of the impact divorce is likely to have on their children, which touches on the mediator's psychoeducational role. Simply passing on the information reviewed above may have salutary effects.

Next, although divorce is intended to sever the relationship among marital partners, it may also have unintended consequences for the parent-child relationship, as fathers or, less often, mothers simply abandon their child(ren). This situation speaks to mediation in various ways, including negotiation around child support as well as the potentially profound psychological effect on the children. Less often noted, but equally noteworthy, is the opposite effect, in which divorce promotes increased paternal involvement among fathers who were previously peripheral in their children's lives. In turn, the choice of custody options is relevant. Among families in which fathers were and remain peripheral, maternal sole custody will be the option of choice. Conversely, where fathers were or show signs of becoming more

consistently involved with their children, a variation on shared parenting or joint custody should be considered.

Finally, despite their best intentions, the distress associated with
divorce may be such as to render previously adequate parents functionally inadequate. Intake assessment of this possibility is central to
the promotion of a workable agreement, but touches too on the ethical
matter of knowingly supporting custody arrangements likely to be
inimical to healthy child development.

7. *Interpersonal Context*. Divorce seldom involves merely the spouses
and their children. More often it involves a variety of others connected
to the family in different ways. Broadly, however, the above review
supports the distinction between personal and institutional others.

Personal others include extended kin (by birth and marriage or
remarriage), friends, and new romantic partners. To the extent that
they are involved in the lives of the spouses, they will necessarily be
involved in mediation. As noted above, this involvement can be positive, as they render social support at a time of great need. However,
their involvement can also be negative, as they "take sides" and in the
process push one or both spouses to take extreme positions they might
not have taken if left on their own. Whether and to what extent
personal others play a role will thus be an important aspect of assessment, including whether or not to include these others directly in one
or more mediation sessions. The latter choice might be necessary for
information purposes alone, given clients who have difficulty articu-
lating their views and might be useful to affirm personal others in their
supportive efforts or to block their additional involvement should
their efforts be at variance with those of the mediator.

Much the same applies to institutional actors,[102] especially legal and
counseling personnel, for both are likely to be central to the mediator's
effort. In all cases, lawyers bring to clients in mediation expert knowledge of statutes and legal procedures without which clients cannot
make informed decisions among the options available. For that reason,
most mediators insist that both spouses retain a lawyer *before* they
enter mediation. For similar reasons, collegial cooperation between
lawyers and mediators may be mutually beneficial. Given their professional socialization, lawyers may be underprepared for some of the
difficulties associated with serving clients in the throes of the divorcing

process. Thus they may find themselves confronted by clients who are highly demanding but who, in light of situational deficits, have no coherent plan. They may similarly find themselves in difficulty as they inadvertently become embroiled in their client's complex family dynamics, which are often exacerbated by the divorcing process. In both respects, mediators' clinical expertise may serve lawyers well by allowing them to concentrate on the use of their legal expertise.

But the reverse also applies. For example, clients may be unwilling to consider a specific option under consideration without the explicit approval of their lawyer. Thus in some situations direct inclusion of the lawyer in mediation may greatly facilitate the mediation process. This is not to suggest that all lawyers take a benign or positive view of mediation. Some may advise clients in ways that are inconsistent with the aims of mediation (see chapter 4). Generally, however, lawyers may best be viewed as allies in the delivery of mediation service.

Much the same may be said of counselors, who can be powerful actors in the lives of clients. The distress of the divorcing process may be such that clients may see their counselor's support as the only thing preventing their total collapse. Consequently, counselors' clinical plans for the course and outcome of treatment may of be importance as part of the assessment process in mediation. Typically, such plans are either congruent with mediation or at least not inconsistent with it. Accordingly, there may be occasions in which the direct involvement of counselors in mediation may need to be considered. More rarely, when their involvement is at cross-purposes with the mediator's service goals, the mediator will likely need to act either to solicit the counselor's cooperation or to block his or her involvement.

8. *Institutional Context.* A closely related context that cannot but affect the divorcing process and thus mediation is the institutional context. Perhaps most immediately relevant is the legal regime. As we have seen, state, provincial, and federal statutes related to divorce vary widely across North America. Although the trend is toward no-fault divorce, it is by no means universal. Similar variation pertains to statutes on such related matters as child custody, child and spousal support, and the division of property. It goes almost without saying that detailed local knowledge of the legal regime will dramatically constrain the range of options to be considered in mediation.

However, there are at least three other sources of institutional constraint. First, each institutional actor operates within statutory and regulatory regimes. Thus, taxation specialists are linked to one statute, medical specialists to another, real estate professionals to another, and so on. It is advantageous for the mediator to know something about the contexts from which these professional originate and thus be able to estimate in advance the likely effect of bringing one or another professional into mediation. Next, whatever the local divorce statutes, they invariably leave considerable room for discretion on the part of local judges, whose task in contested divorce cases is a difficult one. Here, judges and mediators may help each other, the former identifying cases that may benefit from mediation, the latter helping spouses revolve matters that judges would be forced to adjudicate. Even so, as a group, the literature indicates that judges demonstrate biases favoring traditional norms, including a strong preference for maternal sole custody over virtually any other custody option. This knowledge may be critical in sifting between options in mediation.

Finally, the client couple's history of judicial involvement may need to be considered. As we have seen, such involvement tends to push clients to take extreme positions, which often has the effect of exacerbating existing interspousal conflict. Over time, positions can become entrenched and inflexible and thus create family contexts that may be highly problematic for mediation. Although the converse is not necessarily the case—intense conflict can arise without any court involvement—at least such couples are in conflict over issues arising from their marriage and not issues arising from involvement with the court.

By implication, the client's involvement in the court calls attention to their phase in the divorcing process for a second reason: their amenability to mediation. Whereas many separating, divorcing, or divorced couples may benefit from family mediation, this is not always the case. Those in Phases 1 or 2, who have yet to become involved in the adversary system, may be in a good position to respond positively to mediation. Conversely, it may be more difficult for those in Phases 3 or 4, who may have become heavily invested in adversarial procedures and personnel, to do so. Information about their phase in the divorce process, then, is an important part of any assessment.

9. *Marital Status.* The above review calls our attention to a final dimension, marital status, which refers to three aspects of the client couple's marital situation. The first refers to the marital history of the respective spouses. In the past, the rarity of divorce meant that nearly all marriages involved a first marriage for both spouses. Now marriages between spouses with a mixed marital history have become common, for example, between one spouse for whom this is a first marriage and another spouse who has been previously married and divorced. Apparently at highest risk are couples who have both been married and divorced more than once. For purposes of mediation, the couple's marital history speaks to their experience in the divorcing process and possibly their openness to the mediator's suggestions and interventions.

Next, marital status pertains to family form and thus case complexity. Mediation involving a couple with no children or with children who are solely the outcome of their relationship is one thing. Blended families, involving children from previous relationships, are another thing altogether. As we have seen, blended families tend to be considerably more complex, both structurally and functionally, than their first-time counterparts. In turn, they represent different levels of challenge for the mediator.

Finally, marital status can also refer to the divorce history of the parents of client couples. That is, whether clients have been previously divorced is distinct from whether they themselves are the children of divorced parents. This history speaks to the sorts of agendas they bring with them into mediation and especially their explicit as opposed to "hidden" agendas. For those who are children of divorce, the character of their parents' divorce may subtly shape their responses to their own divorce. Those whose parents' divorce was traumatic may come to their own divorce with a sense of fatalism, as if their own divorce were all but inevitable, or alternately may be frozen with fear that history is likely to repeat itself. Conversely, for those whose parents' divorce was benign or even positive, their approach may be quite different, either more positive and hopeful or more weighted by guilt, as they appear not to have learned from their parent's example. In either event, some exploration of the client's parents' divorce history seems warranted.

Issues

Seen individually, the dimensions examined above call attention to specific aspects of mediation practice. Seen collectively, they highlight a series of more general issues, as follows. In reviewing these issues, it will shortly be apparent that the literature reviewed above is more useful for raising issues than resolving them.

Psychoeducational Role. The first issue raised by our discussion of clinically relevant dimensions is the utility of this knowledge base, which more specifically touches on two related issues: the mediator's psychoeducational role and the role of knowledge in clinical practice.

With respect to the former, our review makes clear that spousal relations during the divorcing process are primarily based on the continuity of marital themes. These are often emotionally charged, based on the past or the present, unconcerned with the possible or even the likely consequences of present actions, and uninformed about statutes, procedures, or institutions associated with divorce. In contrast, mediation is intended to reduce the affective charge, help clients think about the future, consider the consequences of preferred choices, and weigh their options in light of information about relevant statutes, procedures, and institutions. A psychoeducational role is central to the mediation process.

In turn, the information that clients need to have to participate meaningfully in mediation should be part of adequate mediation training programs. More specifically, we suggest that information about the divorcing process contributes in at least two ways to delivery of family mediation services. First, it highlights specific areas of risk to adults and children that should inform both the practice of mediation as well as the standards of equity applied to any "final" agreement. Second, it helps mediators understand client behavior that might otherwise appear inexplicable in terms of their recent history of adequate functioning, and suggests ways to respond (or not respond) that allow them to be helpful.

This said, a caution is in order, based on the divergent goals of research and mediation, respectively. The goals of the former are necessarily nomothetic, concerned with the larger picture as it pertains to the population of divorcing families. By contrast, the goals of the latter are necessarily idiographic, concerned with the needs and concerns of the unique couple sitting before them. This divergence, however, cannot be total, for nomothetic data can only arise from idiographic sources, from specific individuals willing to share their experience with an interested researcher. Thus, the nomothetic and the idiographic must overlap. That overlap is our basis for arguing that the above review should be seen to inform rather than direct mediation practice by helping mediators recognize where their specific client diverges from *and* converges with the larger patterns that characterize the divorcing process in North America.

Practitioner Misconduct. Practitioners provide service to those who approach them for help. In responding, mediators necessarily assume a basic level of competence on the part of spouses, for example, to communicate their thoughts, articulate a position, and so forth. As we have seen above, this is not necessarily true of all divorcing spouses. Some may display dysfunction of long standing. Others may do so in response to the situational constraints they find themselves in. Whatever the reason, then, some proportion of divorcing spouses will be incompetent in the above sense. In turn, this raises the issue of practitioner misconduct, specifically, admitting for service couples whose level of dysfunction is such that they are unlikely to benefit from mediation service.

Although the literature implicitly raises this issue, it hardly resolves it, for it is clear that divorcing couples are distributed on a continuum, from highly functional to highly dysfunctional. How far along toward the dysfunctional pole they need to be before they are, in our words, "unlikely to benefit from service" is far from clear.

Safety and Security. It is essential that all mediation clients enter service assured that they will be physically safe and secure as the process unfolds. The literature, however, raises this as a problematic issue. As we have seen, one of the bases of divorce is family violence. Furthermore, such a pattern, once established, may not only continue during the divorcing process, but may escalate, with murder a possible (though rare) outcome. In addition, even when violence was not pre-

viously in evidence, it may spontaneously erupt in response to the
intense pressures and conflicts associated with the divorcing process.
In either event, it seems clear that in an unknown proportion of mediation cases, the safety and security of some clients (mostly female)
cannot automatically be guaranteed. Furthermore, such risks are not
confined to spouses, but extend to children, either as victims of violence, or more typically, as witnesses of violence, with potentially
important long-term consequences for their development. What remains unclear is whether such cases are suitable for mediation, and if
so, how mediators should respond to ensure the safety and security of
those at risk.

Fairness and Equity. A related problem concerns fairness and equity. At
the heart of mediation is the effort to ensure that mediated agreements
are both fair and equitable. The literature presents several dimensions
that make meeting this laudable objective problematic. One example
involves couples in which a history of family violence has rendered the
spouses unequal in power and decision-making authority. Another
concerns ethnicity in which inequality between the spouses may reflect
a cultural tradition. Still a third involves a traditional division of
domestic labor in which wives have most of the responsibility for child
rearing. Although the literature is invaluable in calling our attention
to these sources of inequality, it is of little use in resolving the host of
problems they raise for mediators in their efforts to ensure fairness and
equity.

For illustrative purposes, consider two examples implicit in the
above review. The first concerns the degree of acceptable inequality.
Given variation across spouses on dimensions such as readiness, attachment, distress, and so forth, it is apparent that couples in which
both spouses are exactly equal across all dimensions relevant to mediation will be rare; rather, inequality is the norm. How unequal must
the spouses be before the mediator is likely to feel obliged to intervene?
Furthermore, on whose authority will such intervention be undertaken? In some cases, one or another spouse may perceive his or her
inequality in relation to the other as problematic, thus according the
mediator (if only implicitly) permission to intervene. In other cases,
neither spouse may be aware of inequality or, if they are, will indicate

no pressing need to rectify matters; only the mediator will perceive the inequality and feel the need to intervene. In the latter case, the authority to intervene is based solely on the mediator's standards of fairness and equity, standards that the client couple may or may not share. As will be more apparent in chapter 4, mediators are not all of the same mind on this issue. Some favor absolute neutrality. Others, ourselves included, suggest that mediators cannot afford to be neutral, but must insist on approximate spousal equality. Here the literature is useful in reminding us that divorcing spouses need not attend mediation, but rather have access to the courts and other options; there is no merit in advocating for mediation unless there is good reason to think that the clients in question will benefit from mediation in comparison to available alternatives.

A somewhat different circumstance arises in which spousal inequality has the status of a cultural norm. On the one hand, both spouses may share similar beliefs, even when doing so (typically) places women at a disadvantage compared to their spouses. On the other hand, they have initiated the divorcing process, thus signaling the desire of at least one spouse for a major change. How is the mediator to respond? The mediator's standards may support intervention aimed at promoting equality between the spouses, but this stance may accord with the desires of neither spouse. Furthermore, the standards in question are typically rationalized on the basis of white, middle-class assumptions, assumptions that may be at variance with those of the couple's ethnic group. Indeed, given broad agreement among mediators concerning respect for diversity, interventions inconsistent with couples' fundamental beliefs might be seen as unethical.

Neutrality. The rhetorical questions raised in the previous two examples come into focus as regards neutrality in mediation. Based on the logic of empowerment, mediation stands apart from the adversarial system by returning control over an agreement back to the spouses. In doing so, mediators characterize themselves as neutral, their role solely that of facilitator. As the above review makes clear, this position is difficult to sustain and one that some would argue is unreasonable to strive for. Again, two final examples clarify the point.

One example concerns child custody. Among couples contesting custody, this is an intensely divisive issue, with mothers typically favoring sole custody and fathers typically favoring joint custody or, as we prefer to call it, shared parenting. In this context, the literature suggests that couples and mediators bring different dimensions to bear in determining the best interests of the child(ren). Thus for parents, conflict over the choice of custody option is typically an extension of marital themes, particularly previous involvement in parenting. For the mediator, the issue is more complex, including dimensions such as child age and gender, material resources, parental adequacy, parental psychological state, and so forth. This divergence may be irrelevant when both parents and mediator support a similar custody choice. But what if they do not? Situational parenting inadequacy is typically not something about which the parents in question are aware. In this circumstance, a demand for sole custody may be less in the child's interest than a shared parenting arrangement. Conversely, shared parenting may be unreasonable in the face of parental disengagement or overt parental dysfunction. In either case, mediators are confronted with a series of choices: to remain neutral in the face of an agreement that they perceive as inconsistent with the best interests of the child(ren); to take a position and thus intervene despite client opposition; or to terminate mediation and advise the couple of alternate forms of service.

A related problem arises in the case of spousal abuse. Such couples are by no means homogeneous; they vary across a range of dimensions. Even so, most such couples will be characterized by unequal relationships, with husbands dominant. Under such circumstances, negotiation between the spouses is likely to be a farce, with the final agreement strongly skewed in favor of the husband. Safety and security issues aside (see above), how is the mediator to respond? Again, several options are available. One is to refuse service on the grounds that a fair and equitable agreement is impossible. Another is one of strict neutrality, thus allowing the skewed agreement to stand. However, the obvious objection might be to argue that the agreement itself compromises the mediator's neutrality insofar as the mediator has implicitly abetted the result. A third choice is to intervene to change the balance between the spouses, thus increasingly the likelihood that the agreement will be fair and equitable. In so doing, the mediator's conduct alters the meaning of "neutrality" from absolute to conditional, that is, from one in which the mediator's only concern is with procedural fairness, to one in which the mediator advocates for the interests of neither spouse, but insists on both spousal equality and procedural fairness as the only reasonable basis for substantive fairness and equity.

It will be abundantly clear that thorough knowledge of the research literature is immensely valuable for mediation practitioners. It serves to place a given couple's experience in the context of a spectrum of experience. It highlights key issues in mediation and provides an evidentiary base upon which more discussion can be grounded. And it highlights the range of choices in mediation while grounding them in evidence rather than rhetoric, ideology, or politics; it thus helps keep mediators honest, both to themselves and their clients.

But in achieving these important ends, it simultaneously raises more questions than it answers—questions, moreover, that cannot be answered solely on the basis of data. Rather, the answers require a coherent model of practice that addresses the complex range of pragmatic and ethical issues that routinely arises as mediators help divorcing couples struggle to resolve the painful differences that divide them. It is to such a model that we turn next.

NOTES

1. Ambert (1989), for example, notes the rarity of dyadic data in the divorce research literature, that is, data and analysis involving couples rather than aggregated data comparing male and female spouses.

2. Vaughan (1986, p. 6) observes that, "Uncoupling is complete when the partners have defined themselves and are defined by others as separate and independent of each other—when being partners is no longer a major source of identity. Instead, identity comes from other sources."

3. See also Albrecht, Bahr, and Goodman (1983); Ambert (1990); and Wallerstein and Blakeslee (1989).

4. See also Ambert (1990); Doherty, Su, and Needle (1989); Kitson with Holmes (1992); Kitson and Morgan (1990); and Smith, Mercy, and Conn (1988).

5. In Canada, the most convincing case for an association between divorce and suicide has been provided by Trovato (1987, 1991; Trovato & Lauris, 1989).

6. See Amato (1989), Doherty et al. (1989), Lund (1987), Myers (1989), and Oakland (1984).

7. See also Arnold, Wheeler, and Pendrith (1980); Hetherington et al. (1978); and Shook and Jurish (1992).

8. See Grief (1979), Hetherington et al. (1976), Kelly (1982), Wallerstein and Kelly (1980), and Weiss (1979b).

9. See also Kitson and Sussman (1982), Kitson et al. (1985), Mika and Bloom (1981), and Weiss (1975).

10. See also Albrecht (1980); Baker (1983); and Bloom, Hodges, and Caldwell (1983).

11. See also Bornstein, Clayton, Halikas, Maurice, and Robins (1973) and Crosby et al. (1983).

12. See also Ahrons (1979), Bloom et al. (1978), and Goldsmith (1982).

13. See also Arnold et al. (1980), Hetherington (1987), and Melichor and Chiriboga (1988).

14. See also Hetherington et al. (1976), Wallerstein and Kelly (1980), and Wallerstein and Blakeslee (1989).

15. See also Ahrons and Rodgers (1987), Goldsmith (1980, 1982), and Kurdek and Blisk (1983).

16. See also Folberg and Graham (1981), Hetherington et al. (1976, 1977), Miller (1978), and Spanier and Castro (1979).

17. See also Arnold et al. (1980), Fisher (1982), Kaplan (1977), and Spicer and Hampe (1975).

18. See also Hetherington (1989); Hetherington et al. (1976); Huddleston and Hawkings (1993); Kurdek and Berg (1983); Kurdek and Blisk (1983); McKenry and Price (1991); Mitchell, Billings, and Moss (1982); Pett (1982a); Raschke (1977a); Santrock and Warshak (1979); Vaughan (1986); and Ward, Logan, and Spitze (1992).

19. See also Arnold et al. (1980) and Hetherington et al. (1976).

20. Involvement with a new partner also confers significant psychological benefits, limiting the time and magnitude of adverse consequences of the divorcing process, and in some cases promoting growth and development (Johnston & Campbell, 1988; Kohen, Browen, & Feldberg, 1979; Longfellow, 1979; Weiss, 1979a). It also significantly diminishes the likelihood of reconciliation.

21. See also Ambert (1983, 1988b) and Milardo (1987).

22. Even so, not all kin networks are similarly composed or equally helpful. Isaacs et al. (1986), for example, differentiate between four types of network linking divorcing adults and their parents (local, helpful, disengaged, and directing). Only local networks persisted through time, actively supporting mothers but also frequently infringing on their independence.

23. See also Ahrons and Bowman (1982); Ambert (1988b); Furstenberg and Nord (1985); and Gladstone (1989).

24. However, Cox (1993) notes that in the United States recent statutory changes have sought to strengthen and protect grandparents' visitation rights. For additional discussion of the plight of grandparents, both maternal and paternal, see Johnson (1983); Johnson and Vinick (1981); Kalish and Visher (1981); Matthews and Sprey (1984); and Wood and Robertson (1978). For discussion of the effect of divorce on the extended family more generally, see Fisher (1982).

25. See also Arnold et al. (1980); Beal (1980); and Bloom (1975).

26. See also Holden and Smock (1991); Maudlin (1991); and Weiss and Willis (1989).

27. See also Brandwein, Brown, and Fox (1974); Glasser and Navarre (1965); and Weiss (1979a).

28. See also Duncan and Hoffman (1985); Hoffman and Duncan (1988); and Ozawa (1989).

29. Although the employment income available to divorcing men and women may be unequal, employment per se does appear to confer psychological benefits on both former spouses: Compared to their unemployed counterparts, those who are employed consistently report lower levels of anxiety and depression, fewer emotional problems, greater happiness, and a greater sense of control over their lives (Ambert, 1989; Arnold et al., 1980; Hetherington et al., 1976).

30. See also Beller and Graham (1985, 1988); Buehler (1989); Chambers (1979); Canadian Institute of Law Research and Reform (1981); Duncan and Rodgers (1987); Hetherington (1979); Hoffman (1977); Kitson with Holmes (1992); McCall, Hornick, and Wallace (1988); Ministry of the Attorney General (1992); Paasch and Teachman (1991); Teachman (1991); United States Department of Education (1988); Weiss (1984); and Woolsey (1977).

31. In Ontario, Canada's most populous province, the outstanding child support arrears in 1991 totaled $460 million (Ministry of the Attorney General, 1992); with the average amount in arrears $4,564 (Kitchen, 1992).

32. In addition, Seltzer, Schaeffer, and Charng (1989) show that fathers' willingness to pay child support is related to their pattern of child access and visitation, with fathers who visit regularly more willing than those who do so irregularly or not at all to pay for the privilege.

33. In the United States, this includes mandatory income withholding, interception of tax refunds, access to federal records, late penalties, payment to state agencies, and (in some states) even jail sentences (Cox, 1993; McLanahan and Garfinkel, 1993).

34. See also Albrecht (1980); Ambert (1985, 1990); Bloom and Hodges (1981); Espenshade (1979); Gongla (1982); McLanahan (1983); Nelson (1985); Weitzman (1985); and Zeiss, Zeiss, and Johnson (1980).

35. Sorenson (1992) argues that figures such as this be regarded cautiously in light of the methodological complexities involved in determining the economic consequences of divorce. In her own work, depending on the method used, white women experienced an income decline ranging from 12% to 42% (with a sizable minority actually better off); whereas the income of white men ranged from a decrease of 18% to an increase of 75%.

36. See also Hewlett (1991); Ozawa (1989); Pett and Vaughn-Cole (1986); and Weitzman (1985).

37. See also Bane (1979); Berman and Turk (1981); Brandwein et al. (1974); Esplenshade (1979); Hetherington et al. (1978); Kelly (1982); McConville (1978); and Weiss (1979b).

38. In a related vein, Arendell (1986, 1987) suggests that divorce has "declassed" many women, that is, forced them to move from middle- to lower-class status.

39. Goldberg and Dukes (1985) found that compared to their middle-class counterparts, lower-class black women experienced fewer lifestyle changes associated with the divorcing process. Consequently, they concluded that the financial effects of divorce were less serious for this group.

40. See also Fry and Addington (1985); Kurdek (1981); Long and Forehand (1987); McLanahan (1992); and Santrock (1987).

41. See also Gardner (1974); Nye (1957); Reinhardt (1977); Rosen (1977); Wallerstein and Kelly (1980); Wallerstein and Blakeslee (1989); and Weiss (1979b).

42. See also Arnold et al. (1980); Bernstein and Robey (1962); Goldsmith (1982); Grossman, Shea, and Adams (1980); Lovelene and Lohmann (1978); MacKinnon, Stoneman, and Brody (1984); Richmond-Abbott (1984); Santrock and Warshak (1979); Slater, Stewart, and Linn (1983); and Tuzlat and Hillock (1986).

43. See also Guidubaldi and Perry (1985); Hetherington (1989); Hetherington et al. (1976); Johnston and Campbell (1988); and Wallerstein and Kelly (1980).

44. See also Ambert (1985); Ambert and Saucier (1984); Burgess (1970); Cherlin (1981); Fry and Trifiletti (1983); Glasser and Navarre (1965); Gould (1968); Mitchell (1983); Mueller and Pope (1977); Pitts (1964); Smith (1981); and Wallerstein and Kelly (1980).

45. See also Ambert (1985); Desimone-Luis et al. (1979); Isaacs et al. (1986); Kalter (1977); Johnston and Campbell (1988); Johnston, Kline, and Tschann (1989); Kline et al. (1989, 1991); Kurdek and Berg (1983); and Peterson and Zill (1986).

46. See also Despert (1962); Hodges, Buchsbaum, and Tierney (1984); Kaplan and Pokorny (1971); McDermott (1970); and Wyman, Cowen, Hightower, and Pedro-Carroll (1985).

47. In extreme cases, depression in response to parental divorce may lead to child (Pfeffer, 1986; Rosenthal & Rosenthal, 1984) or adolescent suicide (Curran, 1987; Garfinkel & Northrup, 1991). For Canadian data, see especially Health and Welfare (1987).

48. See also Hagestad, Smyer, and Stierman (1984); Hainline and Feig (1978); Lopez, Campbell, and Watkins (1988); Raschke (1977b); and Slater and Haber (1984).

49. For these adolescents, Hagestad et al. (1984) found that school breaks were especially nightmarish, whereas Farber et al. (1983, cited in Hodges et al., 1984) observed increased problems with studying, disturbances of eating and sleeping, increased social withdrawal, increased dependence on roommates, and increased difficult with intimate relations.

50. See also Dawson (1991); Guidubaldi and Perry (1984); Hetherington (1980); and McLanahan (1985).

51. See also Greenberg and Nay (1982); Hetherington (1972); Landis (1960, 1963); and Wallerstein and Blakeslee (1989).

52. See also Graham-Cambrick, Gursky, and Brendler (1982); and Kalter and Rembar (1981).

53. See also Hetherington (1989); Hetherington et al. (1982, 1985); and Nock (1987).

54. See also Emery (1982); Francke (1984); Frost and Pakiz (1990); Hetherington (1980); Hetherington et al. (1978); Hodges et al. (1984); Kurdek, Blisk, and Siesky (1981); Kurdek and Berg (1983); and Reinhard (1977).

55. See Allison and Furstenberg (1989); and Santrock et al. (1982).

56. Others have made identical observations (Peterson & Zill, 1986; Tschann et al., 1990; see Kelly, 1993).

57. See also Clarke-Stewart (1977); Hetherington (1966, 1979, 1987); Johnston and Campbell (1988); Kurdek and Siesky (1980a, 1980b); Neal (1983); Springer and Wallerstein (1983); Tooley (1976); and Wallerstein and Kelly (1980).

58. See also Rutter (1985, 1987); Werner (1989); and Werner and Smith (1982).

59. See also Arnold et al. (1980); Bane (1979); Fulton (1979); and Sprenkle and Cyrus (1983).

60. See also Black (1959); Hetherington et al. (1976); Jacobson (1978); Kurdek and Berg (1983); Santrock and Warshak (1979); and Wallerstein and Kelly (1980).

61. See also Guidubaldi and Perry (1985); Guidubaldi et al. (1983, 1986); Hetherington, 1987; Hetherington et al. (1978); and Kline et al. (1989).

62. See also Pett (1982b) and Weiss (1979a).

63. This is referred to in the family therapy literature as disruption of the control hierarchy (Abelsohn & Saayman, 1991).

64. This is referred to in the family therapy literature as extremes of cohesion or adaptation (Abelsohn & Saayman, 1991).

65. See also Hetherington (1987); Peterson and Zill (1986); Santrock and Warshak (1979); Santrock et al. (1982); Wallerstein and Kelly (1980); Warshak and Santrock (1983); and Warshak (1986).

66. Even when the children feel closer to their custodial mother than their noncustodial father, Peterson and Zill (1986) found that they still saw their father as a vital part of their life. These data support Ahrons and Rodgers's (1987) contention that the common tendency to describe such custodial arrangements as "single-parent" or "one-parent" families is grossly misleading.

67. A related mechanism may involve maternal identification of sons with their absent fathers, thus seeing sons as targets of maternal hostility. Rita Smith (*Toronto Star*, November 23, 1991, pp. K1, K5), a recently separated mother, describes this process as follows: "I was shocked to discover that despite all my best-intentioned, mature efforts, [my son's] physical resemblance to his father could really get under my skin. For a period of several months we fought almost constantly and on more than one occasion I heard someone saying horrible, hurtful things—only to realize that that someone was me, that those words had actually come out of my mouth. All the anger I felt toward his father, however justified, was now spilling over on to an innocent 7-year-old unfortunate enough to look and sound too much like his dad. Nothing on this planet could justify that."

68. See Kurdek and Berg (1983); Longfellow (1979); Lovelene and Lohmann (1978); Wallerstein and Kelly (1976, 1980); and Weiss (1979a).

69. See also Kurdek (1988).

70. See also Emery (1982, 1988); Fishel and Scanzoni (1989); Furstenberg et al. (1987); Kline et al. (1991); Long (1986); Long et al. (1987); Masheter (1991); Peterson and Zill (1986); Rosen (1979); Shaw and Emery (1987); and Vess et al. (1983).

71. This is especially true as regards spousal violence, particularly if the children are witnesses to such acts (Jaffe et al., 1990).

72. See also Kelly (in press); Koch and Lowery (1984); and Kurdek (1988, 1989).

73. Braver et al. (1991) found that mothers interfered with 20% to 40% of paternal visits to the children. In contrast, a Canadian study by Perry and Associates (1992) found that access denial was not a problem for the majority (70%) of their respondents, with nearly all able to work out problems that arise without resort to the court. That is, in 20% of the cases examined, some informal changes were made in the custody or access arrangements compared to those agreed to at divorce. A recent American study by Mnookin et al. (1990) similarly reports little difficulty around access denial.

74. See also Camara and Resnick (1988); Kurdek (1989); Schwebel et al. (1988); and Slater et al. (1983).

75. See also Santrock and Warshak (1979) and Woody, Colley, Schlegelmilch, Maginn, and Balsanek (1984).

76. See also Lovelene and Lohmann (1978); Rutter (1971); Santrock and Warshak (1979); Stinson (1991); Wallerstein and Kelly (1980); and Wyman et al. (1985).

77. See also Ambert (1989); Colletta (1979); and Marsden (1969, 1973).

78. See also Braver et al. (1989); Buehler, Hogan, Robinson, and Levy (1987); Hodges et al. (1984); Shaw and Emery (1987); and Wallerstein (1987).

79. Specifically, one of three methods has been used. The first method has relied on demographic data, tracking a large cohort of divorced spouses over a period of time (say, 5 to 10 years) using census or survey data (e.g., Allison & Furstenberg, 1989; Furstenberg et al., 1987; Glenn & Kramer, 1987; Morgan, 1991). The second method has relied on retrospective, cross-sectional data, typically comparing the current functioning of adult participants whose parents have or have not been divorced (e.g., Adams et al., 1973; Booth et al., 1984; Fine et al., 1983; Gregory, 1965). The third method has relied on prospective longitudinal data, examining in detail the ongoing experience of divorcing families (and occasionally intact families as well) over 5 to 15 years (e.g., Ambert, 1985, 1989; Block et al., 1986, 1988; Buchanan et al., 1991, 1992; Guidubaldi, 1988; Guidubaldi, Perry, & Nastasi, 1987a, 1987b; Hetherington, 1987, 1989; Hetherington et al., 1989; Hetherington & Arasteh, 1988; Isaacs et al., 1986; Johnston & Campbell, 1988; Wallerstein, 1984, 1985; Wallerstein & Blakeslee, 1989).

80. Recently, subjective accounts have become available concerning what it feels like to grow up in a divorced family (Kalter, 1991) and what it feels like as an adult "child" of divorced parents (Berman, 1992; Berner, 1992).

81. See also Glick (1984b); Moore (1988); and Reiss and Lee (1988).

82. Other, less central factors include: ethnicity (blacks are less likely than whites to remarry after divorce [Coleman & Ganong, 1990; Glick & Lin, 1987; Griffith, Koo, & Suchindran, 1984]) and the number of children (having three or more children reduces the likelihood of remarriage [Folk, Graham, & Beller, 1992]).

83. For a thorough review of this literature, see Pasley and Ihinger-Tallman (1987).

84. Wineberg (1990) reports that of all divorced women who remarry, half will bear one or more children by the new relationship.

85. For example, Oh (1986) reports a negative relationship between education and the likelihood of remarriage. Whereas Bumpass et al. (1990) confirm this for women, for men they found a positive relationship between education and remarriage. Finally, O'Flaherty and Eells (1988) found that although lower-class women remarry more readily than their middle-class counterparts, the reverse was true among men.

86. See also Bane and Ellwood (1986) and Stirling (1989).

87. Across North America, these figures stand at the nexus of two opposing trends: (a) a steady increase in the proportion of marriages between persons one or both of whom have been previously divorced and (b) the slow but steady decline in the rate of remarriage among divorced spouses. As regards the first trend, the proportion of marriages involving divorced spouses has increased in recent years: in the United States from 6% in 1955 to 45% in 1981 to 46% in 1991 (Ahrons & Rodgers, 1987; Cherlin, 1981; Cox, 1993, p. 629; Furstenberg, 1990; Masnick & Bane, 1980); in Canada, from 17% in 1967 to 39% in 1981 to 47% in 1989 (Statistics Canada, 1991); and in the United Kingdom from 9% in 1961 to 33% in 1986 (Stone, 1990). In regard to the second trend, in 1979 of all divorced spouses in the United States, 80% of the men and 75% of the women eventually remarried (Cherlin, 1981); it is the women who, in recent years, have been less willing to remarry and of those who are willing, have extended the time between divorce and remarriage (Norton & Moorman, 1987; for data on the decline in remarriage rates, see Uhlenberg et al., 1990). Similarly, in Canada in the mid-70s, 84% of divorced

men and 76% of divorced women subsequently remarried (Adams & Nagnur, 1989); that is, in recent years both men and women have been less willing to remarry, although the size of the gender difference remains unchanged. Evidence (Ganong & Coleman, 1989; Reiss & Lee, 1988; Stout, 1991; Wilson & Cunningham-Clarke, 1992; see Holland, 1990) suggest this results from a steep rise in the number of divorced spouses who cohabit rather than remarry.

88. See also Glick (1984a); Kitson et al. (1985); and Mueller and Pope (1977).

89. A related result is a small group of what Ambert (1989) has called "marital movers," those who have been married and divorced three or more times (see Morgan, 1991).

90. Finances too continue to play a role. Comparing female and male custodial parents, both Hill (1992) and Wilson and Cunningham-Clarke (1992) found that remarriage was associated with a dramatic decline in child support payments and other benefits (such as insurance) among females but no change among males.

91. See also Glenn and Kramer (1987); Guidubaldi (1988); and McLanahan (1992).

92. See also Farber et al. (1985); Harris, Brown, and Bifulco (1986); and Tennant, Bebbington, and Hurry (1980).

93. See also Glenn and Kramer (1985) and McLanahan (1992).

94. In this regard, Gee (1993, p. 309), following an analysis of Canadian data, notes that, "There are similarities with the results of U.S. research but there are also enough differences to suggest that adult outcomes [of parental divorce] may be bound up with the wider social, economic, and political context of a nation."

95. See also McLanahan (1988); McLanahan and Bumpass (1988); Mueller and Pope (1977); and Pope and Mueller (1979); cf. Gee (1993).

96. The increased risk of divorce is in the order of 5% to 12%.

97. Finkelhor's (1984, chap. 12) review of the evidence for the long-term effects of childhood sexual abuse is more equivocal. "Hard" evidence of such effects are, in fact, extremely thin, whereas clinical evidence is voluminous but notoriously "soft."

98. In addition, Finkelhor (1984, p. 198) argues that, "This preoccupation [with the question of long-term effects] is a kind of ethnocentrism on the part of adults. The impact of an event in childhood itself is treated as less important. It is only 'childhood,' a stage which, after all, everyone outgrows." Rather, speaking about child sexual abuse, he suggests that, "It is a noxious event of childhood, serious for its immediate unpleasantness, if nothing else, not necessarily for its long-term effects."

99. The structural complexity of binuclear family systems is exacerbated by the current ambiguity of the law in regard to such systems (Victor, Robbins, & Bassett, 1991); especially whether parents' first priority should be to the children from their first marriage or to the children and the new spouses of their second marriage (Fine, 1989; Fine & Fine, 1992).

100. See also Bowerman and Irish (1982); Clingempeel and Segal (1986); and Duberman (1973).

101. See also Parish and Dostal (1980); and Parish and Taylor (1979).

102. Other institutional actors might include a combination of the following: medical actors, other legal actors (e.g., the police, probation officers); social assistance actors (e.g., welfare, unemployment insurance, pensions); real estate professionals, taxation consultants, educational actors, and child protection actors.

REFERENCES

Abelsohn, D., & Saayman, G. S. (1991). Adolescent adjustment to parental divorce: An investigation from the perspective of basic dimensions of structural family therapy theory. *Family Process, 30*(2), 177-191.

Adams, B. N. (1979). Mate selection in the United States: A theoretical summarization. In W. R. Burr, R. Hill, F. I. Nye, & I. L. Reiss, (Eds.), *Contemporary theories about the family: Vol. 1: Research-based theories.* New York: Free Press.

Adams, K. S., Lohrenz, J. G., & Harper, D. (1973). Suicidal ideation and parental loss: A preliminary research report. *Canadian Psychiatric Association Journal, 18,* 95-100.

Adams, O., & Nagnur, D. (1989). Marrying and divorcing: A status report for Canada. *Canadian Social Trends, 15,* 24-27.

Ahrons, C. R. (1979). The coparental divorce: Preliminary research findings and policy implications. In A. L. Milne (Ed.), *Joint custody: A handbook for judges, lawyers and counselors.* Portland, OR: Association of Family and Conciliation Courts.

Ahrons, C. R. (1983a). Divorce: Before, during, and after. In H. I. McCubbin & C. R. Figley (Eds.), *Stress and the family. Vol. 1: Coping with normative transitions.* New York: Brunner/Mazel.

Ahrons, C. R. (1983b). Predictors of potential involvement postdivorce: Mothers' and fathers' perceptions. *Journal of Divorce, 6*(3), 55-69.

Ahrons, C., & Bowman, M. (1982). Changes in family relationships following divorce of adult children: Grandmothers' perceptions. *Journal of Divorce, 5,* 49-68.

Ahrons, C. R., & Rodgers, R. H. (1987). *Divorced families: A multidisciplinary developmental view.* New York: Norton.

Ahrons, C., & Wallisch, L. (1986). The relationship between former spouses. In S. Duck & D. Perlman (Eds.), *Close relationships: Development, dynamics, and deterioration.* Beverly Hills, CA: Sage.

Ahrons, C. R., & Wallisch, L. (1987). Parenting in the binuclear family: Relationships between biological and stepparents. In K. Pasley & M. Ihinger-Tallman (Eds.), *Remarriage and stepparenting.* New York: Guilford.

Ainsworth, M., Salter, D., Blehar, M., Walters, E., & Wall, S. (1978). *Patterns of attachment.* Hillsdale, NJ: Lawrence Erlbaum.

Albrecht, S. L. (1980). Reactions and adjustments to divorce: Differences in the experiences of males and females. *Family Relations, 29,* 59-68.

Albrecht, S. L., Bahr, H. M., & Goodman, K. L. (1983). *Divorce and remarriage: Problems, adaptations, and adjustments.* Westport, CT: Greenwood.

Albrecht, S. L., & Kunz, P. R. (1980). The decision to divorce: A social exchange perspective. *Journal of Divorce, 3,* 319-337.

Allen, R. (1991). A survey of child custody laws in Ontario. *Canadian Family Law Quarterly, 9,* 11-42.

Allison, P. D., & Furstenberg, F. F., Jr. (1989). How marital dissolution affects children. *Developmental Psychology, 25,* 540-549.

Amato, P. R. (1989). Long-term implications of parental divorce for adult self-concept. *Journal of Family Issues, 9*(2), 201-213.

Amato, P. R., & Booth, A. (1991). The consequences of divorce for attitudes towards divorce and gender roles. *Journal of Family Issues, 12*(3), 306-322.

Amato, P., & Keith, B. (1991). Parental divorce and adult well-being: A meta-analysis. *Journal of Marriage and the Family, 53,* 43-59.

Amato, P. R., & Partridge, S. (1987). Widows and divorcees with dependent children: Material, personal, family, and social well-being. *Family Relations, 36,* 316-320.

Ambert, A.-M. (1980). *Divorce in Canada.* Toronto: Academic Press.

Ambert, A.-M. (1983). Separated women and remarriage behavior: A comparison of financially secure women and financially insecure women. *Journal of Divorce, 6,* 43-54.

Ambert, A.-M. (1984). Longitudinal changes in children's behavior toward custodial parents. *Journal of Marriage and the Family, 46*(2), 463-467.

Ambert, A.-M. (1985). Custodial parents: Review and a longitudinal study. In B. Schlesinger (Ed.), *The one-parent family in the 1980s: Perspectives and annotated bibliography 1978-1984.* Toronto: University of Toronto Press.

Ambert, A.-M. (1988a). Relationship between ex-spouses: Individual and dyadic perspectives. *Journal of Social & Personal Relations, 5,* 327-346.

Ambert, A.-M. (1988b). Relationship between former in-laws after divorce: A research note. *Journal of Marriage and the Family, 50,* 679-686.

Ambert, A.-M. (1989). *Ex-spouses and new spouses: A study of relationships.* Greenwich, CT: JAI Press.

Ambert, A.-M. (1990). Marital dissolution: Structural and ideological changes. In M. Baker (Ed.), *Families: Changing trends in Canada* (2nd ed.). Toronto: McGraw-Hill Ryerson.

Ambert, A.-M. (1992). *The effect of children on parents.* New York: Haworth.

Ambert, A.-M., & Baker, M. (1984). Marriage dissolution: Structural and ideological changes. In M. Baker (Ed.), *Families: Changing trends in Canada.* Toronto: McGraw-Hill Ryerson.

Ambert, A.-M., & Saucier, J. F. (1983). Adolescents' perception of their parents by parents' marital status. *Journal of Social Psychology, 120,* 101-110.

Ambert, A.-M., & Saucier, J. F. (1984). Adolescents' perception of their parents and parents' marital status. *Canadian Review of Sociology & Anthropology, 21,* 62-74.

Ankenbrandt, M. J. (1986). Learned resourcefulness and other cognitive variables related to divorce adjustment in children. *Dissertation Abstracts International, 47,* 5045B-4046B.

Anspach, D. (1976). Kinship and divorce. *Journal of Marriage and the Family, 38,* 323-330.

Appel, K. W. (1985). *America's changing families: A guide for educators.* Bloomington, IN: Phi Delta Kappa Educational Foundation.

Aquirre, B. E., & Parr, W. C. (1982). Husbands' marriage order and the stability of first and second marriages of white and black women. *Journal of Marriage and the Family, 44,* 605-620.

Ard, B. N., Jr., & Ard, C. C. (Eds.). (1976). *Handbook of marriage counseling* (2nd ed.). Palo Alto, CA: Science & Behavior Books.

Arendell, T. (1986). *Mothers and divorce.* Berkeley: University of California Press.

Arendell, T. J. (1987). Women and the economics of divorce in the contemporary United States. *Signs, 13*(1), 121-135.

Arditti, J. A. (1992). Differences between fathers with joint custody and noncustodial fathers. *American Journal of Orthopsychiatry, 62,* 186-195.

Arnold, R., Wheeler, M., & Pendrith, F. (1980). *Separation and after: A research report.* Toronto: Ministry of Community and Social Services.

Atkeson, B. M., Forehand, R. L., & Rickard, K. M. (1982). The effects of divorce on children. In B. B. Lahey & A. E. Kazdin (Eds.), *Advances in clinical psychology* (Vol. 5). New York: Plenum.

Atkin, E., & Rubin, E. (1976). *Part-time father.* New York: Vanguard.

Atwater, L. (1987, November 30). College students' extramarital involvement. *Sexuality Today,* p. 2.

Bahr, S. J. (1983). Marital dissolution laws: Impact of recent changes for women. *Journal of Family Issues, 4*(3), 455-466.

Baker, M. (1983). Divorce: Its consequences and meanings. In K. Ishwaran (Ed.), *The Canadian family.* Toronto: Gage.

Bala, N. (1987). Family law in the United States and Canada: Different versions of similar realities. *International Journal of Law & the Family, 1*(1).

Bala, N. (1991). Child and family policies for the 1990's: Justice issues. In L. C. Johnson & D. Barnhorst (Eds.), *Children, families and public policy in the 90s.* Toronto: Thompson Educational Publishers.

Bane, M. J. (1979). Marital disruption and the lives of children. In G. Levinger & O. C. Moles (Eds.), *Divorce and separation: Context, causes, and consequences.* New York: Basic Books.

Bane, M. J., & Ellwood, D. T. (1986). Slipping in and out of poverty: The dynamics of spells. *Journal of Human Resources, 21,* 1-23.

Bartz, K. W., & Witcher, W. C. (1978). When fathers get custody. *Children Today, 7,* 2-6.

Beal, E. W. (1980). Separation, divorce, and single-parent families. In E. A. Carter & M. McGoldrick (Eds.), *The family life cycle: A framework for family therapy.* New York: Gardner.

Bean, C. A. (1992). *Women murdered by the men they loved.* New York: Haworth.

Beaujot, R. (1990). The family and demographic change in Canada: Economic and cultural interpretations and solutions. *Journal of Comparative Family Studies, 21*(1), 25-37.

Beller, A. H., & Graham, J. W. (1985). Variation in the economic well-being of divorced women and their children: The role of child support income. In M. David & T. Smeeding (Eds.), *Horizontal equity, uncertainty, and economic well-being.* Chicago: University of Chicago Press.

Beller, A. H., & Graham, J. W. (1988). Child support payments: Evidence from repeated cross-sections. *American Economic Review, Papers and Proceedings, 78*(2), 81-178.

Benjamin, M. (1980). Abused as a child, abusive as a parent: Practitioners beware. In R. Volpe, M. Breton, & J. Mitton (Eds.), *The maltreatment of the school-aged child.* Toronto: Lexington.

Benjamin, M. (1983). General systems theory, family systems theories, and family therapy: Towards an integrated recursive model of family process. In A. Bross (Ed.), *Family therapy: A recursive model of strategic practice.* New York: Guilford.

Berger, J. (1988). A theory of normative control processes. In M. Webster & M. Foschi (Eds.), *Studies in expectation-states theory.* Stanford, CA: Stanford University Press.

Berger, J., Rosenholtz, S., & Zelditch, M., Jr. (1980). Status-organizing processes. *Annual Review of Sociology, 6,* 479-508.

Berman, C. (1992). *Adult children of divorce speak out.* New York: Doubleday.

Berman, W. H., & Turk, D. C. (1981). Adaptation to divorce: Problems and coping strategies. *Journal of Marriage and the Family, 43,* 11-39.

Bernard, C., Ward, R., & Knoppers, B. (1992). Best interests of the child exposed: A portrait of Quebec custody and protection. *Canadian Journal of Family Law, 11,* 57-149.

Bernard, J. (1966). Marital stability and patterns of status variables. *Journal of Marriage and the Family, 28,* 421-439.

Berner, R. T. (1992). *Parents whose parents were divorced.* New York: Haworth.

Bernstein, N. R., & Robey, J. S. (1962). The detection and management of pediatric difficulties created by divorce. *Pediatrics, 16,* 950-956.

Betzig, L. L. (1989). Causes of conjugal dissolution. *Current Anthropology, 30,* 654-676.

Bielby, W. T., & Baron, J. N. (1986). Men and women at work: Sex segregation and statistical discrimination. *American Journal of Sociology, 91,* 759-799.

Bishop, T. A. (1987). The litigation process: Its effective utilization and avoidance. In J. G. McLeod (Ed.), *Family dispute resolution: Litigation and its alternatives.* Toronto: Carswell.

Bisnaire, L., Firestone, P., & Rynard, D. (1990). Factors associated with academic achievement in children following parental separation. *American Journal of Orthopsychiatry, 60,* 67-76.

Black, K. N. (1959). What about the child from a one-parent home? *Teacher, 5,* 24-28.

Block, J., Block, J. H., & Gjerde, P. F. (1988). Parental functioning and the home environment in families of divorce. *Journal of the American Academy of Child & Adolescent Psychiatry, 27,* 207-213.

Block, J. H., Block, J., & Gjerde, P. F. (1986). The personality of children prior to divorce: A prospective study. *Child Development, 57,* 827-840.

Block, J. H., Block, J., & Morrison, A. (1981). Parental agreement-disagreement on child-rearing orientations and gender-related personality correlates in children. *Child Development, 52,* 965-974.

Bloom, B. L. (1975). *Changing patterns in psychiatric care.* New York: Human Sciences Press.

Bloom, B. L., Asher, S. J., & White, S. W. (1978). Marital disruption as a stressor: A review and analysis. *Psychological Bulletin, 85,* 867-894.

Bloom, B. L., & Hodges, W. (1981). The predicament of the newly separated. *Community Mental Health, 7,* 227.

Bloom, B. L., Hodges, W. F., & Caldwell, R. A. (1983). Marital separation: The first eight months. In E. J. Callahan & K. A. McCluskey (Eds.), *Life-span developmental psychology: Non-normative events.* New York: Academic Press.

Blum, H. M., Boyle, M. H., & Offord, D. R. (1988). Single-parent families: Child psychiatric disorder and school performance. *Journal of the American Academy of Child & Adolescent Psychiatry, 27,* 214-219.

Bohannan, P. (1971). Divorce chains, households of remarriage, and multiple divorces. In P. Bohannan (Ed.), *Divorce and after.* Garden City, NY: Anchor.

Bohannan, P. (1985). *All the happy families: Exploring the varieties of family life.* New York: McGraw-Hill.

Booth, A., Brinkerhoff, D. B., & White, L. K. (1984). The impact of parental divorce on courtship. *Journal of Marriage and the Family, 65*(4), 85-94.

Booth, A., Johnson, D. R., White, L., & Edwards, J. N. (1986). Divorce and marital stability over the life course. *Journal of Family Issues, 7,* 421-447.

Bornstein, P. E., Clayton, P. J., Halikas, J. A., Maurice, W. L., & Robins, E. (1973). The depression of widowhood after thirteen months. *British Journal of Psychiatry, 122,* 561-566.

Boss, P. (1977). A clarification of the concept of psychological father presence in families experiencing ambiguity of boundaries. *Journal of Marriage and the Family, 39,* 141-151.

Botwin, C. (1988). *Men who can't be faithful.* New York: Warner.

Bower, D. W., & Christopherson, V. A. (1977). University student cohabitation: A regional comparison of selected attitudes and behavior. *Journal of Marriage and the Family, 39,* 447-453.

Bowerman, C. E., & Irish, D. P. (1982). Some relationships of stepchildren to their parents. *Marriage & Family Living, 44,* 113-121.

Boyd, S. (1989). From gender specificity to gender neutrality? Ideologies in Canadian child custody law. In C. Smaft & S. Sevenhuijsen (Eds.), *Child custody and the politics of gender.* New York: Routledge.

Braid, K. F. (1972). Gross addiction to alcohol and narcotics as evidence of marriage breakdown in Canada. *University of Toronto Faculty of Law Review, 30,* 97-109.

Brandwein, R., Brown, C., & Fox, E. (1974). Women and children last: The social situation of divorced mothers and their families. *Journal of Marriage and the Family, 36,* 498-514.

Brannen, J., & Collard, J. (1982). *Marriages in trouble: The process of seeking help.* London: Tavistock.

Braver, S., Gonzalez, N., Wolchik, S., & Sandler, I. (1989). Economic hardship and psychological distress in custodial mothers. *Journal of Divorce, 12(4),* 19-34.

Braver, S., Wolchik, S., Sandler, I., Forgas, B., & Zvetina, D. (1991). Frequency of visitation by divorced fathers: Differences in reports by fathers and mothers. *American Journal of Orthopsychiatry, 61,* 448-454.

Breunlin, D. C. (1989). Clinical implications of oscillation theory: Family development and the process of change. In C. N. Ramsey, Jr. (Ed.), *Family systems in medicine.* New York: Guilford.

Brice, J. (1982). West Indian families. In M. McGoldrick, J. K. Pearce, & J. Giordano (Eds.), *Ethnicity and family therapy.* New York: Guilford.

Brown, E. (1976). A model of the divorce process. *Conciliation Courts Review, 14(2),* 1-10.

Brown E. M. (1987). The hidden meaning: An analysis of different types of affairs. *Marriage & Divorce Today, 12(44),* 1-2.

Brown, E. M. (1991). *Patterns of infidelity and their treatment.* New York: Brunner/Mazel.

Brown, P., Felton, B. J., Munela, R., & Whitman, V. (1980). Attachment in adults: The special case of recently separated marital partners. *Journal of Divorce, 3,* 303-317.

Brown, P., Felton, B. J., Whitman, V., & Munela, R. (1980). Attachment and distress following marital separation. *Journal of Divorce, 3,* 303-317.

Bryant, S. (1992). Mediation for lesbian and gay families. *Mediation Quarterly, 9(4),* 29-42.

Buchanan, C., Maccoby, E., & Dornbusch, S. (1992). Adolescents and their families after divorce: Three residential arrangements compared. *Journal of Research on Adolescence, 2(3),* 261-291.

Buchanan, C. M., Maccoby, E. E., & Dornbusch, S. M. (1991). Caught between parents: Adolescents' experience in divorced homes. *Child Development, 62,* 1008-1029.

Buehler, C. (1989). Influential factors and equity issues in divorce settlements. *Family Relations, 38,* 76-82.

Buehler, C., Hogan, M. J., Robinson, B., & Levy, R. (1987). Remarriage following divorce: Stressors and well-being of custodial and non-custodial parents. *Journal of Family Issues, 7,* 405-420.

Bumpass, L. L. (1984). Children and marital disruption: A replication and update. *Demography, 21,* 71-82.

Bumpass, L. L., Martin, T. C., & Sweet, J. A. (1991). The impact of family background and early marital factors on marital disruption. *Journal of Family Issues, 12(1),* 22-42.

Bumpass, L. L., & Sweet, J. A. (1972). Differentials in marital instability. *American Sociological Review, 37,* 754-766.

Bumpass, L., Sweet, J., & Castro-Martin, T. (1990). Changing patterns of remarriage. *Journal of Marriage and the Family, 52,* 747-756.

Burchinal, L. G., & Chancellor, L. E. (1963). Survival rates of religiously homogamous and interreligious marriages. *Social Forces, 41,* 353-362.

Burgess, J. K. (1970). The single-parent family: A social and sociological problem. *Family Coordinator, 19,* 137-144.

Camara, K. A., & Resnick, G. (1987). Marital and parental subsystems in mother-custody, father-custody, and two-parent households: Effects on children's social development. In J. Vincent (Ed.), *Advances in family assessment, intervention and research* (Vol. 4). Greenwich, CT: JAI.

Camara, K. A., & Resnick, G. (1988). Interparental conflict and cooperation: Factors moderating children's post divorce adjustment. In E. M. Hetherington & J. D. Arasteh (Eds.), *Impact of divorce, single parenting, and stepparenting on children.* Hillsdale, NJ: Lawrence Erlbaum.

Camara, K. A., & Resnick, G. (1989). Styles of conflict resolution and cooperation between divorced parents: Effects on child behavior and adjustment. *American Journal of Orthopsychiatry, 59,* 560-574.

Canadian Institute of Law Research and Reform. (1981). *Matrimonial support failures: Reasons, profiles, and perceptions of individuals involved.* Edmonton, AL: CILRR.

Carter, H., & Glick, P. C. (1970). *Marriage and divorce: A social and economic study.* Cambridge, MA: Harvard University Press.

Casey, S. (1994). Homosexual parents and Canadian child custody law. *Family and Conciliation Courts Review, 32*(3), 379-396.

Castro-Martin, T., & Bumpass, L. (1989). Recent trends and differentials in marital disruption. *Demography, 26,* 37-51.

Chalfant, H. P. (1985). *Sociology of poverty in the United States: An annotated bibliography.* Westport, CT: Greenwood.

Chambers, D. (1979). *Making fathers pay.* Chicago: University of Chicago Press.

Cherlin, A. J. (1981). *Marriage, divorce, remarriage.* Cambridge, MA: Harvard University Press.

Chiancola, S. P. (1978). The process of separation and divorce: A new approach. *Social Casework, 59*(8), 494-499.

Chiriboga, D. A., Coho, A., Stein, J. A., & Roberts, J. (1979). Divorce, stress, and social supports: A study of help-seeking behavior. *Journal of Divorce, 3,* 121-136.

Chiriboga, D. A., & Cutler, L. (1977). Stress response among divorcing men and women. *Journal of Divorce, 1,* 95-106.

Christensen, D., Dahl, C., & Rettig, K. (1990). Noncustodial mothers and child support: Examining the larger context. *Family Relations, 39,* 388-394.

Christopoulos, C., Cohn, D. A., Shaw, D. S., Joyce, S., Kraft, S. P., & Emery, R. E. (1987). Children of battered women I: Adjustment at time of shelter residence. *Journal of Marriage and the Family, 49,* 611-619.

Clarke-Stewart, A. (1977). *Child care in the family.* New York: Academic Press.

Clingempeel, W. G., & Segal, S. (1986). Stepparent-stepchild relationships and the psychological adjustment of children in stepmother and stepfather families. *Child Development, 57,* 474-484.

Cochrane, M. (1991). *The everyday guide to Canadian family law.* Toronto: Prentice Hall.

Coleman, M. A., & Ganong, L. H. (1990). Remarriage and stepfamily research in the 1980s: Increased interest in an old family form. *Journal of Marriage and the Family,* 52, 925-940.

Colletta, N. D. (1979a). The impact of divorce: Father absence or poverty? *Journal of Divorce, 3,* 27-35.

Colletta, N. D. (1979b). Support systems after divorce: Incidence and impact. *Journal of Marriage and the Family, 41,* 837-846.

Colletta, N. D. (1983). Stressful lives: The situation of divorced mothers and their children. *Journal of Divorce, 6*(3), 19-31.

Colon, F. (1980). The family life cycle of the multiproblem poor family. In E. A. Carter & M. McGoldrick (Eds.), *The family life cycle: A framework for family therapy.* New York: Gardner.

Committee on the Family, Group for the Advancement of Psychiatry. (1981). *Divorce, child custody, and the family.* San Francisco: Jossey-Bass.

Conway, P. M. (1970). To insure domestic tranquility: Reconciliation services as an alternative to the divorce attorney. *Journal of Family Law, 9,* 408-424.

Coogler, O. J. (1977). Changing the lawyer's role in matrimonial practice. *Conciliation Courts Review, 15*(1), 1-8.

Cooney, T., Smyer, M., Hagestad, G., & Klock, R. (1986). Parental divorce in young adulthood: Some preliminary findings. *American Journal of Orthopsychiatry, 56*(3), 470-477.

Cooper, C. L. (1994). Family law: The leave connection. *Family & Conciliation Courts Review, 32*(3), 326-345.

Copeland, A. P. (1985). Individual differences in children's reactions to divorce. *Journal of Clinical Child Psychology, 14*(1), 11-19.

Corey, M. A. (1989). *Why men cheat: Psychological profiles of the adulterous male.* Springfield, IL: Charles C Thomas.

Cox, F. D. (1993). *Human intimacy: Marriage, the family and its meaning* (6th ed.). Minneapolis, MN: West.

Cox, M. J. T., & Cease, L. (1978). Joint custody, what does it mean? How does it work? *Family Advocate, 1*(1), 10-13, 42-44.

Coysh, W. S., Johnston, J. R., Tschann, T., Wallerstein, J. S., & Kline, M. (1989). Parental postdivorce adjustment in joint and sole physical custody families. *Journal of Family Issues, 10*(1), 52-70.

Cramer, D. (1986). Gay parents and their children. *Journal of Counseling & Development, 64,* 504-507.

Crosby, J. F., Gage, B. R., & Raymond, M. C. (1983). The grief resolution process in divorce. *Journal of Divorce, 7,* 3-18.

Cuber, J. F., & Haroff, P. B. (1977). Fives types of marriage. In A. S. Skolnick & J. H. Skolnick (Eds.), *Family in transition* (2nd ed.). Boston: Little, Brown.

Curran, D. K. (1987). *Adolescent suicidal behavior.* New York: Harper & Row.

Cutright, P. (1971). Income and family events: Marital stability. *Journal of Marriage and the Family, 33,* 291-306.

Dawson, D. (1991). Family structure and children's health and well-being: Data from the 1988 National Health Interview Survey of Child Health. *Journal of Marriage and the Family, 53,* 573-584.

Department of Justice. (1987). *Evaluation of the Divorce Act—Phase I: Collection of baseline data.* Ottawa: Queen's Printer for Canada.

Department of Justice. (1990). *Evaluation of the Divorce Act—Phase II: Monitoring and evaluation.* Ottawa: Queen's Printer for Canada.

Department of Justice. (1993). *Custody and access: Public discussion paper.* Ottawa: Ministry of Supply and Services Canada.

Derdeyn, A. P. (1976). Child custody contests in historical perspective. *American Journal of Psychiatry, 133*(12), 1369-1376.

Desimone-Luis, J., O'Mahoney, K., & Hunt, D. (1979). Children of separation and divorce: Factors influencing adjustment. *Journal of Divorce, 3,* 37-42.

Despert, L. (1962). *Children of divorce.* New York: Dolphin/Doubleday.

Devore, W., & Schlesinger, E. G. (1987). *Ethnic-sensitive social work practice* (2nd ed.). New York: Macmillan.

Dickinson, G. E., & Leming, M. R. (1990). *Understanding families: Diversity, continuity, and change.* Boston: Allyn & Bacon.

Doane, J. A., & Cohen, E. L. (1981). Interpersonal help-giving by family practice lawyers. *American Journal of Community Psychology, 9,* 547-558.

Doherty, W. J., Su, S., & Needle, R. (1989). Marital disruption and wellbeing: A panel study. *Journal of Family Issues, 10*(1), 72-85.

Dreyfus, E. A. (1979). Counseling the divorced father. *Journal of Marital and Family Therapy, 5,* 79-85.

Duberman, L. (1973). Step-kin relationships. *Journal of Marriage and the Family, 35,* 283-292.

Dudley, J. R. (1991). Increasing our understanding of divorced fathers who have infrequent contact with their children. *Family Relations, 40,* 279-285.

Duffy, A., & Pupo, N. (1992). *Part-time paradox: Connecting gender, work and family.* Toronto: McClelland & Stewart.

Duncan, G. J., & Hoffman, S. D. (1985). A reconsideration of the economic consequences of marital dissolution. *Demography, 22,* 485-497.

Duncan, G. J., & Rodgers, W. (1987). Single parent families: Are their economic problems transitory or persistent? *Family Planning Perspectives, 19,* 171-178.

Dunn, J., & Plomin, R. (1991). Why are siblings so different? The significance of differences in sibling experiences within the family. *Family Process, 30,* 271-283.

Eastman, S. (1992). Improving outcomes for divorced women. *Canadian Public Policy, 18,* 318-326.

Ebaugh, H. R. F. (1988). *Becoming an ex: The process of role exit.* Chicago: University of Chicago Press.

Economic Council of Canada. (1992). *The new face of poverty: Income security needs of Canadian families.* Ottawa: Ministry of Supply and Services.

Eichler, M. (1993). Lone parent families: An instable category in search of stable policies. In J. Hudson & B. Galaway (Eds.), *Single parent families: Perspectives on research and policy.* Toronto: Thompson Educational Publishers.

Elkin, M. (1977). A counseling model for lawyering in divorce cases. *Notre Dame Law Journal, 53,* 232-265.

Emberson, D., & Gove, W. R. (1989). Parenthood and psychological well-being: Theory, measurement, and stage in the family life course. *Journal of Family Issues, 10*(4), 440-462.

Emery, R. E. (1982). Interparental conflict and the children of discord and divorce. *Psychological Bulletin, 92,* 310-330.

Emery, R. E. (1988). *Marriage, divorce, and children's adjustment.* Newbury Park, CA: Sage.

Emery, R. E., Hetherington, E. M., & DiLalla, L. F. (1984). Divorce, children, and social policy. In H. W. Stevenson & A. E. Siegel (Eds.), *Child development research and social policy.* Chicago: University of Chicago Press.

Emery, R. E., Joyce, S. A., & Fincham, F. D. (1987). The assessment of marital and child problems. In K. D. O'Leary (Ed.), *Assessment of marital discord.* Hillsdale, NJ: Lawrence Erlbaum.

Emery, R. E., & Wyer, M. M. (1987). Divorce mediation. *American Psychologist, 42,* 472-480.

Erickson, S. K. (1988). The legal dimension of divorce mediation. In J. Folberg & A. Milne (Eds.), *Divorce mediation: Theory and practice.* New York: Guilford.

Eshleman, J. R. (1985). *The family: An introduction* (4th ed.). Boston: Allyn & Bacon.

Espenshade, T. J. (1979). The economic consequences of divorce. *Journal of Marriage and the Family, 41,* 615-625.

Everett, C. A. (Ed.). (1987). *The divorce process: A handbook for clinicians.* New York: Haworth.

Everett, C. A. (Ed.). (1988). *Minority and ethnic issues in the divorce process.* New York: Haworth.

Everett, C. A. (Ed.). (1989). *Children of divorce.* New York: Haworth.

Everett, C. A. (1991). *Marital instability and divorce outcomes: Issues for therapists and educators.* New York: Haworth.

Everett, C. A. (Ed.). (1993). *Divorce and the next generation: Effects on young adults' patterns of intimacy and expectations for marriage.* New York: Haworth.

Farber, B. (1964). *Family organization and interaction.* San Francisco: Chandler.

Farber, S. S., Felner, R. D., & Primavera, J. (1985). Parental separation/divorce and adolescents: An examination of factors mediating adaptation. *American Journal of Community Psychology, 13*(2), 171-185.

Federico, J. (1979). The marital termination period of the divorce adjustment process. *Journal of Divorce, 3,* 93-106.

Felner, R. D., Primavera, J., Farber, S. S., & Bishop, T. A. (1982). Attorneys as caregivers during divorce. *American Journal of Orthopsychiatry, 52,* 323-336.

Ferguson, A. (1978). The divorce experience. *Conciliation Courts Review, 16,* 33-34.

Fergusson, D. M. C., Horwood, L. J., & Shannon, F. T. (1984). A proportional hazards model of family breakdown. *Journal of Marriage and the Family, 46,* 539-549.

Fersh, E. A., Jr., & Verling, J. A., III. (1976). Divorce: Legal reports versus psychological realities. In H. Grunebaum & J. Christ (Eds.), *Contemporary marriage: Structure, dynamics, and therapy.* Boston: Little, Brown.

Fethke, C. C. (1989). Life-cycle models of saving and the effect of the timing of divorce on retirement economic well-being. *Journal of Gerontology, 44*(3), 5121-5128.

Fine, M. A. (1989). A social science perspective on stepfamily law: Suggestions for legal reform. *Family Relations, 38,* 53-58.

Fine, M. A., & Fine, D. R. (1992). Recent changes in laws affecting stepfamilies: Suggestions for legal reform. *Family Relations, 41,* 334-340.

Fine, M. A., Moreland, J. R., & Schwebel, A. I. (1983). Long-term effects of divorce on parent-child relationships. *Developmental Psychology, 19*(5), 703-713.

Fineberg, A. D. (1979). Joint custody of infants: Breakthrough or fad? *Canadian Journal of Family Law, 2*(4), 417-454.

Finkel, N. J. (1974). Stress and traumas: An attempt at categorization. *American Journal of Community Psychology, 2,* 265-273.

Finkel, N. J. (1975). Stress, trauma, and trauma resolution. *American Journal of Community Psychology, 3,* 173-178.

Finkelhor, D. (1984). *Child sexual abuse: New theory and research.* New York: Free Press.

Finkelhor, D., Hotaling, G., & Sedlak, A. (1991). Children abducted by family members: A national household survey of incidence and episode characteristics. *Journal of Marriage and the Family, 53,* 805-817.

Finnie, R. (1993). Women, men, and the economic consequences of divorce: Evidence from Canadian longitudinal data. *Canadian Review of Sociology & Anthropology, 30*(2), 205-239.

Fishel, A. H., & Scanzoni, J. (1989). An exploratory study of the post-divorce coparental relationship. *Journal of Divorce, 13*(2), 95-119.

Fisher, E. O. (Ed.). (1982). *Impact of divorce on the extended family.* New York: Haworth.

Fisher, H. E. (1992). *Anatomy of love: The natural history of monogamy, adultery, and divorce.* New York: Norton.

Flavell, J. H. (1979). Metacognition and cognitive monitoring: A new area of cognitive-developmental inquiry. *American Psychologist, 34,* 906-911.

Folberg, J. (1991). Appendix A: Joint custody statutes and judicial interpretations (as of January 1, 1991). In J. Folberg (Ed.), *Joint custody and shared parenting* (2nd ed.). New York: Guilford.

Folberg, J., & Graham, M. (1981). Joint custody following divorce. In H. H. Irving (Ed.), *Family law: An interdisciplinary perspective.* Toronto: Carswell.

Folk, K. F., Graham, J. W., & Beller, A. H. (1992). Child support and remarriage: Implications for the economic well-being of children. *Journal of Family Issues, 13*(2), 142-157.

Foote, C. E. (1988). Recent state responses to separation and divorce in Canada. *Canadian Social Work Review, 5,* 28-43.

Francke, L. B. (1984). The sons of divorce. In O. Pocs & R. H. Walsh (Eds.), *Annual edition: Marriage and family 84/85.* Guilford, CT: Dushkin.

Freed, D., & Walker, T. (1989). Family law in the fifty states: An overview. *Family Law Quarterly, 22*(3), 1-115.

Freed, D., & Walker, T. (1990). Family law in the fifty states: An overview. *Family Law Quarterly, 23*(4), 495-608.

Friedl, E. (1975). *Women and men: An anthropologist's view.* New York: Holt, Rinehart & Winston.

Froiland, D. J., & Hozman, T. L. (1977). Counseling for constructive divorce. *Personnel & Guidance Journal, 55,* 525-529.

Frost, A., & Pakiz, B. (1990). The effects of marital disruption on adolescents: Time as a dynamic. *American Journal of Orthopsychiatry, 60,* 544-553.

Fry, P., & Addington, J. (1985). Perceptions of parent and child adjustment in divorced families. *Clinical Psychology Review, 5,* 141-157.

Fry, P. S., & Trifiletti, R. J. (1983). An exploration of the adolescents' perspective: Perceptions of major stress dimensions in the single-parent family. *Journal of Psychiatric Treatment & Evaluation, 5,* 101-111.

Fulton, J. A. (1979). Parental reports of children's post-divorce adjustment. *Journal of Social Issues, 35,* 126-139.

Furstenberg, F. F., Jr. (1990). Divorce and the American family. *Annual Review of Sociology, 16,* 379-403.

Furstenberg, F. F., Jr., & Cherlin, A. J. (1991). *Divided families: What happens to children when parents part.* Cambridge, MA: Harvard University Press.

Furstenberg, F. F., Jr., Morgan, S., & Allison, P. (1987). Paternal participation and children's well-being after marital dissolution. *American Sociological Review, 52,* 695-701.

Furstenberg, F. F., Jr., & Nord, C. W. (1985). Parenting apart: Patterns of childrearing after divorce. *Journal of Marriage and the Family, 47,* 893-904.

Furstenberg, F. F., Jr., Peterson, J. L., Nord, C. W., & Zill, N. (1983). The life course of children of divorce: Marital disruption and parental contact. *American Sociological Review, 48,* 656-668.

Furstenberg, F. F., Jr., & Spanier, G. B. (1984). *Recycling the family: Remarriage after divorce.* Beverly Hills, CA: Sage.

Gabardi, L., & Rosen, L. A. (1991). Differences between college students from divorced and intact families. *Journal of Divorce & Remarriage, 18*(3/4), 175-191.

Gabardi, L., & Rosen, L. A. (1992). Intimate relationships: College students from divorced and intact families. *Journal of Divorce & Remarriage, 18*(3/4), 25-56.

Gamson, W. (1969). A theory of coalition formation. *American Sociological Review, 26,* 373-382.

Ganong, L. H., & Coleman, M. A. (1984). The effects of remarriage on children: A review of the empirical research. *Family Relations, 32,* 389-406.

Ganong, L. H., & Coleman, M. A. (1989). Preparing for remarriage: Anticipating the issues, seeking solutions. *Family Relations, 38,* 28-39.

Gardner, R. A. (1974). Psychological aspects of divorce. In S. Arieti (Ed.), *American handbook of psychiatry* (2nd ed.). New York: Basic Books.

Garfinkel, I. (1992). Child-support trends in the United States. In L. Weitzman & M. Maclean (Eds.), *Economic consequences of divorce: The international perspective.* Oxford: Clarendon.

Garfinkel, B., & Northrup, G. (1991). *Adolescent suicide.* New York: Haworth.

Garmezy, N. (1981). Children under stress: Perspectives on antecedents and correlates of vulnerability and resistance to psychopathology. In A. Rabin, J. Arnoff, A. Barclay, & R. Zucker (Eds.), *Further explorations in personality.* New York: John Wiley.

Gasser, R. D., & Taylor, C. M. (1976). Role adjustment of single fathers with dependent children. *Family Coordinator, 25,* 397-401.

Gately, D. W., & Schwebel, A. I. (1991). The challenge model of children's adjustment to parental divorce: Explaining favourable postdivorce outcomes in children. *Journal of Family Psychology, 5*(1), 60-81.

Gately, D. W., & Schwebel, A. I. (1992). Favourable outcomes in children after parental divorce. *Journal of Divorce & Remarriage, 18*(3/4), 57-78.

Gecas, V. (1979). The influence of social class on socialization. In W. R. Burr, R. Hill, F. I. Nye, & I. L. Reiss (Eds.), *Contemporary theories of the family* (Vol. 1). New York: Free Press.

Gee, E. M. (1993). Adult outcomes associated with childhood family structure: An appraisal of research and an evaluation of Canadian data. In J. Hudson & B. Galaway (Eds.), *Single parent families: Perspectives on research and policy.* Toronto: Thompson Educational Publishers.

George, V., & Wilding, P. (1972). *Motherless families.* London: Routledge & Kegan Paul.

Gersick, K. (1979). Fathers by choice: Divorced men who receive custody of their children. In G. Levinger & O. C. Moles (Eds.), *Divorce and separation: Contexts, causes, and consequences.* New York: Basic Books.

Gerstel, N. (1988). Divorce, gender, and social integration. *Gender & Society, 2*(3), 343-367.

Gibson, C. (1974). The association between divorce and social class in England and Wales. *British Journal of Sociology, 25*, 79-93.

Gifford, J. (1985). Delivery of family conciliation and mediation services: The B.C. model. *Canadian Journal of Family Law, 4*, 385-411.

Gigy, L., & Kelly, J. (1992). Reasons for divorce: Perspectives of divorcing men and women. *Journal of Divorce & Remarriage, 18*(1/2), 169-187.

Gladstone, J. (1989). Grandmother-grandchild contact: The mediating influence of the middle generation following marriage breakdown and remarriage. *Canadian Journal on Aging, 8*, 355-363.

Glasser, P., & Navarre, E. (1965). Structural problems of the one-parent family. *Journal of Social Issues, 21*, 98-109.

Glenn, N. D., & Kramer, K. B. (1985). The psychological well-being of adult children of divorce. *Journal of Marriage and the Family, 47*, 905-912.

Glenn, N. D., & Kramer, K. B. (1987). The marriages and divorces of the children of divorce. *Journal of Marriage and the Family, 49*, 811-825.

Glenn, N. D., & Supancic, M. (1984). The social and demographic correlates of divorce and separation in the United States: An update and reconsideration. *Journal of Marriage and the Family, 46*, 563-575.

Glick, P. C. (1957). *American families.* New York: John Wiley.

Glick, P. C. (1984a). Marriage, divorce, and living arrangements: Prospective changes. *Journal of Family Issues, 5*, 7-26.

Glick, P. C. (1984b). How American families are changing. *American Demographics, 6*, 20-27.

Glick P. C., & Lin, S. L. (1987). Remarriage after divorce: Recent changes and demographic variations. *Social Perspectives, 30*(2), 162-179.

Goetting, A. (1981). Divorce outcome research: Issues and perspectives. *Journal of Family Issues, 2*, 350-378.

Golan, N. (1981). *Passing through transitions: A guide for practitioners.* New York: Free Press.

Goldberg, M. L., & Dukes, J. L. (1985). Social support in black low-income, single parent families: Normative and dysfunctional patterns. *American Journal of Orthopsychiatry, 55*(1), 42-58.

Goldberg, G., & Kremen, E. (1987). The feminization of poverty: Only in America? *Social Policy, 17*(4), 3-14.

Goldsmith, J. (1980). Relationship between former spouses: Descriptive findings. *Journal of Divorce, 4*(2), 1-20.

Goldsmith, J. (1982). The postdivorce family system. In F. Walsh (Ed.), *Normal family processes.* New York: Guilford.

Goldstein, G., Freud, A., & Solnit, A. J. (1973). *Beyond the best interests of the child.* New York: Free Press.

Gongla, P. A. (1982). Single parent families: A look at families of mothers and children. *Marriage & Family Review, 5*, 5-27.

Goode, W. J. (1949). Problems in post-divorce adjustment. *American Sociological Review, 14*, 394-401.

Goode, W. J. (1956). *After divorce.* New York: Free Press.

Goode, W. J. (1992). World changes in divorce patterns. In L. Weitzman & M. Maclean (Eds.), *Economic consequences of divorce: The international perspective.* Oxford: Clarendon.

Gorlick, C. (1992). The female single parent student. *Canadian Woman Studies, 12*(4), 55-57.

Gould, E. (1968). The single-parent family benefits in parents without partners. *Journal of Marriage and the Family, 30,* 666-671.

Gove, W. R., & Sin, H.C. (1989). The psychological well-being of divorced and widowed men and women. *Journal of Family Issues, 10*(1), 122-144.

Graham-Cambrick, L., Gursky, E. J., & Brendler, J. (1982). Hospitalization of single-parent families of disturbed children. *Family Process, 21,* 141-152.

Grassby, M. (1991). Women in their forties: The extent of their rights to alimentary support. *Reports of Family Law, 30,* 369-403.

Greenberg, E. F., & Nay, W. R. (1982). The intergenerational transmission of marital instability reconsidered. *Journal of Marriage and the Family, 44,* 335-347.

Greenstein, T. N. (1985). Occupation and divorce. *Journal of Family Issues, 6*(3), 347-357.

Greenstein, T. N. (1990). Marital disruption and the employment of married women. *Journal of Marriage and the Family, 52,* 657-676.

Gregory, I. (1965). Anterospective data following childhood loss of a parent: II. Pathology, performance, and potential among college students. *Archives of General Psychiatry, 13,* 110-120.

Grief, J. B. (1979). Fathers, children, and joint custody. *American Journal of Orthopsychiatry, 49,* 311-319.

Grief, G. G., & Hegar, R. L. (1992). Impact on children of abduction by a parent: A review of the literature. *American Journal of Orthopsychiatry, 62,* 599-604.

Griffith, J. D., Koo, H. P., & Suchindran, C. M. (1984). Childlessness and marital stability in remarriages. *Journal of Marriage and the Family, 46,* 577-585.

Grossman, S. M., Shea, J. A., & Adams, G. R. (1980). Effects of parental divorce during early childhood on ego development and identity formation of college students. *Journal of Divorce, 3*(3), 263-272.

Grynch, J. H., & Fincham, F. D. (1990). Marital conflict and children's adjustment: A cognitive-contextual framework. *Psychological Bulletin, 108,* 267-290.

Guidubaldi, J. (1988). Differences in children's divorce adjustment across grade level and gender. In S. Wolchik & P. Karoly (Eds.), *Children of divorce.* Lexington, MA: Lexington Books.

Guidubaldi, J., & Cleminshaw, H. K. (1985). Divorce, family health, and child adjustment. *Family Relations, 34*(1), 35-41.

Guidubaldi, J., Cleminshaw, H. K., Perry, J. D., & McLaughlin, C. S. (1983). The impact of parental divorce on children: Report of the nationwide NASP study. *School Psychology Review, 12,* 300-323.

Guidubaldi, J., Cleminshaw, H. K., Perry, J. D., Natasi, B. K., & Lightel, J. (1986). The role of selecting family environment factors in children's post-divorce adjustment. *Family Relations, 35,* 124-141.

Guidubaldi, J., & Perry, J. D. (1985). Divorce and mental health sequelae for children: A two-year follow-up of a nationwide sample. *Journal of the American Academy of Child Psychiatry, 24,* 531-537.

Guidubaldi, J., Perry, J. D., & Cleminshaw, H. K. (1984). The legacy of parental divorce: A nationwide study of family status and selected mediating variables on children's academic and social competencies. In B. B. Lahey & A. E. Kazdin (Eds.), *Advances in child clinical psychology* (Vol. 7). New York: Plenum.

Guidubaldi, J., Perry, J. D., & Nastasi, B. K. (1987a). Assessment and intervention for children of divorce. In J. P. Vincent (Ed.), *Advances in family intervention, assessment and theory* (Vol. 4). Greenwich, CT: JAI Press.

Guidubaldi, J., Perry, J. D., & Nastasi, B. K. (1987b). Growing up in a divorced family. In S. Oskamp (Ed.), *Annual Review of Applied Social Psychology*. Newbury Park, CA: Sage.

Gurman, A. S. (Ed.). (1982). *Questions and answers in the practice of family therapy* (Vol. 2). New York: Brunner/Mazel.

Gurman, A. S., & Kniskern, D. P. (1981). Family therapy outcome research: Knowns and unknowns. In A. S. Gurman & D. P. Kniskern (Eds.), *Handbook of family therapy*. New York: Brunner/Mazel.

Guttman, J. (1993). *Divorce in psychosocial perspective: Theory and research*. Hillsdale, NJ: Lawrence Erlbaum.

Hagestad, G., Smyer, S., & Stierman, K. (1984). The impact of divorce in middle age. In R. Cohen, B. Cohler, & S. Weissmann (Eds.), *Parenthood: Psychodynamic perspectives*. New York: Guilford.

Hainline, L., & Feig, E. (1978). The correlates of childhood father absence in college-age women. *Child Development, 49*, 37-42.

Hajal, F., & Rosenberg, E. (1978). Working with the one-parent family in family therapy. *Journal of Divorce, 1*, 259-269.

Hanson, S. M. H. (1980). Characteristics of single custodial fathers and the parent-child relationship. *Dissertation Abstracts Index, 40*, M38-A.

Hanson, S. M. H. (1985). Single fathers with custody: A synthesis of the literature. In B. Schlesinger (Ed.), *The one-parent family in the 1980s: Perspectives and annotated bibliography 1978-1984*. Toronto: University of Toronto Press.

Harman, L. (1992). The feminization of poverty. *Canadian Women's Studies, 12*(4), 6-10.

Harris, T., Brown, G. W., & Bifulco, A. (1986). Loss of parent in childhood and adult psychiatric disorder: The role of lack of adequate parental care. *Psychological Medicine, 16*, 641-659.

Hart, N. (1976). *When marriage ends: A study in status passage*. London: Tavistock.

Hart, N. (1978). Marital breakdown as a personal crisis. In M. Corbin (Ed.), *The couple*. London: Penguin.

Health and Welfare Canada. (1987). *Suicide in Canada*. Ottawa: Health and Welfare Canada, National Task Force on Suicide in Canada.

Healy, J., Jr., Malley, J., & Stewart, A. (1990). Children and their fathers after parental separation. *American Journal of Orthopsychiatry, 60*, 531-543.

Heider, F. (1958). *The psychology of interpersonal relations*. New York: John Wiley.

Herzog, E., & Sudia, C. (1973). Children in fatherless families. In B. M. Caldwell & H. N. Ricuiti (Eds.), *Review of child development research. Vol. 3: Child development and child policy*. Chicago: University of Chicago Press.

Hess, R. D., & Camara, K. A. (1979). Post-divorce family relationships as mediating factors in the consequences of divorce for children. *Journal of Social Issues, 35*, 79-96.

Hetherington, E. M. (1966). Effects of paternal absence on sex-typed behaviors in Negro and white preadolescent males. *Journal of Personality & Social Psychology, 4*, 87-91.

Hetherington, E. M. (1972). Effects of father absence on personality development in adolescent daughters. *Developmental Psychology, 7*, 313-326.

Hetherington, E. M. (1979). Divorce: A child's perspective. *American Psychologist, 34*, 851-858.

Hetherington, E. M. (1980). Children and divorce. In R. Henderson (Ed.), *Parent-child interaction: Theory, research, and prospect*. New York: Academic Press.

Hetherington, E. M. (1987). Family relations six years after divorce. In K. Pasley & M. Ihinger-Tallman (Eds.), *Remarriage and stepparenting*. New York: Guilford.

Hetherington, E. M. (1989). Coping with family transitions: Winners, losers, and survivors. *Child Development, 60*, 1-14.

Hetherington, E. M., & Arasteh, J. D. (Eds.). (1988). *Impact of divorce, single parenting, and stepparenting*. Hillsdale, NJ: Lawrence Erlbaum.

Hetherington, E. M., Cox, M., & Cox, R. (1976). Divorced fathers. *Family Coordinator, 25*, 417-428.

Hetherington, E. M., Cox, M., & Cox, R. (1977). Beyond father absence: Conceptualizations of effects of divorce. In E. M. Hetherington & R. Parke (Eds.), *Contemporary readings in child psychology*. New York: McGraw-Hill.

Hetherington, E. M., Cox, M., & Cox, R. (1978). The aftermath of divorce. In J. Stevens, Jr., & M. Matthews (Eds.), *Mother-child father-child relations*. Washington, DC: National Association for the Education of Young Children.

Hetherington, E. M., Cox, M., & Cox, R. (1979). Family interaction and the social, emotional and cognitive development of children following divorce. In V. C. Vaughan & T. B. Brazelton (Eds.), *The family: Setting priorities*. New York: Science & Medicine Publishers.

Hetherington, E. M., Cox, M., & Cox, R. (1982). Effects of divorce on parents and children. In M. E. Lamb (Ed.), *Nontraditional families: Parenting and child development*. Hillsdale, NJ: Lawrence Erlbaum.

Hetherington, E. M., Cox, M., & Cox, R. (1985). The long-term effects of divorce and remarriage on the adjustment of children. *Journal of the American Academy of Child Psychiatry, 24*, 518-530.

Hetherington, E. M., Stanley-Hagan, M., & Anderson, E. R. (1989). Marital transition. *American Psychologist, 44*, 303-312.

Hewlett, S. (1991). *When the bough breaks: The cost of neglecting our children*. New York: Basic Books.

Hill, C. T., Rubin, Z., & Peplau, L. A. (1976). Breakups before marriage: The end of 103 affairs. *Journal of Social Issues, 32*, 147-168.

Hill, M. S. (1992). The role of economic resources and remarriage in financial assistance for children of divorce. *Journal of Family Issues, 13*(2), 158-178.

Hill, R. (1949). *Families under stress*. New York: Harper.

Hiller, D. V., & Philliber, W. W. (1982). Predicting marital and career success among dual-worker couples. *Journal of Marriage and the Family, 44*, 53-62.

Hines, P. M., & Boyd-Franklin, N. (1982). Black families. In M. McGoldrick, J. K. Pearce, & J. Giordano (Eds.), *Ethnicity and family therapy*. New York: Guilford.

Hobart, C. (1988). Relationships in remarried families. *Canadian Journal of Sociology, 13*, 261-281.

Hobart, C. (1991). Conflict in remarriages. *Journal of Divorce & Remarriage, 15*(3/4), 69-85.

Hobart, C., & Brown, D. (1989). Effects of prior marriage children on adjustment in remarriage: A Canadian study. *Journal of Comparative Family Studies, 19/20*, 381-395.

Hodges, W. F. (1986). *Interventions for children of divorce: Custody, access, and psychotherapy*. New York: Wiley-Interscience.

Hodges, W. F. (1991). *Fathers and child custody: A comparative review of interventions for children of divorce: Custody, access and psychotherapy*. New York: John Wiley.

Hodges, W. F. (in press). Problems of visitation post divorce. In W. Witlin & R. Hinds (Eds.), *The child custody handbook*. New York: Irvington.

Hodges, W. F., & Bloom, B. L. (1984). Parent's report of children's adjustment to marital separation: A longitudinal study. *Journal of Divorce, 8*, 33-42.

Hodges, W. F., & Bloom, B. L. (1986). Preventive intervention for newly separated adults: One year later. *Journal of Preventive Psychiatry, 3*(1), 35-49.

Hodges, W. F., Buchsbaum, H. K., & Tierney, C. W. (1984). Parent-child relationships and adjustment in preschool children in divorced and intact families. *Journal of Divorce, 7*, 43-57.

Hoffman, S. (1977). Marital instability and the economic status of women. *Demography, 14*, 67-76.

Hoffman, S. D., & Duncan, G. J. (1988). What are the economic consequences of divorce? *Demography, 25*, 641-645.

Holden, K. C., & Smock, P. J. (1991). The economic costs of marital dissolution: Why do women bear a disproportionate cost? *Annual Review of Sociology, 17*, 51-78.

Holland, W. (1990). *Cohabitation: The law in Canada*. Toronto: Carswell.

Holmes, T. S., & Rahe, R. H. (1967). The social adjustment rating scale. *Psychosomatic Research, 11*, 213-218.

Huber, J., & Spitze, G. (1980). Considering divorce: An expansion of Becker's theory of marital stability. *American Journal of Sociology, 86*, 75-89.

Huddleston, R. J., & Hawkings, L. (1993). The reaction of friends and family to divorce. *Journal of Divorce & Remarriage, 19*(1/2), 195-208.

Hughes, M. (1989). Parenthood and psychological well-being among the formerly married: Are children the primary source of psychological distress? *Journal of Family Issues, 10*(4), 463-481.

Hum, D., & Choudry, S. (1992). Income, work, and marital dissolution: Canadian experimental evidence. *Journal of Comparative Family Studies, 23*, 249-265.

Hunt, M. (1969). *The affair: A portrait of extramarital love in contemporary America*. New York: World.

Iams, H. M., & Ycas, M. A. (1988). Women, marriage and Social Security benefits. *Social Security Bulletin, 51*(3), 3-9.

Irving, H. H. (1979). Post-divorce counselling and access to children. In B. Schlesinger (Ed.), *One in ten: The single parent in Canada*. Toronto: Guidance Centre, Faculty of Education, University of Toronto.

Irving, H. H. (1980). *Divorce mediation: The rational alternative*. Toronto: Personal Library.

Irving, H. H., & Benjamin, M. (1987). *Family mediation: Theory and practice of dispute resolution*. Toronto: Carswell.

Irving, H. H., Benjamin, M., Bohm, P. E., & Macdonald, G. (1981). A study of conciliation counseling in the family court of Toronto: Implications for socio-legal practices. In H. H. Irving (Ed.), *Family law: An interdisciplinary perspective*. Toronto: Carswell.

Irving, H. H., & Bohm, P. E. (1981). An interdisciplinary approach to family dispute resolution. In H. H. Irving (Ed.), *Family law: An interdisciplinary perspective*. Toronto: Carswell.

Irving, H. H., & Irving, B. G. (1974). Conciliation counselling in divorce litigation. *Reports of Family Law, 16*, 257-266.

Isaacs, M. B., & Leon, G. H. (1986). Social networks, divorce, and adjustment: A tale of three generations. *Journal of Divorce, 9*, 1-16.

Isaacs, M. B., Montalvo, B., & Abelson, D. (1986). *The difficult divorce: Therapy for children and families*. New York: Basic Books.

Jacobs, H. (1988). *Silent revolution: The transformation of divorce law in the United States.* Chicago: University of Chicago Press.

Jacobs, J. (1982). The effects of divorce on fathers: An overview of the literature. *American Journal of Psychiatry, 139*(10), 1235-1241.

Jacobson, B. (1987). Family type, visiting patterns, and children's behavior in the stepfamily: A linked family system. In K. Pasley & M. Ihinger-Tallman (Eds.), *Remarriage and stepparenting.* New York: Guilford.

Jacobson, D. S. (1978). The impact of marital separation/divorce on children: Parent child separation and child adjustment. *Journal of Divorce, 1,* 341-360.

Jaffe, P. G., Wolfe, D., & Wilson, S. K. (1990). *Children of battered women.* Newbury Park, CA: Sage.

Johnson, E. S. (1983). Older mothers' perceptions of their child's divorce. *The Gerontologist, 21*(4), 395-401.

Johnson, E. S., & Vinick, B. H. (1981). Support of the parent when an adult son or daughter divorces. *Journal of Divorce, 5,* 69-78.

Johnston, J. R. (1985). Personality attributes and the structure of interpersonal relations. In J. Berger & M. Zelditch, Jr. (Eds.), *Status, rewards, and influence.* San Francisco: Jossey-Bass.

Johnston, J. R., & Campbell, L. E. G. (1988). *Impasses of divorce: The dynamics and resolution of family conflict.* New York: Free Press.

Johnston, J. R., Kline, M., & Tschann, J. M. (1989). Ongoing post-divorce conflict: Effects on children of joint custody and frequent access. *American Journal of Orthopsychiatry, 59,* 576-592.

Jones, C., Marsden, L., & Tepperman, L. (1990). *Lives of their own: The individualization of women's lives.* Toronto: Oxford University Press.

Jones, E. E., & Davis, K. E. (1965). From acts to dispositions: The attribution process in person perception. In L. Berkowitz (Ed.), *Advances in experimental social psychology* (Vol. 2). New York: Academic Press.

Kahn, A. J., & Kamerman, S. B. (Eds.). (1987). *Child support: From debt collection to social policy.* Newbury Park, CA: Sage.

Kalish, R. A., & Visher, E. (1981). Grandparents of divorce and remarriage. *Journal of Divorce, 5,* 127-140.

Kalmuss, D. (1984). The intergenerational transmission of marital aggression. *Journal of Marriage and the Family, 47,* 11-19.

Kalter, N. (1977). Children of divorce in an outpatient psychiatric population. *American Journal of Orthopsychiatry, 47,* 40-51.

Kalter, N. (1991). *Growing up with divorce.* New York: Fawcett.

Kalter, N., Kloner, A., Schreiser, S., & Okla, K. (1989). Predictors of children's postdivorce adjustment. *American Journal of Orthopsychiatry, 59,* 605-618.

Kalter, N., Reimer, B., Brickman, A., & Chen, J. W. (1985). Implications of parental divorce for female development. *Journal of the American Academy of Child Psychiatry, 24,* 538-544.

Kalter, N., & Rembar, J. (1981). The significance of a child's age at the time of parental divorce. *American Journal of Orthopsychiatry, 51,* 85-100.

Kanoy, K. W., & Cunningham, J. L. (1984). Consensus or confusion in research on children and divorce: Conceptual and methodological issues. *Journal of Divorce, 7,* 45-71.

Kaplan, S. (1977). Structural family therapy for children of divorce: Case reports. *Family Process, 16,* 75-83.

Kaplan, H. B., & Pokorny, A. D. (1971). Self-derogation and childhood broken homes. *Journal of Marriage and the Family, 33*, 328-350.

Kaslow, F. W. (1984). Divorce: An evolutionary process of change in the family system. *Journal of Divorce, 7*(3), 21-39.

Kaslow, F. W. (1988). The psychological dimension of divorce mediation. In J. Folberg & A. Milne (Eds.), *Divorce mediation: Theory and practice.* New York: Guilford.

Kaslow, F., & Hyatt, R. (1981). Divorce: A potential growth experience for the extended family. *Journal of Divorce, 5*, 115-126.

Kaslow, F. W., & Schwartz, L. L. (1987). *The dynamics of divorce: A life cycle perspective.* New York: Brunner/Mazel.

Kay, H. H. (1987). Equality and difference: A perspective on no-fault divorce and its aftermath. *University of Cincinnati Law Review, 56*, 4-14, 26-55.

Kay, H. H. (1990). Beyond no-fault: New directions for divorce reform. In S. D. Sugarman & H. H. Kay (Eds.), *Divorce reform at the crossroads.* New Haven, CT: Yale University Press.

Keith, V. M., & Finlay, B. (1988). The impact of parental divorce on children's educational attainment, marital timing and likelihood of divorce. *Journal of Marriage and the Family, 50*, 797-810.

Kelley, H. H. (1973). The processes of causal attribution. *American Psychologist, 28*, 107-128.

Kelly, J. B. (1982). Divorce: The adult experience. In B. Wolman & G. Stricker (Eds.), *Handbook of developmental psychology.* Englewood Cliffs, NJ: Prentice Hall.

Kelly, J. B. (1988). Long-term adjustment in children of divorce: Converging findings and implications form practice. *Journal of Family Psychology, 2*, 119-140.

Kelly, J. B. (1991). Parent interaction after divorce: Comparison of mediated and adversarial divorce processes. *Behavioral Science & the Law, 9*, 387-398.

Kelly, J. B. (1993). Current research on children's postdivorce adjustment: No simple answers. *Family & Conciliation Courts Review, 31*(1), 29-49.

Kelly, J. B. (in press). Developing and implementing postdivorce parenting plans: Does the forum make a difference? In J. Bray & C. Depner (Eds.), *Nonresidential parenting: New vistas in family living.* Thousand Oaks, CA: Sage.

Kelly, J. B., & Duryee, M. A. (1992). Women's and men's views of mediation in voluntary and mandatory settings. *Family & Conciliation Courts Review, 30*(1), 43-49.

Kennedy, L. W., & Dutton, D. G. (1989). The incidence of wife abuse in Alberta. *Canadian Journal of Behavioral Science, 21*, 40-53.

Kephart, W. M. (1972). *The family, society and the individual* (3rd ed.). Boston: Houghton Mifflin.

Kernberg, O. (1967). Borderline personality organization. *Journal of the American Psychoanalytic Association, 15*, 641-687.

Keshet, H. F., & Rosenthal, K. M. (1978). Fathering after marital separation. *Social Work, 23*, 11-18.

Kessler, S. (1975). *The American way of divorce: Prescriptions for change.* Chicago: Nelson · Hall.

Kinard, E. M., & Reinherz, H. (1984). Marital disruption: Effects on behavioral and emotional functioning in children. *Journal of Family Issues, 5*, 90-115.

King, D. B. (1993). Accentuate the positive—eliminate the negative. *Family & Conciliation Courts Review, 31*(1), 9-28.

Kitchen, B. (1992). Framing the issues: The political economy of poor mothers. *Canadian Woman Studies, 12*(4), 10-15.

Kitson, G. C. (with Holmes, W. M.). (1992). *Portrait of divorce: Adjustment to marital breakdown.* New York: Guilford.

Kitson, G. C., Babri, K. B., & Roach, M. J. (1985). Who divorces and why: A review. *Journal of Family Issues, 6*(3), 255-293.

Kitson, G. C., Babri, K. B., Roach, M. J., & Placidi, K. S. (1989). Adjustment to widowhood and divorce: A review. *Journal of Family Issues, 10*(1), 5-32.

Kitson, G. C., & Langlie, J. D. (1984). Couples who file for divorce but change their minds. *American Journal of Orthopsychiatry, 54,* 469-489.

Kitson, G. C., & Morgan, L. A. (1990). The multiple consequences of divorce: A decade review. *Journal of Marriage and the Family, 52,* 913-924.

Kitson, G. C., & Raschke, H. J. (1981). Divorce research: What we know; what we need to know. *Journal of Divorce, 4,* 1-37.

Kitson, G. C., & Sussman, M. (1982). Marital complaints, demographic characteristics and symptoms of mental distress in divorce. *Journal of Marriage and the Family, 44,* 87-102.

Kline, M., Johnston, J. R., & Tschann, J. M. (1991). The long shadow of marital conflict: A model of children's postdivorce adjustment. *Journal of Marriage and the Family, 53,* 297-309.

Kline, M., Tschann, J. M., Johnston, J. R., & Wallerstein, J. S. (1989). Children's adjustment in joint and sole physical custody families. *Developmental Psychology, 25,* 430-438.

Kneisser, T. J., McElroy, M. S., & Wilcox, S. P. (1988). Getting into poverty without a husband and getting out, with or without. *American Economic Association Papers and Proceedings, 78,* 86-90.

Koch, M., & Lowery, C. (1984). Visitation and the noncustodial father. *Journal of Divorce, 8*(2), 47-65.

Kohen, J. A., Browen, C. A., & Feldberg, R. (1979). Divorced mothers: The costs and benefits of female family control. In G. Levinger & O. C. Moles (Eds.), *Divorce and separation: Contexts, causes, and consequences.* New York: Basic Books.

Koo, H. P., Suchindran, C. M., & Griffith, J. D. (1984). The effects on children of divorce and remarriage: A multivariate analysis of the life table probabilities. *Population Studies, 38,* 451-471.

Krantz, S. E., Clark, J., Pruyn, J. P., & Usher, M. (1985). Cognition and adjustment among children of separated or divorced parents. *Cognitive Therapy & Research, 9,* 61-77.

Krause, S. (1979). The crisis of divorce: Growth promoting or pathogenic? *Journal of Divorce, 3*(2), 107-121.

Kressel, K. (1985). *The process of divorce: How professionals and couples negotiate settlements.* New York: Basic Books.

Kressel, K., & Deutsch, M. (1977). Divorce therapy: An in-depth survey of therapists' views. *Family Process, 16,* 413-443.

Kressel, K., Jaffe, N., Tuchman, B., Watson, C., & Deutsch, M. (1980). A typology of divorcing couples: Implications for mediation and the divorce process. *Family Process, 19,* 101-116.

Kronby, M. C. (1991). *Canadian family law* (5th ed.). Toronto: Stoddart.

Kruk, E. (1991). Discontinuity between pre- and post-divorce father-child relations: New evidence regarding parental disengagement. *Journal of Divorce & Remarriage, 16* (3/4), 195-227.

Kruk, E. (1992). Psychological and structural factors contributing to the disengagement of noncustodial fathers after divorce. *Family & Conciliation Courts Review, 30*(1), 82-101.

Kruk, E. (1993). *Divorce and disengagement: Patterns of fatherhood within and beyond marriage.* Halifax, Nova Scotia: Fernwood.

Kruk, E. (1994). The disengaged noncustodial father: Implications for social work practice with the divorced family. *Social Work, 39*(1), 15-25.

Kurdek, L. (1988). Custodial mother's perceptions of visitation and payments of child support by noncustodial fathers in families with low and high levels of preseparation interparent conflict. *Journal of Applied Developmental Psychology, 9,* 315-328.

Kurdek, L. (1989). Children's adjustment. In M. Textor (Ed.), *The divorce and divorce therapy handbook.* New York: Aronson.

Kurdek, L. A. (1981). An integrative perspective on children's divorce adjustment. *American Psychologist, 36,* 856-866.

Kurdek, L. A., & Berg, B. (1983). Correlates of children's adjustments to their parents' divorces. In L. A. Kurdek (Ed.), *Children and divorce.* San Francisco: Jossey-Bass.

Kurdek, L. A., & Blisk, D. (1983). Dimensions and correlates of mother's divorce experience. *Journal of Divorce, 6,* 1-24.

Kurdek, L. A., Blisk, D., & Siesky, A. E. (1981). Correlates of children's long-term adjustment to their parents' divorce. *Developmental Psychology, 17,* 565-579.

Kurdek, L. A., & Siesky, A. E. (1980a). Children's perceptions of their parents' divorce. *Journal of Divorce, 3,* 339-378.

Kurdek, L. A., & Siesky, A. E. (1980b). The effects of divorce on children: The relationship between parent and child perspectives. *Journal of Divorce, 4,* 85-99.

Lamb, M. (1977a). The effects of divorce on children's personality development. *Journal of Divorce, 1,* 163-174.

Lamb, M. (1977b). Reexamination of the infant social world. *Human Development, 20,* 65-85.

Lampe, P. E. (Ed.). (1987). *Adultery in the United States: Close encounters of the sixth (or seventh) kind.* Buffalo, NY: Prometheus.

Landau, B. (1988). Mediation: An option for divorcing families. *Advocate's Quarterly, 9,* 1-21.

Landis, J. T. (1960). The trauma of children when parents divorce. *Marriage & Family Living, 22,* 7-13.

Landis, J. T. (1963). Dating maturation of children from happy and unhappy marriages. *Marriage & Family Living, 25,* 351-353.

Lawrence, W. (1968). Divided custody of children after their parents divorce. *Journal of Family Law 1968, 8,* 58-68.

Lawson, A. (1988). *Adultery: Analysis of love and betrayal.* New York: Basic Books.

Lazarus, A. A. (1981). Divorce counseling or marriage therapy? A therapeutic option. *Journal of Marital & Family Therapy, 7,* 15-22.

Leslie, G. R., & Korman, S. K. (1985). *The family in social context* (6th ed.). New York: Oxford University Press.

Levinger, G. (1965). Marital cohesiveness and dissolution: An integrative review. *Journal of Marriage and the Family, 27,* 19-28.

Levinger, G. (1979a). A social psychological perspective on marital dissolution. In G. Levinger & O. Moles (Eds.), *Divorce and separation: Context, causes, and consequences.* New York: Basic Books.

Levinger, G. (1979b). A social exchange view of the dissolution of pair relationships. In R. L. Burgess & T. L. Huston (Eds.), *Social exchange in developing relationships.* New York: Academic Press.

Levitan, S. A., Belous, R. S., & Gallo, F. (1988). *What's happening to the American family?* Baltimore, MD: Johns Hopkins University Press.

Little, M. (1982). *Family breakups: Understanding marital problems and the mediating of child custody decisions.* San Francisco: Jossey-Bass.

Lochkar, J. (1992). *The narcissistic/borderline couple.* New York: Brunner/Mazel.

Locke, H. J. (1951). *Predicting adjustment in marriage.* New York: Holt, Rinehart & Winston.

London, K. A., & Wilson, B. F. (1988, October). D-i-v-o-r-c-e. *American Demographics*, pp. 22-26.

Long, B. H. (1986). Parental discord vs. family structure: Effects of divorce on the self-esteem of daughters. *Journal of Youth & Adolescence, 15*(1), 19-27.

Long, N., & Forehand, R. (1987). The effects of parental divorce and parental conflict on children: An overview. *Developmental & Behavioral Pediatrics, 8*, 292-296.

Long, N., Forehand, R., Fauber, R., & Brody, G. H. (1987). Self-perceived and independently observed competency of young adolescents as a function of parental marital conflict and recent divorce. *Journal of Abnormal Child Psychology, 15*, 15-27.

Longfellow, C. (1979). Divorce in context: Its impact on children. In G. Levinger & O. Moles (Eds.), *Divorce and separation: Context, causes and consequences.* New York: Basic Books.

Lopez, F. G., Campbell, V. L., & Watkins, C. E., Jr. (1988). The relationship of parental divorce to college student development. *Journal of Divorce, 12*(1), 83-98.

Lovelene, E., & Lohmann, N. (1978). Absent fathers and black male children. *Social Work, 23*, 413-415.

Lowery, C. R., & Settle, S. A. (1985). Effects of divorce on children: Differential impact of custody and visitation patterns. *Family Relations, 34*, 455-463.

Lund, M. (1987). The non-custodial father: Common challenges in parenting after divorce. In C. Lewis & M. O'Brien (Eds.), *Reassessing fatherhood.* London: Sage.

Lupri, E. (1989). Male violence in the home. *Canadian Social Trends, 14*, 19-21.

Maccoby, E. E., Depner, C. E., & Mnookin, R. H. (1988). Custody of children following divorce. In E. M. Hetherington & J. Arasteh (Eds.), *The impact of divorce, single parenting and stepparenting on children.* Hillsdale, NJ: Lawrence Erlbaum.

Maccoby, E. E., Depner, C. E., & Mnookin, R. H. (1990). Coparenting in the second year after divorce. *Journal of Marriage and the Family, 52*, 141-155.

Maccoby, E. E., & Mnookin, R. H. (with Depner, C. E., & Peters, H. E.). (1992). *Dividing the child: Social and legal dilemmas of custody.* Cambridge, MA: Harvard University Press.

MacKinnon, C. E. D., Stoneman, Z., & Brody, G. H. (1984). The impact of maternal employment and family form on children's sex-role stereotypes and mothers' traditional attitudes. *Journal of Divorce, 8*, 51-60.

Macklin, E. D. (1980). Nontraditional family forms: A decade of research. *Journal of Marriage and the Family, 33*, 905-922.

Mahler, M. (1971). A study of the separation-individuation process and its possible application to borderline phenomena in the psychoanalytic situation. *Psychoanalytic Study of the Child, 26*, 403-424.

Marlar, J. A., & Jacobs, K. W. (1992). Differences in the marriage role expectations of college students from intact and divorced families. *Journal of Divorce & Remarriage, 18*(3/4), 93-103.

Marsden, D. (1969). *Mothers alone: Poverty and the fatherless family.* London: Penguin.

Marsden, D. (1973). *Mothers alone.* London: Allen Lane & Pelican Press.

Martin, T., & Bumpass, L. (1989). Recent trends in marital disruption. *Demography, 26,* 37-52.

Mason, M. A. (1993). *From father's property to children's rights: The history of child custody in the United States.* New York: Columbia University Press.

Masheter, C. (1990). Postdivorce relationship between exspouses: A literature review. *Journal of Divorce & Remarriage, 14*(1), 97-122.

Masheter, C. (1991). Postdivorce relationships between ex-spouses: The role of attachment and interpersonal conflict. *Journal of Marriage and the Family, 53*(1), 103-110.

Masnick, G., & Bane, M. J. (1980). *The nation's families: 1960-1990.* Cambridge, MA: Joint Center for Urban Studies of MIT and Harvard University.

Masterson, J. F. (1981). *The narcissistic and borderline disorders.* New York: Brunner/Mazel.

Matthews, S. H., & Sprey, J. (1984). The impact of divorce on grandparenthood: An exploratory study. *The Gerontologist, 24,* 41-47.

McCall, G. (1982). Becoming unrelated: The management of bond dissolution. In S. Duck (Ed.), *Personal relationships. 4: Dissolving personal relationships.* London: Academic Press.

McCall, M. L., Hornick, J. P., & Wallace, J. E. (1988). *The process and economic consequences of marriage breakdown.* Calgary: Canadian Research Institute for Law and the Family.

McConville, B. J. (1978). The effect of non-traditional families on children's mental health. *Canada's Mental Health, 26,* 5-10.

McCubbin, H. I., & Patterson, J. M. (1983). Family transitions: Adaptation to stress. In H. I. McCubbin & C. R. Figley (Eds.), *Stress and the family. Vol. 1: Coping with normative transitions.* New York: Brunner/Mazel.

McDermott, J. F. (1970). Divorce and its psychiatric sequelae in children. *Archives of General Psychiatry, 23,* 421-428.

McDonald, R. J. (1992). Missing children. *Canadian Social Trends, 24,* 2-5.

McGoldrick, M., Pearce, J. K., & Giordano, J. (Eds.). (1982). *Ethnicity and family therapy.* New York: Guilford.

McKenry, P. C., & Price, S. J. (1991). Alternatives for support: Life after divorce—A literature review. *Journal of Divorce & Remarriage, 15*(3/4), 1-19.

McKie, D. C. (1993). An overview of lone parenthood in Canada. In J. Hudson & B. Galaway (Eds.), *Single parent families: Perspectives on research and policy.* Toronto: Thompson Educational.

McKie, D. C., Prentice, B., & Reed, P. (1983). *Divorce: Law and the family in Canada.* Ottawa: Statistics Canada, Research and Analysis Division.

McLanahan, S. (1985). Family structure and the reproduction of poverty. *American Journal of Sociology, 90,* 873-901.

McLanahan, S. (1988). Family structure and dependency: Early transitions to female household headship. *Demography, 25,* 1-16.

McLanahan, S. (1992). Intergenerational consequences of divorce: The United States perspective. In L. Weitzman & M. Maclean (Eds.), *Economic consequences of divorce: The international perspective.* Oxford: Clarendon.

McLanahan, S. S. (1983). Family structure and stress: A longitudinal comparison of two-parent and female headed families. *Journal of Marriage and the Family, 45,* 347-357.

McLanahan, S. S., & Booth, K. (1989). Mother-only families: Problems, prospects and policies. *Journal of Marriage and the Family, 51,* 557-580.

McLanahan, S., & Bumpass, L. (1988). Intergenerational consequences of family disruption. *American Journal of Sociology, 94*, 130-152.

McLanahan, S., & Garfinkel, I. (1991). Mother-only families. In A. Booth (Ed.), *Contemporary families: Looking forward, looking back*. Minneapolis, MN: National Council on Family Relations.

McLanahan, S., & Garfinkel, I. (1993). Single motherhood in the United States: Growth, problems, and policies. In J. Hudson & B. Galaway (Eds.), *Single parent families: Perspectives on research and policy*. Toronto: Thompson Educational.

McLeer, S. V. (1981). Spouse abuse. In G. P. Sholevar (Ed.), *The handbook of marriage and marital therapy*. New York: SP Medical & Science Books.

McPhee, J. T. (1985). Ambiguity and change in the post-divorce family: Towards a model of divorce adjustment. *Journal of Divorce, 8*, 1-15.

Melichor, J. F., & Chiriboga, D. A. (1988). Significance of time in adjustment to marital separation. *American Journal of Orthopsychiatry, 58*, 221-227.

Menaghan, E. (1983). Marital stress and family transitions: A panel analysis. *Journal of Marriage and the Family, 45*, 371-386.

Mendes, H. A. (1976a). Single fatherhood. *Social Work, 21*, 308-312.

Mendes, H. A. (1976b). Single fathers. *Family Coordinator, 25*, 439-444.

Mendes, H. A. (1979). Single parent families: A typology of lifestyles. *Social Work, 24*, 193-200.

Mika, K., & Bloom, B. L. (1980). Adjustment to separation among former cohabitors. *Journal of Divorce, 4*, 45-66.

Milardo, R. M. (1987). Changes in social networks of men and women following divorce: A review. *Journal of Family Issues, 8*, 78-96.

Miller, J. G. (1978). *Living systems*. New York: McGraw-Hill.

Ministry of the Attorney General. (1992). *Automatic wage deduction: A new way to make family support payments* [pamphlet]. Toronto: Ministry of the Attorney General.

Minuchin, S. (1974). *Families and family therapy*. Cambridge, MA: Harvard University Press.

Minuchin, S., Montalvo, B., Guerney, B., Rosman, B., & Schumer, F. (1967). *Families of the slums*. New York: Basic Books.

Mitchell, A. K. (1983). Adolescents' experiences of parental separation and divorce. *Journal of Adolescence, 6*(2), 175-187.

Mitchell, R. E., Billings, A. G., & Moss, R. H. (1982). Social support and well-being: Implications for prevention programs. *Journal of Primary Prevention, 3*, 77-98.

Mnookin, R. H., Maccoby, E. E., Albiston, C. R., & Depner, C. E. (1990). Private ordering revisited: What custodial arrangements are parents negotiating? In S. Sugarman & H. H. Kay (Eds.), *Divorce reforms at the crossroads*. New Haven, CT: Yale University Press.

Moore, M. (1988). How long alone? The duration of female lone parenthood in Canada. *Canadian Social Trends, 10*, 40-42.

Morgan, L. A. (1989). Economic well-being following marital termination: A comparison of widowed and divorced women. *Journal of Family Issues, 10*(1), 86-101.

Morgan, L. A. (1991). *After marriage ends: Economic consequences for midlife women*. Newbury Park, CA: Sage.

Morgan, S. P., Lye, D., & Condran, G. (1988). Sons, daughters, and the risk of marital disruption. *American Journal of Sociology, 94*, 110-129.

Morrison, J. (1974). Parental divorce as a factor in childhood psychiatric illness. *Comprehensive Psychiatry, 15*(2), 95-102.

Moultrup, D. J. (1990). *Husbands, wives, and lovers: The emotional system of the extramarital affair.* New York: Guilford.

Mueller, C. W., & Pope, H. (1977). Marital instability: A study of its transmission between generations. *Journal of Marriage and the Family, 39,* 83-92.

Myers, M. F. (1989). *Men and divorce.* New York: Guilford.

Nadelson, C. C., Polansky, D. C., & Mathews, M. A. (1981). Marriage problems and marital therapy in the middle-aged. In J. G. Howells (Ed.), *Modern perspectives in the psychiatry of middle age.* New York: Brunner/Mazel.

National Institute for Child Support Enforcement. (NICSE). (1986). *History and fundamentals of child-support enforcement* (2nd ed.). Washington, DC: Government Printing Office.

Neal, J. H. (1983). Children's understanding of their parents' divorce. In L. A. Kurdek (Ed.), *Children and divorce.* San Francisco: Jossey-Bass.

Nelson, E., Allison, J., & Sundre, D. (1992). Relationship between divorce and college students' development of identity and intimacy. *Journal of Divorce & Remarriage, 18* (3/4), 121-135.

Nelson, G. (1985). Family adaptation following marital separation/divorce: A literature review. In B. Schlesinger (Ed.), *The one-parent family in the 1980s: Perspectives and annotated bibliography 1978-1984.* Toronto: University of Toronto Press.

Nett, E. M. (1993). *Canadian families: Past and present* (2nd ed.). Toronto: Butterworths.

Newcomb, M. (1986). Sexual behavior of cohabitors: A comparison of three independent samples. *Journal of Sex Research, 22,* 492-513.

Newson, J., & Newson, E. (1976). *Seven years old in the home environment.* London: Pelican.

Neubeck, G. (Ed.). (1969). *Extramarital relations.* Englewood Cliffs, NJ: Prentice Hall.

Noble, J., & Noble, W. (1975). *The custody trap.* New York: Hawthorn.

Nock, S. L. (1987). *Sociology of the family.* Englewood Cliffs, NJ: Prentice Hall.

Norton, A. J., & Glick, P. C. (1976). Marital instability: Past, present and future. *Journal of Social Issues, 32,* 5-20.

Norton, A. J., & Moorman, J. E. (1987). Current trends in American marriage and divorce. *Journal of Marriage and the Family, 49,* 3-14.

Nye, F. I. (1957). Child adjustment in broken and in unhappy unbroken homes. *Marriage & Family Living, 19,* 356-361.

Nye, F. I., & Berardo, F. M. (1973). *The family: Its structure and interaction.* New York: Macmillan.

Oakland, T. (1984). *Divorced fathers.* New York: Human Sciences Press.

Oberlander, H. (1988). *Homelessness and the homeless: Responses and innovations.* Vancouver: University of British Columbia Centre for Human Settlement.

O'Brien, J. E. (1971). Violence in divorce prone families. *Journal of Marriage and the Family, 33,* 692-698.

O'Connel, M., & Rodgers, C. C. (1984). Out-of-wedlock births, premarital pregnancies, and their effect on family formation and dissolution. *Family Planning Perspective, 16,* 157-162.

Offord, D. R., & Boyle, M. H. (1987). Morbidity among welfare children in Ontario. *Canadian Journal of Psychiatry, 32,* 518-525.

O'Flaherty, K. M., & Eells, L. W. (1988). Courtship behavior of the remarried. *Journal of Marriage and the Family, 50,* 499-506.

Oh, S. (1986). Remarried men and remarried women: How are they different? *Journal of Divorce, 9,* 107-113.

Orthner, D., Brown, T., & Ferguson, D. (1976). Single-parent fatherhood: An emerging family lifestyle. *Family Coordinator, 25*, 429-437.

Ozawa, M. N. (1989). *Women's life cycle and economic insecurity: Problems and proposals.* Westport, CT: Greenwood.

Paasch, K. M., & Teachman, J. D. (1991). Gender of children and receipt of assistance from absent fathers. *Journal of Family Issues, 12*(4), 450-466.

Pagels, E. (1988). *Adam, Eve and the serpent.* New York: Vintage.

Parish, T. S., & Dostal, J. W. (1980). Evaluation of self and parent figures by children from intact, divorced, and constituted families. *Journal of Youth & Adolescence, 9*, 347-351.

Parish, T. S., & Taylor, J. C. (1979). The impact of divorce and subsequent father absence on children's and adolescent's self-concept. *Journal of Youth & Adolescence, 8*, 427-431.

Parsons, M. (1990). Lone parent families and the socioeconomic achievement of children as adults. *Journal of Comparative Family Studies, 21*, 353-367.

Pask, D. (1993a). Family law and policy in Canada: Economic implications for single custodial mothers and their children. In J. Hudson & B. Galaway (Eds.), *Single parent families: Perspectives on research and policy.* Toronto: Thompson Educational.

Pask, D. (1993b). Gender bias and child support: Sharing the poverty? *Family Law Quarterly, 10*, 33-260.

Pask, D. E., & McCall, M. L. (1991). *How much and why? Economic implications of marriage breakdown: Spousal and child support.* Calgary: Canadian Research Institute for Law and the Family.

Pasley, K., & Ihinger-Tallman, M. (Eds.). (1987). *Remarriage and stepparenting: Current research and theory.* New York: Guilford.

Payne, J. (1988). *On divorce.* Toronto: Butterworths.

Pearce, D. (1979). Women, work and welfare: The feminization of poverty. In K. W. Feinstein (Ed.), *Working women and families.* Newbury Park, CA: Sage.

Pearson, J., Munson, P., & Thoennes, N. (1982). Legal change and child custody awards. *Journal of Family Issues, 3*(1), 5-24.

Pearson, J., Munson, P., & Thoennes, N. (1983). Children's rights and child custody proceedings. *Journal of Divorce, 7*(2), 1-21.

Perlman, J. L. (1982). Divorce: A psychological and legal process. *Journal of Divorce, 6*, 99-114.

Perry, D., & Associates. (1992). *Access to children following parental relationship breakdown in Alberta.* Calgary: Canadian Research Institute for Law and the Family.

Peters, J. F. (1983). Divorce: The disengaging, disengaged and re-engaging process. In K. Ishwaran (Ed.), *The Canadian family.* Toronto: Gage.

Peters, J. F. (1989). Divorce and remarriage. In G. Ramu (Ed.), *Marriage and family in Canada today.* Scarborough, ON: Prentice Hall.

Peterson, G. W., Leigh, G., & Day, R. (1984). Family stress theory and the impact of divorce on children. *Journal of Divorce, 7*, 1-20.

Peterson, J. L., & Zill, N. (1986). Marital disruption, parent-child relationships, and behavior problems in children. *Journal of Marriage and the Family, 48*, 295-307.

Peterson, R. R. (1989). *Women, work and divorce.* Albany, New York: SUNY.

Pett, M. G. (1982a). Predictors of satisfactory social adjustment of divorced single parents. *Journal of Divorce, 5*, 1-17.

Pett, M. G. (1982b). Correlates of children's social adjustment following divorce. *Journal of Divorce, 5*, 25-39.

Pett, M. A., & Vaughn-Cole, B. (1986). The impact of income issues and social status on post-divorce adjustment of custodial parents. *Family Relations, 35*, 103-111.

Pfeffer, C. R. (1986). *The suicidal child.* New York: Guilford.

Philliber, W. W., & Hiller, D. V. (1983). Relative occupational attainments of spouses and later changes in marriage and wife's work experience. *Journal of Marriage and the Family, 45*, 161-170.

Phillips, R. (1988). *Putting asunder: A history of divorce in western society.* Cambridge, NY: Cambridge University Press.

Pittman, F. S. (1989). *Private lies: Infidelity and the betrayal of intimacy.* New York: Norton.

Pitts, J. R. (1964). The structural functional approach. In E.T. Christensen (Ed.), *Handbook of marriage and the family.* Chicago: Rand McNally.

Pleck, J. S., & Manocherian, J. R. (1988). Divorce in the changing family life cycle. In B. Carter & M. McGoldrick (Eds.), *The changing family life cycle: A framework for family therapy* (2nd ed.). New York: Gardner.

Plunkett, J. W., Schaefer, M., Kalter, N., Okla, K., & Schreier, S. (1986). Perceptions of quality of life following divorce: A study of children's prognostic thinking. *Psychiatry, 49*, 1-12.

Pope, H., & Mueller, C. W. (1979). The intergenerational transmission of marital instability: Comparisons by race and sex. In G. Levinger & O. C. Moles (Eds.), *Divorce and separation.* New York: Basic Books.

Potuchek, J. L. (1992). Employed wives' orientations to breadwinning: A gender theory analysis. *Journal of Marriage and the Family, 54*, 548-558.

Prestrack, J., Martin, D., & Martin, M. (1985). Extramarital sex: An examination of the literature. *International Journal of Family Therapy, 7*, 107-115.

Price-Bonham, S., & Balswick, J. O. (1980). The non-institutions: Divorce, desertion, and remarriage. *Journal of Marriage and the Family, 42*, 959-972.

Raphe, R. H., & Arthur, R. J. (1978). Life changes and illness studies: Past history and future directions. *Journal of Human Stress, 4*, 3-15.

Raschke, H. J. (1977a). The role of social participation in postseparation and postdivorce adjustment. *Journal of Divorce, 2*, 129-140.

Raschke, H. J. (1977b). Family structure, family happiness, and their effect on college students' personal and social adjustment. *Conciliation Courts Review, 15*, 30-33.

Raschke, H. J. (1987). Divorce. In M. B. Sussman & S. K. Steinmetz (Eds.), *Handbook of marriage and the family.* New York: Plenum.

Raschke, H. J., & Raschke, V. J. (1979). Family conflict and children's self-concepts: A comparison of intact and single-parent families. *Journal of Marriage and the Family, 41*, 367-374.

Reinhard, D. W. (1977). The reactions of adolescent boys and girls to the divorce of their parents. *Journal of Clinical Child Psychology, 7*, 21-23.

Reiss, I. L., & Lee, G. R. (1988). *Family systems in America* (4th ed.). New York: Holt, Rinehart & Winston.

Richmond-Abbott, M. (1984). Sex-role attitudes of mothers and children in divorced, single-parent families. *Journal of Divorce, 8*, 61-81.

Riley, G. (1991). *Divorce: An American tradition.* New York: Oxford University Press.

Roach, M. J., & Kitson, G. C. (1989). The impact of forewarning on adjustment to widowhood and divorce. In D. Lund (Ed.), *Older bereaved spouses.* New York: Hemisphere.

Robinson, B. W., & McVey, W. W. (1985). The relative contributions of death and divorce to marital dissolution in Canada and the United States. *Journal of Comparative Family Studies, 16*, 93-109.

Rodgers, R. H., & Conrad, L. M. (1986). Courtship for remarriage: Influences on family reorganization after divorce. *Journal of Marriage and the Family, 48*, 767-775.

Rodgers, S. (1986). Postmarital reorganization of family relationships: A propositional theory. In S. Duck & D. Perlman (Eds.), *Close relationships: Development, dynamics, and deterioration.* Beverly Hills, CA: Sage.

Rogerson, C. J. (1991a). Judicial interpretation of the spousal and child support provisions of the Divorce Act (Part I). *Canadian Family Law Quarterly, 7*, 155-269.

Rogerson, C. J. (1991b). Judicial interpretation of the spousal and child support provisions of the Divorce Act (Part II). *Canadian Family Law Quarterly, 7*, 271-314.

Rosen, R. (1977). Children of divorce: What they feel about access and other aspects of the divorce experience. *Journal of Clinical Child Psychology, 7*, 24-27.

Rosen, R. (1979). Some crucial issues concerning children of divorce. *Journal of Divorce, 3*, 19-25.

Rosenthal, P. A., & Rosenthal, S. (1984). Suicidal behavior by pre-school children. *American Journal of Psychiatry, 141*(4), 520.

Ross, H. L., & Sawhill, I. V. (1975). *Time of transition: The growth of families headed by women.* Washington, DC: Urban Institute.

Rubin, L. B. (1985). *Just friends: The role of friendship in our lives.* New York: Perennial.

Rutter, M. (1971). Parent-child separation: Psychological effects on the child. *Journal of Child Psychology & Psychiatry, 12*, 233-260.

Rutter, M. (1985). Resilience in the face of adversity. *British Journal of Psychiatry, 147*, 598-611.

Rutter, M. (1987). Psychosocial resilience and protective mechanisms. *American Journal of Orthopsychiatry, 57*, 316-331.

Saayman, G. S. & Saayman, R. V. (1989). The adversarial legal process and divorce: Negative effects upon the psychological adjustment of children. *Journal of Divorce, 12*, 329-348.

Sabelli, H. C. (1991). Rapid treatment of depression with selegiline-phenylalanine combination [Letter to the editor]. *Journal of Clinical Psychiatry, 52*, 3.

Sabelli, H. C., Carlson-Sabelli, L., & Javaid, J. I. (1990). The thermodynamics of bipolarity: A bifurcation model of bipolar illness and bipolar character and its psychotherapeutic applications. *Psychiatry, 53*, 346-368.

Salts, C. J. (1979). Divorce processes: Integration of theory. *Journal of Divorce, 2*(3), 233-240.

Sanick, M., & Maudlin, T. (1986). Single versus two parent families: A comparison of mother's time. *Family Relations, 35*, 53-56.

Santrock, J. W. (1987). The effects of divorce on adolescence: Needed research perspectives. *Family Therapy, 14*, 147-159.

Santrock, J. W., & Warshak, R. A. (1979). Father custody and social development in boys and girls. *Journal of Social Issues, 35*, 112-125.

Santrock, J. W., Warshak, R. A., & Elliott, G. L. (1982). Social development and parent-child interaction in father-custody and stepfather families. In M. E. Lamb (Ed.), *Nontraditional families: Parenting and child development.* Hillsdale, NJ: Lawrence Erlbaum.

Saucier, J. F., & Ambert, A.-M. (1983). Adolescents' self-reported physical health and parental marital status. *Canadian Journal of Public Health, 74*, 396-400.

Schlesinger, B. (1977). Children and divorce: A selected review. *Conciliation Courts Review*, 15(1), 36-40.

Schlesinger, B. (1979). Children and divorce in Canada: The Law Reform Commission's recommendations. In B. Schlesinger (Ed.), *One in ten: The single parent in Canada*. Toronto: Guidance Centre, Faculty of Education, University of Toronto.

Schlesinger, B. (Ed.). (1985). *The one-parent family in the 1980s: Perspectives and annotated bibliography 1978-1984*. Toronto: University of Toronto Press.

Schwebel, A. I., Fine, M., Moreland, J. R., & Prindle, P. (1988). Clinical work with divorced and widowed fathers: The adjusting family model. In P. Bronstein & C. Cowen (Eds.), *Fatherhood today: Men's changing role in the family*. New York: John Wiley.

Schwebel, A. I., Gately, D. W., & Milburn, T. (in press). Divorce mediation: An integrative review. In S. M. Fulero & L. Olsen-Fulero (Eds.), *Advances in law and child development*. Greenwich, CT: JAI.

Selleck, L., Draughn, P., Waddle, F., & Buco, S. M. (1989). Attitudes of attorneys and judges towards joint custody and its litigation. *Journal of Divorce, 12*, 103-112.

Seltzer, J. A. (1991). Legal custody arrangements and the child's economic welfare. *American Journal of Sociology, 96*, 895-898.

Seltzer, J. A., & Bianchi, S. M. (1988). Children's contact with absent parents. *Journal of Marriage and the Family, 50*, 663-677.

Seltzer, J. A., & Garfinkel, I. (1990). Inequality in divorce settlements: An investigation of property settlements and child support awards. *Social Science Research, 19*, 82-111.

Seltzer, J. A., Schaeffer, N. C., & Charng, H. W. (1989). Family ties after divorce: The relationship between visiting and paying child support. *Journal of Marriage and the Family, 51*, 1013-1032.

Sev'er, A. (1992). *Women and divorce in Canada: A sociological analysis*. Toronto: Canadian Scholars Press.

Shaw, D. S., & Emery, R. E. (1987). Parental conflict and the adjustment of school-age children whose parents have separated. *Journal of Abnormal Child Psychiatry, 15*, 269-281.

Shaw, L. B. (1983). *Unplanned careers: The working lives of middle-aged women*. Lexington, MA: Lexington Books.

Sheffner, D. J., & Suarez, J. M. (1975). The postdivorce clinic. American *Journal of Psychiatry, 132*, 442-444.

Shook, N. J., & Jurish, J. (1992). Correlates of self-esteem among college offspring from divorced families: A study of gender-based differences. *Journal of Divorce & Remarriage, 18*(3/4), 157-176.

Shover, N. (1973). The civil justice process and societal reaction. *Social Forces, 52*, 169-174.

Shrier, D. K., Simring, S. K., Grief, J. B., Shapiro, E. T., & Lindenthal, J. J. (1989). Child custody arrangements: A study of two New Jersey counties. *Journal of Psychiatry & the Law, 17*, 9-20.

Shrier, D. K., Simring, S. K., Shapiro, E. T., Grief, J. B., & Lindenthal, J. J. (1991). Level of satisfaction of fathers and mothers on joint or sole custody arrangements: Results of a questionnaire. *Journal of Divorce & Remarriage, 16*(3/4), 163-169.

Silver, G. A., & Silver, M. (1981). *Weekend fathers*. Los Angeles: Stratford.

Slater, E. J., & Haber, J. D. (1984). Adolescent adjustment following divorce as a function of family conflict. *Journal of Consulting & Clinical Psychology, 52*, 920-921.

Slater, E. J., Stewart, K., & Linn, M. (1983). The effects of family disruption on adolescent males and females. *Adolescence, 18,* 931-942.

Smith, A. W., & Meitz, J. E. G. (1983). Life-course effect of marital disruption. *Social Indicators Research, 13*(4), 395-417.

Smith, E. J. (1981). Non-judicial resolution of custody and visitation. In H. H. Irving (Ed.), *Family law: An interdisciplinary perspective.* Toronto: Carswell.

Smith, J. C., Mercy, J. A., & Conn, J. A. (1988). Marital status and the risk of suicide. *American Journal of Public Health, 78,* 78-80.

Smith, M. (1987). The incidence and prevalence of woman abuse in Toronto. *Violence & Victims, 2*(3), 173-187.

Smith, S. L. (1991). *Succeeding against the odds: Strategies and insights from the learning disabled.* Los Angeles: Jeremy P. Tarcher.

Smith, T. E. (1990). Parental separation and the academic self-concepts of adolescents: An effort to solve the puzzle of separation effects. *Journal of Marriage and the Family, 52,* 107-118.

Smith, T. E. (1991). Lie to me no more: Believable stories and marital affairs. *Family Process, 30,* 215-225.

Sonkin, D. J., & Durphy, M. (1982). *Learning to live without violence: A handbook for men.* San Francisco: Volcano.

Sonkin, D. J., Martin, D., & Walker, L. E. (1985). *The male batterer: A treatment approach.* New York: Springer.

Sorenson, A. (1992). Estimating the economic consequences of separation and divorce: A cautionary tale from the United States. In L. Weitzman & M. Maclean (Eds.), *Economic consequences of divorce: The international perspective.* Oxford: Clarendon.

Southward, S., & Schwarz, J. C. (1987). Post-divorce contact, relationship with father, and heterosexual trust in female college students. *American Journal of Orthopsychiatry, 57,* 371-382.

Spanier, G. B., & Anderson, E. H. (1979). The impact of the legal system on adjustment to marital separation. *Journal of Marriage and the Family, 41,* 605-613.

Spanier, G. B., & Casto, R. F. (1979). Adjustment to separation and divorce: A qualitative analysis. In G. Levinger & O. C. Moles (Eds.), *Divorce and separation: Context, causes and consequences.* New York: Basic Books.

Spanier, G. B., & Thompson, L. (1984). *Parenting: The aftermath of separation and divorce.* Beverly Hills, CA: Sage.

Spicer, J. W., & Hampe, G. D. (1975). Kinship interaction after divorce. *Journal of Marriage and the Family, 37,* 113-119.

Spitze, G. D., & South, S. J. (1985). Women's employment, time expenditure, and divorce. *Journal of Family Issues, 6,* 307-329.

Sprenkle, D. H., & Cyrus, C. L. (1983). Abandonment: The stress of sudden divorce. In C. R. Figley & H. I. McCubbin (Eds.), *Stress and the family. Vol. 2: Coping with catastrophe.* New York: Brunner/Mazel.

Sprenkle, D. H., & Storm, C. L. (1983). Divorce therapy outcome research: A substantive and methodological review. *Journal of Marital & Family Therapy, 9*(3), 239-88.

Springer, C., & Wallerstein, J. S. (1983). Young adolescents' responses to their parents' divorce. In L. A. Kurdek (Ed.), *Children and divorce.* San Francisco: Jossey-Bass.

Stack, S. (1980). The effect of marital dissolution on suicide. *Journal of Marriage and the Family, 42,* 83-92.

Stack, S. (1990). New micro-level data on the impact of divorce on suicide, 1959-1980: A test of two theories. *Journal of Marriage and the Family, 52*, 119-127.

Statistics Canada. (1991). *Report on the demographic situation in Canada 1991: Current demographic analysis.* Ottawa: Author, Catalogue 91-209E Annual.

Statistics Canada. (1994). *Lone-parent families in Canada.* Ottawa: Author.

Steward, D. G., & Steel, F. M. (1990). *The economic consequences of divorce on families owning a marital home.* Winnipeg, Canada: University of Manitoba.

Stinson, K. M. (1991). *Adolescents, family, and friends: Social support after parents' divorce or remarriage.* New York: Praeger.

Stirling, K. J. (1989). Women who remain divorced: The long-term economic consequences. *Social Science Quarterly, 80*, 549-561.

Stolberg, A. L., Complair, C., Currier, K., & Wells, M. J. (1987). Individual, familial, and environmental determinants of children's post-divorce adjustment and maladjustment. *Journal of Divorce, 11*, 51-70.

Stone, L. (1990). *Road to divorce: England 1530-1987.* Oxford: Oxford University Press.

Stout, C. (1991). Common law: A growing alternative. *Canadian Social Trends, 23*, 18-20.

Survey of American Family Law. (1985). *Family Law Reporter, 11*, 3015.

Tavris, C., & Sadd, S. (1977). *The Redbook report on female sexuality.* New York: Delacorte.

Taylor, G. (1993). Custody, access and abuse. *Vis-a-vis, 10*(3), 4.

Teachman, J. D. (1982). Methodological issues in the analysis of family formation and dissolution. *Journal of Marriage and the Family, 44*, 1037-1053.

Teachman, J. (1991). Who pays? The receipt of child support in the United States. *Journal of Marriage and the Family, 53*, 759-772.

Teachman, J. (1991). Commitment to children by divorced fathers. *Social Problems 38*(3), 358-371.

Teachman, J. D., & Polonko, K. (1990). Negotiating divorce outcomes: Can we identify patterns in divorce settlements? *Journal of Marriage and the Family, 52*, 129-139.

Teleki, J. K. (1983). Parental behavior in divorced and married families. *Dissertation Abstracts International, 43*, 2511B.

Tenov, D. (1979). *Love and limerance: The experience of being in love.* Briarcliff, NY: Stein & Day.

Tennant, C., Bebbington, P., & Hurry, J. (1980). Parental death in childhood and risk of adult depressive disorders: A review. *Psychological Medicine, 10*, 289-299.

Thiriot, T. L., & Buckner, E. T. (1991). Multiple predictors of satisfying post-divorce adjustment of single custodial parents. *Journal of Divorce & Remarriage, 17*(1/2), 27-48.

Thomas, A. M., & Forehand, R. (1993). The role of paternal variables in divorced and married families: Predictability of adolescent adjustment. *American Journal of Orthopsychiatry, 63*(1), 126-135.

Thomlison, R. J. (1984). Something works: Evidence from practice effectiveness studies. *Social Work, 29*(1), 51-56.

Thompson, A. (1984). Extramarital sexual crisis: Common themes and therapy implications. *Journal of Sex & Marital Therapy, 10*, 239-256.

Thompson, A. P. (1983). Extramarital sex: A review of the research literature. *Journal of Sex Roles, 19*(1), 1-22.

Thompson, M. S., & Ensinger, M. E. (1989). Psychological well-being among mothers with school aged children: Evolving family structures. *Social Forces, 67*, 715-730.

Thornton, A., & Rodgers, W. (1987). The influence of individual and historical time on marital disruption. *Demography, 24,* 1-22.

Thurnher, M., Fenn, C. B., Melichar, J., & Chiriboga, D. A. (1983). Sociodemographic perspectives on reasons for divorce. *Journal of Divorce, 6*(4), 25-35.

Todres, R. (1978). Runaway wives: An increasing North American phenomenon. *Family Coordinator, 27,* 17-21.

Tooley, K. (1976). Antisocial behavior and social alienation post-divorce: The man of the house and his mother. *American Journal of Orthopsychiatry, 46,* 33-42.

Toomin, M. K. (1974). The child of divorce. In R. E. Hardy & J. G. Cull (Eds.), *Therapeutic needs of the family.* Springfield, IL: Charles C Thomas.

Touliatos, J., & Lindholm, B. W. (1980). Teachers' perception of behavioral problems in children from intact, single-parent, and stepparent families. *Psychology in the Schools, 17,* 264-269.

Trafford, A. (1982). *Crazy times: Predictable stages of divorce.* New York: Harper & Row.

Trovato, F. (1987). A longitudinal analysis of divorce and suicide in Canada. *Journal of Marriage and the Family, 49,* 193-203.

Trovato, F. (1991). Sex, marital status, and suicide in Canada: 1951-1981. *Sociological Perspectives, 34*(4), 427-445.

Trovato, F., & Lauris, G. (1989). Marital status and mortality in Canada. *Journal of Marriage and the Family, 51*(4), 907-922.

Trussel, J., & Rao, K. V. (1989). Premarital cohabitation and marital stability: A reassessment of the Canadian evidence. *Journal of Marriage and the Family, 51,* 535-544.

Tschann, J., Johnson, J., Kline, M., & Wallerstein, J. (1990). Conflict, loss, change and parent-child relationships: Predicting children's adjustment during divorce. *Journal of Divorce, 13,* 1-22.

Turner, J. R. (1984). Divorced fathers who win custody of their children: An exploratory study. *American Journal of Orthopsychiatry, 54,* 498-501.

Tuzlat, A., & Hillock, D. W. (1986). Single mothers and their children after divorce: A study of those "who make it." *Conciliation Courts Review, 24,* 79-89.

Tzeng, M. S. (1992). The effect of socioeconomic heterogamy and changes on marital dissolution of first marriages. *Journal of Marriage and the Family, 54,* 609-619.

Uhlenberg, P., Cooney, T., & Boyd, R. (1990). Divorce for women after midlife. *Journal of Gerontology: Social Sciences, 45*(1), S3-S11.

Ulrich, D. N. (1986). Mobilizing family resources for constructive divorce. In M. A. Karpel (Ed.), *Family resources: The hidden partner in family therapy.* New York: Guilford.

United States Department of Education. (1988). *Youth indicators 1988: Trends in the well-being of American youth.* Washington, DC: Author, Office of Educational Research and Improvement.

Vanier Institute of the Family. (1991). *Canadian families.* Ottawa: Author.

Vaughan, D. (1985). Uncoupling: The social construction of divorce. In H. Robboy, S. Greenblatt, & C. Clark (Eds.), *Social interaction: Introductory readings in sociology* (3rd ed.). New York: St. Martin's.

Vaughan, D. (1986). *Uncoupling: Turning points in intimate relationships.* New York: Oxford University Press.

Vaughan, P. (1990). *The monogamy myth: A new understanding of affairs and how to survive them.* New York: Newmarket.

Veevers, J. (1988). The real marriage squeeze: Mate selection, mortality and the mating gradient. *Sociological Perspective, 31,* 169-189.

Veevers, J. E. (1991). Traumas versus stress: Paradigms of positive versus negative divorce outcomes. *Journal of Divorce & Remarriage, 15* (1/2), 99-126.

Vess, J. D., Moreland, J., & Schwebel, A. I. (1985). Understanding role reallocation following a death: A theoretical framework. *Omega, 16,* 115-127.

Vess, J. D., Schwebel, A. I., & Moreland, J. (1983). The effects of early parental divorce on the sex role development of college students. *Journal of Divorce, 7*(1), 83-95.

Victor, R. S., Robbins, M. A., & Bassett, S. (1991). Statutory review of third-party rights regarding custody, visitation and support. *Family Law Quarterly, 25,* 19-57.

Visher, E. B., & Visher, J. (1987). *Old loyalties, new ties: Therapeutic strategies with step families.* New York: Brunner/Mazel.

Vogel, E. F., & Bell, N. W. (1968). The emotionally disturbed child as the family scapegoat. In N. W. Bell & E. F. Vogel (Eds.), *A modern introduction to the family.* New York: Free Press.

Volgy, S. S. (Ed.). (1991). *Women and divorce/men and divorce: Gender differences in separation, divorce, and remarriage.* New York: Haworth.

Waite, L. J., Haggstrom, G. W., & Kanouse, D. E. (1985). The consequences of parenthood for the marital stability of young adults. *American Sociological Review, 50,* 850-857.

Walker, T. B., & Elrod, L. H. (1993). Family law in the fifty states: An overview. *Family Law Quarterly, 26*(4), 319-421.

Wallerstein, J. S. (1984). Children of divorce: Preliminary report of a ten-year follow-up of young children. *American Journal of Orthopsychiatry, 54,* 444-458.

Wallerstein, J. S. (1985). Children of divorce: Preliminary report of a ten-year follow-up of older children and adolescents. *Journal of the American Academy of Child & Adolescent Psychiatry, 24,* 545-554.

Wallerstein, J. S. (1987). Children of divorce: Report of a ten-year follow-up of early latency-age children. *American Journal of Orthopsychiatry, 57,* 199-211.

Wallerstein, J. S. (1988a). Foreword. In J. R. Johnston & L. E. G. Campbell (Eds.), *Impasses of divorce: The dynamics and resolution of family conflict.* New York: Free Press.

Wallerstein, J. S. (1988b). Women after divorce: Preliminary report from a ten-year follow-up. *American Journal of Orthopsychiatry, 56,* 65-77.

Wallerstein, J. S. (1991). The long-term effects of divorce on children: A review. *Journal of the American Academy of Child and Adolescent Psychiatry, 30,* 349-360.

Wallerstein, J. S., & Blakeslee, S. (1989). *Second chances: Men, women, and children a decade after divorce.* New York: Ticknor & Fields.

Wallerstein, J. S., & Kelly, J. (1974). The effects of parental divorce: The adolescent experience. In E. Anthony & C. Koupernick (Eds.), *The child in his family: Children at psychiatric risk.* New York: John Wiley.

Wallerstein, J. S., & Kelly, J. (1975). The effects of parental divorce: Experiences of the preschool child. *Journal of Child Psychiatry, 14,* 600-616.

Wallerstein, J. S., & Kelly, J. (1976). The effects of parental divorce: Experiences of the child in later latency. *Journal of Child Psychiatry, 14,* 256-269.

Wallerstein, J. S., & Kelly, J. B. (1980). *Surviving the breakup: How children and parents cope with divorce.* New York: Basic Books.

Ward, R., Logan, J., & Spitze, G. (1992). The influence of parent and child needs on coresidence in middle and later life. *Journal of Marriage and the Family, 54,* 209-221.

Warshak, R. A. (1986). Father-custody and child development: A review and analysis of psychological research. *Behavioral Science & the Law, 4*, 2-17.

Warshak, R. A. (1992). *The custody revolution: The father factor and the motherhood mystique.* New York: Poseidon.

Warshak, R. A., & Santrock, J. W. (1983). The impact of divorce in father-custody and mother-custody homes: The child's perspective. In L. A. Kurdek (Ed.), *Children and divorce.* San Francisco: Jossey-Bass.

Watson, M. A. (1969). The children of Armageddon: Problems of custody following divorce. *Syracuse Law Review, 21*, 55-86.

Webber, M. (1991). *Street kids: The tragedy of Canada's runaways.* Toronto: University of Toronto Press.

Weiss, R. S. (1975). *Marital separation.* New York: Basic Books.

Weiss, R. S. (1976). The emotional impact of marital separation. *Journal of Social Issues, 32*, 135-146.

Weiss, R. S. (1977). The erosion of love and the persistence of attachment. In A. S. Skolnick & J. H. Skolnick (Eds.), *Family in transition* (2nd ed.). Boston: Little, Brown.

Weiss, R. S. (1979a). The adjudication of custody when parents separate. In G. Levinger & O. C. Moles (Eds.), *Divorce and separation: Context, causes, and consequences.* New York: Basic Books.

Weiss, R. S. (1979b). *Going it alone: The family life and social situation of the single parent.* New York: Basic Books.

Weiss, R. S. (1979c). Growing up a little faster: The experience of growing up in a single-parent household. *Journal of Social Issues, 35*, 97-111.

Weiss, R. S. (1979d). The impact of marital dissolution on income and consumption in single-parent households. *Journal of Marriage and the Family, 46*(1), 115-127.

Weiss, Y., & Willis, R. J. (1989). *An economic analysis of divorce settlements.* Chicago: University of Chicago Press.

Weitzman, L. J. (1985). *The divorce revolution: The unexpected social and economic consequences for women and children in America.* New York: Free Press.

Weitzman, L. J. (1992a). Alimony: Its premature demise and recent resurgence in the United States. In L. Weitzman & M. Maclean (Eds.), *Economic consequences of divorce: The international perspective.* Oxford: Clarendon.

Weitzman, L. J. (1992b). Marital property: Its transformation and division in the United States. In L. Weitzman & M. Maclean (Eds.), *Economic consequences of divorce: The international perspective.* Oxford: Clarendon.

Welch, C. E., & Price-Bonham, S. (1983). A decade of no-fault divorce revisited: California, Georgia, and Washington. *Journal of Marriage and the Family, 45*, 411-418.

Werner, E. E. (1989). High-risk children in young adulthood: A longitudinal study from birth to 32 years. *American Journal of Orthopsychiatry, 59*, 72-81.

Werner, E. E., & Smith, B. S. (1982). *Vulnerable but invincible: A study of resilient children.* New York: McGraw-Hill.

Westman, J., Cline, D., Swift, W., & Kramer, D. (1970). Role of child psychiatry in divorce. *Archives of General Psychiatry, 23*, 416-420.

Wheeler, M. (1974). *No-fault divorce.* Boston: Beacon.

White, J. M. (1987). Premarital cohabitation and marital stability in Canada. *Journal of Marriage and the Family, 49*, 641-647.

White, L. (1992). The effect of parental divorce and remarriage on parental support for adult children. *Journal of Family Issues, 12*(2), 234-250.

White, L. K. (1990). Determinants of divorce: A review of research in the eighties. *Journal of Marriage and the Family, 52,* 904-912.

White, L. K., & Booth, A. (1991). Divorce over the life course: The role of marital happiness. *Journal of Family Issues, 12*(1), 5-21.

White, S. W., & Bloom, B. C. (1981). Factors related to the adjustment of divorcing men. *Family Relations, 30,* 349-360.

White, S. W., & Mika, K. (1983). Family divorce and separation: Theory and research. *Marriage & Family Review, 6,* 175-192.

Whitehead, L. (1979). Sex differences in children's responses to family stress: A reexamination. *Journal of Child Psychology & Psychiatry, 20*(3), 247-254.

Whiteside, M. F. (1989). The role of the family therapist in divorce: Benevolent healer or agent of social change? *Family Process, 28,* 357-367.

Whyte, M. K. (1990). *Dating, mating, and marriage.* Hawthorne, NY: Aldine.

Wilcoxon, S. A. (1987). Grandparents and grandchildren: An often neglected relationships between significant others. *Journal of Counseling & Development, 65,* 289-290.

Williams, G. (1983). *Legal negotiations and settlement.* St. Paul, MN: West.

Williams, G. (1984). *Legal negotiations and settlement: A lawyer's handbook for effective negotiation and settlement.* n.p.: National Practice Institute.

Williams, T., & Kornblum, W. (1985). *Growing up poor.* Lexington, MA: Lexington Books.

Wilson, B. F., & Cunningham-Clarke, S. (1992). Remarriage: A demographic profile. *Journal of Family Issues, 13*(2), 123-141.

Wilson, S. J. (1991). *Women, families, and work* (3rd ed.). Toronto: McGraw-Hill Ryerson.

Wineberg, H. (1990). Childbearing after remarriage. *Journal of Marriage and the Family, 52,* 31-38.

Wiseman, R. (1975). Crisis theory and the process of divorce. *Social Casework, 56*(4), 205-212.

Wojtkiewicz, R. A., McLanahan, S., & Garfinkel, I. (1990). The growth of families headed by women. *Demography, 27,* 19-30.

Wolfson, L. H. (1992). *The new family law.* Toronto: Random House.

Wolman, R., & Taylor, K. (1991). Psychosocial effects of custody disputes on children. *Behavioral Sciences & the Law, 9*(4), 399-417.

Wood, V., & Robertson, J. (1978). Friendship and kinship interaction: Differential effect on the morale of the elderly. *Journal of Marriage and the Family, 40,* 367-375.

Woody, J. D., Colley, P. E., Schlegelmilch, J., Maginn, P., & Balsanek, J. (1984). Children's adjustment to parental stress following divorce. *Social Casework, 65,* 405-412.

Woolley, P. (1978). Shared custody: Demanded by parents, discouraged by courts. *Family Advocate, 1*(1), 6-9, 33-34.

Woolley, P. (1980). *The custody handbook.* New York: Summit.

Woolsey, S. H. (1977). Pied piper politics and the child-care debate. *Daedalus, 106,* 127-145.

Wyman, P. A., Cowen, E. L., Hightower, A. D., & Pedro-Carroll, J. L. (1985). Perceived competence, self-esteem, and anxiety in latency-age children of divorce. *Journal of Clinical Child Psychology, 14*(1), 20-26.

Young, D. M. (1983). Two studies of children of divorce. In L. A. Kurdek (Ed.), *Children and divorce.* San Francisco: Jossey-Bass.

Zaslow, M. J. (1988). Sex differences in children's response to parental divorce: 1. Research methodology and post-divorce family forms. *American Journal of Orthopsychiatry, 58,* 355-378.

Zaslow, M. J. (1989). Sex differences in children's response to parental divorce: 2. Samples, variables, ages, and sources. *American Journal of Orthopsychiatry, 59,* 118-141.

Zeiss, A. M., Zeiss, R. A., & Johnson, S. M. (1980). Sex differences in initiation of and adjustment to divorce. *Journal of Divorce, 4,* 21-33.

Zinn, M. B., & Eitzen, D. S. (1990). *Diversity in families* (2nd ed.). New York: Harper & Row.

Zweibel, E. B. (1993). Canadian income tax policy on child support payments: Old rationale applied to new realities. In J. Hudson and B. Galaway (Eds.), *Single parent families: Perspectives on research and policy.* Toronto: Thompson Educational.

PART II

Clinical Practice

Proponents of structural models of mediation recognize that a crucial client task is the negotiation of issues in dispute, without which there can be no agreement. Proponents of therapeutic models of mediation, ourselves included, recognize that there are relational prerequisites without which fair negotiation, and thus agreement, is impossible. Accordingly, they focus as much on relational processes as on negotiation outcomes. They also realize that in the absence of these prerequisites, negotiation is a waste of time, with referral for therapy or to the court better options than mediation.

Part II examines one such model, *Therapeutic Family Mediation* (TFM). On one level, what follows is conventional in all descriptive accounts of a model. That is, chapters 4 and 5 provide an account of the model's basic premises and assumptions, practice principles, and a step-by-step guide to practice. This description is augmented at the end of chapter 4 by a series of case histories that together provide a detailed description of how TFM works and the thinking that guides the interventions of a mediator using the logic of TFM.

On another level, these chapters provide a valuable glimpse into the historical evolution of TFM. Beginning with crude premises based on practice, it has steadily become more sophisticated. On the one hand, this growth reflects the cumulative response to increasing clinical experience in the use of the model. On the other hand, it has changed in response to developments in the literature, in particular, to the feminist critique of mediation. In a literature devoted to the celebration and exploration of mediation, it has been difficult to appreciate that a segment of the audience has come increasingly to oppose its very existence. This response appears so for several reasons: The feminist critique has lacked focus, being scattered in both location and content; there have been only sporadic, unsystematic responses, typically in reply to a specific article or essay; and given their beneficent intentions, mediators as a group have responded with denial to the possibility that a body of opinion should see their efforts as inimical to the fundamental interests of women. In this context, there is the very real temptation to simply dismiss the critique as the hysterical ravings of a band of feminist extremists, most of whom, it might be argued, are legal scholars with no direct knowledge of mediation practice. In chapter 5, we argue that such a reaction would be a mistake. Although we are not uncritical of some feminist arguments, there is much there of substantive value and thus deserving of a thoughtful and constructive response. Ours is a call for collaboration and inclusion rather than more brickbats and invective.

4

Therapeutic Family Mediation

Practice Principles
and Ecosystemic Processes

INTRODUCTION

Following the initial work of Coogler (1978), in the 1980s a spate of publications described various models of family mediation (Blades, 1985; Lemmon, 1985; Moore, 1986). Comparing these models with the knowledge base examined in chapters 2 and 3 supports two conclusions. First, these models consistently emphasize the central importance of negotiation (see also Bahr, Chappell, & Marcos, 1987), which is in keeping with recent evidence indicating that many mediators—though not all (see Sargent & Moss, 1987; Shaw & Phear, 1987)—focus on facts, issues, and positions (Donohue, Lyles, & Rogan, 1989; Kressel, Butler-DeFreitas, Forlenza, & Wilcox, 1989).

Second, these models pay correspondingly little attention to relational variation, either across divorcing couples or across couples in mediation. Among the former, various family "types" have been identified, whose patterns vary from very functional to markedly dysfunctional (Kressel, Jaffe, Tuchman, Watson, & Deutsch, 1980; Little, 1982).

Among the latter, similar pattern variety has been reported (McIsaac, 1987; Walker, 1986). Concomitantly, family "types" or their analogues have proven extremely important clinically, with some "types" of couples highly amenable to family mediation, others less so, and still others contraindicated (Bahr et al., 1987; McIsaac, 1987; Potapchuk & Carlson, 1987; Wallerstein, 1987). In the same vein, recent evidence (see chapter 10) shows that relational processes are precisely the points at which couples get stuck or fail in mediation. Thus, current models of mediation ignore or deemphasize the possibility that some couples seeking mediation are not ready to begin negotiation.

Such a lack of readiness can be traced to two often complementary sources: (a) emotional blockages rooted in dysfunctional patterns of interaction and (b) processes in the ecological context of the families in question, especially their ongoing interaction with a host of others including extended family members, friends and neighbors, judicial actors such as lawyers and judges, and various human service professionals, including those in the fields of mental health, medicine, taxation and accountancy, and real estate. Consequently, couples may benefit from a preliminary intervention designed to alter dysfunctional patterns, block the involvement (and thus the influence) of extrasystemic others, and so increase the couple's readiness to participate meaningfully in negotiation.

In the balance of this chapter, we set out an alternate model of mediation explicitly designed to accommodate the range of client couple interactional variation. Called *therapeutic family mediation* (TFM)—not to be confused with the work of Waldron, Roth, Fair, Mann, and McDermott (1984)—it was developed by Irving (1980) and has undergone significant refinement in the light of clinical experience (Irving & Benjamin, 1987, 1989). The latter has brought the ecosystemic character of the model into sharper focus, which has highlighted the two roots of many difficulties couples encounter in mediation: underlying patterns of couple interaction that remain affectively charged despite separation or divorce and the maintenance or development of dysfunctional patterns in light of new or ongoing involvement of extrasystemic others.

In what follows, we briefly describe our clients, define relevant therapeutic concepts, detail the process of mediation, list the mediator's roles and responsibilities, discuss the model's indications and contraindications, and illustrate operation of the model with a series of short case vignettes.

THE CLIENTS

The first author is in private practice and accepts clients on a fee-for-service basis. Consequently, like the clients of most private services (see Milne, 1983; Pearson, Ring, & Milne, 1983), our clientele, although predominantly middle class, is heterogeneous across dimensions such as employment type and status, religion, and ethnic group.[1] Lawyers and occasionally the courts account for the bulk of referrals, although self-referrals occur.

Compared to clients who receive court-based service (see Irving, Benjamin, Bohm, & Macdonald, 1981; Irving, Bohm, Macdonald, & Benjamin, 1979), our private clients display fewer and less serious presenting problems and complaints. Conversely, they also receive a greater number of mediation sessions, on average between 8 and 16, each lasting approximately 2 hours. On these grounds, TFM is a model of practice that generalizes in varying degrees to different service settings: poorly with respect to court-based services, moderately with respect to clinic settings, and very well with respect to private settings.

Finally, this chapter refers to slightly more than 200 client couples seen over the past 5 years. Of those not referred out as contraindicated (see below), the overall rate of agreement stands at about 70%. However, this rate varied by the course of service provided: Those who initially entered premediation were less likely to reach agreement (45%) than those who moved straight from assessment to negotiation (85%). However, because those who entered service via premediation would likely have been seen as contraindicated by proponents of more conventional models of service, an agreement rate of 45% is not as low as it appears.

GENERAL THERAPEUTIC CONCEPTS

As noted above, TFM is theoretically grounded in an ecosystemic model of the family and operationally involves four phases. Below we address theoretical and clinical notions, respectively.

Theoretically, TFM draws selectively on communication (Bodin, 1981), structural (Aponte, 1981), and especially strategic (Stanton, 1981) models of family therapy as well as the conceptual work of Benjamin (1983) and recently Elkaim (1990). In turn, these models provide support for a range of ecosystemic assumptions that underpin the model, including the following:

- Interaction among family members is organized or patterned.
- These patterns are extremely potent, constraining and shaping interaction on the levels of behavior, communication, affect, and meaning.
- The operation of these patterns is typically outside the awareness of family members.
- Across any population of families, family patterns distribute across a continuum, from highly functional or "healthy" to highly dysfunctional or "unhealthy."
- Following marital separation, families systems undergo major structural change; although such change may produce concomitant changes in various patterns of interaction, these two sorts of change are only weakly coupled, such that prevailing patterns of interaction, especially marital interaction, may persist.
- Apart from the immediate family, family patterns may encompass others with whom family members come into regular or routine contact.
- Including in these patterns persons outside the system—a process known as "induction"—invariably operates to stabilize the patterns in question or to promote the evolution of new and typically dysfunctional patterns and thus is typically inconsistent with the goals of professional others such as mediators.

With respect to mediation, the significance of these assumptions is fourfold: (a) they suggest that a proportion of families that enter mediation will display patterns at the dysfunctional end of the continuum; (b) the mediator must be continually on guard against induction, both of himself or herself as well as of other professionals involved in the case; (c) unless the mediator can block or otherwise neutralize the influence of "outsiders" inducted into the system, the likelihood of changing those patterns of couple interaction inconsistent with the requirements of negotiation will be low; and, (d) unless the mediator can change or neutralize dysfunctional behaviors inimical to negotiation, the likelihood that the client couple will encounter an impasse in negotiation is high.

TFM represents our clinical response to these interactional bases of mediation failure. As noted, this model conceives of the mediation process in terms of four phases, namely, *assessment, premediation, negotiation,* and *follow-up.* These phases are most easily displayed graphically, as in Figure 4.1.

The model's key terms are defined as follows. *Assessment* denotes a screening process on the basis of which client couples are initially judged for their readiness to enter mediation. Here, three levels of functioning are distinguished: clients who are contraindicated for mediation, those who are immediately ready to enter negotiation, and those who are likely to be capable of negotiation following a course of premediation (see Indications and Contraindications, p. 172).

Premediation refers to a treatment process applied to client couples judged amenable to mediation but whose relational dysfunction renders them unable to enter fruitful negotiation. Entry into premediation may directly follow assessment or happen one or more times during negotiation should a blockage occur that is judged to be rooted in the clients' relational problem(s). *Negotiation* is that process whereby client couples seek to reach agreement on various issues in dispute between them. If successful—with or without premediation—the resulting terms and conditions are used to prepare a formal agreement. If unsuccessful, they are referred out for treatment or processing via the court. Finally, *follow-up* involves a routine "check-up" about 6 weeks after termination. It is intended to monitor the couple's progress and evaluate the utility of their current agreement, thus whether it should remain as is, be modified, or be abrogated entirely. If necessary, a brief return to premediation or negotiation may be indicated.

Thus each phase of TFM involves different forms of intervention and has correspondingly divergent clinical goals (see Goals and Responsibilities, p. 169). Furthermore, no phase occurs independently of any other, for each is linked to the others by a series of feedback loops. Indeed, in accordance with the model's ecosystemic emphasis, the characteristic form of mediation based on TFM is a series of recursive loops.

In formal terms, *feedback* refers to a process in which a portion of a system's output is reintroduced as input, thus providing the system with news of a "difference" between its present status and its intended

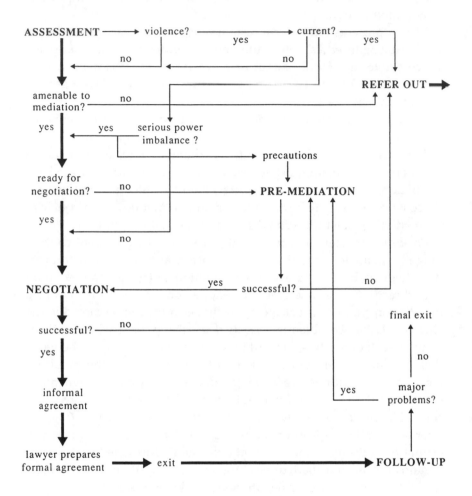

Figure 4.1. The Decision-Making Process of Therapeutic Family Mediation

goal(s). Such information allows a well-functioning system to "correct" this "error" by reducing the "difference" between where it is and where it wants to be by changing its behavior, intended goal(s), or both.

Many of the couples who seek our service use such a feedback process positively, with negotiation a means of reducing conflict about one or more substantive issues, thus increasing the likelihood that mediation will result in a successful and mutually satisfying outcome. Among a minority of couples, however, this process goes awry, with a "vicious cycle" setting in that amplifies rather than reduces "error," thus locking them into conflictual positions from which they can neither see escape nor conceive of viable alternative(s). The recursive character of TFM is designed to disrupt such vicious loops at whatever stage of mediation they appear, thus promoting conflict resolution and a successful outcome.

We now turn to a detailed examination of each phase of TFM.

THE PROCESS OF INTERVENTION

Existing models of mediation arbitrarily distinguish between four and 12 stages or phases of mediation. The four stages of TFM are substantively comparable to existing models, with three exceptions: TFM's greater emphasis on assessment, the selective application of premediation, and the recursive linkage between phases.

The Assessment Process

Of the four phases of TFM, the assessment phase may well be the most demanding clinically, for a great deal of information must be assembled over a comparatively short period of time. Based on the knowledge base (see chapters 2 and 3) and our clinical experience, this phase encompasses seven areas of concern that are broadly predictive of outcome success or failure:

1. *Postdivorce Spousal Functioning.* Conceptually, this functioning refers to the ability of former spouses to solve problems and resolve differences through discussion and negotiation. Operationally, it encompasses at least nine components of marital interaction:

   - Communication: the ability of each spouse to communicate his or her concerns clearly and coherently (Walker, 1986)
   - Conflict: the extent, intensity, and manner in which spouses seek to resolve differences (Barsky, 1983)

- Violence: whether, to what extent, and when one spouse has been violent with his or her partner (Kitson, Babri, & Roach, 1985), especially wife abuse, including physical violence, marital rape, and verbal abuse such as threats or intimidation

- Trust: the extent to which each spouse perceives the other as trustworthy, a dimension critical to effective negotiation (Milne, 1983)

- Repertoire: the interactional flexibility of the spouses, separately and together (Benjamin, 1983)

- Pattern: the dominant pattern(s) that characterize family interaction, especially relations between spouses (McIsaac, 1987; Potapchuk & Carlson, 1987)

- Attachment: the extent to which the client spouses have fully accepted the end of their marital relationship and concomitantly have ceased to be involved affectively and behaviorally with the other spouse (Bahr et al., 1987)

- Divorce readiness: the extent to which each spouse is prepared for the decision to separate and in particular whether their respective levels of readiness are congruent or divergent (Wallerstein, 1987)

- Plan for the future: the extent to which either spouse has begun to formulate a plan for the future, another dimension critical, in our experience, to their ability to negotiate

2. *Parental Functioning.* Conceptually, this refers to the capacity of both spouses, separately and together, to care for and control their children. Operationally, six components can be distinguished.

   - Parenting adequacy: the extent to which each spouse cares for their children in keeping with the latter's developmental and physiological needs; includes the perception by each spouse of the parenting ability of the other

   - Parenting involvement: the degree to which each spouse is actively involved in the provision of care to their children (Kitson et al., 1985)

   - Change in parenting involvement: the extent to which parenting involvement has changed since the marital separation

   - Child attributes: specifically, the number, age, and genders of the children

   - Child information: whether and how the children were informed of their parents' divorce

- Child reaction: how and to what degree the children have manifested signs of distress after the separation of their parents
- Parent-child relationship: the quality of the relationship between each spouse and their children, including feelings of closeness and love, and their opposites (McIsaac, 1987; Wallerstein, 1987), including child abuse

3. *Resources.* Conceptually, the extent and adequacy of a range of resources. Operationally, it involves at least three components.

  - Demand: the level of stress experienced by each spouse, together with their judgment of the stress being experienced by the children (Wallerstein & Kelly, 1980)
  - Coping: how each spouse is coping with their perceived level of demand, separately and together (Wallerstein, 1987)
  - Resources: broadly, the resources available to each spouse, including financial, emotional, and social resources (Walker, 1986)

4. *Ethnicity.* Conceptually, the extent to which each spouse identifies with a specific ethnic group, together with beliefs and practices specific to that belief system. Operationally, this dimension concerns the manner in which ethnicity plays out across all aspects of family life. Because ethnic identification varies widely, ethnicity may be critical or irrelevant to the divorce experience. In addition, three aspects of ethnicity may be especially important in assessing readiness for family mediation.

  - Cultural diversity: whether and to what extent certain group-specific beliefs and practices are central to the client couple, including religious beliefs and degree of observance. These issues may be of particular importance in cases involving intermarriage.
  - Immigration status: whether one or both spouses has immigrated within the past 5 years, and if so, their current immigration status
  - Language: to what extent either spouse and the children have a working knowledge of English

5. *Interpersonal Context.* Conceptually, this refers to others outside of the immediate family with whom one or more family members routinely interact, and who thus may influence the course of mediation. Operationally, it involves three components:

- New partner(s): the presence and duration of a new romantic partner in the life of one or both spouses
- Extended kin and friendship network: the identity and degree of involvement of extended kin (especially grandparents) and friends
- Institutional others: the identity and degree of involvement of institutional others, especially lawyers and counselors or therapists

6. *Court Involvement.* Whether and over what duration the client couple has been involved in adversarial proceedings. In our experience, the more extensive and longer the involvement, the less amenable couples are to mediation.

7. *Marital Status.* Finally, whether either or both spouses have previously been married or lived common law and then divorced or separated and, if so, how many times. In our experience, this factor operates on two levels. One level concerns the expectations of the spouses and the extent to which those expectations are explicit or take the form of a hidden agenda. The other level concerns the structural complexity of the client family, that is, whether it involves parents and children or various degrees of stepkin, with the latter representing a greater challenge than the former for the mediator.

These data are so central to our subsequent practice that the assessment process typically involves three sessions, one with each spouse seen alone and the third a joint session.[2] In form these sessions most resemble the problem assessment process in family therapy (see Bross & Benjamin, 1983; Minuchin & Fishman, 1981) and are similarly explained to clients, that is, as the basis for identifying key problems and deciding how they might best be resolved. In turn, this process gives the mediator the scope to ask questions covering the areas of concern noted above.

The initial choice of individual sessions is intended to establish trust, encourage frankness, and provide individualized support. This time in the client's life is often one when much is happening all at once, such that many clients are in considerable distress. This state makes it crucial that the mediator become involved and establish a relationship of trust quickly. However, this relationship must include not only each spouse separately, but both spouses as a couple. Accordingly, the conjoint session is booked as soon after the last individual session as possible. The conjoint session also serves as a forum in which to restate the goals, purposes, and methods of family mediation.

Assessment data thus generated are used to address three questions: Is this couple interested in reconciliation? Is this couple amenable to mediation? If so, are the spouses ready to enter directly into negotiation? The answers to the last two questions turn on the couple's level of functioning (see Indications and Contraindications, p. 172) expressed as a configuration that takes account of all the above areas of concern. Based on this assessment, couples may be referred out for long-term treatment or litigation or may be assigned to negotiation or premediation.

It is important to note that the assignment of couples to premediation or negotiation is provisional and thus subject to change based on the couple's subsequent performance. On occasion, assessment errors occur (see Bross & Benjamin, 1983). Dysfunction thought problematic vis-à-vis negotiation may respond well to premediation intervention or be less troubled than initially perceived. Premediation may thus be brief, with clients entering negotiation sooner than planned. Conversely, among couples who enter negotiation directly, areas of dysfunction may be missed on assessment only to produce impasses during negotiation: Conflict, subdued at first, may gradually become unmanageable; preliminary flexibility may gradually be transformed into positions of extreme rigidity involving few options, and so on. In such cases, exposure to premediation would be likely. TFM thus requires that practitioners continually read the feedback in an effort to provide an optimal match between service and client requirements.

Systemic and Extrasystemic Processes

What we here call systemic and extrasystemic processes move beyond assessment to encompass the three phases of mediation—premediation, negotiation, and follow-up—directed toward disruption of dysfunctional patterns of interaction, conflict resolution, construction of a viable agreement, and its subsequent maintenance.

The Premediation Process

Premediation is intended to produce a change in patterns of relating between former partners consistent with the requirements of negotiation. Toward this end, it is useful to distinguish between systemic processes, extrasystemic processes, and family resources.

Systemic Processes

As in family therapy, desired changes can involve an array of family processes. Unlike family therapy, they are restricted by the ultimate goal, fruitful negotiation, such that intervention is highly selective, in some cases leaving various forms of dysfunction untouched. Thus, selective targets for intervention, based on the requirements of negotiation as well as the prediction of outcome success, may include the following:

- Cognitive recognition and affective acceptance that the marital relationship is at an end and that planning for the future needs to commence
- Commitment to the mediation process, thus ignoring or resisting the disruptive influence of relatives, friends, and others who may unwittingly have become embroiled in the client couple's unsuccessful efforts at dispute resolution (see Extrasystemic Processes, p. 159)
- Information dissemination so that clients have the basis on which to make informed choices about their future course, including the choice of mediation as opposed to litigation as the method most likely to achieve their ends
- Communication training sufficient to allow clients to get their message across clearly, to assert their rights, interests, and concerns and, in short, to become effective negotiators
- Rules and procedures put in place to ensure the safety and security of both spouses and thus be useful for all couples (e.g., regarding the use of threats or intimidation), but critical for those who have a history of marital violence[3]

Toward these ends, the mediator's primary concern is to identify the systemic processes that block or prevent the couple from entering negotiation while maintaining an impasse. Such blockages, in our clinical experience, typically involve one or a combination of the following systemic components:

- Individuals may be so distressed by the separation as to become immobilized, a response that may reflect individual variation in responsiveness or sensitivity

- Spousal dysfunction, either in the form of continuing attachment to the other spouse or a pattern of interaction that makes negotiation impossible (e.g., sustained and uncontrolled conflict in the absence of closure)
- Parent-child relations, often in the form of a cross-generational coalition, say, between a mother and son, which excludes the father
- The entire family system may be the locus of the blockage, especially in enmeshed families in which there are no clear boundaries separating the marital and child subsystems (Johnston & Campbell, 1988; McIsaac, 1987, chap. 3)

In this context, we caution again linear explanations that place blame for a blockage in mediation on one or the other spouse. Kressel, Butler-DeFreitas, Forlenza, and Wilcox (1989), for example, in a series of case studies, found that husbands were far more likely than wives to adopt rigid and inflexible positions. Although we do not question their observations, in our experience their explanation is insensitive to the ecosystemic character of the family systems in question. Such a perspective, although it enjoins the observer to consider the entire system, does not preclude explanations that place greater emphasis on one member than another. Encompassed in the notion of the *leading part*, this view acknowledges that some family members may be more influential than others in sustaining certain patterns of interaction, but simultaneously notes the participation of all members for the production and maintenance of the pattern in question. Thus blockages in mediation are not the result of processes at any specific level of such systems; rather, across client couples, the primary source of the blockage may occur at the level of the individual, the couple, or the entire system. Each suggests a different ecosystemic pattern of interaction, which, in turn, has direct implications for intervention.

Extrasystemic Processes

Extrasystemic elements may additionally complicate the picture. Here, four sets of others may be distinguished: (a) lawyer(s), (b) new intimate partner(s), (c) therapist(s), and (d) relatives and other intimates (see also Johnston & Campbell, 1988, chap. 2). In each case, the involvement of one or both client spouses with one or more of these extrasystemic others may facilitate the process of mediation or, more typically, may actively interfere with it. In this section, we address the latter outcome, reserving our comments about the former outcome for the next section (see Family Resources, p. 163; also Johnston & Campbell, 1988, chap. 3).

Lawyers. Lawyers are generally supportive of family mediation and work well with mediation practitioners. However, despite their best intentions, they may inadvertently block the process of mediation, typically as the result of two processes. In the first, lawyers may become emotionally involved and thus overprotective of their clients. Like a parent intervening on behalf of a hurt child, lawyers may seek to do everything for their client. Although this response is understandable under the circumstances, it may not only hinder clients in working emotionally through the divorcing process, but prevents them from discovering and asserting their own concerns, intentions, and plans in mediation. In the second process, lawyers and mediators may be unaware that they have divergent agendas. Consequently, they may miscommunicate about specific issues; such misunderstandings undermine what would usually be a fruitful working relationship. With experience working together on cases, such misunderstandings usually clear up on their own.

Even so, such experience makes clear that lawyers, whether they know it or not, are active participants in mediation cases and as such typically affect the course of mediation, usually positively (see Family Resources, p. 163), but sometimes negatively. In the latter instance, the mediator's responsibility is to encourage lawyers to cooperate or to block behavior that might undermine the course of mediation.

New Partner. The presence of one or more new intimate partners may similarly act to derail the mediation process. In this context, the key problem typically centers on the feelings of threat engendered in one spouse when the other spouse enters a relationship with a new partner who is seen as stealing not only the spouse, but also the affection of the child(ren), which is experienced as intolerable. In such cases, Johnston and Campbell (1988, p. 28) are correct in observing that new partners are frequently "not the primary instigators and their role [is] not central; rather, the real drama [is] between the formerly married. In this respect, the new partners serve . . . as puppets, pawns, trophies, or merely weapons in the continuing marital dispute."

Although this situation is typical, in a minority of cases, the new partner(s) can take a more active role and thus can act in important ways to stabilize or exacerbate ongoing marital conflict. Having seen the other spouse only through the conflict-distorted eyes of their new partner, the new partner may encourage that partner to take unrealistic or extreme positions, refuse to consider compromise suggestions and, in effect, obliterate the other spouse in a zero-sum game, thus confirming the threat noted above.

Therapist. A third group that may block mediation are the therapists with whom one or both client spouses may be involved concurrent with mediation. This involvement may lead to two sorts of complications: The interventions of the therapist(s) may conflict with the related efforts of the mediator and the therapist(s) may become emotionally involved with the family system, thus sustaining dysfunction. (Mediators too may be vulnerable to induction in this way.)

The former complication typically derives from involvement with only one spouse and thus knowledge of the family system in general and the other spouse as perceived by that spouse. This necessarily distorted view may lead to well-intentioned intervention—having the spouse in question assert his or her autonomy by declining to talk with the other spouse—which has the unintended consequence of undermining mediation.

The latter complication typically represents evidence of induction, in which the therapist completes the pattern disrupted by the separation-related departure of the former. Thus a wife accustomed to a passive-dependent stance in relation to an authoritarian husband may enter a relationship with a male therapist who, confronted by her apparent helplessness, is encouraged to tell her what to do. The upshot of this process is to stabilize the very pattern the mediator is attempting to disrupt.

Extended Family. Finally, extended family members (especially grandparents) as well as other intimates, such as friends or neighbors, represent a final and extremely potent source of interference. Such involvement is by no means automatic and can often be benign or positive (see Family Resources, p. 163). However, when such involvement acts to disrupt the mediation process, two variations can be distinguished.[4] The first involves cross-generational coalition—often between a grandparent and a spouse or a child (see Haley, 1976). The second involves side-taking in which, for example, friends, relatives, or neighbors side with one spouse and accordingly counsel a course of action that is typically inconsistent with that recommended by the mediator pursuant to a negotiated agreement.

In both cases, family relations can be enormously complicated by ethnicity. Intergenerational conflict, for example, can evolve from circumstances in which parents (and grandparents) support traditional values, whereas the children (especially adolescents) have been assimilated into the dominant culture and thus view their parents' position as out of step with modern life. In a similar vein, extended kin may insist on rejection of a given proposal on the grounds of family honor (e.g., in Asian families) or respect (e.g., in Hispanic families) when the spouse in question might otherwise be inclined to accept a proposal.

Furthermore, both cases involve the formation of coalitions or alliances that are double-edged in character. On the one hand, they provide support: emotional support for a spouse at a time of stress and support and validation for a position typically at odds with the position of the other spouse. On the other hand, that support is not without cost in the form of a series of obligations and counterdemands, polarizing already conflictual relations while in many cases inserting into the dispute a new hidden agenda. Such processes thus stabilize often dysfunctional patterns of spousal relating while escalating conflict by supporting extreme or unrealistic positions as well as introducing extraneous issues that do not truly belong to the couple.

Taken together, these various sources of extrasystemic influence emphasize the potency of an ecosystemic perspective. Technically external to the couple in dispute, such sources of influence often are excluded from explicit consideration in the mediation process. This omission makes perfect sense from the perspective of many of the models noted above, which rely on an economic model of practice. In turn, however, it restricts their efficacy to client couples where the involvement of such extrasystemic elements is excluded or minimal; where such influences are important, the probability of outcome failure is high. In contrast, TFM assumes that the likelihood of such involvement is high, especially among couples that have been in conflict for some time, and thus it builds in mechanisms to deal with them. Specifically, in each case we suggest that blocking such involvement—or at least curtailing it significantly—is a prerequisite to successful negotiation. Consequently, the range of clients seen as amenable to mediation is considerable, as ecosystemic sensitivity translates into clinical flexibility.

Family Resources. Finally, resources—financial, emotional, and social— may act to block or facilitate family mediation, especially negotiation. Financial resources refer to assets, liquid and otherwise. If abundant, such resources make available options—for example, establishing two households, hiring additional child care support, and so forth—that may be ruled out for partners (especially women) with meager assets.

Emotional resources refer to the coping capacity of each spouse [5] and the extent to which they report feeling OK or at the "end of their tether." Those in the former group can be expected to handle the exigencies of negotiation in a fashion very different from those in the latter group.

Finally, our comments above might be taken to suggest that the involvement of others in the lives of client couples invariably has negative consequences for the mediation process. In fact, that is clearly not the case; rather, it is the character of that involvement that is critical because members of one or more of the four groups cited above, acting as social resources, may be important, if not central, to family mediation. Extended family members, friends, and neighbors may provide client spouses with a source of support that helps see the clients through a very difficult period in their lives and encourage conciliatory positions. Key individuals, for example, grandparents, may also assist by lending their often considerable authority to the mediator. New partners may help by making clear that they pose no threat to the other spouse, especially in regard to the ongoing relationship between that spouse and the child(ren). Finally, therapists and lawyers can be enormously helpful insofar as they act in accord with the mediation process rather than in opposition to it. Therapists, for example, may facilitate the mediation process by providing their clients with needed support and affirmation, helping them be clear in their own minds about what they want from mediation (and how this may differ from what their children need), and selecting interventions congruent with those in use by the mediator. For example, passive-dependent spouses or spouses who have been abused will typically need help in achieving autonomy and asserting their rights and preferences. Finally, lawyers in the case may be helpful in a number of ways, including selective referral of clients suitable for mediation; avoidance of client induction, thus forcing clients to confront their problems in mediation; vigilance over their client's rights and self-interests, thus keeping the mediator honest; forcing the mediator to stick to his or her own agenda, thus preventing mediation from drifting into therapy; making available the lawyer's fund of knowledge of the law, negotiation, fair dealing, and clear communication; and, where warranted, lending their authority to the mediation process, especially in the face of client misbehavior (e.g., lying or intimidation).

Thus TFM confronts mediators with two challenges. First, they must find a way to use the client couple's ecosystem to best advantage, blocking or minimizing the disruptive influence of extrasystemic elements and intervening to alter dysfunctional patterns of marital relating likely to be inconsistent with negotiation, while capitalizing on available system resources. Second, all or, more typically, some of these premediation processes need to be accomplished relatively quickly, in four to eight sessions. Throughout, careful reading of the feedback usually indicates whether the mediator is on the right track. For example, indications of change in the right direction include evidence of spouses who have begun to talk with each other, cooled down emotionally, accepted that their marital relationship is over, and begun to consider what the future may hold and to think and speak in terms of the welfare of their children rather than their own pain.

Following this effort, if none of the goals of premediation has been met or evidence suggests that they can be met only after prolonged therapy, the couple is referred either for therapy or to their lawyers for judicial processing.

THE NEGOTIATION PROCESS

In all formal models of mediation, including TFM, negotiation is based on four premises, namely, that the spouses in question:

- Think and act rationally
- Have a relatively clear idea of the issues in question
- Have a good sense of what they would regard as a satisfying or at least acceptable outcome
- Can articulate and assert their position, even in the face of opposition by their spouse

In this context, it is useful to distinguish between negotiation principles and mediation practices.

Negotiation Principles

Broadly, two conceptual approaches to negotiation can be distinguished: positional bargaining (Gifford, 1985) and principled negotiation (Fisher, Ury, & Patton, 1991; Ury, 1991).

As its name suggests, positional bargaining encourages spouses to take a justified position and defend it against attack. It is basically adversarial in nature because it assumes that

- The interests of the spouses necessarily diverge
- Maintenance of an ongoing relationship between the spouses is not an issue
- Negotiation involves a zero-sum game in which anything one spouse gains, the other spouse loses

Thus in negotiation using this approach, there is a tendency for spouses to adopt entrenched positions as they resist demands for concessions by the other spouse. Furthermore, the focus is exclusively on substantive issues and problems, with little regard for relational processes, past or present.

That said, three variations on this approach are noteworthy. In competitive bargaining, one spouse forces the other to settle by a combination of the strength of their arguments, the superiority of their resources and the skillfulness of their tactics, all of which convince the other spouse to settle for less than they had planned. In cooperative bargaining, concessions by one spouse foster trust, thus encouraging the other spouse to make reciprocal concessions. Settlements achieved using this approach are perceived by both spouses as fair and equitable, though efforts to maximize individual gains remain fundamental to the goals of both spouses. Finally, in integrative bargaining, concessions are given and received while deliberately searching for creative problem-solving solutions, thus increasing both the likelihood of settlement and the perception of receiving mutual benefits.

All three variations may be contrasted with principled negotiation. The latter focuses on interests rather than positions and assumes that

- Although some interests of the spouses may diverge, insofar as resolution of the problem benefits them both, in a fundamental sense their interests necessarily converge
- Maintenance of an ongoing relationship between the spouses is a central issue
- Negotiation involves a process intended to satisfy the underlying interests of both spouses

Accordingly, in principled negotiation every effort is made to separate relational and substantive issues. Various options are explored before a course of action is selected and the terms of any agreement are assessed against objective standards to avoid arbitrary results.

Given the fundamentally cooperative aims of family mediation and the therapeutic character of TFM, we are much more likely to base our practice on principled negotiation than positional bargaining, although the latter continues to have its place under specific circumstances.

Mediation Practices

Selection of an approach to negotiation creates the structure that frames the negotiation process. However, it fails to specify the techniques needed to carry the process to dispute resolution. The first of these, usually accomplished in the assessment or premediation stages, is the collection of information needed to

- Identify what each spouse perceives as the issue(s)
- Discover the position of each spouse on each issue, or, failing that
- Ascertain that one or both spouses does not know their own mind
- Organize and evaluate the amount and accuracy of the information that each spouse has about their respective positions

- Uncover the affective charge associated with each position
- Investigate the extent to which each spouse's position and individual interests coincide
- Establish the extent to which both spouses think it possible to achieve a fair and equitable agreement
- Develop a sense of the assumptions and presuppositions that underlie each spouse's approach to mediation
- Assist the couple in setting out the terms and conditions of an informal agreement

These concerns are what negotiation is actually about. With these understandings in place, the mediator brings to bear a variety of practice techniques whose collective purpose is to help couples negotiate fruitfully and, if possible, come to a fair and equitable agreement.

These practice methods derive from two primary sources, neither one new, namely, the clinical literature in mediation (Felstiner & Williams, 1978; Haynes, 1981) and family therapy (de Shazer, 1986; Fisch, Weakland, & Segal, 1982), and an extensive literature on dispute resolution in labor-management and community relations (Anderson, 1982; Bomers & Peterson, 1982; Raiffa, 1982).

The latter entails a wide range of techniques and procedures aimed at maintaining the flow of negotiation and avoiding impasses. A partial list includes the following:

- Setting the agenda
- Exploring the consequences of alternatives
- Encouraging full disclosure of information
- Maximizing similarities and synchronizing negotiating readiness, both as means of balancing power
- Indicating when one spouse has the floor
- Providing emotional support when negotiation becomes especially difficult—often around emotionally charged issues, such as custody or access—and moving them forward
- Setting a pace within the couple's response capacity but not so slow that they get bored or lose concentration
- Breaking (or "fractionating") large issues into smaller ones, those that open up room to maneuver

- Keeping the conflict fluid by focusing on several issues rather than on the one on which the spouses appear to be stuck
- Placing items for negotiation in reverse order of importance, with the less important issues first, critical issues last, to establish a "yes set" (Zeig, 1980), and thus positive momentum, with agreement on minor issues encouraging hope that the larger issues are resolvable
- Exploring "what if" scenarios
- Consolidating gains, noting each successfully negotiated issue, and occasionally summarizing gains as a way of minimizing conflict around more serious issues
- Broadening the alternatives available to the couple by citing options that have worked for other couples
- Ordering brief "time outs" to give the spouses the chance to get control of their feelings
- Premature closure of one or more sessions, with each spouse sent home to formulate a plan for discussion at the next session

Family mediation and family therapy also involve a long list of relatively standard techniques and procedures. Having discussed these in detail in Irving and Benjamin (1987), no purpose would be served by repeating that discussion here. However, in the light of the cases that follow, two such methods merit a brief note. The first method is reframing, whereby statements and behaviors are reinterpreted to change their meaning from negative to positive. An example is the use of superordinate mutual goals to constrain uncontrolled marital conflict, particularly the spouses' mutual commitment to the welfare of the children. Should this and other methods fail and an impending deadlock rooted in relational issues be assessed, the second method involves calling a time out while one or both spouses return for limited premediation. This method seeks to deal with the relational issue before returning the couple to negotiation around the remaining substantive issues.

THE FOLLOW-UP PROCESS

We automatically arrange to see couples who have reached agreement about 6 weeks after termination to assess the durability of their agreement and help them resolve conflictual issues that may have arisen in the interval. This session typically includes a detailed review of the terms of their agreement with respect to how well or poorly the terms continue to serve what the spouses see as their present interests, an exploration of concomitant relations between family members, especially the spouses, including important changes in their life circumstances (e.g., employment, residence, relationships) and changes in their involvement with any extrasystemic others discussed above, and discussion of other problems they wish to explore or which the mediator felt during service might become a source of tension or conflict.

Depending on the couple in question, subsequent follow-up contacts may also be scheduled for what are, in effect, periodic family life check-ups. This procedure is especially relevant to premediation couples where areas of relational dysfunction are known to prevail. Furthermore, we routinely close with a preempting maneuver in which couples are told to expect difficulties that, having gone through mediation, they can now handle themselves without having to go to court. Finally, we make clear that the door to mediation is always open; should they encounter problems, for example, around renewed spousal conflict or the threat of violence, that they do not seem able to resolve by themselves, they can always return for short-term assistance.

GOALS AND RESPONSIBILITIES

It will now be apparent that each phase of TFM involves different forms of intervention and, as colored by the model's sensitivity to ecosystemic issues, has correspondingly divergent clinical goals. As noted, the first phase of mediation is assessment. As used in the literature, the term has acquired two slightly different meanings. For proponents of the available formal models, for example, it is synonymous with "intake" (Haynes, 1984). Encompassing initial telephone contact and the first mediation session, it refers to the mediator's sense of the clients presenting disputes and their habitual means of addressing them. More rarely, assessment refers to a process in which client functioning is evaluated against a set of standard criteria, with these data used as the basis for planning subsequent intervention (e.g., Walker, 1986).

As we use the term, it overlaps with this second usage but also includes three additional meanings:

- The use of assessment data as the basis for a key clinical decision, whether to refer clients to premediation or negotiation

- The use of assessment data as a screening device, referring some clients out, as contraindicated for family mediation (see Indications and Contra-indications, p. 172)

- The use of assessment data to formulate a clinical plan based on judgments about the spouses' individual strengths and weaknesses, the extent to which their typical patterns of interaction are dysfunctional, and the ecosystemic context within which the couple is operating, especially in regard to the involvement of a range of extrasystemic others

This takes us to the second phase of mediation, premediation. Here there is ongoing debate in the literature about the extent to which family mediation should and does involve a frankly therapeutic component. Some suggest that mediation and therapy, although bearing a superficial resemblance, are in fact quite different (Gold, 1985; Kelly, 1983). Others argue that therapeutic change is often a necessary part of mediation (Gadlin & Ouellette, 1987; Waldron et al., 1984). Furthermore, even among those advocating for what Milne (1983) calls a "therapeutic model," there is disagreement about what constitutes "therapy." For some it refers to change in individual behavior based on insight (Weaver, 1986), whereas others interpret it more in terms of relational change (Sargent & Moss, 1987; Shaw & Phear, 1987).

TFM shares the latter view and suggests that there is no inconsistency about using frankly therapeutic methods in the interests of dispute resolution. This view is based on the simple observation that failure in mediation can often be traced to relational dysfunction. This said, TFM is, as far as we know, unique in three respects: the extent to which an explicitly ecosystemic understanding of family processes guides clinical practice (cf. Saposnek, 1985); the extent to which therapy is integral to the model; and the selective application of such methods so as to produce the maximum benefit to the widest possible array of clients.

More broadly, TFM requires the mediator to develop a systemic understanding of the client couples and their larger social context and to incorporate that understanding into clinical conduct. Intervention is thus rationalized by the need to create those minimal relational conditions in client systems (including extrasystemic others) such that they have at least some reasonable hope of emerging from negotiation with a workable agreement.

Following premediation (where applicable), the third phase of mediation involves negotiation. Within TFM, the negotiation process is intended to be facilitative, with these specific goals: to encourage cooperation and mutual trust; to establish a context in which both spouses can achieve a fair and equitable agreement; and to identify, clarify, and extend the number and variety of options that spouses brought with them.

In this context, the mediator has three major roles in the negotiation process. The first is to establish a structure within which the spouses can proceed by directing the flow of interaction. The second is that of advisor. Whereas nearly all client couples are new to both divorce and mediation, the mediator will typically have gone through it many times before. There is consequently every likelihood that an issue that the couple find difficult to resolve is one with which the mediator is familiar. The third role is to monitor the affective states and patterned behavior of both spouses as the process unfolds. Although blockages in the negotiation process can occur on purely substantive grounds, such events more likely occur because they tap an underlying affective process which, in turn, is enacted by the reappearance of dysfunctional patterns of interaction. If so, some intervention will be required to move negotiation forward (see Saposnek, 1985).

Finally, follow-up, the fourth and last phase of mediation, has as its primary goal ongoing monitoring of family functioning, both with respect to various patterns of interaction (including the involvement of extrasystemic others) as well as adherence to the terms and conditions of the agreement negotiated during mediation. Accordingly, the role of the mediator is that of friendly advisor, noting difficulties the family may encounter and suggesting ways of going around these problems or resolving them without resort to litigation. Should serious difficulties be observed, a limited return to mediation, especially premediation, may be recommended.

INDICATIONS AND CONTRAINDICATIONS

In TFM, after assessment, clients are assigned to one of three levels of functioning, described below. This assignment will have immediate consequences for the subsequent course of mediation.

Level 1

In the past 5 years, 20% of the couples who sought entry into family mediation with us were assessed as functioning at Level 1 and thus were contraindicated for mediation. These couples were characterized by a combination of the following key attributes, each of which is known (see Introduction) to predict outcome failure:

1. Intense stress, often experienced as overwhelming
2. Obsessive preoccupation with the rejecting spouse
3. Extreme rigidity in expectations and plans, often coupled with a very restricted response repertoire
4. Intense anger, sometimes to the point of rage, often coupled with uncontrolled conflict
5. The pervasive involvement of extrasystemic others, especially when short-term efforts (i.e., one to four sessions) to block such involvement have a limited chance of success, as in the intensely enmeshed family
6. Current and ongoing family violence, whether in the form of child abuse (physical, sexual, or neglect) or spousal abuse (physical or psychological and directed toward the wife or the husband) and, rarely
7. Severe cognitive or affective dysfunction of one or both spouses

Each of these attributes would typically be identified in the assessment process. These cases were referred out for individual or family treatment or judicial resolution. Such a decision is represented to clients in a nonjudgmental manner and often as a measure of the mediator's limitations (e.g., "I don't believe I can be helpful to you at this time."). It is also explained that at a later point the client couple may wish to reapply to mediation.

Level 2

Approximately 50% of our clients were assessed as functioning at Level 2. These couples, with the exception of #6 or #7, above, displayed one or more of the characteristics of Level 1 couples, but to a significantly lesser degree. Accordingly, they were seen as having the potential to develop the attributes required by the negotiation process, with premediation a requisite to the realization of that potential. The shift from assessment to premediation is not signaled in a formal way. Rather, it is rationalized simply as carrying on with the process of solving the problems presented in assessment (e.g., "I think it would be helpful if I saw Jeff for a few sessions to deal with his feelings of anger."). As such, although one or both spouses may object to the delay, few challenge the mediator's authority to suggest such a course of practice, especially because one or both spouses is typically in considerable distress.

Level 3

Finally, about 30% of our clients were assessed as functioning at Level 3. These were couples who had completed or at least begun the emotional and organizational transition to single personhood but were unable to resolve one or more substantive issues pursuant to a divorce settlement. For example, they were able to formulate their positions clearly and coherently and to plan for the future, demonstrated reasonable flexibility, and so on. Consequently, they were ready to go straight into the negotiation phase of mediation. Such a view is typically conveyed to clients in a very positive and optimistic manner, suggestive of the possibility of a relatively speedy resolution of their difficulties. However, this view is always accompanied by a preempting maneuver (see Bross & Benjamin, 1983) in which clients are warned that should some snags be encountered along the way, it may be necessary to pause in the negotiation process (i.e., enter premediation) to deal with them. This framing is typically acceptable to clients.

CASEBOOK: THREE VIGNETTES

Use of TFM is hard to visualize in the absence of case material. Accordingly, three brief vignettes are presented, from assessment through premediation to negotiation and follow-up. Throughout, emphasis is placed on the importance of an ecosystemic perspective in sensitizing the mediator to ongoing processes as well as specific points of intervention.

Case 1: Jeanne and Garth Jansen: 13 Sessions[6]

Jeanne Jansen contacted our office on her lawyer's recommendation. She and her husband, Garth, were still living in the same house but were in the process of separating. Their primary concern was the custody, access, and support of their 9-year-old son, Eric, and division of property and assets. Each wanted sole custody, she said, and was willing to give the other liberal visiting rights. However, tension was high. It was hard for her to assert herself with Garth. She felt overpowered by his anger. She hoped mediation would help Garth understand that his attitude was detrimental and help her to better state her opinions. Garth was agreeable to mediation and she would ask him to call as well. He called the following day.

Assessment: Five Sessions

Individual Interview: Jeanne. In the first individual interview, Jeanne, a bilingual Francophone, presented as soft-spoken, stressed and anxious, but articulate. At age 43, she was a primary school teacher. Neither spouse had family locally and they had only a very small circle of friends. Her salary was in the middle income range. The couple was debt free, owned two cars, and lived in their own home. Jeanne said that she had initiated the marital separation. She felt Garth had been dominant in the marriage and that she had deferred to him. In his family, the male was the head of the family. This was acceptable to her for the first part of the marriage, as Garth was also protective and attentive. He was strenuously opposed to the separation and very angry about it.

When Jeanne began evaluating her marriage, she had sought out a therapist at Family Services. She was finding therapy helpful in dealing with her guilt and anger and, although she was anxious about it, was beginning to stand up to her husband. She had discussed mediation with her therapist and had consulted her regarding several mediators recommended by her lawyer.

When the mediator inquired about reconciliation, Jeanne stated clearly that the marriage was over for her and that she needed to get on with her life. She was still living with Garth to ensure that she had a good chance of obtaining custody. When asked about Garth's dominant character and the potential for violence, she indicated that there had been no violence in the past and, although Garth could be angry and abrupt with her, she did not feel he would ever be physically aggressive.

At that point, the mediator asked about Eric's reaction to the tension in the household and the ensuing separation. This question was intended to focus Jeanne's attention on one of the key purposes of mediation, namely, to secure an arrangement that would be in Eric's best interests. Jeanne described a negative change in Eric's attitude and performance at school, his testing the limits at home, and his having nightmares. Eric had been pampered by both his parents in the past. However, Jeanne was concerned that since the decision to separate, Garth was catering to the child, openly blaming her for the separation, and making comments about "boys needing to live with their father." Jeanne was worried about Garth's manipulative behavior and hoped that he would "hear out" a neutral party. She had trusted his parenting in the past; both parents had adhered to routine and structure. She said Garth and Eric were particularly close.

Individual Interview: Garth. The following day, Garth came for his initial interview. A 55-year-old accountant, bilingual, and of Armenian extraction, he presented himself as rational, controlling, and a bit guarded. He had a responsible position in an accounting firm, with a salary higher than Jeanne's. Garth had agreed to come to mediation because his lawyer had recommended it, and he hoped it would cut time and expense. When Jeanne asked him if he would meet with the therapist at Family Services, he refused, saying that she was "her therapist." Besides, he was not interested in therapy, but in settling issues.

When asked how the decision to separate came about, Garth became less self-assured. It was clear he was quite angry and distraught. He thought their personalities had worked well together, he being the decision maker because she was so easygoing. He would have been willing to work on their marriage had she only talked with him before coming to the decision to separate. Because her mind was made up, he just wanted to ensure that he would not lose his son.

Asked to describe Eric and his reactions to the situation, Garth spoke at some length about his involvement with his son, his parenting style, and his previous confidence in Jeanne's parenting skills. Garth was concerned about Eric's shaky adjustment.

The mediator turned next to Garth's stress level (high), and especially the (few) supports and resources available to him.

In these two sessions, the mediator's goals were to assess each parent's level of functioning as well as to engage each of them and thus encourage the development of trust that would be essential later in the case.

One more session was held with each partner, partly centered on the conflict assessment protocol used as a way of helping to understand how the couple made decisions, managed conflict, and expressed anger (see Girdner, 1990). It contributed to the assessment effort, but would also be helpful in setting the stage for negotiations, especially in helping prepare them for their continued relationship as parents.

Joint Interview. The following week, the Jansens came for a joint interview. The mediator began by reviewing the details of mediation, including the mediator's role and expectations, the ground rules clients are expected to follow, the closed and confidential nature of mediation, the fee structure (each spouse would pay proportionate to income), the parties' responsibility for decision making, and the nature of a mediated agreement.

To keep the process transparent and avoid having either spouse thinking the mediator privy to the other spouse's secrets, the mediator asked each spouse to talk again about how they saw their marital difficulties, how they got started, and what they expected to get out of mediation. When asked who wanted to go first, Garth jumped in immediately, blaming Jeanne for not telling him about her concerns much earlier.

With the mediator's support and encouragement, Jeanne was able to tell about feeling unheard and overruled by Garth. Both were asked to consider how these feelings might affect mediation, thus using this opportunity to pursue both spouses' bottom line, their perception of the process of mediation, and the couple's responsibility for the outcome. Again, Garth expressed anger, but was able to say that he would make an effort to be reasonable during the mediation process.

Each spouse was asked to spend some time talking about Eric—how each parented him and how each saw the other spouse's parenting. Subsequent discussion included their daily routines, such as mealtimes and bedtimes, and the couple's expectations of their son. The mediator provided background information about the typical reaction of children to parental separation and the child's need for consistency and protection from parental conflict. The mediator also asked the couple to distinguish among their needs and distress as separating spouses, their ongoing parental roles, and their son's needs. The mediator emphasized the spouses' common interest in parenting the child they both loved dearly.

At that point, because they seemed ready to begin mediation, the mediator had them sign the standard mediation contract, which specified the expected rules of conduct, the fee-splitting arrangement, and the understanding that they were responsible for a settlement, which would be ratified by their lawyers rather than by the mediator. In preparation for the next session, the mediator asked them to start thinking about the family's future, especially care of Eric and how they saw their respective roles.

Assessment indicated that the Jansens were good candidates for mediation at Level 2, that is, negotiation would need to be preceded by premediation to resolve several outstanding relational issues. Given Garth's anger at his wife and his "closeness" to his son, I thought that we should begin with individual sessions. The goals would be to help him accept the end of his marriage, establish himself as a single person, and clearly differentiate between his parental and marital roles. Similarly, individual sessions with Jeanne were intended to provide support in asserting herself and to determine whether her therapist needed to be included in mediation.

More generally, assessment indicated an enmeshed couple with a narrow social circle, with Eric consequently given inordinate attention.

Each would likely have had a hard time sharing Eric. Furthermore, their marital relationship had been characterized by dominance and submission, with only very recent changes since Jeanne started therapy. It thus confirmed a power imbalance and called for the mediator to take a position of focal neutrality (see chapter 5). In addition, the mediator would need to be aware of issues where Jeanne would need support to assert her position.

Premediation: Four Sessions

Three sessions with Garth focused on past marital relationship patterns and gave him an opportunity to express anger at Jeanne. Emphasis throughout was on helping him understand that his reactions were normal and reinterpreting his experience to allow him to see it as an opportunity for growth, both as a person and as a parent. In particular, the mediator repeatedly asked Garth how he intended to parent Eric in the future. This focus emphasized his common cause with Jeanne. We explored specific parenting skills, separating his needs from those of Eric. Through time, Garth's anger gradually became more diffused. He began to think how he planned to parent Eric, yet not be in complete charge of him. His growing ability to focus on future plans and on his parenting were indications that he was ready to move to the next stage of mediation.

Turning to Jeanne, we spent a long but fruitful session together providing support in dealing with the stress of cohabitation and checking on her level of comfort during the previous joint session. Jeanne felt that the ongoing sessions with her therapist were very helpful and she agreed that the mediator could communicate with the therapist if Jeanne felt it necessary. Then, as with Garth, the mediator discussed with Jeanne how she and Garth intended to parent Eric. This discussion emphasized the importance of separating her feelings for Garth from the shared work they needed to do as parents. That she was able to do so boded well for the next stage of mediation. Furthermore, a call to her therapist indicated that she was working along lines helpful to mediation, namely, assertiveness and communication training as well as providing support in Jeanne's transition to single parenthood.

Negotiation: Three Sessions

With this extensive preparation in place, negotiation was relatively brief and not unusually complicated. At the start of the first session, the mediator stressed the importance of cooperation and mutual trust by asking Jeanne and Garth to recall past experiences when they had worked together successfully on issues concerning parenting. In response, the couple came up with several examples, thus helping to establish a positive tone.

As negotiation proper began, the mediator first established a structure for the spouses, for example, by setting the agenda. The spouses agreed that their main concern was custody, access, and child support. However, previous discussion made clear that these were emotionally charged issues and would likely be difficult. In contrast, Garth indicated that property division was less important to him, although Jeanne expressed some apprehension about equity in this area, because her salary was less than Garth's. Here we had a chance of easy and early success, so that item was placed on the top of the agenda. This assessment proved correct. Both partners were able to discuss their wishes and agreed that the family home would be sold and the proceeds divided proportionately. They agreed on the division of the furniture, with each keeping the car they now used. Pension funds and Garth's investments would be divided proportionately. Thus the first session saw some significant movement toward a final agreement. As the session ended, the mediator sought to consolidate these gains by emphasizing how well the couple had worked together to arrive at these reasonable and fair decisions, expressed confidence that they would continue to so, and asked them to confer with their lawyers on these matters.

The next session focused on custody issues. To avoid conflict, much time was spent clarifying and extending the spouses' custody options. This process involved exploring the success other couples had had with shared parenting, the values that typically underpinned this choice, and what it might entail on a day-to-day basis. As expected, the partners had a variety of questions. The session ended with the mediator asking them to think carefully about their specific options and the likely consequences of each and to bring their ideas to the next session.

At the final session, the partners agreed to a trial parenting plan to last 6 months. Eric would live with one parent 4 days per week and with the other Wednesdays and weekends. This arrangement would be alternated every 2 weeks. Garth was looking for an apartment, while Jeanne would remain in the home until it was sold. Garth agree to pay his share of the costs of maintenance and repair work needed to ready the house for sale. Discussion throughout was relatively cordial, even positive. Although Garth had to be reminded to give Jeanne equal air time, and Jeanne needed occasional support in expressing her views, this area did not prove to be the problem that assessment data suggested it might have been.

In closing, the mediator asked the spouses to write out a draft agreement in their own words, which was forwarded to their respective lawyers, and called each lawyer to explain the process by which the agreement was arrived at and its intent. With only minor amendments, the lawyers approved the agreement. Jeanne's lawyer translated it into legal terminology and this version was signed by both spouses.

Follow-Up: One Session

At follow-up, 6 months later, despite minor changes the agreement was still basically intact and seemed to be working well. Jeanne and Garth had been able to resolve minor parenting disagreements by themselves. As at the end of negotiation, the mediator closed with a preempting maneuver, telling them to expect occasional difficulties in the future but expressing confidence that they now had the ability to handle it on their own. However, should they encounter more serious difficulties, they could be assured that the door was always open to them.

Discussion

We began with the Jansens because their case is relatively typical of many we see. Had we followed a traditional course and brought this couple straight into negotiation, failure would have been likely. However, extensive assessment and brief but focused premediation allowed the negotiation phase to go smoothly because their underlying relational issues had first been addressed. In addition, despite the relational emphasis, the mediation process had a clear and specific form that accorded major responsibility for all final decisions to the spouses. Nevertheless, it was necessary for the mediator to maintain control of that process and occasionally intervene for this couple to realize their potential for agreement and so that spousal issues did not overwhelm parenting matters.

Case 2: John and Angelina Richardson: 16 Sessions

The Richardson family consisted of John, age 45, of English extraction, his wife Angelina, age 39, of Italian extraction, and their two daughters, Roselina, age 12, and Jenetta, age 9. The couple was referred for family mediation by Angelina's lawyer following her decision to separate from John; John's lawyer concurred. They had been married 15 years, during most of which they had maintained a relatively affluent lifestyle based on John's considerable income as a neurologist.

Assessment: Three Sessions

The thrust of assessment was to develop a systemic understanding, first, of their marital relationship and, second, of the family's ecosystemic context.

As to the first, it revealed a couple in a state of flux. Throughout much of their married life, relations between John and Angelina were characterized by a pattern of dominance and submission. John, based on his personality and professional socialization, was accustomed to being in charge. This fit neatly with Angelina's upbringing in a strict Catholic home and her comparatively limited education as a medical secretary (they had met when Angelina worked in John's office as a "temp"). Accordingly, she had been content to let John make all the major decisions and satisfied to concentrate her efforts on the care and feeding of two bright and active children.

Changes in this arrangement began when the younger child entered first grade and Angelina had a good deal of time on her hands. She became restless and began taking courses at a nearby community college in business administration. The result, following additional studies at the university level, was that as Angelina's confidence, assertiveness, and verbal sophistication increased, so did her dissatis-faction with John in a dominant position. Furthermore, her increas-ingly insistent efforts to move their relationship to one in which they were more equal had failed.

In turn, John too was dissatisfied. Away from home much of the time and only peripherally involved in raising his daughters, he was at first annoyed and then shocked by the gradual change in his wife. Mild and later more forceful efforts to reestablish the status quo had only pro-duced escalating conflict, including a brief but unsuccessful attempt by John to physically intimidate his wife, although actual violence did not occur then or since. This stage culminated in Angelina's declaration that she wanted a divorce.

As to their ecological context, John and Angelina were very differ-ently involved with others outside their immediate family. Although John was well known and generally liked within the medical commu-nity, these connections were collegial rather than intimate; Angelina was his only close friend. In addition, both his parents were deceased and contact with his one elder brother was infrequent and emotionally distant. By contrast, Angelina's involvement with her extended kin, especially her aged parents, was intense and ongoing. She spoke with her mother several times a week and she and the children saw her parents at least once every 2 weeks. Moreover, both parents had been against her marriage to John because he was neither Catholic nor Italian and they continued to feel emotionally cut off from him. An-gelina also had a close and supportive relationship with her two older sisters, whom she saw regularly, and she had developed several friends among the students in the MBA program in which she was enrolled at the point of intake.

Thus John and Angelina were very differently prepared for An-gelina's demand for a divorce. Having considered it for nearly 2 years before her announcement, she was well prepared for it, both emotionally and socially. Conversely, John, faced with the collapse of his marriage, only then realized how much he depended on Angelina for emotional support; he went to pieces. Totally unprepared for the news of the breakup, he pleaded with Angelina for a second chance. Failing that, he accused her of being selfish and confidently promised to sue for sole custody of the children. Angelina would not budge; her demand for divorce was the outcome of a long process of emotional separation from John.

Thus, assessment supported several conclusions:

- Despite their affluence and education, this couple had an extremely limited repertoire
- Over time, Angelina had gradually increased her communication skills, so that she now was on a par with John, a fact that was intensely threatening to him
- Marital conflict had steadily increased to the point that it had become intractable and destructive, both in terms of their relationship as well as in relation to the children
- Both spouses were competent parents, though John was largely untested in this area because the bulk of the child care responsibilities had always been Angelina's
- John appeared to be coping the least well of the two and he would have to undergo the most change before negotiation would become viable
- There was an indication that the involvement of Angelina's parents, especially her mother, was an important complicating factor

Accordingly, the goals of premediation were as follows:

- To help John accept the reality of his impending divorce, encourage him to develop and sustain a positive relationship with his children, and disempower him in order to create a level playing field in relations between him and Angelina
- To help Angelina plan for the future without excluding John as her children's father
- To help reduce the extent and intensity of both spouse's affective response so that both could fruitfully begin the negotiation process
- If necessary, to block or curtail the negative involvement of Angelina's parents, especially her mother

Premediation: Five Sessions

Premediation involved five sessions, three with John, one with Angelina, and one joint. With respect to John, his newfound desire to become a good parent provided a powerful lever for change. Repeatedly, his negative statements about his wife were juxtaposed with questions about his positive feelings for his children or the ways in which what he wanted was distinct and different from what the children needed. In effect, he was asked to consider their welfare rather than his own and how his wife might help him achieve this end.

John was also asked to accept personal responsibility by taking control over his own life. Slowly, John came to the painful realization that much as he wanted Angelina to change her plans for divorce, all he could ultimately do was to gain better control over his choices, especially in regard to caring for two children. In the process, John's anger and preoccupation with marital issues dissipated and his attention shifted from the past to the future. His emotional intensity also lessened significantly.

With respect to Angelina, her thinking was already less affectively charged than her husband's and oriented primarily toward the future. This outlook involved two major issues: her vision of John's involvement with the children and how she was going to support her children while earning a limited income as a graduate student. Premediation sought to defuse her anger while shifting her focus from John as husband to John as parent. Here her concern for proper parenting and John's cooperation in providing regular child support became levers for change. Thus her uncertainty about John's parental adequacy was reinterpreted in terms of her children's love and concern for him. For her children's sake as well as John's, John would need to become a good father, something he could do only with her help. Similarly, she and John would need to stop fighting and begin to interact more cooperatively, so that John would have a reason to provide them with needed financial support. Gradually, her position softened as she increasingly focused on her children to the point where she was willing to admit that her children did love their father and would be very unhappy to be apart from him. She would consider an arrangement that would permit his continued contact with them. She would also try to control her anger and get along with John as they, together, planned for the future.

At the joint session the mediator indicated that he thought they were now ready to begin negotiation. He reviewed the purpose and methods of mediation and explained the fee schedule. Their respective lawyers were also informed of their decision to proceed.

Negotiation: Five Sessions

Two initial sessions were held with John and Angelina separately. These were intended to clarify their positions across a range of issues. For example, Angelina expressed concern about financial issues, including child support and division of the assets represented by the matrimonial home. Both were willing to sell the home and divide the proceeds. However, child support hinged on the other major issue, namely, custody of the two girls. Here, to our surprise, both spouses insisted on sole custody, which represented a considerable hardening of their respective positions at the close of premediation. Exploration indicated that it derived from different sources for each spouse: for John, a threat to the core of his identity as a father, an underlying fear that Angelina would take the children away from him forever, and a last effort to punish Angelina for deserting him; for Angelina, strenuous objections on the part of her parents that she share any part of the children with John.

Subsequent efforts during session three to negotiate this issue failed, as conflict quickly got out of hand. To prevent reaching an impasse, a range of practical issues around the division of property was rapidly dispensed with. When return to the custody issue proved impractical, a brief return to premediation was indicated, a decision that proved pivotal to successful resolution of the case and exemplifies the importance of being vigilant about the involvement of extrasystemic others.

Accordingly, at the fourth session, both the grandparents and the children were invited to attend. Both children strongly expressed the desire to spend time with John and, most important, did so in front of their grandparents. As for the latter, the mediator supported the grandmother's concern for the welfare of the children but expanded it to include the beneficial effects of having both parents actively involved in the care of the children. The grandmother was also asked to lend some of her wisdom and authority to her daughter so that she might do what she thought best for the children. Blocking the involvement of the grandparents in this way allowed Angelina to follow her initial inclination to allow John reasonable access, which lessened John's fear.

Subsequent return to negotiation, during sessions four and five, proved more successful, with John and Angelina agreeing to a shared parenting arrangement. Specifically, the children would stay with

Angelina during weekdays and alternate weekends with John; they would alternate major holidays, such as Christmas and Easter. Given his income, John agreed to pay the bulk of child care expenses until Angelina's graduation. Thereafter, a new arrangement would be negotiated. These and other details were duly translated into a draft agreement that John and Angelina prepared themselves. It was forwarded to Angelina's lawyer, who prepared a formal agreement that the spouses signed in his presence.

Follow-Up: Three Sessions

Given the difficulties in reaching agreement in this case, the mediator contracted with the couple for three follow-up sessions over the next 3 months. One year following termination no serious problems had arisen. Periodic follow-up sessions continued with fruitful results, including increasing access so that the children now stay with John every weekend as well as one month during the summer holiday.

Discussion

This case was selected because, although it is less common than the Jansens', it displays well the complexities that can arise in family mediation and how they were handled using TFM. Three aspects of practice account for the successful outcome: first, the correct assessment of the patterns that characterized the interaction between the spouses; second, the careful reading of the feedback during premediation and negotiation phases; third, and perhaps pivotally, awareness of the critical importance of the involvement of extrasystemic elements, in this case Angelina's parents. This case highlights the clinical utility of an ecosystemic perspective while conversely making clear that, in this case at least, moving directly from assessment to negotiation, as would happen in most formal models, would have been a disaster.

Case 3: Adele and Gord Watkins: 12 Sessions

The couple was originally referred by their lawyers for custody and access mediation about their 7-year-old daughter, Margaret. Assessment over three sessions suggested a couple at Level 3, that is, imme- diately ready to proceed with negotiation. Both seemed mature, ratio- nal, and fully aware that their marriage was finished. Each respected the other's parenting ability, and each had a good relationship with Margaret. The shared parenting concept was eagerly accepted by each spouse and an arrangement was worked out whereby Margaret would live with her mother for 1 week, her father for 1 week, and split vacation time equally. The child would attend the same school, since she was doing well there and it was roughly halfway between both parents' homes. Similarly, all child care costs would be shared equally, because both parents had well-established careers (he as a civil engi- neer, she as a university professor of English literature) and earned roughly the same income. The parents came in to see the mediator (not the authors) for periodic review of their shared parenting agreement.

Over the next 6 months, the agreement functioned well. The parents talked regularly in a friendly way to discuss Margaret's welfare and the logistics of their situation. Then Adele met and fell in love with Richard. Over the next several months, they decided to live together. Adele and her friend, Richard, were willing to continue with shared parenting. Richard did not feel he had a right or the need to interfere.

Gord Watkins's reaction was quite different. When Adele told him that she and Richard had decided to live together in her home, he became terrified that another man would replace him as Margaret's father and jealous of Richard's relationship with Adele. Because his relationship with Adele had been friendly and functional around par- enting issues over the past year, from time to time he fantasized about the possibility of a future reconciliation. His fears and resentments about Richard's relationship with Adele expressed themselves in a plan to apply for sole custody of Margaret. Adele's commitment and confidence in shared parenting were shaken. Concerned that the only reason her former husband had agreed to shared parenting initially was to stay involved with her, she too planned to apply for sole custody.

As for Margaret, she had adjusted extremely well to shared parent- ing. However, in the face of these recent troubles, she began having difficulty sleeping and repeatedly asked why her parents couldn't live together again.

In an effort to resolve these difficulties the Watkins returned to mediation, this time with us (their previous mediator was unavailable, having moved to a new location). We close with this case because it is unusual in at least two respects: the occurrence of serious difficulties in follow-up and the parents' agreement that their sessions be audio-recorded, hence the inclusion of transcript excerpts in what follows. In addition, although the entire case involved 10 sessions and ended with an agreement, only the first two are discussed, because they provide an opportunity to display how a TFM-trained mediator deals with impasses based on relational issues.

Joint Session

Given the serious likelihood of an impasse in this case, we felt it crucial to connect with the couple as quickly as possible. Accordingly, after the usual opening pleasantries, the mediator began with a remark designed with this in mind:

Mediator: I've been doing mediation for a number of years and have a particular interest in helping people come up with cooperative parenting arrangements. And I was really pleased to find out that you have been one of those group of pioneers who went into shared parenting, were able to make it work and who now have come to, I guess, a situation where it's not workable, and knowing that the two of you are so committed to your child that you want to come back here and make it work again really makes me feel good. I see so many terrible, conflictual situations with parents grabbing their children, manipulating their children, that it's a relief to have this kind of a situation and I compliment you on the fact that you have the ability to try this and I want you to know that I'm going to do whatever I can to help the two of you.

Reinterpretation or reframing was also used to move the couple away from their marital difficulties and to make parenting a central issue. We often do this by asking the spouses questions such as, "Describe Margaret to me, tell me what she looks like." As is usually the case, the couple not only pictured their daughter as lively, intelligent, affectionate, and attractive, but emphasized how much each loved her and wanted only the best for her, sentiments that became powerful levers for change. To consolidate the point, the mediator noted how much the couple had accomplished and how much they stood to lose should they be unable to resolve their present difficulties.

Mediator: Could you see that as, I guess in some ways, a commentary on what the two of you have been able to do? Because usually kids whose parents go through divorce have a much more difficult time. It sounds like you two must have done something for her to do as well as she did.

Although subsequent questioning established both parents' respect for each other's parenting ability, it also revealed what was to be the first of three central stumbling blocks in the case—the father's continued attachment to his former wife:

Gord: Well, she's [the daughter] a lot like her mother in many ways. Like I would agree with that. She's very nice, very pleasant to be with.

The second concerned the father's fear that the shift in Adele's romantic situation would eventually involve loss of contact with his daughter. This fear only became apparent gradually as the mediator sought to reinterpret the issue of child custody from a marital issue to a parenting issue, with the emphasis on Margaret's likely experience:

Mediator: What if we said to her now, "Okay, Margaret, now there's going to be a shift, and Dad's going to have all the time with you and Mom will visit occasionally. And Dad will make all the decisions and Mom won't make very many, if any." I wonder how, how do you think she would see that?
Adele: I don't think she would like that.

Next, it became clear that Adele was seeking only sole custody because Gord was doing so; she would have preferred to continue their shared parenting arrangement, because it had been working well. As would Gord; it was Richard's presence, the second stumbling block, that was causing him grief:

Gord: I think what's happening now is that there is the influence of Richard. I think that we're kind of talking as if everything is normal here, but you know we have to understand the impact of having this other man, not only to be seen privately with Adele, but also the impact of this man being in the house. He's not just going to sit in the corner. I know for a fact that he's going to become involved in telling some things to Margaret. I know for a fact he has in fact an influence on Margaret, even now.

Later, he made his fear crystal clear:

Gord: Well, in a lot of these cases, you know, I mean, when there is a stepparent that moves in, and I think you know that, and you'll agree with me, in a lot of these cases that the father's role becomes next to none.

Efforts to explain Adele's new arrangement as commonplace failed, as Gord rejected any such suggestion for himself:

Mediator: Okay, let's forget about Richard for a moment, and think about somebody that you might decide to live with in the future.

Gord: You have to maybe respect the fact that I don't have that interest.

The third stumbling block was Gord's sense of anger and betrayal that Adele hadn't discussed with him her relationship with Richard, so that Gord would have been better prepared when she decided to live with Richard:

Gord: . . . is that it's a private matter, their relationship. The problem comes in the fact that for the other person it comes as an unexpected, and there's no discussion about that, because there's the element of privacy that comes into play. And you don't want to be intruding and sort of saying, "Well, but really there's need for there to be some discussion in terms of what that will mean." And we'd have this. And we used to have this with Margaret.

This series of stumbling blocks was rooted in the past, in Gord's continuing attachment to Adele and his fantasy that one day perhaps they could reconcile. Because this line of reasoning would inevitably lead to impasse, much of the balance of the session was directly toward repeatedly reinterpreting the issues in parental rather than marital terms. At one point, this focus was stated succinctly:

Mediator: How can the two of you continue to be good parents and give her everything she deserves?

Realizing that this shift would require more work than could be accomplished in one session, the mediator used the last few minutes of the session to set up the next series of individual sessions, especially those with Gord. He did this in two steps. First, the mediator reinterpreted Gord's objections in parental terms:

Mediator: I must admit, I don't know how you feel about it, but I think it does show a lot of strength on Gord's part to be as concerned as he is about his daughter. Would you agree?
Adele: Yeah, I do respect his concern for Margaret.

Second, the mediator suggested that only more discussion would unearth the real issues underlying the current problem, including the views of the other players in this drama, Margaret and Richard:

Mediator: What I would like to do, if it makes sense, because I don't know enough about this situation, and I don't know enough about you, and I feel that even in this afternoon's session that I am feeling a little bit pulled here. And that I would like to get together with you . . . individually, to explore a little more. I think I could get a little closer to your real concerns if I saw you individually. So I would like to begin with that. I would also like your permission to meet with Margaret because she's the one that probably has some questions. Obviously there is something going on because she's not feeling as good as she did about the situation, and I always see the third party [Richard] because I feel that I have a responsibility to the child. You [Adele] may not like it, and you [Gord] may not like it, and he [Richard] may not like it, but if you're going to work with me I have to see the third party.

Individual Session: Gord

In this session, the mediator had three goals: to get Gord to explicitly articulate the stumbling blocks hinted at in the first session, to reinterpret them as his problem, and to juxtapose this personal problem against his daughter's needs.

The first goal was easily accomplished, as Gord readily admitted to continuing emotional investment with Adele.

Mediator: How come you were so positive? What I don't understand is you seemed to be quite positive before. Were you hoping that maybe you and Adele could get back together? Was that one of the things you thought about?

Gord: I think any human being who had the kind of relationship I had with Adele doesn't stop hoping. Ah, I'd only be kidding myself.

He also readily acknowledged his anger and disappointment in Adele:

Gord: Right now, we're not able to reach agreement. And I don't want to put blame, but if Richard hadn't moved in. I know, obviously, he must be important to her, but if he hadn't been in the picture, I really think we wouldn't have had these problems. I'm even prepared to say that if he hadn't come on so suddenly, if it had been more gradual, let's say, if the dating had been spread over a longer period of time. If Adele would've sat down and said, "Gord, we've gotta talk. I'm concerned about the impact of this . . . how we're going to approach it."

Mediator: It might have been a lot easier for you.

The second goal required an interpretation that shifted Gord's reaction to Adele's relationship as *his* problem, specifically one of loss and mourning:

Mediator: You know what's happening to you? What's happening to you is that there's been a sort of delay. Like, initially, when people are confronted with the fact that their marriage may be over they feel the pain and the emptiness and the hurt and the sorrow. And I think in the beginning, it probably didn't hit you as hard. But

now I think you're going through the. . . . You look very unhappy
to me. You look sad. Are you sad?

Gord: I am sad, yeah. I am unhappy.

Mediator: It's been a real loss to you.

Gord: And now we're having the daughter. How about that?

Mediator: Let's talk about the loss for you of Adele.

Gord: If we're talking about the loss of Adele, we're talking about the
loss of my daughter, too. My daughter reminds me of her.

Mediator: And the house. You had to move out of that house, which
I'm sure meant something to you, too.

Gord: That's right. We have a nice arrangement of sharing back and
forth.

Mediator: So it's almost like your whole world is . . .

The final goal proved more difficult. To get at it, the mediator posed
a question that emphasized the separation between marital and parenting issues:

Mediator: There are two things that you need to work out. One is how
you're going through this hurtful, painful situation of disengaging from your wife. How are you going to be able to do that and
be a good parent like you have been. That's the challenge. How
can you do these two things?

Initially, Gord resists, seeing the two as tied together:

Gord: Well, I think that some time you reach a point in your life when
you go for broke [re: sole custody]. I think maybe I'm going for
broke.

In response, the mediator persisted in separating the issues, implying too that linking them the way Gord had done had made it increasingly difficult for Gord to continue to be the good parent he was
striving to be.

Mediator: Let's not discuss sole custody right now. Let's talk about
the two things. The disengaging emotionally from Adele, that
that's over, and being a good parent. How are you going to do
that?

Gord: I thought I was doing that. You're saying to me I'm not, obviously, you're sensing that I'm not.

Mediator: You seem very hurt by this. I have a feeling, and I may be wrong about this, that a lot of your energy is being tied up in this sadness, and that you can't do as much as you'd like to do.

Gord: Um-hum.

Mediator: For example, it's not [like] you really to fight for sole custody and try to remove your wife from the situation as a mother. That doesn't sound like you, right? So, something's getting in the way. What's getting in the way I think is the ending of the marriage that is now there. And you're having a hard time, and I think it's OK to have a hard time. There's nothing wrong with that.

As Gord slowly begins to think about what had, to this point, been the unthinkable, the mediator consolidated Gord's movement by posing a question and offering to help him find an answer:

Mediator: Would you like it if you had the ability, and you may not have it now, but would you like to be able to say, "I've got to be able to begin a new life, and as much as I would like it, it's not going to happen. She's not coming back. And I have got to begin a new life, for myself and for my daughter." Is that what you would like to be able to do?

Gord: Yeah.

Mediator: OK, would you like me to help you try and do that?

Gord: How would you help me do it?

Mediator: I don't know yet. But would you like me to help you? So the two of us try. . . .

Gord: What happens in the meantime? Life goes on.

Mediator: In the meantime, you will continue to be a good parent.

Gord: What does that mean, "continue to be a good parent?"

Mediator: And Adele is going to continue to be a good mother. Well, one thing would be to stop the lawsuit and stop fighting about who should have sole custody. That would be one thing in my opinion. And to give as much attention as you can to your daughter without being preoccupied with Richard and Adele. Those would be two things. And there may be other things. But, you're gonna get through this. And you've got to get through it with the least amount of damage to yourself and your daughter. And I think that, you know, maybe between the two of us we can do that. Are you willing to give it a shot?

Gord: You're telling me that this is the way it would work. That this is going to work, isn't it? That is going to . . . with the lawyer, I've already started a suit.

Mediator: I know that, but I feel strongly that you value, that you really value Adele as a parent, and you value yourself as a parent, and I don't really want to upset that by going through a court case and fighting over who the better parent is. And I think what is getting in the way is the hurt and the loss of the marriage ending and that's what I want to help you to do. OK?

Gord: OK.

Discussion

Were this case reported in a text on individual or family therapy, it would be unremarkable, even routine. The fact that this is a text on mediation makes it noteworthy. Gord's words convey on a visceral level what the previous two cases have only indicated on an intellectual level, that many impasses in mediation are rooted in interpersonal processes and it is only when those processes have been dealt with that agreement on the substantive issues becomes possible, at least with any hope of durability.

DISCUSSION

In light of this review of the phases of TFM, the fully recursive or ecosystemic character of the model should be clear. As a function of the degree of success of the couple at entry, mediation involves a succeeding series of *feedback loops.*

- One loop represents couples who come to mediation ready to negotiate and succeed by reaching an informal agreement, which is then formally ratified by their respective lawyers as the couple exits to follow-up.
- A second loop is identical to the first but consists of couples who enter mediation via premediation and are similarly successful.

- A third loop involves couples who begin negotiation but encounter serious difficulties, require limited premediation, return to negotiation, succeed, then exit.
- A fourth loop involves couples who begin with premediation, are unable to resolve their difficulties and thus are referred out.
- Finally, a fifth loop describes couples who enter premediation, go to negotiation, are unable to resolve their differences, return to premediation where again they encounter intractable problems, and so are ultimately unable to reach agreement and are referred out.

Note, moreover, that each loop has both an entry and an exit point. Those couples who succeed in developing an agreement can always return to mediation, based on follow-up assessment, should they later encounter intractable difficulties. Similarly, couples judged not amenable to mediation on first contact may, following outside treatment, reapply to enter mediation. The same applies to couples whose problem(s) are judged serious and who, following brief contact (i.e., one or two sessions), are sent to their lawyers for processing through the courts. Breakdown of that process or their later desire to relitigate a court-imposed settlement may make them eligible once again for family mediation.

Such fluidity is the hallmark of TFM and of the ecosystemic perspective that underpins it, thus accenting the ability of its practitioners to match the service they provide with the mediator's judgment of what is required to move client couples to agreement. Moreover, the model's circular or systemic quality signifies that the distinction between processes of assessment, premediation, negotiation, and follow-up, although useful for expository purposes, is in practice an arbitrary way of punctuating an ongoing, highly variable process.

CONCLUSION

Separated couples face a complex task in attempting to reestablish their lives as single individuals. Most, with much effort and some pain, accomplish this task without difficulty and without assistance. Some cannot and, wishing to avoid a traumatic and expensive court battle, seek the assistance of family mediation.

Such a request for service represents a challenge for the mediator. These are typically couples in flux, with much happening in their lives. They are often under tremendous stress, likely feeling alternately depressed and angry, and face an uncertain future with understandable apprehension. This condition is complicated by the ecosystemic contexts in which they live. On the one hand, their characteristic patterns of family interaction may vary on a continuum from functional to dysfunctional; these patterns in turn may apply in differential fashion across the various subsystems that compose the family unit. Furthermore, the influence of each family member in the organization of these patterns may vary substantially; some may be considerably more influential than others. On the other hand, the family is simultaneously embedded in a larger social context potentially concerning a host of extrasystemic others whose involvement in the conflict between the spouses may vary from none to considerable. In turn, dysfunctional patterns of family relating and the involvement of extrasystemic others form what is in effect a higher-order feedback loop, each stabilizing the other, and both typically interfering with the spouses' ability to think and behave rationally, essential attributes to fruitful involvement in negotiation.

Any inflexible model of mediation practice will fail with some proportion of these couples simply because something other than negotiation must happen before they are ready to negotiate. Therapeutic family mediation, by its emphasis on an ecosystemic sensitivity and understanding of client couples and their social contexts, seeks to establish the optimum fit between the needs of client couples and the mediation techniques available to assist them in reaching an amicable and durable agreement. In this sense, TFM stresses process over outcome and ecosystem over issue, for only genuine resolution of underlying emotional issues ensures an agreement likely to remain intact and functioning despite the many predictable vicissitudes of client postdivorce adjustment.

The heart of TFM, then, is its ecosystemic flexibility, seeking continually to match the clinical behavior of the mediator with the behavior of client couples to move them to the point where they are ready to meaningfully enter into negotiation which, in turn, is maintained until a mutually satisfactory and sustainable agreement is achieved. Toward this end, the model *must* address both interactional and substantive

issues. In doing so, it is thus necessarily a therapeutic model of mediation, for in the process client couples are not only provided assistance
in achieving their objectives, but the potential is always present for
mediator-induced change in patterns of behaving, thinking, and feeling. The balance between assistance and therapy is not defined in
advance but in the process of doing mediation, for only through such
interaction can the most appropriate "fit" between clinical action and
client requirements be discovered and sustained. In turn, we suggest
that achieving such a fit substantially increases the likelihood of a
successful outcome despite the interactional diversity of the mediation
client population.

NOTES

1. In part, this reflects the increasing popularity of mediation. However, it also
reflects recent changes in legal policy that allow mediators to accept legal aid funds paid
to the client's lawyers.
2. Although useful for heuristic purposes, this clean separation of assessment and
intervention does not hold in practice, where the two may overlap.
3. Couples with a history of spousal abuse invariably require careful assessment to
determine to what extent that history is likely to affect mediation. In turn, although
those in which abuse occurred months or years in the past might be considered for
service, those in which it is current and ongoing are invariably regarded as *absolutely*
contraindicated for mediation.
4. Both variations involve the formation of coalitions or alliances. Johnston and
Campbell (1988, chap. 2) call attention to a third variation, "tribal warfare," which is
organized along ethnic or racial lines, often among mixed marriages.
5. Johnston and Campbell (1988, chaps. 4 and 5) extend this notion by arguing that
intractable conflict as well as blockages in mediation derive from a combination of three
sources: patterns of marital interaction, the involvement of extrasystemic elements, and
various forms of intrapsychic conflict, including, in extreme cases, individual psychopathology.
6. Prepared by Lilianne Denis and used with permission. In all cases, the names are
fictitious.

REFERENCES

Anderson, J. C. (1982). Determinants of collective bargaining impasses: Effects of
    resolution procedures. In G. B. J. Bomers & R. B. Peterson (Eds.), *Conflict manage-
    ment and industrial relations.* Norwell, MA: Kluwer-Nijhoff.

Aponte, H. J. (1981). Structural family therapy. In A. S. Gurman & D. P. Kniskern (Eds.), *Handbook of family therapy.* New York: Brunner/Mazel.

Bahr, S. J., Chappell, C. B., & Marcos, A. C. (1987). An evaluation of a trial mediation program. *Mediation Quarterly, 18,* 37-52.

Barsky, M. (1983). Emotional needs and dysfunctional communication as blocks to mediation. *Mediation Quarterly, 2,* 55-66.

Benjamin, M. (1983). General systems theory, family systems theories, and family therapy: Towards an integrated recursive model of family process. In A. Bross (Ed.), *Family therapy: A recursive model of strategic practice.* New York: Guilford.

Benjamin, M., & Bross, A. (1983). Family therapy: A typology of therapist error. In A. Bross (Ed.), *Family therapy: A recursive model of strategic practice.* New York: Guilford.

Blades, J. (1985). *Family mediation: Cooperative divorce settlement.* Englewood Cliffs, NJ: Prentice Hall.

Bodin, A. M. (1981). The interactional view: Family therapy approaches of the Mental Health Institute. In A. S. Gurman & D. P. Kniskern (Eds.), *Handbook of family therapy.* New York: Brunner/Mazel.

Bomers, G. B. J., & Peterson, R. B. (Eds.). (1982). *Conflict management and industrial relations.* Norwell, MA: Kluwer-Nijhoff.

Bross, A., & Benjamin, M. (1983). Family therapy: A recursive model of strategic practice. In A. Bross (Ed.), *Family therapy: A recursive model of strategic practice.* New York: Guilford.

Coogler, O. J. (1978). *Structured mediation in divorce settlement.* Lexington, MA: Lexington Books.

de Shazer, S. (1986). An indirect approach to brief therapy. *Family Therapy Collections, 19,* 48-55.

Donohue, W. A., Lyles, J., & Rogan, R. (1989). Issue development in divorce mediation. *Mediation Quarterly, 24,* 19-28.

Elkaim, M. (1990). *If you love me, don't love me: Constructions of reality and change in family therapy* (H. Chubb, Trans.). New York: Basic Books.

Felstiner, W. L. F., & Williams, L. A. (1978). Mediation as an alternative to criminal prosecution. *Law and Human Behavior, 2*(3), 223-244.

Fisch, R., Weakland, J. H., & Segal, L. (1982). *The tactics of change: Doing therapy briefly.* San Francisco: Jossey-Bass.

Fisher, R., & Brown, S. (1988). *Getting together: Building relationships as we negotiate.* Boston: Houghton Mifflin.

Fisher, R., Ury, W., & Patton, B. (1991). *Getting to yes: Negotiating agreement without giving in* (2nd ed.). Boston: Houghton Mifflin.

Gadlin, H., & Ouellette, P. A. (1987). Mediation Milanese: An application of systemic family therapy to family mediation. *Mediation Quarterly, 14/15,* 101-118.

Gifford, L. (1985). A context-based theory of strategy selection in legal negotiation. *Ohio State Law Journal, 41,* 45-58.

Gold, L. (1985). Reflections on the transition from therapist to mediator. *Mediation Quarterly, 9,* 15-26.

Haley, J. (1976). *Problem-solving therapy: New strategies for effective family therapy.* San Francisco: Jossey-Bass.

Haynes, J. M. (1981). *Divorce mediation: A practical guide for therapists and counselors.* New York: Springer.

Haynes, J. M. (1984). Mediated negotiations: The function of the intake. *Mediation Quarterly, 6,* 3-15.

Irving, H. H. (1980). *Divorce mediation: The rational alternative.* Toronto: Personal Library.

Irving, H. H., & Benjamin, M. (1987). *Family mediation: Theory and practice of dispute resolution.* Toronto: Carswell.

Irving, H. H., & Benjamin, M. (1989). Therapeutic family mediation: Fitting the service to the interactional diversity of client couples. *Mediation Quarterly, 7*(2), 115-131.

Irving, H. H., Benjamin, M., Bohm, P., & Macdonald, G. (1981). *A study of conciliation counseling in the family court: Implications for socio-legal practice.* Toronto: Welfare Grants Directorate, Health and Welfare Canada, and the Ontario Ministry of the Attorney General, Demonstration Project 25555-1-65.

Irving, H. H., Bohm, P., Macdonald, G., & Benjamin, M. (1979). *A comparative analysis of two family court services: An exploratory study of conciliation counseling.* Toronto: Welfare Grants Directorate, Health and Welfare Canada, and the Ontario Ministry of the Attorney General, Demonstration Project 25555-1-65.

Johnston, J. R., & Campbell, L. E. G. (1988). *Impasses of divorce: The dynamics of family conflict.* New York: Free Press.

Kelly, J. B. (1983). Mediation and psychotherapy: Distinguishing the differences. *Mediation Quarterly, 1,* 33-44.

Kitson, G. C., Babri, K. B., & Roach, M. J. (1985). Who divorces and why: A review. *Journal of Divorce, 6,* 255-293.

Kressel, K., Deutsch, M., Jaffee, N., Tuchman, B., & Watson, C. (1977). Mediated negotiations in divorce and labor disputes: A comparison. *Conciliation Courts Review, 15*(1), 9-12.

Kressel, K., Jaffe, N., Tuchman, B., Watson, C., & Deutsch, M. (1980). A typology of divorcing couples: Implications for mediation and the divorce process. *Family Process, 19,* 101-116.

Kressel, K., Butler-DeFreitas, F., Forlenza, S. G., & Wilcox, C. (1989). Research in contested custody mediation: An illustration of the case study method. *Mediation Quarterly, 24,* 55-70.

Lemmon, J. A. (1985). *Family mediation practice.* New York: Free Press.

Little, M. (1982). *Family breakups: Understanding marital problems and the mediating of child custody decisions.* San Francisco: Jossey-Bass.

McIsaac, H. (1987). Toward a classification of child custody disputes: An application of family systems theory. *Mediation Quarterly, 14/15,* 39-50.

Milne, A. L. (1978). Custody of children in a divorce process: A family self-determination model. *Conciliation Courts Review, 16,* 1-10.

Milne, A. L. (1983). Divorce mediation: The state of the art. *Mediation Quarterly, 1,* 15-31.

Milne, A. L. (1986). Divorce mediation: A process of self-definition and self-determination. In N. S. Jacobson & A. S. Gurman (Eds.), *Clinical handbook of marital therapy.* New York: Guilford.

Minuchin, S. (1974). *Families and family therapy.* Cambridge, MA: Harvard University Press.

Minuchin, S., & Fishman, H. C. (1981). *Family therapy techniques.* Cambridge, MA: Harvard University Press.

Moore, C. W. (1986). *The mediation process: Practical strategies for resolving conflict.* San Francisco: Jossey-Bass.

Pearson, J., Ring, M., & Milne, A. (1983). A portrait of divorce mediation services in the public and private sector. *Conciliation Courts Review, 21,* 1-24.

Potapchuk, W., & Carlson, C. (1987). Using conflict analysis to determine intervention techniques. *Mediation Quarterly, 16,* 31-43.

Raiffa, H. (1982). *The art and scisence of negotiations.* Cambridge, MA: Harvard University Press.

Saposnek, D. T. (1985). *Mediating child custody disputes: A systematic guide for family therapists, court counselors, attorneys, and judges.* San Francisco: Jossey-Bass.

Sargent, G., & Moss, B. (1987). Ericksonian approaches in family therapy and mediation. *Mediation Quarterly, 14/15,* 87-100.

Shaw, M. L., & Phear, W. P. (1987). New perspectives on the options generation process. *Mediation Quarterly, 16,* 65-73.

Stanton, M. D. (1981). Strategic approaches to family therapy. In A. S. Gurman & D. P. Kniskern (Eds.), *Handbook of family therapy.* New York: Brunner/Mazel.

Ury, W. (1991). *Getting past no: Negotiating with difficult people.* New York: Penguin.

Waldron, J. A., Roth, C. P., Fair, P. H., Mann, E. M., & McDermott, J. F., Jr. (1984). A therapeutic mediation model for child dispute resolution. *Mediation Quarterly, 3,* 5-20.

Walker, J. A. (1986). Assessment in divorce conciliation: Issues and practice. *Mediation Quarterly, 11,* 43-56.

Wallerstein, J. S. (1987). Psychodynamic perspectives on family mediation. *Mediation Quarterly, 14,* 7-21.

Wallerstein, J. S., & Kelly, J. B. (1980). *Surviving the breakup: How children and parents cope with divorce.* New York: Basic Books.

Weaver, J. (1986). Therapeutic implications of divorce mediation. *Mediation Quarterly, 12,* 75-90.

Zieg, J. K. (Ed.). (1980). *A teaching seminar with Milton H. Erickson, M.D.* New York: Brunner/Mazel.

5

Toward a
Feminist-Informed Model
of Therapeutic Family Mediation

INTRODUCTION

As we have seen in chapter 4, under certain circumstances women in mediation can be at risk, both in terms of their physical safety and the fairness and equity of agreements arrived at through this approach. Both concerns have been uppermost in the minds of feminist critics and observers of family mediation. However, their subsequent response has been less than unanimous, a function of the complex state of modern feminism.

At present, feminism is not a monolithic perspective, but rather involves several divergent schools or factions (Luepnitz, 1988, p. 15; Wilson, 1991, p. 8). One of the central notions of some feminist proponents is in patriarchy, that social arrangement in which domination by

AUTHORS' NOTE: This chapter was originally published as Benjamin, M., and Irving, H. H. (1992). Towards a feminist-informed model of therapeutic family mediation. *Mediation Quarterly, 10*(2), 129-153. This modified version is published with permission.

men has left women in subordinate positions. This inequity remains, proponents argue, in all spheres, including social institutions such as mental health and family law. Feminist views of psychiatry (Chesler, 1972, 1986; Mowbray, Lanir, & Hulce, 1985) and family therapy (Goldner, 1985a, 1985b) reveal both as reproducing patriarchal assumptions, and thus sharply, if implicitly, biased against women. Similarly, feminist criticism (Brophy & Smart, 1985; Fineman, 1988; Menkel-Meadow, 1985) and research (National Council on Welfare, 1990; Weitzman, 1985) suggest that existing family law statutes are inequitable, leading to the "feminization of poverty" (Pearce, 1979); patriarchal bias inheres in the adversarial system, with male judges and lawyers tending to advance characteristically "male" solutions to problem of divorce, emphasizing conflict, competition, and "winning"; and women are consequently typically rendered passive, dependent observers in their own cases.

In this context, family mediation might be seen as an attractive alternative to litigation in divorce. Indeed, Rifkin (1984) argues that mediation reflects what she understands as a feminist analysis, one that stresses cooperation, negotiation, equity, and especially participation and ownership. In short, mediation would appear to provide one basis for resolving divorce disputes that gives women back their "voice."

Despite early feminist support for mediation, by the mid-1980s the tide of feminist opinion had turned sharply and decisively negative (Ange, 1985; Bottomley, 1985; Leitch, 1986; Lerman, 1985; Summers, 1985; Woods, 1985). With few exceptions (Corcoran & Melamed, 1990; Neumann, 1992), if anything, more recent views have hardened in their opposition to mediation (Grillo, 1991; Hart, 1990; Majury, 1991).

The ensuing debate between supporters and opponents of family mediation has been curious in at least two respects. Although the feminist critique of mediation has grown steadily from the 1980s to the present, there has yet to be a definitive statement of the feminist position. Rather, given the diversity of views that are broadly feminist, each author has struck out on his or her own, thus generating a wide range of opinion, albeit uniformly negative in tone. Similarly, proponents of mediation have only recently recognized the critique and begun to respond to it (Kelly & Duryee, 1992; Thoennes & Pearson, 1992), thus far in only piecemeal fashion. As a result, the debate has often been unproductive, promoting extreme positions and mutual misunderstanding (see Landau, 1992). In the spirit of mediation, then, two things seem to be needed: first, a more systematic and comprehensive treatment of both positions; second, discussion leading to the development of feminist-informed models of family mediation. Here, we address the second. What follows is divided into two sections, the first briefly summarizing the feminist critique of mediation, the second exploring three issues (neutrality, empowerment, and violence) to show how TFM can be feminized. Simply put, our position is that family mediation is currently designed to help couples resolve their difficulties in such a way as to benefit both parties, especially the weaker spouse (typically female). Enlarging that approach by sensitizing it to feminist concerns extends current trends and thus can only benefit all concerned.

Finally, to avoid misunderstanding, it is important to distinguish between the feminist critique of mediation and the feminist literature per se, despite some overlap between the two. In what follows, our remarks are directed exclusively to the former.

THE FEMINIST CRITIQUE

At the risk of oversimplification, our reading of the literature suggests that the feminist critique of family mediation resolves into four general arguments (neutrality, equality, rights, and practice standards) that translate into 10 specific assertions, as follows.

1. *The failure of neutrality.* Mediator conduct that deviates from absolute neutrality constitutes a failure of neutrality. Insofar as mediators cannot be value-free, any action on their part may "propagate certain value judgements [so that] what is actually a blend of informal adjudication with an element of party control is legitimated by the appearance of greater [party] control than is evident in practice" (Bottomley, 1985, p. 175). That being so, mediators are apt to "replicat[e] existing conditions of inequality supported by patriarch" (Leitch, 1986, p. 169).

2. *Bias favoring shared parenting.* Bruch (1988) and others (e.g., Advisory Committee, 1989, p. 35; Bailey, 1989; Pagelow, 1990) advance a three-part argument: (a) mediators routinely encourage couples to select shared

parenting as a custody option; (b) this option, especially legal joint custody, often places women in a subordinate position; and thus (c) it replicates the patriarchal character of society at large (Delorey, 1989).

3. *Patriarchal power and inequality.* Recognizing "women's oppression in patriarchal social systems" (Leitch, 1986, p. 165), the feminist critique takes the form of a logical syllogism: If women in the larger patriarchal society are unequal to men and if mediation cannot or will not redress this imbalance, women in mediation will similarly be in a subordinate position (Grillo, 1991; Majury, 1991).

4. *Failure of empowerment.* Given an unequal power balance on entry into mediation, the onus is on the mediator to recognize indicators of such an imbalance and correct it by empowering the female spouse. On both counts, mediators typically fail (Grillo, 1991; Shaffer, 1988) in that "regardless of the issues presented, the disputants are accorded mutual responsibility" (Lerman, 1985, p. 86).

5. *Mediation and family violence.* In the feminist literature, wife abuse is pictured as involving severe, repeated, and enduring violence (Clark, 1989; Ellis, 1987, 1990). The invariable result is a massive power imbalance between husband and wife, rendering the latter unable to advocate either for her own rights or those of her child(ren) (Hart, 1990; Hilton, 1991). When such women are forced into mediation (see Marks, 1988), resulting agreements are likely to be anything but fair and equitable (Arsenault, 1990). Accordingly, Majury (1991, p. 135) argues that "gender inequality can render unconscionable a separation agreement that seriously disadvantages the systematically weaker party, the wife"; such cases are better handled through the courts (Hart, 1990; Stallone, 1984).

6. *Coercive mediation and equality.* Mandatory mediation serves to perpetuate female inequality by failing to differentiate between (a) divorcing couples who are or are not amenable to mediation (Advisory Committee, 1989, p. 36; Marks, 1988) and (b) those who have or have not been abused (Hart, 1990; Pagelow, 1990). Consequently, any settlement will typically have been arrived at under duress, the woman in question having been forced to deal on a face-to-face basis with her abuser (Germane, Johnson, & Lemon, 1985; Shaffer, 1988).

7. *Mediation a lesser forum.* "In light of the substantial gains women have made in family law in recent years, family mediation trivializes family law issues by relegating them to a lesser forum. It diminishes the public perception of the relative importance of laws addressing women's and children's rights in the family by placing these rights outside society's key institutional system of dispute resolution—the legal system. . . .

Only the legislatures and courts create, develop, expand and enforce women's rights" (Woods, 1985, pp. 435-436). Thus a key objection to mediation is that it privatizes rights and obligations whose recognition and protection is best accomplished in the public domain.

8. *No enforcement mechanism.* Adversarial proceedings are able to protect the rights and interests of women by the presence of formal enforcement mechanisms (e.g., discovery, compliance, and review) to discourage lying, manipulation, and the like. By contrast, family mediation, by virtue of its informality, lacks such mechanisms and is correspondingly less able to protect women's rights and thus ensure them a fair and equitable settlement (Advisory Committee, 1989, pp. 34-35, 46; Arsenault, 1990; Grillo, 1991).

9. *Sensitivity to "hidden" family violence.* Critics, especially Hart (1990), Pagelow (1990), and Shaffer (1988), note that many mediators (a) have received no specialized training in family violence; (b) are relatively insensitive to family violence and fail to actively seek to uncover it; (c) use unreasonably "high" standards for severe violence; (d) tend to disregard female reports of previous violence; (e) employ no special techniques or procedures with violent as opposed to nonviolent cases; and, (f) in consequence, may unwittingly endanger the lives of the women and children involved, including an increased risk of postseparation violence (Ellis, 1987, 1990; see Stallone, 1984).

10. *Mediator not accountable.* Finally, whereas lawyers are accountable for their professional conduct, mediators are not, given the absence of state requirements of accreditation or licensing (Advisory Committee, 1989, pp. 35, 46; Shaffer, 1988). Consequently, an unknown proportion of mediators may be incompetent or at least biased, thus providing a level of service below that available through the adversarial system. Supportive evidence involves a series of anecdotal case reports (e.g., Arsenault, 1990; Grillo, 1991).

FEMINIST-INFORMED FAMILY MEDIATION

Taken together, these arguments suggest only three future courses: (a) abandon family mediation as inherently inimical to the interests of women; (b) carry on as usual, judging the feminist critique as having little to contribute of practical value; or (c) regard family mediation as a valid alternative to litigation (Astor, 1991; Gale, 1989), providing it listens to criticism (Girdner, 1987), especially feminist criticism (Leitch, 1986). We regard the last choice as the most reasonable because we judge that feminist critics have something important to say that can only enrich mediation practice. Listening to the critics in this sense, however, means nothing less than the creation of a feminist-informed family mediation.

This said, such a creation is not a simple matter. Much of the existing critique is written by feminist legal scholars who argue on the basis of principle, logic, and evidence, rather than clinical experience. Even feminist mediators have not, with few exceptions (see Girdner, 1990; Neumann, 1992), addressed issues of clinical practice. Our solution is to integrate the advice of selected mediation practitioners with that of feminist family therapists (e.g., Avis, 1991; Carter, 1992; Doherty, 1991), for it is the latter who continue to struggle with the critical problem of translating feminist theory into clinical practice.

Although we think this the best solution, we simultaneously acknowledge that it is far from ideal. As noted above, modern feminism is represented by an array of schools and positions. Consequently, whatever positions we support will necessarily fail to satisfy some feminists. In the same vein, as Luepnitz (1988, p. 20) notes, feminism is a body of theory, not a specified set of techniques. Thus it provides clinicians who agree with this school of feminism with a sensibility and conscious purpose, but fails to specify how this purpose is to be accomplished. Perhaps most salient, our reading of the feminist family therapy literature must necessarily be selective and subject to various translation errors. This result is unavoidable given that family therapy and mediation have divergent goals. The former seeks to produce enduring change while leaving the integrity of the family system intact. The latter seeks to alter marital interaction only insofar as this promotes viable negotiation between relatively equal parties (Irving & Benjamin, 1987a, pp. 53, 81).

Furthermore, just as there is no single feminism, so there is no single family mediation. Rather, contemporary family mediation is characterized by extraordinary diversity, including variation across dimensions such as location (court-based versus private practice), model of practice (legal versus clinical and neutral versus interventionist), and substantive focus (custody and access versus comprehensive). Development of a feminist-informed family mediation is a complex task in its own right; adaptation of such a model to the diversity of mediation forms is beyond the purview of this chapter. Accordingly, our reformulation will be confined to TFM (Irving & Benjamin, 1989; see chapter 4).

Finally, working through 10 arguments is beyond the available space. Accordingly, our remarks will be limited to the three concerns we see as the core of the critique, namely, neutrality (#1), empowerment (#4), and violence (#5).

Neutrality

Neutrality concerns the presuppositions that frame what the mediator does or does not do, when, how, and with whom. Such presuppositions deserve careful consideration, because "unexamined presuppositions lead to sexist therapy" (Luepnitz, 1988, p. 12).

In this context, Bernard, Folger, Weingarten, and Zumeta (1984) suggest that mediators distribute on a practice continuum (see also Silbery & Merry, 1986). At one end are those who take a neutral stance, facilitating the process of mediation but voicing no opinions on substance. Midrange mediators suggest alternative options or provide supplementary information. At the other end are those who actively intervene to shape the agreement, making it acceptable to clients and consistent with the mediator's values of fairness and equity.

Our selective review of feminist family therapy suggests that a feminist-informed mediation would favor interventionist strategies and values consistent with mutuality, collaboration, and equity. With regard to the former, feminist therapists emphasize enduring power imbalances in gendered human relations, both within the family (Carter, 1992) as well as in the world beyond (Ganley, 1990), which can only be altered through intervention (Dienhart & Avis, 1990). Such imbalance is manifest in client behavior and deeply internalized beliefs (Avis, 1991), traced to their early socialization (Goldner, Penn, Sheinberg, & Walker, 1990) and replicated in the history of women's subordination (Leitch, 1986; Luepnitz, 1988, p. 7). Given such a history, Leitch (1986) argues that systematic subordination can only be balanced by superordination, although Goldner (1988, p. 30) notes that therapists have clear limits on how much change they can induce insofar as "not all, or even most failures in treatment are therapist-generated, nor can someone else's more artful interview necessarily save a marriage."

In turn, such views support a series of value positions in keeping with an androgynous model of mental health (Ganley, 1990; Luepnitz, 1988, p. 15), including individual responsibility (autonomy), equality in role relations, and collaboration among equals (Ganley, 1990); creating increased options for change (Dienhart & Avis, 1990); validation and respect for women's views and opinions and their need for connection (Doherty, 1991); conscious control over areas of life over which clients have some power (Avis, 1991); ownership of change through insight (Leitch, 1986); the importance of challenging distorted beliefs, creation of a "holding environment" (of safety and trust), the selection of interventions in keeping with feminist theory (i.e., leaving families less patriarchal and less father absent), helping mothers to better care for themselves and allow themselves to be cared for by others, the role of empathy and caring, special attention given to issues concerning gender (and social class), and the validation of affect and its expression (Luepnitz, 1988, pp. 7, 20-22, 183, 189, 194, 230, 262).

Such values cast feminist comments about mediator neutrality in a new light, suggesting that mediators should be neutral in regard to the parties but clearly biased in favor of *feminist values* which, in turn, affect the nature and direction of service delivery. This view is likely to be problematic for proponents of absolute neutrality. It is much less so for proponents of TFM. For example, elsewhere (Irving & Benjamin, 1987a, pp. 84-85) we have argued that: (a) absolute neutrality is a luxury family mediators can ill afford; (b) different family members as well as various interested others (such as lawyers and mediators) have different interests; (c) the most appropriate position of the mediator ought to be one of "focal neutrality" such that their conduct is case- and context-specific, with different interests deserving priority at different points in the same case; and (d) such a bias ought to be enacted, not by advocating on behalf of one spouse against the other, but by intervening in the relations between spouses, including responding to one spouse differently than to the other spouse (see Empowerment, p. 210).

Although such a view is consistent with feminist-informed mediation, it remains unclear on what principled or ethical basis intervention should occur, thus avoiding both the appearance and the reality of arbitrariness. This problem has yet to be satisfactorily resolved. However, Zygmond and Boorhem (1989), mindful of feminist concerns, make a convincing case in favor of Kitchener's model of ethical decision making. This model assumes that ethical decisions are situational and proposes a hierarchically tiered process involving four levels. Decision making begins at the intuitive level, which allows prereflexive action. As situations become more complex, rules or prescribed standards are applied, as might be contained in existing codes of ethics. As case complexity increases, ethical principles are brought to bear, specifically: autonomy (freedom of action), nonmaleficence (do no harm), beneficence (contribute to the health and welfare of others), fidelity (faithfulness, loyalty, respect), and justice (fairness and equity). Finally, if all else fails, ethical theory is used, specifically, the notions of universalizability (can the intended action be unambiguously generalized to all similar cases?) and balancing (do the least avoidable harm to all involved, even if this course limits the benefits that accrue to the parties). Applied to family mediation, such an approach provides a systematic basis for a mediation model sensitive to the values noted above, balanced as to the mutual and competing interests of the various parties (including the mediator) while intervening to promote fairness in process and outcome.

Empowerment

Feminist critics argue that spousal inequality is such that women's interests are best served by forceful legal representation. We agree that many marital arrangements are imbalanced and that reasonable and fair negotiation between these spouses can only occur if the women in question are empowered by the mediation process. Accordingly, the critical question concerns how this mediation might be done in a way that is feminist informed, although three qualifications are in order.

First, although there is evidence that empowerment is necessary for many women, this is not necessarily the case for all. For example, Ricci (1985, p. 52), a feminist family therapist and family mediator, observes that, "Some career homemakers, firmly rooted in daily necessities and realities of running a household, are superb negotiators with a solid sense of their own entitlements and clear goals."

Similarly, the mediation research literature (Irving & Benjamin, 1987b; Kressel & Pruitt, 1989; see chapter 10) shows that the majority of mediation clients, both men and women, were satisfied with the terms of their agreements and adhered to them at least as often as did litigation clients.

Second, the feminist position on divorce (Leitch, 1986) is that it is primarily a legal, political, and financial problem, not merely an emotional one (see Bailey, 1989). We agree but see no contradiction in also recognizing its emotional basis. On the one hand, there is ample evidence that divorcing couples are not homogeneous, but involve a variety of types that vary considerably in terms of spousal equality (Little, 1982; Montalvo, 1982), and thus are likely to benefit differentially from empowerment. On the other hand, there is equally good evidence that some patterns of marital interaction make fair negotiation impossible (Johnston & Campbell, 1988; Ricci, 1985), although some patterns may change through premediation and thus ultimately be amenable to mediation (Fuhr, 1989; Irving & Benjamin, 1989).

Third, critics argue that the only way to protect women's interests involves competent legal representation (Bailey, 1989). We agree that all clients, men and women, should be represented by a lawyer. However, the question remains of whether such representation alone is necessarily the best choice for all women. There is ample evidence that some forms of legal involvement disempower clients, especially women. For example, in regard to the 90% of divorce cases that do not involve litigation, Bishop (1987, p. 13) argues that

> in the vast majority of cases which statistics show as having been "settled," the outcomes have, in fact, been determined by the attorneys, with their clients more or less "going along with" what their lawyers have told them they should do to avoid a trial. The process in which a lawyer determines the outcome is essentially no different from one in which a judge determines the outcome and has all the attributes which characterize the litigation process.

Following the work of Kruk (1992) on the abandonment of children by some noncustodial fathers, the "attributes" to which Bishop (1987) refers include creating conflict where it did not exist and escalating it where it did; prohibiting direct communication between the spouses;

undercutting previous parenting plans; promoting a competitive and hostile atmosphere; shaping client expectations regarding (limited) access; providing uniform legal advice despite client differences; and contributing to client feelings of powerlessness and (for noncustodial fathers) hopelessness. Although disempowerment may thus apply to men, it more typically applies to women. As Marlow and Sauber (1990, p. 477) note, men's greater financial resources often mean they are more likely to have access to high quality legal representation. In our experience, some men are more likely to use that representation to delay the process until their spouse's resources are exhausted, thus rendering her more amenable to a settlement favoring his interests.

As for divorce cases that proceed to trial, Marlow and Sauber (1990, p. 109) describe the current situation this way:

> The idea that the wife's problems will all be over once she turns to adversarial proceedings, and that the lion that her husband was in mediation now becomes a lamb, is simply a myth, albeit a convenient one. The myth aside, the parties have no power whatsoever in traditional adversarial divorce proceedings. The only power they have is to initiate them.

Similarly, Thoennes and Pearson (1992, p. 142) argue that feminist critics appear to apply fundamentally different standards of equity in their (implicit) comparison of litigation and mediation. In their words, "it would be inequitable to place no demands on the adversarial system beyond the generation of a settlement, while expecting successful mediation to demonstrate improved child adjustment, parental cooperation, compliance with settlements, and no additional litigation." Finally, Folberg (1992, pp. 3, 11) confesses that

> I get impatient with those who romanticize the courts, which have not always had a great track record in behalf of women, minorities and the poor. . . . Mediation may not be cheaper, more fair or more equalizing than its alternatives, but it does tend to be more rational, more healing, more inclusive, less divisive and, ultimately, more satisfying than the alternatives.

We do not suggest that legal representation can be dispensed with or is unimportant. On the contrary, as proponents of TFM we insist on it; those clients who reach complete or partial agreement sign a memorandum of understanding that only becomes a formal agreement once it has been vetted and ratified by their legal representatives. Thus in TFM we see lawyers not as opponents, but as critical members of our team who work with us throughout the process of mediation.

These comments support two conclusions: There is no simple solution to disputes between divorcing spouses and, for those who choose the mediation option, efforts to empower female spouses are often necessary. Movement toward a feminist-informed mediation, then, turns on two related questions: Under what circumstances is empowerment required and by what means should it be effected?

Empowerment Required. Feminist family therapists are vague about the circumstances under which empowerment is required. Rather, they assume that power imbalances are typical (Goldner, 1988) and routinely assess the degree of imbalance. Carter (1992), for example, routinely asks about how money is handled. In cases where divorce is likely, she advises the transfer of assets *before* the divorce until the wife feels financially secure enough to negotiate emotional issues as an equal. Luepnitz (1988, pp. 13, 20) looks for evidence of mother-blaming and father abdication from parenting. Ganley (1990) examines family sex roles, whereas Dienhart and Avis (1990) focus on the division of domestic labor as well as the distribution of power and rewards. Avis (1991) looks for beliefs supporting female subordination, especially in regard to marital decision making.

Mediators too approach this issue indirectly. Davis and Salem (1984), Mayer (1987), and Ricci (1985), for example, suggest intervening to ensure that both parties:

1. Have all relevant information
2. Have the opportunity to be heard
3. Can articulate their feelings and interests (as well as those of the child[ren])
4. Can differentiate between their short- and long-term interests
5. Can participate without fear, intimidation, or retaliation
6. Have entered mediation voluntarily and with informed consent
7. Can negotiate with roughly equal skill

8. Are fully aware of the consequences of agreements, both current and future
9. Adhere to the ground rules set by the mediator
10. Are equally committed to mediation
11. Show no evidence of destructive patterns of interaction (the wife accepts all blame or blames everything on her spouse) (see also Johnston & Campbell, 1988; Smart, 1987)

From a feminist perspective, the only contentious criterion may be #8, because it may give rise to agreements that, although acceptable to the parties, may be patently unfair. Here is where the mediator's presuppositions become critical. Mayer (1987) and Davis and Salem (1984) remain neutral; if each party gives informed consent, the mediator has no right to intervene, especially if there are no better options. We agree that the issue turns on consent and available options, with the choices open to low-income couples especially restricted. However, following Ricci (1985), too often consent is based on emotion rather than information and better options may well exist, if not in mediation, then through litigation. Hence the importance of concurrent legal representation. Under such circumstances, we suggest the mediator either empower the "weaker" party and try again or terminate mediation and refer the couple to litigation or counseling.

Empowerment Techniques. Ricci (1985) cites an unpublished paper by Becker-Haven (1983) indicating four categories of intervention: normative/evaluative, rational/analytic, therapeutic, and educational. Feminist family therapists have tended to emphasize therapeutic and psychoeducational approaches to empowerment. Carter (1992), for example, encourages female clients to engage experts who can teach them the skills they need to negotiate effectively. She also intervenes to counteract both mother-blaming and father abdication from parenting. Dienhart and Avis (1990) use reframing and relabeling to confront an inequitable power structure and present clients with a complex set of alternatives for change. Doherty (1991) validates female concerns for connection and caring, supports female challenges of the therapist, and stresses the negotiation of meaning. Avis (1991) confronts patriarchal beliefs, communicates an empowering attitude, and encourages women to take action on their own behalf. Luepnitz (1988, pp. 22,

187-189) stresses the creation of a "holding environment," while encouraging change through insight. Goldner et al. (1990) use coaching techniques to induce change.

Mediators too have technical suggestions. Mayer (1987), Davis and Salem (1984), and Neumann (1992) agree that mediators can best empower the parties by controlling the process of mediation, including the following:

1. Setting ground rules
2. Asking the right questions
3. Helping the parties to think through their respective interests (including delays while they consult experts, legal and otherwise)
4. Blocking disruptive behavior (e.g., intimidation, threats) inimical to the process
5. Ensuring that all appropriate institutional safeguards are being used (including support services, female mediators, and comediation)
6. Compensating (in caucus) for one party's skill deficiencies (including additional information and explicit coaching for effective negotiating techniques)
7. Encouraging insight into the parties' (destructive) patterns of interaction
8. The use of proxies to stand in place of a spouse
9. Controlling who attends mediation sessions

Ricci (1985) addresses #6, 7, and 8 by stressing the importance of "traded assurances" and "interactional monitoring." The former refers to training either or both parties in techniques of effective negotiation. The latter refers to explicit comments by the mediator on the character of ongoing interaction, especially behavior inimical to effective negotiation (see Smart, 1987). A final option concerns using a proxy to stand in place of a female who is unable to negotiate effectively; failing that, she suggests terminating mediation as not in the woman's best interests. As for #9, our most recent study (see chapter 7) showed that of all sessions in private mediation, only 20% involved the two spouses seen together (with or without their children); the balance involved a single spouse, seen alone or with a combination of others, including his or her lawyer. (Mediators may also want to use standardized instruments, such as the Feminist Family Therapy Behavior Checklist

[Chaney & Piercy, 1988] or the Feminist Family Therapy Scale [Black & Piercy, 1991] to monitor the extent to which their conduct is consistent with feminist theory.)

Thus, in the words of Davis and Roberts (1989, p. 306), "perhaps the main challenge to the feminist critique of mediation as perpetuating a power imbalance between men and women lies in this control over the mediation process . . . [by] controlling the ebb and flow of negotiation; in some cases, the 'weaker' party d[oes], indeed, feel empowered." However, Davis and Roberts (1989, p. 305) note an important gender difference, because, "What the man s[ees] as unnecessary interference and control, the woman may have experienced as protection and support."

Combining the above structural and technical subsections suggests that for TFM to become feminist-informed would require two modifications in terms of empowerment: (a) to expand its assessment procedures to routinely explore spousal power balance and (b) to expand current techniques to include measures expressly designed with power balancing in mind.

Expanded assessment would include explicit questions about both objective (e.g., employment status, income, control over assets) and subjective (e.g., perceived power balance, feeling of powerlessness, beliefs regarding the proper place of women) aspects of power balance. In our experience, these assessment efforts can usefully be supplemented by the use of one or more of a growing array of standardized instruments including the Conflict Tactics Scale (Straus, 1979), Conflict Assessment Protocol (Girdner, 1990), Feminist Family Therapy Behavioral Checklist (Chaney & Piercy, 1988), and Assessment of Patterns of Dangerousness (Stuart & Campbell, 1989). The utility of such instruments is that they are sensitive to feminist concerns while simultaneously locating client behavior on a continuum (from "ordinary" conflict to life-threatening violence) and so help decide whether the couple in question is amenable to mediation and, if so, whether they ought first to enter premediation or negotiation.

Expanded intervention would concentrate on mediator control over the process of mediation, including the use of individual caucusing sessions for skills training and personal validation and the use of conjoint sessions to encourage patterns of interaction consistent with effective negotiation.

Violence

Feminist authors who write about wife abuse characterize it in complex, multileveled terms (Bograd, 1984; Ylö & Bograd, 1988). Such complexity is not evident in our reading of feminist critics of mediation (Hilton, 1991; Majury, 1991) who characterize marital violence as (a) necessarily severe and prolonged, (b) invariably resulting in long-standing psychological (if not physical) damage, (c) involving an extreme power imbalance and, as such, (d) *never* amenable to family mediation. Lerman, Kuehl, and Brygger (1989, p. 23) advance a generalization that is only slightly less sweeping. In their view, "victims" of domestic violence may enter mediation *only* under five conditions, namely: (a) the woman's "request for mediation [is] free from intimidation"; (b) "the last incident of violence has occurred more than two years ago"; (c) "none of the critical risk factors exist which identify the abuse as current"; (d) she be referred first "to a battered women's advocate for consultation"; and (e) she understands "why mediation still may be inappropriate." Recent evidence supports the more complex view and in turn significantly qualifies the critics' conclusion that most, if not all, abused women are inappropriate for mediation.

With respect to abuse itself, feminist family therapists Goldner et al. (1990, p. 344) say of their approach toward violent marriages that

> we tried to get beyond the reductionist view of men as simply abusing their power, and of women as colluding in their own victimization by not leaving. This description casts men as tyrants and women as masochists, which deprives both of their humanity while simultaneously capturing a piece of the truth.

Reviews of the research literature (Koss, 1990; Steinmetz, 1987) support their more complex view, which includes variations on dimensions such as the following: (a) duration (some women never leave, some leave after one episode of violence); (b) severity (from no physical injury to death; from no psychological harm to severe damage); (c) frequency (from daily to annually or longer); (d) onset (from before marriage to a later period); (e) abuse of alcohol (from abstinence to alcoholism); (f) psychiatric disorder (from "normal" to psychotic); and (g) other family dysfunction (from none to multiproblem, including child abuse). Thus some abused wives remain with their spouses for long periods but others do not; some abused wives suffer severe injury but others do not; and some abused wives are severely damaged psychologically but others are not.

These findings support three conclusions: (a) the experience of abused women distributes across a series of continua; (b) they appear to distribute similarly across a range of outcomes, including the degree of "psychological damage" (however defined); and, accordingly, (c) some (perhaps many) are contraindicated for mediation, whereas others (proportion unknown) will be amenable to it, especially entry into premediation (see also below).

Lerman, Kuehl, and Brygger (1989, p. 11) refute the final conclusion, citing the case of a court-based mediation service (the Citizen's Dispute Settlement Project) in Minneapolis that "was required by the judges of Hennepin County to stop mediation of domestic violence cases after twelve years of providing that service when it became evident that the mediated contracts were not ending the violence."

In contrast, there is ample evidence in the clinical literature that mediation has been and continues to be used effectively with cases involving domestic violence. Corcoran and Melamed (1990), for example, based on a review of the literature and their experience, indicate the extent to which mediation can be tailored to the specialized needs of abused women. This adaptation includes individual caucusing so that face-to-face contact is minimized; the presence of a victim advocate or lawyer to ensure that the woman's rights are protected and her position clearly articulated; refusal to disclose sensitive information; a requirement that one or both spouses be involved concurrently with rehabilitative counseling; access to the usual array of legal protections (e.g., restraining and consent orders), but tailored in mediation to fit the circumstances of the case and thus containing provisions not normally attended to by judges; and insistence that failure to comply with such protections or any rules established in mediation will automatically terminate mediation. These protections are applied only if abuse is detected following careful screening before service delivery.

Girdner (1990), a feminist mediator, conceptualizes screening in terms akin to medical triage, thus separating couples into three groups: those who show no evidence of violence and would benefit from mediation "as usual"; those who show evidence of violence and would benefit from mediation only with special safeguards; and those who show evidence of extreme ongoing violence and who should be excluded from mediation. Client categorization is based on their responses to Girdner's assessment instrument, the Conflict Assessment Protocol.

Chandler (1990) reports on a Hawaii-based mediation program serving about 300 couples annually, with serious violence detected in 10% of the total. Following mediation, he reports an overall agreement rate of 60%, higher among violent (69%) than nonviolent (53%) couples, despite the fact that violent cases were rated clinically more complex. As to the quality of the agreements, although differences between violent and nonviolent couples were noted, across an array of dimensions not less than 60% of violent couples judged their agreement fair (66%), durable (62%), workable (75%), and comprehensive (66%) (see also Marthaler, 1989).

Erickson and McKnight (1990), based on clinical experience with more than 1,400 cases (half involving emotional or physical abuse), argue that the question is not whether to mediate spousal abuse cases but what special steps must be taken when abuse is detected. They note that such cases tend to be complex and may be more suitable for highly experienced as opposed to novice mediators. Furthermore, they argue in favor of joint sessions as a means of teaching cooperative modes of interaction, the need to validate and empower the abused spouse's concerns, and cooperation with related therapeutic and legal systems.

Finally, the authors cited in the last several paragraphs (especially Corcoran and Melamed [1990]) all note the failure of the judicial system to effectively protect the rights and interests of abused women. The police, for example, have traditionally treated domestic violence calls as trivial, involving nonproductive work while exposing them to a heightened risk of injury and, in rare instances, death; they have typically been reluctant to press charges when restraining orders are violated. Should abusive spouses be arrested, prosecutors have often applied exaggerated tests of sincerity in light of a client dropout rate in excess of 50% and have proceeded only in cases associated with compelling evidence. In cases that actually go to trial, juries have often been reluctant to convict even when they believe the wife; judges have emphasized the rights of defendants and, even when finding them guilty, have typically applied light sentences, thus leaving abused spouses in future jeopardy. (The press has recently reported several United States cases in which abusive husbands, jailed for their behavior, have vowed to kill their spouses and on parole have done just that, despite repeated pleas by the victim for police protection.)

As applied to a feminist-informed TFM, these data suggest the need for a three-step decision-making process involving the following changes:

1. *Primary decision:* expansion of our assessment procedure to include explicit inquiry of each spouse seen in caucus about the recent and regular occurrence of violent or inappropriate acts (e.g., sexual touching by one spouse directed at the other spouse or child[ren]), including the supplementary use of the standardized instruments cited above

2. *Secondary decision:* in cases where a history of violence or other inappropriate conduct was confirmed, additional inquiry would be required to determine if violence is current and ongoing or was terminated in the past; given a history of violence, in light of the admission criteria noted above, we would still need to determine if mediation was indicated or contraindicated; if contraindicated, the couple would be referred out (to a lawyer, counselor, or women's advocate); if indicated, the couple would routinely be seen initially in premediation in light of the previous discussion of empowerment, and as an additional hedge against the possibility of an assessment error; finally, if violence is current and ongoing (regardless of its severity), our experience is that these couples always fail to meet our admission criteria and so are routinely referred out.

3. *Tertiary decision:* in cases judged appropriate for mediation, a final decision concerns which (if any) special precautions (safety plans) are needed for the process to be fair and hold out the reasonable likelihood of an equitable and workable agreement; such special precautions are tailored to fit the needs of the couple in question, but will typically include one or some combination of the following:

   • Who would be present during mediation sessions: special precautions might mean including in each session the woman's lawyer, a women's advocate or another person or persons deemed relevant to protect the woman's best interests

- Routine procedures: whether individual caucusing, joint sessions, or a combination of both would be appropriate; it might also include the timing of sessions to ensure, for example, that the spouses do *not* meet or arranging for an escort for the woman to and from her car to avoid unexpected confrontations in the parking lot before and after sessions
- Extraordinary procedures: rules tailor-made for a given couple to reduce the likelihood of intimidation, either in session (e.g., no interruptions, yelling, demeaning words or phrases, veiled or explicit threats toward the spouse, children, or a third party, violent acts directed at a person or an object) or between sessions (e.g., no contact by telephone or in person; no contact between the abusive spouse and the children except under supervision)
- Concurrent legal procedures: these may include various legal instruments (e.g., peace bonds, restraining orders, other court orders), with adherence to such instruments on the understanding that their contravention would result in immediate termination of mediation. It may also include other matters, such as confidentiality (including withholding certain information from the abusive spouse or his or her representative(s): for example, the address and telephone number of the female spouse) and other programs (including concurrent participation in other therapeutic procedures [e.g., group treatment for abusive men; treatment for alcohol abuse; psychiatric treatment; drug treatment; separation therapy])

CONCLUSION

Rendering TFM feminist informed would involve a variety of important changes: (a) expansion of our value base to incorporate feminist values, including an ethical basis for systematic intervention; (b) expansion of our assessment procedures to involve routine, explicit inquiry into spousal power balance and the presence and extent of violence, including the use of standardized instruments to both of these ends; (c) expansion of our intervention techniques to include approaches explicitly designed to empower the weaker party, typically the female spouse, including several in which women in caucus are trained in the methods of effective negotiation; and (d) inclusion of a three-step decision-making procedure expressly designed to ensure that cases involving wife abuse that have made it through screening procedures have a reasonable likelihood of achieving a fair and work-able agreement (see Figure 4.1 in chapter 4).

In evolving these insights, we were repeatedly reminded, in keeping with the spirit of mediation, of the fact that feminist critics, women's advocates, judicial actors (lawyers, judges) and family mediators ulti-mately share the common concern that all parties to divorce emerge from whatever process they choose with a minimum of harm and with appropriate regard for their respective rights and interests (as well as those of the child[ren]). The changes to TFM proposed above provide the basis for arguing that this end is best served when the groups in question work together, not in opposition. As we see it, family media-tion in divorce must necessarily be a team effort; the mediator cannot be effective when acting alone (Yellott, in press). With Neumann (1992) and others, then, we see no contradiction in the construction of a model of family mediation that is feminist informed.

REFERENCES

Advisory Committee on Mediation in Family Law. (1989). *Report of the attorney general's advisory committee on mediation in family law.* Toronto: Ministry of the Attorney General.

Ange, G. M. (1985). Mediation: Panacea or placebo? *New York State Bar Journal, 57*(4), 6.

Arsenault, M. (1990). Mediation and abused women: Who's looking out for their safety? *Vis-à-Vis, 8*(2), 5-6.

Astor, H. (1991). Feminist issues in ADR. *Law Institute Journal, 65,* 69-71.

Avis, J. M. (1991). Politics and empowerment in my therapy. *Journal of Feminist Family Therapy, 3*(1/2), 141-153.

Bailey, M. J. (1989). Unpacking the "rational alternative": A critical review of family mediation movement claims. *Canadian Journal of Family Law, 8*(1), 61-94.

Becker-Haven, J. F. (1983). *Analyzing the process of child custody mediation: An heuristic model.* Unpublished manuscript.

Benjamin, M., & Adler, S. (1980). Wife abuse: Implications for socio-legal policy and practice. *Canadian Journal of Family Law, 3*(4), 339-367.

Benjamin, M., & Irving, H. H. (1992). Towards a feminist-informed model of therapeutic family mediation. *Mediation Quarterly, 10*(2), 129-153.

Bernard, S. E., Folger, J. P., Weingarten, H. R., & Zumeta, Z. R. (1984). The neutral mediator: Value dilemmas in divorce mediation. *Mediation Quarterly, 4,* 61-74.

Bishop, T. A. (1987). The litigation process: Its effective utilization and avoidance. In J. G. McLeod (Ed.), *Family dispute resolution: Litigation and its alternatives.* Toronto: Carswell.

Black, L., & Piercy, F. P. (1991). A feminist family therapy scale. *Journal of Marital & Family Therapy, 17*(2), 111-120.

Bograd, M. (1984). A family-systems approach to wife battering: A feminist critique. *American Journal of Orthopsychiatry, 54*, 558-568.

Bottomley, A. (1985). What is happening to family law? A feminist critique of concili-ation. In J. Brophy & C. Smart (Eds.), *Women-in-law: Explorations in law, family and sexuality.* London: Routledge.

Brophy, J., & Smart, C. (Eds.). (1985). *Women-in-law: Explorations in law, family and sexuality.* London: Routledge.

Bruch, C. S. (1988). And how are the children? The effects of ideology and mediation on child custody law and children's well-being in the United States. *International Journal of Law and the Family, 2*(1), 106-126.

Carter, B. (1992, January/February). Stonewalling feminism. *The Family Therapy Net-worker,* pp. 64-69.

Chandler, D. B. (1990). Violence, fear, and communication: The variable impact of domestic violence on mediation. *Mediation Quarterly, 7*(4), 331-346.

Chaney, S. E., & Piercy, F. P. (1988). A feminist family therapy behavior checklist. *American Journal of Family Therapy, 16*(4), 305-318.

Chesler, P. (1972). *Women and madness.* Garden City, NY: Doubleday.

Chesler, P. (1986). *Mothers on trial.* Toronto: McGraw-Hill.

Clark, M. L. (1989). Feminist perspectives on violence against women and children: Psychological, social service, and criminal justice concerns. *Canadian Journal of Women and the Law, 3*, 421-431.

Corcoran, K. O., & Melamed, J. C. (1990). From coercion to empowerment: Spousal abuse and mediation. *Mediation Quarterly, 7*(4), 303-316.

Davis, A. M., & Salem, R. A. (1984). Dealing with power imbalances in the mediation of interpersonal disputes. *Mediation Quarterly, 6*, 17-26.

Davis, G., & Roberts, M. (1989). Mediation and the battle of the sexes. *Family Law, 19*, 305-306.

Delorey, A. M. (1989). Joint legal custody: A revision to patriarchal power. *Canadian Journal of Women and the Law, 3*, 33-44.

Dienhart, A., & Avis, J. M. (1990). Men in therapy: Exploring feminist-informed alterna-tives. *Journal of Feminist Family Therapy, 2*(3/4), 25-49.

Doherty, W. J. (1991). Can male therapists empower females in therapy? *Journal of Feminist Family Therapy, 3*(1/2), 123-137.

Ellis, D. (1987). Postseparation woman abuse: The contribution of lawyers as "bar-racudas," "advocates" and "counsellors." *International Journal of Law and Psychia-try, 10*(4), 403-411.

Ellis, D. (1990). Marital conflict mediation and postseparation wife abuse. *Law and Inequality, 8*(2), 317-339.

Emery, R. E., & Jackson, J. (1989). The Charlottesville Mediation Project: Mediated and litigated child custody disputes. *Mediation Quarterly, 24*, 3-18.

Erickson, S. K., & McKnight, M. S. (1990). Mediating spousal abuse divorces. *Mediation Quarterly, 7*(4), 377-388.

Fineman, M. (1988). Dominant discourse, professional language and legal change in child custody decisionmaking. *Harvard Law Review, 101*(4), 727-774.

Folberg, J. (1992). Confessions of a mediator: Seven pitfalls in getting from here to there. *Resolve (Publication of Family Mediation Canada), 7*(1), 3, 10-11.

Fuhr, J. (1989). Mediation readiness. *Family and Conciliation Courts Review, 27*(2), 71-74.

Gale, S. (1989). [Review of the article, "Divorce mediation: A feminist perspective" by Martha Shaffer (1988)] *Canadian Journal of Family Law, 8*, 212-214.

Ganley, A. (1990). Feminist therapy with male clients. *Journal of Feminist Family Therapy,* 2(3/4), 1-23.

Germane, C., Johnson, M., & Lemon, N. (1985). Mandatory custody mediation and joint custody orders in California: The danger for victims of domestic violence. *Berkeley Women's Law Journal,* 1(1), 175-200.

Girdner, L. K. (1987). A critique of family mediators: Myths, themes, and alliances. *Mediation Quarterly,* 18, 3-8.

Girdner, L. K. (1990). Mediation triage: Screening for spouse abuse in divorce mediation. *Mediation Quarterly,* 7(4), 365-376.

Goldner, V. (1985a). Feminism and family therapy. *Family Process,* 24, 31-47.

Goldner, V. (1985b). Warning: Family therapy may be dangerous to your health. *The Family Therapy Networker,* 9, 19-23.

Goldner, V. (1988). Generation and gender: Normative and covert hierarchies. *Family Process,* 27, 17-31.

Goldner, V., Penn, P., Sheinberg, M., & Walker, G. (1990). Love and violence: Gender paradoxes in volatile attachments. *Family Process,* 29, 343-364.

Grillo, T. (1991). The mediation alternative: Process dangers for women. *Yale Law Journal,* 100(6), 1545-1610.

Hart, B. J. (1990). Gentle jeopardy: The further endangerment of battered women and children in custody mediation. *Mediation Quarterly,* 7(4), 317-330.

Hilton, N. Z. (1991). Mediating wife assault: Battered women and the "new family." *Canadian Journal of Family Law,* 9(2), 29-53.

Irving, H. H., & Benjamin, M. (1987a). *Family mediation: Theory and practice of dispute resolution.* Toronto: Carswell.

Irving, H. H., & Benjamin, M. (1987b). Family mediation research: Critical review and future directions. In Vermont Law School (Author), *The role of mediation in divorce proceedings: A comparative perspective (United States, Canada and Great Britain).* South Royalton: Vermont Law School.

Irving, H. H., & Benjamin, M. (1989). Therapeutic family mediation: Fitting the service to the interactional diversity of client couples. *Mediation Quarterly,* 7(2), 115-131.

Johnston, J. R., & Campbell, E. G. (1988). *Impasses of divorce: The dynamics and resolution of family conflict.* New York: Free Press.

Kelly, J. B., & Duryee, M. A. (1992). Women's and men's views of mediation in voluntary and mandatory settings. *Family and Conciliation Courts Review,* 30(1), 43-49.

Koss, M. P. (1990). Violence against women. *American Psychologist,* 45, 374-380.

Kressel, K., Jaffe, N., Tuchman, B., Watson, C., & Deutsch, M. (1980). A typology of divorcing couples: Implications for mediation and the divorce process. *Family Process,* 19, 101-116.

Kressel, K., & Pruitt, D. G. (Eds.). (1989). *Mediation research: The process and effectiveness of third-party intervention.* San Francisco: Jossey-Bass.

Kruk, E. (1992). Psychological and structural factors contributing to the disengagement of noncustodial fathers after divorce. *Family and Conciliation Courts Review,* 30(1), 82-101.

Landau, B. (1992). Point/counterpoint. *Resolve (Publication of Family Mediation Canada),* 7(1), 5-7.

Leitch, M. L. (1986). The politics of compromise: A feminist perspective on mediation. *Mediation Quarterly,* 14, 163-175.

Lerman, L. (1985). Mediation of wife abuse cases: The adverse impact of informal dispute resolution on women. *Harvard Women's Law Journal,* 7, 57-113.

Lerman, L., Kuehl, S., & Brygger, M. (1989). *Domestic abuse and mediation: Guidelines for mediators and policy makers.* Washington, DC: National Women Abuse Prevention Project.

Little, M. (1982). *Family breakups: Understanding marital problems and the mediating of child custody decisions.* San Francisco: Jossey-Bass.

Luepnitz, D. A. (1988). *The family interpreted: Feminist theory in clinical practice.* New York: Basic Books.

Majury, D. (1991). Unconscionability in an equality context. *Family Law Quarterly, 7,* 123-153.

Marks, L. A. (1988, Winter). Mandatory mediation of family law and domestic violence cases. *Voice,* pp. 18-22.

Marlow, L., & Sauber, R. S. (1990). *The handbook of divorce mediation.* New York: Plenum.

Marthaler, D. (1989). Successful mediation with abusive couples. *Mediation Quarterly, 23,* 53-66.

Mayer, B. (1987). The dynamics of power in mediation and negotiation. *Mediation Quarterly, 16,* 75-86.

Menkel-Meadow, C. (1985). Portia in a different voice: Speculations on a women's lawyering process. *Berkeley Women's Law Journal, 1,* 740-764.

Montalvo, B. (1982). Interpersonal arrangements in disrupted families. In F. Walsh (Ed.), *Normal family processes.* New York: Guilford.

Mowbray, C. T., Lanir, S., & Hulce, M. (1985). (Eds.). *Women and mental health: New directions for change.* New York: Harrington Park.

National Council on Welfare. (1990). *Women and poverty revisited.* Ottawa: Minister of Supply and Services.

Neumann, D. (1992). How mediation can effectively address the male and female power imbalance in divorce. *Mediation Quarterly, 9,* 227-239.

Pagelow, M. D. (1990). Effects of domestic violence on children and their consequences for custody and visitation agreements. *Mediation Quarterly, 7*(4), 347-363.

Pearce, D. (1979). Women, work and welfare: The feminization of poverty. In K. W. Feinstein (Ed.), *Working women and families.* Beverly Hills, CA: Sage.

Ricci, I. (1985). Mediator's notebook: Reflections on promoting equal empowerment and entitlements for women. *Journal of Divorce, 8*(3-4), 49-61.

Rifkin, J. (1984). Mediation from a feminist perspective: Promise and problems. *Law and Inequality, 2*(2), 21-31.

Shaffer, M. (1988). Divorce mediation: A feminist perspective. *University of Toronto Faculty of Law Review, 46*(1), 162-200.

Silbery, S., & Merry, M. E. (1986). Mediator settlement strategies. *Law and Policy, 8*(1), 7-32.

Smart, L. (1987). Mediator strategies for dealing with dirty tricks. *Mediation Quarterly, 16,* 53-63.

Stallone, D. R. (1984). Decriminalization of violence in the home: Mediation in wife battering cases. *Law and Inequality, 2,* 493-519.

Steinmetz, S. K. (1987). Family violence: Past, present and future. In M. B. Sussman & S. K. Steinmetz (Eds.), *Handbook of marriage and the family.* New York: Plenum.

Straus, M. A. (1979). Measuring intrafamilial conflict and violence: The Conflict Tactics (CT) Scale. *Journal of Marriage and the Family, 41,* 75-88.

Straus, M. A., & Gelles, R. J. (1986). Societal changes and change in family violence from 1975 to 1985 as revealed in two national surveys. *Journal of Marriage and the Family, 48,* 465-479.

Stuart, E., & Campbell, M. (1989). Assessment patterns of dangerousness with battered women. *Issues in Mental Health, 10,* 245-260.

Summers, D. C. (1985). The case against lay divorce mediation. *New York State Bar Journal, 57*(4), 7, 13.

Thoennes, N., & Pearson, J. (1992). Response to Bruch and McIsaac. *Family & Conciliation Courts Review, 30*(1), 142-143.

Weitzman, L. (1985). *The divorce revolution: The unexpected social and economic consequences for women and children in America.* New York: Free Press.

Wilson, S. J. (1991). *Women, families, and work* (3rd ed.). Toronto: McGraw-Hill Ryerson.

Woods, L. (1985). Mediation: A backlash to women's progress on family law issues. *Clearinghouse Review, 19*(4), 431-436.

Yellott, A. (in press). Mediation and domestic violence: A call for collaboration. *Mediation Quarterly.*

Yllö, K., & Bograd, M. (Eds.). (1988). *Feminist perspectives on wife abuse.* Newbury Park, CA: Sage.

Zygmond, M. J., & Boorhem, H. (1989). Ethical decision making in family therapy. *Family Process, 28,* 269-280.

PART III

Child Custody

If they really want to fight, divorcing couples can fight about just about anything. In practice, some aspects of their experience are more emotionally charged than others. Couples can fight about money, but most divorcing couples have little, some none at all. Their possessions and especially the matrimonial home are sources of conflict, not so much because of their survival value, but because they have become imbued with symbolic meaning. Such meaning makes the relationship between the spouses an especially salient source of conflict. With marriage's inherent expectations of fidelity, loyalty, closeness, and trust, divorce is an all-too-public failure for many couples whose pain quickly transforms into anger. But it is the presence of children, more than any other aspect of marriage, that is the focus of the most intense feelings and, in some cases, the most intense conflict. Expectations of protection, support, caring, and love encourage divorcing couples to see parenting as an explosive issue. This makes parenting a blank screen onto which spouses can project all the feelings toward their former partner they might be unable to express directly. It also makes parenting a killing field when one (or both) spouse perceives—realistically or fantastically—that the other constitutes a real threat to the welfare of their children.

With such feelings in play and with the stakes so high, it is not hard to understand why child custody has been the focus of much strident rhetoric in the literature, none more so than the literature of joint custody or *shared parenting*. Indeed, until recently, heated rhetoric was about all there was in the literature. Happily that situation has changed and it is that change that prompted the two chapters that make up Part III.

Starting from the premise that debate is empty without data, chapter 6 provides the most complete review of the shared parenting research literature available. Having all of these data in one place—being able to see the sweep of the findings across the entire literature—is critical. Authors of single-sample studies have repeatedly been tempted to generalize from their local data to the nation at large. Addressing the various issues associated with shared parenting with all available data invariably places such generalizations in perspective, sometimes providing support, sometimes denying credibility. The larger context is essential if we are to formulate sociolegal policy that is more than merely the rhetorical reflection of one or another ideological stances.

Chapter 7 summarizes the findings of a study unusual in its use of a large sample of shared parents. Large sample size is critical for analytical purposes. It allows us to answer some questions with confidence that cannot be addressed at all with the small, descriptive (rather than comparative) samples that still typify the research literature. In this case, the data make one thing at least abundantly clear: The problems and issues raised by child custody are not amenable to quick fixes or easy solutions; there is no one right option for all divorcing parents, shared parenting included.

6

Shared Parenting

Critical Review
of the Research Literature

INTRODUCTION

In recent years traditional practices of child custody have been called in question. Over the past half century in North America, in the majority of divorce cases involving minor children, maternal sole custody (SC) has been awarded (Nett, 1993; Teachman & Polonko, 1990). Of the remainder, an increasing proportion has involved a joint custody or *shared parenting* (SP) award, in which care and control of the child(ren) are shared equally between both parents (Folberg & Graham, 1981).

As of 1984, more than 30 American states had legislation that recognized, presumed, or mandated SP (Folberg, 1984a, 1984b). Since then, additional states have enacted such legislation (Coller, 1988; Robinson, 1985). Consequently, by 1991, 44 states made SP either optional (25 [50%]), presumed (12 [24%]), or mandated (7 [14%]); it is not favored or is precluded in only six (12%) states (Folberg, 1991, appendix A). Under such statutes, SP may involve *legal* SP, with care and control shared but with a primary residence (typically maternal), or *physical* SP, the child(ren) moving between households in the absence of a primary residence.

This bias favoring SP has meant a slow but steady rise in the proportion of all custody awards involving some version of SP. For example, a national survey done in the early 1980s found that 3% of the sample was involved in an SP arrangement (Furstenberg, Peterson, Nord, & Zill, 1983). A recent study suggested a national average of about 7% (Donnelly & Finkelhor, 1993). Such data, however, obscure considerable variation across American states. Glaser (1989), for example, noted an SP rate of 2% in Michigan compared to 16% in California. Similarly, recent studies in different counties in California report SP rates ranging from 7% to 33% (Kelly, in press; Mnookin, Maccoby, Albiston, & Depner, 1990; Teachman & Polonko, 1990), whereas Kelly (1993, p. 42) observes that joint legal custody is "now the norm in California." Related estimates suggest that across states SP rates vary from 2% to 30% (Furstenberg & Nord, 1985; Weitzman, 1985), most involving legal SP (see Coller, 1988).

In contrast, as of the early 1980s, Canada resisted SP, with case law indicating considerable hesitance on the part of the judiciary (Payne, 1979; Payne & Patrick, 1979). However, as Ingram (1989) has observed, "during the past decade both trial and appellate courts have ordered or allowed joint custody with increasing frequency," even against joint parental opposition. Consequently, current legislation (in Ontario, Manitoba, New Brunswick, and Prince Edward Island) allows custody to be awarded to more than one person; in only the Yukon Territory is SP formally recognized (Ingram, 1989; Payne & Edwards, 1991). As a result, the Canadian SP rate has steadily risen and is now estimated at 14% (Department of Justice, 1993, p. 13).

As for the literature, interest in SP has had two consequences. First, it has increased the number of articles debating the merits of SP, both in favor (Colman, 1989; Ferreiro, 1990; Ricci, 1989) and opposed (Fidler, Saunders, Freedman, & Hood, 1989; Kuehl, 1989; Opie, 1993), with feminist legal scholars especially bitter in their opposition to legal SP (Bruch, 1988; Delorey, 1989; Fineman, 1988), particularly when it is imposed on an unwilling parent (Holmes, 1987; Singer & Reynolds, 1988).[1] Second, such interest has increased the number of articles reviewing the research literature (Clingempeel, Shuvall, & Heiss, 1988;

Coller, 1988; Felner & Terre, 1987).[2] The former highlight the salient issues. The latter should systematize the literature, subject it to critical appraisal, and integrate what is known about the subject. We say "should" because existing reviews have failed to do justice to the SP research literature in at least three respects: They have omitted available reports; given little attention to theoretical or methodological issues, focusing instead on practice or policy; and taken a global approach, thus ignoring much important detail.

Accordingly, this article reviews the 38 published studies[3] that constitute the SP research literature (see also Benjamin & Irving, 1985, 1989; Irving & Benjamin, 1987). The discussion is divided into five sections concerned respectively with theory, methodology, analysis, substantive results, and global evaluation. We conclude by exploring implications for theory, research, and sociolegal policy. However, for those unfamiliar with SP, we begin with a brief case vignette that provides a sense of what SP means for families on a day-to-day basis.

CASEBOOK: SHARED PARENTING

The following case vignette illustrates one variation on SP available: shared parenting in which both parents have legal custody, but the children physically reside with one parent. In this case, the court award corresponds to reality. However, according to Mnookin et al. (1990), it is important to note that this situation is often not the case. The child(ren) may spend roughly equal amounts of time with each parent when in fact only one has been awarded physical custody. Alternately, they may spend most of their time with one parent when in fact both have been awarded physical custody.

Jill and Sam Dworkin: Shared Legal Custody, Maternal Physical Custody

In college, Jill and Sam met and fell in love. They married soon after graduation and set about establishing themselves in their respective careers—he as a manager in a large computer software firm, she as a graphic designer. Over the next 5 years, they both became well established in their respective careers, enabling them to maintain a comfortable lifestyle. In turn, that security was the basis on which the Dworkins had two children, Andy and Sara, in quick succession.

Despite their heavy commitments to work, both were devoted and loving parents who shared this important task more or less equally. Over the next 5 years, however, their involvement in work and parenting took their toll. Both seemed to assume that if their life was good in other respects, then surely their marriage would be good too. In fact, they gradually drifted apart, neither noticing their growing distance because their many other concerns absorbed all their time and energy. By the time they did notice, it was too late, both agreeing that perhaps it was best if they both went separate ways.

But that left unclear how to continue to provide the high quality care they had always provided for their children. Unable to conceive of not being involved in parenting on a regular basis, they were unable to work out an arrangement that pleased them both. They were preparing to fight it out in court when Jill's lawyer suggested family mediation. That is how they came to us. Over the course of eight sessions, three of them in premediation, the Dworkins were able to agree. The text of that agreement (except for the financial terms), written by Jill and Sam themselves, was as follows:

> We, Jill and Sam, have prepared the following draft Parenting Plan. In preparing this plan, we were guided by what we thought would be best for the children, Andy and Sara. We have devised a plan that will give them the opportunity to spend a substantial period of time with both parents with the least possible amount of disruption.
>
> We, Jill and Sam, agree that we are both involved, committed, and loving parents who would like our children, Andy and Sara, to continue to have a meaningful relationship with each of us.
>
> We have always shared in the responsibility of raising Andy and Sara and we continue to trust and respect each other as parents. We agree that our children will benefit from a positive relationship with each of us and are committed to a shared parenting plan.
>
> We agree that the children's primary residence will be with Jill and that they will spend time with Sam according to the following 2-week schedule. During week 1, Sam will pick up the children Thursday after school, keep them overnight, and return them to school Friday morning. He will also drive them to school on two mornings. During week 2, Sam will pick up the

children Thursday after school and they will live with him until he returns them to school Monday morning.

We agree that there shall be full disclosure between us in all matters touching the welfare of Andy and Sara. We will confer as often as necessary to consider any matter requiring discussion, any problem or difficulty touching the welfare of the children.

We agree to discuss and make decisions together on all major issues relating to the children. Such issues shall include, but not be limited to, religious upbringing; education and choice of schools, health, and recreational activities; and attendance at any special events.

We agree that day-to-day decisions for the children will be the responsibility of the parent with whom they are residing, free of any interference from the other parent. We agree that although the parent with whom the children are residing has full responsibilty in making day-to-day medical decisions, the other parent is to be involved in all major decisions and promptly consulted and advised about illnesses or accidents.

We agree that we will attempt to maintain consistency with respect to major household rules but will otherwise honor one another's parenting style, privacy, and authority. We agree not to interfere in the parenting style of the other parent nor will we make plans or arrangements that would impinge on the other parent's authority or times with the children without expressed agreement of the other parent. We agree to encourage Andy and Sara to discuss their grievances with a parent directly with the parent in question.

We agree that we shall each have 2 weeks during the summer holidays to spend with Andy and Sara, the exact dates to be discussed and agreed on between us. We will share time with the children on all other holidays according to a schedule to be discussed and agreed on between us. We agree that neither of us will move our permanent residence outside of the immediate jurisdiction.

We agree that we will work together to resolve any disputes that may arise in regard to the provisions of this agreement. If any disputes arise that we cannot resolve, we agree to enter mediation before seeking a solution in court.

THEORY

One of the prime functions of scientific research is to develop theory that explains selected natural phenomena. This theory may be explicit or, as in the SP literature, left implicit. In neither case, however, can the effort escape the constraints of theory. As Harris (1970, p. 202) explains, "theoretical conceptions permeate the entire process of thinking, and facts always involve interpretation, so that no sharp distinction can be drawn between theory and observation."

Accordingly, inspection of the SP research literature indicates that authors operate within one of three theoretical frames of reference. The first involves a clinical model characterized by (a) concern with intra-psychic phenomena, especially affective states; (b) interest in the dis-covery of pathology, particularly problems with individual adjust-ments; (c) reliance on qualitative data, typically the clinical interview; and (d) use of the individual as the unit of analysis.

The second model may be characterized as *social psychological* in character (see Webster, 1975). This approach is characterized by (a) concern with intrapsychic states, especially subjective representations of role relations (e.g., parental attachment); (b) interest in interpersonal behavior, albeit from the individual's perspective; (c) heavy reliance on quantitative data, especially the use of standardized instruments, and (d) use of the individual as the unit of analysis.

The final model is that of *family systems theory* (see Benjamin, 1983). This approach is characterized by (a) concern with interpersonal be-havior, including associated affective and cognitive processes; (b) use of both qualitative and quantitative methods; and (c) reliance on a dyadic or triadic unit of analysis.

The distribution of authors by their theoretical preference is dis-played in Table 6.1. Most authors favor a social psychological approach (74%), with the clinical approach next in frequency (21%), and the systems approach least common (5%). This distribution is significant, for it immediately delineates the sorts of issues and questions deemed relevant and those excluded from examination. For example, it sug-gests that the primary unit of analysis is the individual respondent and that his or her perception of and response to particular people and situations is the prime subject of inquiry. From a systemic perspective, these analytic concerns are highly problematic, with individual re-sponses seen to reflect the larger family system of which respondents are members and within which their behavior is meaningful. It follows that, in the absence of data about that larger context, individual re-sponses become difficult to interpret.

TABLE 6.1 Theoretical Models Implicit in the Shared Parenting Research
Literature

Author(s)[a]	Year	Theoretical Models Clinical	Social/Psychological	Family Systems
1. Keshet & Rosenthal[b]	1978		X	
2. Abarbanel[c]	1979		X	
3. Ahrons[d]	1979			X
4. Gersick [e]	1979		X	
5. Grief [f]	1979a		X	
6. Nehls [g]	1979		X	
7. Steinman	1981		X	
8. Watson	1981		X	
9. White & Bloom	1981		X	
10. Ilfeld et al.	1982		X	
11. Awad	1983	X		
12. Rothberg	1983		X	
13. D'Andrea[h]	1983		X	
14. Phear et al.	1984		X	
15. Steinman et al.[i]	1985	X		
16. Frankel	1985	X		
17. Richards & Goldenberg[j]	1986	X		
18. Shiller[k]	1986a		X	
19. Luepnitz[l]	1986		X	
20. Isaacs et al.	1987	X		
21. McKinnon & Wallerstein[m]	1987	X		
22. Brotsky et al.	1988	X		
23. Koel et al.	1988		X	
24. Sandler et al.[n]	1988		X	
25. Coysh et al.	1989		X	
26. Glover & Steele	1989		X	
27. Kline et al.[o]	1989	X		
28. Nelson	1989		X	
29. Neubauer	1989		X	
30. Maccoby et al.[p]	1990		X	
31. Crosbie-Burnett[q]	1991		X	
32. Irving & Benjamin[r]	1991			X
33. Pearson & Thoennes[s]	1991		X	
34. Shier et al.[t]	1991		X	
35. Buchanan et al.[u]	1992		X	
36. Arditti[v]	1992a		X	
37. Donnelly & Finkelhor[w]	1993		X	
38. Kelly[x]	1993 [y]		X	
TOTAL		8	28	2
PERCENT		21	74	5

(Continued)

TABLE 6.1 (Continued)

NOTES: a. Shared parenting has been the subject of graduate work research, including: Cowen
  (1982, cited in Shiller, 1986b), Handley (n.d., cited in Ingram, 1989), Nunan (1980),
  cited in Richards & Goldenberg (1986), Pojman (1981, cited in Ilfeld et al., 1982), and
  Shavin (1976, cited in Grief, 1979a).
  b. See Rosenthal and Keshet (1978, 1981).
  c. Publication based on author's PhD thesis.
  d. See Ahrons (1980a) and Bowman and Ahrons (1985).
  e. Publication based on author's PhD thesis.
  f. See Grief (1979b).
  g. See Morgenbesser and Nehls (1981) and Nehls and Morgenbesser (1980).
  h. Publication based on author's PhD thesis.
  i. See Zemmelman, Steinman, and Knoblauch (1987).
  j. See Richards and Goldenberg (1985).
  k. Publication based on author's PhD thesis; see Shiller (1986b).
  l. See Luepnitz (1982).
  m. See also Kolata (1988).
  n. See Wolchik, Braver, and Sandler (1985).
  o. See Johnston and Campbell (1988) and Johnston, Kline, and Tschann (1989).
  p. See Albiston, Maccoby, and Mnookin (1990); Maccoby, Depner, and Mnookin (1988);
  Maccoby and Mnookin, in press; and Mnookin, Maccoby, Albiston, and Depner (1990).
  q. See Crosbie-Burnett (1989).
  r. Irving, Benjamin, and Trocme (1984); Irving and Benjamin (1986, 1989); and Benjamin
  and Irving (1990).
  s. See Pearson and Thoennes (1988, 1990).
  t. See Shier, Simring, Grief, Shapiro, and Lindentahl (1989).
  u. See Buchanan, Maccoby, and Dornbusch (1991).
  v. See Arditti (1992b).
  w. See Donnelly and Finkelhor (1992).
  x. See Kelly and Duryee (1993) and Kelly, Gigy, and Hausman (1988).
  y. See Kelly (in press).

More generally, like the divorce literature itself, the bulk of the SP research literature is, with few exceptions (Irving & Benjamin, 1991; Isaacs, Leon, & Kline, 1987; Kline, Tschann, Johnston, & Wallerstein, 1989; see also Tschann, Johnston, Kline, & Wallerstein, 1990) atheoretical. Rather, research has largely been driven by policy-related questions about identification (Donnelly & Finkelhor, 1993), logistics (Maccoby, Depner, & Mnookin, 1990), adjustment (Brotsky, Steinman, & Zemmelman, 1988) and litigation (Pearson & Thoennes, 1991). This point is not meant to belittle the importance of the issues in question, but to highlight the fact that custody choice per se cannot be separated from the larger processes associated with divorce. A theoretical model of the latter would presumably illuminate the relationship between divorce and custody (see chapter 2). Failure to address this relationship in the SP literature makes it less valuable than it otherwise might be.

METHODOLOGY

If the development of theory is one cornerstone of scientific research, another concerns the scientific method (Denzin, 1978). Operationally, methodology translates into a concern for study design and data analysis. Study design, in turn, involves study sample (size, recruitment procedure), operational definition of SP (i.e., sampling criteria), and the presence or absence of one or more comparison groups. Additional concerns specific to the SP debate include the use of clinical or normative samples and whether SP groups involve legal or physical SP. These data are displayed in Table 6.2.

Several aspects of this table stand out. First, sample sizes have tended to be small, generally ranging from 5 to 50. Furthermore, in the past, studies with large samples used cases drawn from court or clinic records. The problem with "case" data is that it was originally constructed for judicial or clinical purposes and so may be subject to a variety of unspecified biases when used for research purposes. In contrast, the last five years have seen a slow but steady increase in the number of studies with samples in excess of 100 and using instruments expressly designed for research purposes.

Second, study designs are markedly heterogeneous, varying in terms of the parental status of the respondents, the recruiting method used, and the use of clinical versus nonclinical respondents. For example, although a substantial minority of studies has concentrated on parents (without regard for gender; 42%), others have focused on fathers alone (21%), children alone (8%), or entire families (21%). In addition, researchers have relied on court (37%) or clinical (16%) records to recruit respondents or have used convenience or snowball samples (39%). Such varied sampling methods have been compounded by studies that focus on clinical (26%) or nonclinical (74%) families, but not both, that is, clinical and nonclinical samples have not been directly compared despite evidence of sharp differences between such groups in the divorce literature (Abelsohn & Saayman, 1991). Such variation is important because it reduces study comparability and in turn makes it difficult to use the findings of any one study to comment generally about SP as a custody option.

Third, heterogeneity is again evident in terms of the operational definition of SP, with the same result. In some cases, researchers

TABLE 6.2 Research Design in the Shared Parenting Research Literature

| | | | | Research Methods | | | | |
| | Sample[a] | | | Define | | | | Groups |
Author(s)	Subjects	Recruit	CL	s	c	a	CS	Comp.
1. Keshet & Rosenthal	29/128 Fa	N/I	N	X	-	X	-	No
2. Abarbanel	4 Fam	N/I	N	-	-	X	P	No
3. Ahrons	41 Par	Court	N	-	-	X	P+	No[b]
4. Gersick	15/40 Fa	Court	N	-	-	X	L	Yes
5. Grief	8/40 Fa	Snowball	N	-	-	X	P+	No
6. Nehls	18 Par	Court	N	-	X	-	P+	No
7. Steinman	24 Fam	Snowball	N	-	-	X	P	No
8. Watson	11/17 Par[c]	Court	N	-	X	-	P+	Yes
9. White & Bloom	3/40 Fa	Court	N	-	-	X	P	Yes
10. Ilfeld et al.	138/414 Ca	Court	N	-	X	-	P+	Yes
11. Awad	100 Ca	Clinic	Y	-	-	X	L	No[d]
12. Rothberg	30 Par	Snowball	N	-	-	X	P	No
13. D'Andrea	24/46 Fa	Snowball	N	-	-	X	P+	Yes
14. Phear et al.	109/500 Ca	Court	N	-	X	-	L	Yes
15. Steinman et al.	48 Par	Clinic	Y	-	-	X	P+	No
16. Frankel	32 Par	Clinic	Y	-	-	X	P	No
17. Richards & Goldenberg	10 Fa	Court	Y	-	-	X	P	No
18. Shiller	20/40 Par	Snowball	N	-	-	X	P+	Yes
19. Luepnitz	11/43 Fa[e]	Snowball	N	-	-	X	P+	Yes
20. Isaacs et al.	85/202 Par[f]	Clinic	N	-	-	X	L/P	Yes
21. McKinnon & Wallerstein	25 Fam	Clinic	Y	-	-	X	P+	No
22. Brotsky et al.	48 Fam	Snowball	Y	X	-	-	P	No[g]
23. Koel et al.	219/700 Fam	Court	N	-	X	-	L/P	Yes
24. Sandler et al.	44/158	Child	N	-	X	-	P	Yes
25. Coysh et al.	101/298 Par	Snowball	Y	X	-	-	P	Yes
26. Glover & Steele	8/24 Par	Snowball	N	X	-	-	P	Yes
27. Kline et al.	100 Fam	Clinic	Y	X	-	-	L/P	No
28. Nelson	34/121 Fam	Snowball	Y	X	-	-	P	Yes
29. Neubauer	6/40 Child	Snowball	N	-	-	-	P	Yes
30. Maccoby et al.	170/664 Par[h]	Court	N	-	-	X	L/P	Yes
31. Crosbie-Burnett	18/84 Par	Snowball	N	-	X		L	Yes
32. Irving & Benjamin	201/395 Par	Snowball	N	X	-	-	P+	Yes
33. Pearson & Thoennes	153/418 Par	Snowball	N	-	-	X	L/P	Yes
34. Shier et al.	35/105 Par	Court	N	-	X	-	L/P	Yes
35. Buchanan et al.	51/517 Child	Court	N	X	-	-	P+	Yes
36. Arditti	41/212 Fa	Snowball	N	-	X	-	P	Yes
37. Donnelly & Finkelhor	42/320 Fam	Random[i]	N	X	-	-	L[j]	No
38. Kelly	155/421 Par	Court	Y	X	-	-	P	Yes

(Continued)

TABLE 6.2 (Continued)

	Subjects	Recruit	CL s c a	CS	Comp.
TOTAL (%)	Fa 08 21%	N/I 02 05%	Y10 10 08 20%	P 14 37%	N 15 39%
	Fam 08 21%	Ct 14 37%	26% 26% 21% 53%	P+ 12 31%	Y 23 61%
	Par 16 42%	CL 06 16%	N28	L 05 13%	
	Ca 03 08%	Sn 15 39%	74%	L/P 06 16%	
	Ch 03 08%	Ran 01 03%		- 01 03%	

KEY: Fa = father, Par = parent; Fam = family; Ca = case (based on court or clinic records); CL = clinical case; Y = yes; N = no; Define = author definition of SP (s = defined by subject; c = defined by court; a = defined by author); CS = custody status (L = legal SP [primary residence]; P = physical SP [no primary residence]; P+ = more than 50% of subjects physical SP); Group Comp. = groups compared.

NOTES: a. Sample size is described in terms of the number of SP respondents, the larger sample total of which they were a part (if applicable), and their parental status (see Key).
b. Three different forms of custody are differentiated: SP, alternating custody, and split custody.
c. Sample includes three children of the parents: one sole custody, one SP, and one split custody.
d. Two variants of SP are distinguished: nonalternating SP (one residence, typically maternal) with or without dispute between parents, and alternating SP (two residences with or without dispute between the parents).
e. Includes both maternal and paternal sole custody.
f. Includes 41 physical SP, 28 mother legal SP, and 16 father legal SP.
g. Compare within group: successful, stressed, and failed SP.
h. Total sample: 1,620 parents in 1,128 families; sample used varies across publications.
i. Based on a crossnational random survey of households.
j. Authors recognize both formal and informal legal SP.

accepted respondents' perception that they were involved in an SP arrangement (26%), although closer examination of the 10 studies in question indicates that additional criteria (such as the absence of a primary residence, the presence of minor children, separated or divorced parents) were given the status of default values. In an additional minority of studies (21%), definition by the courts was used. This standard is problematic, because legal definitions of SP tend to vary across North American jurisdictions (see Folberg, 1991; Ingram, 1989). Most often, authors developed their own idiosyncratic selection criteria (53%). These varied from the default values noted above (Abarbanel, 1979), to highly specific definitions (Steinman, 1981), to de facto definitions (Maccoby et al., 1990) based on the number of transitions between homes or number of hours per week in each home.

Fourth, most authors have relied on respondents involved in a physical SP arrangement (37%) or with more than 50% of respondents in such an arrangement (35%). The emphasis on physical SP is noteworthy for two reasons. First, it misrepresents the preponderence of legal SP cases in North America and thus what SP *really* means in practice (see Weitzman, 1985). Second, early studies of legal SP samples (Phear, Beck, Hauser, Clark, & Whitney, 1984), because of their reliance on secondary data, have been limited in the questions addressed; only recently has a handful of studies appeared using primary data that included both legal and physical SP subsamples (13%), including an unpublished study by Walsh and Kalter (1986) using a normative sample (see below).

Finally, a bare majority of studies (61%) have directly compared SP and SC groups, most of them published within the past 5 years. As important, several of these studies are questionable in terms of "fairness." Those employing "case" data (Ilfeld, Ilfeld, & Alexander, 1982; Phear et al., 1984) are, as previously noted, both limited in extent and vulnerable to charges of bias. Several studies focus exclusively on fathers (Arditti, 1992a; D'Andrea, 1983; Luepnitz, 1986), useful for illuminating their experience but problematic because the experience of mothers and fathers differs markedly between SP and SC samples (Irving & Benjamin, 1991). Finally, several studies (Awad, 1983; Brotsky, Steinman, & Zemmelman, 1988; Irving & Benjamin, 1991; Luepnitz, 1986) suggest that both SP and SC groups are not internally homogeneous; rather, subtypes *within* each group may reliably be differentiated, in turn calling in question the studies that failed to make such distinctions.

These design characteristics render this literature methodologically suspect, despite improvements in rigor in recent years. Small sample size, for example, tends to limit generalizability whereas heterogeneity reduces comparability and reliability (Campbell & Stanley, 1963). Similarly, the infrequent use of comparison groups and the dearth of studies that both compare across groups and differentiate subtypes within groups all serve to weaken any claims—positive or negative—about the viability or efficacy of the SP alternative.

ANALYSIS

Given a sample of respondents, the next step in the research process involves collecting and analyzing the data (Anderson & Zelditch, 1968). The data collection and analysis procedures in use in the SP literature are displayed in Table 6.3.

Table 6.3 demonstrates that data analysis in SP research has undergone major change since its inception. Early studies concentrated on "weak" statistical measures and relied inordinately on the interview method. For example, of the 24 studies published before 1989, only eight (33%) used any statistical test, typically the chi square test. Although the latter is better than simple means or percentages, it can be problematic in the absence of measures of strength (such as gamma or lambda) without which spurious findings may be given weight (Nie, Hull, Jenkins, Steinbrenner, & Bent, 1975). Similarly, among the same set of studies, clinical or questionnaire-guided interviews were a standard means of data collection; 12 studies (50%) supplemented interviews with data from standardized instruments. Although we have no quarrel with the interview method, such data are notoriously vulnerable to charges of bias. It follows that the use of independent measures can only strengthen whatever claims are advanced. Here the utility of "triangulation" (Denzin, 1978; see Baker & Schulberg, 1973) to guard against bias has been well demonstrated. Conversely, variability across interviewers using clinical techniques has reliably been demonstrated (see Sartorius, Jablensky, Stromgren, & Shapiro, 1978). Thus the data analysis in the early SP literature can fairly be characterized as "weak."

This characterization stands in sharp contrast to the work published from 1989 on. Of the 14 studies in question, the majority (57%) used interviews supplemented with one or more standardized instruments, with two (14%) relying on standardized measures alone. Similarly, all but one of these studies used one or more statistical tests, typically analysis of variance or multivariate analysis. In short, the level of rigor in the analysis of data has markedly improved in the past 6 years.

TABLE 6.3 Data Collection and Analysis in the Shared Parenting Research Literature

	Data Collection		Statistics
	Interview	Instrument(s)	N D Ts
1. Keshet & Rosenthal	Xb	-	X - -
2. Abarbanel	Xa	-	X - -
3. Ahrons	Xb	Xs	- X -
4. Gersick	-	Xs	- X X
5. Grief	Xb	-	- X X
6. Nehls	-	X	- X -[a]
7. Steinman	Xa	X	- X -
8. Watson	Xb	-	- X -
9. White & Bloom	Xb	X	- X -[b]
10. Ilfeld et al.	-	-[c]	- X -
11. Awad	-	-[d]	X - -
12. Rothberg	Xa	-	- X -
13. D'Andrea	Xb	Xs	- X X
14. Phear et al.	-	-[e]	- X -
15. Steinman et al.	Xb	Xs	- X X
16. Frankel	-	-[f]	X - -
17. Richards & Goldenberg	Xb	-	- X -
18. Shiller	Xb	Xs	- X X
19. Luepnitz	Xb	Xs	- X X
20. Isaacs et al.	-	X	- X X
21. McKinnon & Wallerstein	Xa	-	- X -
22. Brotsky et al.	Xb	Xs	- X -
23. Koel et al.	-	-[g]	- X -
24. Sandler et al.	-	Xs	- X X
25. Coysh et al.	Xa	Xs	- X X
26. Glover & Steele	-	X	- X X
27. Kline et al.	Xa	Xs	- X X
28. Nelson	Xa	Xs	- X X
29. Neubauer	Xb	X	- X -
30. Maccoby et al.	Xb	-	- X X
31. Crosbie-Burnett	-	X	- X X
32. Irving & Benjamin	Xb	-	- X X
33. Pearson & Thoennes	Xb	Xs	- X X
34. Shier et al.	Xb	-	- X X
35. Buchanan et al.	Xb	Xs	- X X
36. Arditti	Xb	Xs	- X X
37. Donnelly & Finkelhor	Xb	-	- X X
38. Kelly	Xb	Xs	- X X
TOTAL (%)	- 11 29%	- 16 42%	N 04 11%
	Xa 07 18%	X 07 18%	D 34 89%
	Xb 20 53%	Xs 15 39%	Ts 21 55%

(Continued)

TABLE 6.3 (Continued)

KEY: Interview: Xa = yes, clinical, Xb = yes, questionniare guided, either stuctured or semistruc-
tured; Instrument(s): X = yes, either a standardized measure of some variable or one created
especially for the study in question, Xs = two or more instruments used; Statistics: N = none (no
numerical analysis), D = descriptive (e.g., mean, median, mode, standard deviation, frequency, and
simple percentage) only, Ts = one or more statistical tests (statistical procedures intended to meet a
conventional alpha of .05, including chi square, t test, analysis of variance (ANOVA), and regression
or multivariate analysis).

NOTES: a. The author refers to the use of the Mann-Whitney "U" test, but reports no such data
              in the published report.
         b. The authors employ both cluster analysis and analysis of variance, but these do not
              apply to the SP subsample because of the small sample size ($n = 3$).
         c. No instrument was employed here other than a data collection form used to tabulate
              court records.
         d. The author reports his "clinical impressions" only.
         e. No instrument was employed here other than a data collection form used to tabulate
              court records.
         f. No instrument was employed here other than a data collection form used to tabulate
              psychiatric records.
         g. No instrument was employed here other than a data collection form used to tabulate
              court records.

RESULTS

Our final concern is with the findings of SP research, which involves
two issues: the substantive areas of inquiry that are the foci of data
collection and the findings in these areas. The first issue is important,
for it speaks to the degree of consensus about matters deserving
attention. The second issue is important for a different reason. Given
the methodological deficiencies in this literature, it is impossible for a
single study to speak in a definitive sense to the viability or efficacy of
SP. The same may not be true of the literature *taken as a whole.* From this
perspective, methodological heterogeneity is (paradoxically) an advantage: If similar findings are consistently reported despite methodological variation, these findings may be given considerable weight.

Data about areas of inquiry are displayed in Table 6.4, which indicates that attention is primarily centered on six topic areas. Furthermore, coverage of these areas has been markedly uneven, ranging
from a high of 61% about "satisfaction" to a low of 42% about "parent-
child relations"; only five studies (13%) have addressed all six issues
(Abarbanel, 1979; Irving & Benjamin, 1991; McKinnon & Wallerstein,
1987; Pearson & Thoennes, 1991). Noteworthy is the fact that less than

TABLE 6.4 Areas of Substantive Inquiry in the Shared Parenting Research
Literature

		Substantive Area				
	Parents	Child	Co-P	P-C	Log	Sat
1. Keshet & Rosenthal	X	-	X	X	X	-
2. Abarbanel	X	Xd	X	X	X	X
3. Ahrons	-	-	X	-	X	X
4. Gersick	X	-	-	-	-	X
5. Grief	X	-	-	X	-	X
6. Nehls	-	Xi	-	-	X	X
7. Steinman	-	Xd	X	-	X	X
8. Watson	-	Xi	X	X	X	X
9. White & Bloom	X	-	X	-	X	X
10. Ilfeld et al.	-	-	-	X	X	
11. Awad	-	-	-	-	-	-
12. Rothberg	X	-	X	X	X	X
13. D'Andrea	X	-	-	X	-	X
14. Phear et al.	-	-	-	-	X	X
15. Steinman et al.	X	-	X	-	X	X
16. Frankel	-	-	X	-	-	-
17. Richards & Goldenberg	X	-	X	X	X	X
18. Shiller	X	Xd	-	X	-	-
19. Luepnitz	X	Xd	X	-	-	-
20. Isaacs et al.	-	Xd	-	X	X	-
21. McKinnon & Wallerstein	X	Xd	X	X	-	X
22. Brotsky et al.	X	Xd	-	X	-	-
23. Koel et al.	-	-	X	-	-	-
24. Sandler et al.	X	Xd	-	-	-	-
25. Coysh et al.	X	-	X	-	-	-
26. Glover & Steele	-	Xd	-	X	-	-
27. Kline et al.	X	Xd	X	X	-	-
28. Nelson	X	-	X	-	X	-
29. Neubauer	-	Xd	-	-	-	-
30. Maccoby et al.	-	Xi	X	-	X	X
31. Crosbie-Burnett	X	-	X	-	-	X
32. Irving & Benjamin	X	Xi	X	X	X	X
33. Pearson & Thoennes	X	Xi	X	X	X	X
34. Shier et al.	X	-	-	-	X	X
35. Buchanan et al.	-	Xd	-	-	X	X
36. Arditti	-	-	-	-	X	X
37. Donnelly & Finkelhor	-	-	X	-	X	-
38. Kelly	X	Xi	X	X	X	X

(Continued)

TABLE 6.4 (Continued)

		Substantive Area				
	Parents	Child	Co-P	P-C	Log	Sat
TOTAL	22	18	22	16	22	23
PERCENT	58	48	58	42	58	61
		Xi 06 16%				
		Xd 12 32%				

KEY: Parents = parental adjustment; Child = child(ren)'s experience, the data either obtained directly (d), by interviewing or testing the child(ren) or indirectly (i) based on parental reports; Co-P = coparental relations; P-C = parent-child interaction (e.g., parental involvement); Log = logistics (e.g., scheduling); Sat = parental satisfaction.

half of the studies in question (48%) have addressed the issue of child adjustment and only 12 (32%) report data taken directly from child respondents. Given that custody awards are primarily intended to safeguard the "best interests" of children, and given the controversy that still surrounds the SP option, such scant interest in the experience of SP children is remarkable.

As for the substantive findings, their summarization below is organized on the basis of the same six topic areas plus an "other" category.

Parental Adjustment

SP parents have been examined in one of three ways: their social and psychological adjustment to separation or divorce; their feelings about themselves as persons and as parents; and the extent to which they differ on either basis from SC parents.

In all three respects, there was considerable consensus. Separation or divorce was universally experienced as a difficult, stressful, and emotionally painful experience. For this reason, parents who encountered no adjustment problems after the dissolution of their marriage were rare, although the issues perceived by parents as problematic tended to vary by sex. Fathers, for example, reported feelings of guilt, anger, and depression as well as loneliness and a sense of loss. Mothers had to cope with many of the same feelings as well as the need to find employment (if they had not already done so) and the danger of becoming overburdened with simultaneous vocational and child care responsibilities.

Furthermore, Gersick (1979) notes that the more fathers felt betrayed by the divorce, the more likely they were to seek child custody for the "wrong" reasons: anger and revenge. Irving and Benjamin (1991) report similar findings among "dissatisfied" SP parents, especially mothers, whereas Maccoby et al. (1990) report that divorcing parents, especially fathers, may use custody as a bargaining ploy, with a minority of parents requesting SP when they really only wanted SC. Grief (1979a) found that as the frequency of father-child contact increased, the rapidity of fathers' emotional adjustment also increased. Related evidence comes from Rothberg (1983) and Irving and Benjamin (1991), both of whom found first that cordial relations between former spouses promoted parental adjustment, and second that the involvement of new intimate partners was either neutral or promoted adjustment. In addition, Crosbie-Burnett (1991) found that among remarried stepfathers, SP was associated with greater role ambiguity and under some circumstances greater competition between them and their biological counterparts.

SP parents appeared to fare somewhat better than their SC counterparts. On the one hand, this result relates to parental attributes prior to divorce. D'Andrea (1983) and Steinman et al. (1985), for example, found higher self-esteem among SP than SC parents. On the other hand, parental adjustment appears directly attributable to the child custody arrangement. Several authors (Irving & Benjamin [1991]; Steinman, Zemmelman, & Knoblauch [1985]; Shiller [1986a]) found that SP as opposed to SC parents reported less anger, guilt, and depression and were more satisfied with the continuity of parent-child and parent-parent contact. Although most fathers with physical SP had to make some adjustment to new parenting responsibilities, both their former wives and their children were available to assist them. Similarly, whereas mothers continued as before, the burdens associated with child care were now shared, providing them with more time alone.

Exceptions to these findings are reported. White and Bloom (1981) found that their SP fathers adjusted poorly compared to SC custodial or noncustodial fathers. Given a sample size of $n = 3$, however, it is hard to know how much weight to give these findings. Richards and Goldenberg (1986) report that fathers involved in physical SP had problems with role overload and hostile relations with their former spouses. In addition to caveats associated with sample size ($n = 10$), the authors' findings are qualified: spousal hostility did not interfere with father-child relations, which, in turn, reduced or eliminated a sense of loss or abandonment. Both Coysh, Johnston, Tschann, Wallerstein, and Kline (1989) and Pearson and Thoennes (1991) report high continuity between pre- and postdivorce parental attributes, but found no difference in parental adjustment based on custody type. McKinnon and Wallerstein (1987) and Kline, Tschann, Johnston, and Wallerstein (1989) report both poor adjustment among SP parents and a direct relationship between parental and child adjustment. Indeed, Kline et al. (1989) found that although the majority of the parents in their sample functioned well before their divorce, at the time of testing 64% showed evidence of a personality disorder. However, both sets of findings derive from clinical samples, which may be expected to have more problems than their nonclinical counterparts. Indeed, McKinnon and Wallerstein (1987) support such an interpretation by agreeing with Irving, Benjamin, and Trocme (1984) about the existence of dissatisfied SP parents.

Child(ren)

Two findings are consistent among the studies that report child data: A minority of children exhibit some degree of difficulty in adjusting to the demands of SP; and the proportion of such children and the severity of their problems were *never* worse than those reported by SC children, and were sometimes better.

For example, several authors note "good" SP child adjustment coupled with "high" SP child satisfaction and only "minor" transition difficulties (Buchanan, Maccoby, & Dornbusch, 1992; Neubauer, 1989; Pearson & Thoennes, 1991). The difficulties expected to arise from moving between households and living with parents having divergent lifestyles simply did not materialize in *most* cases. Most researchers attribute child adjustment to the closeness of these children's relationship with the residential parent (Buchanan et al., 1989; Neubauer, 1989).

Of the minority of SP children who experienced difficulty, Steinman (1981) found that 30% ($n = 32$) were "hyperloyal" and 25% were confused by residential transition; in general, 30% felt "overburdened" by the demands of SP. Shiller (1986a), who compared 20 SP and 20 SC boys, found that although both groups were above test norms on the Achenbach Child Behavior Checklist, SP children exhibited fewer problems, a finding consistent with parent and teacher reports. McKinnon and Wallerstein (1987), who explored the experience of 26 preschool SP children, found that four out of seven (57%) of the youngest children, and three out of 19 (16%) of the older children, showed evidence of "distress," with more severe distress among the older children. Kline et al. (1989), who explored the experience of 100 children in severely conflicted divorcing families, found that the majority were multisymptomatic around episodes of transition, especially among the younger children. Finally, Irving and Benjamin (1991), relying on parental reports, showed that first, only a minority of SP children were dissatisfied (10% to 25%); and second, parental perception of child satisfaction was directly related to parental satisfaction with SP; dissatisfied SP parents were significantly more likely than their satisfied counterparts to perceive that their children were dissatisfied with their custody arrangement.

Four factors appeared to predict child adjustment: continuity and closeness of parent-child interaction; regularity and predictability of child movement between households; coparental cooperation; and child age, with older children more likely than younger children to report distress associated with disruption of their peer relations together with enduring fantasies of parental reconciliation. Although there is consensus about the relevance of these factors, some disagreement persists about their relative salience. Luepnitz (1986), for example, found that a low-conflict family climate was critical to the adjustment of the 91 children in her sample and that child adjustment was independent of custody type.

Finally, in regard to the comparative merits of SP versus SC, authors using normative or clinical samples drew related conclusions. Among the latter, McKinnon and Wallerstein (1987) suggest that just as there is no evidence that SP protects children from the stress of divorce, so there is no evidence that children are better served by SC. Similarly, Kline et al. (1989) suggest that SP is probably contraindicated among families characterized by intense conflict. Among the former, both Luepnitz (1986) and Irving and Benjamin (1991) suggest that SP at its best serves the end of child adjustment better than SC at its best. Moreover, Donnelly and Finkelhor (1993) and Irving and Benjamin (1991) add that SP is not a panacea, because both SP and SC can fail; under such circumstances, neither serves the best interests of the children. The primary advantage of SP, based on available evidence, is that it is less likely to fail and thus provides a positive postdivorce experience to a greater proportion of the children involved in it.

Coparental Relationships

Both SP and SC promote interaction among divorced spouses, which suggests the possibility that ongoing mutual dissatisfaction may undermine their ability to cooperate with respect to child care. Here there is considerable agreement that coparental cooperation is more likely among SP as opposed to SC parents. Abarbanel (1979), for example, notes SP parental agreement around scheduling, child rearing values, and mutual support. Ahrons (1979) and Rothberg (1983) report SP joint decision making, information sharing, and general cordiality. Pearson and Thoennes (1991) and Steinman (1981) found SP parents friendly, tolerant of differences, nonviolent, and respectful of each other's parenting skills, with mutual anger kept away from the children (see also Richards and Goldenberg [1986]). Similarly, comparative studies such as Koel, Clark, Phear, and Hauser (1988), Irving and Benjamin (1991), Pearson and Thoennes (1991), and Steinman et al. (1985) report less conflict, greater mutuality, and more cooperation among SP as opposed to SC parents.

Exceptions include Frankel (1985), McKinnon and Wallerstein (1987), and Nelson (1989), all of whom report intense conflict among the SP parents in their clinical samples. However, the generalizability of these findings may be limited to the 17% of dissatisfied SP parents reported by Irving and Benjamin (1991) (see Benjamin & Irving, 1990). In accordance with this view, Maccoby et al. (1990) found that the nonclinical families in their sample distributed across four categories based on coparental cooperation rather than custody type: disengaged (29%), conflicted (34%), cooperative (25%), and mixed (11%).

Finally, cordiality among SP parents appears related to three factors: low predivorce conflict; intense commitment to child rearing; and continuity in parent-child involvement. The first factor implies a typological difference between SP and many SC families (see below). It may also relate to the finding that SP parents report fewer and less severe predivorce marital problems than SC parents (Irving & Benjamin, 1991). The second factor suggests greater mutuality regarding the salience and direction of child rearing values, what Irving and Benjamin (1991) call a "child orientation." The third factor may be the most important, for it eliminates care and control of the children as a bone of contention, especially among SC parents (Irving & Benjamin, 1987).

Parent-Child Relations

Three aspects of the parent-child relationship have been the focus of SP research. The first, already noted, concerns the greater likelihood of a "child orientation" among SP as opposed to SC parents (Irving & Benjamin, 1991), evidenced by the fact that choice of custody option is more likely to be mutual among SP parents (Gersick, 1979; Koel, Clark, Phear, & Hauser, 1988; Watson, 1981).

The second is an extension of the first: the level of predivorce parenting involvement, especially among fathers. Here there is near unanimity that SP fathers were highly involved in parenting before the divorce (Grief, 1979a; Richards & Goldenberg, 1986) and that this was more likely of SP as opposed to SC fathers (Irving & Benjamin, 1991). In addition, both Pearson and Thoennes (1991) and Shiller (1986a) note that SP compared to SC mothers were more likely to perceive their former spouses as understanding and supportive and to respect their parenting skills.

Finally, the third issue concerns the level of postdivorce parenting involvement, especially among fathers. Again, near unanimity is apparent: SP fathers demonstrate high levels of postdivorce parenting involvement (Grief, 1979a), and significantly more so than their SC counterparts (Arditti, 1992a; Coysh et al., 1989; Irving & Benjamin, 1991; Nelson, 1989; see Bowman & Ahrons, 1985). Indeed, continuity of parenting involvement appears to be the norm (Grief, 1979a).

In a related vein, D'Andrea (1983) notes that SP as opposed to SC parents were more knowledgeable about their children, more influential in their lives, and more satisfied with their level of child influence; the likelihood of physical SP was directly related to the level of parental involvement. Irving and Benjamin (1991), Luepnitz (1986), and

Pearson and Thoennes (1991) all note the greater likelihood that SP compared to SC mothers report a reduction in their child care burden. Shiller found that SP as opposed to SC children were likely to feel comfortable expressing their feelings (both positive and negative) and were less preoccupied by reconciliation fantasies. Isaacs, Leon, and Kline (1987), using the Draw-A-Family Test, report that SP as opposed to SC children were much less likely to omit the nonresident parent and were much more likely to perceive that both parents were responsible for their care. Glover and Steele (1989) found that SP children had a more positive relationship with their mothers than children in SC or intact homes. Buchanan et al. (1992) found no evidence of loyalty conflicts among children in SP families. They also noted that under conditions of high coparental conflict SP and SC children were equally likely to feel caught between parents; however, when coparental interaction was cooperative, SP children were less likely to feel "caught." Arditti (1992a) found that the higher contact between fathers and SP as opposed to SC children was associated with fathers' feelings of closeness to the child(ren) in question, adding that such closeness could arise *after* divorce when it had not been present before divorce.

Two exceptions were Kline et al. (1989) and Donnelly and Finkelhor (1993). The former, using a high conflict clinical sample, found that SP children indeed had more contact with their fathers than their SC counterparts, but that this level was also associated with an increase in behavior problems. Even so, they noted that SP fathers were less likely than their SC counterparts to abandon their children. The latter, Donnelly and Finkelhor (1993), found that the level of parent-child conflict was no different in SP and SC families and that conflict was best predicted by the level of coparental cooperation rather than custody type.

Logistics

SP is a logistically complex custody arrangement—including the movement of children between residences, variations in scheduling, and the sharing of parenting responsibilities—that invariably places great demands on SP parents.

Research has focused on three concerns: the nature of the child sharing schedule; the extent to which it is a source of conflict; and the identification of factors that may facilitate or impede the demands associated with SP.

The expectation that physical SP necessarily involves a 50-50 split has received little support. Rather, child sharing schedules vary widely (Irving & Benjamin, 1991). Indeed, Ingram (1989) notes two Canadian cases in which SP was awarded despite the fact that the parents in question lived on two different continents. This said, a weekly schedule is the single most common arrangement (Maccoby et al., 1990; Pearson & Thoennes, 1991; Richards & Goldenberg, 1986; Shiller, 1986a; Steinman et al., 1981).

Furthermore, there is general agreement around two additional findings: First, scheduling is the most contentious issue among SP parents (Irving & Benjamin, 1991; Nehls, 1979; Rothberg, 1983); and second, SP parents are characterized by flexibility and informal problem-solving (exception: McKinnon & Wallerstein, 1987). Similarly, conflict over scheduling seldom involves litigation (Ahrons, 1979; Maccoby et al., 1990; Steinman, 1981). Given the intensity of conflict typical among SC parents (see Irving & Benjamin, 1987), it is noteworthy that SP parents were significantly less likely than SC parents to perceive scheduling as a "serious problem" (Irving & Benjamin, 1991; see Benjamin & Irving, 1990). In this regard, Pearson and Thoennes (1991) found that 30% of divorced families with children reported some problems with visiting, but that was equally likely among SP and SC families.

Finally, there is agreement that residential proximity is a central facilitating factor (McKinnon & Wallerstein, 1987; Rothberg, 1983; Steinman, 1981; Watson, 1981). Irving and Benjamin (1991) found that residential proximity was directly related to the *absence* of a primary residence, that is, among those children reporting no primary residence, 55% lived "close" to each other compared to 33% who lived "far" apart. Although important, this trend should not be construed to mean that residential distance contraindicates SP. On the contrary, Irving and Benjamin (1991) report that most of the minority of SP parents (and most of their children) in their sample who lived some distance apart were "very satisfied" with their arrangements. Moreover, the benefits of proximity for the SP arrangement may involve other hidden costs, including limits to parental vocational advancement (Richards & Goldenberg, 1983). We will return to the issue of "primary residence" in a later section.

Satisfaction

The issue of satisfaction among SP parents and children has been widely explored. The consensus is that both SP parents and children report a "high" degree of satisfaction, with proportions ranging from 67% (Rothberg, 1983) to 84% (Ahrons, 1979; Irving & Benjamin, 1991; Neubauer, 1989).

In addition, SP parents are significantly more satisfied than SC parents (Ahrons, 1979; Crosbie-Burnett, 1991; D'Andrea, 1983; Grief, 1979a; Shier, Simring, Shapiro, Grief, & Lindentahl, 1991). Whereas Irving and Benjamin (1991) found no difference in overall satisfaction between the SP and SC parents in their sample, SP parents reported many fewer problems and less severe problems. Furthermore, Irving and Benjamin (1991) and Arditti (1992a) found that SP fathers were significantly more satisfied than their SC counterparts, with Irving and Benjamin (1991) noting that those able to establish a working arrangement in a year or less were much more likely to be satisfied than those who required more than a year or who had yet to achieve a working arrangement; child satisfaction was highly correlated with parental satisfaction. Crosbie-Burnett (1991) reports similar results among remarried SP families, especially those with female children. Maccoby et al. (1990) confirm that noncustodial SC and nonresidential SP parents were less satisfied than their custodial and residential counterparts, however, this feeling turned on coparental cooperation rather than custody type. Thus SP parents were most satisfied when coparental relations were cooperative and least satisfied when they were conflictual.

Finally, SP parents and children were often satisfied for different reasons. Parents were satisfied because SP was a voluntary as opposed to a court-imposed choice, and in light of joint decision making, helped with positive child postdivorce adjustment and was a relief from the burden of sole parenting. In contrast, children were satisfied because of the continuity of peer relations, reduction in tension in the home, and relief that they were no longer part of the marital battle (Neubauer,

1989). There was, however, one reason on which both parents and children concurred: parenting continuity. For SP fathers, this meant continuity of parental involvement in child care. Indeed, Kruk (1992) found that disruption of child contact was one of the main reason for child abandonment among SC fathers who had previously been highly involved in child care. For SP children, it meant feeling wanted and perceiving that both parents were involved in their care on an ongoing basis. Consequently, the majority of SP parents and children recommended SP to others in similar circumstances (Irving & Benjamin, 1991; Neubauer, 1989; Rothberg, 1983).

Other

Finally, five additional issues are noteworthy, but fit neatly into none of the above categories: (a) compliance in regard to child- and spousal-support payments; (b) the long-term durability of SP; (c) typological variation among SP families; (d) socioeconomic status; and (e) primary residence.

Support

Among women with SC, absent or irregular support payments are a common problem (Wallerstein & Blakeslee, 1988; Weitzman, 1985) and contribute to poverty among a significant proportion of these women and their children (see chapter 2). For this reason a number of jurisdictions across North America have established programs in which paternal support payments are made directly to the court, which passes them on to the SC mothers in question. Concomitantly, the court is empowered to pursue fathers who default or are in arrears.

In contrast, most studies of SP parents report consist paternal support (Luepnitz, 1986; Pearson & Thoennes, 1991; Steinman, 1981), although it can be a source of conflict (Rothberg, 1983). Irving and Benjamin (1991), for example, found that SP compared to SC parents were more likely to report "consistent" support payments (fathers: 88% versus 61%; mothers: 83% versus 61%). Similarly, Pearson and Thoennes (1991) found that SP as opposed to SC fathers were more likely to make their child support payments in full and on time. Indeed, they note that a number of parents selected SP with no child support against legal advice. Related findings are reported by Ilfeld, Ilfeld, and Alexander (1982), who found that over a 2-year period SP parents had a relitigation rate (16%) half that of their SC counterparts (32%) (see Luepnitz, 1986). Even when SP was ordered without the consent of both parents, their relitigation rate (33%) was no different than that of SC parents. Similarly, Irving and Benjamin (1991) report that SP parents were more likely to arrive at their custody arrangement through mutual agreement and, once the arrangement was in place, were more likely to alter its terms informally rather than through litigation (see Maccoby et al., 1990). Exceptions include the work of Koel, Clark, Phear, and Hauser (1988) and Phear et al. (1984), with both studies reporting that SP and SC parents exhibited similar relitigation rates. The basis of the difference between these findings and those of Ilfeld et al. (1988) is not clear, although variation in the distribution of SP subtypes may reduce their comparability. For example, nearly all of Phear et al.'s cases, based in Massachusetts (SP optional), involved legal SP, whereas Ilfeld et al.'s cases, based in California (SP preferred or presumed), may have involved an unknown but possibly greater proportion of physical SP. Only the cases examined by Koel et al. (1988), also based in Massachusetts, involved both legal and physical SP.

Durability

In the absence of longitudinal data, the absolute or relative durability of SP arrangements remain unclear. Only scattered data exist. Steinman et al. (1985) and Brotsky et al. (1988), for example, assessed 48 clinical SP families based on level of coparental cooperation. After 1 year of a 3-year study, Steinman et al. (1985) found that SP parents fell into three categories: successful (25%), stressed (42%), and failed (31%). On follow-up, Brotsky et al. (1988) found successful and failed groups unchanged whereas stressed SP families were "much improved." Within 1 year, 75% of Frankel's (1985) "cases" returned to court, whereas McKinnon and Wallerstein (1987) found that coparental cooperation was "rare." All three studies are suspect, because their clinical samples were likely biased in favor of SP dissatisfaction.

Such is not the case with Buchanan et al. (1992), who found that the likelihood of return to court varied by custody type, with SP arrangements more stable than paternal SC but less stable than maternal SC.

In contrast, Irving and Benjamin (1991) found that only a minority of their nonclinical SP parents were dissatisfied with their arrangement (17%) and of these only two families (5% of the dissatisfied subsample, less than 1% of the total sample) had returned to court seeking SC.

With ongoing longitudinal studies reported by Maccoby et al. (1990) and Kelly (1993), more information should soon be forthcoming on the important matter of durability.

Typological Variation

Most studies fail to distinguish typological variation *within* SP families. This omission is curious given recent publications in the divorce literature (see Ahrons & Rodgers, 1987; Vaughan, 1986). There are, however, a few exceptions. Awad (1983) distinguishes between four "types" of child custody: type 3 refers to "nonalternating joint custody" (that is, legal SP) whereas type 4 refers to "alternating joint custody" (that is, physical SP). In both types, parents in agreement or dispute are additionally distinguished. Although Awad's results indicate that type 3 parents fared better than type 4, the findings are problematic given the small sample size (SP $n = 12$) and the clinical character of his "cases." Similarly, Phear et al. (1984) found few differences between SP and SC cases, with 70% virtually identical. Although problematic given the use of court records and sparse in the range of variables examined, the data at least call attention to the difference between legal and physical SP.

Only recent studies allow for comparison of legal and physical SP subsamples. For example, in an unpublished study, Walsh and Kalter (1986) compared the experience in Michigan of 30 legal (maternal) SP and 30 maternal SC children, all seven to 12 years of age and equally split as to gender (18 boys, 12 girls). The authors found few differences between the two groups, either among the children (both were within the normal range, with about a third of each group "depressed") or the mothers (both groups reported equal levels of [high] coparental hostility), whereas the differences that were found were unrelated to custody type and were better explained in terms of predivorce parental differences. These results bear some resemblance to Luepnitz's (1986) finding that child adjustment was better predicted by the quality of postdivorce coparental and parent-child relations than by custody type (physical SP, paternal SC, maternal SC).

Other examples include Isaacs, Leon, and Kline (1987), who examined a group of 202 children divided into five custody groups: SP physical, maternal SP legal, paternal SP legal, maternal SC, and paternal SC; Koel et al. (1988), who used legal case data to compare 199 SP legal, 20 SP physical, and 479 SC families; Kline et al. (1989), who examined 100 clinical families, all of whom had legal SP but were otherwise distinguished by child residence: dual, maternal, or paternal; Maccoby et al. (1990), who distinguished between five groups (mother physical/legal [maternal SC], mother physical/joint legal, joint physical/legal [physical SP], father physical/joint legal, father physical/ legal [paternal SC]; Pearson and Thoennes (1991), who reanalyzed data from four previous studies and in turn reclassified respondent families as either SC, SP legal, or SP physical; and Shier et al. (1991), who recognized four custody types: SC (maternal, paternal) and SP (maternal, paternal), with SP either legal, physical, or both and either voluntary or court-ordered (involuntary).

With several of these studies ongoing, the thrust of the findings to date is similar to those of Walsh and Kalter (1986), that is, whereas major differences emerge between SP and SC families, there are comparatively few difference between legal and physical SP subtypes. For example, Koel et al. (1988) found that 71% of mothers who got legal SP also got physical SP, whereas this result was much less common (14%) among fathers. Kline et al. (1989) found that nonresidential SP fathers were more likely than their SC counterparts to abandon their children, although those who remained made contact with their children more frequently. Maccoby et al. (1990) found that although only 30% of their families exhibited high conflict about custody, SP physical was more likely than mother physical/joint legal to be a source of such conflict, despite which nearly all cases were resolved through negotiation rather than trial. Pearson and Thoennes (1991) report that physical SP parents were more positive than their legal SP counterparts who, in turn, were more positive than SC parents across a range of measures. For example, parenting responsibilities were seen as overwhelming by 40% of SC respondents, 30% of mother/SP legal respondents, and 13% of physical SP respondents.

Finally, Irving and Benjamin (1991) report three findings of special interest: first, that satisfied and dissatisfied SP parents differed systematically across a range of variables (see Benjamin & Irving, 1990); second, satisfied as opposed to dissatisfied SP parents were more likely to live in close proximity and to report no primary residence (i.e., physical SP); and, third, that typologically distinct groups emerged when custody type, gender, and satisfaction were interacted. The result of this analysis was a hierarchical array, with satisfied SP mothers and fathers at the top and dissatisfied SC fathers at the bottom.

Socioeconomic Status

Patterson (1982), using population data about household costs, projected additional expenses associated with SP ranging from $12,354 to $15,617. This finding implies that SP may be restricted to middle- to upper-class families. Support for this inference comes from several studies (Arditti, 1992a; Buchanan et al., 1992; Donnelly & Finkelhor, 1993) that consistently show that SP more than SC families are characterized by high income and education and low family size. This said, it is important to put these data in perspective. Among *both* higher and lower income families, SC is still the majority choice, and although SP is preferred by more high income than low income families, the SP arrangement can nevertheless be found among both groups. For example, Irving and Benjamin (1991) indicate that one third of their sample reported annual incomes below $20,000, with family income and outcome satisfaction unrelated among both SP or SC group. Moreover, Koel et al. (1988), based on data from Massachusetts, advance a conclusion that may apply across North America, namely, that as the SP option becoming increasingly popular, those who select it are also becoming more heterogeneous across a range of dimensions, including income and education.

Primary Residence

Finally, feminist authors have repeatedly charged that legal SP is unjust, giving fathers rights without corresponding responsibilities and effectively saddling mothers with care of the children (Delorey, 1989). In turn, researchers have begun to compare formal legal labels that would accompany a court-based custody award with de facto residency patterns, the number of hours per week children spend in the home of either parent. These efforts (Irving & Benjamin, 1991; Kelly, 1993; Maccoby et al., 1990; Shier et al., 1991) have yielded three findings: first, between 65% and 80% of children in divorced families with a formal SP award actually live with their mothers; second, between 20% and 35% of such children have no primary residence, spending between 35% and 50% of their time with one parent and the remainder with the other, especially among boys between 7 and 12 years of age (Maccoby et al., 1990; see also Donnelly & Finkelhor, 1993); and, third, such discrepancies apply to *all* formal custody labels, with Maccoby et al. (1990) reporting that 11% of maternal SC, 23% of paternal SC, and 43% of SP children actually move between residences, for an overall rate of de facto dual residence of 16%. The significance of de facto dual residence is that it is arrived at informally, through coparental negotiation, typically with the support of their children, and independent of the court. In this context, the rhetorical debate in the literature about whether SP is just or viable is moot; it is a reality, reflecting how a minority of divorced parents in North America choose to care for their children on a daily basis.

GLOBAL EVALUATION

Finally, in light of our methodological reservations about the SP research literature, we suggest it makes little sense to rely too heavily on any one study, but rather to examine the literature as a whole. The substantive summary, above, is one such approach. We also adopted an alternate approach, giving each study a global rating based on whether on balance the findings characterize the experience of SP respondents as positive, negative, or no different than their SC counterparts. The results are displayed in Table 6.5, which shows that two thirds of the studies were positive, one fourth were negative and one tenth showed no difference. Of the studies showing "no difference," two (Donnelly & Finkelhor, 1993; Phear et al., 1984) used weak measures, the third (Maccoby et al., 1990) is a longitudinal study that may yield positive or negative findings, and the final study (Coysh et al., 1989) used a clinical sample. Of the "negative" studies, seven of nine

TABLE 6.5 Global Rating of Studies in the Shared Parenting Research
            Literature

	Positive	Negative	No Different
		Global Rating	
1. Keshet & Rosenthal	X		
2. Abarbanel	X		
3. Ahrons	X		
4. Gersick	X		
5. Grief	X		
6. Nehls	X		
7. Steinman	X		
8. Watson	X		
9. White & Bloom		X	
10. Ilfeld et al.	X		
11. Awad		X	
12. Rothberg	X		
13. D'Andrea	X		
14. Phear et al.			X
15. Steinman et al.		X	
16. Frankel		X	
17. Richards & Goldenberg	X		
18. Shiller	X		
19. Luepnitz	X		
20. Isaacs et al.	X		
21. McKinnon & Wallerstein		X	
22. Brotsky et al.		X	
23. Koel et al.	X		
24. Sandler et al.	X		
25. Coysh et al.			X
26. Glover & Steele	X		
27. Kline et al.		X	
28. Nelson		X	
29. Neubauer	X		
30. Maccoby et al.			X
31. Crosbie-Burnett		X	
32. Irving & Benjamin	X		
33. Pearson & Thoennes	X		
34. Shier et al.		X	
35. Buchanan et al.	X		
36. Arditti	X		
37. Donnelly & Finkelhor			X
38. Kelly	X		
TOTAL (%)	25 66%	09 24%	04 10%

used clinical samples, with the remaining two (Awad, 1983; White & Bloom, 1981) both methodologically very weak. Finally, of the positive studies, these combine early studies that were methodologically suspect with current studies, most of them methodologically rigorous.

Thus the overall thrust of the SP research literature is positive, with some evidence of negative experience among clinical samples and additional evidence that for some dimensions, custody type per se including SP may be less salient than other factors, such as coparental relations.

DISCUSSION

Having reviewed the SP research literature and summarized the substantive evidence, we close by exploring the implications of these data in three areas: theory, research, and sociolegal practice.

Theory

Of the deficiencies in the SP research literature, none is more significant than the absence of *explicit* effort at theory building. Virtually none of the studies examined, including ours, seeks either to include an existing model or to derive a model by induction. This absence maintains SP research on the periphery of the social sciences and restricts the sophistication of the research designs in use. It follows that such theoretical efforts should be a primary future concern of SP researchers.

This point is not intended to belittle the practical concerns of policymakers and legal and human service personnel. The desire for guidance in legal decision making, counseling services, or fiscal expenditure is important. We contend, however, that theory development and these pragmatic interests are complementary. New theoretical formulations can only contribute to the interests of service personnel by reducing the level of "indeterminacy" in the social sciences, which Mnookin (1975) correctly sees as particularly problematic for them.

Research

If theoretical deficits are most significant, methodological deficiencies are most prominent. Here a half dozen changes are urgently required, some of them already underway, albeit on a small scale.

First, generalizability is hampered by small sample sizes, the absence of measures of reliability and validity, and reliance on basic methods of data analysis. All of this needs to change, as this field of study traverses the same course as the divorce literature, from exploratory to analytical efforts. Happily, this is one area in which some recent studies show good improvement.

Second, both family and couples research tend to get short shrift. The typical use of individual measures cannot subsequently be employed as ad hoc measures of family process without serious distortion (Reiss, 1981).

Similarly, more effort is required in selecting samples of couples rather than data derived from "parents" or "mothers/fathers." The importance of such work is underscored by Ahrons (1981), who reports that divorced spouses not only maintain an ongoing relationship, but their respective perceptions of that relationship tend to diverge (see also chapter 8).

Third, as Irving and Benjamin (1991) and Steinman et al. (1985) demonstrate, parent and child adjustment takes time, which points to the salience of longitudinal studies. Interaction processes, for example, may vary significantly over time as a function of child and parent development, the addition of new family members (through birth or remarriage) or their loss (through serial divorce or the departure of older children), the complications associated with forming binuclear family systems, and even statutory changes as SP families increase in prevalence. Ahrons (1980b) and a handful of others (cited above) are pursuing this line of inquiry. More such work is needed.

Fourth, if couples' data can only be derived from research samples containing both former spouses, the same is true with respect to child data. Too often, researchers have taken the easy (and less costly) route, relying on secondary parental reports rather than primary child data. This choice is curious, for the research instruments with which to conduct such efforts are plentiful (Kanoy & Cunningham, 1984).

A related concern is the merits of self-report measures versus those based on third-party observation. The former are widely favored over the latter. This choice is defensible. The experimental approach is much more complex than the use of a questionnaire or the completion of a face-to-face interview. That observational methods should be less widely used than their self-reporting counterparts is thus hardly surprising. Whether the results are comparable is another issue. Apart from the pitfalls attendant on questionnaire or interview methodologies (see Sartorius et al., 1978), it remains doubtful whether family members can accurately report on their interaction processes when they themselves may not be consciously aware of them. It follows that observation may be the only means to obtain such data.

Fifth, the comparison group design, although recently in more common use, still represents only a bare majority of the literature. This proportion is understandable in early exploratory work; single group designs are no longer defensible. Concomitantly, future concern should *not* be with the viability of SP, which has been demonstrated, but should address the more challenging task of examining the extent to which SP and SC are similar or different. Such specificity will require two forms of comparison group design. The first involves the comparison of SP and SC groups *matched* on demographic and social indicators. The second, more potent design will first identify specific SP (e.g., contested versus noncontested) and SC (e.g., maternal versus paternal custody) variants and compare them, both across and within *matched* groups. This approach would seek to identify the intervening and predictive variables with respect to both.

Finally, whereas existing studies are hypothesis-generating, more attention is required to make such hypotheses explicit and to subject them to empirical tests. Accumulation in science does not consist merely of additional findings, but includes a selective process that eliminates unprofitable lines of inquiry and classes of research question. Such ongoing refinement of formulations and designs profits us all by reducing wasted effort and making it unnecessary for researchers to reinvent the wheel.

Turning to analysis, we note an inordinate reliance on single methods and descriptive statistics. Both trends need to change and indeed appear to be doing so. Here, we echo Clingempeel and Repucci's (1982) call for more studies using multioperational and multidimensional methods. In this context, a word about the intersection between statistical methods and theoretical formulations is in order. All statistical procedures make specific assumptions about linear causality. Because these assumptions accord with the assumptions underlying the social psychological formulation, there is little trouble about "fit" between the two. Such is not the case with family systems formulations. Its recursive assumptions are simply not amenable to existing statistical procedures such that authors (such as Ahrons, 1979; Irving & Benjamin, 1991) are forced to employ linear causal models in their statistical analysis. This supports the use of multioperationalism, for only some combination of quantitative and qualitative methods will provide the data to substantiate the claims of systems theory proponents.

Similarly, the interpretation of results relates to the database in use. SP reviewers (such as Derdeyn & Scott [1984] and Steinman [1983]) have typically focused on the individual study. Moving the analysis up a level to the body of literature *taken as a whole* yields a different result, as we show above. Here, the literature's heterogeneity becomes an advantage. The logic of triangulation holds that if studies using divergent samples, focusing on different variables and employing different methods *all* generate similar findings, confidence is warranted in the empirical trends thus revealed. Despite our caveats about methodological variation in the SP research literature, reliable trends in the substantive findings are unmistakable, in turn providing a secure empirical base from which to draw conclusions. The same interpretation holds with regard to our global ratings.

Sociolegal Policy

Among *nonclinical* families with an SP custody arrangement, the reliable trends noted above include the following:

- High coparental agreement about child-rearing values and the salience of child rearing
- High parental involvement in child rearing
- High parenting continuity

- Good postdivorce parental adjustment
- Good postdivorce child adjustment
- High coparental cooperation on child care issues
- High compliance on scheduling and child support
- Informal resolution of disputed issues, including a low relitigation rate
- High parental and child satisfaction

These trends point to an optimal pattern of postdivorce spousal and parent-child relating. Although this pattern does not describe all SP families, it does establish an ideal against which all custodial arrangements may be assessed. In turn, we suggest that existing sociolegal policy be consistent with such an ideal. At present relevant statutes vary widely across North American jurisdictions. On the basis of earlier reviews, we argued in favor of a presumption of shared parenting (Benjamin & Irving, 1989; Irving & Benjamin, 1987). In light of more recent data, reviewed above, we now suggest that a uniform sociolegal policy should have the following features: (a) a philosophical bias favoring SP but (b) eschewing any presumptions, (c) a detailed and specific parenting plan, (d) a specified trial period, and (e) the routine provision of support services during the latter period. We conclude by elaborating on these changes.

Bias Favoring Shared Parenting

Evidence consistently indicates that most parents and children adjust well to an SP arrangement. Consequently, they make fewer demands on the state in terms of court or other costs associated with failure to provide child and spousal support. Moreover, comparative data indicate that SP *at its best* is at least as good as and often better than SC. On these bases, we continue to believe that SP would likely be the option of choice, other things being equal.

Absence of Presumption

That said, we have nevertheless moved away from a rebuttable presumption of SP, unlike Coller (1988) and Schwartz (1984). The basis of this shift is contained in the phrase "other things being equal," for in practice they seldom are. Instead, as seen in chapters 2 and 3, divorcing families display remarkable diversity. Such diversity carries over, as one would expect, to the area of child custody. Thus, as we have seen above, although many SP families adjust well, some do not, especially those toward the dysfunctional end of the parenting continuum. Furthermore, SP in specific subgroups of divorcing parents would conflict with the principle of the child's best interests. Accordingly, we now judge the presumption of SP as too confining, with specific classes of parental conduct particularly contraindicated. Elkin (1987) and Coller (1988) tender the following list:

- Inability to care for the child(ren), whether mentally, emotionally, or physically
- Significant substance abuse
- Physical or emotional abuse of spouse or child
- Intractable overt hostility over time between spouses despite mediation
- Great geographic distance in the case of very small children, making frequent changes of residences unmanageable
- Expressed desire of parents not to participate in SP

We concur, although we find the last item problematic (see below). Nor do we deny Coller's (1988) argument that judges have historically preferred SC (see Kelly, 1984 and note 1). However, the evidence reviewed above and in chapter 2 suggests that those preferences are changing, with SP becoming common in an increasing number of jurisdictions, although still in the minority. In turn, these changing preferences obviate the need to limit judicial discretion by imposing a statutory presumption. Rather, our preference is to increase such discretion, but only in combination with the additional features of our proposal discussed below.

Parenting Plan

Debate often centers on the viability or efficacy of SP versus SC. Data reviewed above indicate that in the majority of cases SP is both viable and comparatively more efficacious than SC. However, this line of argument misses the point, for the data also show that physical SP, legal SP, and SC (with or without access) all serve well the best interests of *some* children. Thus, the critical issue concerns not a statutory preference for one custody option over another, but rather *creating a parenting plan that best matches the needs of the child(ren) in question* (cf. Emery, 1994; Weitzman, 1985).

We suggest a preferred hierarchy of parenting arrangements or *plans*, with both physical and legal SP first, legal SP only second, and SC (with or without access) third. Matching plan to family should be guided by *both* best interest and the above parenting ideal: maximum parental involvement, parenting continuity, and mutual decision making about child care.

Parenting plans, although practical, also address an ideological objective: to replace the legal notion of "custody" with one that highlights the integral character of the parent-child relationship. Parents do not *own* their children and so should not be forced to struggle over who gets custody of them (Everett, 1984). Nor should parenting be decided on the basis of support for one ideological position or another. Rather, what is at stake is the relationship between family members and the sort of postdivorce relationship that serves the children's best interests. It is that relationship that is specified by a parenting plan, *not* the strength of each parent's claim to child ownership ("custody"). On a similar basis, we would place little faith in custody claims based solely on the number of hours devoted to child care, except as one among several indicators of parental involvement.

Trial Period

Related issues concern (a) whether SP should be *restricted* to voluntary couples or *extended* to those in which one or both partners prefer SC and (b) how to deal with inappropriate behavior by one or both SP parents.

Scarce evidence about the first issue suggests that the extended option may operate as well as or better than SC. Recall Ilfeld et al.'s (1982) finding that the relitigation rate of SP and SC parents were the same. In our work, although dissatisfied SP and SC fathers did not differ in most respects, the former alone maintained parenting continuity. Furthermore, Williams (1988), based on his clinical experience,

argues that "joint custody provides one of the best methods of stimulating a degree of significant and meaningful cooperation in warring
parents," adding "that cooperation should not be a criteria for joint
custody vs. sole custody schedules for children." Finally, Kelly (1983)
adds that

> some women legitimately refuse joint physical custody because they have
> lived with men who have emotionally or physically abused their children.
> And some seek relief from physical spousal abuse or harassment. Others
> who refuse, however, are angry and rejected women who seek revenge and
> a reinstatement of self-esteem by using their children to punish a spouse
> who has terminated the marriage. There are also women whose identities
> are so bound up in their role as full-time mother that they cannot envision
> sharing the parental role with the father without undue anxiety and fear for
> their own well-being. Furthermore, there are emotionally disturbed women
> who, due to their own pathology, vigorously fight a father's desire to be
> involved in the children's lives. Some additional women have been advised
> by friends or parents not to allow the father anything more than traditional
> every-other-weekend visitation. In these various instances, there may be no
> legitimate reasons based on the father's capacity to parent for refusing to
> consider joint custody. Yet the children of such women would be denied
> more generous access to their father despite the real possibility that in-
> creased contact could be more psychologically beneficial.

Thus, contraindicated parents excepted, and noting that fathers too
may resist SP for all of the reasons Kelly observes, *imposing* SP on
reluctant parents will at worst likely do *no more harm* than SC while
offering some parents an unexpectedly positive custody experience. It
is likely, however, that involuntary couples will be at higher risk than
voluntary couples of an unsatisfying arrangement. Accordingly, all
couples judged appropriate to an SP arrangement, whether voluntary
or involuntary, should enter SP for a trial period of between 6 and 12
months. At the end of that time, their experience should be reviewed
and SP either made permanent, modified, or abandoned.

As to inappropriate parental behavior, a trial period would provide
the opportunity to adjust terms and conditions in response to parental
complaints—which is what parents appear to do informally anyway—
with the court available to adjudicate intractable conflict. More impor-

tant, with the exception of contraindicated couples, SP should first be *seen to fail* before SC is regarded as an appropriate option.

Support

Finally, having become involved in SP, at present couples are more or less on their own. With respect to voluntary couples, this independence poses no problem; within 12 months most will have a working arrangement. For "at-risk" couples, the absence of support may prove more problematic. In turn, this situation suggests that SP be routinely coupled with some form of support. Although several options come to mind, our bias favors the use of family mediators (see Irving & Benjamin, 1987). They would serve three functions: to monitor the couple's progress during the trial period; to intervene as needed (e.g., by helping them work through conflict); and to report to the court the operation of the SP parenting plan and to recommend its continuation, modification, or replacement.

NOTES

1. Alternately, they look with favor on the primary caretaker presumption, whereby child custody is awarded to the parent who attends to most of the child's day-to-day needs "subject to the non-custodial parent's visitation rights" (Bruch, 1988; Neely, 1984; cf. Boyd, 1990).

2. It has also given rise to growing interest in judicial attitudes and behaviors regarding SP (see Belleck, Draughn, Waddell, & Buco, 1989; Racusin, Albertini, Wishik, Schurr, & Mayberry, 1989; Reidy, Silver, & Carlson, 1989; Settle & Lowery, 1982).

3. In some cases, a given study has yielded more than one publication. Thus the total number of research studies is 38 but the number of publications is 71 (see Table 6.1).

REFERENCES

Abarbanel, A. (1979). Shared parenting after separation and divorce: A study of joint custody. *American Journal of Orthopsychiatry, 49,* 320-329.

Abelsohn, D., & Saayman, G. S. (1991). Adolescent adjustment to parental divorce: An investigation from the perspective of basic dimensions of structural family therapy theory. *Family Process, 30*(2), 177-191.

Ahrons, C. R. (1979). The coparental divorce: Preliminary research findings and policy implications. In A. L. Milne (Ed.), *Joint custody: A handbook for judges, lawyers, and counselors*. Portland, OR: Association of Family Conciliation Courts.

Ahrons, C. R. (1980a). Joint custody arrangements in the postdivorce family. *Journal of Divorce, 3*, 189-205.

Ahrons, C. R. (1980b). A crisis of family transition and change. *Family Relations, 29*(4), 533-540.

Ahrons, C. R. (1981). The continuing coparental relationship between divorced spouses. *American Journal of Orthopsychiatry, 51*, 415-428.

Ahrons, C. R., & Rodgers, R. H. (1987). *Divorced families: A multidisciplinary developmental view*. New York: Norton.

Anderson, T. R., & Zelditch, M., Jr. (1968). *A basic course in statistics: With sociological application* (2nd ed.). New York: Holt, Rinehart & Winston.

Arditti, J. A. (1992a). Differences between fathers with joint custody and noncustodial fathers. *American Journal of Orthopsychiatry, 62*(2), 186-195.

Arditti, J. A. (1992b). Factors related to custody, visitation, and child support for divorced fathers: An exploratory analysis. *Journal of Divorce & Remarriage, 17* (3/4), 23-42.

Awad, G. A. (1983). Joint custody: Preliminary impressions. *Canadian Journal of Psychiatry, 28*, 41-44.

Baker, F., & Schulberg, H. L. (1973). A system model for evaluating the changing mental hospital. In F. Baker (Ed.), *Organizational systems*. Homewood, IL: Irwin.

Belleck, L. R., Draughn, P. S., Waddell, F., & Buco, S. M. (1989). Attitudes of attorneys and judges towards joint custody and its litigation. *Journal of Divorce, 12*(4), 103-116.

Benjamin, M. (1983). General systems theory, family systems theories, and family therapy: Towards an integrated model of family process. In A. Bross (Ed.), *Family therapy: A recursive model of strategic practice*. New York: Guilford.

Benjamin, M., & Irving, H. H. (1985). Shared parenting: A critical review of the research. *Canadian Social Work Review, 84*, 13-29.

Benjamin, M., & Irving, H. H. (1989). Shared parenting: Critical review of the research literature. *Family and Conciliation Courts Review, 27*(2), 21-35.

Benjamin, M., & Irving, H. H. (1990). Comparison of the experience of satisfied and dissatisfied shared parents. *Journal of Divorce & Remarriage, 14*(1), 43-61.

Bowman, M. E., & Ahrons, C. R. (1985). Impact of legal custody status on fathers' parenting postdivorce. *Journal of Marriage and the Family, 47*, 481-488.

Boyd, S. B. (1990). Potentialities and perils of the primary parent presumption. *Canadian Family Law Quarterly, 7*, 1-30.

Brotsky, M., Steinman, S., & Zemmelman, S. (1988). Joint custody through mediation: A longitudinal assessment of the children. *Conciliation Courts Review, 26*(2), 53-58.

Bruch, C. S. (1988). And how are the children? The effects of ideology and mediation on child custody law and children's well-being in the United States. *International Journal of Law and the Family, 2*(1), 106-126.

Buchanan, C. M., Maccoby, E. E., & Dornbusch, S. M. (1991). Adolescents' experience in divorced homes. *Child Development, 62*(5), 1008-1029.

Buchanan, C. M., Maccoby, E. E., & Dornbusch, S. M. (1992). Adolescents and their families after divorce: Three residential arrangements compared. *Journal of Research on Adolescence, 2*(3), 261-291.

Campbell, D. T., & Stanley, J. C. (1963). *Experimental and quasi-experimental designs for research*. Chicago: Rand McNally.

Clingempeel, W. G., & Repucci, N. D. (1982). Joint custody after divorce: Major issues and goals for research. *Psychological Bulletin, 91*, 102-107.

Clingempeel, W. G., Shuvall, M. A., & Heiss, E. (1988). Divorce and remarriage: Perspectives on the effects of custody arrangements on children. In S. A. Wolchik & P. Karoly (Eds.), *Children of divorce: Empirical perspectives on adjustment*. New York: Gardner.

Coller, D. R. (1988). Joint custody: Research, theory, and policy. *Family Process, 27,* 459-469.

Colman, G. C. (1989). Joint custody: Recent developments. *Canadian Family Law Quarterly, 4,* 1-38.

Coysh, W. S., Johnston, J. R., Tschann, J. M., Wallerstein, J. S., & Kline, M. (1989). Parental postdivorce adjustment in joint and sole physical custody families. *Journal of Family Issues, 10*(1), 52-71.

Crosbie-Burnett, M. (1989). Impact of custody arrangement and family structure on remarriage. *Journal of Divorce, 13*(1), 1-16.

Crosbie-Burnett, M. (1991). Impact of joint versus sole custody and quality of coparental relationship on adjustment of adolescents in remarried families. *Behavioral Science & Law, 9*(4), 439-449.

D'Andrea, A. (1983). Joint custody as related to paternal involvement and paternal self-esteem. *Conciliation Courts Review, 21*, 81-87.

Delorey, A. M. (1989). Joint legal custody: A reversion to patriarchal power. *Canadian Journal of Women and the Law, 3,* 33-44.

Denzin, N. K. (1978). *The research act* (2nd ed.). New York: McGraw-Hill.

Derdeyn, A. P., & Scott, E. (1984). Joint custody: A critical appraisal. *American Journal of Orthopsychiatry, 54,* 199-209.

Donnelly, D., & Finkelhor, D. (1992). Does equality in custody arrangement improve the parent-child relationship? *Journal of Marriage and the Family, 54,* 837-845.

Donnelly, D., & Finkelhor, D. (1993). Who has joint custody? Class differences in the determination of custody arrangements. *Family Relations, 42,* 57-60.

Elkin, M. (1987). Joint custody: Affirming that parents and families are forever. *Social Work, 32,* 18-24.

Emery, R. E. (1994). *Renegotiating family relationships: Divorce, child custody, and mediation.* New York: Guilford.

Everett, W. J. (1984). Shared parenthood in divorce: The parental covenant and custody law. *Journal of Law and Religion, 2,* 85-99.

Felner, R. D., & Terre, L. (1987). Child custody dispositions and children's adaptation following divorce. In L. Weithorn (Ed.), *Psychology and child custody determination.* Lincoln: University of Nebraska Press.

Ferreiro, B. W. (1990). Presumption of joint custody: A family policy dilemma. *Family Relations, 39*(4), 420-426.

Fidler, B. F., Saunders, E., Freedman, E., & Hood, E. (1989). Joint custody: Historical, legal, and clinical perspectives with emphasis on the situation in Canada. *Canadian Journal of Psychiatry, 34,* 560-568.

Fineman, M. (1988). Dominant discourse, professional language and legal change in child custody decision-making. *Harvard Law Review, 101*(4), 727-774.

Folberg, J. (1984a). Custody overview. In J. Folberg (Ed.), *Joint custody and shared parenting*. Washington, DC: Bureau of National Affairs and Association of Family and Conciliation Courts.

Folberg, J. (1984b). Joint custody statutes and judicial interpretations (as of January 1, 1984). In J. Folberg (Ed.), *Joint custody and shared parenting*. Washington, DC: Bureau of National Affairs and Association of Family and Conciliation Courts.

Folberg, J. (1991). Appendix A: Joint custody statutes and judicial interpretations (as of January 1, 1991). In J. Folberg (Ed.), *Joint custody and shared parenting* (2nd ed.). New York: Guilford.

Folberg, J., & Graham, M. (1981). Joint custody of children following divorce. In H. H. Irving (Ed.), *Family law: An interdisciplinary perspective*. Toronto: Carswell.

Frankel, S. A. (1985). Joint custody awards and children: A theoretical framework and some practical considerations. *Psychiatry, 48*, 318-328.

Furstenberg, F. F., Jr., & Nord, C. W. (1985). Parenting apart: Patterns of child rearing after marital disruption. *Journal of Marriage and the Family, 47*, 893-904.

Furstenberg, F. F., Jr., Peterson, J. L., Nord, C. W., & Zill, N. (1983). The life course of children of divorce: Marital disruption and parental contact. *American Sociological Review, 48*, 656-668.

Gersick, K. E. (1979). Fathers by choice: Divorced men who receive custody of their children. In G. Levinger & O. C. Moles (Eds.), *Divorce and separation: Contexts, causes, and consequences*. New York: Basic Books.

Glaser, S. (1989). Joint custody: Is it good for the children? *Editorial Research Reports, 39*, 58-68.

Glover, R. J., & Steele, C. (1989). Comparing the effects on the child of post-divorce parenting arrangements. *Journal of Divorce, 12*(2/3), 185-201.

Grief, J., & Simring, S. (1982). Remarriage and joint custody. *Conciliation Courts Review, 20*, 9-14.

Grief, J. B. (1979a). Joint custody: A sociological study. *Trial, 15*(5), 32-33, 65.

Grief, J. B. (1979b). Fathers, children, and joint custody. *American Journal of Orthopsychiatry, 49*, 311-319.

Harris, E. (1970). *Hypotheses and perception: The roots of scientific methods*. New York: Humanities.

Holmes, S. (1987). Imposed joint legal custody: Children's interests or parental rights? *University of Toronto Faculty Law Review, 35*, 300-321.

Ilfeld, F. W., Jr., Ilfeld, H. Z., & Alexander, J. R. (1982). Does joint custody work? A first look at outcome data or relitigation. *American Journal of Psychiatry, 131*(1), 62-66.

Ingram, A. P. (1989, March 4). *Joint custody since Baker and Kruger*. Institute of Continuing Legal Education. Toronto: Canadian Bar Association (Ontario).

Irving, H. H., & Benjamin, M. (1987). *Family mediation: Theory and practice of dispute resolution*. Toronto: Carswell.

Irving, H. H., & Benjamin, M. (1991). Shared parenting project: Overview and implications. In J. Folberg (Ed.), *Joint custody and shared parenting* (2nd ed.). New York: Guilford.

Irving, H. H., Benjamin, M., & Trocme, N. (1984). Shared parenting: An empirical study utilizing a large data base. *Family Process, 23*, 561-569.

Isaacs, M. B., Leon, G. H., & Kline, M. (1987). When is a parent out of the picture? Different custody, different perceptions. *Family Process, 26*(1), 101-110.

Johnston, J. R., & Campbell, L. E. G. (1988). *Impasses of divorce: The dynamics and resolution of family conflict*. New York: Free Press.

Johnston, J. R., Kline, M., & Tschann, J. M. (1989). Ongoing postdivorce conflict: Effects on children of joint custody and frequent access. *American Journal of Orthopsychiatry, 59*(4), 576-592.

Kanoy, K. W., & Cunningham, J. L. (1984). Consensus or confusion in research on children and divorce: Conceptual and methodological issues. *Journal of Divorce, 7*(4), 45-71.

Kelly, J. (in press). Developing and implementing postdivorce parenting plans: Does the forum make a difference? In J. Bray & C. Depner (Eds.), *Nonresidential parenting: New vistas in family life.* Thousand Oaks, CA: Sage.

Kelly, J. B. (1984). Examining resistance to joint custody. In J. Folberg (Ed.), *Joint custody and shared parenting.* Washington, DC: Bureau of National Affairs and Association of Family and Conciliation Courts.

Kelly, J. B. (1988). Long-term adjustment in children of divorce: Converging findings and implications from practice. *Journal of Family Psychology, 2,* 119-140.

Kelly, J. B. (1993). Current research on children's postdivorce adjustment: No simple answers. *Family and Conciliation Courts Review, 31*(1), 29-49.

Keshet, H. F., & Rosenthal, K. M. (1978). Fathering after marital separation. *Social Work, 23*(1), 11-18.

Kline, M., Tschann, J. M., Johnston, J. R., & Wallerstein, J. S. (1989). Children's adjustment in joint and sole physical custody families. *Developmental Psychology, 25*(3), 430-438.

Koel, A., Clark, S. C., Phear, W. P. C., & Hauser, B. B. (1988). A comparison of joint and sole custody agreements. In E. M. Hetherington & J. D. Arasteh (Eds.), *Impact of divorce, single parenting, and stepparenting on children.* Hillsdale, NJ: Lawrence Erlbaum.

Kruk, E. (1992). Psychological and structural factors contributing to the disengagement of noncustodial fathers after divorce. *Family and Conciliation Courts Review, 30*(1), 82-101.

Kuehl, S. J. (1989). Against joint custody: A dissent to the General Bullmoose theory. *Family and Conciliation Courts Review, 27*(2), 37-45.

Luepnitz, D. (1982). *Child custody: A study of families after divorce.* Lexington, MA: Lexington Books.

Luepnitz, D. (1986). A comparison of maternal, paternal, and joint custody: Understanding the varieties of post-divorce family life. *Journal of Divorce, 9*(3), 1-12.

Maccoby, E. E., Depner, C. E., & Mnookin, R. H. (1988). Custody of children following divorce. In E. M. Hetherington & J. D. Arasteh (Eds.), *Impact of divorce, single parenting, and stepparenting on children.* Hillsdale, NJ: Lawrence Erlbaum.

Maccoby, E. E., Depner, C. E., & Mnookin, R. H. (1990). Coparenting in the second year after divorce. *Journal of Marriage and the Family, 52,* 141-155.

Maccoby, E. E., & R. H. Mnookin (in press). *Custody after divorce: The social and legal dilemmas of custody.* Cambridge, MA: Harvard University Press.

McKie, D. C., Prentice, B., & Reed, R. (1983). *Divorce: Law and the family in Canada.* Ottawa: Statistics Canada, Research and Analysis Division.

McKinnon, R., & Wallerstein, J. S. (1986). Joint custody and the preschool child. *Behavioral Science and Law, 4*(2), 169-183.

McKinnon, R., & Wallerstein, J. S. (1987). Joint custody and the preschool child. *Conciliation Courts Review, 25,* 39-47.

Mnookin, R. H. (1975). Child custody adjudication: Judicial functions in the face of indeterminacy. *Law & Contemporary Problems, 39*(3), 226-293.

Mnookin, R. H., Maccoby, E. E., Albiston, C. R., & Depner, C. E. (1990). Private ordering revisited: What custodial arrangements are parents negotiating? In S. D. Sugarman & H. H. Kay (Eds.), *Divorce reform at the crossroads*. New Haven, CT: Yale University Press.

Neely, R. (1984). The primary caretaker parent rule: Child custody and the dynamics of greed. *Yale Law and Policy Review, 3*, 168-186.

Nehls, N. H. (1979). Joint custody of children: A descriptive study. In A. L. Milne (Ed.), *Joint custody: A handbook for judges, lawyers, and counselors*. Portland, OR: Association of Family & Conciliation Courts.

Nehls, N. H., & Morgenbesser, M. (1980). Joint custody: An exploration of the issues. *Family Process, 19*, 117-125.

Nelson, R. (1989). Parenting hostility, conflict and communication in joint and sole custody families. *Journal of Divorce, 13*(2), 145-157.

Nett, E. M. (1993). *Canadian families: Past and present* (2nd ed.). Toronto: Butterworths.

Neubauer, R. (1989). Divorce, custody, and visitation: The child's point of view. *Journal of Divorce, 12*(2/3), 153-168.

Nie, N. H., Hull, C. H., Jenkins, J. G., Steinbrenner, K., & Bent, D. H. (1975). *Statistical package for the social sciences* (2nd ed.). New York: McGraw-Hill.

Opie, A. (1993). Ideologies of joint custody. *Family and Conciliation Courts Review, 31*(3), 313-326.

Patterson, M. (1982). The added cost of shared lives. *Family Advocate, 5*(2), 10-13, 46.

Payne, J. D. (1979). Co-parenting revisited. *Family Law Review, 2*, 243-252.

Payne, J. D., & Edwards, B. (1991). Cooperative parenting after divorce: A Canadian legal perspective. In J. Folberg (Ed.), *Joint custody and shared parenting* (2nd ed.). New York: Guilford.

Payne, J. D., & Patrick, J. B. (1979). Divided opinion on joint custody. *Family Law Review, 2*(3), 163-172.

Pearson, J., & Thoennes, N. (1988). Supporting children after divorce: The influence of custody in support levels and payments. *Family Law Quarterly, 22*, 319-319.

Pearson, J., & Thoennes, N. (1990). Custody after divorce: Demographic and attitudinal patterns. *American Journal of Orthopsychiatry, 60*(2), 233-249.

Pearson, J., & Thoennes, N. (1991). Child custody and child support after divorce. In J. Folberg (Ed.), *Joint custody and shared parenting* (2nd ed.). New York: Guilford.

Phear, W., Beck, J., Hauser, B., Clark, S., & Whitney, R. (1984). An empirical study of custody agreements: Joint versus sole legal custody. In J. Folberg (Ed.), *Joint custody and shared parenting*. Washington, DC: Bureau of National Affairs and Association of Family and Conciliation Courts.

Racusin, R. J., Albertini, R., Wishik, H. R., Schurr, P., & Mayberry, J. (1989). Factors associated with joint custody awards. *Journal of the American Academy of Child and Adolescent Psychiatry, 28*(2), 164-170.

Reidy, T. J., Silver, R. M., & Carlson, A. (1989). Child custody decisions: A survey of judges. *Family Law Quarterly, 23*, 75-87.

Reiss, D. (1981). *The family's construction of reality*. Cambridge, MA: Harvard University Press.

Ricci, I. (1989). Mediation, joint custody and legal arrangements: A time to review, revise and refine. *Family and Conciliation Courts Review, 27*(1), 47-55.

Richards, C. A., & Goldenberg, I. (1985). Joint custody: Current issues and implications for treatment. *Journal of Family Therapy, 13*, 33-40.

Richards, C. A., & Goldenberg, I. (1986). Fathers with joint physical custody of young children: A preliminary look. *American Journal of Family Therapy, 14*, 154-162.

Robinson, H. (1983). Joint custody—An idea whose time has come. *Journal of Family Law, 21*, 641-685.

Robinson, H. (1985). Joint custody: Constitutional imperatives. *Cincinnati Law Review, 54*, 27-65.

Rosenthal, K. M., & Keshet, H. F. (1978). The impact of child care responsibilities on part-time and single fathers. *Alternative Lifestyles, 1(4), 465-491.*

Rosenthal, K. M., & Keshet, H. F. (1981). *Fathers without partners: A study of fathers and the family after marital separation.* Totowa, NJ: Roman & Littlefield.

Rothberg, B. (1983). Joint custody: Parental problems and satisfaction. *Family Process, 22*, 43-52.

Sandler, I. N., Wolchik, S. A., & Braver, S. L. (1988). The stressors of childrens' postdivorce environments. In S. A. Wolchik & P. Karoly (Eds.), *Children of divorce: Empirical perspectives on adjustment.* New York: Gardner.

Sartorius, N., Jablensky, A., Stromgren, E., & Shapiro, R. (1978). Validity of diagnostic criteria across cultures: A preliminary report from the international pilot study of schizophrenia. In L. C. Wynne, R. L. Cromwell, & S. Mathysse (Eds.), *The nature of schizophrenia.* New York: John Wiley.

Schwartz, S. F. G. (1984). Towards a presumption of joint custody. *Family Law Quarterly, 18*, 225-246.

Settle, S. A., & Lowery, C. R. (1982). Child custody decisions: Content analysis of a judicial survey. In E. O. Fisher & M. S. Fisher (Eds.), *Therapists, lawyers, and divorced spouses.* New York: Haworth.

Shier, D. K., Simring, S. K., Grief, J. B., Shapiro, E. T., & Lindenthal, J. J. (1989). Child custody arrangements: A study of two New Jersey counties. *Journal of Psychiatry & Law, 17*, 9-20.

Shier, D. K., Simring, S. K., Shapiro, E. T., Grief, J. B., & Lindenthal, J. J. (1991). Level of satisfaction of fathers and mothers in joint and sole arrangements: Results of a questionnaire. *Journal of Divorce & Remarriage, 16(3/4)*, 163-169.

Shiller, V. M. (1986a). Joint versus maternal custody for families with latency age boys: Parent characteristics and child adjustment. *American Journal of Orthopsychiatry, 56*, 486-489.

Shiller, V. M. (1986b). Loyalty conflicts and family relationships in latency age boys: A comparison of joint and maternal custody. *Journal of Divorce, 9(4)*, 17-38.

Singer, J., & Reynolds, W. (1988). A dissent on joint custody. *Maryland Law Review, 47*, 497-523.

Steinman, S. B. (1981). The experience of children in a joint custody arrangement: A report of a study. *American Journal of Orthopsychiatry, 51*, 403-414.

Steinman, S. B. (1983). Joint custody: What we know, what we have yet to learn, and the judicial and legislative implications. *University of California at Davis Law Review, 16*, 739-762.

Steinman, S. B., Zemmelman, S. E., & Knoblauch, T. M. (1985). A study of parents who sought joint custody following divorce: Who reaches agreement and sustains joint custody and who returns to court. *Journal of the American Academy of Child Psychiatry, 24*, 545-554.

Teachman, J. D., & Polonko, K. (1990). Negotiating divorce outcomes: Can we identify patterns in divorce settlements? *Journal of Marriage and the Family, 52*, 129-139.

Tschann, J. M., Johnston, J. R., Kline, M., & Wallerstein, J. S. (1989). Family process and children's functioning during divorce. *Journal of Marriage and the Family, 51,* 431-444.

Tschann, J., Johnston, J., Kline, M., & Wallerstein, J. (1990). Conflict, loss, change and parent-child relationships: Predicting children's adjustment during divorce. *Journal of Divorce, 13,* 1-22.

Vaughan, D. (1986). *Uncoupling: Turning points in intimate relationships.* New York: Oxford University Press.

Wallerstein, J. S., & Blakeslee, S. (1988). *Second chances: Men, women, and children a decade after divorce.* New York: Ticknor & Fields.

Walsh, M. C., & Kalter, N. (1986). *Joint legal custody versus sole maternal custody: A comparison of the effects of custody arrangements on the post-divorce adjustment of children.* Paper presented at the Annual Conference of the American Orthopsychiatric Association.

Watson, M. A. (1981). Custody alternatives: Defining the best interests of the children. *Family Relations, 30,* 474-479.

Webster, M., Jr. (1975). *Actions and actors: Principles of social psychology.* Cambridge, MA: Winthrop.

Weitzman, L. J. (1985). *The divorce revolution: The unexpected social and economic consequences for women and children in America.* New York: Free Press.

White, S. W., & Bloom, B. C. (1981). Factors related to the adjustment of divorcing men. *Family Relations, 30,* 349-360.

Williams, F. S. (1988, January). Child custody and parental cooperation. *Joint Custodian,* pp. 1-5.

7

Shared Parenting and Sole Custody

A Complex Comparative Analysis

INTRODUCTION

From an overview of the shared parenting literature (chapter 6), we turn to our original research. To place it in context, consider that the history of research in divorce and child custody has been one of successive refinement and differentiation. As seen in chapter 2, early divorce research was consumed with the issue of the pathological consequences of divorce. This monolithic view (Sprenkle & Cyrus, 1983) rationalized research that was primarily cross-sectional and unidimensional (Clingempeel & Reppucci, 1982). More recent efforts have come to see divorce as a complex phenomenon. Consequently, differential analyses have become the order of the day, with research characterized by multidimensional explorations of subgroups of divorcing couples (Little, 1982; Montalvo, 1982).

AUTHORS' NOTE: This is a modified version of a chapter originally published as Irving, H. H., & Benjamin, M. (1991). Shared parenting project: Overview and implications. In J. Folberg (Ed.), *Joint custody and shared parenting* (2nd ed.). New York: Guilford. Reproduced with permission.

The study of child custody has followed a roughly similar developmental course, but offset by perhaps a decade (Atkeson, Forehand, & Rickard, 1982; Kanoy & Cunningham, 1984). Early efforts concentrated on the pathological consequences of divorce among children (Burgess, 1970; Gardner, 1974). Typically, researchers relied on parental reports rather than data drawn from children themselves (Kurdek & Blisk, 1983). Later efforts again came to the realization that child custody was more complex than was first thought. Researchers now carefully distinguish between child age (Kurdek, 1981; Wallerstein & Kelly, 1980), child sex (Arnold, Wheeler, & Pendrith, 1980; Hetherington, 1980; Kurdek & Berg, 1983), and the relationship between the children and their same-sex or opposite-sex custodial or noncustodial parent (Hess & Camara, 1979; Hetherington, 1979).

Recently, an additional categorical distinction has gained increasing attention, that of custody type (Luepnitz, 1982; Phear, Beck, Hauser, Clark, & Whitney, 1984). For much of this century, custody type was not problematic, because 90% of all dependent children were given into the custody of their mothers (Cherlin, 1981; McKie, Prentice, & Reed, 1983). This situation changed in the 1970s with the appearance of a new custody option, joint custody or *shared parenting* (SP) in which care and control of the child(ren) was the responsibility of both parents, legally or physically. As we have seen in chapters 2 and 6, SP has become the norm in some states and has come to represent a substantial minority of all custody awards in many states and provinces.

In this context, much of the debate about the desirability and efficacy of shared parenting has been largely ideological, with proponents (Grief & Simring, 1982; Kelly, 1983, 1984; Morgenbesser & Nehls, 1981) and critics (Caroll, 1982; Gardner, 1982; Patterson, 1982; Weitzman, 1985) arguing vehemently, but largely in the absence of data (Clingempeel & Reppucci, 1982). More recently, a small but rapidly expanding research literature has arisen. Among other things, our review demonstrates that these research efforts followed the same developmental course as previous studies of child custody and divorce. That is, until very recently most studies were purely descriptive; relied on small, unrepresentative samples; used weak or unreliable measures; and examined a narrow range of variables. For example, with respect to the latter, although a proportion of dissatisfied shared parents was routinely noted (Irving & Benjamin, 1987), no study until about 1989 had explored in detail the basis for the satisfaction or dissatisfaction of shared parents.

To compensate for some of these deficiencies and on the assumption that it is as important to know how shared parenting fails as how it succeeds, we undertook the Toronto Shared Parenting Project.[1] To date only partial accounts of the results have been published (Irving & Benjamin, 1986; Irving, Benjamin, & Trocme, 1984). In what follows, we present a comprehensive summary. Beginning with a brief statement of the project's objectives and methodology, the findings will be reported followed by a discussion of their implications for legal policy and clinical practice.

OBJECTIVES AND METHODOLOGY

The objectives of the Toronto Shared Parenting Project were (a) to derive a large sample of divorced couples with dependent children who were involved in either sole (maternal) custody or shared parenting; (b) to examine these sample populations in terms of a broad range of variables selected on the basis of a detailed review of the relevant literature (see chapter 6); (c) to compare and contrast these samples to identify the variables, variable clusters, or interaction effects that significantly differentiate between them; and (d) to derive from these data implications relevant to policy and practice.

Achieving these ends, however, proved problematic. Shared parenting is not legally recognized as such in Canada. Consequently, there is no simple way of discovering its incidence or distribution. This situation precluded random sampling by means of the public record; nor did we have the resources to undertake random sampling on a household basis. The alternative involved snowball sampling targeted on several specific sources, including appeals in the media (both newspaper and radio), personal contacts, and a letter sent to more than 20 child care or parenting groups.

Sampling criteria included (a) residence within metropolitan Toronto (population: 2.5 million); (b) English-language proficiency; and (c) the perception by both parents that they shared care and control of their child(ren). The last criterion was intended as the rough equivalent of legal joint custody in the United States (cf. Steinman, 1983).

The final sample consisted of 395 respondents: 201 shared and 194 maternal sole custody parents. Both subsamples were evenly divided between men and women. SP respondents encompassed 75 couples (75% of the total subsample) and 51 individuals. Sole custody respondents included 42 couples (43% of the total subsample) and 112 individuals. Limited resources restricted data gathering to adult respondents.

Respondents were interviewed for 1.5 to 2 hours using a 114-item questionnaire specifically designed and pretested for the present study. The questionnaire combined Likert-type questions with open-ended or probe questions. The final database encompassed 268 variables together with additional items derived from the open-ended questions. In all cases, the questionnaire was administered in the respondents' home. Statistical analysis relied on chi square using an alpha of .05 and a gamma (a strength coefficient) of .20.

The results indicated that of a sample of 201 shared parents, 167 (83%) were classified as satisfied and 34 (17%) as dissatisfied. Respondents were so classified by means of a 12-item satisfaction index. Constituent items were as follows: satisfaction with the process of shared parenting (V124); parent satisfaction with the visitation schedule (V171); child satisfaction with the visitation schedule (V172); the effect of shared parenting on the children (V173); change in the level of satisfaction among parents (V174); change in the level of satisfaction among children (V175); satisfaction with the shared parenting arrangement (V179); the quality of the shared parenting experience (V180); time to a smooth working shared parenting arrangement (V181); parent satisfaction with shared child-rearing responsibilities (V251); child satisfaction with shared child-rearing responsibilities (V252); and recommend shared parenting (V268).

Derivation of the satisfaction index used principal component analysis, which involved three steps. First, principal component analysis was applied to generate a scale incorporating the common elements of constituent items, with the weight of each component a function of how much it shared with the other items. In addition, missing values for each item were replaced by their mean score to maximize the number of respondents included in the analysis.[2] Next, intercorrelations were run between each item and the scale which, together with the principal component analysis, revealed high consistency and thus good internal validity.[3] Finally, the scale was collapsed into two categories—satisfied and dissatisfied—based on the distribution of responses to its constituent items. On inspection of this distribution, the cutoff point was set at 3.59.

THE FINDINGS

The findings will be reported in four parts concerned respectively with shared parents, sole custody (SC) parents, comparison *within* the shared parenting subgroup, and comparison *across* the two SP and SC subgroups.

Shared Parents

The majority of SPs were in the age range 30 to 39 years and lived a middle-class lifestyle, with most men service, technical, or teaching professionals. SPs typically had two children between the ages of 1 and 12 in what was the first marriage for both partners. The majority were nonpracticing Protestants.

In the majority of cases, the wife initiated the marital separation, which had been in place at the time of testing for an average of 3 years. Value differences and communication problems were the major bases for the separation, with most respondents describing the level of marital conflict as mild to moderate. One third of these respondents were remarried or living common-law; whereas the remainder lived alone, 65% reported involvement in a new intimate relationship that had been in place from 6 months to 3 years. Among former spouses, the majority lived less than five miles from each other, many only a "short walk" apart.

SP was usually suggested by fathers, family friends, or a third party, either a clinician or a lawyer. Most couples reported little previous knowledge of it and most selected it for one of three reasons: It best reflected their mutual investment in child rearing; it was thought best for the child(ren); or it appeared the best way to minimize the trauma of the divorce for the child(ren). Friends and relatives were perceived as hostile to this custody choice. In only 60% of couples was a lawyer directly involved in drafting their separation agreement. Lawyers were

typically seen as supportive of a shared parenting arrangement, although fewer than half actually recommended it. Overall, 60% of
lawyers were rated "helpful."

At the time of testing, respondents had been involved in an SP
arrangement for an average of 3 years. In the majority of couples, care
and control of the child(ren) was mutual and in 40% no primary
residence for the children was cited, that is, the child(ren) moved
between residences on a prearranged schedule. This arrangement was
related to the distance between residences: among those who lived
close together, mutual care and control was typical whereas maternal
control was much more likely among those who lived far apart. Nevertheless, all SPs saw themselves as having mutual responsibility for the
children (whether or not there was a primary residence) and all perceived their arrangement as "different" from a sole custody arrangement.

Once established, their SP agreement was usually maintained without disruption. In addition to shared responsibility for child care, this
agreement stipulated cost sharing and the child-sharing schedule. As
to costs, most respondents reported either a 50-50 or a 75-25 arrangement, with husbands bearing the major cost burden in the latter case.
These arrangement were typically maintained without incident. As to
child care, the majority of respondents reported a weekly child-sharing
schedule (weekdays with one parent, weekends with the other) on the
grounds that it was thought best for the child(ren). Although both
parents reported a high level of child-rearing involvement prior to
their divorce, only fathers reported a significant increase in such involvement following the initiation of SP.

Coparental relations were described by most respondents as
"friendly," with communication typically positive but restricted to
child-rearing issues. In most cases, the involvement of former spouses
in a new intimate relationship was seen as having either a positive
effect or no effect on their SP arrangement.

Finally, as noted above, 83% of respondents reported satisfaction
with their shared parenting arrangement and almost 90% recommended it to parents in a similar situation. Satisfaction was directly
related to the length of time it took to achieve a smooth working
relationship, with those who reached this state in less than a year

significantly more likely to report satisfaction than those who took more than a year.

Sole Custody Parents

Although the *absence* of sex differences characterized SPs, the *presence* of such differences was typical of sole custody respondents.

The majority of sole custody parents were in the age range 30 to 39 years, lived a middle-class lifestyle, were usually nonpracticing Protestants, and had been married for 9 or more years when they separated. However, the men had significantly more income and education than the women.

At the time of testing, most couples had been separated for 5 or more years. About a third of respondents were either remarried or living common-law, which was more common among men than women. Although the remainder lived alone, the majority had been involved in a new intimate relationship for several years. In most cases, the separation was initiated by the wife, although husbands were more likely to recall it as having been a mutual decision. Differences in personal values and communication as well as violence and alcohol abuse were typically cited as the reasons for the marriage failure, with the last two grounds more often cited by women than men. Women were also more likely to report ongoing feelings of hostility toward their former spouses.

Respondents had been involved in a sole custody arrangement for more than 3 years at the time of testing. Most, especially the women, had responded positively to the idea of this arrangement and it received the support of relatives, friends, and the lawyers for both spouses. About half of all respondents reported having some previous information about sole custody. Most selected it because they thought it best for the child(ren), it was seen as the only possible choice, or it was a way to punish the former spouse. In almost all cases, the agreement was prepared with the aid of their lawyers, most of whom were seen as "helpful."

As to their custodial agreement, it specified both child visitation and child care costs. In 70% of cases all child care costs were assumed by the men, with twice-monthly visits the norm. Women were far more likely than men to report noncompliance with payment or visitation.

Coparental relations were usually described as "friendly," although women were more likely to report that sole decision making was a burden and that the child(ren) were upset after a visit with their father. In contrast, men were more likely to report a significant reduction in parenting involvement following divorce. As for their involvement in a new intimate relationship, women and men saw it differently. Men reported that it had a positive effect whereas women felt that it had no effect on their custody arrangement.

Finally, 71% of sole custody respondents reported satisfaction with their custody arrangement, although it was significantly more likely among women than men. Dissatisfied respondents reported a range of problems, especially financial or the burden of sole decision making. In addition, women complained of the lack of time for themselves, whereas men were dissatisfied with the lack of time with the children. Dissatisfied respondents were also those most likely to still be struggling with their arrangement more than a year after its inception and were significantly more likely than their satisfied counterparts to relitigate.

Comparative Analysis: Satisfied versus Dissatisfied Shared Parents

Analysis compared the responses of satisfied and dissatisfied shared parents in five areas: sociodemographics, marital separation, the initiation of shared parenting, the shared parenting agreement, and the coparental relationship.

Sociodemographics

Satisfied and dissatisfied SPs were entirely comparable with respect to most of the indices examined. Both groups were in the age range 30 to 39, lived a middle-class lifestyle, had two children, were typically Protestants, and most had been married once (80%). Typically, the wife initiated the end of the marriage (70%), which had been in place for an average of 9 years. Respondents had lived apart for an average of 3 years at the time of testing and the majority (57%) reported mild to moderate marital conflict. Although 65% of respondents lived alone (with their children), the majority of these (65%) were involved in a new intimate relationship, which had been in place from 6 months to 3 years. Most respondents (78%) resided within five miles of each other, with many (45%) only a "short walk" apart.

Satisfied SPs, however, had a narrower range of income ($20,000 to $50,000, Canadian) and more education (completed university) than their dissatisfied counterparts. In addition, satisfied SPs were significantly *less* likely to report that their own parents had been divorced (11% versus 27%) and *more* likely to indicate that they lived within a short distance of their former spouses.

Marital Separation

Satisfied SPs were more likely than their dissatisfied counterparts to describe the preseparation relationship with their former spouses in "positive" terms. For example, satisfied parents were *more* likely to use descriptors such as "caring," "reasonable," "supportive," and "cooperative" and *less* likely to use the descriptor "bitter." In a similar vein, satisfied parents were more likely to describe their degree of marital conflict as "mild" or "moderate" (23% versus 12%), compared to dissatisfied parents, who were more inclined to use the descriptor "extreme" (39% versus 64%). Finally, satisfied as opposed to dissatisfied parents were more likely to judge that their marital separation had *not* adversely effected the child(ren).

Initiation of Shared Parenting

For parents with children, marital separation is necessarily associated with the choice of a custody option. In this context, satisfied SPs were more likely than their dissatisfied counterparts to have selected SP jointly. Concomitantly, the former as opposed to the latter were much more likely to have reacted positively to the suggestion of shared parenting (81% versus 56%) and were less likely to have experienced a change of heart with increasing experience. Indeed, of those parents who reported a change in their response to the notion of SP, satisfied as opposed to dissatisfied parents were significantly more likely to indicate that their opinion had become "more positive" or "much more positive."

Related differences were apparent on inspection of open-ended items. Satisfied and dissatisfied parents had divergent reasons for selecting SP. Among satisfied parents, SP was selected because it was in the best interests of their children or it normalized child rearing following divorce. By contrast, dissatisfied parents did so because they felt they had been coerced, in the interests of obtaining a cheap divorce, as a way of increasing the likelihood of reconciliation, as a way of avoiding another traumatic confrontation, or as a way of ensuring contact with the child(ren).

Furthermore, among dissatisfied parents, whereas wives were more likely than husbands to suggest termination of the marital relationship, for child custody husbands were more likely than wives to express a preference for SP. The open-ended responses of wives suggest that they often conceded to SP because of guilt over the effects of separation on the child(ren) or as a concession to pressure by their former spouse. In short, many dissatisfied wives saw the choice of SP as in some sense coerced. Ironically, dissatisfied husbands preferred SP because of the coercion they felt was implied in sole custody, especially in regard to child access and visitation.

Returning to the quantitative data, although many in both groups had engaged a lawyer, for a larger proportion of satisfied as opposed to dissatisfied parents the choice of custody option and the creation of the agreement with respect to this selection was made *without* the involvement of a lawyer. Satisfied parents were also more likely than their dissatisfied counterparts to rely on a verbal as opposed to a written agreement. Similarly, the former were much more likely than the latter to report satisfaction with the process of arranging their SP agreement.

Shared Parenting Agreement

The result of the above process was an SP arrangement, which may be characterized in several ways, each of which differentiates between satisfied and dissatisfied parents.

First, satisfied as opposed to dissatisfied parents were much more likely to have an arrangement in which there was no primary residence for the child(ren) (42% versus 12%); children simply moved between residences. Open-ended responses suggest that the presence of a primary residence was an important source of resentment and bitterness among dissatisfied parents. Wives, who typically provided primary child care, felt angry that not only were their former spouses not burdened in the same way, but nevertheless continued to have a major say in child-rearing decisions. Husbands, who typically lived apart from the child(ren), feared that major child-rearing decisions might be made without their participation and that future loss of child contact was a real possibility.

Second, satisfied as opposed to dissatisfied parents were more likely to have a formal, written schedule concerning the movement of children between homes. The creation of this schedule was less likely to have involved a lawyer among the former than the latter. Conversely, the schedule was more likely to be a source of satisfaction among the former than the latter; this difference was similarly true of their respective views of their child(ren). Consequently, not only were satisfied as opposed to dissatisfied parents more likely to perceive SP as having had a "positive" effect on their child(ren), among those whose level of satisfaction had changed, it was more likely to have become "more positive" among the former than the latter.

Again, these findings were reflected in open-ended responses. Among satisfied parents, there was sufficient congruence among husbands' and wives' descriptions that a coherent picture of the details of their child sharing schedule was not difficult to assemble. Such was not the case among the dissatisfied parents. Indeed, the lack of congruence was so striking and so consistent as to render their accounts typically incomprehensible. In turn, the child-sharing schedule was the single most frequent source of complaint among dissatisfied parents.

Third, satisfied as opposed to dissatisfied parents were more likely to describe shared parenting in terms of mutuality, both between former spouses as well as in terms of their relationship with their child(ren). Thus the former were significantly more likely than the latter to associate SP with joint decision making, shared responsibility (71% vs. 35%), shared cost, regular interaction with their former spouses, joint parenting, parenting continuity, increased parental participation in child rearing, access of the child(ren) to both parents, and increased opportunity for personal privacy.

Fourth, satisfied as opposed to dissatisfied parents were more likely to adhere to agreed-on financial and child sharing schedules. Concomitantly, return to court for purposes of adjusting their agreement was significantly *less* likely among the former than the latter. Similarly, there was a trend ($p < .08$) indicating that satisfied parents were more likely than their dissatisfied counterparts to have sustained their initial agreement through time.

These differences were reflected in open-ended responses. Many dissatisfied parents reported that their agreement had undergone numerous negotiated revisions since its inception and now bore little resemblance to its original form. Indeed, a handful of these respondents were then in the process of relitigation in an effort to secure a sole custody arrangement. It was not surprising, then, that many dissatisfied parents identified the legal processes associated with obtaining and maintaining their SP arrangement as highly problematic.

The consequences of these various features of their SP agreement were twofold. On the one hand, satisfied as opposed to dissatisfied parents were able to establish a working arrangement much sooner; indeed, many dissatisfied parents were still struggling more than a year after the inception of their agreement. On the other hand, divergent descriptions of the advantages and disadvantages of SP emerged. Satisfied parents reported advantages such as shared responsibility, a feeling of achievement, the ability to remain flexible, support for a desired lifestyle, enjoyment associated with shared parenting, more time for oneself, and child(ren) who were perceived to like the proximity of both parents, felt comfortable with the child-sharing schedule, and generally felt secure with their current custody arrangement. By contrast, dissatisfied parents were more likely to highlight a range of disadvantages, including inconvenience, lack of time, transition difficulties, frequent separations, the feeling of being emotionally and physically drained (17% versus 62%), recurrent problems, the need to make major shifts in personal identity, the possibility of decisions about the child(ren) being made without the participation of one of the spouses, and spouses who failed to abide by the terms of their shared parenting agreement.

Coparental Relationship

Shared parenting necessarily entails the maintenance of some sort of coparental relationship. In this area, too, satisfied and dissatisfied parents differed markedly. The thrust of these differences concerned the degree of mutuality among the former as opposed to the latter.

Thus, compared to their dissatisfied counterparts, satisfied parents were more likely to report that joint decision making was the norm; their former spouse could always be contacted when needed; communication with their former spouse was "warm" and "friendly" (74% versus 21%), and personal differences in lifestyle rarely affected their relationship with their former spouse. Similarly, among satisfied as opposed to dissatisfied parents, such issues as child-rearing decisions, daily routine, child-rearing approaches, personality differences, finances, and the frequency of child sharing were *not* problematic. Satisfied parents were even able to discuss matters other than the child(ren), at least some of the time, particularly mutual friends and their careers.

This quantitative impression was confirmed by respondents' qualitative remarks. Dissatisfied parents typically characterized their relationship with their former spouse in terms of poor communication and pervasive feelings of bitterness; indeed, several respondents stated that they could no longer tolerate *any* contact with their former spouse. Consequently, repeated contact between such spouses was experienced as highly problematic and becoming increasingly so.

Turning to the children, much the same picture emerges. Satisfied parents were more likely than their dissatisfied counterparts to indicate that the child(ren) were rarely upset following shifts between homes. Furthermore, the former were more likely than the latter to associate SP with increased postseparation parenting involvement, with the result that they now felt closer to their child(ren) than before. They were also more likely to perceive that the child(ren) were satisfied with their current child-rearing arrangement.

Finally, we explored respondents' feelings concerning the reciprocal effects of combining a new intimate relationship with a SP arrangement. Both subgroups agreed that SP had little effect on a new romantic relationship. Satisfied parents, however, were more likely than their dissatisfied counterparts to indicate that involvement in a new intimate relationship had a "positive" effect on their effort to create and maintain a working shared parenting arrangement. This indication was confirmed in open-ended responses in which dissatisfied parents indicated that a new intimate partner—especially one involving a live-in partner (i.e., a common law or marital relationship)—was typically experienced as an additional source of tension and conflict. Not surprisingly, satisfied as opposed to dissatisfied parents were far more likely to recommend SP as a custody option of choice.

Comparative Analysis: Shared Versus Sole Custody Parents

Direct comparison between SP and SC subgroups involved three phases. Phase 1 compared these sets of parents *at the group level*. Phase 2 combined custody status with (a) sex *or* (b) satisfaction. Finally, Phase 3 explored the combination of custody status, sex, *and* satisfaction. Furthermore, the latter analysis was restricted to nine subgroups of particular clinical interest. In addition, insofar as analysis of Phase 1 showed that certain variables were especially potent predictors of outcome, analysis in subsequent phases was restricted to six clusters of variables—referred to here for convenience as the *selected process profile* (SPP)—encompassing a total of 23 variables.[4]

Phase 1

The central finding was that SPs exhibited a significantly more positive SPP than their sole custody counterparts. This profile included, for example, more agreement about marital separation and custody choice, less preseparation marital conflict, more child-sharing contact, more joint decision making, more adherence to the financial aspects of their agreement, a more positive coparental relationship, greater parental involvement in child rearing, less time to reach a smooth working arrangement, and a greater number of issues about which they reported satisfaction (e.g., shared parenting responsibility).

Phase 2A: Sex

The first part of the analysis in Phase 2 focused on the relationship between custody status and sex. This showed that SPs consistently exhibited a more positive SPP than their sole custody counterparts. This outcome was expected *within* sex; we correctly predicted that SP women would display a more positive profile than sole custody women. What was surprising was that these findings held *across* sex:

Not only did SP women display a more positive SPP than sole custody men, but the same was true for SP men relative to sole custody women.

Phase 2B: Satisfaction

The second part of the analysis in Phase 2 examined the relationship between custodial status and satisfaction. Although the same trends were evident as are reported above for sex, the findings were some-what more heterogeneous. Satisfied SPs exhibited a more positive SPP than satisfied or dissatisfied sole custody parents. Although there was no difference between groups when both were *dissatisfied*, dissatisfied SPs still exhibited a more positive SPP than *satisfied* sole custody parents.

Phase 3

The findings of Phase 2, at the group level, suggest that all custodial parents do not experience their arrangement in the same way; rather, their adjustment distributes along a continuum from highly positive among satisfied SPs to highly negative among dissatisfied sole custody men. Analysis in Phase 3, at the individual level, yielded a still more complex picture involving three distinct patterns of difference.

First, when both sets of spouses were satisfied, SPs consistently exhibited a more positive SPP than their sole custody counterparts, both men and women. For example, satisfied SP women reported more sources of satisfaction than their satisfied sole custody counterparts.

Second, satisfied spouses always exhibited a more positive SPP than dissatisfied spouses, irrespective of custody option or sex. Satisfied sole custody women, for example, reported greater satisfaction with their visitation schedule than their dissatisfied SP counterparts.

Finally, when both sets of spouses were dissatisfied, sex was a critical differentiating variable: dissatisfied men showed no differences, irre-spective of their custody status; however, among dissatisfied women, SP women displayed a more positive profile (e.g., more frequent child sharing contact) than their sole custody counterparts.

These data suggest that custody status, sex, and satisfaction combine in complex ways to determine the adjustment of parents and children to their particular custodial arrangement.

DISCUSSION

In the majority of cases, when it worked well, SP offered parents and children an optimal arrangement that only improved through time. Although it offered superior benefits to a smooth working sole custody arrangement, that too could be quite satisfying, especially for the women and children. Finally, although *both* SP and sole custody could yield intensely troublesome and unhappy arrangements, the former alone at least offered the solace of continual contact between the child(ren) and both their parents.

Thus, although SP is not for everyone, it offers a range of distinct advantages for those who select it. The choice of SP appears especially indicated among couples who exhibit a combination of the following attributes:

- Low to moderate levels of preseparation conflict
- Child-centered orientation to parenting
- Mutuality with respect to the decision to end their marital relationship and to select SP
- Motivation among both parents to accept and overcome the day-to-day exigencies and complications invariably associated with SP

IMPLICATIONS:
POLICY AND PRACTICE

These findings hold a range of implications for both legal policy and clinical practice. In closing, we briefly mention a handful of examples in each category.

Legal Policy

The policy implications center on change of existing child custody statutes and the attitudes of lawyers and judges. The first and most central is the universal recognition of a general principle: Following divorce, it is in the best interests of children that they maintain frequent, reliable, and ongoing contact with both their parents (see Isaacs, 1988).

The existing judicial preference for sole custody is rooted in a historical context that favors an adversarial approach centered on the individual. Both facets of this preference have become increasingly problematic. The adversarial system, with its emphasis on "winner take all," tends to promote protracted conflict rather than the spirit of compromise (Schwartz, 1984) crucial to solutions in keeping with the best interests of the child. Similarly, the focus on individual rights, responsibilities, and obligations promotes a conception of the family seen as a collection of individuals and too often transforms the children into pieces of property over whose ownership or control parents may struggle. This attitude flies in the face of the family systems literature, which holds that the organization of family systems is independent of the members taken one at a time; such systems shape the manner in which members perceive and experience both each other and the external world; and the patterned relationships that constitute family life bond members together and provide a context within which members' behavior is meaningful (Benjamin, 1983; Reiss, 1981).

From this perspective, the fact that sole custody disrupts the relationship between the children and the noncustodial parent (usually the father) violates one aspect of the child(ren)'s sense of self. Given that concern for the best interests of the child is a universally accepted second general principle (Derdeyn, 1976a, 1976b), it follows that child custody statutes should rest on a parenting plan best suited to the needs of the children and the circumstances of the family. Given the above findings, we suspect that, more often than not, that will involve some form of shared parenting. By comparison with sole custody, SP promotes joint coparental involvement and decision making as well as fiscal responsibility and encourages maximum contact between the child(ren) and both parents. As we have seen, the split need not be 50-50, either in time or in money, to be satisfying for all parties. Nor, in most cases, do distance or movement between residences prove to be insurmountable problems.

Given the high level of mutuality among most SPs, this implication may not be problematic so long as parents agree. But what if they do not and child custody becomes a matter of contention between them? We still believe that SP makes good sense *on a provisional basis*. Our data show that even when SPs are unhappy with their situation, there is still a greater degree of parent-child contact within SP as opposed to a sole custody arrangement. Recall too that SP fathers were far more likely than their sole custody counterparts to become actively and extensively involved in parenting despite the fact that both reported comparable levels of parenting before the divorce (see Kelly, 1983).

This option would require that judges have the authority to order SP even when the parents disagree. In this view, parents' rights to care for their child(ren) and child(ren)'s rights to maintain their relationship with both parents are not lost in divorce and then "won back" through the courts. Rather, these respective rights can be lost or limited only for just cause. Accordingly, the onus is on the judge to state explicitly why in a given case he or she developed the parenting plan in question, including the reasons that SP was not an appropriate choice (Everett, 1984).

The possibility that parents will fail to agree about custody disposition suggests a third implication about the role of third-party assistance, particularly that of family mediation. Divorce can be characterized as a family crisis. During this time, family systems may be more amenable to change than at any other time (Bross & Benjamin, 1983). The direction of change will depend in large part on the nature of the intervention to which they are subjected. Advice from a lawyer about a fight for or acquiescence to sole custody constitutes one type of intervention. Advice from a family mediator about involvement in an SP plan constitutes a different type of intervention.

Although this way of characterizing the involvement of lawyers and family mediators does not apply in all instances, it is typical in our experience (see Irving & Benjamin, 1987) and salient in two respects. First, mediation may be useful not only in helping couples select a custody option, but also in terms of identifying underlying family problems, differentiating between appropriate and inappropriate reasons for making such a selection, and maintaining ongoing contact and thus assisting with problem solving as required. Second, there appear to have been a fair number of sole custody parents in our sample who, if advised differently, might have opted for SP. Similarly, there appear to have been a small number of dissatisfied SPs who might have avoided this outcome with appropriate intervention.

These findings speak to the potential usefulness of family mediation in the choice and maintenance of an SP arrangement. Its use finds additional support in a restricted literature that demonstrates the outcome effectiveness of this approach (Emery & Wyer, 1987; Irving & Benjamin, 1987; Koopman & Hunt, 1988). This literature implies that custody statutes that support SP as an option of preference should simultaneously support the use of mediation services, perhaps on a mandatory basis in cases in which SP has been ordered against parental opposition.

Finally, we turn from statutory reform to attitudinal change among judicial actors. Although many lawyers have come to see the wisdom of SP (Miller, 1979), the present study demonstrates that substantial opposition still exists. Similar opposition among an equal proportion of judges seems likely.

Like the statutes they administer, judges' preference for sole custody (Fineberg, 1979; Scott & Derdeyn, 1984), we suggest, is rooted in adherence to an adversarial model of judicial action and an individualistic model of the family. Nothing is more symbolic of these perspectives than the language of custody law. "Petitioners" and "respondents," "contested" and "noncontested cases," "litigated settlements" and "judicial decrees"—this is the language of combat, opponents locked in struggle, championed by their respective lawyers, in which the winner takes the child(ren) as the prize. Similarly, "custodial" and "noncustodial" parents, "visitation" and "access" rights, and "care and control" orders are all ways of conceiving of a family split into its constituent elements, with remaining linkages among them formalized in legal ritual.

In our view, none of these attitudes is appropriate to the continuing relationship between parents and children. Although one may choose to "visit" the hospital or a funeral parlor to see a sick or deceased friend or relative (Everett, 1984), it is entirely wrongheaded to speak of "visiting" one's own child(ren), a point noncustodial fathers have been making for some time (Roman & Haddad, 1978). In this context, the language of "parenting plans," "shared parenting," "negotiated agreements," and "coparental cooperation" does not merely involve a change of terminology; it represents a paradigmatic or "second order" shift (Watzlawick, Weakland, & Fisch, 1974), from an adversarial to a cooperative model of judicial action and from an individualistic to a relational model of the family (Everett, 1984).

Given the rising incidence of SP (see chapters 2 and 6) and accompanying statutory changes, such a shift seems inexorable. But change is hard for most of us; we resist it because it is new and threatens long and sincerely held beliefs. Thus the erosion of opposition to SP among lawyers and judges may be a long and gradual process. If, as this study demonstrates, SP is in the best interests of many (though *not* all) children, some way must be found to accelerate the acceptance of parenting plans tailored to promote committed, responsible parenting by both spouses, including shared parenting. One obvious answer is through education, including the widespread dissemination of current and ongoing research efforts in this area.

Such information will not quell all doubt, nor should it, for many questions about SP have yet to be addressed (Kelly, 1983; Steinman, 1983). What it should do, however, is stimulate serious debate among a group of people known for their intelligence and practicality, debate not only about SP per se, but more importantly about parenting plans, the full range of options that might entail (including variations on both SP and SC), and the criteria that might be used in their selection and tailoring to suit the needs of children.[5] In such an undertaking, we are convinced that the movement toward SP cannot but benefit, which in turn benefits us all, especially the thousands of children who in coming years will, we hope, become participants in the process of divorce rather than its victims.

Clinical Practice

The final area to which our study speaks is practice. Practitioners in this area help parents and child(ren) accept this change in their lives and cope with the transition difficulties it inevitably brings (Beal, 1980; Keshet & Mirkin, 1985). Increasingly, practitioners are coming to realize that divorce is not an anomalous event, but a normative one, much like birth, death, or leaving home (Carter & McGoldrick, 1980; McCubbin & Figley, 1983). As such, practitioners must become aware of the special exigencies and stresses that characterize this process to be most helpful to clients going through it.

What the present study makes clear is that child custody appears to represent a discrete subphase within the larger process of divorce. This subphase includes not only the interactional bases for selecting a SP option, but also the subsequent processes it sets in train, as parents and children struggle to cope with the day-to-day problems and joys of living within a SP arrangement.

In short, SP represents a new family form about which parents, children, and practitioners have much to learn if they are to prosper. The present study calls special attention to four aspects of the SP experience.

First, although most divorcing couples appear well suited to the SP option, some are not and should be directed to a sole custody arrangement. The problem for practitioners is acquisition of the necessary assessment skills to differentiate between these two groups. Here we can do no better than to reiterate those inclusion criteria noted already: mutuality, cooperation, circumscription, and motivation. Given some evidence of the presence of these attributes, the couple in question will likely be good to excellent candidates for SP and should be so advised. Conversely, as the number of opposite attributes increases, SP is increasingly contraindicated.

Second, a commonly accepted clinical principle is that the better prepared one is for a given event, the better one will be able to cope with its demands and the less disorganizing will be its consequences. In this regard, practitioners can provide an important psychoeducational service. For many clients, SP will be totally new, its meaning and exigencies opaque. Recall too that for many satisfied SPs, smooth adjustment was anything but automatic; it required hard work, lasting more than a year in some cases. If a couple's choice of SP is to be fully informed, practitioners need to know this and more so that they may pass on this information to the appropriate clients.

Third, as in any transitional period, the problems associated with it are most pressing while it is still new and strange. Here, practitioners not only need to be vigilant of early difficulties, but will be most helpful in a support capacity. This study makes clear that the logistical and relational demands of SP can be significant. We speculate that this is especially true in the initial period—say, the first 6 months—when considerable adjustment is required to achieve a workable SP arrangement. However careful and detailed a couple's agreement, it cannot possibly foresee all contingencies. Consequently, during this period the family is most vulnerable to getting caught up in a "vicious cycle" of conflict and recrimination leading to outcome failure. By providing needed support during periods of particular stress or crisis, practitioners may help ensure that client families derive the maximum benefits from a SP arrangement.

Finally, practitioners need sufficient knowledge of SP to suggest practicable alternatives to the problems couples are likely to encounter. The present study indicates that scheduling, finances, and coparental decision making represent those areas in which conflict is most likely. Here, satisfied SPs displayed no single best solution; rather, they were characterized by flexibility, willingness to compromise, and a single-minded focus on the best interests of the child(ren). In our clinical experience, it is the latter that is the practitioner's most powerful lever for change, with vestiges of the marital relationship the central underlying problem. Thus, effective intervention with SP families not only requires generic clinical skills, but also in-depth substantive knowledge concerning the typical developmental course of couples who enter into a shared parenting arrangement.

NOTES

1. From 1983 to 1986, this research was funded by the Social Science and Humanities Research Council (Ottawa, Canada), Grant 498-83-0017.

2. The first principal component analysis accounted for 45% of the variation among the 12 items composing the scale.

3. Correlations between the scale and its constituent items (i.e., first principal eigenvector) were as follows: V124 0.22; V171 0.34; V172 0.32; V173 0.27; V174 0.26; V175 0.19; V179 0.37; V180 0.31; V181 0.26; V251 0.29; V252 0.30; and V268 0.30.

4. The six variable sets in question concerned preseparation marital relationship; custody choice; child-sharing or visitation schedule and child care costs; parent-child relationship; coparental relationship; and outcome satisfaction.

5. Parenting plans of the sort we envisage are currently in use in Washington state, although related legislation also exists in Florida and Maine.

REFERENCES

Arnold, R., Wheeler, M., & Pendrith, F. (1980). *Separation and after: A research report.* Toronto: Ministry of Community and Social Services.

Atkeson, B. M., Forehand, R. L., & Rickard, K. M. (1982). The effects of divorce on children. In B. B. Lahey & A. E. Kazdin (Eds.), *Advances in clinical psychology* (Vol. 5). New York: Plenum.

Beal, E. W. (1980). Separation, divorce, and single-parent families. In E. A. Carter & M. McGoldrick (Eds.), *The family life cycle: A framework for family therapy*. New York: Gardner.

Benjamin, M. (1983). *General systems theory, family systems theories, and family therapy: Towards an integrated model of family process*. In A. Bross (Ed.), *Family therapy: A recursive model of strategic practice*. New York: Guilford.

Bross, A., & Benjamin, M. (1983). Family therapy: A recursive model of strategic practice. In A. Bross (Ed.), *Family therapy: A recursive model of strategic practice*. New York: Guilford.

Burgess, J. K. (1970). The single-parent family: A social and sociological problem. *Family Coordinator, 19*, 137-144.

Caroll, C. (1982). Ducking the real issues of joint custody. *Family Advocate, 5*(2), 18-23.

Carter, E. A., & McGoldrick, M. (1980). The family life cycle and family therapy: An overview. In E. A. Carter & M. McGoldrick (Eds.), *The family life cycle: A framework for family therapy*. New York: Gardner.

Cherlin, A. J. (1981). *Marriage, divorce, remarriage*. Cambridge, MA: Harvard University Press.

Clingempeel, W. G., & Reppucci, N. D. (1982). Joint custody after divorce: Major issues and goals for research. *Psychological Bulletin, 91*, 102-127.

Derdeyn, A. P. (1976a). A consideration of legal issues in child custody contests: Implications for change. *Archives of Geneneral Psychiatry, 33*(2), 165-171.

Derdeyn, A. P. (1976b). Child custody contests in historical perspective. *American Journal of Psychiatry, 133*(12), 1369-1376.

Emery, R. E., & Wyer, M. M. (1987). Child custody mediation and litigation: An experimental evaluation of the experience of parents. *Journal of Clinical & Consulting Psychology, 55*, 179-186.

Everett, W. J. (1984). Shared parenthood in divorce: The parental covenant and custody law. *Journal of Law and Religion, 2*, 85-99.

Fineberg, A. D. (1979). Joint custody of infants: Breakthrough or fad? *Canadian Journal of Family Law, 2*(4), 417-454.

Gardner, R. A. (1974). Psychological aspects of divorce. In S. Arieti (Ed.), *American handbook of psychiatry* (2nd ed., vol. 1). New York: Basic Books.

Gardner, R. A. (1982). Joint custody is not for everyone. *Family Advocate, 5*(2), 6-9.

Grief, J., & Simring, S. (1982). Remarriage and joint custody. *Conciliation Courts Review, 20*(1), 9-14.

Hess, R. D., & Camara, K. A. (1979). Post-divorce family relationships as mediating factors in the consequences of divorce for children. *Journal of Social Issues, 35*, 79-96.

Hetherington, E. M. (1979). Divorce: A child's perspective. *American Psychologist, 34*, 851-858.

Hetherington, E. M. (1980). Children and divorce. In R. Henderson (Ed.), *Parent-child interaction: Theory, research, and prospect*. New York: Academic Press.

Irving, H. H., & Benjamin, M. (1986). Shared parenting in Canada: Questions, answers, and implications. *Canadian Family Law Quarterly, 1*, 79-103.

Irving, H. H., & Benjamin, M. (1987). *Family mediation: Theory and practice of dispute resolution*. Toronto: Carswell.

Irving, H. H., Benjamin, M., & Trocme, N. (1984). Shared parenting: An empirical analysis utilizing a large data base. *Family Process, 23*, 561-569.

Isaacs, M. B. (1988). The visitation schedule and child adjustment: A three-year study. *Family Process, 27*, 251-256.

Kanoy, K. W., & Cunningham, J. L. (1984). Consensus or confusion in research on children and divorce: Conceptual and methodological issues. *Journal of Divorce, 7*, 45-71.
Kelly, J. B. (1983). Further observations on joint custody. *University of California at Davis Law Review, 16*, 762-770.
Kelly, J. B. (1984). Examining resistance to joint custody. In J. Folberg (Ed.), *Joint custody and shared parenting*. Washington, DC: Bureau of National Affairs and Association of Family and Conciliation Courts.
Keshet, J. K., & Mirkin, M. P. (1985). Troubled adolescents in divorced and remarried families. In M. P. Mirkin & S. L. Roman (Eds.), *Handbook of adolescents and family therapy*. New York: Gardner.
Koopman, E. J., & Hunt, E. J. (1988). Child custody mediation: An interdisciplinary synthesis. *American Journal of Orthopsychiatry, 58*, 379-386.
Kurdek, L. A. (1981). An integrative perspective on children's divorce adjustment. *American Psychologist, 36*, 856-866.
Kurdek, L. A., & Berg, B. (1983). Correlates of children's adjustments to their parents' divorces. In L. A. Kurdek (Ed.), *Children and divorce*. San Francisco: Jossey-Bass.
Kurdek, L. A., & Blisk, D. (1983). Dimensions and correlates of mothers' divorce experience. *Journal of Divorce, 6*, 1-24.
Little, M. (1982). *Family breakups: Understanding marital problems and the mediating of child custody decisions*. San Francisco: Jossey-Bass.
Luepnitz, D. (1982). *Child custody: A study of families after divorce*. Lexington, MA: Lexington Books.
McCubbin, H. I., & Figley, C. R. (1983). Introduction. In H. I. McCubbin & C. R. Figley (Eds.), *Stress and the family. Vol. 1: Coping with normative transitions*. New York: Brunner/Mazel.
McKie, D. C., Prentice, B., & Reed, P. (1983). *Divorce: Law and the family in Canada*. Ottawa: Statistics Canada, Research and Analysis Division.
Miller, D. J. (1979). Joint custody. *Family Law Quarterly, 13*(3), 345-412.
Montalvo, B. (1982). Interpersonal arrangements in disrupted families. In F. Walsh (Ed.), *Normal family processes*. New York: Guilford.
Morgenbesser, M., & Nehls, N. M. (1981). *Joint custody: An alternative for divorcing families*. Chicago: Nelson-Hall.
Patterson, M. (1982). The added cost of shared lives. *Family Advocate, 5*(2), 10-13, 46.
Phear, W. P. C., Beck, J. C., Hauser, B. B., Clark, S. C., & Whitney, R. A. (1984). An empirical study of custody agreements: Joint versus sole legal custody. In J. Folberg (Ed.), *Joint custody and shared parenting*. Washington, DC: Bureau of National Affairs and the Association of Family and Conciliation Courts.
Reiss, D. (1981). *The family's construction of reality*. Cambridge, MA: Harvard University Press.
Roman, M., & Haddad, W. (1978). *The disposable parent*. New York: Holt, Rinehart & Winston.
Schwartz, S. F. G. (1984). Towards a presumption of joint custody. *Family Law Quarterly, 18*, 225-246.
Scott, E., & Derdeyn, A. (1984). Rethinking joint custody. *Ohio State Law Journal, 45*, 455-498.
Sprenkle, D. H., & Cyrus, C. L. (1983). Abandonment: The stress of sudden divorce. In C. R. Figley & H. I. McCubbin (Eds.), *Stress and the family. Vol. 2: Coping with catastrophe*. New York: Brunner/Mazel.

Steinman, S. (1983). Joint custody: What we know, what we have yet to learn, and the judicial and legislative implications. *University California at Davis Law Review, 16,* 739-762.

Wallerstein, J. S., & Kelly, J. B. (1980). *Surviving the breakup: How children and parents cope with divorce.* New York: Basic Books.

Watzlawick, P., Weakland, J., & Fisch, R. (1974). *Change: Principles of problem formation and problem resolution.* New York: Norton.

Weitzman, L. J. (1985). *The divorce revolution: The unexpected social and economic consequences for women and children in America.* New York: Free Press.

PART IV

Special Topics

The history of family mediation in North America is characterized by opposing tendencies of exclusion and inclusion. Exclusion means that family mediation is less likely to accommodate the needs of some groups than others. Like all "talking therapies," family mediation is implicitly modeled on middle-class, white, Anglo-Saxon client couples. In our experience, for example (we know of no national data on this matter), most mediators fit this description. Whether public or private, services are centralized (clients must travel to the agency's office), offered during business hours only, and with some exceptions (e.g., the state of Louisiana and the province of Quebec), usually delivered in English. Moreover, clients are referred to mediation through legal (their lawyer or the court) or service (their counselor) channels and thus assumed to address their marital difficulties through formal, institutional means. Finally, in the increasingly voluminous mediation literature, the identity of the target clientele is almost universally left unspecified, that is, to borrow a computer analogy, middle class, white, and Anglo is the default or "standard" condition.

The obvious problem with this portrait is that it does not correspond to a substantial minority of either the general or the divorcing population. Indeed, should current demographic trends continue, today's "visible minorities" (blacks, Hispanics, Asians, Native Americans) are likely to become tomorrow's majority. Moreover, since the likelihood of divorce is inversely related to social class and several of the groups in question are more likely to be poor than affluent, a sizable proportion of all potential mediation clients are neither middle class, white, nor Anglo.

That said, the historical tendency for mediation to have largely ignored ethnicity appears wrongheaded in at least two respects: It fails to exploit a large population of potential clients and, even more important, it repels potential clients, is seen as irrelevant by them, provides them with inadequate service or actually does harm.

That said, it remains unclear how service might need to change with increasing sensitivity to and awareness of ethnic clients. Chapter 8 addresses this issue with a detailed profile of three of the groups noted above (blacks, Hispanics, and Asians) as well as a fourth group, Jews, included for comparative purposes. The result is a fascinating glimpse into issues that, although largely absent from the mediation literature, are likely a daily reality for many mediation practitioners across North America.

From exclusion, we turn to inclusion. Historically, mediation has centered almost entirely on two areas of practice: Labor mediators and arbitrators concentrated on labor-management relations, whereas family mediators focused on separated and divorcing couples. Consistent success in mediation in these fields, however, has not gone unnoticed in other areas characterized by interpersonal conflict. Thus through the efforts of individual pioneers, mediation as a generic approach to conflict resolution has become increasingly inclusive. For example, other areas of practice include: business and corporate (i.e., conflict among business partners or between different levels of management); community and neighborhood (i.e., conflict between neighbors or identified groups in a community); school (i.e., conflict between children, often involving peers trained as mediators); civil (e.g., conflict between landlords and tenants); and, most recently, child welfare (i.e., between protection workers and parents accused of abuse). Given its very recent history, it is hardly surprising that little is known about child welfare mediation. Chapter 9 provides a comprehensive overview of this new form of mediation: what it is, how it works, and what it can and cannot do.

More generally, mediation can remain healthy only by changing and adapting to meet the changing needs of its clientele. These chapters have been included because we think they reflect two aspects of the future of family mediation in North America.

Finally, the sorts of change likely to shape the future of mediation have been driven by two related processes. One, alluded to above, concerns changing client demand. The other, the subject of chapter 10, concerns ongoing research on family mediation. Here, two processes can be distinguished. While mediation sought to join the mainstream, outcome research was the order of the day, justifying and legitimizing confidence in mediation by clients, but also by legal actors, politicians, and funding agents. Now that mediation has joined the mainstream, the focus is beginning to shift from outcome to process, that is, how mediators conduct themselves in session and what seems to work best with what sorts of clients. Both sorts of data are helpful to the practitioner, hence the critical review that follows.

8

Family Mediation and Ethnicity

A Critical but Neglected Dimension of Practice

INTRODUCTION

The size of the population of divorcing couples in North America (see chapters 2 and 3) is such that we can take for granted diversity among those who seek mediation service. In most of the mediation literature, however, such diversity is assumed to vary in circumscribed ways, around a common mean centered on white, middle-class couples. Accordingly, it is widely seen as reasonable to talk about mediation clients in generic terms. Although appropriate to many clients, such talk ignores systematic sources of variation, notably ethnicity.

Ethnicity may be defined as membership in a "human group that entertains a 'subjective belief' in its common descent because of similarities of physical type or customs or both, or because of memories of colonization and migration" (Alba, 1985, p. 17; see Alba, 1990). These factors include race, religion, and national or geographic origin (Yinger, 1985). The profound impact of these shared beliefs cannot be overemphasized, for they pervade all aspects of members' lives. In the words of McGoldrick (1988, p. 69), [ethnicity] plays a major role in determining what we eat, how we work, how we relate, how we celebrate holidays and rituals, and how we feel about life, death, and illness. We see the world through our own cultural filters and we often persist in our established views in spite of evidence to the contrary.

In short, ethnicity helps establish the fundamental bases on which we relate to ourselves and others in the world, with much of this perspective typically beyond awareness (Schwartzman, 1982).

The family therapy and social work literatures have only recently begun to give prominence to ethnicity in discussions of clinical practice (McAdoo, 1993; McGoldrick, Garcia-Preto, Hines, & Lee, 1989). In contrast, our reading, together with available bibliographies (see Stone, 1991), indicates that concurrent concern with ethnicity in family mediation has not occurred, with few exceptions (LeResche, 1992; Meierding, 1992). This chapter seeks to redress this imbalance. What follows is divided into three parts, concerned with core dimensions, a detailed profile of five ethnic groups (African Americans, Caribbean Canadian blacks, Hispanics, Asians, and Jews) and discussion of the implications of these data for clinical practice, with particular reference to TFM (see chapter 4).

Before proceeding, however, three caveats are in order. First, the following profiles rely heavily on American sources. Although descriptive Canadian data are available, they are hardly abundant. There appear to be two main reasons for this disparity: population size and scholarly interest. As seen in Table 8.1, "visible" minority groups make up a much larger proportion of the population in the United States compared to Canada, and, with local exceptions, are likely to do so for the foreseeable future. In practice, this difference has meant that ethnicity has received both less and different attention in Canada. For example, Peters (1990) and Tavuchis (1989) have noted the meager character of the Canadian ethnicity literature in regard to size and (narrow) range, with the emphasis on history and demography as opposed to family life. By contrast, in the United States, Buenker and Ratner (1992, p. 232) observe that "the explosion of ethnic studies in every discipline over the past quarter century has produced a flood of literature, and the torrent is not likely to crest in the near future." In part, this "flood" reflects the much greater abundance of academic

TABLE 8.1 Ethnic Minority Population in Canada and the United States

| | Census Data (in millions) | | | |
| | United States (1990) | | Canada (1991)* | |
Group	No.	%	No.	%
Blacks	30.0	12.1	0.34	1.3
Hispanics	22.4	9.0	0.16**	0.6
Asians	7.3	2.9	1.62	6.0
Natives	2.0	0.8	0.47	1.7
Total Population	251.0***	100.0	27.00	100.0
Minority Population	61.7	24.8	2.59	9.6
Projection to 2001[a]	78.6	35.0	5.68	17.7

a. SOURCES: United States: Dana (1993); Canada: Samuel (1992, cited in Toronto Star, May 30, 1992, pp. A1-A2).
  * Includes single origins only representing 70% of the total; multiple origins are distributed across 14 categories that distinguish only between British, French, Canadian, and "other."
 ** Based on reported mother tongue, single responses only.
*** Total population in 1993 (in millions): United States 255.1, Canada 28.7.

programs in the United States devoted to ethnic concerns, with more than 300 programs, for example, concerned exclusively with Jewish life, 27 of them at the doctoral level (Silberman, 1985). In light of these differences, despite every effort to balance American and Canadian data, Canadian readers are advised to examine the profiles to follow with caution as to their local applicability.

Second, for two reasons, substantive limitations on our treatment of the topic were unavoidable. The first reason relates to the collective size of the literatures in question, which requires that comprehensive treatment necessarily be encyclopedic in size. Because the intent of this chapter is more modest, the following profiles provide coverage that is at best selective. The second reason concerns the criteria used to select the groups to be profiled, namely: (a) visible minority group status, (b) group size relative to the North American context, and (c) the availability of literature describing fundamental beliefs (attitudes and values), family practices, and help-seeking behavior. Concern with visible minority status derives from our concern to select groups likely to be at some variance from the white majority. Reliance on American sources explains the use of a North American rather than an exclusively American or Canadian context. And reasons for our concern with specific substantive content will shortly be apparent in discussing profile dimensions (see below). In combination, these selection criteria dramatically limited the groups that could be included in the profiles. For example, the profile of Asians deliberately omitted consideration of several large and important subgroups, notably the South Asians of India, Pakistan, and Bangladesh. Similarly glaring is the omission of North America's aboriginal groups: native Indians, Metis, Inuit, and Alaskan natives.

Third, as will become clear, each of the groups in question is heterogeneous, constituted of multiple subgroups that, in turn, vary in size, social class distribution, religious affiliation, and so on. Given this complex reality, any set of profiles such as those found below is at risk of stereotyping the groups described. Conversely, systematic attention to such heterogeneity would similarly risk losing sight of general trends by the sheer weight of detail. By carefully specifying the dimensions to be used in creating the profiles that follow, we try to strike a balance between the general and the specific. That is, these profiles should be seen as general descriptions that will apply to varying degrees to any given member of the groups in question. On the one hand, this consideration means that these profiles do not lessen in any way the importance of assessment data as the basis for subsequent intervention. On the other hand, they should profoundly shape the nature of the assessment procedure when dealing with ethnic couples.

CORE DIMENSIONS

The mediation literature displays little consensus about preferred intervention practices (Donohue, Lyles, & Rogan, 1989; Landau, Bartoletti, & Mesbur, 1987). That being so, it is unclear how these practices need to vary when dealing with client families across ethnic groups. A profile of the groups in question would help clarify what mediation practice might mean in the context of ethnic diversity. It may also highlight our unconscious biases, given "the power of culture to make us relatively oblivious to the limitations of our own perspectives, behaviors, and values" (Patton, 1985, p. 1).

However, it is still unclear what dimensions to use in constructing such profiles, because a large number of pertinent dimensions readily come to mind. Following Devore and Schlesinger (1987), McAdoo (1993), and McGoldrick, Garcia-Peto, Hines, and Lee (1989), the profiles to follow will be based on six dimensions selected for the extent to which they capture the core meaning and behavioral systems of the groups in question: modal social class, definition of the family, life cycle, husband-wife relations, parent-child relations, and perspectives on treatment.[1] Each core dimension will be briefly described, including its salience for TFM.

Modal Social Class

Social class, based on available resources and completed education, plays a central role in shaping life experience. Compared to the impoverished, the affluent eat better, live in families that are better organized, have access to better health care, and live longer (see Aponte, 1976, 1986). Thus it is unreasonable to speak about a given ethnic group without simultaneously specifying the social class of those being described. This distinction is so central that Gordon (1964) has coined the term "ethclass" to refer to the intersection between class and ethnicity, the underlying assumption being that both dimensions together are needed to gain a sense of the perspective of those being described.

That said, comprehensive data on the intersection between the four ethnic groups of interest here and at least three social classes (upper, middle, and lower/working) simply do not exist. Rather, researchers have tended to concentrate on a modal class that accounts for a majority of those in the group in question. That practice will be followed here.

With respect to TFM, social class speaks to a client family's opportunity structure, that is, their resources for such things as clothing, housing, travel, food, alternative child support, and the like. Generally, the fewer the resources, the fewer the opportunities and thus the fewer the options around which mediated negotiation can meaningfully occur.

Definition of the Family

Across ethnic groups, great variation exists about the definition of who is inside and who is outside the family. At one extreme, family boundaries may be tightly defined, so that family refers to the immediate family and no others. At the other extreme, family boundaries may be loosely defined, so that family includes extended family members, living and dead, as well as close family "friends."

Such definitions have practical consequences, for example, in regard to whom one might turn to for support in times of need or what happens to children when their biological parents experience difficulty caring for them, both common problems confronting parents undergoing divorce (see chapter 2). It thus speaks directly to mediation, for example, in terms of who must be included in mediation sessions and who can be excluded.

Life Cycle

A closely related dimension concerns variation in life cycle phases. That is, ethnic groups vary widely in regard to all aspects of life cycle processes, including the number of phases that are recognized, their respective duration and salience, and the markers used to signify transition between stages, say from the status of adolescent to that of adult. As Fulmer (1988) makes clear, this variation is not solely a function of ethnicity, but is importantly shaped by social class, with affluent professional families typically displaying an "elongated" life cycle compared to their lower-income counterparts, whose life cycle is typically "compressed." The former may spend many years completing the educational requirements of a professional degree and thus a corresponding numbers of years in the "young adult" phase of the life cycle, in which they remain single and financially dependent on their parents. This phase is thus "elongated" relative to others in "average" middle-class families. By contrast, their lower-income counterparts may leave education early, marry, become parents, and take full-time employment (if they can find it), all before their 21st birthday. In their case, the "young adult" phase is "compressed," again relative to others in "average" middle-class families.

Such information bears directly on TFM, for it speaks to the sorts of solutions to divorced-related problems that clients are likely to see as "fair" and "reasonable." Mediated solutions in keeping with culturally approved norms are likely to be seen as acceptable and adhered to when mediation is completed. However, the reverse is likely to be true should solutions be advanced that are in keeping with white norms but inconsistent with client cultural beliefs. Indeed, in our experience, ethnic couples confronted in this way by a mediator who is white are likely to terminate service abruptly.

Marital Relations

Another way in which ethnic groups vary is in terms of their perspective on appropriate relations between marital partners (whether heterosexual, homosexual, or lesbian). This variance turns on two issues. First is the relative salience of spousal relations in comparison to parent-child relations. Some groups regard spousal relations as primary or at least concurrent with parent-child relations, whereas other groups accord it secondary or tertiary place, with parent-child relations taking precedence. Second, groups vary in their perception of how marital partners should relate to each other. Some groups expect that one spouse should be in charge (often the husband in heterosexual arrangements), with the other spouse (the wife) submissive and conforming in response. Others see the marital partners as equal in most, if not all respects.

Clearly, this dimension is central to TFM, for its seeks to capture the patterns of interaction that led to the divorce, which in turn predicts the spouses likely conduct in negotiation and may or may not be the focus of premediation intervention.

Parent-Child Relations

In addition to the salience of the parent-child relationship, groups vary also in terms of both the character of parent-child relations and the responsibility for child care. As to the latter, some groups take literally the adage that "children should be seen and not heard" whereas others adopt a more democratic stance (see Yip, 1985). Furthermore, in some groups child care is seen as the mother's responsibility (perhaps shared with other females in the extended family), whereas in others fathers are expected to participate to varying degrees.

This dimension is also important to TFM. Unlike family therapy, in which relational continuity is a key lever for change, in mediation the provision of child care is one of the central bases on which client spouses are encouraged to reach agreement. It follows that assessment efforts inquire in detail about the nature of the client couple's parenting beliefs and arrangements.

Perspectives on Treatment

Finally, of special relevance to mediation practice, groups vary widely in regard to treatment, that is, they way in which they define illness (physical or psychological) and their attitude toward help-seeking. In this respect, some groups find somatic illness acceptable as the basis for help-seeking, whereas others legitimize both physical and mental complaints. Similarly, some groups are very reluctant to seek help, seeing it as an admission of weakness, and so typically go for treatment only after the problem in question is serious and well advanced. Others go for treatment readily, often when the problem in question is at an early stage in its typical course. Either strategy yields differential prognostic results and has divergent social consequences. Finally, groups differ in their preferred relationship with the caregiver, ranging from formal and authoritarian to familiar and informal.

Such information is important to TFM in at least two respects. First, it specifies for the mediator the sort of relationship and the types of intervention that are possible and likely to be most effective. Second, it provides a window on the conduct of the mediator. Both Devereux (1967) and Stein (1985), for example, point to variation among psychotherapists in regard to cultural-based value filters that shape the way in which they interact with clients who are ethnically "different" from themselves. As Pedersen (1984, p. 340) explains, "cultural differences introduce barriers to understanding in those very areas of interaction that are most crucial to the outcomes of therapy, through discrepancies between counselor and client experiences, beliefs, values, expectations and goals."

PROFILES OF FOUR ETHNIC GROUPS

Below we profile four ethnic groups: blacks, Hispanics, Asians, and Jews. In each case, the profile is summarized in a table, followed by elaboration in the text.

Blacks

Blacks, like each of the groups to be profiled, represent a heterogeneous group, drawing members from North America, the Caribbean,
Africa, and South America, with each subgroup distinctively different
from the others (see Allahan, 1993; Kasinitz, 1992). This profile will
focus on two groups: African Americans (hereafter referred to as
blacks) and Canadian Caribbean blacks (hereafter referred to as Caribbean blacks). Blacks are those originally brought here as slaves
(Pinderhughes, 1982). They have received the most attention in the
literature (Boyd-Franklin, 1993; Dana, 1993; Dickson, 1993; Edelman,
1993; McAdoo, 1988, 1993; Staples & Johnson, 1993). For quick reference, the profile of North American blacks is summarized in Table 8.2
with detailed description in the text.

There are at least three reasons that this portrait of the blacks in the
United States does not generalize well to their counterparts in Canada,
that is, Afro-Canadian blacks and Caribbean blacks: Canadian blacks
have a very different history (Walker, 1980); Caribbean blacks represent
a much higher proportion of the black population in Canada (27%)
than in the United States (5%) (Kasinitz, 1992); and Caribbean blacks
remain a distinct subgroup of the larger black community in Canada,
as a result of both self-identification (Walker, 1984) and language,
specifically, the use of dialect.

In light of these various differences, in all that follows we will
systematically distinguish between blacks and Caribbean blacks. This
solution is not ideal. Although Afro-Canadian blacks warrant equal
attention, the paucity of material about them (see Clairmont & Magill,
1987; Govia, 1988) offers no alternative. Rather, it suggests the need to
develop a separate profile of Caribbean blacks. For quick reference,
that profile is summarized in Table 8.3, with detailed description in the
text.

Modal Social Class

Blacks. Despite major advances in equality and equity in recent years
(Farley, 1984; Fisher, 1992), North America remains a relatively hostile
environment for blacks (Wilkinson & Spurlock, 1986). A glimpse at
current demographic data reveals just how hostile. In the United

TABLE 8.2 Summary Profile of Blacks in the United States

Modal social class:	lower/working
Definition of the family:	multigeneration informal extended, including "kept" children and "fictive" kin
Life cycle:	compressed, three phases, with emphasis on adulthood
Husband-wife relations:	role flexibility, matrilocal
Parent-child relations:	authoritarian; corporal punishment
Perspective on treatment:	community sources of help preferred, especially kin and church pastor

TABLE 8.3 Summary Profile of Caribbean Blacks in Canada

Modal social class:	lower middle
Definition of the family:	modified "Christian" or nuclear family, including child lending
Life cycle:	no information
Husband-wife relations:	role segregation, matrilocal
Parent-child relations:	authoritarian; corporal punishment
Perspective on treatment:	community sources of help preferred, especially kin and church pastor

States, for example, on average, employed black males earn only 58% of the income of their white counterparts (Dickson, 1993). Forced male underachievement (Giddings, 1985) and chronic unemployment (Boyd-Franklin, 1989; Farley, 1984) remain commonplace. The majority (76%) of married black women with children work (Piotrkowski & Hughes, 1993) in jobs characterized by low pay, unskilled menial work, and close supervision (Tomaskovic-Devey, 1993). Indeed, single mothers represented 56% of all black families in 1990 (Walsh, 1993). Of these, 70% reported incomes below the poverty line (Billingsley, 1988). The result is that 35% of black families in the United States report incomes below the poverty line and an additional 20% earn only slightly more (Dickson, 1993; see Massey & Eggers, 1990). In short, the majority of American blacks are lower/working class (Bonacich, 1990), including a significant minority who belong to the "underclass" (Marks, 1991; Wilson, 1987).

Caribbean Blacks. Although the evidence is slim and not always clear, it appears that Caribbean blacks come closer than blacks to income parity with whites. For example, Moreau (1991), using data from the 1986 census for the Toronto Census Metropolitan area, compared men and women in three ethnic groups ("black," Chinese, and Indo-Pakistani) across a range of dimensions. Among other things, this data showed that blacks were twice as likely to be poor (26%) as whites (12%).

Similarly, Sev'er, Isajiw, and Driedger (1993), based on data from the late 1970s, found that of seven ethnic groups studied, "West Indian" and Italian men had the lowest level of education and income, the lowest overall level of occupational status, and the highest level of anomie, that is, of perceived powerlessness. In contrast, other investigators using data gathered in the early 1980s found evidence of income close to parity, especially among Caribbean black women (Breton, Isajiw, Kalbach, & Reitz, 1990). Recently, using data from the 1986 census, DeSilva (1992) found no difference in the average incomes of Caribbean blacks and whites when years of education and work experience in Canada were controlled.

These data support two conclusions. Although there does appear to be a disparity between Caribbean blacks and whites in terms of income, it is not nearly as great as that reported between blacks and whites in the United States. Furthermore, despite the higher proportion of poor Caribbean blacks compared to whites, the modal class of Caribbean blacks is likely to be within the middle-class range.

Definition of the Family

Blacks. Among blacks, the basic family unit is the multigeneration informal extended family (Edelman, 1993), including parents, biological children, extended kin, family friends regarded as fictive kin (Ogbu,

1986), informally adopted children (Hill, 1977), and visiting relatives (Hill, 1977). Relations in such family systems are based on expectations of loyalty and mutual support (Hines & Boyd-Franklin, 1982; McGoldrick, 1988) and represent an adaptive response to the confluence of three long-standing structural processes: poverty, the scarcity of eligible males, and the degraded status of males. Poverty places the very survival of the family at continual risk (Boyd-Franklin, 1993).

Evidence of poverty has been noted above. As for the scarcity of males, in some regions of the United States the ratio of men to women may be as high as one to seven (Dickson, 1993). This scarcity results from the fact that black men are much more likely than either black women or whites (men or women) to die young (in the age range 15 to 24) because of elevated rates of illness (such as heart disease, hypertension, sickle-cell anemia), suicide, and murder or because they are simply unavailable, the result of a comparatively high rate of imprisonment. Unable to find eligible men, black women are more willing to accept a common-law relationship and to bear children in that relationship (Staples & Johnson, 1993) but less willing to consider abortion or formal adoption (McGoldrick, 1982). In some cases, then, each of several children may have different fathers (Fulmer, 1988; Hunter & Ensinger, 1992). Black women who marry tend to do so younger, have more children, and wait less time between marrying and having their first child (Halli, Trovato, & Driedger, 1990; Spanier & Thompson, 1985). Finally, the degraded status of black men contributes to families that are often female centered (Sanua, 1985). Although respected as the head of the household, men are more vulnerable than women to job loss, given employment characterized by low stability, racial discrimination, and what Franklin (1992) has called the "invisibility factor," the tendency of whites to perceive black men as hostile and dangerous and thus to react in encounters with them as if they were invisible.

Consequently, women frequently have the primary responsibility for supporting the family. They are thus more likely than their white counterparts to be employed (Beckett, 1976) and to see work as a family obligation (Leggon, 1983). Additional processes accentuate the focus on women. The emphasis on informal solutions to problems may mean long periods of informal marital separation leaving mothers to provide child care (Hines & Boyd-Franklin, 1982). The involvement of nonresident fathers is additionally discouraged by welfare regulations that may cut off support on evidence of male involvement. This situation labels women as heads of their households and officially renders men peripheral to the family (Franklin, 1992). The result is that in 1990, female-centered households represented 61% of all black families with children (Dickson, 1993).

In turn, attitudes toward work and education have been affected. Although black parents have high aspirations for their children (Nora, 1993), their daily reality limits the likelihood that those aspirations will be achieved. Black children perform less well than their white counterparts at all levels of schooling, from public (Entwisle & Alexander, 1993) to high school (Coleman, 1990) to university (Beaudry, 1992). In light of such experience, black parents are less likely than whites to perceive the benefits of educational achievement (Davis, 1992).

As for work, black attitudes are mixed. Although black parents stress the importance of hard work and success (Devore & Schlesinger, 1987; McGoldrick et al., 1989), black experience at work is often negative. Their overall commitment to work, then, especially among the young, may be ambivalent (Staples & Johnson, 1993).

Caribbean Blacks. The generalizability of this portrait to Caribbean blacks is limited by culture and immigration. At the risk of oversimplification, life in the Caribbean islands may be characterized as poor, authoritarian, and matriarchal. The basic unit family falls somewhere between the white nuclear family and the black extended family (Brice, 1982; Christiansen, Thornley-Brown, & Robinson, 1982). It is embedded in a rich support network, with family boundaries sufficiently diffuse that acceptance of "child lending," an arrangement during hard times in which children may temporarily live with relatives or family friends is widespread. Given those hard times, husbands are often absent for extended periods in search of work, with hard work and "thrift" as central cultural values. Consequently, women, many of whom work, are expected to be self-sufficient, strong, and resourceful. Moreover, a history of British colonization means that authority is hierarchical, based on age. This value is especially evident in island schools in the respectful and dependent way in which students interact with teachers. Such behavior also highlights education as another central cultural value.

These processes are complicated by immigration. For example, immigration may involve extended separations between parents and children (Christiansen et al., 1982). Family support systems must be abandoned. Although many immigrants live with or near relatives (Moreau, 1991) and prefer to live in neighborhoods with high concentrations of Caribbean blacks (Breton et al., 1990), the web of reciprocal relations that typifies island life takes generations to reconstruct. However, one problem confronted by black women, the shortage of black men, does not apply to their Caribbean counterparts. Moreau's (1991) study of Metropolitan Toronto found that men made up 48% and 45% of the white and black populations, respectively. Such figures must be placed in the context of assimilation, one aspect of which concerns intermarriage. Ram (1990), for example, found that (in 1981) between 22% (among Trinidadians) and 34% (among Jamaicans) of Caribbean blacks married someone not of the same national origin. The comparable rate among American blacks appears to be between 5% and 10% (Bruce & Rodman, 1973; Heer, 1974).

Finally, although black and Caribbean black children both encounter problems in education, they do so for very different reasons (Anderson & Grant, 1987). Caribbean black children have been socialized by a school system in which most students are black, schools are small, language includes elements of dialect, and instruction involves a dependent relationship in which teachers issue detailed instruction for students to follow; disobedience is typically dealt with severely. By contrast, their Canadian experience is likely to be characterized by minority status, large school size, instruction in standard English, and a teaching process designed to foster child independence. Consequently, Caribbean black public and high school students in and around Toronto, for example, do less well than their white counterparts (Cheng, Tsuji, Yau, & Ziegler, 1989). A recent Canadian study tracking the movement of these students to university showed that at the end of their first year, Caribbean black students performed on a par with their white counterparts (Grayson, 1994).

Life Cycle

Blacks. Following Fulmer (1988) and Hines (1988), the life cycle of lower/working class black families tends to be compressed and accelerated compared to their middle-class counterparts. Whereas the life cycle of middle-class black families is elongated in light of the need for extended education, that of poor black families is shaped in response to the demands of survival in a dangerous and hostile environment with meager resources. The result is a three-phase process in which adolescence early fades into adulthood, often ambiguously marked by parenthood, especially among girls (Furstenberg, 1986; Gibbs, 1989a, 1989b). Furthermore, child care and other demands mean that there may be no clear demarcation between adulthood and old age. The experience of being overburdened as young women supports the view that struggle, sacrifice, and the denial of personal satisfaction are inevitable (Hines, 1990). Confirmed by later experience, such attitudes are simply carried over into old age. Thus, despite support from their adult children (Taylor, 1986), the elderly often continue to work, either in the home or in paid employment, despite ill health, with the result that males in particular are at risk of premature death, either before or shortly after retirement (Hines, 1988). Given the harshness of their lives, release through death is seen as an extremely important transitional event whose celebration can often be costly and elaborate (McGoldrick, 1988).

Caribbean Blacks. No comparable data are available with regard to Caribbean blacks. It is consequently unclear how to characterize their life cycle processes.

Husband-Wife Relations

Blacks. As implied above, an array of structural forces operates against the maintenance of stable marital relations among lower- and working-class blacks. In addition to those noted, another concerns the manner in which marriage is often initiated, through pregnancy (Devore & Schlesinger, 1987).

Female adolescents are pushed to grow up fast, with motherhood widely seen as essential to becoming a woman (Hines, 1990). Male adolescents may be encouraged to father babies (Stack, 1974) as a test of manhood but without social fatherhood (Aschenbrenner, 1975). Indeed, Wilson (1987) argues that lacking a sense of a secure future fosters in men especially an approach to life that is present centered and pleasure oriented. Conversely, both parents and the church frown on premarital sex. Mothers may perceive that they have little control over whether their daughters become pregnant and among their sons may feel powerless to counteract the pull of the street (McGoldrick, 1982b). The result is a high adolescent pregnancy rate (Gibbs, 1989a, 1989b)[2] combined, in the absence of paternal involvement, with mothers often caring for their daughters' children (McGoldrick, 1993). In turn, this situation may initiate a series of relatively transient romantic relationships, thus creating a household of several generations of women and their respective children (Fulmer, 1988).

Although commonplace, this scenario is only one of several variants on the extended family. Boyd-Franklin (1989) calls attention to three additional family forms: (a) the subfamily, involving two partners without children or with children living elsewhere; (b) family with a secondary member(s), that is, an extended or a nuclear family form but including other relatives (children or the elderly) as well as family friends; and (c) the augmented family, that is, an extended or nuclear family form but including nonrelated others such as informally "adopted" children as well as boarders or lodgers.

All of these variants can represent well functioning families (Billingsley, 1988). Marital relations in poor black families are often characterized by more balanced and flexible gender roles than would be expected among their white counterparts (Allen, 1978). Black fathers, for example, are more likely to help out with household and child care tasks (Gary, 1981). Poverty encourages reliance on the "underground" or informal economy in which barter and mutual aid stand in place of cash, thus indirectly promoting community solidarity. Nearly universal spirituality among blacks (Boyd-Franklin, 1989, 1993) means that the church is a central source of solace, practical support and self-help (Daniel, 1985).

Such flexibility notwithstanding, the pressures on black families are such that families are at considerable risk of dysfunction. Black couples, for example, are at greater risk of separation or divorce than their white counterparts (Dickson, 1993). Mothers may become overburdened (Boyd-Franklin, 1989). Informal adoptions may become family secrets or sources of conflict resembling custody battles following divorce. Intergenerational conflict may erupt when teenage mothers, growing older, assert the desire to begin to parent their children only to find that their mothers, who had previously cared for the grandchildren, refuse to relinquish control. Parental disciplinary consistency may be impossible when daily confronted with life circumstances that are unpredictable (Aponte, 1976); children may not have their own room or their own bed (Hunter & Ensinger, 1992). Under these conditions, several adaptive responses are possible. Parents may inadvertently encourage the emergence of one or more parental children, typically female (Hines, 1988). Other adults, especially women, from among extended kin may be asked to take one or more of the children (Stack, 1974). Here, child-keeping may be seen as an adaptive response to family distress (Stack, 1974), although it means that some children may spend at least part of their childhood in the care of adults who are unrelated to them (Davis, 1992). And the efforts of well-meaning but intrusive service (welfare, counseling) and control (police, parole) agencies can make matters worse rather than better.

Caribbean Blacks. Brice (1982) and Christiansen et al. (1982) note one source of similarity between blacks and Caribbean blacks. Specifically, both Caribbean black and black women place equal importance on motherhood as the key to both femininity and adulthood, although there is no evidence of high rates of teenage births among Caribbean black adolescents.

These authors also note two areas of difference. Caribbean families are characterized by a much wider range of family variation, from "Christian marriage" (the nuclear family) to "faithful concubinage" (cohabitation). Across forms, relations between spouses are typified by role segregation, with household chores and child rearing largely a female responsibility. Separation between the sexes is similarly played out in the importance accorded privacy in the Caribbean black community, with extensive family secrets, even between spouses, not uncommon.

Christiansen et al. (1982) describe the second source of difference, namely, the marrying of religion, spirituality, and magic, especially among poor Caribbean blacks. Many Caribbean blacks are deeply religious. To this is added a belief in the reality of human spirits who are thought to live on after death. In turn, these spirits are thought to play an important role in human affairs, particularly in the form of dreams, visions, prophecies, and spirit possession. Accordingly, like blacks but for very different reasons, it is essential that on death an individual be given a proper funeral to ensure that his or her spirit is sent off properly.

Parent-Child Relations

Blacks. Child care practices among blacks vary by child age and gender (Boyd-Franklin, 1989). Parents tend to be relatively indulgent with infants but strict, even authoritarian, with older children, including corporal punishment (McGoldrick, 1993; Scanzoni, 1971). Children are expected to obey parental commands immediately, and are not permitted to talk back, question parental authority, or have angry tantrums (McGoldrick, 1993). Feelings, both positive and negative, tend to be expressed openly, although nurturance is more likely to take the form of verbal praise rather than physical affection (McAdoo, 1981). Consequently, children are raised to be assertive, independent, and positively self-accepting (McGoldrick et al., 1989). Child rearing also varies by child gender. Although daughters usually share household tasks, sons are seen as harder to control and may be lost to the streets relatively early. Indeed, recent evidence indicates that sons make independent decisions much earlier (at 13 years) than daughters (at 17 years; Dornbusch et al., 1985).

Furthermore, given the focus on parental as opposed to marital roles, black families are more inclined to see child behavior as opposed to adult conduct as a particular source of difficulty (Hines & Boyd-Franklin, 1982). In turn, this perspective highlights the special role of the elderly, especially elderly women, in black culture. By virtue of their survival to old age, the elderly are viewed with respect, as sources of good advice, wisdom, and stability (McGoldrick et al., 1989). The complexities of black family life mean that elderly women seldom experience an empty nest, as their help is needed and valued in child care. Indeed, they may head a three- or four-generation family (Hines, 1988).

Caribbean Blacks. As for Caribbean blacks, their attitudes toward child rearing have much in common with their black counterparts (Christiansen et al., 1982), although they are sustained in a different cultural context. For Caribbean blacks, children are seen as a gift from God. Consequently, contraception, abortion, and formal adoption are all strongly prohibited.

Despite such regard, children are typically seen as extensions of their parents, and thus not seen as having individual rights, perceptions, or feelings. Child socialization stresses obedience and passivity, with strong prohibitions against behavior labeled rude (impertinent). Disobedience may be severely punished by scolding, threats, or flogging (spanking) severe enough to produce welts. In this context, the independence and expressiveness that Canadian public schools seek to foster may conflict with parental norms and become a key source of intergenerational conflict. Similarly, Caribbean standards of discipline directly conflict with community standards in Canada, with charges of child abuse sometimes resulting from this discrepancy.

This accent on propriety is especially apparent in relations between mothers and daughters. Daughters are taught housekeeping and child rearing but little about sex. This socialization prepares them for the helping professions (such as nursing or teaching), but for neither menstruation nor sexual relations within marriage. More generally, this approach stresses emotional control, such that women have fewer emotional outlets than men for dealing with frustration, conflict, and trauma.

Perspectives on Treatment

Blacks. Finally, faced with monetary, psychological, or interpersonal troubles, the first response of blacks is to seek advice either from members of their extended family or the church (Daniel, 1985). Thus, formal help-seeking reflects the absence of alternatives or referral to treatment by an agency upon which they depend for resources (Boyd-Franklin, 1989). Blacks have traditionally underutilized mental health services (Cleary & Demone, 1988), based on bitter experiences (Logan, Freeman, & McDay, 1990) or lack of both money and health insurance (Amaro, Beckman, & Mays, 1987). Consequently, they often have no idea of why they have been referred, what to expect, how the process is likely to be helpful, or the nature of the relationship between their therapist and the other agencies with whom they are simultaneously involved (Hines, 1988). In addition, service providers are overwhelmingly white (Lassiter, 1990) and have been inclined to misdiagnose blacks (Pavkov, Lewis, & Lyons, 1990).

Accordingly, blacks typically approach treatment by being inarticulate or belligerent (Daniel, 1985). However, once trust has been established using an informal style, blacks often prove realistic, emotionally aware, and comfortable with their feelings (Boyd-Franklin, 1989). In turn, they respond best to an approach that is short-term, highly structured, and problem-focused (Boyd-Franklin, 1989). Even so, blacks have a high dropout rate and, given an approach to time that accords it less salience than do whites, they may often be late for scheduled appointments or fail to show up (Wilkinson & Spurlock, 1986).

Caribbean Blacks. Like blacks, Caribbean blacks faced with troubles are likely to turn first to family, friends, and the church. They too have historically been reluctant to seek formal assistance (Christiansen et al., 1982), although, again, for different reasons that have to do with culture and language. Self-sufficiency and privacy, so highly valued in Caribbean culture, support a prohibition against help-seeking, with service providers likely to be seen as just plain nosey (*jus' wan' fas' in a mi business*). Similarly, referral for "counseling" is likely to be misinterpreted, because in dialect "counseling" variously refers to "scolding," "instructing," or "preaching," misconceptions easily sustained in the absence of direct experience. However, once Caribbean blacks have been induced to attend, the counselor, Christiansen et al. (1982) stress, needs to respect family hierarchy by seeing only the parents at first and delaying direct parent-child confrontation. They also commend the effort to combine religious parables and stories with psychological notions.

More generally, all that has been said above about Caribbean blacks supports a counterintuitive conclusion, namely, that although blacks and Caribbean blacks may look and often act alike, these similarities hide fundamental differences in culture.

Hispanics

Hispanics are a heterogeneous group made up of Spanish-speaking peoples from Mexico, Puerto Rico, Cuba, the Caribbean, Spain, and Central and South America. In the United States, Mexicans (Latinos)

TABLE 8.4 Summary Profile of Hispanics

Modal social class:	lower/working
Definition of the family:	informal extended, including godparents and "lent" children
Life cycle:	compressed, six phases, with elongation of adolescence and middle adulthood
Husband-wife relations:	patriarchal, with clear role segregation
Parent-child relations:	authoritarian; double standard
Perspective on treatment:	community sources of help preferred, including spiritual healers

(Dana, 1993; Valdivieso & Davis, 1988) are the largest subgroup (62%), followed by Puerto Ricans (*Puertoriquenos*) (13%), Cubans (*Cubanos*) (5%), Central and South Americans (12%), and others (8%). In Canada, most Hispanics originate from Central and South American (Hartzman, 1991; Logan, 1991).

In both countries, Hispanic subgroups are characterized by different histories, traditions, and beliefs (Devore & Schlesinger, 1987; Garcia-Preto, 1982). Our discussion focuses on the Latinos and the Puerto Ricans, newly arrived and long resident, because they have received the most attention in the literature (Bean, 1987; Bean & Tienda, 1987; Keefe & Padilla, 1987; Rodriguez, 1992). The profile of Hispanics is summarized in Table 8.4, with detailed description in the text. In the absence of evidence to the contrary, no effort is made to distinguish between American and Canadian populations.

Modal Social Class

The history of Hispanics in North America is typically one of migration—sometimes legal, sometimes not (Bean, 1983)—of a mostly rural, agricultural people seeking a better life for themselves and their children in urban, industrialized North America (Massey & Schnabel, 1983; McGoldrick et al., 1989). Data on a range of demographic indicators (Dana, 1993; Valdiveso & Davis, 1988) tell a story not unlike that examined above for the blacks.

The majority of Latinos (54%) and Puerto Ricans (67%) have a high school education or less, although the lower educational level is more likely among recent immigrants (Duryea & Gundison, 1993). Although 90% of native-born Hispanics speak English, comparable proportions among recent immigrants vary between 35% and 65%, with 80% reporting some language difficulty (Portes & Truelove, 1987). The immigration status of many Hispanics is uncertain, with a substantial minority likely to be "undocumented aliens" (Bean et al., 1983; Dana, 1993). Out of financial necessity, the labor force participation rate among Hispanics is high, both among men and women (Pedraza, 1991). However, in light of the above, the majority of Latinos and Puerto Ricans are forced to accept unskilled or semiskilled clerical, service, or seasonal jobs characterized by low prestige and pay, and high rates of turnover and underemployment (Rodriguez & Melendez, 1992; Safa, 1984). This situation explains the fact that among Hispanics 26% of intact families and 47% of single parent families report income below the poverty line, with another 20% in both groups classed as working poor (Dana, 1993). Thus, the majority of Hispanics are lower or working class.

Definition of the Family

Among Hispanics, the family is the multigenerational informal extended family (Griffith & Villavicencio, 1985; Sabogal, Marin, Otero-Sabofal, VanOss Martin, & Perez-Sable, 1989). This structure explains their distinction between the immediate (*la casa*) and the extended kinship network (*la familia*). Such networks expand vertically and laterally to include grandparents, uncles and aunts, cousins (to the third and fourth generation), godparents (*compadres, comadres*) and close family friends (*amistad, cuatismo*). Even relations with nonfamily members are family-like in intensity (Murillo, 1976). In times of crisis, family boundaries are sufficiently flexible and the norms of mutual support (*confianza en confianza*) sufficiently strong to sanction child lending (Garcia-Preto, 1982) as well as taking in relatives for varying lengths of time.

Relations within kinship systems may be variously characterized by personalism, familism, hierarchical organization, honor, and cohesion (Taylor & Sanchez, 1991). Personalism refers to a meaning system in which members are encouraged to see the world in terms of personal relationship with others (Mindel, 1980). Thus time is seen as flexible, based on interpersonal priorities. Tasks have no inherent salience apart from the relationships from which they emerge. In short, the importance of relating to others stands as a cornerstone of the Hispanic meaning system. In turn, social relations among Hispanics may be typified as friendly, spontaneous, emotional, and unorganized (Duryea & Gundison, 1993). A variety of patterns of relating supports this approach, including residential closeness, frequent contact, social bonds (*personalismo*) based on informal friendliness and affection (*simpatia*), and a warm and accepting atmosphere (*ambiente*). Such relations are epitomized by a comfortable chat (*platicando*) (Triandis, Marin, Lisansky, & Betancourt, 1984). Furthermore, in behavioral terms, these preferences distinguish Hispanics from their white (*Anglo*) counterparts. As Keefe (1984, p. 68) observes,

> For Mexican Americans, it is important to see relatives regularly face-to-face, to embrace, to touch, and to simply be with one another, sharing the minor joys and sorrows of daily life. For Anglos, these things are integral to nuclear family life but less important with regard to extended family ties.

Familism stresses the importance of interdependence and mutual aid (*compadrazgo*) (Taylor & Sanchez, 1991) and discourages autonomy and independent achievement. In particular, confrontation and competition are strongly prohibited, with indirect means (*indirectas*) of dealing with conflict strongly preferred. Accordingly, Hispanics have evolved elaborate methods to ensure control (*controlarse*) of sexual and aggressive impulses (Cohen, 1985). This control relates to the social character of the "self" in Hispanic culture. As Hall (1959, 1976) explains, Hispanics are caught in a dilemma of being exquisitely sensitive to insult or criticism, but prohibited from direct confrontation. On occasion, the result is that without warning there is likely to be a violent response; confrontations can be bitter and, rejecting third-party intermediaries, prolonged. Thus in handling conflict, Hispanics are characterized by a short, rapid escalation of steps; reliance on social rather than personal inhibitions; and an emphasis on control over social situations or processes rather than individuals.

A key mechanism for achieving such control is respect (*respecto*) for authority (Falicov, 1982). Hispanic kinship systems are hierarchical, with older males dominant. Hence, such systems are patriarchal and patrilocal and exemplified by related notions of *machismo* and honor. Machismo applies only to males and may be loosely translated as manliness, courage, and virility. However, it is better understood as an expression of the relationship between authority and responsibility (Davenport & Yurich, 1991). According to group norms, males are obliged to protect and provide for their kin.

However, this obligation can only be understood in cultural context, in beliefs about personalism and familism as well as fatalism (*resignarse*) and strength in the face of the inevitability of hard times (*aguantarse*). Hence, Hispanics typically take a lighthearted approach to work that emphasizes living for today (*chotao*). Although married men are expected to be dignified and hardworking, they do not see work as having value in and of itself (Murillo, 1976); its worth arises from associated social processes.

Finally, in comparison with whites, Hispanic kinship systems are extraordinarily close and cohesive (Dana, 1993; Delgado, 1985). Families within the kinship system often live in close proximity. Feelings of mutual emotional involvement are often intense and visiting frequent, occasioned by all life cycle transitions (such as baptism) as well as a variety of religious ceremonies and festivals (such as Christmas Eve [*Noche Buena*]). Strong ties among siblings and cousins are encouraged, whereas contact with nonfamily members is discouraged (Falicov, 1982). In part, this familial closeness explains a low rate of intermarriage (Fitzpatrick & Gurak, 1979). It also suggests that members can become extremely distressed should such support be absent or the system begin to malfunction (Keefe, Padilla, & Carlos, 1979), as in divorce.

Life Cycle

Falicov and Karrer (1980) describe the Hispanic family life cycle, in comparison with whites, as composed of six stages: an extended childhood, a shortened adolescence, a prolonged courtship, a brief couple stage, an elongated middle age, and a shortened old age.

The cultural emphasis on the group means that child dependence is encouraged, with children seen as extensions of parents (Garcia-Preto, 1982). Young children are indulged, with discipline becoming increasingly strict with advancing age, and focused on obedience and respect for authority (McGoldrick, 1988). With adolescence, a double standard becomes increasingly evident. Whereas *machismo* reflects community expectations of boys, *marianismo* is the equivalent for girls, emphasizing modesty, submissiveness, and virginity. Thus the onset of menstruation marks an important change among Hispanic girls, for the family's honor is now linked to her virtue (Falicov, 1982). In contrast, restrictions on boys begin to ease, with special privileges associated with the position of eldest son. Boys are expected to come to marriage with some sexual experience whose acquisition serves as a rite of passage and one basis for reputation among their social group (*palomillas*) (Murillo, 1976).

The shift from adolescence to adulthood comes with early marriage (Falicov & Karrer, 1980), with childbearing expected soon (Devore & Schlesinger, 1987). Because most Hispanics (90%) are Roman Catholic (Dana, 1993), large families are preferred (Bean, 1987), placing emphasis on parental as opposed to marital functions. In turn, this stress highlights the prolongation of child rearing, the frequent absence of an "empty nest" phase (Falicov, 1982), and approval of a level of closeness that would be regarded as dysfunctional in white families (Zayas & Bryant, 1984).

Such processes also bring into focus Hispanic attitudes toward education. Like blacks, Hispanics' experience of education has often been far from positive. Obstacles to success include limited English language proficiency and attendance at underresourced and sometimes dangerous inner-city schools. Especially important, however, are life cycle norms that (a) associate work with adult pursuits and school with childhood concerns (Falicov, 1982) and that (b) emphasize cooperative behavior at the expense of individual striving (Koss-Chioino & Vargas, 1992). Consequently, Hispanic involvement with education has been problematic at all levels (Mow & Nettles, 1990).

Husband-Wife Relations

Married woman are expected to be strong, flexible, and self-sacrificing in the face of troubles (*hembrismo*) (Comas-Diaz, 1989). This expectation implies a traditional power imbalance favoring husbands (Meierding, 1992) and spousal relations organized around a gender-based division of authority and labor (McGoldrick et al., 1989). However, following Cromwell and Ruiz (1979), Davenport and Yurich (1991), and Takash and Zavella (1993), it is more useful to distinguish between social fiction and social reality.

The fiction is that husbands exercise complete authority over their wives, who are expected to be humble, submissive, compliant, and respectful (McGoldrick et al., 1989). Furthermore, with the emphasis on parenting, relations between spouses can be somewhat formal (Falicov, 1982); neither deep intimacy nor overt conflict is expected (Garcia-Preto, 1982). Given prohibitions against overt conflict, marital problems, should they arise, are typically handled indirectly (Duryea & Gundison, 1993). That is, no effort may be made to clarify issues. Rather, dealing with them may be indefinitely postponed in the common hope that time will heal differences. If discussion of these issues occurs, it will be confined to family members and extended kin, never with children or strangers. Alternately, marital problems may be displaced as concerns over the children. Indeed, lingering parental concerns about child rebelliousness or failure to show respect may suddenly take on special significance (McGoldrick, 1988).

The reality is more varied, as Vazquez-Nuttall, Romero-Garcia, and DeLeon (1987) demonstrate. Although wives may remain respectful of their husbands' authority in public, they may be quite powerful behind the scenes, based especially on their alliance with the children (Comas-Diaz, 1989). Relations between spouses likely distribute on a continuum, from husband dominant to husband submissive to egalitarian (Hawkes & Taylor, 1975). This difference appears related to three factors (Vazquez-Nuttall et al., 1987): time in the United States or Canada, education level, and employment status. The longer their duration in North America, the greater their acculturation, achieved education, and employment status, the greater the likelihood of a shift from "traditional" to "liberal" attitudes. For example, the fact that many Hispanic women work outside the home means that they have a source of financial independence. In turn, this situation may significantly shift the balance of power in the marital relationship (Duryea & Gundison, 1993; Mizio, 1974), challenging traditional male authority, in some cases up to and including divorce.

Parent-Child Relations

Parent-child relations are clearly hierarchical. Although parents may be friendly, they are in charge and not friends (Preto, 1990). The nurturant role of mothers is central, whereas fathers, the occasional role of enforcer aside, are not expected to help with child rearing (McGoldrick et al., 1989). Relations between mothers and children are very close, but differentiated by gender. Mother-son relations are mitigated by expectations of machismo, whereas mother-daughter relations are more reciprocal, because mothers are expected to teach daughters all they need to know to become wives and mothers. This task not only includes modesty and maternal self-sacrifice, but also a passive approach to sexuality (but in the absence of any sexual instruction).

Thus the thrust of child socialization combines gender-specific skills and attitudes with a generic respect for authority. Although discipline may involve spanking, it more typically relies on shame, threats, and belittling (Falicov, 1982). Parents typically take a very relaxed approach to child achievement of developmental milestones or self-reliance. Although adolescents are encouraged to help out around the house, they are not encouraged to work outside the home. In addition, the control function of fathers becomes more obvious as children reach adolescence, when an intergenerational struggle may erupt if children seek to assert their independence (McGoldrick, 1988). This situation is complicated in new immigrant families by the issue of language (Duryea & Grundison, 1993). Unable to speak English, parents may become dependent on their children to translate. In turn, this development accords children much greater power than they would have "back home," thus encouraging them to defy traditional parental authority. The resulting parent-child conflict can be explosive, in extreme cases leading to complete rupture, the children spurning their parents for the street and thus a life of delinquency and drug abuse.

Perspectives on Treatment

Hispanic perspectives on treatment are shaped by beliefs such as machismo, social selves, privacy, and spirits. Machismo enjoins men to resolve problems by the imposition of their will (*sobreponerse*). This value makes it difficult to admit to failure and rationalizes delaying help-seeking until no alternative is available. It also legitimizes somatic complaints. Thus, help-seeking, if it occurs, is more likely to involve medical rather than psychiatric or psychological complaints (McGoldrick, 1982) and explains why mental health services tend to be underused (Solomon, 1988).

Moreover, behavior is explained in terms of situations rather than personalities (Hall, 1976). The idea that a person is mentally ill (*enfermidad mental*) is foreign. Although a person may behave strangely under certain circumstances, the solution is to keep them away from circumstances in which this behavior is likely to arise; the notion that the problem may be "inside" the person is not considered. This attitude explains why Hispanics tend to delegate responsibility for their presenting problems to others (Evans, Acosta, Yamamoto, & Hurwicz, 1986).

Moreover, we have alluded to norms about privacy that prohibit discussion of intimate family matters in front of children or strangers. Thus, wives are likely to feel highly ambivalent about voicing complaints about their spouses to strangers and more comfortable discussing such matters with relatives, *compadres*, friends, or priests.

In addition, many Hispanics continue to believe that illness is the result of extrahuman forces (Dana, 1993), either because troubles may cause the persons's spirit or soul to leave their body (*susto*) or bad spirits may be willfully used to attack a person, typically as a result of jealousy or vengeance, by means of hexes (*mal puesto*), the evil eye (*mal ojo*), and the like (Delgado, 1985). Thus in explaining illness, Hispanics who hold such beliefs make no distinction between natural, supernatural, and superstitious causes. In turn, they are likely to seek relief by consulting folk healers (Delgado, 1988).

Finally, Garcia-Preto (1982) warns that Hispanics who seek formal therapy are likely to take an informal approach to appointments, prefer home visits, seek service only in crisis, and drop out as soon as the crisis appears to have passed. Falicov (1982, in press) adds that

TABLE 8.5 Summary Profile of Asians

Modal social class:	middle
Definition of the family:	formal extended, including deceased ancestors
Life cycle:	elongated, six phases, especially adolescence and early adulthood
Husband-wife relations:	patriarchal, with clear role segregation
Parent-child relations:	hierarchical interdependence
Perspective on treatment:	informal and community-based sources of help preferred

of various forms of mental health service, family therapy is likely to be the most acceptable, especially if it is brief, highly structured, conducted in Spanish, and employs indirect techniques such as allusion and storytelling. If successful, through time, family behavior is likely to gradually shift from the formality expected when interacting with a stranger to the informal friendliness expected when dealing with kin.

Asians

Asians in North America comprise 32 distinct groups (Dana, 1993). In 1990, in the United States they distributed as follows: Chinese, 23%; Filipino, 19%; South Asian (Indian), 16%; Japanese, 12%; Korean, 11%; Indochinese (from Myanmar [formerly Burma], Cambodia, Laos [including the H'mong people], Thailand and Vietnam), 8%, and "other," 16% (Porter & Washington, 1993). In 1991, in Canada they distributed differently: Chinese, 42%; South Asian (Indian), 30%; Filipino, 11%; Indochinese, 8.5%; Japanese, 3.5%; Korean, 3.1%; and "other," 1.9%.

Our discussion concentrates on the Chinese and Japanese—both newly arrived and long-resident—because they have received the most attention in the literature (Dana, 1993; Fugita & O'Brien, 1991; Kitano, 1976; Kitano & Daniels, 1990; Portes & Rumbaut, 1990), although occasional reference will be made to other subgroups. The profile of Asians is summarized in Table 8.5, with detailed description in the text.

Given substantial evidence of similarity (see below), no effort will be made to distinguish between American and Canadian populations.

Modal Social Class

In North America, the social status of Asians has been shaped by six interrelated processes: history, immigration, education, language, employment, and cultural values.

Historically, Asians have been subject to unremitting discrimination, racism, and oppression (Adachi, 1991; Li, 1988; Takaki, 1989). In the late 19th century, for example, Chinese men were recruited as cheap, disposable manual laborers (Boswell, 1986). The result was "bachelor" communities (Thompson, 1989) where men worked and died under appalling conditions (Ong, 1981). Later, women were allowed entry, but their numbers were few and, although more likely than men to be accepted into mainstream society (Kitano & Yeung, 1982), they were confronted by sexist stereotypes (McGoldrick et al., 1989).

In part, this treatment reflected the relatively small numbers of Asian immigrants allowed into North America. Changes in immigration policies mean that what was once a trickle has become a flood, with Asians now representing the largest of the various national groups streaming into North America in record numbers (Logan, 1991). The result has been dramatic, changing the shape of subgroup communities and rendering Asians a dynamic force (Aldrich & Waldinger, 1990). Among the Chinese, for example, the immigrant influx is largely responsible for a dramatic shift from a "bachelor" to a family-based community and, with it, the proliferation of Chinatowns in major cities across North America (Godfrey, 1988; Lai, 1988; Thompson, 1989).

An additional factor shaping the status striving of Asians has been their outstanding educational attainment, second only to the Jews in North America (Breton et al., 1990; Fugita & O'Brien, 1991). In the United States, for example, Asians have been dramatically more successful in higher education than blacks or Hispanics and at least on par with whites (Levine & Rhodes, 1981; Nagasawa & Espinoza, 1992).

In part, this achievement may reflect their level of proficiency in English (McDowell, 1992). English proficiency is clearly related to how long they have lived in North America, with recent immigrants at a distinct disadvantage. For example, in the United States, Tsang (1989) estimates that 65% of Asians speak a language other than English at home and 5 or more years after immigration 20% have acquired very limited English proficiency. By contrast, Fugita and O'Brien (1991) observe that among the *Yonsei* (fourth generation) Japanese, virtually all are fluent in English and indeed more than half do not speak Japanese, a fact that can occasion considerable intergenerational conflict. In both the United States and Canada, such proficiency may, at least in part, account for two facts about the Japanese: a high rate of intermarriage (at or above 50%; Fugita & O'Brien, 1991; Ram, 1990) coupled with a low rate of residential segregation (Breton et al., 1990; Fugita & O'Brien, 1991).

Another facet of the status picture concerns employment, especially self-employment. With respect to the former, among recent immigrants (especially women) and specific subgroups (especially the Indo-Chinese), language barriers, restricted skills and education, and various degrees of discrimination have meant that they are confined to low-level employment characterized by long hours and low wages (Boyd, 1990; Cabesas & Kawaguchi, 1986). In contrast, among immigrants who have been in North America for generations or those who arrived recently but with professional skills and education, the majority have been concentrated in high-status, white-collar employment (Breton et al., 1990; Moreau, 1990). Such status has been associated with a low rate of fertility (Halli, 1987a, 1987b). As for self-employment, Asians, especially Chinese, Japanese, and Koreans, have been pushed into small business, at which they have been very successful, which accounts for self-employment rates of 21% and 20% among the Koreans (Light & Bonacich, 1988) and *Sansei* (third generation) Japanese (Fugita & O'Brien, 1991), respectively.

Finally, their success is based on yet another dimension: culture, which involves three interlocking elements (Fugita & O'Brien, 1991): economic adaptations in response to exclusion from mainstream economic activity (see above); socialization into middle-class family life; and, perhaps most important, a supportive cultural milieu. Middle-class socialization includes values emphasizing hard work, deferred gratification, and a future orientation, with the roots of these values in a particular kinship system (see below) and a legacy of labor-intensive agriculture (Thompson, 1989).

The cultural milieu involves a complex, multifaceted belief system. At the heart of this system is support for what has variously been described as "ascriptive ties" (Light, 1972) or "structural intimacy" (Kiefer, 1971), that is, the belief that Asians are ethically bound to behave honorably in financial dealings with other Asians. In related fashion, they show a propensity to buy and sell to and from each other, in part because of a shared, nonassertive interactional style. Historically, this interaction has been assisted by their development of small-scale, community-based financial institutions (such as the *tanomosho* among the Japanese or the *hui* among the Chinese) designed to assist small businesses (Fugita & O'Brien, 1991). Furthermore, Asians are characterized by a high level of participation in voluntary community organizations dedicated to promoting harmonious interpersonal relations (Fugita & O'Brien, 1991). This reflects a collective orientation (see below) emphasizing group preservation, even at the expense of individual interests (Hall, 1976). Accordingly, Asians tend to see and treat other Asians as quasi-kin (Hall, 1976). Finally, and paradoxically, Asians have found a way to balance high levels of acculturation with equally high levels of group identification, based on a strong and abiding sense of "peoplehood" (Haglund, 1984). Indeed, various authors have argued that Asian business success has been a critical factor in promoting community solidarity (Makabe, 1979; Wong, 1982).

In combination, these various factors account for steady upward mobility, with the majority of second and later generation Asians middle class (Li, 1992; Nee & Wong, 1985).

Definition of the Family

Asians emphasize the collectivity (Cushman, 1990; Sampson, 1988). Thus, the individual is coextensive with and superseded by the family (Tamura & Lau, 1992). Indeed, among the Japanese, Roland (1988) refers to a "familyself." In turn, the family extends in both place and time (Li, 1988), going beyond the nuclear unit to include all blood relations (Yung, 1986) and beyond the present to include deceased ancestors (Chao, 1990).

In this context, Asian families are organized hierarchically, based on age, gender, and rank (Lau, 1986). However, it will be useful to distinguish between traditional and acculturated expressions. Among the

Japanese, the historical prototype for such an arrangement is the *iemoto*, literally, the "origin of the household or the household root" (McGill, 1987), which prescribes a superior-subordinate quasi-kin relationship among all members of the nation, from the emperor to the lowest peasant farmer. Among the Chinese, the counterpart is filial piety (Shon & Ja, 1982) whereby every family member is obliged to honor and obey those above one in the hierarchy.

Furthermore, kinship ties are traditionally highly structured in accordance with patriarchal principles and formalized rules. Inheritance is patrilineal, both property and rank passing from father to eldest son (McGoldrick et al., 1989). Authority and obligation are reciprocal (Shon & Ja, 1982) and characterized by restraint, dependence, and interpersonal sensitivity (Korean: *nunch'i*; Japanese: *ki*; Tamura & Lau, 1992). Accordingly, interaction emphasizes helpfulness, kindness, sensitivity, consensus, and harmony (Korean: *hwa hae*) (Yum, 1988). Based on rank, members are expected to defer to others, devalue their individual importance, and avoid confrontation (Devore & Schlesinger, 1987); direct conflict reflects the inability to maintain harmony (LeResche, 1992), and is thus a source of shame or loss of face (Chinese: *mentz*; Japanese: *haji*; Korean: *chaemyun*; Filipino: *hiya*; Li, 1988). Such shame highlights the central importance of family honor, the improper behavior of any member causing the whole family to lose face.

Note that the authors cited above present their accounts in the present tense, implying their contemporary relevance. There is, however, reason to think they may be only partly right. In the United States, for example, Fugita and O'Brien (1991) argue that the Japanese show few signs of *iemoto* because it is inconsistent with American norms of casual egalitarianism and discouraged by the small size of many Japanese communities. Instead, it is easier to create horizontal peer relations within generations whose key expression is the voluntary organization. In Canada, Maykovich (1980), in an old but useful study, makes similar observations. The study found that Japanese in Toronto were widely dispersed and upwardly mobile. Although a group orientation remained common, it was by no means universal, with many preferring to identify themselves as "Canadians" rather than "Japanese." Parents remained influential, but adult children were more inclined to emphasize marital obligations than filial piety. The main language in the home, at least among *Sansei* (third generation) Japanese, was English.

These observations suggest that authors have erred in failing to make distinctions on the basis of ethnic group, generation, and immigration. Asian families across North America are likely to vary on a spectrum in their commitment to traditional norms (Lee, 1989). The above portrait will be most relevant to families at the traditional end of the spectrum: recent immigrants, elderly parents, and families who find this approach philosophically appealing. The majority, in contrast, will likely have moved to the acculturated end of the spectrum, where many aspects of culture will have fallen away, including language, religion, dress codes, strict hierarchical divisions, and food preferences. What is left is quintessentially Asian in its emphasis on harmonious and consensual social relations, and its strong self-identification with subgroup culture, but is otherwise indistinguishable from white, middle-class families. This spectrum, then, qualifies all that follows.

Life Cycle

The life cycle of the Asian family is shaped and elongated by concerns with achievement and mutual dependence (Japanese: *amae*). Following Fulmer's (1988) description of the "professional family," the phases of adolescence and young adulthood are expanded to meet the needs first of education and later of occupational or professional achievement (Shon & Ja, 1982). Such behavior illuminates Asian attitudes to time and work, sacrificing the present for the future (Shon & Ja, 1982) while enduring pain to ensure success (Thompson, 1989).

As for dependence, childhood is elongated by a positive view of mutual dependence (Suzuki, 1980). Thus Japanese mothers typically assume that children are born in a state of independence and must be drawn, through persuasion and reasoning, into dependence (Kitano, 1980). Accordingly, child passivity, submissiveness, and dependence are encouraged (Sanua, 1985), with normal development seen to proceed from immature to mature dependence (Colman, 1986).

Mature dependence is achieved only in middle adulthood associated with marriage and childbearing (Shon & Ja, 1982). Subsequently, life is oriented to work and parenting rather than marital intimacy (McGoldrick et al., 1989), whereas old age brings with it the respect accorded high rank (Yu, 1984). Accordingly, aging parents or other relatives need not fear abandonment because they will be involved in paid employment or child care or be cared for in the home of an adult child (McGoldrick, 1988).

Husband-Wife Relations

Historically, marriage had nothing to do with the spouses (McGoldrick et al., 1989). Rather, aided by a go-between (Japanese: *baishakunin)* or middleman (Japanese: *nakohdo;* Vogel, 1967), it was an arrangement between families or clans to recruit a female into the male line. The past half century has brought significant change. However, the character of spousal relations depends on their position on the traditional-acculturated spectrum discussed above. Among the minority of traditional families, marriages are still semiarranged (Lau, 1986). Among the acculturated majority, marriage for love is the norm. The expression of such intimacy, however, is mitigated both by norms emphasizing emotional control and the salience of parenting. Thus feelings of love and concern are more likely be expressed by caring for the other's physical needs—by good food and pleasant surroundings—than by words (Tseng & Wu, 1985). Similarly, wives seldom talk spontaneously or discuss opinions or feelings with their husbands (Tseng & Hsu, 1991).

Such separateness is also encouraged by role segregation (Duryea & Gundison, 1993), which accords wives and husbands very different rights and responsibilities. Wives, for example, are in control of the home and associated household monies. Household activities remain their domain, with the generous assistance of other women in the kin system. In contrast, husbands are responsible for dealings with the outside world and are not expected to help with household chores or child care. Those who fail to fulfill their material obligations (through unemployment or illness) risk shame and dishonor (Shon & Ja, 1982). Extramarital relations continue to be viewed indulgently for men but are prohibited for women. Although both parties can now initiate divorce (McGoldrick et al., 1989), divorce rates remain comparatively low (Cox, 1993; Sev'er, 1993). This fact relates to three processes: the centrality of family life as an organizing norm; the fact that divorce continues to be seen as a source of disgrace and dishonor, especially for women (Chin & Associates, 1993); and the restraining influence of extended kin (Lai & Yue, 1990).

In addition to providing child care, extended kin continue to be important in other areas. For example, for financial reasons, brides still often move in with the family of the groom (patrilocality) and mothers-in-law still carry much authority. Thus that relationship can be fraught with tension, sometimes mitigated by alliances between brides and their sisters-in-law (Lau, 1986). Even so, parents and other extended kin would likely be involved with both spouses in dealing with serious family problems (Lai & Yue, 1990), including marital difficulties. This involvement not only reflects the esteem with which older, and thus higher status, family members are held, but also the reluctance of spouses to deal directly with such difficulties among themselves (Duryea & Gundison, 1993; Tseng & Hsu, 1991).

Finally, changes related to immigration and mobility have begun to undermine the traditional stability of Asian marriages. Among families newly arrived in North America, the traditionally subservient position of wives can be significantly mitigated by immigration (Duryea & Gundison, 1993), with the one to arrive in North America first often in a dominant position, because he or she knows better than the spouse how things work.

Among Asian families resident in North America over generations, the single most important change has been women's increased status by virtue of their involvement in higher education and subsequently in white-collar work (McGoldrick et al., 1989). In the work context, contrary to traditional norms, women are expected to be effective and assertive. Their success in such efforts has brought them considerable economic freedom, but with double-edged consequences. On the one hand, in many Asian families, spousal relations have become much more egalitarian than would be expected among their traditional counterparts (Devore & Schlesinger, 1987). On the other hand, changing standards have sparked spousal conflict, including increased rates of family violence and divorce (McGoldrick et al., 1989).

Parent-Child Relations

In Asian families, fathers, mothers, and children have different roles to play. Children's lives are, in contrast to their white counterparts, fully integrated with those of their parents and other adults in the kin network. In the words of Tseng and Wu (1985, p. 128), "[the child] is not the center of the social world but is only part of a social network of individuals who are intimate yet variously dominant." In practical terms, this position means, for example, that there are likely to be few restrictions on children when they make noise in the presence of adults (Tseng & Hsu, 1991).

Fathers tend to be associated with discipline and can be distant from their children (Sue & Morishima, 1982), whereas mothers take deep satisfaction from child care (Morsbach, 1978). The mother-child relationship is a very special one. It is the only one that permits the open expression of love. It can also represent a covert form of power, with mothers forming alliances with their children that can extend well past adolescence. Given the approval of stoicism in the face of adversity (Japanese: *shitagtanai* [water under the bridge]), admissions of adult distress are associated with a loss of face (Shon & Ja, 1982). Accordingly, child rather than adult behavior is much more likely to be seen as problematic. This attitude applies especially to issues of academic success and demonstrations of obedience and respect for adults.

However, such processes can be complicated through exposure to the dominant culture, with its emphasis on autonomy and individualism (Fong, 1973; Muzny, 1989). The result can be intergenerational conflict, with parents distressed by their children's failure to show gratitude (Aranas, 1983) or their refusal to learn the family's native language (Ho, 1992a). Similarly, Lau (1986) indicates that more serious, indeed explosive, consequences can follow cultural conflict between the generations. Furthermore, these sources of conflict extend into the school. There, it can place Asian youth in a bind, being "too Asian" for their peers and "too American" or "too Canadian" for their parents (Chao, 1990). Finally, children's educational experience can provide yet another source of parent-child conflict. With a traditional emphasis on prosperity and financial support for the elderly, Asian parents may place intense pressure on their children to pursue a professional career in such areas as medicine, law, engineering, computer science, or commerce. Consequently, children whose aspirations lead them toward careers in the arts are likely to encounter considerable parental hostility (Duryea & Gundison, 1993).

Perspectives on Treatment

Finally, the Asian approach to illness and help-seeking is shaped by two interlocking belief systems. The first involves a humoral model of illness and disease. This posits that health requires a balance of good and bad (Chinese: *yin-yang*) or hot and cold (Vietnamese) forces or energies (Chinese: *chi*; Chao, 1990). This belief accords greater respectability to somatic complaints and resists recognition of psychological or psychiatric problems (Devore & Schlesinger, 1987; Lin et al., 1978). Indeed, based on a stark dichotomy between "normal" and "crazy" (Shon & Ja, 1982), those admitting to psychiatric disorder may be heavily stigmatized by their peers (Health & Welfare Canada, 1988).

The humoral model of illness is complemented by a spiritual view of mind. Thus, Tamura and Lau (1992) suggest that Asians tend to deal with problems by internalizing rather then externalizing them. This reaction, they suggest, can be traced to the Buddhist belief that each person has a "true" voice, one that is always good. Distress or illness thus reflects failure to listen to that voice, often because of the loss of harmony in social relations (LeResche, 1992). This view is also consistent with two observations by Hall (1976): that the Chinese deal with minor problems by pretending they do not exist, for to acknowledge them would require some action, which is very serious; and that the Japanese make no distinction between active and inactive, so that what a Western person might see as "just plain sitting," a Japanese person would see as doing something useful.

The upshot of these perspectives on illness involves two related forms of treatment. Active forms of treatment involve measures designed to restore balance, including the use of acupuncture, medicinal herbs, "coining" (massage using the edge of a coin), moxibustion (burning a cone of herbs placed along acupuncture points), and "cupping" (a glass container, evacuated by heat, used to draw blood to the surface of the skin; Chao, 1990; Health & Welfare Canada, 1988). Passive or "quiet" forms of treatment (Reynolds, 1980) are also used, especially solitary meditation and contemplation (LeResche, 1992).

In this context, it is hardly surprising that Asians tend to underuse mental health services (Murase, Egawa, & Tashima, 1985; Yamamoto, 1982). Indeed, families may delay seeking treatment so long that a condition has advanced to the point of psychosis (Sanua, 1985). When they do eventually seek mental health services, cultural biases among white service providers may significantly distort mental health assessments (Sue, 1981). Conversely, Asian clients tend to approach service providers differently than do their white counterparts. The Japanese, for example, tend to view therapists as teachers (*sensei*) and expect them to be active, even authoritative, while connecting with and caring for the family, thus justifying family informality, as if they were family "insiders" (Tamura & Lau, 1992).

Accordingly, therapy with Asians, especially recent immigrants, should involve some combination of the following (Chao, 1990; Ho, 1992a, 1992b). Therapists should adopt a relatively authoritarian stance, based on their status as knowledgeable experts. Therapy should be directive, whereas communication should be indirect, with no effort made to hurry the process. Harmony rather than independence or self-realization should be the goals of treatment, and no effort should be made to encourage or force the expression of feelings. Discussion of topics such as sexuality or aggression should be avoided. And, whereas family therapy is an acceptable treatment modality, it should focus on activity rather than insight. Conversely, the use of standard forms of service with Asians has proven ineffective (Mokuan, 1987; Tsui & Schultz, 1985).

Jews

For comparative purposes, the final ethnic group to be examined is Jews. Jews are a heterogeneous group, including Sephardic Jews from the Iberian Peninsula, western Asia and North Africa, and Ashkenazi Jews from Eastern and Central Europe (Taieb-Carlen, 1992). In North America, the latter represent about 75% of the total Jewish population (Herz & Rosen, 1982), with the majority having lived in North America for three or more generations. Furthermore, Ashkenazi Jews can be distinguished in terms of their degree of religious orthodoxy, ranging from liberal (Reform) to conservative (Conservative) to orthodox (Orthodox, Ultra-Orthodox [e.g., *Hassidim*]).

In the United States in 1990, Jews numbered about 7 million (Waxman, 1992) or 2.7% of the general population. In Canada in 1991, Jews numbered 246,000 or just under 1% of the general population. Our discussion concentrates on long-resident Ashkenazi Jews because

TABLE 8.6 Summary Profile of Jews

Modal social class:	middle
Definition of the family:	nuclear family
Life cycle:	elongated, six phases, especially adolescence and early adulthood
Husband-wife relations:	egalitarian
Parent-child relations:	democractic, permissive, emphasis on child success
Perspective on treatment:	formal sources of help preferred

they have received the most attention in the literature (Devore & Schlesinger, 1987; Tavuchis, 1989). The profile of Jews is summarized in Table 8.6, with detailed description in the text. Given substantial evidence of similarity (see below), no effort will be made to distinguish between American and Canadian populations.

Modal Social Class

Two facets of the history of the Jews helps explain much of what follows in describing them: study and persecution.

Study refers to a traditional reverence for intellectuality and educational pursuits (Abella, 1990). Historically, the Jews of Eastern Europe highly valued the pious, sedentary life of the scholar devoted to religious study (Stein, 1985), a vocation open only to men. This value left the family in chronic poverty and the women with much training in the practical art of making do with very little (Zborowski & Herzog, 1952). The modern consequence of this tradition has been a people who value education, complex verbal reasoning, and direct emotional expression, logical and critical thought, openness to new ideas, problem solving through discussion, analysis and inquiry, respect for "experts," and the importance of insight and understanding. Conversely, they are likely to be suspicious of things physical (Devore & Schlesinger, 1987).

Persecution refers to traditional adaptations to suffering. Historically, in Europe Jews were not permitted to travel, own land, gain higher education, or enter the professions, thus institutionalizing their chronic poverty. They were subject to periodic murderous attacks (*pogroms*) culminating in the Holocaust associated with World War II (Epstein, 1979). The Holocaust had several immediate consequences (Benkin, 1978): Forced into ghettos, Jews came to think of themselves as "outsiders"; the objects of hatred, they became unusually self-reliant, especially in terms of forming and operating voluntary self-help organizations; excluded from the mainstream economy, they became expert in the few areas open to them, especially business and finance; the latter required routine dealings with non-Jews (*goys*), and they preferred to buy from and sell to each other; and toward the end of the 19th century, they were highly motivated to escape to North America (among other destinations) through emigration.

In North America, during the first half of this century, Jews confronted conditions that, although less extreme, were familiar, including virulent antisemitism (Abella, 1990; Herz & Rosen, 1982). Their response was to apply the same solutions that had helped them survive in Europe: an emphasis on self-employment (Goldscheider & Kobrin, 1980; Perlman, 1983) within the context of an ethnic enclave (Rischin, 1962); reliance on voluntary self-help organizations (Benkin, 1978; Turner & Bonacich, 1980); a propensity to buy from and sell to each other (Bonacich, 1973) within an urban ghetto (Gendrot & Turner, 1983); and a sense of what Rose (1959) calls "dual cultural membership" (see Fowler, 1977), that is, skills allowing comfortable interaction with Jews or non-Jews.

In characterizing Jews in the present, it is useful to distinguish between general and specific outcomes. Among the general consequences are a people who fear persecution; deal with problems by intensifying closeness and interaction; are extremely flexible and adaptive; see suffering as inevitable and thus to be shared and borne with pride rather than overcome; identify with the poor; sustain a belief in philanthropy and see good works (*tzedaka*) (Sklare, 1972) as a religious obligation and a blessing (*mitzvah*); feel a driving need to achieve material success (Fernando, 1986); and place inordinate emphasis on food (Braverman, 1990; Tuchman & Levine, 1993).

More specific outcomes, seen in comparative perspective, include the following. Jews have higher levels of educational achievement (Shamai, 1992) than any group examined above, including overrepresentation in professional occupations such medicine and law

(Braverman, 1990; Breton et al., 1990); higher levels of residential segregation (Breton et al., 1990; Silberman, 1985) than blacks, Caribbean blacks, or Hispanics, and much higher than Asians. Jews have an intermarriage rate of about 25% (McGoldrick, 1982; Silberman, 1985), higher than blacks and Hispanics, on par with Caribbean blacks, but lower than Asians. Their (high) level of ethnic identification (Kallen, 1976; Silberman, 1985) is on par with other groups, but unlike those of other groups, has declined very little across generations (Breton et al., 1990). Their (low) fertility rate (Braverman, 1990; Halli, Trovato, & Driedger, 1990; Tavuchis, 1989) is on par with Asians and Caribbean blacks, lower than blacks, and much lower than Hispanics. Finally, the average income (Breton et al., 1990; Heilman & Cohen, 1989; Tavuchis, 1989) of Jews is on a par with Asians, higher than Caribbean blacks, and much higher than blacks and Hispanics.

It seems safe to conclude that the majority of Jews fall into the middle class.

Definition of the Family

Like Hispanics, Jews are characterized by familism, which emphasizes the central importance of family life (Zuk, 1978). Marriage is seen as a duty (Birnbaum, 1975), and celibacy is condemned (Herz & Rosen, 1982). Husbands are expected to be good spouses, fathers, and providers; wives are expected to be good spouses as well as the mother of intelligent children. Thus unlike any of the groups examined thus far, the Jewish focus is on the nuclear as opposed to the extended family. The extended family is important, but not central.

Life Cycle

Following Fulmer (1988), the Jews are a classic example of the elongated life cycle typical of the professional family. At an early age, parents, especially mothers, are deeply invested in child academic achievement (Sanua, 1978), and are ready to make any sacrifices necessary to translate existing talents into concrete achievements. Later, the *bar mitzvah* (for boys at the age of 13) or the *bas mitzvah* (for girls at the age of 12) are special rituals that reflect the value placed by Jews on intellectual development (McGoldrick, 1988).

Next, higher education coupled with graduate or professional school are typically taken for granted (Herz & Rosen, 1982), delaying marriage and childbearing. Leaving home may also be delayed (McGoldrick, 1988). As McGoldrick (1988) suggests, such leaving may be characterized by "ambivalent closeness," that is, distance mitigated by guilt at going, coupled with the expectation of ongoing, intimate interaction with parents.

Later still, parenting is complicated by the rigors of consolidating a professional career and being involved in the larger community, especially in voluntary self-help organizations (Silberman, 1985). Finally, following an empty nest period, old age may be characterized by caregiving by an adult child. However, unlike the other groups examined above, Jews see institutional care as an acceptable solution (McGoldrick, 1988), a fact exemplified by an extensive network of community-funded charities and residential and nursing homes (Devore & Schlesinger, 1987).

Husband-Wife Relations

The character of husband-wife relations turns on the family's position on the spectrum of religious belief.

Among orthodox families (Bulka, 1986; Irving & Benjamin, 1992), marriage and family life is organized in accord with Jewish law (halakhah), with the goal of achieving marital satisfaction (shalom bayit). Arranged marriage, often with the aid of a marriage broker (shadkhan), is still common. The marriage ceremony itself, foreshadowing what is to follow, involves complete gender segregation. In turn, married life is shaped by strict adherence to an array of prescriptions or commandments (taryag mitzos)—613 in all—drawn from the first five books of the Old Testament (the torah) or the accumulated commentaries about the latter (the Talmud), which regulates virtually all aspects of life, including dress, diet, religious observance, community relations, and married life. Men grow beards and earlocks (payess). They wear skullcaps (yarmulkes) and garments made only of natural fibers (sha'atnez), including special tasseled undershirts (tzitzits). Women wear extremely modest clothing and no makeup, shave their heads, and wear wigs. Monthly, they go to a ritual bath (mikveh). Dietary laws (kashrut, kosher) dictate that milk and meat never be mixed, and forbid the consumption of foods seen as unclean (*trayf*), especially pork. Religious observance not only includes a variety of festivals (*yomtovim*), but organizes daily life, with prayer required three times daily. Prayer on the Sabbath, which extends from Friday sundown to Saturday sundown, is not only segregated by gender, but forbids 39 kinds of work. Good works and charity may entail donating up to 10% or more (*maaser*) of a family's annual income.

Finally, married life is characterized by role segregation, with religious tradition specifying (by written contract [*ketuvah*]) the rights and obligations of each spouse. For example, both spouses are seen as having a right to sexual satisfaction, such that the frequency of sexual relations is regulated. In turn, childbearing is an obligation, with birth control strictly forbidden; families with 6 to 12 or more children are not uncommon. Orthodox culture is patriarchal (Baum, Hyman, & Michael, 1975), with most authority accruing to older males. As wives, women are expected to be patient and submissive; as mothers they are expected to be self-sacrificing and devoted to child care and housekeeping. As husbands, men are expected to be faithful and prosperous; as fathers they are expected to help with discipline and instruction. Given these specialized requirements, orthodox families often form small, relatively segregated, homogeneous communities.

In contrast, Reform Jewish families are, in many ways, indistinguishable from what is typical among dual-career families in the dominant culture. Marriage is seen as extremely important, with much effort on the part of the family to ensure good, stable marriages between daughters and successful, prosperous husbands (Herz & Rosen, 1982). In turn, marriage is based on love. Relations among the spouses are democratic and egalitarian, with both agreeing on the primacy of family life (McGoldrick, 1988) and birth control (Silberman, 1985). Both parents share child care and housekeeping tasks, although the balance still often tilts toward women, who thus must juggle family and career responsibilities. Consequently, not only is the marriage rate high, but the divorce rate is correspondingly low (Herz & Rosen, 1982; Vigod, 1984).

However, even in divorce, Orthodox and Reform Jewish families can be distinguished (Irving & Benjamin, 1992; Syrtash, 1992). Although both groups necessarily seek divorce through the civil courts, only the Orthodox also seek divorce through the rabbinical court (*Beth Din*).

Because under Jewish law marriage is entered into voluntarily and without coercion, it can only be dissolved in the same way, indicated by the giving and receiving of formal notice of consent (*get*). However, here the spouses are not equal, for only husbands can give a get; wives can only receive one. This inequity has four consequences. First, it speaks to child custody. Under the age of 6, male children are traditionally given into the custody of the father, whereas female children go to the mother; the case of older children is decided individually, on the basis of child best interest. Next, it addresses child support. Under Jewish law, fathers are obliged to support their daughter(s) to the age of majority (even should a former wife remarry) and son(s) to the age of 6; after 6, should the son(s) be given into the custody of the mother, the responsibility for his support becomes hers. Third, in couples whose marriage was the product of religious intermarriage, typically between a Christian and a Jew, it can create serious problems around child education and upbringing. In such cases, the Christian partner may have converted to Judaism. On divorce, some revert back to Christianity. The court is thus confronted by a couple, one of whom insists that the child(ren) be raised as Orthodox Jews and the other of whom is equally adamant that they be raised as Christians. Finally, it creates a situation unique among Orthodox Jews, for a husband may refuse to give his wife a *get*. This refusal transforms her into an *agunah*, a chained woman, one who does not live with her husband, receives no support from him, but cannot be divorced from him, and so is forbidden to remarry or live with another man. If she does so anyway, she risks being branded an adulteress and any children of the union are considered bastards who, as adults, may only marry others who are the product of a similarly illicit relationship.

Parent-Child Relations

Parent-child relations also turn on the level of religious commitment. Among Orthodox families, child care is often shared among the women. Child socialization is directed toward fostering intellectual achievement, autonomy, and religious faith. However, most parenting tasks are distributed along gender lines. Thus, the training, instruction, and discipline (based solely on reason) of boys is left almost exclusively to fathers. Although the formal education of boys and girls is similar, they are sent to different private schools, although both meet all state educational requirements. Schools for boys, however, attend equally to language and religious instruction, making for a demanding educational course (Helmreich, 1986). Schools for girls are similar but stress skills related to female roles in the home (*yiddishkeit*).

In contrast, among Reform families, child care is shared by both parents. Child socialization stresses intellectual achievement, independence, emotional development, and social skills (McGoldrick, 1988). Moreover, compared to blacks or Hispanics, Jewish children are allowed so much more latitude that they might appear spoiled (*zelosen*) (Blau, 1974). As Silberman (1985, p. 138) explains, "Jewish parents traditionally have seen their children as extensions of themselves rather than separate, still less subordinate, creatures; . . . children are their parents' *nachas*—a hard-to-translate term that means that children provide their parents with honor and fulfillment as well as with joy." He adds, however, that indulgence is coupled with high expectations and rigorous standards in keeping with demanding and ambitious parents; thus, no one is spared, neither children nor parents (Blau, 1974; Braverman, 1990).

This standard is exemplified in education. Educated in the public school system, children may receive supplementary instruction in languages and religion after school (Devore & Schlesinger, 1987). Academic success is emphasized (McGoldrick, 1988) and can be a major source of parent-child conflict (Radetsky, Handelsman, & Browne, 1984). However, parenting is often permissive and democratic, with discipline based on reasoning rather than corporal punishment; children are often free to challenge parental beliefs and are included in family problem-solving (Herz & Rosen, 1982). Until very recently, even in such families boys had special status, burdened with the responsibility of being successful and thus ensuring the transmission of Jewish values (Silberman, 1985). Ironically, the later price of their success may be a feeling of relative impotence and lack of appreciation in the face of a powerful wife and demanding children (Herz & Rosen, 1982).

Perspectives on Treatment

Finally, unlike the ethnic groups examined above, Jews do not equate illness with weakness. Rather, they are extremely sensitive to signs of illness, quick to seek medical treatment and voluble about their pain (Greenblum, 1974; Sanua, 1985). Although tolerant of deviant thinking (Wylan & Mintz, 1976), they view psychotherapy positively and seek services early (Srole, Langer, Michael, Opler, & Rennie, 1962). Consequently, compared to other groups, they display a much higher rate of outpatient treatment but a much lower rate of serious impairment (Sanua, 1985; Silberman, 1985).

In addition, problems with children may bring them into treatment (Herz & Rosen, 1982). Once in treatment, their concern with logic and understanding may immobilize them, whereas family enmeshment may block change. Conversely, these concerns mean that Jews value talking therapies oriented toward insight. Typically bright and verbally sophisticated, they tend to use anger, criticism, argument, self-deprecating humor, and the direct expression of feelings as ways of dealing with problems. Thus they are likely to recognize complex levels of meaning (McGoldrick, 1982) and favor complex solutions to presenting problems (Herz & Rosen, 1982).

DISCUSSION

These profiles of blacks, Caribbean blacks, Hispanics, Asians, and Jews make abundantly clear that diverse solutions exist for such universal challenges as birth, child rearing, marriage, work, and education (see Table 8.7). In turn, these sources of divergence hold profound implications for a range of issues central to family mediation practice. Below, we address five such issues.

Relevance of Client Ethnicity to Practice

Clearly, the first issue concerns the relevance of knowledge of ethnic variation to mediation practice. Here opinions are split. One position advises that practitioners adopt a generic perspective. Family therapists Montalvo and Gutierrez (1983, p. 15) put it this way:

In dealing with the possibility of being distracted by cultural masks, it helps if therapists orient themselves beyond the elements making this family a member of a particular ethnic group. This means searching for what is basic

TABLE 8.7 Comparison of Five Ethnic Groups

Attribute	Black	Caribbean Black	Hispanic	Asian	Jew
Family:					
Social Class	Working	Middle	Working	Middle	Middle
Family Defined	Extended	Nuclear	Extended	Extended	Nuclear
Life Cycle	Compressed	Elongated	Compressed	Elongated	Elongated
Marital Relations	Matrilocal	Matrilocal	Patriarchal	Patriarchal	Egalitarian
Parent-Child Relations	Autocratic	Autocratic	Autocratic	Autocratic	Democratic
Family Size	High	Low	High	Low	Low
English Proficiency	NA	NA	Low	Low	NA
Marriage Age	Young	Older	Young	Older	Older
Child Lending	Yes	Yes	Yes	No	No
Intermarriage	Low	Moderate	Low	High	Moderate
Divorce Rate	High	NK	Low	Low	Low
Teen Parents	High	Low	Low	Low	Low
Sex Parity	No	Yes	Yes	Yes	Yes
Work:					
Income Parity	No	Yes	No	Yes	Yes
Unemployment	High	Low	High	Low	Low
Work Type	Skilled	Professional	Skilled	Professional	Professional
Self-Employment	Low	Moderate	Low	High	Moderate
Mother Work	High	High	High	High	Moderate
Higher Education:					
Enrollment	Low	NK	Low	High	High
Academic Success	Low	NK	Low	High	High
Attrition Rate	High	NK	High	Low	Low
Other:					
Self-Help	Yes	Yes	Yes	Yes	Yes
Spirituality	High	High	High	Moderate	Low
Self-Identification	High	Moderate	High	High	High
Time Sense	P-time	P-time	P-time	P-time	M-time
Residential Segregation	High	Moderate	High	Low	High
Help-Seeking	Informal	Informal	Informal	Informal	Formal

NOTE: NA = not applicable; NK = not known.

to families rather than what are idiosyncratic cultural dimensions that tend to make the family alien to the therapist. . . . The therapist's goal must be a generalized flexibility rather than specialized sensitivities toward a particular ethnic group.

The alternate view is expressed well by psychologist Dana (1993, p. vii) who argues that, "culturally competent assessment services stem from efforts to understand persons who differ in the realities that they have constructed to endow their lives with meaning and dignity and to offer respect to varied solutions to basic problems of living." He builds on the observation by Sue and Zane (1987, p. 44) that premature termination of service by ethnic clients derives primarily from "a series of frustrations, misunderstandings, distortions, and defensive reactions . . . [that include] language problems, role ambiguities, misinterpretations of behavior, [and] differences in priorities of treatment."

From our perspective, both views are complementary. That is, following Ivey, Ivey, and Simek-Morgan (1993) and Pedersen (1984, 1985, 1988, 1991), mediation practitioners require at least four levels of competence. The first of these, clinical competence or skill, comes closest to Montalvo and Gutierrez in stressing generic clinical skills of the sort described in Part II of this volume. The second concerns substantive competence, by which we mean detailed, current expertise in the various knowledge bases about mediation, including the law and legal practice as well as research such as that described in Part I of this volume. Finally, this chapter suggests two additional levels of competence. One of these Dana (1993, p. vii) calls "cultural competence," which includes knowledge of the ways in which various ethnic groups are similar to and different from each other and the dominant culture. The other involves what we call "personal" competence, that is, awareness of one's cultural biases and assumptions likely to affect one's perception of and interaction with clients who are culturally different from oneself.

The practitioner's failure to achieve these levels of mastery exposes clients to two consequences. The first is clear: inadequate service delivery to clients in need. In our experience, this inadequacy is evidenced by three outcomes: clients who, without warning, simply drop out of service; clients who become increasingly uncooperative as their level of anxiety, frustration, and confusion begin to mount; and clients who passively comply with the demands of the mediator, but who subsequently abandon the terms of "their" agreement, thus muddling through on their own or eventually returning to court. The second consequence is that it robs ethnic client groups of the mediation option. They are then dependent on the court, where they have fared poorly, and subject to various moral and racial biases that favor traditional solutions to divorce-related problems (Syrtash, 1992). These poor outcomes apply both to their lack of comprehension of court proceedings and in their subsequent rejection of court judgments, which are often perceived as inconsistent with their cultural norms and values.

Assessment

As stressed in Part II, thorough assessment is central to the TFM model of mediation practice. Our ethnic profiles (see Table 8.7) suggest that at least two aspects of assessment are crucial when dealing with ethnic clients (see also Clinical Issues, p. 357).

The first aspect concerns the level of group identification. As we have repeatedly seen, visible minority status alone says little *by itself* of the degree to which couples identify with the beliefs and values stereotypically attributed to the group to which they belong. *Issei* (first generation) Japanese may have lived in North America for 60 years yet speak no English, behaving as if they had never left Japan. In contrast, their *Yonsei* (fourth generation) great-grandchildren may speak no Japanese and may espouse values and beliefs consistent with those in the dominant culture. Indeed, in couples characterized by ethnic or religious intermarriage, value and attitudinal differences, rooted in culture, may be at the crux both of their divorce and postdivorce conflict. Accordingly, some indication is necessary as to couples' degree of group identification before it becomes clear what knowledge from this chapter, if any, is relevant to the provision of culturally competent mediation service.

In this context, to the meticulous attention we normally pay to assessment, we add a protocol (see Table 8.8) we have found helpful in locating former spouses on the traditional-acculturated spectrum. In turn, such information has proven invaluable in helping the practitioner select the most appropriate interactional style (democratic versus authoritative, formal versus informal, passive versus active) and

TABLE 8.8 Ethnic Group Client Protocol: 15 Assessment Questions

1. Where were you born? When did you come to (the United States or Canada) and under what circumstances (as a voluntary immigrant or a refugee)?

2. What is your current immigration status (undocumented alien, landed immigrant or citizen)?

3. What does it mean to you be (black, Caribbean black, Hispanic, Asian, Jewish)?

4. Has this changed at all during the course of your marriage?

5. Have you ever suffered from discrimination because you are (black, Caribbean black, Hispanic, Asian, Jewish)?

6. Have you encountered any problems in your marriage because you are (from one ethnic group or religion) and your partner is (from a different ethnic group or religion)?

7. What is your mother tongue and what language do you now use at home?

8. How often do you visit with your in-laws? Do you live close to them? How close emotionally do you feel to them?

9. How close are you to other members of your family (grandparents, aunts and uncles, cousins)? Do you have a close circle of friends?

10. Have you discussed with your partner how each of you plans to raise the children (as regards religion, language, and cultural values)?

11. In your view, what is the proper way a (mother or father) should relate to their children?

12. Has living here (in the United States or Canada) made it difficult to be a proper parent to your children, because their friends, the school, and the media have given them a very different sense of what proper parenting should be?

13. To what extent have you relied on others outside your immediate family in caring for your children?

14. How involved have you been with the social and community organizations in your community, including the (church or synagogue)?

15. What has been your experience in dealing with professionals in your community (lawyers, doctors, teachers, social service workers)? What proportion have been (black, Caribbean black, Hispanic, Asian, Jewish) like yourself?

the best approach to intervention, both in terms of content (strategic versus insight oriented, direct versus indirect, supportive versus confrontational, verbal versus behavioral) as well as timing. It has also helped us orient to the couple's ecological field, especially regarding the clinical decision to include or exclude extended family members, real or fictive, in session.

The second aspect of ethnicity relevant to assessment concerns migration status, especially level of assimilation. This aspect applies to all clients, but has differential application depending on whether they are native born or first-generation immigrants. With respect to the former, immigration is relevant in two senses: Family memories of immigration may continue to shape current interaction processes; and based on socialization experience, it speaks to degree of group identification, discussed above. As for the latter, immigration can often be a traumatic experience that places enormous strain on those involved and may be the proximate basis for the divorce action. Spouses may have had quite different reasons for leaving their home country and, in turn, may have very different experiences on arrival. Under the stress of adaptation, their relationship may crumble, leaving the detritus on the mediator's doorstep. The couple's immigration history and subsequent efforts at assimilation thus become crucial aspects of intake assessment.

Clinical Issues

A variety of clinical issues affects all clients in one way or another; many have been discussed in Part II. There is, however, a handful of issues that our review suggests are likely to be more prominent among ethnic clients. The following incomplete list is offered for illustrative purposes.

Intermarriage

Table 8.7 makes clear that groups vary widely in their propensity to intermarry. This fact is relevant to mediation in two senses. The first and most obvious is that cultural differences may lie at the heart of the divorce decision. Intermarried couples confront an uphill battle in making their marriages work. They may lack support from extended kin, may be rejected by their respective communities while grappling with fundamental differences concerning marriage and parenting. In the end, despite their initial bravery in making this difficult marital choice, they may be unable to make it work. In turn, such cases are likely to be clinically complex because at the very least they require of the practitioner some knowledge of *both* cultures to understand the stresses they are under and the issues in dispute and thus help move them toward a mediated resolution. For example, the ongoing involvement of extended family kin, real and fictive, needs to be carefully considered with couples from most groups. Indeed, as seen in Johnston and Campbell (1988), such involvement may not only have actively contributed to the divorce, but may continue to fuel ongoing postdivorce disputes.

Such knowledge is also be crucial in orienting such couples to current trends in case adjudication by the courts. As noted above, Syrtash's (1992) review of Canadian case law makes abundantly clear that judges have favored traditional interpretations of cases and thus have not always been sensitive to multicultural realities. Such realities are salient in helping such couples reach agreements that are reasonable in light of how they are likely to be viewed by the court.

Intergenerational Conflict

As we have seen, new immigrants come to North America filled with hopes and dreams of a new life. Many of them find it, at least in economic terms, only to discover that in the process they have become estranged from their children. The latter, although reared in their parents' home, have absorbed through their peers and the media the values, beliefs, behaviors, and language of the dominant culture. The resulting conflict can be intense and extremely divisive, the ultimate consequence of which will be divorce. This source may be apparent in assessment, or it may not, as spouses concentrate on marital issues. In the latter case, mediators are advised to examine and rule out intergenerational conflict as an issue before they move on to other things; failure to do may result in a later unexplained blockage in negotiation. As noted in the profiles, clients may be initially reluctant to share information about family problems with a stranger, their presence in mediation notwithstanding. Later, however, when such reserve has dissipated in the light of client trust, intergenerational conflict may appear as a crucial issue, for example, as a covert mother-child alliance acts to promote child disrespect for father and, in turn, heightened marital conflict.

Cross-generational Conflict

A variation on the same theme concerns cross-generational conflict, for example, between parents and grandparents. Here, two variations are prominent. One is typical of dysfunctional families and involves a cross-generational coalition between grandparents and children against parents. The second, more typical of ethnic families, concerns conflict around a range of family issues between second-generation parents and their first-generation parents. Grandparents, for example, may intrude on the grounds that their children are not raising their children correctly, that is, with proper respect for older adults. Alternately, one spouse may be closer to his or her parents than the other, thus sparking conflict between the spouses over how one treats parents. Still a third variation involves communication barriers created by the fact that the older generation may speak only the native language, whereas the younger generation may speak only English or may be in the process of losing their native tongue.

In our experience, such conflict is seldom at the heart of the divorce, but it can render the mediator's task enormously more complicated. In essence, it means that such cases often involve multiple agendas, some overt, others covert. Furthermore, as seen in the case histories in chapters 3 and 4, because several groups accord status to older generations, they have a considerable capacity to undermine the efforts of the mediator.

Religious Observance

Degree of religious orthodoxy stands as a surrogate for group identification. Among couples for whom religious observance is not central to their identity, issues that arise from it, such as child education, are typically no more problematic than might be found among couples from the dominant culture. Among orthodox couples, however, traditional views are absolutely central to the mediation process, and moreover demand considerable knowledge on the part of the mediator. Meierding (1992), for example, notes that among orthodox Jews, religious observance and religious education are highly contentious issues, especially so when the parents are split on these issues, one parent having become more or less observant than the other. For these couples, resolving conflict around child custody and education will be central to case resolution. More generally, orthodox couples, irrespective of their religion, will likely represent clinically demanding cases. One the one hand, their belief systems dramatically constrain the range of acceptable solutions to the issues in conflict; lack of flexibility is typical of such clients. On the other hand, considerable knowledge of their belief system is required to understand the reasoning that underpins their decision-making process and choice preferences.

Spousal Relations

As seen in Table 8.7, groups vary systematically in their expectations of proper spousal relations. Important issues thus arise about power and gender (see also Meierding, 1992). In groups in which men are expected to make all the important decisions and women are expected to be submissive, wives may literally be unable to assert their own needs or may be fearful of opposing the wishes of their more powerful spouses. At the very least, they will probably experience considerable discomfort when asked to discuss sources of marital conflict. Similarly, taboo topics such as sex and violence may represent potential stumbling blocks for practitioners who routinely inquire into such matters. Furthermore, such matters are complicated by the possible divergence between social fiction and social reality, with the former initially presented and accepted because it conforms to stereotypes in the dominant culture.

In our view, none of this should distract mediators from their central goal, namely, a fair and equitable solution. The means to that end, however, require not only painstaking assessment, but also a relationship of trust with the couples in question, an issue we address in more detail later.

Social Class

As noted previously, family mediators typically operate with a middle-class clientele in mind. This assumption is relevant in two senses. First, as LeResche (1992) makes clear, it assumes that clients have knowledge of the law and the resources to pay for service, will attend during normal business hours, will have no difficulty finding transportation, will be fluent in English, and so on. As we have seen, above, few (if any) of these attributes are likely to be true of poor families, including poor blacks and Hispanics. For family mediation to proceed, then, requires the creation of a supportive infrastructure, including, suggest Taylor and Sanchez (1991), day care services, transportation to and from the mediator's office, translators, office hours in the evenings and weekends, and services paid for by the state. In addition, mediation services per se may need to be augmented by a significant educational component, because reasonable knowledge of individual rights and obligations under the law is a prerequisite to fair negotiation.

There is, however, a second sense in which class is important, namely, the manner in which it intersects with race and racism. Asians, Hispanics, and especially blacks will likely bring to mediation expectations of service based on their experience of racism in other settings. Such experience needs to be acknowledged explicitly. Allaying fears and correcting beliefs will need to be part of the rapport and trust-building process, beginning soon after intake.

Clinical Style

Trust-building will also relate to the mediator's clinical style. As we have seen, clinical observers caution that some groups are amenable to insight-oriented approaches, whereas other groups respond best to behavioral approaches. In a similar vein, groups vary in regard to such matters as long-term versus short-term service; problem-focused versus relationship-focused techniques; indirect versus more direct, confrontative methods; and the involvement or noninvolvement of extended kin. In our experience, here is where Sue and Zane's (1987) "misinterpretations" are likely to arise and where group-specific knowledge is critical. The match between clinical approach and group-based client needs must be exact or premature dropout is likely. These complexities advise the practitioner to proceed cautiously, and accent the salience of careful assessment as well as intervention tailored to the group in question. In particular, groups that stress the centrality of extended kin are likely to present as complex cases more suitable for experienced as opposed to novice practitioners. They may also be less appropriate in court-based mediation as opposed to private mediation, where time is not so pressing a constraint.

Considerations such as these also recommend the advantages associated with moving *away* from the notion of the solitary practitioner and moving *toward* a view of mediation as a team or group effort. When practitioners lack intimate knowledge of the client couple's ethnic group, the greatest practice risk is that of inadvertent error through ignorance—of blindly breaking cultural taboos, contradicting sacred beliefs, and contravening traditional rules of conduct. The alternative is to act in partnership with someone who does have knowledge of the group in question. This partner may be in one of a variety of positions—colleagues (lawyers, social workers, family therapists, doctors, clergy, etc.) who may or may not be a member of the group in question. Alternately, he or she may be a layperson or a friend or relative of the client couple. What matters most is having intimate knowledge of the group in question such that the partner can advise the practitioner in conduct compatible with group norms and values. This is not to suggest that the practitioner must never confront these belief systems if he or she feels they contribute to blockage in the case. But this confrontation should be intentional rather than accidental and with advance knowledge of the potential consequences, both positive and negative.

Culture-Specific Issues

Although some issues are generic to all families and others are more prominent among ethnic groups, still others are group specific. The above review provides a number of examples.

Among Asians, the issue is shame, captured in the idea of "face." At the heart of the culture is the Confucian injunction toward harmony between people and with nature. Conflict and associated behaviors—

confrontation, jealousy, hatred, personal pride, violence—are seen as unnatural and thus sources of shame. This issue puts in relief the meaning of divorce as a source of public pain.

Among Hispanics, the issue is pride, the necessity of strength and endurance in the face of inevitable troubles. It is the residue of an agricultural people whose sense of time is thus geological. It is the center of individual identity, though it takes different forms in men and women. In turn, it is the basis of personal dignity and respect. Divorce places this central value in jeopardy, as evidence of public failure before people and before God.

Among Jews, especially the Orthodox, the issue is the Law. Going back some 6,000 years, the Law is at the heart of all matters seen as important. It is prescriptive, specifying a variety of duties, obligations, and rights. It is not to be forsworn or transgressed in any particular. In this context, divorce is the undoing of a complex contract, requiring due process of law and having clear consequences for the future; the personal pain is superfluous.

Among the Caribbean blacks, the issue is privacy, each spouse standing separately before God. Adversity demands strength and personal integrity and success can only be achieved through hard work and dedication. Both processes admit support from kin and others; grief and pain can be shared. But in the end, the future is likely to be preordained and thus can only be accepted with equanimity. Thus divorce, although it affects all family members, is first and foremost a personal trial.

Among African American blacks, the issue is danger. The inner-city ghetto is no place for the weak. Survival requires strength and perseverance in the face of inevitable troubles. It is easier managed in groups than alone and it gives an extra meaning to the idea of marriage. Yet danger can never be ignored. The streets sound a siren call to the children. Men stay but they also leave. The world, certainly the white world, is against you and yours. And marriages die, victims of a structural threat that is too big for any one couple to withstand.

These are the specific realities that each of these groups brings with them into the mediator's office. They represent important sources of complexity in service delivery and they can only be addressed effectively by culturally competent practitioners.

Client Identity

Finally, groups vary in terms of the likelihood that they will seek mediation service. As seen above, only African American blacks have a relatively high divorce rate; the divorce rate among Caribbean blacks, Hispanics, Asians, and Jews is relatively low, with that among ultraorthodox Jews vanishingly small. Cultural norms within the black community also sanction common-law relations and separation with no recourse to the courts, thus reducing the likelihood of blacks seeking service. The same is true among Hispanics, whose knowledge of the law and thus of family mediation is likely to be very limited, and whose preference is to handle marital separation informally. Only Jews view service positively; the other groups view treatment with suspicion bordering on loathing, with Hispanics and Asians attaching a stigma to public evidence of family breakdown.

The above characteristics of these ethnic groups support three conclusions. First, acceptance of traditional ethnic beliefs and values is likely to be inversely related to the frequency of requests for mediation service; the more traditional a group's belief system, the less likely its members are to turn to the court or to mediation for relief from marital distress. Second, ethnic white client groups are more likely to demand services than their visible minority counterparts. This fact relates to the likelihood that the experience of visible minority clients with white institutions, such as the courts or the welfare system, has been negative. Finally, the involvement of ethnic groups with mediation services likely reflects degrees of acculturation or deviation, that is, they come from subgroups of ethnic communities who identify with the dominant culture or who hold views or beliefs contrary to the larger ethnic community to which they belong. The former points to the adult children or grandchildren of immigrant parents who have moved some distance away from traditional views. The latter points to those who, because of beliefs or circumstances, have moved to the periphery of the communities in question. In short, this movement predicts that ethnic families who seek services will display a complex mix of dominant and ethnic cultures and in that sense they represent a considerable challenge to the practitioner.

FINAL WORD

Ethnicity, then, should be regarded as another dimension of family life routinely considered by mediation practitioners, both in assessment and intervention. Those who already do so may see this chapter as confirmation and support of what we see as wise practice. Conversely, those who have yet to do so should see this chapter as notice of change in the prevailing trends that characterize modern family mediation practice and thus an advisory of the need for change in their routine practice conduct.

NOTES

1. Although these five dimensions stand at the core of a group's identity, their impact can be significantly mitigated by a variety of additional factors. Our reading of the literature suggests that six such factors warrant careful attention as part of the assessment of a case: immigration, degree of group identification, intermarriage, gender, age or generation, and degree or level of family functioning.

2. Gibbs (1989a, 1989b) reports a birth rate among black teenage girls (in 1985) of 163 per 1,000 pregnancies—twice the comparable rate (of 83 per 1,000) among whites. This rate means that of all teenagers under 15 years of age who gave birth in that year, 60% were black (Ho, 1992b).

REFERENCES

Abella, I. (1990). *A coat of many colours: Two centuries of Jewish life in Canada*. Toronto: Lester & Orpen Dennys.

Adachi, K., with Findley, T. (1991). *The enemy that never was: A history of Japanese Canadians* (Updated ed.). Toronto: McClelland & Stewart.

Alba, R. D. (1985). *Italian-Americans: Into the twilight of ethnicity*. Englewood Cliffs, NJ: Prentice Hall.

Alba, R. D. (1990). *Ethnic identity: The transformation of white America*. New Haven, CT: Yale University Press.

Aldrich, H., & Waldinger, R. (1990). Ethnicity and entrepreneurship. *Annual Review of Sociology, 16*, 111-135.

Allahan, A. L. (1993). Unity and diversity in Caribbean ethnicity and culture. *Canadian Ethnic Studies, 25*(1), 70-84.

Allen, W. R. (1978). Black family research in the United States: A review, assessment and extension. *Journal of Comparative Family Studies, 9*, 166-188.

Amaro, H., Beckman, L. J., & Mays, V. M. (1987). A Comparison of black and white women entering alcoholism treatment. *Journal of Studies on Alcohol, 48*, 220-228.

Anderson, W. W., & Grant, R. W. (1987). *The new newcomers*. Toronto: Canadian Scholars' Press.

Aponte, H. (1976). Underorganization in the poor family. In P. Guerin (Ed.), *Family therapy: Theory and practice*. New York: Gardner.

Aponte, H. (1986). If I don't get simple, I cry. *Family Process, 25*(4), 531-548.

Aranas, M. Q. (1983). *The dynamics of Filipino immigrants in Canada*. Edmonton, AL: Coles.

Aschenbrenner, J. (1975). *Lifelines: Black families in Chicago*. Prospect Heights, IL: Waveland.

Baum, C., Hyman, P., & Michael, S. (1975). *The Jewish woman in America*. New York: Dial.

Bean, F. D., King, A. G., & Passel, J. S. (1983). The number of illegal immigrants of Mexican origin in the United States: Sex ratio-based estimates for 1980. *Demography, 20*(1), 99-109.

Bean, F. D., & Tienda, M. (1987). *The Hispanic population of the United States*. New York: Russell Sage.

Beaudry, J. S. (1992). Synthesizing research in multicultural teacher education: Findings and issues for evaluation of cultural diversity. In A.-M. Madison (Ed.), *Minority issues in program evaluation: New directions for program evaluation* (Vol. 53). San Francisco: Jossey-Bass.

Beckett, J. O. (1976). Working wives: A racial comparison. *Social Work, 21*, 463-471.

Benkin, R. L. (1978). Ethnicity and organization: Jewish communities in Eastern Europe and the United States. *Sociological Quarterly, 19*, 614-625.

Billingsley, A. (1988). *Black families in America*. New York: Simon & Schuster.

Birnbaum, P. (1975). *A book of Jewish concepts* (Rev. ed.). New York: Hebrew Publishing.

Blau, Z. S. (1974). The strategy of the Jewish mother. In M. Sklare (Ed.), *The Jews in American society*. New York: Behrman House.

Bonacich, E. (1973). A theory of middleman minorities. *American Sociological Review, 38*, 583-594.

Bonacich, E. (1990). Inequality in America: The failure of the American system for people of color. In G. E. Thomas (Ed.), *U.S. race relations in the 1980s and 1990s: Challenges and alternatives*. New York: Hemisphere.

Boswell, T. E. (1986). A split labor market analysis of discrimination against Chinese immigrants, 1850-1882. *American Sociological Review, 51*, 352-371.

Boyd, M. (1990). Immigrant women. In S. S. Halli, F. Trovato, & L. Driedger (Eds.), *Ethnic demography: Canadian immigrant, racial and cultural variations*. Ottawa: Carleton University Press.

Boyd-Franklin, N. (1989). *Black families in therapy: A multisystem approach*. New York: Guilford.

Boyd-Franklin, N. (1993). Race, class, and poverty. In F. Walsh (Ed.), *Normal family processes* (2nd ed.). New York: Guilford.

Braverman, L. (1990). Jewish mothers. *Journal of Feminist Family Therapy, 2*(2), 9-14.

Breton, R., Isajiw, W. W., Kalbach, W. E., & Reitz, J. G. (1990). *Ethnic identity and equality: Varieties of experience in a Canadian city*. Toronto: University of Toronto Press.

Brice, J. (1982). West Indian families. In M. McGoldrick, J. K. Pearce, & J. Giordano (Eds.), *Ethnicity and family therapy*. New York: Guildford.

Bruce, J. D., & Rodman, H. (1973). Black-white marriages in the United States: A review of the empirical literature. In I. R. Stuart & L. Edwin (Eds.), *Interracial marriage: Expectations and realities*. New York: Grossman.

Buenker, J. D., & Ratner, L. A. (1992). Bibliographical essay. In J. D. Buenker & L. A. Ratner (Eds.), *Multiculturalism in the United States: A comparative guide to acculturation and ethnicity.* Westport, CT: Greenwood.

Bulka, R. P. (1986). *Jewish marriage: A Halakhic ethic.* New York: KTAV.

Cabezas, A., & Kawaguchi, G. (1986). Empirical evidence for continuing Asian American income inequality: The human capital model and labor market segmentation. In G. Y. Okihiro, S. Hune, A. A. Hansen, & J. M. Liu (Eds.), *Reflections on shattered windows: Promises and prospects for Asian American studies.* Pullman: Washington State University Press.

Chao, C. M. (1992). The inner heart: Therapy with Southeast Asian families. In L. A. Vargas & J. D. Koss-Chioino (Eds.), *Working with culture: Psychotherapeutic interventions with ethnic minority children and adolescents.* San Francisco: Jossey-Bass.

Cheng, M., Tsuji, G., Yau, M., & Ziegler, S. (1989). *The every secondary student survey, fall, 1987.* Toronto: Toronto Board of Education, Research Services, Report No. 191.

Chin, J. L., & Associates. (1993). *Transference and empathy in Asian American psychotherapy: Cultural values and treatment needs.* New York: Praeger.

Christiansen, J. M., Thornley-Brown, A., & Robinson, J. A. (1982). *West Indians in Toronto: Implications for helping professionals.* Toronto: Family Service Association of Metropolitan Toronto.

Clairmont, D. H., & McGill, D. W. (1987). *Africaville: The life and death of a Canadian black community* (Rev. ed.). Toronto: Canadian Scholars' Press.

Cleary, P. D., & Demone, H., Jr. (1988). Health and social service needs in a northeastern metropolitan area: Ethnic group differences. *Journal of Sociology & Social Welfare, 15*(4), 63-76.

Cohen, L. (1985). Controlarse and the problems of life among Latino immigrants. In W. A. Vega & M. R. Miranda (Eds.), *Stress and Hispanic mental health: Relating research to service delivery.* Rockville, MD: National Institutes of Mental Health.

Coleman, J. (1990). *Equality and achievement in education.* Boulder, CO: Westview.

Colman, C. (1986). International family therapy: A view from Kyoto, Japan. *Family Process, 25,* 651-664.

Comas-Diaz, L. (1989). Culturally relevant issues and treatment implications for Hispanics. In D. R. Koslow & E. P. Salett (Eds.), *Cross cultures in mental health.* Washington, DC: SIETAR International.

Cox, F. D. (1993). *Human intimacy: Marriage, the family and its meaning* (6th ed.). Minneapolis, MN: West.

Cromwell, R., & Ruiz, R. (1979). The myth of macho dominance in decision making with Mexican-American and Chicano families. *Hispanic Journal of Behavioral Science, 1,* 355-373.

Cushman, P. (1990). Why the self is empty: Towards a historically situated psychology. *American Psychologist, 45*(5), 599-611.

Dana, R. H. (1993). *Multicultural assessment perspectives for professional psychology.* Boston: Allyn & Bacon.

Daniel, J. H. (1985). Cultural and ethnic issues: The black family. In E. H. Newberger & R. Bourne (Eds.), *Unhappy families: Clinical and research perspectives on family violence.* Littleton, MA: PSG.

Davenport, D. S., & Yurich, J. M. (1991). Multicultural gender issues. *Journal of Counseling and Development, 70*(1), 64-71.

Davis, J. E. (1992). Reconsidering the use of race as an explanatory variable in program evaluation. In A.-M. Madison (Ed.), *Minority issues in program evaluation: New directions for program evaluation* (Vol. 53). San Francisco: Jossey-Bass.

Delgado, M. (1985). Natural support systems in the Puerto Rican community. In E. H. Newberger & R. Bourne (Eds.), *Unhappy families: Clinical and research perspectives on family violence*. Littleton, MA: PSG.

Delgado, M. (1988). Groups in Puerto Rican spiritism: Implications for clinicians. In C. Jacobs & D. D. Bowles (Eds.), *Ethnicity and race: Critical concepts in social work*. Silver Springs, MD: National Association of Social Work.

DeSilva, A. (1992). *Earnings of immigrants: A comparative analysis*. Ottawa: Minister of Supply and Services.

Devereux, G. (1967). *From anxiety to method in the behavioral sciences*. The Hague, Netherlands: Mouton.

Devore, W., & Schlesinger, E. G. (1987). *Ethnic-sensitive social work practice* (2nd ed.). New York: Macmillan.

Dickson, L. (1993). The future of marriage and family in black America. *Journal of Black Studies, 23*(4), 472-491.

Donohue, W. A., Lyles, J., & Rogan, R. (1989). Issue development in divorce mediation. *Mediation Quarterly, 24,* 19-28.

Dornbusch, S., Carlsmith, J. M., Bushwall, S., Ritter, P., Leiderman, H., Hastorf, A., & Gross, R. (1985). Single parents, extended households, and the control of adolescents. *Child Development, 56,* 326-341.

Duryea, M. L., & Gundison, J. B. (1993). *Conflict and culture: Research in five communities in Vancouver, British Columbia*. Victoria, BC: UVic Institute for Dispute Resolution.

Edelman, M. W. (1993). The black family in America. In L. Tepperman & S. Wilson (Eds.), *Next of kin*. Englewood Cliffs, NJ: Prentice Hall.

Entwisle, D. R., & Alexander, K. L. (1993). Entry into school: The beginning school transition and educational stratification in the United States. *Annual Review of Sociology, 19,* 401-423.

Epstein, H. (1979). *Children of the Holocaust*. New York: Putnam.

Evans, L. A., Acosta, F. X., Yamamoto, J., & Hurwicz, H. L. (1986). Patient requests: Correlates and therapeutic implications for Hispanic, black, and Caucasian patients. *Journal of Clinical Psychology, 42,* 213-221.

Falicov, C. (in press). *Latino families in therapy*. New York: Guilford.

Falicov, C. J. (1982). Mexican families. In M. McGoldrick, J. K. Pearce, & J. Giordano (Eds.), *Ethnicity and family therapy*. New York: Guildford.

Falicov, C. J., & Karrer, B. M. (1980). Cultural variations in the family life cycle: The Mexican-American family. In E. A. Carter & M. McGoldrick (Eds.), *The changing family life cycle: A framework for family therapy*. New York: Gardner.

Farley, F. (1984). *Blacks and whites: Narrowing the gap?* Cambridge, MA: Harvard University Press.

Fernando, S. (1986). Depression in ethnic minorities. In J. L. Cox (Ed.), *Transcultural psychiatry*. London: Croom Helm.

Fisher, S. (1992). *From margin to mainstream: The social progress of black Americans* (2nd ed.). Lanham, MD: Rowman & Littlefield.

Fitzpatrick, J., & Gurak, D. (1979). *Hispanic intermarriage in New York City*. New York: Fordham University Hispanic Research Center.

Fong, S. L. M. (1973). Assimilation and changing roles of Chinese Americans. *Journal of Social Issues, 29,* 115-127.

Fowler, F. J. (1977). *1975 community survey: A study of the Jewish population of Greater Boston.* Boston: Combined Jewish Philanthropies of Greater Boston.

Franklin, A. J. (1992). Therapy with African-American men. *Families in Society, 73*(6), 350-355.

Fugita, S. F., & O'Brien, D. J. (1991). *Japanese American ethnicity: The persistence of community.* Seattle: University of Washington Press.

Fulmer, R. H. (1988). Lower-income and professional families: A comparison of structure and life cycle process. In B. Carter & M. McGoldrick (Eds.), *The changing family life cycle: A framework for family therapy* (2nd ed.). New York: Gardner.

Furstenberg, F. (1986). Teen mothers 17 years later: They've recovered but their children are maladjusted. *Professional Newsletter of Family Therapy Practitioners, 46,* 11.

Garcia-Preto, N. (1982). Puerto Rican families. In M. McGoldrick, J. K. Pearce, & J. Giordano (Eds.), *Ethnicity and family therapy.* New York: Guildford.

Gary, L. (Ed.). (1981). *Black men.* Beverly Hills, CA: Sage.

Gendrot, S., & Turner, J. (1983). Ethnicity and class: Politics on Manhattan's Lower East Side. *Ethnic Groups, 5,* 79-108.

Gibbs, J. T. (1989a). Black adolescents and youth: An update on an endangered species. In R. Jones (Ed.), *Black adolescents.* Berkeley, CA: Cobb & Henry.

Gibbs, J. T. (1989b). Black American adolescents. In J. T. Gibbs, L. Huang, & Associates (Eds.), *Children of color: Psychological intervention with minority youth.* San Francisco: Jossey-Bass.

Giddings, P. (1985). *When and where I enter: The impact of black women on race and sex in America.* New York: Bantam.

Gilbert, D., & Kahl, J. A. (1987). *The American class structure: A new synthesis.* Homewood, IL: Dorsey.

Godfrey, B. J. (1988). *Neighborhoods in transition: The making of San Francisco's ethnic and nonconformist communities.* Berkeley: University of California Press.

Goldscheider, C., & Kobrin, F. E. (1980). Ethnic continuity and the process of self-employment. *Ethnicity, 7,* 256-278.

Gordon, M. M. (1964). *Assimilation in American life.* New York: Oxford University.

Govia, F. (1988). *Blacks in Canada: In search of the promise: A bibliographic guide.* Edmonton: Harambee Centres Canada.

Grayson, J. P. (1994). *Race on campus: Outcomes of the first year experience at York University.* Toronto: Institute for Social Research.

Greenblum, J. (1974). Medical and health orientations of American Jews: A case of diminishing distinctiveness. *Social Science Medicine, 8,* 127-134.

Griffith, J. E., & Villavicencio, S. (1985). Relationship among acculturation, socio-demographic characteristics, and social support in Mexican American adults. *Hispanic Journal of Behavioral Sciences, 7,* 75-92.

Haglund, E. (1984). Japan: Cultural considerations. *International Journal of Intercultural Relations, 8,* 61-76.

Hall, E. T. (1959). *The silent language.* New York: Fawcett.

Hall, E. T. (1976). *Beyond culture.* Garden City, NY: Anchor.

Halli, S. S. (1987a). Minority group status and fertility of Chinese and Japanese in Canada. *Canadian Ethnic Studies, 19*(2), 44-66.

Halli, S. S. (1987b). *How minority status affects fertility.* Westport, CT: Greenwood.

Halli, S., Trovato, F., & Driedger, L. (1990). The social demography of ethnic groups. In S. Halli, F. Trovato, & L. Driedger (Eds.), *Ethnic demography: Canadian immigrant, racial and cultural variations.* Ottawa, Canada: Carleton University Press.

Hartzman, C. A. (1991). *Not yet Canadians: The Latin American immigrant in Nova Scotia.* Halifax, Nova Scotia: International Education Centre, St. Mary's University.

Hawkes, G., & Taylor, M. (1975). Power structure in Mexican and Mexican American farm labor families. *Journal of Marriage and the Family, 31,* 807-811.

Health and Welfare Canada. (1988). Canada Task Force in Mental Health Issues Affecting Immigrants and Refugees. *Review of the literature on migrant mental health.* Ottawa: Supply and Services Canada.

Heer, D. M. (1974). The prevalence of black-white marriage in the United States, 1960 and 1970. *Journal of Marriage and the Family, 36,* 246-258.

Heilman, S., & Cohen, S. M. (1989). *Cosmopolitan parochials: Modern Orthodox Jews in America.* Chicago: University of Chicago Press.

Helmreich, W. B. (1986). *The World of the Yeshiva: An intimate portrait.* New Haven, CT: Yale University Press.

Herz, F. M., & Rosen, E. J. (1982). Jewish families. In M. McGoldrick, J. K. Pearce, & J. Giordano (Eds.), *Ethnicity and family therapy.* New York: Guilford.

Hill, R. (1977). *Informal adoption among black families.* Washington, DC: National Urban League.

Hines, P. M. (1988). The family life cycle of poor black families. In B. Carter & M. McGoldrick (Eds.), *The changing family life cycle: A framework for family therapy* (2nd ed.). New York: Gardner.

Hines, P. M. (1990). African American mothers. *Journal of Feminist Family Therapy, 2*(2), 23-32.

Hines, P. M., & Boyd-Franklin, N. (1982). Black families. In M. McGoldrick, J. K. Pearce, & J. Giordano (Eds.), *Ethnicity and family therapy.* New York: Guilford.

Ho, M. K. (1992a). Differential application of treatment modalities with Asian American youth. In L. A. Vargas & J. D. Koss-Chioino (Eds.), *Working with culture: Psychotherapeutic interventions with ethnic minority children and adolescents.* San Francisco: Jossey-Bass.

Ho, M. K. (1992b). *Minority children and adolescents in therapy.* Newbury Park, CA: Sage.

Hunter, A. G., & Ensinger, M. (1992). The diversity and fluidity of children's living arrangements: Life course and family transitions in an urban, Afro-American community. *Journal of Marriage and the Family, 54,* 239-248.

Irving, H. H., & Benjamin, M. (1992). *Family mediation in Canada and Israel: A comparative analysis.* Occasional Paper #11. Jerusalem: The Hebrew University of Jerusalem.

Ivey, A. E., Ivey, M. B., & Simek-Morgan, L. (1993). *Counseling and psychotherapy: A multicultural perspective* (3rd ed.). Boston: Allyn & Bacon.

Johnston, J. R., & Campbell, L. E. G. (1988). *Impasses of divorce: The dynamics of family conflict.* New York: Free Press.

Kallen, E. (1976). Family lifestyles and Jewish culture. In K. Ishwaran (Ed.), *The Canadian family* (Rev ed.). Toronto: Holt, Rinehart & Winston.

Kasinitz, P. (1992). *Caribbean New York: Black immigrants and the politics of race.* Ithaca, NY: Cornell University Press.

Keefe, S. E. (1984). Real and ideal extended familism among Mexican-Americans and Anglo-Americans: On the meaning of "close" family ties. *Human Organization, 43,* 65-70.

Keefe, S. E., & Padilla, A. M. (1987). *Chicano ethnicity.* Albuquerque: University of New Mexico Press.

Keefe, S. E., Padilla, A. M., & Carlos, L. M. (1979). The Mexican-American extended family as an emotional support system. *Human Organization, 38,* 144-152.

Kiefer, C. W. (1971). Notes on anthropology and the minority elderly. *The Gerontologist,* *1,* 94-98.

Kitano, H. H. L. (1976). *Japanese Americans: The evolution of a sub-culture* (2nd ed.). Englewood Cliffs, NJ: Prentice Hall.

Kitano, H. H. L., & Daniels, R. (1990). *Asian Americans: Emerging minorities.* Englewood Cliffs, NJ: Prentice Hall.

Kitano, H. H. L., & Yeung, W.-T. (1982). Chinese interracial marriage. *Marriage & Family Review, 5,* 35-48.

Koss-Chioino, J. D., & Vargas, L. A. (1992). Through the cultural looking glass: A model for understanding culturally responsive psychotherapies. In L. A. Vargas & J. D. Koss-Chioino (Eds.), *Working with culture: Psychotherapeutic interventions with ethnic minority children and adolescents.* San Francisco: Jossey-Bass.

Lai, D. C. (1988). *Chinatown: Towns within cities in Canada.* Vancouver: University of British Columbia Press.

Lai, M. C., & Yue, K. M. K. (1990). The Chinese. In N. Waxler-Morrison & Associates (Eds.), *Cross-cultural caring.* Vancouver: University of British Columbia Press.

Landau, B., Bartoletti, M., & Mesbur, R. (1987). *Family mediation handbook.* Toronto: Butterworths.

Lassiter, J. F. (1990). A minority experience of private practice. In E. A. Margenau (Ed.), *The encyclopedic handbook of private practice.* New York: Gardner.

Lau, A. (1986). Family therapy across cultures. In J. L. Cox (Ed.), *Transcultural psychiatry.* London: Croom Helm.

Lee, E. (1989). Assessment and treatment of Chinese-American families. *Journal of Psychotherapy & the Family, 6,* 99-122.

Leggon, C. (1983). Career, marriage and motherhood: "Copping out" or coping. In C. E. Obudho (Ed.), *Black marriage and family therapy.* Westport, CT: Greenwood.

LeResche, D. (1992). Comparison of the American mediation process with a Korean-American harmony restoration process. *Mediation Quarterly, 9*(4), 323-339.

Levine, G., & Rhodes, C. (1981). *The Japanese American community: A three generation study.* New York: Praeger.

Li, P. S. (1988). *The Chinese in Canada.* Toronto: Oxford University Press.

Li, P. S. (1992). Ethnic enterprise in transition: Chinese business in Richmond, B.C., 1980-1990. *Canadian Ethnic Studies, 14*(1), 120-138.

Light, I. (1972). *Ethnic enterprise in America.* Berkeley: University of California Press.

Light, I., & Bonacich, E. (1988). *Immigrant entrepreneurs: Koreans in Los Angeles.* Berkeley: University of California Press.

Lin, T. Y., Tardiff, K., Donetz, G., & Goresky, W. (1978). Ethnicity and patterns of help-seeking. *Culture, Medicine & Psychiatry, 2,* 3-13.

Logan, R. (1991). Immigration during the 1980s. *Canadian Social Trends, 20,* 10-13.

Logan, S. M. L., Freeman, E. M., & McDay, R. G. (Eds.). (1990). *Social work practice with black families.* White Plains, NY: Longman.

Makabe, T. (1979). Ethnic identity scale and social mobility: The case of the Nisei in Toronto. *Canadian Review of Sociology & Anthropology, 16*(2), 136-146.

Marks, C. (1991). The urban underclass. *Annual Review of Sociology, 17,* 445-466.

Martinez, J. L., & Mendoza, R. N. (1984). *Chicano psychology* (2nd ed.). New York: Academic Press.

Massey, D. S., & Eggers, M. (1990). The ecology of inequality: Minorities and the concentration of poverty. *American Journal of Sociology, 95*(5), 1153-1188.

Massey, D. S., & Schnabel, K. M. (1983). Recent trends in Hispanic immigration to the United States. *International Migration Review, 17*(2), 212-244.

Mata, F. (1985). Latin American immigration to Canada: Some reflections on the immigration statistics. *Canadian Journal of Latin American & Caribbean Studies, 10,* 27-42.

Maykovich, M. K. (1980). Acculturation versus familism in three generations of Japanese-Canadians. In K. Ishwaran (Ed.), *Canadian families: Ethnic variations.* Toronto: McGraw-Hill Ryerson.

McAdoo, H. P. (Ed.). (1981). *Black families.* Beverly Hills, CA: Sage.

McAdoo, H. P. (Ed.). (1988). *Black families* (2nd ed.). Newbury Park, CA: Sage.

McAdoo, H. P. (Ed.). (1993). *Family ethnicity.* Newbury Park, CA: Sage.

McDowell, C. L. (1992). Standardized tests and program evaluation: Inappropriate measures in critical times. In A.-M. Madison (Ed.), *Minority issues in program evaluation: New directions for program evaluation* (Vol. 53). San Francisco: Jossey-Bass.

McGill, D. (1987). Language, cultural psychology, and family therapy: Japanese examples from an international perspective. *Contemporary Family Therapy, 9,* 282-293.

McGoldrick, M. (1982). Normal families: An ethnic perspective. In F. Walsh (Ed.), *Normal family processes.* New York: Guilford.

McGoldrick, M. (1988). Ethnicity and the family life cycle. In B. Carter & M. McGoldrick (Eds.), *The changing family life cycle: A framework for family therapy* (2nd ed.). New York: Gardner.

McGoldrick, M. (1993). Ethnicity, cultural diversity, and normality. In F. Walsh (Ed.), *Normal family processes* (2nd ed.). New York: Guilford.

McGoldrick, M., Pearce, J. K., & Giordano, J. (Eds.). (1982). *Ethnicity and family therapy.* New York: Guilford.

McGoldrick, M., Garcia-Preto, N., Hines, P. M., & Lee, E. (1989). Ethnicity and women. In M. McGoldrick, C. M. Anderson, & F. Walsh (Eds.), *Women in families: A framework for family therapy.* New York: Norton.

Meierding, N. R. (1992). The impact of cultural and religious diversity in the divorce mediation process. *Mediation Quarterly, 9*(4), 297-305.

Mizio, E. (1974). Impact of external systems on the Puerto Rican family. *Social Casework, 55,* 76-83.

Mokuan, N. (1987). Social worker's perceptions of counseling effectiveness for Asian American clients. *Social Work, 32,* 331-335.

Montalvo, B., & Gutierrez, M. (1983). A perspective for the use of the cultural dimension in family therapy. In J. C. Hansen & C. E. Falicov (Eds.), *Cultural perspectives in family therapy.* Rockville, MD: Aspen Systems.

Moreau, J. (1991). Changing faces: Visible minorities in Toronto. *Canadian Social Trends, 23,* 26-28.

Morsbach, H. (1978). Aspects of Japanese marriage. In M. Corbin (Ed.), *The couple.* London: Penguin.

Mow, S. L., & Nettles, M. T. (1990). Minority student access to, and persistence and performance in, college: A review of trends and research literature. In J. C. Smart (Ed.), *Higher education: Handbook of theory and research* (Vol. 6). New York: Agathon.

Murase, K., Egawa, J., & Tashima, N. (1985). Alternative mental health services models in Asian/Pacific communities. In T. C. Owan (Ed.), *Southeast Asian mental health treatment, prevention services, training, and research.* Washington, DC: National Institutes of Mental Health.

Murillo, N. (1976). The Mexican-American family. In R. A. Martinez (Ed.), *Hispanic culture and health care: Fact, fiction, folklore*. St. Louis, MO: C. V. Mosby.

Muzny, C. C. (1989). *The Vietnamese in Oklahoma City: A study of ethnic change*. New York: AMS Press.

Nagasawa, R., & Espinosa, D. J. (1992). Educational achievement and the adaptive strategy of Asian American college students: Facts, theory, and hypotheses. *Journal of College Student Development, 33*, 137-142.

Nee, V., & Wong, H. Y. (1985). Asian American socioeconomic achievement. *Sociological Perspectives, 28*, 281-306.

Nora, A. (1993). Two-year colleges and minority students' educational aspirations: Help or hindrance? In J. C. Smart (Ed.), *Higher education: handbook of theory and research* (Vol. 9). New York: Agathon.

Ogbu, J. (1986). The consequence of the American caste system. In U. Neisser (Ed.), *The school achievement of minority children: New perspectives*. Hillsdale, NJ: Lawrence Erlbaum.

Ong, P. (1981). An ethnic trade: The Chinese laundries in early California. *Journal of Ethnic Studies, 8*, 95-113.

Patton, M. Q. (1985). Editor's notes. In M. Q. Patton (Ed.), *Culture and evaluation: New directions for program evaluation* (Vol. 25). San Francisco: Jossey-Bass.

Pavkov, T. W., Lewis, D. A., & Lyons, J. S. (1990). Psychiatric diagnosis and racial bias: An empirical investigation. *Professional Psychology, 20*, 364-368.

Pedersen, P. (1984). The intercultural context of counseling and therapy. In A. J. Marsella & G. M. White (Eds.), *Cultural conceptions of mental health and therapy*. Dordrecht, Holland: Reidel.

Pedersen, P. (1985). *Handbook of cross-cultural counseling and therapy*. Westport, CT: Greenwood.

Pedersen, P. (1988). *A handbook for developing multicultural awareness*. Alexandria, VA: American Association for Counseling and Development.

Pedersen, P. (1991). Multiculturalism as a generic approach to counseling. *Journal of Counseling & Development, 70*(1), 6-12.

Pedraza, S. (1991). Women and migration: The social consequences of gender. *Annual Review of Sociology, 17*, 303-325.

Perlman, J. (1983). Beyond New York: The occupations of Russian Jewish immigrants in Providence, R.I., and other small Jewish communities, 1900-1915. *American Jewish History, 72*, 369-394.

Peters, J. (1990). Cultural variations: Past and present. In M. Baker (Ed.), *Families: Changing trends in Canada* (2nd ed.). Toronto: McGraw-Hill Ryerson.

Pinderhughes, E. (1982). Afro-American families and the victim system. In M. McGoldrick, J. K. Pearce, & J. Giordano (Eds.), *Ethnicity and family therapy*. New York: Guilford.

Piotrkowski, C. S., & Hughes, D. (1993). Dual-earner families in context: Managing family systems and work systems. In F. Walsh (Ed.), *Normal family processes* (2nd ed.). New York: Guilford.

Porter, J. R., & Washington, R. E. (1993). Minority identity and self-esteem. *Annual Review of Sociology, 19*, 139-161.

Portes, A., & Rumbaut, R. (1990). *Immigrant America: A portrait*. Berkeley: University of California Press.

Portes, A., & Truelove, C. (1987). Making sense of diversity: Recent research on Hispanic minorities in the United States. *Annual Review of Sociology, 13*, 359-385.

Preto, N. G. (1990). Hispanic mothers. *Journal of Feminist Family Therapy*, 2(2), 15-21.

Radetsky, D. S., Handelsman, M. M., & Browne, A. (1984). Individual and family environment patterns among Jews and non-Jews. *Psychological Reports, 55,* 787-793.

Ram, B. (1990). Intermarriage among ethnic groups. In S. S. Halli, F. Trovato, & L. Driedger (Eds.), *Ethnic demography: Canadian immigrant, racial and cultural variations.* Ottawa, Canada: Carleton University Press.

Reynolds, D. K. (1980). *The quiet therapies: Japanese pathways to personal growth.* Honolulu: University of Hawaii Press.

Rischin, M. (1962). *The promised city.* Cambridge, MA: Harvard University Press.

Rodriguez, C. E. (1992). *Puerto Ricans: Born in the USA.* Boston: Unwin Hyman.

Rodriguez, C. E., & Melendez, E. (1992). Puerto Rican poverty and labor markets: An introduction. *Hispanic Journal of Behavioral Science, 14,* 4-15.

Roland, A. (1988). *In search of self in India and Japan: Toward a cross-cultural psychology.* Princeton, NJ: Princeton University Press.

Rose, P. I. (1959). *Strangers in their midst: A sociological study of the small-town Jew and his neighbors.* Unpublished doctoral thesis, Cornell University, Ithaca, NY.

Sabogal, F., Marin, G., Otero-Sabogal, R., VanOss Martin, B., & Perez-Sable, E. J. (1989). Hispanic familism and acculturation: What changes and what doesn't? *Hispanic Journal of Behavioral Science, 9,* 397-402.

Safa, H. I. (1984). Female employment and the social reproduction of the Puerto Rican working class. *International Migration Review, 18*(4), 1168-1187.

Sampson, E. E. (1988). The debate on individualism: Indigenous psychologies of the individual and their role in personal and social functioning. *American Psychologist, 43,* 15-22.

Sanua, V. D. (1978). The contemporary Jewish family: A review of the social science literature. In G. Babis (Ed.), *Serving the Jewish family.* New York: KTAV.

Sanua, V. D. (1985). The family and sociocultural factors of psychopathology. In L. L'Abate (Ed.), *The handbook of family psychology and therapy* (Vol. 2). Homewood, IL: Dorsey.

Scanzoni, J. (1971). *The black family in modern society.* Boston: Allyn & Bacon.

Schwartzman, J. (1982). Normality from a cross-cultural perspective. In F. Walsh (Ed.), *Normal family processes.* New York: Guilford.

Sev'er, A., Isajiw, W. W., & Driedger, L. (1993). Anomie as powerlessness: Sorting ethnic group prestige, class, and gender. *Canadian Ethnic Studies, 25*(2), 84-99.

Shamai, S. (1992). Ethnicity and educational achievement in Canada, 1941-1981. *Canadian Ethnic Studies, 14*(1), 43-57.

Shon, S. P., & Ja, D. Y. (1982). Asian families. In M. McGoldrick, J. K. Pearce, & J. Giordano (Eds.), *Ethnicity and family therapy.* New York: Guilford.

Silberman, C. E. (1985). *A certain people: American Jews and their lives today.* New York: Summit.

Sklare, M. (1972). *American Jews.* New York: Random House.

Solomon, P. (1988). Racial factors in mental health service utilization. *Psychosocial Rehabilitation Journal, 11,* 3-12.

Spanier, G. B., & Thompson, L. (1984). *Parenting: The aftermath of separation and divorce.* Beverly Hills, CA: Sage.

Srole, L., Langer, T. S., Michael, S. T., Opler, M. K., & Rennie, T. A. C. (1962). *Mental health in the metropolis: The midtown Manhattan study.* New York: McGraw-Hill.

Stack, C. (1974). *All our kin: Strategies for survival in a black community.* New York: Harper & Row.

Staples, R., & Johnson, L. B. (1993). *Black families at the crossroads*. San Francisco: Jossey-Bass.

Stein, H. F. (1985). Values and family therapy. In J. Schwartzman (Ed.), *Families and other systems: The macrosystemic context of family therapy*. New York: Guilford.

Stone, G. P. (1991). *Family and interpersonal mediation: A bibliography of the periodical literature 1980-1989*. Guelph: Family Mediation Canada.

Sue, D. W. (1981). *Counseling the culturally different: Theory and practice*. New York: John Wiley.

Sue, S., & Morishima, J. K. (1982). *The mental health of Asian Americans: Contemporary issues in identifying and treating mental problems*. San Francisco: Jossey-Bass.

Sue, S., & Zane, N. (1987). The role of culture and cultural techniques in psychotherapy: A critique and reformulation. *American Psychologist, 42*(1), 37-45.

Suzuki, B. H. (1980). The Asian American family. In M. Fantini & R. Cardenas (Eds.), *Parenting in a multicultural society*. White Plains, NY: Longman.

Syrtash, J. T. (1992). *Religion and culture in Canadian family law*. Toronto: Butterworths.

Taieb-Carlen, S. (1992). Monocultural education in a pluralist environment: Ashkenazi curricula in Toronto Jewish educational institutions. *Canadian Ethnic Studies, 14*(3), 75-86.

Takaki, R. (1989). *Strangers from a different shore: A history of Asian Americans*. Boston: Little, Brown.

Takash, P. C., & Zavella, P. (Eds.). (1993). Social construction of gender in U.S. Latino communities. *Urban Anthropology*, Special Issue, *23* (3-4).

Tamura, T., & Lau, A. (1992). Connectedness versus separateness: Applicability of family therapy to Japanese families. *Family Process, 31*(4), 319-340.

Tavuchis, N. (1989). Ethnicity and the family. In G. N. Ramu (Ed.), *Marriage and the family in Canada today*. Scarborough, Ontario: Prentice Hall.

Taylor, R. (1986). Receipt of support from family among black Americans: Demographic and familial differences. *Journal of Marriage and the Family, 48*, 67-77.

Taylor, A., & Sanchez, E. A. (1991). Out of the white box: Adapting mediation to the needs of Hispanic and other minorities within American society. *Family and Conciliation Courts Review, 29*(2), 114-127.

Thompson, R. H. (1989). *Toronto's Chinatown: The changing social organization of an ethnic community*. New York: AMS.

Tomaskovic-Devey, D. (1993). Labor process inequality and the gender and race composition of jobs. *Research in Social Stratification & Mobility, 12*, 215-247.

Triandis, H. C., Marin, G., Lisansky, J., & Betancourt, H. (1984). Simpatia as a cultural script of Hispanics. *Journal of Personality & Social Psychology, 47*, 1363-1375.

Tsang, C. L. (1989). Informal assessment of Asian Americans. In B. Gifford (Ed.), *Test policy and test performance: Education, language, and culture*. Boston: Kluwer.

Tseng, W.-S., & Hsu, J. (1991). *Culture and family: Problems and therapy*. New York: Haworth.

Tseng, W.-S., & Wu, D. Y. H. (Eds.). (1985). *Chinese culture and mental health*. New York: Academic.

Tsui, P., & Schultz, G. L. (1985). Failure of rapport: Why psychotherapeutic engagement fails in the treatment of Asian clients. *American Journal of Orthopsychiatry, 55*, 561-569.

Tuchman, G., & Levine, H. G. (1993). New York Jews and Chinese food: The social construction of an ethnic pattern. *Journal of Contemporary Ethnography, 22*(3), 382-407.

Turner, J. H., & Bonacich, E. (1980). Toward a composite theory of middleman minorities. *Ethnicity, 7,* 144-158.

Valdivieso, R., & Davis, C. (1988). *U.S. Hispanics: Challenging issues for the 1990s.* Washington, DC: Population Reference Bureau.

Vazquez-Nuttall, E., Romero-Garcia, I., & DeLeon, R. (1987). Sex roles and perceptions of femininity and masculinity of Hispanic women: A review of the literature. *Psychology of Women Quarterly, 2,* 409-425.

Vigod, B. L. (1984). *The Jews in Canada.* Ottawa: Canadian Historical Association.

Vogel, E. (1967). The go-between in a developing society: The case of the Japanese marriage arranger. *Human Organization, 20,* 112-120.

Walker, J. W. St. G. (1980). *A History of blacks in Canada: A study guide for teachers and students.* Ottawa: Minister of Supply and Services.

Walker, J. W. St. G. (1984). *The West Indians in Canada.* Ottawa: Canadian Historical Association.

Walsh, F. (1993). Conceptualization of normal family processes. In F. Walsh (Ed.), *Normal family processes* (2nd ed.). New York: Guilford.

Waxman, C. I. (1992). Are American Jews experiencing a religious revival? *Qualitative Sociology, 15*(2), 203-211.

Wilkinson, C. B., & Spurlock, J. (1986). The mental health of black Americans. In C. B. Wilkinson (Ed.), *Ethnic psychiatry.* New York: Plenum Medical Books.

Wilson, W. J. (1987). *The truly disadvantaged: The inner city, the underclass, and public policy.* Chicago: University of Chicago Press.

Wong, B. (1982). *Economic adaptation and ethnic identity of the Chinese.* New York: Holt, Rinehart & Winston.

Wylan, L., & Mintz, M. (1976). Ethnic differences in family attitudes towards psychotic manifestations, with implications for treatment programmes. *International Journal of Social Psychiatry, 22,* 86-95.

Yamamoto, J. (1982). Japanese Americans. In A. Gaw (Ed.), *Cross-cultural psychiatry.* Boston: John Wright-PSG.

Yinger, M. (1985). Ethnicity. *Annual Review of Sociology, 11,* 151-180.

Yip, G. (1985). *Cross-cultural childrearing: An annotated bibliography.* Vancouver: Centre for the Study of Curriculum and Instruction, University of British Columbia.

Yu, L. C. (1984). Acculturation and stress within Chinese-American families. *Journal of Comparative Family Studies, 15,* 77-94.

Yum, J. O. (1988). The impact of Confucianism on interpersonal relationships and communication patterns in East Asia. *Communication Monographs, 55*(4), 374-388.

Yung, J. (1986). *Chinese women of America: A pictorial history.* Seattle: University of Washington Press.

Zayas, L. H., & Bryant, C. (1984). Culturally sensitive treatment of adolescent Puerto Rican girls and their families. *Child & Adolescent Social Work, 1*(4), 235-253.

Zborowski, M., & Herzog, E. (1952). *Life is with people.* New York: Schocken.

Zuk, G. H. (1978). A therapist's perspective on Jewish family values. *Journal of Marriage & Family Counseling, 4,* 101-111.

9

Mediation in
Child Protection Cases

Allan E. Barsky

INTRODUCTION

In the past, family mediation generally referred to the mediation of child custody, access, and financial matters arising from separation and divorce. In recent years, mediation has been used with families in which child abuse or neglect has occurred. This chapter will show how mediation can be adapted and applied to child protection cases (CPCs).

The child protection system is designed to safeguard children from maltreatment. Ideally, this protection is accomplished in ways that are least intrusive to families and children (Solnit, Nordhaus, & Lord, 1992) by working with families on a voluntary and consensual basis. In contrast, one of the main concerns about the child protection system are that some parents may be disempowered and alienated by it and thus may feel resentful and angry at child protection workers (CPWs). If so, it can be difficult, if not impossible, for parents and CPWs to work together on a truly voluntary basis. In appropriate CPCs, mediation can remedy some of these problems.

In what follows, I first examine the sociolegal context for CPC mediation, then provide an overview of the CPC mediation process.

Next, I turn to the role of CPC mediators and the techniques and strategies they can use in providing assistance. I then analyze the values that can come into conflict in this type of mediation and conclude by discussing implications for future policy and practice.

THE CONTEXT OF CHILD PROTECTION

Parents are responsible for meeting the basic needs of their children. What happens when they fail in this task? State responses in North America have varied through time. Not long ago, children were viewed as the property of their parents. Although most provided for their children's needs, they were still free to abuse, neglect, or exploit their children without state interference (Bala, Hornick, & Vogl, 1991, p. 2). More recently, the state began to assume the role of parent when it was thought necessary to "rescue" children from parental maltreatment (Cohen, 1992, p. 18; Rothery & Campbell, 1990). It has even become possible for the state to cut all ties between parents and their children. Although current attitudes support neither extreme, the challenge of how to reconcile the divergent values represented by these positions continues to confront state authorities (Maidman, 1984).

Despite jurisdictional variation, most child protection systems are guided by the same basic principles. Such systems are legislatively mandated to secure children against parental abuse and neglect. This goal is balanced by the needs to support the family's integrity and autonomy and where intervention is required to do so using the least disruptive means (Bala et al., 1991, p. 18). When parents and CPWs agree on a course of action, these values can be balanced without conflict. Conflict arises when the parties have different views concerning the child(ren)'s welfare.

Agency concern about the welfare of a particular child is usually based on reports from the community. The agency is then mandated to investigate through the authority vested in CPWs and subject to court sanction (Palmer, 1983, p. 122). Under this system, CPWs frequently enact conflicting roles. On the one hand, CPWs are given legal responsibility to safeguard children from harm, with duties that including investigating, informing the court of their findings, cooperating with police, acting as witnesses, and monitoring court orders for enforcement (Mayer, 1987a, p. 6). On the other hand, in their roles of counselor, case manager, and service provider, CPWs value client self-determination and cooperative relationships. They also seek to provide clients with a range of possible responses, which may alleviate stress and reduce the future risk of maltreatment (Maidman, 1984). Despite these concerns, CPWs are frequently seen by parents as agents of the state.

An alliance between the family and the CPW is not just a professional ethic, but a necessary condition for effective intervention (Maidman, 1984; Mayer, 1987a). Research shows that a worker's use of authority can be an obstacle to such an alliance or a potential source of positive change (Shulman, 1991). The way that authority is used determines whether its impact is positive or negative (Maidman, 1984). Authority used to foster trust can produce beneficial results (Shulman, 1991). Authority used to inhibit trust will make effective intervention difficult. Accordingly, some writers recommend that CPWs negotiate their relationship with clients, rather than intervene directly or impose authority unilaterally (Cingolani, 1984; Murdoch, 1980).

Levels of compliance are higher when clients see the CPW's authority as legitimate. Treated unfairly, there are many ways in which clients can "resist" help, including testing the limits of the CPW's sanctioning ability. Parents' use of such nuisance power can place CPWs in a difficult position; whenever possible, arrangements with parental consent are preferred over involuntary interventions (Bala et al., 1991, pp. 41-43).

More generally, Palmer (1983) suggests that a CPW's authority is not a fact of child protection, but is essential to practice in this field. She argues that use of authority can be an expression of "caritas" or caring, rather than coercion and as such is a form of love, "which is not only accepting, but critical and able to transform what it loves" (Palmer, 1983, p. 121; Siporin, 1975, p. 70). Thus the use of authority is justified and necessary to facilitate client change and growth (Gourse & Chescheir, 1981, p. 69). Reluctant to seek help on their own, parents in turmoil may feel relieved when intervention is imposed by legal authority (Murdoch, 1980, p. 460; Palmer, 1983, p. 121).

In contrast, it seems hard to argue that the family's right to self-determination, choice, and autonomy are not being compromised. Even if involuntary intervention is necessary, there is still a measure of paternalistic control. CPWs' authority gives them significantly greater power than parents. Indeed, parents who do not cooperate "voluntarily" face powerful sanctions. Power imbalances also reflect differences in education, income, and language and communication skills. Families charged with abuse are disproportionately poorer and otherwise disadvantaged (Maidman, 1984), and many believe the system is against them and that consequently CPWs cannot be trusted.

Clients face other informational and cultural barriers. When CPWs try to "educate" parents about community parenting norms, CPWs draw on moral and expert power sources (Maidman, 1984, p. 39). CPWs have the advantage of agency resources, unilateral access to records, and prior experience in CPCs. CPWs, unlike most clients, are familiar with the law and protection process. In is hardly surprising, then, that many clients feel they are fighting the entire system by themselves (Callahan, 1991).

The addition of lawyers and court procedures simply exacerbates the power imbalance. Formal procedures and technical language (Auerbach, 1983, p. 117) increase parents' fear and anger (Maidman, 1984, p. 52), and leave them feeling alienated and less capable of full participation. Having a lawyer may help some parents feel empowered; the lawyer can explain the process and advocate on their behalf, whereas the trial itself may be open to public and judicial accountability (cf. Mnookin & Kornhauser, 1979).

However, any existing conflict tends to become entrenched by the trial process. Although judges may encourage voluntary settlement, they retain the authority to make final decisions. Furthermore, dispositions available to judges are limited by statute, which does not give the court broad powers. Judicial choices, then, may be more limited than if the parties negotiate a settlement out of court.

Although the foregoing suggests that CPWs and courts have significant power, parents are far from powerless. Their legal rights and freedoms are augmented by protective legislation and the Canadian Constitution, which place limits on state intervention (cf. Burak, 1988) and, in favoring the status quo, place the onus on CPWs to demonstrate the need for intrusive measures. In addition, the protection system values parental autonomy and recognizes the likely negative impact of removing children from their homes. There is good reason then to think that CPC mediation may have a useful role to play.

THE BASICS OF MEDIATION
IN CHILD PROTECTION CASES

Given the above framework, in what follows I examine the who, what, when, where, and why of applying CPC mediation. The framework of child protection mediation presented in this chapter is based in part on a model developed by June Menesca, Joanne Wildgoose, and their associates at the Child and Family Mediation Centre, Toronto.

Who Are the Parties?

The parties to be included in mediation depend on who is involved in the presenting conflict and whose inclusion will be necessary for conflict resolution. Frequently, mediation is confined to parents and the CPW, who typically have different views about how to ensure child safety. Sometimes a new worker or a supervisor can be included to mitigate past emotional baggage.

Conflict may also include other parties, such as the child, foster parents, members of the extended family, and other social service workers. For example, the CPW and the parents may agree that the child should return home, but the parents and the child may be in conflict around house rules such as curfew and discipline. In this case, bringing the child into mediation is likely to be helpful.

Inclusion of lawyers depends on a number of factors. Including one lawyer requires that both attend, although their presence is subject to the limits of their clients' resources. Lawyers' involvement may help clients focus on the legal issues and possible solutions. However, allowing parents and the CPW to work together without lawyers present may allow them to deal with nonlegal issues such as the underlying emotional issues and may encourage disclosure and open communication between parties who need to interact for some time after mediation. I recommend confining mediation to CPWs and parents initially; lawyers may be invited later and only if their involvement will be helpful.

Even when lawyers do not attend, both lawyers should regularly be apprised of what is going on, so that they can advise their clients while negotiation is ongoing. Parents in particular should have legal representation from the outset and especially before any agreement is finalized. Without such legal involvement, all the efforts that have gone into mediation can go for naught if one lawyer simply vetoes the proposed settlement.

What Is CPC Mediation and What Is Mediatable?

CPC mediation can be defined as a problem-solving process in which a third party professional assists parties involved in a child protection proceeding to resolve differences between them. Mediated issues include (a) types of service to be provided, (b) types of service parents will use, (c) conditions that must be satisfied before child returns home, (d) alternative child care options, (e) the terms of parent-child visitation, (f) appropriate nonviolent responses to family conflict, (g) other parenting practices, and (h) termination of parental rights and voluntary, open adoption (if permitted by local laws).

In offering service, mediators must deal with both the presenting issues and underlying concerns. Parents seeking affirmation of their parenting skills or who need to know that temporary placement will not jeopardize their parenting relationship may manifest these underlying concerns by insisting that their child be returned home immediately, despite realizing that is not in the child's best interest.

CPC mediation begins with an initial contact from one party, usually a CPW or a lawyer, because they are more likely than parents to be familiar with mediation. The mediator then meets with each party alone to explain the process and evaluate their suitability for mediation. The mediator may prefer to meet with the CPW first, because the CPW may be better able to explain the family involvement in protection proceedings. However, the mediator must guard against allying with the CPW, thus causing parents to question the mediator's impartiality. Rather, mediators must clarify their independence and demonstrate that they have no interest in any specific outcome.

If the case is appropriate and the parties agree, the mediator will arrange for a joint session at which he or she reviews the ground rules and identifies each party's presenting issues. Each party may be asked to recount the issues they have already explained to the mediator in private. The mediator explains that hearing it all again helps him or her better understand the situation and the parties themselves may see the issues differently when involved in collaborative problem solving.

Throughout, the mediator should encourage open and constructive communication and help the parties identify areas of mutual interest, especially the child's welfare and the obvious benefits of amicable resolution. If the parties are able to agree, the mediator prepares a memorandum of understanding. The parties, with their lawyers, then formalize this understanding by returning to court to request an "order of consent" or by drafting a "voluntary provision of service agreement," also known as a "voluntary plan of care."

Follow-up mediation can be built into the agreement to deal with changing circumstances. To build trust, the mediator may encourage the parties to make arrangements in stages and build on each success. Rather than decide whether a child should return home, the parties may agree to successive interim plans in which parents spend more and more time with the child. As trust increases, they work toward having the child return home full time. If that goal is not realistic, at least the parents will know that they have tried, and must come to accept this reality. The parties may also deal with underlying issues. Parents may agree to foster placement, but later ask to have the child back. Apparently intent on regaining custody, the parents' underlying issue may be trouble working out sufficient access and time with the child.

These processes illustrate the difference between CPC mediation and the mediative functions of CPWs, lawyers, and judges. Although CPWs may mediate between parents and systems in the client's environment, this is mitigated by the nonvoluntary aspects of the parent-CPW relationship, as enshrined in existing protection statutes. CPWs may try to resolve protection issues consensually; however, if these efforts fail, CPWs' authority allows them to use nonvoluntary measures, including child removal. This ability creates a tendency for CPWs and parents to act as partisans in negotiating with one another. Similarly, lawyers may seek nonadversarial case settlements. However, such efforts are limited by the fact that lawyers must advocate for parties (CPWs, parents, children) with divergent interests.

Judges too may strive for consensual agreement at various pretrial stages. However, the court still retains decision-making authority in CPCs (see Saunders, Baker-Jackson, Flicker, & McIsaac, 1991; Shaw & Phear, 1991).

Thus although CPWs, lawyers, and judges may perform mediative functions, mediation is not their primary mandate. To distinguish such efforts from those of CPC mediators, the role of the latter can be characterized as follows: (a) mediators represent none of the parties, but act to facilitate advancement of each of their interests; (b) although mediators are bound by legal and ethical obligations (see below), these obligations are different than those that apply to CPWs; (c) mediation is "closed" for court purposes, because the mediator has no decision-making authority and advances neither case assessment judgments nor recommendations; (d) although mediators seek to promote positive interaction between the parties in dispute (cf. Donohue, Lyles, & Rogan, 1989; Irving & Benjamin, 1987, 1991), primary responsibility for dispute resolution rests with the parties; and (e) mediators are responsible for control over the mediation process.

Where Mediation Is Held

There are three considerations in selecting the site for CPC mediation: accessibility, neutrality, and informality. An accessible location is important because parents often have limited travel resources. Although access is not a significant issue for CPWs, their heavy workload makes travel time a factor.

Mediation may be conducted in agency offices or the parents' home. The risk in doing so is that the party not on "home turf" may see the other party as having a tactical advantage. Choosing a neutral site can also help establish the mediator as independent of the parties. Court-based offices may serve as a neutral venue, but may suggest to the parties that the mediator is a judicial decision maker.

Finally, creating an informal atmosphere encourages the parties to open up and work collaboratively. Where conflict has been high, special care should be taken to ensure that the mediation room looks different from court or agency offices to put the parties at ease and avoid unpleasant reminders or ill feelings.

An important but often forgotten consideration is where the child will be during mediation. Although older children may participate directly, child care facilities (a room, toys, and a supervisor) may be needed for younger children. In the absence of such facilities, the parents' only option may be to stay home or come to mediation with child in arms.

When Mediation Is Appropriate

Mediation can be used at any stage in CPCs so long as certain minimum eligibility criteria are met (Barsky, 1992a, 1992b; Maresca, Savage, & Wildgoose, 1990): (a) the child is in no immediate danger; (b) there are legitimate, child protection concerns about the child; (c) participation (and termination) are based on voluntary consent of all parties; (d) all parties are competent to negotiate for themselves, taking into account any uncontrolled mental illness, substance abuse problems, significant retardation, language impediment, or significant family violence; (e) there are no outstanding criminal charges related to the issues under negotiation; and (f) there are no ongoing family assessments.

It is critical to the process that parents have accepted that there is a legitimate child protection concern. CPC mediation should not be used to debate whether child abuse or neglect is taking place. If either abuse or neglect occurs, mediation is terminated and traditional child protection mechanisms are used to ensure the child's safety. Initially, parents may deny the CPW's safety concerns, making the case inappropriate (at that stage) for mediation. The CPW may help parents acknowledge the need for intervention. Failing that, a court order may be needed to validate the CPW's concerns. Thus a case that is inappropriate for mediation at one stage may be appropriate at another, when the parties recognize that concern about the child's welfare is appropriate.

Children benefit from stability and reduced parental conflict. Accordingly, early settlement and permanency planning are important. From this perspective, mediation can be useful at early stages of the protection process to resolve issues quickly before the parties become too entrenched in conflict or antagonism and mistrust resulting from court involvement.

In practice, the parties may not consider early mediation. The parents may know little about child protection or mediation. Rather, they will likely be referred by a lawyer or other professional. Although CPWs may know about mediation, they may justifiably prefer to try to resolve the case on their own. In turn, some CPWs may reject mediation as a duplication of their efforts or as a tacit admission of failure. However, the more CPWs know about and experience mediation, the less intimidating it will be. Such CPWs select mediation if they believe it can help families make their own work easier.

Both CPWs and parents may be more willing to consider mediation in cases headed for trial. The parties may be referred to mediation by their lawyer or a judge as a way of avoiding the time, costs, emotional stress, and risks of going to court. Mediation offers the parties more room for compromise and the possibility of at least a partial win. To paraphrase one parent, "If I had my druthers, my children would be home and I'd have nothing to do with Children's Aid. In court we had a 20% chance of winning. At least in mediation, the odds are 50-50." Even so, during premediation meetings, the mediator should inform all parties that they are under no pressure to participate.

Why Mediation Is Justifiable

Although mediation is not a panacea, there are several reasons it should be considered in CPCs (cf. Center for Policy Research, 1992; Palmer, 1989; Wildgoose, 1987; see Benjamin, 1991, p. 243): (a) Its accent on consent makes it congruent with protection system procedures and existing statutes; (b) by emphasizing common interests, it can help maintain reasonable relations between CPWs and parents; (c) it is less intimidating than court and allows fuller participation by family members; (d) by encouraging the parties to develop their own agreement, it enhances parents' rights of self-determination; (e) it stresses agreements that are individualized, future-oriented, and subject to future amendment; (f) in accord with permanency planning, it leads to more timely resolution than litigation; (g) given consensual agreements, it encourages parties to comply with them; (h) it can accommodate the participation of a wide range of parties in the decision-making process; and (i) it offers direct savings to families and court diversion for the justice system.

Some of these arguments are debatable (Wildgoose, 1989). Bush (1989), for example, argues that cost savings is a weak rationale for the use of mediation. Success defined in terms of cost gives mediators an incentive to force parties to agree quickly, sacrificing fairness. More generally, opponents of mediation suggest that because it is based on compromise and negotiation, the process may be unable to protect children, respect parental rights, ensure fair negotiation, or prevent duplication of earlier settlement efforts (Center for Policy Research, 1992, p. 101). One safeguard, noted above, is to ensure ongoing legal representation. The fact that 60% to 85% of CPC mediations end in agreement provides compelling evidence that mediation is not redundant (Hogan, 1993).

Negotiations in CPCs involve CPWs and parents, not just lawyers (Murdoch, 1980). Thus Thoennes (1991, p. 248) argues that the value of mediation lies in its promotion of "careful bargaining with all of the relevant parties represented." Ultimately, the value of CPC mediation should be similarly judged in terms of whether it leads to better outcomes for children and families. Both anecdotal reports and empirical studies are promising (Shaw & Phear, 1991; Thoennes, 1991, 1993).

THE ROLE OF A
CHILD PROTECTION MEDIATOR

From a basic description of CPC mediation, I turn to a more detailed look at what mediators can, should, and should not do, and under what circumstances. Mediators draw on a broad repertoire of techniques and strategies. How they use them will depend on the dynamics of the case (Center for Policy Research, 1992). In what follows, analysis of the mediator's role begins with a look at a structural issue: the mediator's mandate and authority. I then explore interventions in terms of power and other aspects of the CPW-parent relationship.

Mandate and Authority

Although the roles of CPWs are mandated by statute, few jurisdictions even mention mediation. Even where it is mentioned, there is little guidance as to the mediator's mandate and authority (see Saskatchewan's Child & Family Service Act [1989-90]). In jurisdictions that do not explicitly allow for the use of CPC mediation, it may be inferred that mediation is intended to resolve protection concerns consensually. Mediation would thus be preferred to more intrusive measures so long as the child is not at risk. In turn, some protection agencies have added mediation to their checklist of options for consideration. Unless there is contrary legislation, mediation should not be mandatory, that is, a prerequisite to court access or other alternatives (see Charbonneau, 1993).

Thus the bulk of CPC mediation's mandate derives not from statute, but from the protection agency, its governing bodies, and its funding sources. Protection services can operate under various auspices: court-affiliated programs, community based services, or private practitioners (either certified or on a registry). Funding can be through government financing, charitable donations, fee for service, or a combination. Whatever the arrangements, mediation services must devise their own mandate and standards of practice. The codes of ethics and standards of practice of mediation associations across North America have not addressed CPC mediation, and their voluntary status means they have no authority to license mediators.

Unable to specify the CPC mediators' mandate, I can at least say what it is not, namely, it cannot be the same as that of a CPW, judge, or assessor. It is crucial for CPC mediators to distinguish their role from that of other professionals involved in CPCs. CPWs, judges, and assessors must each form an opinion of the child's best interests. In contrast, there are several reasons for mediators' neutrality: (a) they are not trained in family assessment; (b) they do not have the means that other professionals have to gather information on which to base their opinion; (c) mediators offer no recommendations or decisions, for to do so would render them interested parties in the conflict; and (d) mediator assessment would not only render them biased, but would duplicate the CPW's role.

Furthermore, insofar as mediation is voluntary and consensual, there is an inherent contradiction in the notion of a "mandate for mediation," because it is not something that can only be imposed from above. In contrast, "authority" is transactional; although it can be asserted, it must first be accepted to be meaningful and effective (Sloan, 1992). Thus, "authority for mediation" refers to the terms under which the parties agree to mediate.

This authority is reflected in the "agreement to mediation," a document signed by all the parties before service begins. It sets out expectations and ground rules, defines the mediator's role, lists the issues to be dealt with, whether independent legal advice is recommended or required (see Bush, 1989), the scope of confidentiality (see Bala et al., 1991), the identity of the parties, how sessions will be arranged and paid for, and how mediation can be terminated (with or without an agreement).

By signing an agreement to mediate, the parties give the mediator authority over the process. In designing such a document, mediators and agencies should address the following: the type(s) of authority vested in the mediator, the degree to which they should be facilitative or directive, the limits (if any) on the permissible outcomes of mediation, and the role of the mediator. Although there are a number of ways the role of the mediator can be framed, mediators are typically given discretion to use both facilitative and directive methods. In the following, I detail how mediators can use authority to be facilitative and when they can be more directive.

Power, Facilitation, and Direction

Having a mediator come between CPW and parents affects the power balance between them. Although mediators have no authority to impose specific outcomes, they can affect outcomes. For example, authorized to establish ground rules, the mediator gains considerable control over the process. Such procedural power may be as simple as agreement that each party will be allowed to speak without interruption. The parties are likely to accept such rules because they are so "obviously" fair (cf. Rifkin, Millen, & Cobb, 1991, p. 152). Though facilitative, this rule can have a significant effect on power and outcome. Consider that a CPW with advanced language and communication skills will have an advantage over less articulate parents. The no-interruption rule reduces the power imbalance, leaving the parents in a better position to convey viewpoints, interests, and options (Thoennes, 1991, p. 252). Consequently, the final settlement may be very different from what it might have been without a mediator. Similar effects can be achieved by choice of a neutral meeting site and mediator control over seating arrangement, pace, formality, and ground rules (Bercovitch, 1992).

Power also derives from the mediator's expertise. His or her experience helps the parents peek into what might happen if the case is not resolved through mediation (cf. Feuille, 1992, pp. 139-140). Although mediators cannot provide legal advice, they can do reality testing with a party whose position is patently unreasonable and can help a party explore whether its interests are more likely to be achieved through mediation or by an alternative process (Fisher & Ury, 1981, p. 101).

Consider the mother who insists that her child be returned home but is unwilling to take precautions so that her boyfriend, who abused the child, does not do so again. Here the mediator might tell the mother that in similar cases neither the agency nor the court would allow return of the child. The mediator might then explore other options such as ways of preventing the boyfriend from having contact with the child or inviting him to join the mediation process. In facilitating these insights, the mediator uses directive techniques to help the mother decide whether to pursue settlement through mediation or take another course of action. It is the mother who chooses which path to take, even if the mediator believes that there is a better alternative.

The following strategies illustrate the range of potential interventions designed to affect power dynamics:

Bring Other People Into the Negotiating Process (Benjamin, 1991, p. 240). For parents intimidated by their CPW, the mediator may ask the parents' lawyer, friend, or others to join the process to provide support, reduce parental anxiety, and lessen the CPW's advantage. When the parties come from different cultures, a cultural interpreter can be helpful as someone who can translate between languages and help each party understand the other's beliefs, values, and customs.

Encourage Constructive and Discourage Destructive Negotiating Behavior. CPWs' use of coercive power and parents' use of nuisance power are examples of destructive negotiating behaviors. To reduce their use, the mediator can instruct the parties on how to constructively express their thoughts and advance their interests. This instruction can be particularly useful with parents with limited language or communication skills (Thoennes, 1991, p. 252). Conversely, mediators can help CPWs understand how parental cooperation can be enhanced by refraining from displaying their authoritative power (Palmer, 1983, p. 122).

Provide Information. Parents typically have less knowledge than do CPWs of the protection system. Mediators can help parents overcome this disadvantage by providing information (Girdner, 1989, p. 150; Thoennes, 1991, p. 251), or helping access information through task prescriptions (cf. Sloan, 1992). With this information, parents may be able to access social services from the voluntary service sector or come to an agreement that minimizes interaction with protection agencies. Mediators can also encourage CPWs to share their knowledge with parents in words that even an "ignorant mediator" can understand.

Help Parents Make Reasonable Requests (Thoennes, 1991). Parents who advance patently unreasonable demands hurt their ability to negotiate solutions that are in their best interest. For example, a parent may suggest that whenever she goes out, she could drop the child off at the agency to be looked after. The mediator can challenge the feasibility of this suggestion and assist her to formulate a more reasonable position, such as that the agency provide respite child care at specific times.

Conflict Management Strategies

Additional techniques are used to help parties resolve differences, including the underlying causes of conflict. The analysis that follows compares the process with and without a mediator.

To preempt problems and deal with nonconstructive beliefs, mediators need to be aware of each party's perspective. CPWs may respond defensively if they think the mediator is questioning their professional judgment. Parents may ignore joint problem solving so long as they are trying to convince the mediator. Types of nonconstructive beliefs include (Hogan, 1993): (a) that all options have already been considered; (b) the refusal to make exceptions for fear of setting a precedent; (c) negative feelings in the present are based solely on past negative experiences; and (d) plans that have not previously been considered may mean more work for the CPW or place him or her at risk with the agency.

In most CPCs, parents and CPWs agree that the child's best interests are paramount (Thoennes, 1991, p. 255). Conflict arises because they have different understandings of what best interest means under the circumstances. Employed parents may see nothing wrong with leaving a 10 year old alone in the house after school, whereas the CPW may see it as neglect. The mediator's role is not to judge who is right, but rather to help the parties achieve mutual understanding. In this case, he or she might have the parties explore the child's needs and how they can best be met.

CPC mediation stands in sharpest contrast with litigation. The latter requires a judge to adjudicate rights and declare an outcome. CPC mediation emphasizes consensual and personalized decision making. If there is a single attribute that distinguishes mediation from litigation it is the mediator's capacity to encourage the parties to exercise self-determination, choice, and autonomy (Bush, 1989). Although some writers argue that mediation is empowering insofar as it places responsibility on participants for decision making, others take a broader view. Kelly and Gigy (1988) argue that mediation offers a way of enhancing participants' confidence and ability to stand up for themselves, be responsible for managing their own affairs, understand the other party's viewpoint, and identify important issues and problems (Barsky, 1992a; Girdner, 1989; cf. Torre, 1986). Techniques mediators can use to realize these outcomes are described below.

Both CPWs and mediators prefer to deal with parents in ways that (Maidman, 1984): (a) encourage them to be responsible for their own affairs; (b) allow them to direct their own destinies; (c) keep children out of care or enable them to reunite quickly (Hegar & Hunzeker, 1988, p. 501); (d) help them explore all options; (e) foster a relationship with the CPW based on respect and empathy (Bush, 1989, p. 274); and (f) ensure the child's safety.

A crucial difference between mediators and CPWs is their respective mandates, authority, and power. To ensure safety, a CPW may involuntarily apprehend a child. Alternately, a CPW may negotiate a "voluntary agreement with parents using varying levels of coercion" (cf. Badami, 1990, p. 186). Parents know that failure to agree will mean going to court, having the child removed from the home, or other intrusive measures. Mediators have no such mandate and must rely instead on their communication skills and techniques. If they are unable to help the parties on a consensual basis, their only recourse is to terminate service; they are unable to impose a solution. Being nonthreatening in this way enhances their ability to gain the parties' trust and confidence.

In mediation, CPWs retain their power and authority, checked by the mediator's control over the process. A CPW who threatens to remove the child can be blocked by the mediator in various ways. The mediator can emphasize the "mutuality of the disputants, reminding them that it will take free and conscious consent of both to craft a fair agreement" (Sloan, 1992, p. 8). Furthermore, meeting alone with the CPW, the mediator can pose a number of questions such as: (a) Is the parents' continued involvement important to the child? (b) If the case went to court, would the judge block access between parent and child? and (c) Is the parents' cooperation important, whether or not the child is placed in foster care?

In addition, CPWs know that even when a parent has abused a child, it is legally difficult totally to deny parents access, and the amount of control CPWs can enforce through the protection system is limited. Sanctioning power tends to produce only public compliance and requires ongoing monitoring for compliance to endure (Robbins, 1979); consensual agreement is more likely to engender acceptance and compliance (Mayer, 1984, 1987a). The mediator's task is to help parties see that cooperative problem solving can lead to a "win-win-win" outcome for the parents, CPW, and child.

These premises are not new to CPWs. However, mediators enable the parties to achieve outcomes they might be unable to achieve alone by helping: (a) CPWs step back and reappraise whether cooperative problem solving can be established; (b) parents express fear and anger about past abuse by authority (Maidman, 1984, pp. 38-40; Palmer, 1983, p. 123), correct misperceptions of the present CPW (Foren & Bailey, 1968, pp. 23, 283) and focus on the future; (c) the parties separate "personality clashes" from underlying problems; (d) CPWs "save face" when they need to back down from previous positions that are no longer tenable (Thoennes, 1991, p. 255); (e) the parties "go around" impasses by changing their expectations and making compromises they had not previously considered; and (f) CPWs demonstrate to parents that they are acting out of genuine concern for the family, which has perhaps been concealed by professional training directed at controlling emotional displays.

Returning to self-determination, various techniques can advance this value. In helping the parties define the issues, mediators encourage them to identify common issues and interests. If a party frames an issue in provocative terms, the mediator can help him or her reframe it more positively. Parents who say the CPW treats them "like crap" can be helped to reframe this as their desire to be treated "with respect." Such respect can be one of the first issues upon which the parties can agree and can extend to the CPW's role as a professional, the parents' rights of self-determination, and the family's right to autonomy. By focusing on mutual and future-oriented interests, mediators open the door to an array of solutions and choices.

Mediation can also enhance the parties' choices by the use of option generating strategies, the most common being brainstorming. Both parties generate possible solutions that are recorded and saved for subsequent evaluation.

Additional choices arise by having the parties focus on underlying interests rather than positions. The CPW's position may be that there should be supervised access to the child, whereas the underlying interest is to secure the child's welfare. By focusing on the latter, parents who demand unsupervised access have the opportunity to rethink their plan in ways that meet the child's needs. The CPW's real concern might be that the parents feed an infant improperly. Structured access might be arranged so that the foster parent is present only during feeding but not otherwise, a less intrusive option. The mediator might suggest additional choices the parties might not have considered.

In two respects, service termination is similar whether or not a mediator is involved: Any agreement is formalized in a written contract; and should agreement prove impossible, the parties can resort to other alternatives. However, there is another way in which mediated termination is distinctive. In CPW-parent negotiation, the CPW controls the process, including an agreement. In mediation, the mediator seeks to ensure that the interests of both parties are represented in an agreement and that it is written in language that is nonjudgmental, mutual, and future-oriented (Maidman, 1984, pp. 48-51). Rather than say that the parent "will stop using beatings to discipline the child," a mediated agreement would list the disciplinary methods parents can use.

VALUE DILEMMAS IN PRACTICE

The above illustrations reflect only a small sample of the techniques available in CPC mediation. In what follows, I turn to the question of values and how they help define the mediator's roles. Mediator neutrality and party's right of self-determination are two values central to mediation. However, the meaning of neutrality is ambiguous when questions are raised about fairness and the safety of children. Similarly, parental self-determination is problematic when parents are negotiating with a CPW backed by legal sanctioning power. Below, I suggest a framework for dealing with these issues.

Neutrality, Fairness, and Safety

Mediator neutrality is essential to the mediation process (Palmer, 1989; Zartman & Touval, 1985). This statement is based on the premise that a "biased mediator," one allied with one party, would create an unfair process. Although mediators may declare themselves neutral, their interventions defy this notion to varying degrees (Rifkin et al., 1991). Welton and Pruitt (1987) question whether neutrality is really critical. Their data show that "mediator bias tends to erode readiness to accept and be influenced by the mediator" (p. 124), whereas "the greater the disputant power over the mediator, the less impact will mediator bias have over readiness to accept and be influenced by the mediator" (p. 124).

In reference to CPC mediation, the parties' power over the mediator derives from several sources: parties may withdraw from mediation, publicly praise or censure the mediator, or choose to be cooperative or difficult (cf. Murdoch, 1980, p. 460; Welton & Pruitt, 1987). In addition, parents may miss or be late for appointments and CPWs or their agency may refuse to mediate in the future.

Given these factors, CPWs may be willing to trust a mediator who, from time to time, seems to be allying with parents. In contrast, parents who see a mediator allying with the CPW may be less willing to extend their trust and may resist, rebel, or disengage from the process. For CPWs and parents, then, the mediator needs to demonstrate his or her impartiality to gain their trust.

That said, there are several bases for believing that for a CPC mediator, unconditional neutrality is untenable. For one thing, even "simple" choices present neutrality issues, including which party will be asked to speak, confront, or caucus first. Second, mediators enter the process with certain professional values such as the importance of open communication and mutual decision making. Ideally, these values are identified in the agreement to mediate (cf. Ontario Association for Family Mediation, n.d., p. 5). Although these values do not inherently favor one party over another, they have unequal effects depending on circumstances. For example, the CPW or the parents may be withholding information the mediator will encourage them to disclose (cf. Rifkin et al., 1991, p. 153). Finally, for mediation to be fair, each party must be able to advance their interests free of fear, coercion, or exploitation. In situations where the process becomes unfair, the mediator cannot be neutral (Haynes, 1981, pp. 62-63). Rather, he or she must be able to take steps to redress unfairness or terminate mediation.

Ideally, questions of fairness are identified at intake. The mediator meets with each party to see if they meet minimal eligibility required, listed above, especially the party's ability to negotiate. When there are significant disparities between the parties, there are various ways the mediator can help those with weaker skills negotiate effectively, such as slowing down the process, using clarifying questions, bringing in support persons, and so on—short of the mediator himself or herself becoming an advocate. Consider the CPW who is inexperienced or relatively low skilled (Thoennes, 1991, p. 25). Allowed to negotiate freely, the CPW may accept an agreement that puts the child at risk. The mediator might act as the child's defender, but would displace the CPW. Rather than allow this situation to arise, the mediator should terminate service (cf. Corcoran & Melamed, cited in Girdner, 1990, p. 314).

Some writers question whether mediators should "be the embodiment and protectors of community norm" (Folberg, 1983, p. 13; Greatbatch & Dingwall, 1989, p. 614; Stulberg, 1981), whereas others argue that mediators should (Haynes, 1981, p. 123) or should not (McRory, 1981; Stulberg, 1981) act "forcibly" to prevent agreements that negatively affect children. Those, as with Saskatchewan's Child and Family Services Act (1989-90), who think that mediators should be "representative of community standards," effectively turn mediators into CPWs. Although mediators can have the parties discuss their respective views of the child's interests (cf. Stulberg, 1981, p. 116) and can halt mediation when faced with a poor CPW, the mediator has neither the authority, the training, nor the information to assess or represent the child's interests (cf. Girdner, 1989, p. 148). Rather, mediators must distinguish between confrontation and advocacy. Although it is appropriate for a mediator to confront each party with the arguments of the other, the mediator may not advocate his or her personal opinions (Stulberg, 1981, p. 105).

As for concerns about coercion, procedural fairness may require mediators to ally with one party to avoid abuses of power (Sloan, 1992). That is, fairness requires equitable treatment, not equal treatment. Although some writers view mediators' efforts to rebalance power as legitimate, the issue remains contentious (Girdner, 1989; Ricci, 1985; Thoennes, 1991). Mediation cannot redress many disadvantages of poor parents (Mayer, 1987b, pp. 83-84), but it can significantly affect the dynamics of power (Bush, 1989, pp. 260-266). The key issue is normally not how mediators may exert power, but rather how to limit its use (Sloan, 1992, p. 8).

On the question of the extent to which mediators should be facilitative or directive, a "least intrusive" standard is appropriate. Ideally, directive intervention is not required because the parties negotiate fairly; only facilitative intervention is then needed. However, ideal cases are rare. Mediators must be free to be more directive when negotiation becomes unfair, the parties lose sight of the child's interests, or both. Indeed, the balance between facilitative and directive intervention varies by circumstances. The parties may negotiate fairly until a critical issue creates an impasse. At this point, the mediator may become directive to resolve the impasse and keep the process on track. Note that being directive is still less intrusive than imposing a solution on the parties (Blades, 1984, p. 71).

In some cases, rather than allow one party to be coerced, mediation may need to be halted because power disparities become too great. It is not possible to specify with precision when this halting should be done. However, mediation ceases to be useful when power imbalances become "so severe that no mediator can balance the scale without destroying the mediator's *credibility* and *base of authority*" (Sloan, 1992, p. 7, emphasis added). Mediators can also discuss alternative options with the parties and refer them to their lawyers for advice (cf. Charbonneau, 1993).

In a similar vein, mediators must be accountable so that they do not abuse their power (Bush, 1989; Greatbatch & Dingwall, 1989; McRory, 1981, p. 64; Susskind, 1981). Analysis of this issue goes beyond the scope of this chapter. However, options include judicial review, administrative review, and investigations or hearings by mediation associations.

Self-Determination, Choice, and Autonomy

Mediators' efforts to promote client self-determination are problematic. Consider that insofar as CPWs represent the state, CPC mediation may be seen as a form of social control. Mediators' neutrality may be taken to mean that child abuse is negotiable or that parents' "voluntary" participation is a sham given the alternative. Below, I address these issues in turn.

Social Control. Although mediation is conducted within a statutory framework (Saunders et al., 1991, p. 262), CPWs' mandate requires them to advocate for their view of the child's needs. This leads Greatbatch and Dingwall (1989, p. 614) to argue that

> much of the enthusiasm about mediation reflects the influence of libertarian arguments against state intervention. Private ordering is accordingly seen as more efficient and morally superior to determination by some public authority.
>
> In its pure form, however, private ordering brings with it the possibility of the strongest disputant imposing a settlement that seems grossly unfair when measured against some external measure of justice or that infringes on the rights of third parties, such as the state, as a provider of income support or children with their needs for economic and psychological security.

However, CPC mediation is paradoxical. Strictly speaking, it does not advance private ordering, because the CPW is a state agent. Thus, mediation can be said to encourage parents to submit to social control.

Although the argument is valid, the point of comparison is crucial. Mutuality and joint problem solving can limit parents' right of self-determination (cf. Gourse & Chescheir, 1981, p. 68). But this is only true in comparison with no state intervention. More relevant is the comparison to CPW-parent negotiation. As noted above, mediation can significantly affect the dynamics of CPCs. Only additional research can determine whether mediation actually fosters self-determination compared to the alternatives.

Child Abuse Negotiable. I argue above that mediators do not judge the child's interests, but encourage a future focus and the avoidance of blame. However, in CPCs there is still right and wrong. A mediated agreement that puts a child at risk is a bad agreement; a court-imposed solution is preferred (cf. Rifkin et al., 1991). Thus mediation can be an instrument for social injustice "bypassing the safeguards of a formal judicial process" (Chupp, 1991, p. 5) and undermining the effectiveness of criminal law accountability (Menard & Salius, cited in Girdner, 1990, p. 298).

My response is threefold. First, the use of mediation does not preclude the use of institutional safeguards (Mayer, 1987b; Pearson, Thoennes, Mayer, & Golten, 1986, p. 320), including the discretionary use of nonvoluntary interventions. Second, CPCs are concerned with protecting children, not finding fault or exacting retribution. Mediation addresses the protection concern (Benjamin, 1991, p. 230). When retribution is deemed appropriate, the case should be processed through the criminal justice system (Menard & Selius, cited in Girdner, 1990, p. 295), although it is very limited as a mechanism to protect children (Benjamin, 1991, p. 232). Finally, mediators help the parties define the child's interests. CPWs retain their protection mandate, thus allowing mediators to remain neutral.

Voluntary Choice. If it is recommended to them by a professional, parents may have a hard time refusing mediation. How can this situation be seen as truly voluntary given the alternative? (Hart, cited in Girdner, 1990). Even if they do not feel threatened, parents may feel uncertain because they may know nothing about mediation or may confuse it with "meditation."

These concerns are real. Precautions must be taken to ensure that mediation is as voluntary a choice as possible. Referral sources can be trained to present mediation as a real choice and can explain it in concrete terms. Once a referral has been made, mediators can screen for coercion and ensure that an agreement to mediate involves free and informed consent. Mediators can also check that parents have legal advice and remind the parties during mediation that either party is free to terminate.

Even more important may be how parents feel on termination of mediation (Girdner, 1989, p. 143). There is significant evidence that most participants come away satisfied (Mayer, 1987a; Pearson et al., 1986), although more work is needed to determine the effect of mediation on client self-determination (Eddy, 1992; Smith et al., 1992; Wildgoose & Maresca, 1994).

CONCLUSION

Proponents of CPC mediation advance strong claims about its desirability in terms of empowerment, timely settlement, individualized and durable solutions, and participant satisfaction. Critics charge that it puts children at risk, insidiously imposes social control, and duplicates the CPW role. Resolution of this debate depends on how CPC mediation is defined and implemented. The above description demonstrates some of the positive aspects of CPC mediation.

In particular, CPC mediation needs to be distinguished from CPW clinical practice. Unlike CPWs, mediators emphasize collaborative problem solving as the parties negotiate to determine the best substantive outcome (Mayer, 1989, p. 92). To this end, CPC mediators use a range of techniques. For facilitators, these techniques include procedures that help the parties (Bush, 1989; Mayer, 1987b, p. 81) access relevant information, ensure each has been heard, understand each other's positions, generate creative solutions, evaluate these options, consider the costs and benefits of alternatives to mediation, and reach agreements that are mutually acceptable, clearly stated, comprehensive, and feasible.

CPWs must reconcile their roles as state agents and helping professionals. Parents can feel disempowered, confronting an alien system threatening intrusion into their family. Mediators need to help CPWs with role conflict and empower parents.

In this context, mediators derive their authority from the parties. Mediation is voluntary and consensual and relies on mediators to secure the parties' trust. That outcome is possible only if parties see mediators as fair and empathic. Only then can mediators offer parties hope that the process will lead to agreement. Thus mediators must treat the parties equitably, rather than equally, in light of power and other disparities between the parties. Recognizing these dynamics, mediators use a wide range of techniques and strategies.

Mediators face ethical dilemmas dealing with power imbalances. If these dilemmas are ignored, the process can become grossly unfair. Mediator attempts to redress power imbalances can lead to charges of mediator bias. Preferred interventions depend on the types of power being exerted. The parties will tolerate unequal treatment if it is seen as legitimate. They are thus likely to accept ground rules designed to discourage coercive tactics or procedures that encourage disclosure. Throughout, mediators must remain neutral as to specific outcomes.

Finally, CPC mediation has a number of limitations. It is inappropriate when either party is unable to negotiate for his or her interests. It cannot redress all types of power imbalance and cannot guarantee that children will not be put at risk, for it is not intended to replace the protection system. Indeed, additional study is needed to identify the types of cases best suited to mediation, and development of codes of conduct is still needed to ensure mediator accountability. However, where CPC mediation has been used, most parties report high satisfaction with the results. Although funding and statutory recognition are still wanting, there is growing interest across North America in this new application of mediation. As of this writing, its future seems promising as part of a larger trend toward the use of consensual and collaborative dispute resolution.

AGREEMENT TO MEDIATE (Sample)

BETWEEN:_____

AND

BETWEEN:_____

1. **The parties** named above,

_____

wish to attempt to settle the dispute between them through mediation with [name of mediation service provider].
The issues to be settled are summarized as follows:

_____
_____
_____

2. Role of Mediator

The parties acknowledge that the mediator is an impartial third party who represents none of the parties. The parties further acknowledge that although the mediator is a lawyer, the mediator cannot and will not represent any of them. The role of the mediator is to assist the parties to negotiate a voluntary settlement of the issues outlined in paragraph one above, based on full and frank disclosure between them. The primary responsibility of resolving the disputes rests with the parties, with the mediator acting as facilitator only. Nevertheless, the mediator will at all times promote a settlement that is fair and equitable and in the best interests of the children.

3. Independent Legal Representation

The parties understand that the mediator will not give them legal advice or a legal opinion. They each further acknowledge that the mediator has strongly advised and encouraged each of them to obtain independent legal advice from the outset of mediation.

The parties further understand that if one of both of them choose to proceed to mediate a settlement without independent legal advice, they risk making decisions without being fully informed of their legal rights and obligations, and with full knowledge of the possibility that any agreement reached between them may not later be enforced by a court of law.

In the event that the parties or one of them refuse to obtain independent legal advice, he/she/they agree to indemnify and save the mediator harmless from any and all liabilities arising out of the mediated agreement.

4. Confidentiality

The parties agree that the mediation will be conducted on a partially confidential basis. The mediator will not voluntarily disclose to anyone who is not a party to the mediation anything said or any materials submitted to the mediator, *except:*

 a. To the lawyers for the parties, at such times as deemed necessary by the mediator
 b. To the counsel for the child(ren)
 c. For research or educational purposes, on an anonymous basis
 d. Where ordered to do so by a judicial authority or where required to do so by the law
 e. Where the information suggests an actual or potential threat to human life or safety

The parties agree that the mediator shall not be called as a witness to give any evidence or make any report in any legal proceedings, whether current or contemplated. The parties themselves are not bound by confidentiality, and any admissions, or any communication made in the course of mediation, may be disclosed *by the parties* in any current or any future litigation.

5. Third-Party Involvement

The parties agree that the mediator may speak to and involve significant third parties in the mediation process where, in the opinion of the mediator, such involvement is necessary to the furtherance of the resolution of the dispute. The mediator agrees to advise the parties of his or her intention to involve a third party. The parties agree that it may be necessary to seek information and advice from other professionals in the resolution of the dispute. The mediator shall seek the written consent of the parties to obtain such information and advice.

6. Disclosure of Information

The parties agree to make full and complete disclosure of all relevant facts, reports, documents, or other written or oral information regarding the issues to be mediated.

7. Mediation Sessions

The mediator will schedule the time and place of the mediation sessions with the parties. Sessions may be canceled without penalty by either of the parties or the mediator on 24 hours' notice. Generally, the mediator will meet with both parties in joint sessions. However, occasionally the mediator may wish to meet with one or the other of the parties in individual sessions. In such cases, the mediator will have the right to disclose the content of the individual session(s) to the other party, if, in his or her own opinion, it is significant for the mediation process.

8. Conclusion of Mediation

Each of the parties has the right to withdraw from the mediation process at any time prior to agreement on notice to the mediator and the other party. The mediator has the right to suspend or terminate the mediation process at any time where in his or her opinion continuation of the process would result in harm or prejudice to one or more of the participants. The parties or their counsel will draft any agreement reached with the assistance of the mediator. Such agreement will not be binding until reviewed by each party's independent counsel.

9. Further Undertakings and Acknowledgments

The parties agree that neither of them will initiate or take any fresh steps in any legal proceedings between them while the mediation is in progress. Should any further legal action be required to protect the child(ren), the mediation process will first be terminated.

Each of the parties and the mediator acknowledge that he or she has read this agreement and agrees to proceed with mediation on the terms set out above.

DATED THIS _____DAY OF_____19__. _____

DATED THIS _____DAY OF_____19__. _____

DATED THIS _____DAY OF_____19__. _____

DATED THIS _____DAY OF_____19__. _____

NOTE: Printed with permission of Joanne Wildgoose and June Maresca, Child and Family Mediation Centre, Toronto.

REFERENCES

Auerbach, J. S. (1983). *Justice without law?* Toronto: Oxford University Press.

Badami, S. (1990). Constitutionally recognizing court mandated arbitration: Paradise found of problems abound. *Journal of Dispute Resolution, 1990*(1), 179-180.

Bala, N., Hornick, J. P., & Vogl, R. (1991). *Canadian child welfare laws.* Toronto: Thompson Educational.

Barsky, A. E. (1992a). *Enfranchisement as a rationale for the use of mediation in child protection cases.* Unpublished doctoral paper, Faculty of Social Work, University of Toronto.

Barsky, A. E. (1992b). *Mediation in child protection cases: Managing "mandate, authority and power" with "self-determination, choice and autonomy."* Unpublished doctoral paper, Faculty of Social Work, University of Toronto.

Benjamin, R. D. (1991). Mediative strategies in the management of child sexual abuse cases. *Family and Conciliation Courts Review, 29,* 221-245.

Bercovitch, J. (1992). Mediators and mediation strategies in international negotiations. *Negotiation Journal, 8,* 99-112.

Blades, J. (1984). Mediation: An old art revisited. *Mediation Quarterly, 3,* 59-98.

Burak, S. (1988). The power of social workers: A comparative analysis of child protection legislation. *Canadian Journal of Family Law, 7,* 117-130.

Bush, R. A. B. (1989). Efficiency and protection, or empowerment and recognition? The mediator's role and ethical standards in mediation. *Florida Law Review, 41,* 253-286.

Callahan, M. (1991). *Empowering women in child welfare.* Russel Joliffe Lecture. Toronto: Ryerson Polytechnic University.

Center for Policy Research, Denver. (1992). *Alternatives to adjudication in child abuse and neglect cases.* Alexandria, VA: State Justice Institute.

Charbonneau, P. (Ed.). (1993). *Report from the Toronto forum on woman abuse and mediation.* Toronto: Women's Law Association.

Chupp, M. (1991). When means and ends come together. *MCS Conciliation Quarterly,* 4-5.

Cingolani, J. (1984, September/October). Social conflict perspectives on work with involuntary clients. *Social Work,* 442-446.

Cohen, N. A. (1992). *Child welfare: A multicultural approach.* Toronto: Allyn & Bacon.

Donohue, W. A., Lyles, J., & Rogan, R. (1989). Issue development in divorce mediation. *Mediation Quarterly, 24,* 19-28.

Eddy, W. A. (1992). *Mediation in San Diego's Dependency Court: A balancing solution for a system under fire?* Unpublished paper, San Diego School of Law.

Feuille, P. (1992). Why does grievances mediation resolve grievances? *Negotiation Journal, 8,* 131-145.

Fisher, R., & Ury, W. (1981). *Getting to yes: Negotiating without giving in.* Boston: Houghton Mifflin.

Folberg, J. (1983). Mediation overview: History and dimensions of practice. *Mediation Quarterly, 1,* 3.

Foren, R., & Bailey, R. (1968). *Authority in social casework.* Oxford: Pergamon.

Gibelman, M., & Demone, H. W. (1989). The social worker as mediator in the legal system. *Social Casework,* 28-36.

Girdner, L. K. (1989). Custody mediation in the United States: Empowerment or social control? *Canadian Journal of Women and the Law, 3,* 134-154.

Girdner, L. K. (Ed.). (1990). Mediation and spouse abuse. *Mediation Quarterly, 7*(4).

Gourse, J. E., & Chescheir, M. W. (1981). Authority in treating resistant families. *Social Casework*, 67-73.

Greatbatch, D., & Dingwall, R. (1989). Selective facilitation: Some preliminary observations on a strategy used by divorce mediators. *Law & Society Review, 23,* 613-641.

Haynes, J. M. (1981). *Divorce mediation*. New York: Springer.

Hegar, R. L., & Hunzeker, J. M. (1988). Moving toward empowerment-based practice in public child welfare. *Social Work, 33,* 499-502.

Hogan, J. L. (1993). *Mediating child welfare cases*. Unpublished paper, Geneva, Illinois.

Irving, H. H., & Benjamin, M. (1987). *Family mediation: Theory and practice of dispute resolution*. Toronto: Carswell.

Kelly, J. B., & Gigy, L. L. (1989). Client Assessment of Mediation Services (CAMS): A scale measuring client perceptions and satisfaction. *Mediation Quarterly, 19,* 43-52.

Lederach, J. P. (1986). *Mediation in North America: An examination of the profession's cultural premises*. Unpublished doctoral paper, University of Denver.

Maidman, F. (1984). *Child welfare: A sourcebook of knowledge and practice*. New York: Child Welfare League of America.

Maresca, J., Savage, H., & Wildgoose, J. (1990). *Program proposal, Centre for Child and Family Mediation*. Toronto: Laidlaw Foundation.

Mayer, B. (1984). Conflict resolution in child protection and adoption. *Mediation Quarterly, 9,* 69-81.

Mayer, B. (1987a). *Mediation and compliance in child protection*. Unpublished doctoral dissertation, University of Denver (UMI Dissertation Services, No. 8802810).

Mayer, B. (1987b). The dynamics of power in mediation and negotiation. *Mediation Quarterly, 16,* 57-86.

Mayer, B. (1989). Mediation in child protection cases: The impact of third-party intervention on compliance attitudes. *Mediation Quarterly, 24,* 89-106.

McRory, J. (1981). The mediation puzzle. *Vermont Law Review, 61*(1), 85-117.

Mnookin, R., & Kornhauser, L. (1979). Bargaining in the shadow of the law: The case of divorce. *Yale Law Journal, 88,* 960-997.

Murdoch, A. D. (1980, November). Bargaining and persuasion with non-voluntary clients. *Social Work,* 458-461.

Ontario Association for Family Mediation. (n.d.). *Code of professional conduct*. Guelph, Ontario: Author.

Palmer, S. E. (1983, March/April). Authority: An essential part of practice. *Social Work,* 120-125.

Palmer, S. E. (1989). Mediation in child protection cases: An alternative to the adversarial system. *Child Welfare, 68,* 21-31.

Pearson, J., Thoennes, N., Mayer, B., & Golten, M. M. (1986). Mediation in child welfare cases. *Family Law Quarterly, 20,* 303-320.

Ricci, I. (1985). Mediator's notebook: Reflections on promoting equal empowerment and entitlements for women. *Journal of Divorce, 3,* 49-61.

Rifkin, J., Millen, J., & Cobb, S. (1991). Toward a new discourse for mediation: A critique of neutrality. *Mediation Quarterly, 9,* 151-164.

Robbins, S. P. (1979). *Organizational behavior*. Englewood Cliffs, NJ: Prentice Hall.

Rothery, M., & Cameron, G. (Eds.). (1990). *Child maltreatments: Expanding our concept of helping*. Hillsdale, NJ: Lawrence Erlbaum.

Saunders, C., Baker-Jackson, M., Flicker, B., & McIsaac, H. (1991). Mediation in the Los Angeles Superior Court, Juvenile Dependency Court: An approach to designing a program that meets the interests and concerns of all parties. *Family and Conciliation Courts Review, 29,* 259-269.

Shaw, M., & Phear, W. P. (1991). Innovation in dispute resolution: Case status conferences for child protection and placement proceedings in the state of Connecticut. *Family and Conciliation Courts Review, 29,* 270-290.

Shulman, L. (1991). *Interactional social work practice: Toward an empirical theory.* Itasca, IL: Peacock.

Siporin, M. (1975). *Introduction to social work practice.* New York: Macmillan.

Sloan, G. (1992). Power: Its use and abuse in mediation. *Interaction, 4*(1), 7-8.

Smith, R., Maresca, J., Duffy, M., Banelis, N., Handelman, C., & Dale, N. (1992). *Mediation in child protection: Limited or limitless possibilities.* Unpublished paper, Children's Aid Society of Metropolitan Toronto.

Solnit, A., Nordhaus, B. F., & Lord, R. (1992). *When home is no haven.* New Haven, CT: Yale University Press.

Stulberg, J. B. (1981). The theory and practice of mediation: A reply to Prof. Susskind. *Vermont Law Review, 6*(1), 49-116.

Susskind, L. (1981). Environmental mediation and the accountability problem. *Vermont Law Review, 6*(1), 1-48.

Thoennes, N. (1991). Mediation and the dependency court: The controversy and three courts' experiences. *Family and Conciliation Courts Review, 29,* 246-258.

Thoennes, N. (1994). Child protection mediators in the juvenile court. *The Judge's Journal, 33*(1), 14-19, 40-43.

Torre, D. A. (1986). *Empowerment: Structured conceptualization and instrument development.* Unpublished doctoral dissertation, Cornell University, Ithaca, NY.

Welton, G. L., & Pruitt, D. G. (1987). The mediation process: The effects of mediator bias and disputant power. *Personality & Social Science Bulletin, 13*(1), 123-133.

Wildgoose, J. (1987). Alternative dispute resolution of child protection cases. *Canadian Journal of Family Law, 6,* 61-84.

Wildgoose, J., & Maresca, J. (1994). *Report on the Centre for Child and Family Mediation, Toronto.* Kitchener, Ontario: The Fund for Dispute Resolution.

Zartman, I. W., & Touval, S. (1985). International mediation: Conflict resolution and power politics. *Journal of Social Issues, 41,* 27-46.

10

Research in Family Mediation

An Integrative Review

INTRODUCTION

For family mediation practitioners, research is useful both as a reality check and a guide to practice. The dedication required of the practitioner is such that it creates a bias favoring belief in one's own efficacy. Conversely, of late family mediation has been the focus of much criticism (Benjamin & Irving, 1992; Bryan, 1994). In both cases, research relates opinions to facts, confronting practitioners with the outcomes of their efforts and forcing critics to acknowledge the successes as well as failures of mediation.

That said, an overview of that expanding literature is not readily available. Although several collections of such research have been published recently (Folberg & Milne, 1988; Kelly, 1989a; Kressel & Pruitt, 1989), integrative reviews are either dated (Irving & Benjamin, 1987; Kressel, 1985, 1987a; Kressel & Pruitt, 1985), deal only peripherally with family mediation (Carnevale & Pruitt, 1992) or are published in journals that are not widely available (Clement & Schwebel, in press). The integrative review that follows is thus timely and appropriate. It is divided into three parts: studies of the process of providing service; studies reporting the outcomes of service; and studies of the predictors of mediated agreement. We then discuss the implications of the findings for researchers, policymakers, and practitioners.

Before proceeding, two qualifications are in order. First, the 50 studies reviewed below, although representative of the literature, are by no means comprehensive, because our search has largely been confined to published works in English in North America. Second, the results of this literature must be interpreted with caution, because comparability across studies remains low, which reflects the heterogeneous character of family mediation. Major variation obtains across at least *five* dimensions. The key dimension is what Pearson (1991) calls "dispute resolution forum," court-based versus private mediation. Compared to private mediation, court-based services offer fewer hours of service and fewer sessions, but at no charge. Additional sources of variation include the characteristics of client groups; the model of mediation practice in use; the local statutory regime; and the identity and training of the mediation practitioners providing service. Thus, although two services may look the same on paper, they may provide very different services to very different client groups using very different service models and differently trained mediators and they may operate in very different legal environments. Such variation does *not* make it impossible to reach general conclusions, but it argues for caution in applying generalizations to local practices.

RESEARCH IN FAMILY MEDIATION:
A REVIEW

The review that follows (see Table 10.1) groups research studies into three categories or parts. Part 1 focuses on process studies, Part 2 on outcome studies, and Part 3 on studies about predictors of successful mediation.

Part 1: Process Studies

Ideally, process studies should indicate what sorts of behaviors on the part of mediators have what sorts of effects with what sorts of client

(Text continued on page 412)

TABLE 10.1 Research Studies of Family Mediation in Divorce

Author(s)	Date	Location	Clients	Data
Margolin	1973	—	75 Ct/DM	I
			75 Control	
Salius	1977	Connecticut	577 Ct/DM	I
Dunlop	1978	Kingston, ON	49 Ct/DM	I & R
			19 Ct	
Caron & Doyle	1979	Minneapolis, MN	700	DM or Ct
Irving et al.	1979[a]	Toronto, ON	106 Ct/DM	I & T
			228 Ct Intake	
Parker	1980	Atlanta, GA	— Ct/DM	I & R
		Winston-Salem, NC	— Ct/DM	
		Charlotte, NC	— Ct	
Irving et al.	1981	Toronto, ON	193 Ct/DM	I & T
Gaybrick & Brymer	1981	Arlington, VA	— Ct/DM	I
Gardner	1981	Kingston, ON	— Ct/DM	R
			— Ct	
Bahr	1981a[b]	Virginia	19 P/DM	R
	1981b	U.S., Can., Australia	N/A	L
Pearson[c]	1982	Los Angeles, CA	500+ Ct/DM Spouse	I & R
		Minneapolis, MN		
		Connecticut		
		Minneapolis, MN	Ct/DM or Ct	I/f
		Colorado	Ct only	
Gaughan	1982	Washington, DC	— P/DM	I
Johnson	1984	San Bernardino, CA	50 Ct/DM success	R
			50 Ct/DM fail	
Koopman et al.	1984	Piedmont, CA	31 Ct/DM agree	R
			31 Ct/non-DM agree	
Saposnek et al.	1984	California	— Ct/DM	I/f
Waldron et al.	1984	—	13 Ct/DM	I
FFRS[d]	1984	Kingston, ON	— Ct/DM	I & R
Pearson & Thoennes[e]	1985	Denver, CO	200 Ct/DM accept	I & T
			100 Ct/DM reject	
			100 Ct	

(Continued)

TABLE 10.1 (Continued)

Author(s)	Date	Location	Clients	Data
Yates	1985	U.K.	— P/DM	R
Johnston et al.[f]	1985	California	80 P/DM	I & I/f
Weingarten & Douvan	1985	U.S.	24 M[g]	I
Gifford	1985	British Columbia	503 Ct/DM	R
Girdner	1985	U.S.	—	I & O
Matheson & Gentleman[h]	1986	Bristol, U.K.	— P/DM	I
Dingwall	1988	Bristol, U.K.	15 P/DM	TA
Richardson	1988	Canada[i]	2055 Ct/DM or Ct	I & R
Davis & Roberts	1988	Bristol, U.K.	169 P/DM	I & R
Ogus et al.[j]	1989	U.K.	225 Ct/DM	I & R
			220 P/DM	
			911 Ct	
Emery & Jackson[k]	1989	Charlottesville, NC	35 Ct/DM	I
			36 Ct	
Jones	1988	—[l]	18 Ct/DM agree	A/V
			18 Ct/DM no-agree	
Donohue et al.[m]	1989	—[n]	10 Ct/DM agree	TA
			10 Ct/DM no-agree	
Kressel et al.	1989	New Jersey	12 Ct/DM	R
Kelly[o]	1989b	California	212 P/DM	I & R
			225 Ct	
Chandler	1990	Hawaii	300 P/DM	R
Paquin	1990	California	124 M	Q
Camplair & Stolberg	1990	Virginia	36 Ct/DM	Q, T, R
Wagner[p]	1990	Maine	503 Ct/DM	R
Depner et al.[q]	1991	California	979 Ct/DM	I
Cohen	1991	San Diego, CA	— Ct/DM/M	R
Irving & Benjamin[r]	1992	Toronto, ON	72 P/DM	I & I/f
Mathis & Yingling	1992[s]	U.S.	51 Ct/DM	T
Pearson	1991	U.S.	302 DM, Other	Q
Kelly & Duryee	1992	California	184 Ct/DM/M or Ct/DM	I & I/f
Slater et al.	1992	California	557 Ct/DM	Q

(Continued)

TABLE 10.1 (Continued)

Author(s)	Date	Location	Clients	Data
Duryee	1992	California	49 Ct/DM	Q
Meierding	1993	California	94 P/DM	R & Q
Magna & Taylor	1993	California	— Ct/DM	R
Whiting[t]	1994	U.S.	38 P/DM	R
			68 P/non-DM	
Kressel et al.	1994	New Jersey	32 Ct/DM	R, I & A/V
Donohue et al.	1994	Indiana[u]	20 Ct/DM	TA

Total Studies: 50

KEY: DM = family mediation in divorce; Ct = adversarial proceedings in court; Ct/DM – court-based divorce mediation; Ct/DM/M = court-based mediation, mandatory; P/DM = private, fee-for-service divorce mediation, either for profit or not-for-profit; M = mediator; I = interview; O = observation; I/f = follow-up interview; Q = mail-out questionnaire; R = records; T = tests; L = literature; TA = transcript of session audiotapes; A/V = audiotapes and/or videotapes. Unless specified otherwise, all numbers refer to client couples.

NOTES: a. See also Irving and Benjamin (1983, 1984).
　　　　b. See also Bahr et al. (1987).
　　　　c. See also Little et al. (1985), Lyon et al. (1985), Cauble et al. (1985), Pearson and Thoennes (1982a, 1982b, 1984b), and Pearson et al. (1983).
　　　　d. This refers to the Frontenac Family Referral Service. The reference in question summarizes a series of studies conducted from 1978 to 1984. See also FFRS (1979).
　　　　e. See also Pearson and Thoennes (1984a, 1984c, 1988a, 1988b, 1989), Pearson et al. (1982), Slaikeu et al. (1985a, 1985b, 1988), Thoennes and Pearson (1985), and Vanderkooi and Pearson (1983).
　　　　f. See Campbell (1988).
　　　　g. Only some of the respondents (numbers unspecified) were family mediators. The balance were involved in diverse settings, including international trade and labor-management, environmental, academic, and church conflicts.
　　　　h. See also Matheson (1985).
　　　　i. Specifically, data were collected in four cities: Saskatoon, Winnepeg, Montreal, and St. John's.
　　　　j. See Ogus et al. (1990) and Walker (1987, 1989).
　　　　k. See also Emery and Jackson (1989), Emery and Wyer (1987a, 1987b), Emery et al. (1987, 1991, 1994), Peterson and Emery (1988), and Emery (1994).
　　　　l. Data were drawn from Pearson (1982).
　　　　m. See also Burrell et al. (1988), Donohue (1989, 1991), Donohue and Weider-Hatfield (1988), and Donohue et al. (1984, 1985, 1988).
　　　　n. Data were drawn from Pearson (1982).
　　　　o. See also Kelly (1990), Kelly et al. (1988), and Kelly and Gigy (1988, 1989).
　　　　p. See also Orbeton and Charbonneau (1988).
　　　　q. See Depner et al. (1994).
　　　　r. See Irving and Benjamin (1988).
　　　　s. See also Mathis and Yingling (1990, 1991).
　　　　t. See Whiting (1992).
　　　　u. Data drawn from an unpublished study by Thoennes and Pearson (1991, cited in Donohue et al., 1994).

couples in what sorts of contexts. Available studies fall short of this ideal, but have gone some way to help us understand what actually occurs in mediation.

Pearson (1982) and Pearson and Thoennes (1985) examined audio-tapes of court-based mediation (see Slaikeu et al., 1985a). Their research showed that "successful" mediators were active and directive, playing a major role in structuring the process of mediation, spent much time discussing possible solutions, and were assisted by clients with good communication skills. In cases where agreement was not reached, mediators focused more on facts and their efforts were undermined by poor client communication skills.

Donohue and his colleagues (1989) reanalyzed these data and showed that "successful" mediators were characterized by flexible control over the mediation process. They allowed clients to express their views but blocked the polarization of positions. Intervention frequency increased or decreased as spousal conflict varied. Thus mediators shaped communication in directions likely to produce agreement while disrupting clients' attack-defend cycles. They focused more on facts and interests than on relationships and values "because of the lack of time afforded them by the court's constraints" (p. 335; see Jones, 1988) and because such a focus produced agreement.

A recent replication (Donohue, Drake, & Roberto, 1994) confirmed these findings, adding that their court-based mediators failed to help clients with deeper relational problems, especially evident in couples that did not reach agreement. Donohue et al. (1994) suggest that this failure to address relational issues may reflect state law, which constrains what court-based mediators may discuss (see Donohue, 1991). In our view, it may also be related to the fact that the mediators in question were lawyers who had received 40 hours of training and thus were likely ill-equipped to cope with complex, conflictual marital interaction. Donohue et al. (1994, p. 274) concluded that "it is our view that agreement in mediation is not so much affected by the number of interest issues . . . but rather by the number and intensity of the relational issues [mediators] must confront. If those relational issues are numerous and severe, then reaching agreement . . . will be more difficult."

Whiting (1991) compared family mediation and other mediation (e.g., neighborhood mediation) cases. He found that family mediation was more likely to end in agreement, with these clients characterized by having ongoing relations (i.e., with children in common) and multiple issues in dispute, which accorded mediators more flexibility than single-issue cases (see also Dingwall [1988], Girdner [1985], and Paquin [1990]).

Irving and Benjamin (1992) and Kressel et al. (1994) attended to mediator behavior. Irving and Benjamin (1992), using mediator self-reports in private mediation, found that mediators emphasized passive forms of intervention, including support, clarifying, and active listening. Kressel et al. (1994) found, also in private mediation but using case audiotapes and videotapes, that mediators fell into settlement-oriented or problem-solving categories. The former were strictly neutral and settlement oriented. The latter were more structured and active, interested in the causes of the conflict and thus prepared to depart from strict neutrality when conflict was fueled by the destructive behavior of one spouse. The problem-solving approach yielded more and more durable agreements, and clients found it more satisfying.

It will now be clear that the handful of process studies available are only weakly comparable. However, by their consistency and taken together, these studies support at least two necessarily tentative conclusions. First, although mediator practice styles vary, "successful" mediators tend to intervene actively in couple interaction, encouraging productive exchanges and discouraging destructive conflict. They avoid fixed or inflexible practice structures, instead responding flexibly to couple interaction.

Second, practice setting makes a difference, whether mediation is public or private, and depending on local statutory regime. Setting seems to act as an important constraint, shaping what mediators do or do not do and with what frequency. Court-based mediators stick to facts and issues, a reasonable practice given their time constraints and professional socialization. However, given the different predelictions of private mediators, these findings raise questions about issues such as case selection, case referral, client satisfaction, client outcomes, and mediator training. For example, on what basis are divorcing couples referred for court-based as opposed to private mediation and does the route into mediation make any difference to process or outcome? Other things being equal, is case complexity likely to affect the process or the outcome if the case in question is handled through court-based as opposed to private mediation?

At present, these and other questions are unanswerable, which speaks to the methodological and, we would argue, conceptual limitations of available studies and hints at the untapped future potential of a process approach to the study of family mediation.

Part 2: Outcome Studies

Nearly all the studies listed in Table 10.1 provide data about one or more of *six* indicators of outcome: (a) agreement rate, (b) client satisfaction, (c) gender differences, (d) coparental relations, (e) cost, and (f) follow-up. Below we address each of these indicators in turn.

1. *Agreement Rate.* One measure of outcome effectiveness concerns the rate at which clients reach agreement, with respect to all (complete agreement) or some (partial agreement) of the issues in dispute. The overall agreement rate is the combination of these two client groups.

In this context, it serves little purpose to review the findings of individual studies. Rather, across studies, rates vary between 40% and 60% for complete agreement and between 10% and 20% for partial agreement. Thus overall agreement rates varied between 50% and 80%, typically the latter. Furthermore, these rates were consistent, whether involving court-based (Irving et al. [1981]; Pearson & Thoennes [1985]; Richardson [1988]; Wagner [1990]) or private mediation (Davis & Roberts [1988]; Irving & Benjamin [1992]; Kelly [1989b]; Pearson [1991]), voluntary (Camplair & Stolberg [1990]; Slater, Shaw, & Duquesne [1992]) or mandatory cases (Cohen [1991]; Duryee [1992]; Kelly & Duryee [1992]) and couples with a history of marital violence (Chandler [1990]) or intense marital conflict (Johnston, Campbell, & Tall [1985]).

In addition, several studies report that mediation clients were more likely to reach voluntary agreement than their counterparts in litigation, both in the United States (Emery & Wyer [1987a]; Pearson & Thoennes [1985]) and Great Britain (Dingwall [1988]; Ogus, Walker, & Jones-Lee [1989]) and to do so in fewer sessions and less time (Emery & Wyer [1987a]; Kelly [1989b]; Parker [1980]). Furthermore, compared to their litigated counterparts, mediated agreements were both different and better (cf. Emery & Wyer [1987a]; Pearson [1991]). For example, Koopman, Hunt, and Stafford (1984) found that mediated agreements were more comprehensive and more likely to favor shared parenting.

These data are noteworthy in at least four respects: They suggest that family mediation is efficient and effective, contributes to court diversion (however, see Follow-Up Studies, p. 419), and yields agreements that are comparatively complete and comprehensive. Moreover, court-based and private mediation appear equally effective.

2. *Client Satisfaction.* Mediation is distinguished from litigation insofar as it seeks to empower clients, so that they themselves fashion the agreements that will shape their futures (Irving & Benjamin, 1993). Another facet of outcome, then, is client satisfaction, whether addressed directly or indirectly.

Direct measures ask clients at termination to indicate to what extent they are satisfied. Of the studies in question, 60% to 80% of clients report high satisfaction with both service and outcomes (Depner, Cannata, & Simon [1991]; Kelly [1989b]; Kelly & Duryee [1992]; Parker [1980]; Pearson & Thoennes [1985]; Waldron et al. [1984]). A few studies report rates above or below this range (Davis & Roberts [1988]; Irving & Benjamin [1992]; Kressel et al. [1989]).

Common sense suggests that client satisfaction and outcome success should be related. Available data support this expectation, with outcome satisfaction more likely among agreeing than nonagreeing couples (Emery & Wyer [1987a]; Pearson & Thoennes [1985]; Richardson [1988]). However, the opposite was not necessarily true; 40% to 60% of clients who did not agree also reported satisfaction (Depner et al. [1991]; Kelly [1989b]; Kressel et al. [1989]; Meierding [1993]).

Indirect measures ask clients to evaluation their mediation experience. Although results varied, collectively they indicated that most clients were satisfied. For example, Chandler (1990) found that across an array of dimensions not less than 60% of violent couples judged their agreement fair (66%), durable (62%), workable (75%), and comprehensive (66%). Similar findings have been reported by others (Gaughan [1982]; Irving & Benjamin [1992]; Kelly [1989b]; Meierding [1993]; Saposnek, Hamburg, Delano, & Michaelson [1984]).

These data support the following conclusion by Kressel (1985, p. 187) that "these levels of user satisfaction are comparable [to] and perhaps even higher than, those reported for public satisfaction with other types of professional services." These include satisfaction rates of 60% to 85% for divorce counseling and 65% for legal services in divorce.

3. *Gender Differences.* Given the feminist critique of mediation (Benjamin & Irving, 1992; Bryan, 1994), researchers have taken a recent interest in the satisfaction of husbands and wives. The results suggest that both are treated fairly in mediation.

In a much hailed experimental study, Emery and Wyer (1987a) found that women in litigation felt that they had won more and lost less than their counterparts in mediation. More recent work by Emery and colleagues (see Table 10.1, note k) has qualified these results by showing that in litigation women's satisfaction rose through time, whereas men's declined. In contrast, in mediation women's satisfaction, already very high on entry, changed little, whereas men's increased through time. On the whole, then, women in mediation more than litigation expressed satisfaction with both process and outcome.

Similar findings have been reported by others. Davis and Roberts (1988), Kelly (1989b), and Pearson (1991) all found that women were more likely than men to judge their mediated agreements fair. Kelly and Duryee (1992) found that wives preferred mediation because it allowed them to express their views, put aside their anger, focus on their children, and develop self-confidence; accordingly, they were more satisfied (see Mathis & Yingling [1992]; Parker [1980]; Pearson & Thoennes [1985]). Others have noted few, if any, differences between men and women in mediation (Meierding [1993]; Richardson [1988]), whereas Kelly (Table 10.1, note o) found that women who dropped out of service did so for the "right reasons," namely, feeling unempowered or overwhelmed (cf. Bohmur & Ray [1994]).

Taken together, these data provide a potent rejoinder to the feminist critique of mediation. Bryan (1994), for example, has recommended that lawyers routinely accompany female clients into mediation because mediators cannot be relied on to protect their rights. The studies examined above paint a different picture, namely, that the majority of women most of the time prefer mediation over litigation because it affords them a more equitable and sensitive process. This preference does not diminish the feminist critique. Although the negative experiences cited in Bryan (1994) may be atypical, they are real and represent a challenge with which mediation must grapple. However, the data reviewed above make clear that mediators have heard women's complaints and have responded in ways that protect the rights of both women and men.

4. *Coparental Relations.* In mediation, the reduction of spousal conflict may be indispensable to fruitful negotiation. Here the findings are mixed, with some studies demonstrating such changes whereas others fail to do so.

Irving and Benjamin (1992) found that 60% to 76% of their respondents reported improvement in coparental relations, including decreased conflict, improved communication, and a reduction in the number of problems judged "serious." Furthermore, agreeing clients said that mediation was the main reason for the change. Others report similar changes (Camplair & Stolberg [1990]; Emery & Wyer [1987a]; Girdner [1985]; Johnston et al. [1985]; Kelly [1989b]; Pearson & Thoennes [1985]; Waldron et al. [1984]).

Studies by others report limited or no change in coparental relations. Mathis and Yingling (1992), for example, found that husbands more than wives changed their views during the course of service. Before mediation, husbands were more dissatisfied with their coparental relationship. After mediation, the same was still true, although husbands were more satisfied whereas their wives had not changed. Similar findings have been reported by others (Davis & Roberts [1988]; Pearson [1991]; Richardson [1988]).

It is unclear why some studies report coparental change but others do not. Two possibilities come to mind, both related to differences between court-based and private mediation. The first argues that different service settings attract clients with divergent attributes. Court-based services attract clients with few resources and more serious problems, whereas the reverse is true for private services. This situation suggests that court-based clients are less amenable than their private counterparts to major relational changes. Evidence for this self-selection argument is mixed. Irving and Benjamin (1992), Pearson (1991), and Pearson and Thoennes (1985) show that court-based clients display serious problems. However, the same can be true in private mediation (Chandler [1990]; Johnston et al. [1985]).

The other possibility focuses on client hours of service. Relationship change takes time and intent. Only services that employ a therapeutic model of service and that intend to effect such changes and have the time to do so are likely to report change in coparental relations. Support for this therapeutic argument comes from Donohue et al. (see Table 10.1, note m), who show that court-based services offer fewer than four hours of service, during which mediators avoid relational processes. Conversely, Johnston et al. (1985), Kressel et al. (1994), and Matheson and Gentleman (1986) all document the focus of private mediators on relationship change.

At present, there is no basis on which to prefer one explanation over the other. Like many of the issues raised in this review, resolution must rely on additional research.

5. *Cost.* The majority of divorcing couples have few assets (see chapters 2 and 3). The cost of divorce proceedings is therefore an important issue. Proponents of mediation argue that mediated settlements cost less than their litigated counterparts. The research literature generally supports this claim. Pearson and Thoennes (1985) found that the average cost of mediation among agreeing clients was $1,630, compared to $2,360 for litigation clients. They estimated that the public saves between $5,610 and $27,510 per 100 cases sent to mediation rather than litigation. Bahr (1981a) found that private mediation cost an average of $565 *less* per case than litigation (see Kelly, 1989b), with comparable savings contrasting court-based mediation and litigation (see Parker, 1980). Ogus et al. (1989) in Great Britain and Richardson (1988) in Canada found that although private mediation and court-based mediation respectively were slightly *more* costly than litigation, mediation was more effective. Such data led Kressel (1985) to estimate that projected on a national basis such figures translated into annual savings in the United States of between $79.5 million and $159 million.

Although most studies examined above focus on efficacy, these data speak to efficiency. Here two measures have been used: time to settlement and cost. Data regarding the former, reported above, show that in agreeing cases, mediation requires fewer sessions and fewer service hours than litigation. Above, cost data support a similar conclusion.

6. *Follow-Up Studies.* Whereas most studies in this literature are cross-sectional, a handful are longitudinal. Such efforts have focused on four outcomes: satisfaction, compliance, postdivorce adjustment, and relitigation.

Studies of satisfaction show that up to 2 years later, 40% to 60% of mediation clients remain satisfied. Davis and Roberts (1988), for example, found that 64% of custodial mothers compared to 40% of noncustodial fathers were satisfied with their visitation arrangement. Studies involving follow-up at 4 months (Margolin, 1973), 6 months (Duryee, 1992), 1 year (Kelly [1989b]; Irving et al. [1981]; Irving & Benjamin [1992]; Meierding [1993]; Pearson & Thoennes [1985]; Waldron et al. [1984]), and 2 years (Pearson [1991]) *all* found that mediation clients were more satisfied than their litigation counterparts and judged the mediation process "fairer" (cf. Emery & Wyer, 1987a).

Common sense suggests that such satisfaction should be related to greater compliance with the terms of the agreement, as it was in a number of studies (Bahr [1981a, 1981b]; Emery & Wyer [1987a]; Irving & Benjamin [1992]; Johnston et al. [1985]; Pearson & Thoennes [1985]; Waldron et al. [1984]). In addition, several studies noted that 40% to 65% of clients had consensually made changes to the terms of their agreements (Davis & Roberts [1988]; Emery & Wyer [1987a]; Irving & Benjamin [1992]; cf. Johnston et al. [1985]).

These findings imply greater positive changes through time in coparental relations among mediation as opposed to litigation clients. In fact, the findings are mixed. Several studies report such changes (Bahr, 1987; Irving & Benjamin, 1992; Margolin, 1973; Pearson & Thoennes, 1985), although others do not (Emery & Wyer, 1987a; Pearson, 1991; Waldron et al., 1984). Indeed, Johnston et al. (1985) found among their conflictual and dysfunctional couples that although there was overall reduction in coparental conflict and hostility, 40% showed no obvious improvement and another 15% had deteriorated.

Finally, as to the relitigation rate, the data show a lower rate among mediation than litigation couples. For example, among Johnston et al.'s (1985) clients, relitigation was 18%, with another 18% returning to mediation rather than the court. Others reported rates that were lower still (Irving & Benjamin, 1992, 10%; Margolin, 1973, 12%; Meierding, 1993, 7%; Pearson & Thoennes, 1985, 4%), and considerably lower than comparable rates among litigation clients (Margolin, 1973, 79%; Pearson & Thoennes, 1985, 15%; cf. Emery & Wyer, 1987a).

These data are noteworthy in at least three senses. They speak in unequivocal terms to mediation efficacy in regard to agreement durability, compliance, and satisfaction. They also continue the debate about coparental relations, with divergent findings the norm. Finally, they address court diversion, with low relitigation rates suggesting that few mediated couples who reach agreement return to court, in sharp contrast to their litigation counterparts.

Part 3: Predictors of Mediated Agreement

Finally, there is no consensus among researchers as to the best predictors of mediated agreement. Rather, their efforts distribute on a continuum, from the simple to the complex. Toward the simple end of the spectrum are studies that focus exclusively on client attributes. Camplair and Stolberg (1990), for example, found that agreement is related to the content of disputes, their relative importance to the spouses, and the spouses' willingness to compromise. Emery and Wyer (1987a) saw as critical the extent to which husbands accept the end of their marital relationship; those who failed to do so were much less likely than those who did to reach agreement in mediation. Irving and Benjamin (1992) found that clients with moderate problems and a limited number of issues in dispute were more likely to reach agreement in private mediation because these attributes gave mediators room to maneuver. Kelly (1989b) reported that agreement was more likely with couples with relatively equal financial acumen, a clear commitment to divorce, and emotional stability in both. Paquin (1990) found that agreement was associated with client communicative competence, especially rates of interruption, statements of feeling, alternatives proposals, and the use of "I" statements. Depner et al. (1991) found that clients with less education and income were most likely to rate their court-based service as helpful and to value services in which mediators do *not* forward recommendations to the judge.

Toward the complex end of the spectrum are studies that found that agreement was predicted best by the interaction *between* client and mediator attributes. Donohue et al. (1989), for example, showed that agreement was related to the interaction between mediator communicative competence and client attributes. Mediators' flexible control over the process with couples who had relatively few relational issues in dispute was most likely to achieve agreement in court-based mediation. Johnston et al. (1985) found that client personality attributes (especially personality disorders), extended family involvement, and intense coparental conflict all reduced the likelihood of reaching agreement. However, these attributes interacted with the mediation model in use, with group mediation proving more effective than individual mediation in private practice. Kressel et al. (1994) found that "problem-solver" mediators were more effective than "settlement oriented" mediators. Finally, Pearson and Thoennes (1985) found that several variables, alone and in interaction, helped predict the likelihood of reaching an agreement. These variables included mediator conduct, client characteristics, and the nature of client disputes. Agreement was most likely when clients perceived that the mediator could help them gain insight into feelings, their own and those of other members of their family; among clients with relatively recent and less severe disputes; and among clients with good communication skills who were willing to cooperate with each other.

These efforts help delineate the best fit between attributes of clients, mediators, and settings. Thus they suggest that certain constellations of variables identify clients who are and are not amenable to mediation. That said, it will now be apparent that these efforts are at a rudimentary stage of development and are as yet of limited practical utility.

SUMMARY

Family mediation is a service technology intended to help divorcing couples resolve their differences. The past 20 years have seen mediation become increasingly prominent, moving, in our view, from the periphery into the mainstream. In turn, that prominence has occasioned increased research scrutiny. The result is a growing research literature, the results of which are reviewed above.

The research shows, first, that mediation is highly effective. The majority of clients (both women and men) reach agreement (in whole or in part), report satisfaction, consider it fair and responsive, and, on follow-up, tend to comply with their agreement and resolve difficulties informally.

Second, mediation is also efficient, requiring limited time and expense to reach settlement.

Third, compared to litigation, mediation clients (both women and men) are more likely to reach voluntary agreement, do so more quickly and cheaply, generate more comprehensive agreements, and find it fairer and more sensitive to their needs and thus more satisfying. Whether and to what extent mediation or litigation affect coparental relations remains unclear. Similarly, although practice setting emerges as an important factor, its precise effects remain unclear.

Finally, we still know very little about what actually takes place in mediation and have a limited capacity to predict what constellation of client, mediator, and setting attributes is most likely to yield agreement. That said, some progress is being made on both fronts, with process studies holding great but as yet unrealized promise.

DISCUSSION

These trends are subject to multiple interpretations. Pearson (1991), on the basis of her data, concludes that family mediation is no better and no worse than litigation. Although it offers advantages in areas of satisfaction and cost, it fails to disrupt troubled coparental relations or to promote positive postdivorce relations. Rather, she argues that the quality of coparental relations and child custody arrangements provides better explanations than does settlement mechanism of variation in client outcomes.

Clement and Schwebel (in press), based on their review, conclude that family mediation has extraordinary promise in helping divorcing couples in conflict resolve their disputes. They note that this resolution requires a mix of different service models and is most suitable for clients who are well motivated, display manageable levels of conflict, and are provided service by mediators willing to intervene actively.

Our view falls somewhere between the two. Based on our extensive review of the divorce literature (see chapters 2 and 3), we agree with Pearson (1991) that family patterns in divorce tend to be extraordinarily stable and thus difficult to disrupt. However, it is unreasonable to assume that all forms of mediation are equally interested in changing such patterns. Nor is it clear how the double standard to which Thoennes and Pearson (1992) refer has arisen, with litigation only expected to produce settlement, although mediation—in some cases, only 2 *hours* long—is also expected to transform intense marital conflict into affectionate cooperation, and intense distress into positive postdivorce family adjustment. A key distinction, then, is among various mediation forums, with private mediation models such as Therapeutic Family Mediation (see chapter 4) much more likely to claim explicitly therapeutic objectives than their court-based counterparts.

A related distinction derives from our discussion of predictors of outcome, which supports a multivariate model of mediation. That is, mediation involves the interaction among several classes of variables. These include the following:

- The personality and other individual characteristics of clients
- The prevailing patterns of family interaction, especially patterns of conflict resolution and the number, nature, and severity of the issues in dispute
- The demographic characteristics of client families, especially social class and ethnicity (see chapter 8)
- The characteristics of the mediation forum, that is, whether it operates in the public or private domain and its espoused model of service, including objectives of service (agreement about child custody and access or a comprehensive agreement), the number of service sessions and hours of service, and, as in TFM, the number and types of service phases
- The characteristics of the mediation practitioners offering service, especially whether their professional training was primarily in the law or the mental health or human services fields, whether service is offered by a single practitioner or takes the form of comediation, and whether service is offered to a single couple or groups of couples
- The local statutory regime, especially the extent to which it constrains the range of options open to mediation practitioners

- The characteristics of other actors involved with the family at the time of intake, such as new partners, extended kin, and various professionals, especially the extent to which they take sides in the dispute between the spouses

Based on the interaction among these classes of variables, the processes and outcomes of mediation are likely to be highly variable. That the mediation programs that have been studied in fact yield relatively consistent positive outcomes is a testament to the great promise to which Clement and Schwebel (in press) refer and with which we concur. Thus to conclude that mediation is no better and no worse than litigation is true, but only in some configurations of these classes of variables; in other configurations, mediation has at least the potential to be notably better.

IMPLICATIONS

In closing, we explore the implications of the preceding review for researchers, policymakers, and practitioners.

Researchers

For researchers, we draw three implications from the above review. The first concerns the model of mediation driving any given research effort. All researchers use a model of some sort, because all such efforts examined above collect data selectively. However, the models of mediation implicit in such efforts have tended to be quite simple and thus do not do justice to the complexity of the services in question. This is especially evident in the many studies that employ essentially a "black box" model of service, in which data gathering is confined to client characteristics on intake and agreement rates on termination, with no meaningful way to relate these two data sets. The classes of variables discussed above suggest one basis for future research efforts.

Second, we need to know a great deal more about what practitioners actually do in various dispute resolution forums. As seen before, although we are making some headway in understanding what court-based mediators do, our understanding is incomplete. There is need not only for more studies of service processes, but also a greater reliance on audio and video taping to provide an observational database that will not leave us as dependent as we now are on client and practitioner self-reports (see Tan, 1988, 1991; White, 1985). In a similar vein, we know very little about what actually happens in cases that are litigated in family court. This knowledge is critical because it is on such data that claims about the comparability of mediation and litigation presumably rest. The absence of such data is curious, because criminologists have subjected the same processes in the criminal court to detailed and systematic scrutiny over the past half century.

Finally, given a multidimensional model of mediation, we need to know a great deal more about client families *before* they enter mediation. Although rudimentary baseline data is part of most of the studies examined above, it is usually confined to various demographic indicators and self-report measures of marital conflict. However, just as observational studies of mediation processes are rare, so thorough assessments of mediation clients before intake are virtually absent. Again, this situation is curious. Elsewhere, our discussion of TFM (Irving & Benjamin, 1993; see chapter 4) heavily emphasizes the salience of thorough intake assessment across a range of dimensions. In comparison, existing research protocols are restricted and thus provide a very incomplete basis for assessing the extent or the direction of change, either at service termination or on follow-up.

Policymakers

Early research in mediation was, in part, intended to sell mediation to policymakers, for whom it was still novel and untested. That is no longer true. The critical policy question now is *not* whether mediation is useful, but rather how to use it to best advantage. In this context, the preceding review holds three implications.

First, the most effective use of mediation involves matching clients amenable to it with the particular service model best suited to their needs. In contrast, the above review makes clear that that is not how mediation works now. In voluntary systems, as exist in many states and across Canada, clients self-select into mediation. In mandatory systems, as exist in several American states, divorcing couples who cannot agree must go through mediation before they can have access to the court. In both systems, clients are neither screened for their amenability to mediation nor are they matched, either with the mediation forum or the practice model best suited to their needs. Admittedly, as seen above, our knowledge of the bases on which to screen potential clients is incomplete. But the little we do know can make a big difference to outcomes. In our early work (Irving et al., 1979, 1981), for example, shifting from blanket acceptance to selected acceptance into court-based family mediation increased the agreement rate from 22% to 70%. Similarly, we have noted above that one interpretation of available data is that private mediation may be more useful in achieving settlement with clients whose problems are severe or complex. In the United States, this interpretation suggests the need to move away from an automatic mandatory system to make more selective use of available mediation resources. Across North America, it recommends coupling a screening process with referral to services best suited to clients' assessed needs. Although such an approach would obviate some of the current cost savings over the short term, the result would likely save money in increased effectiveness over the long run.

Second, we note that governments currently fund court-based mediation services, whereas clients must pay their own way in private mediation. Assuming that court diversion is important, such funding arrangements are short-sighted. One interpretation of the evidence reviewed above is that court-based mediation is inadequate for complex cases. Providing that such cases are judged amenable to mediation at all, such use of mediation is wasteful; such cases ought to be referred to private mediation. However, case complexity is not confined to any one social class. Although low-income divorcing couples may be unable to afford private mediation, some couples will be able to avoid litigation only through its use. It follows that for such couples *only*, we suggest that legal aid plans be expanded to include both lawyers and family mediators as recipients of payment.

Finally, research agendas in mediation have, in part, been driven by policy-based funding. This relationship is problematic because policy-makers have traditionally had very restricted interest in outcomes, for example, the focus on agreement rate. If we are to pursue the research agenda outlined above, a critical distinction will need to be made between pragmatic and fundamental research. As we noted in the introduction, the former provides a useful reality check. Thus descriptive studies will continue to be useful. However, they are not designed to address the more fundamental questions that need to be addressed if family mediation is to realize its full potential; only fundamental research can do that. In turn, such research will only take place with government funding.

Practice

For practitioners, questions of research design and policy making may seem remote from their day-to-day practice. Nevertheless, the above review holds at least three implications for them, too.

First, in the course of their practice, experienced mediators learn that family mediation is likely to be useful for some clients but not others. Many rely on that experience to guide case assessment and thus the later decision as to whether to proceed with a given couple. Such an approach probably yields good results much of the time. It remains problematic, however, because it is likely to vary widely across mediators. The utility of the research reviewed above is that it identifies a series of criteria of amenability based on empirical data across a series of studies. In some cases, this data may simply confirm what individual practitioners already know; in others, it will be counterintuitive. In either case, it will be reliable and thus a useful place on which to base assessment practice. That said, as Pearson and Thoennes (1989) note, such data are valid only at the group level; they may or may not apply to individual client couples. Thus the research literature can only supply general guidelines; the practitioner must decide whether the literature is useful in any individual case.

Second, although our knowledge of mediation processes remains incomplete, the literature makes increasingly clear that passive neutrality aimed at settlement—what Kressel et al. (1994) call a settlement-oriented approach—often serves clients poorly. Rather, active, directive, and flexible intervention seems to produce better results. At first glance, this approach may strike some practitioners as ill-advised because it appears to violate the neutrality that stands at the heart of mediation. However, as we have noted elsewhere in our discussion of TFM (Irving & Benjamin, 1993; see chapter 4), this view obscures the critical distinction between mediator control over process as opposed to content. Active mediators can only intervene in issues that clients are willing to put on the table. They can help clients negotiate only those solutions that they, the clients, find acceptable. And, as Kelly and Gigy (1989) note, clients always have the option of terminating service if they feel overwhelmed or pressured into accepting terms that they think are unfair. For practitioners accustomed to more passive forms of service, accepting the utility of an active approach involves a significant shift in emphasis. Such acceptance also has significant implications for mediation training (see Koopman & Hunt, 1988).

Finally, the research reviewed above suggests the need to redefine "success" in mediation and thus move away from what Kressel et al. (1989) call "settlement mania." Traditionally, mediation has been seen as successful *only* if client agreement is achieved. However, the above research indicates that (a) up to 20% of clients reach only partial agreement; (b) even those who fail to reach agreement may nervertheless derive significant benefits from the experience; and (c) a substantial proportion of clients who fail nevertheless say they were satisfied with the mediation process. Conversely, several studies show that agreement per se is no guarantee of reduced coparental conflict or improved postdivorce adjustment. Thus the key to success in mediation is change: greater confidence in one's ability to negotiate; the opportunity to fully explore one's grievances and examine the full range of settlement options; encountering a receptive ear and a soft shoulder when all else is hostility and demand. If this process leads to agreement, well and good. If it does not and clients still come away with a positive experience, then the mediation process will still have succeeded.

REFERENCES

Bahr, S. (1981a). An evaluation of court mediation: A comparison in divorce cases with children. *Journal of Family Issues, 2,* 39-60.

Bahr, S. (1981b). Mediation is the answer: Why couples are so positive about this route to divorce. *Family Advocate, 3*(4), 32-35.

Bahr, S. J., Chappell, C. B., & Marcos, A. C. (1987). An evaluation of a trial mediation program. *Mediation Quarterly, 18,* 37-52.

Benjamin, M., & Irving, H. H. (1992). Towards a feminist-informed model of therapeutic family mediation. *Mediation Quarterly, 10*(2), 129-153.

Bohmur, C., & Ray, M. L. (1994). Effects of different dispute resolution methods on women and children in divorce. *Family Law Quarterly, 28*(2), 223-245.

Bryan, P. E. (1994). Reclaiming professionalism: The lawyer's role in divorce mediation. *Family Law Quarterly, 28*(2), 177-222.

Camplair, C. W., & Stolberg, A. L. (1990). Benefits of court-sponsored divorce mediation: A study of outcomes and influences on success. *Mediation Quarterly, 7*(3), 199-213.

Carnevale, P. J., & Pruitt, D. G. (1992). Negotiation and mediation. *Annual Review of Psychology, 43,* 531-582.

Chandler, D. B. (1990). Violence, fear, and communication: The variable impact of domestic violence on mediation. *Mediation Quarterly, 7*(4), 331-346.

Clement, J. A., & Schwebel, A. I. (in press). A research agenda for divorce mediation: The creation of second-order knowledge to inform legal policy. *Ohio State Journal on Dispute Resolution.*

Cohen, L. (1991). Mandatory mediation: A case of any alter none. *Mediation Quarterly, 9*(1), 33-46.

Davis, G., & Roberts, M. (1988). *Access to agreement.* Milton Keyes, UK: Open University Press.

Depner, C., Cannata, K., & Ricci, I. (1994). Client evaluations of mediation services: The impact of case characteristics and mediation service models. *Family & Conciliation Courts Review, 32*(3), 306-325.

Depner, C. E., Cannata, K. B., & Simon, M. B. (1991). Building a uniform statistical reporting system: A snapshot of California Family Court Services. *Family & Conciliation Courts Review, 30,* 185-206.

Dingwall, R. (1988). Improvement or enforcement? Some questions about power and control in divorce mediation. In R. Dingwall & J. Eekalaar (Eds.), *Divorce mediation and the legal process.* Oxford, UK: Open University Press.

Donohue, W. A. (1989). Communicative competence in mediators. In K. Kressel, D. G. Pruitt, & Associates (Eds.), *Mediation research: The process and effectiveness of third-party intervention.* San Francisco: Jossey-Bass.

Donohue, W. A. (1991). *Communication, marital dispute, and divorce mediation.* Hillsdale, NJ: Lawrence Erlbaum.

Donohue, W. A., Allen, M., & Burrell, N. (1985). Communication strategies in mediation. *Mediation Quarterly, 10,* 75-89.

Donohue, W. A., Allen, M., & Burrell, N. (1988). Mediator communicative competence. *Communication Monographs, 55,* 104-119.

Donohue, W. A., Diez, M. E., & Weider-Hatfield, D. (1984). Skills for successful bargainers: A valence theory of competent mediation. In R. N. Bostrom (Ed.), *Competence in communication.* Beverly Hills, CA: Sage.

Donohue, W. A., Drake, L., & Roberto, A. J. (1994). Mediator issue intervention strategies: A replication and some conclusions. *Mediation Quarterly, 11*(3), 261-274.

Donohue, W. A., Lyles, J., & Rogan, R. (1989). Issue development in divorce mediation. *Mediation Quarterly, 24,* 19-28.

Donohue, W. A., & Weider-Hatfield, D. (1988). Communication strategies in mediation. In J. Folberg & A. Milne (Eds.), *Divorce mediation: Theory and practice.* New York: Guilford.

Duryee, M. (1992). Mandatory court mediation: Demographic survey and consumer evaluation of one court service—executive summary. *Family & Conciliation Courts Review, 30*(2), 260-267.

Emery, R. E. (1994). *Renegotiating family relationships: Divorce, child custody, and mediation.* New York: Guilford.

Emery, R. E., & Jackson, J. A. (1989). The Charlottesville Mediation Project: Mediated and litigated child custody disputes. *Mediation Quarterly, 24,* 3-18.

Emery, R. E., Matthews, S. G., & Kitzman, K. M. (1994). Child custody mediation and litigation: Parents' satisfaction and functioning one year after settlement. *Journal of Consulting & Clinical Psychology, 62*(1), 124-129.

Emery, R. E., Matthews, S. G., & Wyer, M. M. (1991). Child custody mediation and litigation: Further evidence on the differing views of mothers & fathers. *Journal of Consulting & Clinical Psychology, 59,* 410-418.

Emery, R. E., Shaw, D. S., & Jackson, J. A. (1987). A clinical description of a model of child custody mediation. In J. P. Vincent (Ed.), *Advances in family intervention, assessment and theory* (Vol. 4). Greenwich, CT: JAI Press.

Emery, R. E., & Wyer, M. M. (1987a). Child custody mediation and litigation: An experimental evaluation of the experience of parents. *Journal of Consulting & Clinical Psychology, 55,* 179-186.

Emery, R. E., & Wyer, M. M. (1987b). Divorce mediation. *American Psychologist, 42,* 472-480.

Folberg, J., & Milne, A. (Eds.). (1988). *Divorce mediation: Theory and practice.* New York: Guilford.

Frontenac Family Referral Service. (1979). *Couples in crisis: The Kingston mediation model.* Kingston, Ontario: Frontenac Family Referral Service.

Frontenac Family Referral Service. (1984). *Couples in crisis II: The Kingston mediation model.* Kingston, Ontario: Frontenac Family Referral Service.

Gaughan, R. A. (1982). The family mediation service. In H. Davidson & Associates (Eds.), *Alternative means of family dispute resolution.* Washington, DC: American Bar Association.

Girdner, L. K. (1985). Adjudication and mediation: A comparison of custody decision-making processes using third parties. *Journal of Divorce, 8*(3/4), 33-47.

Irving, H. H., & Benjamin, M. (1983). Outcome effectiveness of conciliation counseling: An empirical study. *Conciliation Courts Review, 21*(2), 61-70.

Irving, H. H., & Benjamin, M. (1984). A study of conciliation counselling in the Family Court of Toronto: Implications for socio-legal practice. In J. M. Eekelaar & S. N. Katz (Eds.), *The realities of family conflict: Comparative legal perspectives.* Toronto: Butterworths.

Irving, H. H., & Benjamin, M. (1987). Family mediation research: Critical review and future directions. In Vermont Law School, *The role of mediation in divorce proceedings: A comparative perspective (United States, Canada and Great Britain).* South Royalton: Vermont Law School.

Irving, H. H., & Benjamin, M. (1988). Divorce mediation in a court-based fee for service agency: An empirical study. *Conciliation Courts Review, 26,* 43-47.

Irving, H. H., & Benjamin, M. (1992). An evaluation of process and outcome in a private family mediation service. *Mediation Quarterly, 10*(1), 35-55.

Irving, H. H., & Benjamin, M. (1993). Therapeutic family mediation: Ecosystemic processes and the linkage between pre-medation and negotiation. In M. Rodway & B. Trute (Eds.), *The ecological perspective in family-centered therapy.* Lewiston, NJ: Edwin Mellen.

Irving, H. H., Benjamin, M., Bohm, P., & Macdonald, G. (1981). A study of conciliation counseling in the Family Court of Toronto: Implications for socio-legal practice (Abridged). In H. H. Irving (Ed.), *Family law: An interdisciplinary perspective.* Toronto: Carswell.

Irving, H. H., Bohm, P., Macdonald, G., & Benjamin, M. (1979). *A comparative analysis of two family court services: An exploratory study of conciliation counseling.* Toronto: Welfare Grants Directorate, Health and Welfare Canada, and the Ontario Ministry of the Attorney General, Demonstration Project 25555-1-65.

Johnston, J. R., & Campbell, E. G. (1988). *Impasses of divorce: The dynamics and resolution of family conflict.* New York: Free Press.

Johnston, J. R., Campbell, L. E. G., & Tall, M. C. (1985). Impasses to the resolution of custody and visitation disputes. *American Journal of Orthopsychiatry, 55,* 112-129.

Jones, T. S. (1988). Phase structures in agreement and no-agreement mediation. *Communication Research, 15*(4), 470-495.

Kelly, J. B. (Ed.). (1989a). *Empirical research in divorce and family mediation.* San Francisco: Jossey-Bass.

Kelly, J. B. (1989b). Mediated and adversarial divorce: Respondents' perceptions of their processes and outcomes. *Mediation Quarterly, 24,* 71-88.

Kelly, J. B. (1990). Is mediation less expensive: Comparison of mediated and adversarial divorce costs. *Mediation Quarterly, 8*(1), 15-26.

Kelly, J. B., & Duryee, M. A. (1992). Women's and men's views of mediation in voluntary and mandatory settings. *Family and Conciliation Courts Review, 30*(1), 43-49.

Kelly, J. B., & Gigy, L. L. (1988). Client Assessment of Mediation Services (CAMS): A scale measuring client perceptions and satisfaction. *Mediation Quarterly, 19,* 43-52.

Kelly, J. B., & Gigy, L. L. (1989). Divorce mediation: Characteristics of clients and outcomes. In K. Kressel, D. G. Pruitt, & Associates (Eds.), *Mediation research: The process & effectiveness of third-party intervention.* San Francisco: Jossey-Bass.

Kelly, J. B., Gigy, L., & Hausman, S. (1988). Mediated and adversarial divorce: Initial findings from a longitudinal study. In J. Folberg & A. Milne (Eds.), *Divorce mediation: Theory and practice.* New York: Guilford.

Koopman, E. J., & Hunt, E. J. (1988). Child custody mediation: An interdisciplinary synthesis. *American Journal of Orthopsychiatry, 58,* 379-386.

Koopman, E. J., Hunt, E. J., & Stafford, V. (1984). Child related agreements in mediated and non-mediated divorce settlements: A preliminary examination and discussion of implications. *Conciliation Courts Review, 22*(1), 19-25.

Kressel, K. (1985). *The process of divorce: How professionals and couples negotiate settlements.* New York: Basic Books.

Kressel, K. (1987a). Research on divorce mediation: A summary and critique of the literature. In Vermont Law School (Ed.), *The role of mediation in divorce proceedings: A comparative perspective (United States, Canada and Great Britain).* South Royalton: Vermont Law School.

Kressel, K. (1987b). Clinical implications of existing research on divorce mediation. *American Journal of Family Therapy, 15*(1), 69-74.

Kressel, K., Butler-DeFreitas, F., Forlenza, S. G., & Wilcox, C. (1989). Research in contested custody mediations: An illustration of the case study method. *Mediation Quarterly, 24,* 55-70.

Kressel, K., Frontera, E., Forlenza, S., Butler, F., & Fish, L. (1994). The settlement-orientation versus the problem-solving style in custody mediation. *Journal of Social Issues, 50*(1), 67-83.

Kressel, K., Jaffe, N., Tuchman, B., Watson, C., & Deutsch, M. (1980). A typology of divorcing couples: Implications for mediation and the divorce process. *Family Process, 19,* 101-116.

Kressel, K., & Pruitt, D. G. (1985). Themes in the mediation of social conflict. *Journal of Social Issues, 41*(2), 179-198.

Kressel, K., Pruitt, D. G., & Associates (Eds.). (1989). *Mediation research: The process and effectiveness of third-party intervention.* San Francisco: Jossey-Bass.

Margolin, F. M. (1973). *An approach to resolution of litigation disputes postdivorce: Short-term counseling.* Doctoral dissertation, United States International University, San Diego, CA.

Matheson, S., & Gentleman, H. (1986). *The Scottish Family Conciliation Service (Lothian): Report of an assessment of the first two years of service.* Edinburgh: Scottish Office Central Research Unit.

Mathis, R. D., & Yingling, L. (1990). Family functioning level and divorce mediation outcome. *Mediation Quarterly, 8*(1), 3-13.

Mathis, R. D., & Yingling, L. (1991). Discriminant function analysis and FACES III and Family Satisfaction questionnaires to predict outcome in divorce mediation. *American Journal of Family Therapy, 19*(4), 367-377.

Mathis, R. D., & Yingling, L. C. (1992). Analysis of pre and posttest gender differences in family satisfaction of divorce mediating couples. *Journal of Divorce & Remarriage, 17*(3/4), 75-85.

Meierding, M. R. (1993). Does mediation work? A survey of long-term satisfaction and durability rates for privately mediated agreements. *Mediation Quarterly, 11*(2), 157-170.

Ogus, A., Jones-Lee, M., Cole, W., & McCarthy, P. (1990). Evaluating alternative dispute resolution: Measuring the impact of family conciliation on costs. *Modern Law Review, 53*(1), 57-74.

Ogus, A., Walker, J., & Jones-Lee, M. (1989). *Report of the Conciliation Project Unit, University of Newcastle Upon Tyne, to the Lord Chancellor on the costs and effectiveness of conciliation in England and Wales.* Newcastle Upon Tyne, UK: University of Newcastle Upon Tyne.

Orbeton, J., & Charbonneau, P. G. (1988). Comparing the results of mediated domestic relations cases. *Mediation Quarterly, 22,* 61-67.

Paquin, G. W. (1990). Mediators' perceptions of the effect of the couples' behavior in child custody mediation. *Journal of Divorce & Remarriage, 14*(2), 79-90.

Parker, A. O., Jr. (1980). *A comparison of divorce mediation vs. lawyer adversary processes and the relationship to marital separation.* Doctoral dissertation, University of North Carolina, Chapel Hill.

Pearson, J. (1982). An evaluation of alternatives to court adjudication. *Justice System Journal, 7,* 420-444.

Pearson, J. (1991). The equity of mediated divorce settlements. *Mediation Quarterly, 9,* 179-197.

Pearson, J., Ring, M. L., & Milne, A. (1983). A portrait of divorce mediation in the public and private sector. *Conciliation Courts Review, 21*(1), 1-24.

Pearson, J., & Thoennes, N. (1982a). Divorce mediation: Strengths and weaknesses over time. In H. Davidson, L. Ray, & R. Horowitz (Eds.), *Alternative means of dispute resolution.* Washington, DC: American Bar Association.

Pearson, J., & Thoennes, N. (1982b). The mediation and adjudication of divorce disputes: Some costs and benefits. *Family Advocate, 4,* 3.

Pearson, J., & Thoennes, N. (1984a). A preliminary portrait of client reactions to three court mediation programs. *Mediation Quarterly, 3,* 21-40.

Pearson, J., & Thoennes, N. (1984b). Mediating and litigating custody disputes: A longitudinal evaluation. *Family Law Quarterly, 17*, 497-524.

Pearson, J., & Thoennes, N. (1984c). Custody mediation in Denver: Short and longer term effects. In J. M. Eekelaar & S. N. Katz (Eds.), *The resolution of family conflict: Comparative legal perspectives*. Toronto: Butterworths.

Pearson, J., & Thoennes, N. (1985). A preliminary portrait of client reactions to three court mediation programs. *Conciliation Courts Review, 23*(1), 1-14.

Pearson, J., & Thoennes, N. (1988a). Divorce mediation research results. In J. Folberg & A. Milne (Eds.), *Divorce mediation: Theory and practice*. New York: Guilford.

Pearson, J., & Thoennes, N. (1988b). Mediating parent-child postdivorce arrangments. In S. A. Wolchik & P. Karoly (Eds.), *Children of divorce: Empirical perspectives on adjustment*. New York: Gardner.

Pearson, J., & Thoennes, N. (1989). Divorce mediation: Reflections on a decade of research. In K. Kressel, D. G. Pruitt, & Associates (Eds.), *Mediation research: The process and effectiveness of third-party intervention*. San Francisco: Jossey-Bass.

Pearson, J., Thoennes, N., & Vanderkooi, L. (1982). The decision to mediate: Profiles of individuals who accept and reject the opportunity to mediate contested child custody and visitation issues. *Journal of Divorce, 6*, 17-35.

Peterson, S. E., & Emery, R. E. (1988). Acceptance of marital termination and outcome in mediation. *Group Analysis, 21*, 37-46.

Richardson, C. J. (1988). *Court-based divorce mediation in four Canadian cities: An overview of research results*. Ottawa: Department of Justice Canada.

Salius, A. J. (1977). *Annual report*. West Hartford, CT: Family Division, Superior Court.

Saposnek, D. T., Hamburg, J., Delano, C. D., & Michaelson, H. (1984). How has mandatory mediation fared? Research findings of the first year's follow-up. *Conciliation Courts Review, 22*(2), 7-19.

Slaikeu, K. A., Culler, R., Pearson, J., & Thoennes, N. (1985). Process and outcome in divorce mediation. *Mediation Quarterly, 10*, 55-74.

Slaikeu, K. A., Pearson, J., Luckett, J., & Myers, F. C. (1985). Mediation process analysis: A descriptive coding system. *Mediation Quarterly, 10*, 25-53.

Slaikeu, K. A., Pearson, J., & Thoennes, N. (1988). Divorce mediated behaviors: A descriptive system and analysis. In J. Folberg & A. Milne (Eds.), *Divorce mediation: Theory and practice*. New York: Guilford.

Slater, A., Shaw, J., & Duquesne, J. (1992). Client satisfaction survey: A consumer evaluation of mediation and investigative services—executive summary. *Family & Conciliation Courts Review, 30*(2), 252-259.

Sprenkle, D. H., & Storm, C. L. (1983). Divorce therapy outcome research: A substantive and methodological review. *Journal of Marital & Family Therapy, 9*, 239-258.

Tan, N. T. (1988). Developing and testing a family mediation assessment instrument. *Mediation Quarterly, 19*, 63-67.

Tan, N. T. (1991). Implications of the Divorce Mediation Assessment Instrument for mediation practice. *Family & Conciliation Courts Review, 29*(1), 26-40.

Thoennes, N., & Pearson, J. (1985). Predicting outcomes in divorce mediation: The influence of people and process. *Journal of Social Issues, 41*, 115-126.

Thoennes, N., & Pearson, J. (1992). Response to Bruch and McIsaac. *Family & Conciliation Courts Review, 30*(1), 142-143.

Vanderkooi, L., & Pearson, J. (1983). Mediating divorce disputes: Mediator behaviors, styles and roles. *Family Relations, 32*, 557-566.

Wagner, R. V. (1990). Mediated divorces last—At least to the bench. *Negotiation Journal,* 6(1), 47-52.

Waldron, J. A., Roth, C. P., Fair, P. H., Mann, E. M., & McDermott, J. F., Jr. (1984). A therapeutic mediation model for child custody dispute resolution. *Mediation Quarterly, 3,* 5-20.

Walker, J. (1987). Divorce mediation—Is it a better way? In Vermont Law School (Ed.), *The role of mediation in divorce proceedings: A comparative perspective (United States, Canada and Great Britain).* South Royalton: Vermont Law School.

Walker, J. A. (1989). Family conciliation in Great Britain: From research to practice to research. *Mediation Quarterly, 24,* 29-54.

Weingarten, H. R., & Douvan, E. (1985). Male and female visions of mediation. *Negotiation Journal, 1*(4), 349-358.

White, J. H. (1985). Developing an instrument to measure satisfaction in mediation. *Mediation Quarterly, 10,* 91-98.

Whiting, R. A. (1992). The single-issue, multiple-issue debate and the effect of issue number on mediated outcomes. *Mediation Quarterly, 10*(1), 57-74.

Whiting, R. A. (1994). Family disputes, nonfamily disputes, and mediation success. *Mediation Quarterly, 11*(3), 247-260.

Yates, C. (1985). NFCC research project: The latest findings. *National Conciliation Council Newsletter, 8,* 4-6.

PART V

Closing Thoughts

11

Closing Thoughts

Thematic Issues and the Future of Family Mediation

INTRODUCTION

This volume has carefully considered four themes central to family mediation practice: the divorcing process, mediation practice, child custody, and new developments. In the process, we have sifted through an immense amount of information and considered a variety of options, scenarios, and contemporary issues. In this final chapter, we pull back from fine-grained analysis in an effort to distill, identify, and discuss the key trends and implications for each theme that we believe will collectively shape the future of family mediation in North America over the next decade or so.

THEME 1: DIVORCE

1. *The rate of divorce will gradually decline.* The past 35 years have witnessed an explosion in the rate of divorce. This rate peaked in the late 1980s and has since gradually declined. Our reading of the

evidence suggests that over the next decade that slow decline is likely to continue.

The increase in the divorce rate resulted from the interaction among a variety of factors. Technological change, increased productivity, the globalization of trade, and increased trade competition were all at the heart of the single major social change over the past half century: the tremendous influx of women into the labor market. For middle-class women, the primary beneficiaries of this evolution, this influx changed the dynamics of the relations between spouses and accorded women greater financial resources and concomitant autonomy than they had ever experienced. In contrast, these same processes also disenfranchised the poor, both men and women, as the rich got richer and the poor got poorer. Included here are increasing rates of out-of-wedlock pregnancy, adolescent abortion, and early marriage (formal or common-law).

Furthermore, such changes were part of what fueled a related social process, the feminist movement, with its emphasis on equality, women's rights, and requisite statutory change. On the whole, we have all benefited, which is witnessed by significant statutory reform in several areas. But many people are also no longer willing to endure unsatisfying marital relationships "for the sake of the children." In addition, as the divorce rate rose, it acquired a momentum of its own, with the stigma previously attached to divorce one of its first victims. In the eyes of many, divorce (and remarriage [see below]) has now become a normative aspect of the family life cycle. Thus the rising rate of divorce has been the dynamic product of the combination of structural, attitudinal, and behavioral changes.

More recently has appeared a series of countervailing forces. Two of these are again structural. The demographic shape of the North American population has changed. Moving from a pyramid weighted in favor of the young, the aging of the baby boom generation has produced a diamond weighted in favor of middle-aged adults. Many of those who are likely to divorce have already done so and there are simply fewer of the young, those traditionally at the highest risk of divorce. In a similar vein, the decade of the 1990s has and will continue to be one characterized by hard times. Unemployment is up, real earnings (controlling for inflation) are down, and so on. At such times, there is a natural tendency to hold on for dear life, including keeping a marital relationship that is less than ideal. Related trends are in the same direction: a steady rise in religious fundamentalism; an increasing concentration of wealth wedded to rising conservatism; in some quarters, a return to "family values"; the rise of environmentalism, with its emphasis on preservation, care, concern for the future, and more generally, commitment to goals larger than the self; and, on the darker side, the perception that the world, especially city life, is becoming increasingly inhospitable and unpredictable, thus supporting a survival mentality characterized by conservatism. Thus, moderating trends in the divorce rate have been the result of a very different set of structural, attitudinal, and behavioral changes than those that produced the rate increase. The millennium is likely to see North America in a different place than it is now, including a somewhat lower rate of divorce.

2. *The direction of statutory reform, toward increasing equality between the sexes, will continue.* Although the specifics of statutory reform have varied widely from one jurisdiction to another, the general trend is clear, favoring increasing liberalization of divorce and related statutes. This liberalization is especially evident in the trend favoring no-fault divorce and the relaxation of rules and procedures concerning waiting times and grounds for divorce. As noted in chapter 2, this process is hardly complete. In many states and Canada, fault-based holdovers from the past remain in place. Similarly, various legal observers, especially feminist legal scholars, have trenchantly noted the various ways in which women remain unequal before the law, at least as it operates in practice.

It is noteworthy, however, that statutory changes in the past decade have consistently been in the same direction, toward increasing equalization. Examples include recognition of joint custody or shared parenting; increasing attention to economic inequality between husbands and wives and the need (in some cases) for spousal support, not necessarily of wives by husbands; gradual implementation of programs designed to make the collection of child support the responsibility of the state rather than individual spouses; gradual recognition of the rights of extended relatives, especially grandparents; increasing respect for the rights and opinions of children, especially those of an age where they can express clear and informed preferences about their future; and so on. There is every reason to think that these and related measures will continue to chip away at entrenched inequalities in the law, with child and spousal support likely the area of greatest urgency.

That said, a caution is in order. The law cannot get too far ahead of the society it is intended to reflect. True equality before the law can only occur in tandem with various structural changes intended to achieve the same end in society at large. So long as women earn only 60% to 70% of what their equally qualified male counterparts earn, formal equality before the law, both now and in the future, has little practical significance. Happily, these wider economic changes are occurring; women have made real, substantive gains in recent years. So long as this process continues, increasing equalization before the law in the area of divorce is inevitable. Should this process be halted or diverted, the future direction of change in divorce statutes will be much less certain.

3. *Dysfunctional divorce represents a real threat to child development.* Much has been written about the effect of the divorcing process on children. This material has been problematic in at least two respects. The first concerns the changing thrust of the literature. The early literature was darkly judgmental. Divorce was considered evil and necessarily destructive of children. Later the literature became cautiously optimistic. Most children eventually adjusted to the disruption, some did very well and those that did poorly did no worse than some children in unhappy but intact families. The most recent literature is more confused than ever. Some studies indicate that some children do just fine whereas others are at serious developmental risk, with the impact of divorce considered by some to continue for much longer than previously thought. The major culprit here appears to be not divorce per se, but rather postdivorce conflict between former spouses. Similarly, much of the literature has been the product of research in psychology which, ironically, appears to operate with an implicit model of what is called "the normal person." This model not only attends more to intrapersonal states as opposed to interpersonal processes, but treats all such processes as variations around a normal mean. Thus self-esteem, anxiety, anger, and so forth may be characterized as "high"

or "low" but always within a hypothetical "normal" range. This model is clearly at variance with the daily experience of many lawyers, judges, and mental health professionals who recognize that divorcing families distribute on a continuum, from the highly functional to the highly dysfunctional.

This continuum is useful here in two respects. First, it becomes a basis for clearing up some of the confusion evident in the divorce literature. There is no such thing as *the* divorcing individual or *the* divorcing family. Divorce involves a complex process that is necessarily social. Rather, it is more useful (although much more awkward) to say that all individuals are members of one of several different family types, each of which locates somewhere on the function/dysfunction continuum and that all are engaged in the divorcing process. On the one hand, this model suggests that psychological statements about individuals going through divorce are largely meaningless without concomitant information about their family contexts, particularly the patterns of relating that characterize their families. On the other hand, this model implies that all locations on the continuum are not equally pernicious in regard to child development. As one moves toward families at the dysfunctional end of the continuum, presumably the risk to child development increases.

Whether this risk is conditional on the patterns characteristic of the family's type is unclear. Although a case can be made about the destructive potential of interparental conflict, such a claim remains problematic. Not only is "conflict" a very simpleminded way of describing something as complex as a family's interaction pattern, it has, as far as we know, never been paired with "family type." For example, not only may "high" conflict be expressed in a variety of ways, but its impact on child development may be a function of a variety of factors, including the compensating effect of a supportive relationship with a grandparent, teacher, or friend. Thus the function/dysfunction continuum alone does not eliminate the confusion. However, it points in a promising direction, and it clearly has face validity in light of the daily experience of many types of practitioners regularly in contact with divorcing families. Similarly, it points to the potential benefits of greater dialogue between researchers and practitioners, hardly a new thought but one worth repeating.

The function/dysfunction continuum is useful in another way, for it bears on the limitations of current legal practice. The law is designed with the "reasonable" person in mind, that is, one who is competent, rational, informed, logical, and calm. For the same reason, legal training is biased in favor of facts, rules, and procedures that presumably reflect such "reasonable" clients. And so long as real-life clients more or less conform to such expectations, the adversarial system works well. In the area of divorce, however, it runs afoul of the function/ dysfunction continuum. Because the law is not designed with dysfunctional families in mind and because such families patently do not conform to the expectations of the law, the fit between them is likely to be poor. For the same reason, all lawyers who specialize in family law are routinely confronted by clients who, despite their lawyers' best efforts to protect their rights and entitlements, persist in doing things that are not in their best interest, driving their lawyers crazy in the process. Yet there is no one at fault here. Rather, there are two systems whose compatibility varies from very good to very poor. The function/ dysfunction continuum helps make clear that their compatibility is not likely to change and recognizes that despite the indispensability of the law, it has inherent limitations.

4. *Family mediation is likely to become increasingly important as one of the mechanisms for dealing with divorcing families.* The limitations of the legal system make clear why family mediation is likely to increase in importance over the next decade. Whereas the law begins with a model of the "reasonable" person, family mediation, especially therapeutic models of mediation, start with a much more varied and thus more practicable model of divorcing families. In short, whether they articulate it or not, they start with some version of the function/dysfunction continuum and actively assess client couples to locate their position on that continuum. In turn, mediation practitioners are trained to deal with clients across the continuum, although even they find clients at the dysfunctional end more difficult and challenging than their counterparts at the functional end.

None of this means to imply that family mediation holds the solution to every legal problem. The majority of divorcing couples neither needs nor wants mediation for a variety of reasons: They may have little to fight over, may have resolved any differences between them, may prefer to rely on a lawyer, or may want more than anything to punish the "errant" partner by taking him or her to court.

However, for the remainder, family mediation stands in contrast to adversarial proceedings by offering the opportunity to fit the service to the needs of clients. In future, the demand for such service is likely to be shaped by two final trends.

The first trend concerns public awareness. As family mediation has moved from the fringe into the mainstream, public awareness of its availability and the character of the services it offers has inevitably increased. This awareness appears to reflect the simultaneous impact of three processes: word of mouth, as the cumulative number of clients served increased; public education efforts by mediation organizations at the national and state or provincial levels; and, in some jurisdictions, the efforts of government to reduce the caseload burden on the courts. As to the latter, in California and several other states, mediation is mandatory before a disputing couple can proceed to court. In Canada, lawyers in divorce matters are now obliged by law to inform their clients of the availability and location of mediation services.

The final trend concerns remarriage and divorce. As noted in chapters 2 and 3, the rising divorce rate has been associated with a marriage rate that has diminished only slightly. In practice, this trend means that an increasing proportion of those seeking mediation services will involve remarried couples. In the majority of cases, their demand for service will involve a second or later divorce. On the one hand, because blended families are structurally more complex than their first-time counterparts, such cases are likely to be more difficult and clinically demanding. On the other hand, because these couples will have experienced a previous divorce, they may be more inclined to a mediated settlement as opposed to one arrived at through negotiation between their lawyers. Indeed, by virtue of their age and maturity alone, they may be less willing than younger couples to remain passive while their fate is arranged by others; for such couples the empowerment offered by mediation may be especially appealing.

However, in a minority of cases, their demand for service may involve requests for prenuptial agreements. Precisely because of their divorce experience, they may wish to protect themselves in the event of divorce, while, ironically, making divorce easier and less contentious should it later come to pass. This possibility is especially likely if their first divorce was mediated and it proved a satisfying experience.

THEME 2: MEDIATION PRACTICE

In the wake of steadily rising visibility, the increasing demand for and popularity of family mediation is double-edged. On the one hand, our prediction of a steadily increasing demand for mediation services implies a bright future for the profession, as demand and supply feed back on each other. On the other hand, increased visibility also means increased critical scrutiny. Feminist observers increasingly reject mediation as inimical to the interests of divorcing women in general and women subjected to abuse in particular. Our reading of Part II suggests that, over the next decade, the profession will face a series of important challenges. What follows is our sense of the three most central of these challenges.

Achieving Professional Status. In recognized professions, such as law and medicine, professional status is understood to mean three things: a recognized body of specialized knowledge; universal standards of service and training such that all practitioners have exceeded a minimum level of practice expertise; and *internal* control over accreditation and licensing, including state-ceded authority to dispense and withdraw licenses to practice. Similar attributes characterize newer professions, such as psychology and family therapy. Recent trends suggest that family mediation is steadily moving in the same direction: New training programs are springing up across North America as increasing numbers of practitioners are attracted to mediation; the clinical literature continues to expand, with several professional journals now dedicated to mediation issues (*Mediation Quarterly; Family & Conciliation Courts Review*); mediation organizations now exist at national, provincial or state, and local levels; debate is ongoing about ethical and practice standards; and practitioners now regularly share their expertise at conferences and colloquia. Extending these trends into the near future suggests that mediation is undergoing transformation from its status as a service movement to a recognized profession. In practice, this shift will likely mean four things: some form of accreditation, universal standards of practice, university-accredited training, and professional liability.

Accreditation. Much of the force of the feminist critique stems from the fact that at present virtually anyone can assume the title of family mediator. In most cases, this title is legitimate, typically based on professional training as a human service provider or a lawyer coupled with specialized training in mediation. However, specific jurisdictions excepted (e.g., California), neither form of training is absolutely required to begin accepting clients. Thus, great variation in the skills of practicing mediators is assured, in turn, providing evidence in support of critics of various stripes. This issue will diminish in importance only with some form of accreditation, so that clients can readily discriminate between mediators who meet accreditation standards and those who do not. Although the exact form accreditation will take remains unclear, we favor a system resembling that in place in family therapy and represented by the American Association of Marriage and Family Therapists. In mediation, such a system might be administered by existing national organizations, such as Mediation Canada.

Ethical Standards. Before ethical standards can be achieved, several obstacles must be overcome. One is the absence of universal standards of practice and ethics. Although all mediation organizations have developed such standards, they vary across organizations. Only a unified standard would lend credibility to an accreditation plan.

Training Programs. Next, as in psychology and social work, accreditation must be tied to university-based training programs. At present, mediation training across North America varies widely across dimensions such as setting (private versus public), course content, number of training hours, clinical hours (none versus some), and clinical supervision (none versus some). Furthermore, in the absence of data, we suspect that many practitioners simply assume that their professional qualifications in the law or a helping profession automatically generalize to mediation. The result, we imagine, is that were some universal standard of competence to be applied to all practitioners, they would distribute on a continuum. This result is unacceptable and certainly not what the public expects from other professions. Only when *all* mediators have received training in an accredited program will mediators' claim to professional status be legitimate.

Professional Liability. Finally, despite every effort at screening and even the highest standards of training, in every profession a small proportion conducts itself inappropriately. In doing so, however, its members leave themselves open to professional liability, up to and including revocation of their license to practice. Thus established professions protect themselves from public criticism and such should be the case for family mediation. At present, clients who are dissatisfied or claim damages resulting from mediation service have only two recourses, to professional organizations if the practitioner is a member, or to civil litigation if not. Accreditation would give a third alternative. Professional status requires public accountability by means of a mediation organization. Just as mediation accreditation may be granted on demonstration of practice competence, so it must be revokable for cause.

Developing a Multidisciplinary Approach. Traditionally, disciplines have militantly protected their boundaries from incursion. Sociologists speak a singular language and are typically unable to converse (and uninterested in conversing) with their psychologist counterparts. The same applies to the law, with lawyers, judges, and others acquiring membership in the profession by virtue of their mastery of the esoteric language of the law. Family mediation represents a major challenge to such disciplinary isolation.

Simple mediation cases involve a mediator, typically trained in a helping profession, and two lawyers, one for each divorcing spouse. More complex cases may also involve personnel trained in medicine (medicine, psychiatry), finance (accounting, real estate, taxation, pensions, insurance, business), engineering (property assessment), human services (social work, psychotherapy), and the law (probation, corporate law). In addition, mediation draws practitioners across a variety of disciplines, from law to pastoral work. Dialogue, based on mutual respect and substantive insight, is essential in the interests of service to the client.

A variety of routes to such dialogue is possible and will become increasingly urgent over the next decade. Four routes are likely to become important, although we suspect they are more likely to occur in combination than alone.

Curricula. One route involves changing mediation curricula to include cross-disciplinary training. Dealing with lawyers, for example, involves more than just a thorough knowledge of the law. It helps to know how they are trained, the issues under debate in the legal literature, and the shaping effects of the adversarial system in which they operate. In current mediation curricula, such knowledge is presented in piecemeal fashion. In future, we expect that such efforts will become much more systematic.

Cross-Training. Another route is more specialized, cross-training. Here, students take courses in two different faculties and earn a specialized degree reflecting their particular training. Cross-training programs, now in sparse supply (e.g., at the University of Toronto), are gradually becoming more available across North America. These programs typically combine training in law with training in a helping profession such as social work or psychology. Graduates are particularly suited to family mediation, having become fluent in the languages of service and law. If, indeed, demand for mediation continues to rise, such programs are likely to become increasingly available and popular. We suggest that these graduates represent a new breed of practitioner who is able to bridge the traditional gap between disciplines.

Team Approach. Another route that we especially favor involves the team approach to the disciplinary dilemma. Adversarial systems tend to divide people, because each sees himself or herself as representing a divergent set of interests. In contrast, mediation systems are intended to bring people together by emphasizing cooperation and constructive negotiation. This intent does not deny that spouses may have divergent interests. Rather, it insists that they always share a higher-order interest, namely, achieving an equitable solution to issues in dispute. This focus serves the short-term concerns of their children and their own long-term concern with getting on with their lives. However, traditionally, mediation focuses exclusively on client family members. All others are seen as extraneous to the case and are treated accordingly. In the team approach, other professionals are regarded as integral to service delivery such that where relevant they are encouraged to become actively involved in the case, with the mediator acting as team leader. This approach typically involves periodic consultation between the mediator and others. However, under some circumstances, one or more of these professionals can be invited to participate in one or more mediation sessions. Having been through this process a few times, professionals become enthusiastic participants and develop a much more positive attitude toward mediation than they held previously. This approach is a powerful means of debunking stereotypes, eliminating misunderstandings, and creating and sustaining dialogue', as professionals share information in their effort to serve client needs. As the supply of mediators expands, we suspect that this route to dialogue will become increasingly routine. The same is true of the increasing interest in mediation directed toward comprehensive agreements as opposed to agreements restricted to child custody issues. However, it continues to be an uphill battle, because it is initially foreign to the practice style in which most professionals and many mediators were socialized in their professional training.

Comediation. A final route to multidisciplinary practice involves co-mediation, in which mediation is conducted by two (or more) mediators, typically a man and a woman. The disadvantages of this approach are that it is a complex form of practice, expensive, and takes a good deal of experience to do well. However, in our experience, the advantages are significant. For example, it gives equal attention to "male" and "female" perspectives, and the "voices" attendant on gender-based experience. It makes it possible for each spouse to identify with his or her same-sex mediator counterpart and thus more difficult for the other spouse to feel "ganged up on." And it gives free rein to the combined creativity of the comediators, including the opportunity to model clear communication. However, in the present context, what may be most salient is that in addition to representing both sexes, comediators may also represent different disciplines, notably human services and law. This interweaving of divergent sources of expertise makes it less likely that a problem or issue will arise for which the comediators are unprepared and thus optimizes the likelihood of achieving an equitable and mutually satisfying agreement.

Maintaining Service Flexibility. Dissatisfaction with the adversarial system is centered on its inflexibility. Based on fixed procedures, complex rules, and arcane language, the system forces clients to its requirements; the system will not change to meet their needs. By intention, the opposite is true of mediation systems, hence the emphasis in the literature on client empowerment, self-determination, and so on. Recent critiques of mediation, however, make painfully clear that maintaining service flexibility over the next decade will require significant reform in areas such as the following.

Case Selection. Existing models of mediation tend to take a "black box" approach to service delivery. Not only do they place more emphasis on outcome as opposed to process, but they assume that mediation will be equally amenable to all divorcing couples. Experienced practitioners know differently. Clients vary widely in their ability to communicate clearly, negotiate effectively, put their children's interests before their own, plan for the future—in short, all of the skills that characterize clients suitable for mediation. Such experience highlights the importance of case selection through informed referral and careful screening. Such effort would represent a necessary shift in the public image of family mediation, from a universal alternative to adversarial procedures to one among an array of mechanisms for managing the multiple transitions from marriage to divorce to remarriage.

Client Access. Case selection is complicated by problems associated with service access. In theory, because court-based mediation is offered free of charge, it is universally accessible. In practice, universal accessibility is neither practical nor desirable. Seen as an adjunct to the divorcing process, court-based mediation facilities are typically small and thus limited in the number of clients they can serve. Consequently, an unknown proportion of divorcing spouses who might like to enter mediation is prevented from doing so. As important, court-based mediation is not equally suited to the range of clients seeking service. Such service is usually brief, highly structured, and limited to substantive issues. Complex cases, cases where conflict has become entrenched, and cases where relationship processes block agreement, for example, are unlikely to succeed given the constraints of court-based mediation. Conversely, private mediation may better meet the needs of such clients, but the fact that it is offered on a fee-for-service basis may make it inaccessible to many divorcing couples who would otherwise be interested in and responsive to mediation.

This situation stands in contrast to the logic underpinning legal services. On the assumption that all citizens deserve access to the courts, divorcing couples who cannot afford to hire a lawyer will have one provided to them by the state under various legal aid plans. The state assures universal but not equal access to legal services. Because such plans pay lawyers between one half and one third of their usual fee rate, only some lawyers choose to accept clients under the plan. This may mean that legal aid clients have access to lawyers who are less experienced than their private practice colleagues.

However, at least this approach ensures access. As we argued in chapter 10, divorcing couples deserve similar access to the full range of mediation services. Ensuring such access would require two changes in policy: first, that the state recognize both legal and mediation services for inclusion under legal aid plans; and second, that both legal and mediation practitioners be eligible, on a voluntary basis, to accept legal aid for their respective services.

Special Cases. The professionalization of family mediation implies universal standards of service, but it does *not* require standardized procedures for the delivery of service. On the contrary, in the interests of flexibility, it is critical that mediators recognize that special cases require special mechanisms and procedures. A case in point, to be explored with respect to theme 4, concerns ethnicity. Another, to be briefly examined here, concerns divorcing couples with a history of violence.

As feminist critics correctly stress, families with such a history—whether involving child or spousal abuse—are characterized by massive power imbalances. In consequence, they conclude that in such cases, mediation is automatically contraindicated. As noted in chapter 5, we disagree. In cases where violence is no longer ongoing, specialized training and appropriate safeguards ensure that mediation with such couples *can* be fair, equitable, and safe.

However, much of this debate misses the larger issue, which centers on service flexibility. The dynamic potential of mediation resides in its ability to shape its service to meet the needs of clients, whatever those needs might be. With regard to couples with a history of violence, whether specific couples prove amenable to mediation will depend, as it does with nonviolent couples, on the results of intake assessment, thus their suitability for mediation. However, only momentary consideration suggests a wide range of additional groups that might have specialized needs, including divorcing couples who are poor, handicapped, blended, elderly, and gay or lesbian. As the demand for mediation slowly rises, more and more couples with specialized needs will present for service. It is our job to be ready for them when they do.

Multidoor Centers. Finally, one possibility in keeping with the notion of service flexibility is the multidoor center. Initially suggested by Frank Zandor, it seeks to apply the notion of one-stop shopping to the area of divorce. Thus centers would be created that would house under one roof a range of professionals whose services might be required across the population of divorcing couples. Above, we have listed some of those professionals.

The general point is that the divorcing process is a complex one. It extends through time, involves transitions across a variety of phases, includes multiples actors (both familial and nonfamilial) and is responded to in different ways by different family types. In light of such complexity, it is unreasonable to create a single system to which all families must fit themselves. Indeed, existing critiques of contemporary adversarial systems precisely reflect this lack of fit. Rather, systems must be created whose flexibility is such that they can shape and reshape themselves to fit the diverse and changing requirements of divorcing families. Family mediation provides the model for such a system, but it cannot stand alone. The contribution of legal, financial, medical, psychological, and other professionals is indispensable. Indeed, only the integration of the varied skills represented by these professions would possess the level of flexibility required. The multidoor center is one model of the sort of flexible system that will be required over the next decade.

THEME 3: CHILD CUSTODY

Child custody is by far the most contentious and emotionally charged issue among divorcing spouses with children. It is also the topic most likely to generate heated rhetoric in the literature, with observers from traditionalists to radical feminists ready to trumpet their ideological positions. Such debate makes it difficult to separate facts from opinions; any views we advance are sure to be the target of criticism from one quarter or another. Even so, the issues raised in Part III seem to fall into two categories: demographic trends and shared parenting.

Demographic Trends. In their rush to stake out positions on the proper disposition of the children of divorce, observers seem to have overlooked the fact that the world is changing. We refer in particular to the demographic shape of the North American population. From 1950 to the present, the age distribution has shifted from a pyramid, emphasizing the presence of children, to a diamond, stressing the preponderance of adults. Simply put, the average number of children per family has steadily declined to its current level of 1.7, well below the replacement level of 2.1. The next decade is likely to see this trend continue.

This decline is in response to various interacting trends. Global recession, the rising cost of living, increasing urbanization, the massive movement of women into the labor force, the scarcity of alternative child care options, and the rising cost of child rearing have all placed a premium on small families. Similarly, the globalization of trade coupled with the technological revolution have meant that the minimal educational requirements for employment have steadily risen. In turn, couples have either abandoned plans for children in favor of lifestyle advantages or have significantly delayed having children in the interests of completing educational requirements. However, fertility is inversely related to age. Consequently, an increasing proportion of parents report fertility problems or must settle for only one child when they would have preferred more.

In short, the salience of the custody issue is significantly mitigated by demographic trends that will see fewer children in the population and, as we noted earlier, a gradual decline in the divorce rate. Over the next decade, this trend is likely to mean three things.

First, it suggests increasing family heterogeneity, more adults who choose not to marry, more common-law relationships, more dual-earner and dual-career families, more childless couples, more gay and lesbian couples seeking to have children, more never-married parents, more emphasis on fertility through the laboratory, and so on.

Next, this trend predicts that the proportion of divorcing couples for whom child custody is a problematic issue is likely to decline. Just as the range of family forms has increased, so too has the range of available custody options. Where once maternal sole custody was, for practicable purposes, the only choice, now legal and physical shared parenting have produced a spectrum of choices. Thus, maternal or paternal sole custody may stand alone, be coupled with maternal or paternal legal shared parenting, be replaced by physical shared parenting, or, under special circumstances, be replaced by split custody. Indeed, in the case of blended families, several or all of these options may be exercised simultaneously. The salience of this range of options is that it increases the likelihood of finding a suitable match with the particular needs of any given family.

That said, the proportion of divorcing couples for whom child custody is a serious problem is likely to increase. This notion follows from two arguments. The first argument concerns the composition of couples who decide to divorce. If we are correct in thinking that the divorce rate is likely to decline, that suggests that those who divorce will include a somewhat higher proportion of couples toward the dysfunctional end of the function/dysfunction continuum. The second argument concerns the changing meaning of parenthood. If we are correct in thinking that there are likely to be fewer children born in the near future, that suggests that those that are born are likely to be viewed by their parents as extraordinarily precious, such that child custody is likely to be an even more emotionally charged issue than it is today. The two arguments point to a future in which the divorcing population is likely to involve an increased proportion of dysfunctional couples with spouses each of whom is heavily invested in "winning" the battle for custody of their only child.

Shared Parenting. Our treatment of shared parenting in Part III supports a short series of thematic statements, as follows.

1. *Physical shared parenting is a viable custody option.* Shared parenting has been the focus of a range of ideological arguments and thus has garnered an extraordinary amount of critical attention. The plain fact is that some parents choose it voluntarily and like what it does for them and their children. That said, this option is logistically and emotionally complex and some parents' judgment or judges' decisions regarding what they and the children need will be unrealistic. Consequently, in a minority of cases it may break down. In such cases, there may be harm done in the process, to either the parents or the children. However, in the majority of cases it succeeds, with significant benefits to all concerned. This result likely comes from preselection variables, another way of saying that those who prefer physical shared parenting are probably already located toward the functional end of the function/dysfunction continuum and so are flexible enough and with sufficient resources to discover a way around rough spots and make this option work.

2. *Physical shared parenting is not the option of choice for all divorcing families with children.* Although many parents who chose physical shared parenting eventually make it work for them, not all divorcing parents with children should be forced to try it, on two grounds. First, the demands it makes on families are such that those with neither flexibility nor resources required will be at high risk of failing, which explains why studies using clinical samples reported such negative results. Even so, it is still not entirely clear what the critical variables are—personal, interpersonal, or circumstantial—that predict who is and who is not going to succeed. A great deal more research is required here. Second, throughout the literature, alternate custody options, including sole custody, work fine for some parents, although again the variables that discriminate consistently between and among each group are not well understood. In short, on the evidence, physical shared parenting is not and never was a panacea for all the custody problems that can arise.

3. *Success should be defined in terms of patterns of parenting, not configurations of ownership.* The usual conventions of psychological and socio-

logical research focus attention on sharp differences between groups. In the shared parenting literature, we think it equally, if not more, important to attend to instances where there are not differences between groups. A case in point concerns the "value added" assumptions underpinning much of this research. That is, various researchers have explored the view that if shared parenting is as good as its proponents say it is, then children living in that option should show significant developmental gains compared to those in a sole custody arrangement. That no such differences have been found has been interpreted to mean that shared parenting is no better than sole custody and thus the latter should be preferred.

What seems to have been forgotten is that "shared parenting" and "sole custody" are simply legal labels helpful only in apportioning parenting responsibilities. They say literally nothing about the character of the relations between and among the key actors: mothers, fathers, and children, but also extended family members, friends, and neighbors. In other words, developmental effects attach to relationships and not to labels. More specifically, when children are in particular sorts of relationships with the significant people in their lives, they develop well. As to the particular relations in question, that remains controversial. Typically, the research highlights parental relationships characterized by consistency, involvement, and support, and marital relationships featuring low to moderate conflict, good cooperation, and clear communication. The question is an important one and deserves continued attention. We suspect the findings will eventually show that a wide range of parenting arrangements will work, a tribute to the flexibility and resilience of children. In turn, what seems to be important is the relationship and not the label, so that the lack of difference is from this perspective both predictable and positive and thus underscores the salience of divorcing parents' voluntary and informed choices.

4. *Legal shared parenting is an important addition to the spectrum of custody options.* That said, some have cast doubt on the degree to which legal shared parenting is truly voluntary and informed. They have made much, for example, of findings showing that when legal shared parenting and maternal sole custody are compared, women in both options still end up with the bulk of the child care burden. Arguing

moreover that rights and responsibilities should be tied together, they conclude that fathers that do not share the latter should lose the former, with maternal sole custody the fairer option. Others counter by pointing to the maternal biases built in to current legal procedures, which push men into accepting maternal sole custody and thus a necessarily secondary role in their children's lives.

The legalistic way in which we have framed these arguments is entirely intentional and speaks to our earlier comment about relationships. Although both positions have some merit, they miss the larger issue, namely, how to encourage parents, both men and women, to do their very best by their children at a time when either or both may be in real distress. The evidence suggests that in the majority of cases, both parents are deeply committed to what they see as their children's best interests. It shows too that fathers who are regularly involved in their children's upbringing play an enormously important role in their children's long-term development. Unfortunately, the way in which society is currently organized makes it harder for fathers to remain involved and easier for them to discover other options. For the minority of fathers who do not care about their children, the state is helpless to intervene. For the remaining majority, we see as positive anything that is likely to encourage fathers to continue to be actively involved with and committed to their children. There is evidence that legal shared parenting appears to help in this respect—although, paradoxically, it is physical shared parenting that has gotten the bulk of the research attention—and thus it remains an important custody option. In turn, future research into this option needs to pay more attention to the quality of parent-child relations and the meaning of parenting and less on the number of hours expended.

5. *Decisions about child custody should involve a standardized process rather than a standard principle.* When arrangements about the custody of children reflect agreement between divorcing parents, the courts have been inclined to let them stand. When such parents do not agree or when their agreements pertain to arrangements that appear wildly inappropriate, judicial decision makers have two problems: What is the right arrangement for the children in question and on what basis should such a decision be made? Traditionally, these decision makers have favored maternal sole custody, especially when younger children

are involved. In the same vein, the decision-making principle in common use has been that of "child best interest."

In recent years, some have called this principle in question. In essence, this view holds that in bending over backward to be fair, decision makers have, in practice, been unfair insofar as in many cases both parents do not contribute equally to the care and control of the children. Rather, women are much more likely than men to provide the bulk of child care. In recognition of this fact, the "primary parent" principle, they argue, makes more sense. Accordingly, where this unequal contribution applies, the parent who contributes the most (typically women) should be awarded sole custody.

In light of our previous comments about parenting, we take a rather different position, for we believe that no standard principle, however broad or generic, is sufficiently flexible to accommodate the incredible diversity of divorcing families. Indeed, the sociodemographic trends discussed above suggest that this point is likely to be increasingly so, as the range and variety of family forms continue to proliferate over the next decade. Such diversity argues that "custody orders" be replaced by "parenting plans" tailor-made to the unique configuration and circumstances of the divorcing families in question.

In turn, to ensure that derivation of such plans would be fair and reasonable, what is required is a standardized evaluation process that would involve several components. The first would concern evidence that the parents really cannot agree. Indeed, one of the premises on which family mediation was founded was the notion that what starts out as a firm "no" in the hands of lawyers intent on conflict can often turn first into a tentative "maybe" and then a relieved "yes" in the hands of a skilled mediator. Assuming even after mediation that the answer remains "no," the wishes of family members, both parents and children (providing they are old enough to express their wishes), must be consulted. Additional inquiry would explore such matters as the degree of parental involvement in child care and control, parental emotional commitment, degree of personal and interpersonal resources, and family position on the functional continuum. In short, assessment would seek to identify the family's positive and negative features, including those contraindicative of shared parenting (see chapters 6 and 7). Then, and only then, after considering this range of factors, would an interim parenting plan be evolved and applied for a trial period of about 12 months. The plan's success would be evaluated and finalized or modified.

Furthermore, here is where mediation can be relevant, as an ideal context in which to help parents think through clearly and in detail what sort of arrangement is likely to best suit their circumstances and the individual needs of their children in the present and the future. In dealing with custody and access cases, many mediators already do something like this. We are merely suggesting that in future it be seen as integral to their mandate.

THEME 4: NEW DEVELOPMENTS

Finally, we have explored three new developments in family mediation: ethnicity, child welfare mediation, and research. We consider each in turn.

1. *Ethnocultural sensitivity is likely to become a standard feature of mediation training and practice.* In a broad sense, everyone reading these words is a member of an ethnic group. Of course, this identification varies; some identify much more strongly than others with an ethnic group. But all ultimately derive from one group or another and even in vestigial form retain traces of that background in their attitudes, food preferences, assumptions about work, and so on. Moreover, it is increasingly impossible to escape identifying with a group. In the United States by the turn of the century in some states visible minority groups will represent a majority of the population and in turn the majority of the divorcing subpopulation. In Canada, these demographics will not be the case for the foreseeable future. Nevertheless, Canada has traditionally pursued a policy of multiculturalism whose purpose is to support and celebrate the cultural distinctiveness of the variety of groups that collectively constitute its society. Accordingly, members of such groups can reasonably expect that their group-specific views will be respected, whether or not they are consistent with the dominant culture.

The relevance of this issue will vary depending on whether it is seen from the perspective of mediators or clients. For mediators, the relevance of ethnicity is often immediate and dramatic: It affects practice delivery. In our experience, a class of interventions that works well with clients from one group may consistently fail with those from another group; worse, used unwittingly, they may do harm or promote the premature termination of service. For example, as a group, Asians are likely to respond poorly to confrontational tactics, preferring indirect approaches to conflict resolution. Hispanics and orthodox Jews, given their religiosity and assumptions about female modesty, will find discussions of sexuality and violence highly problematic. Caribbean blacks, given highly developed norms of privacy, need some time to get to know the mediator before sensitive topics can be broached; they are likely to respond poorly when service is time limited. African Americans are typically forthright about sex and violence, but tend to respond better to behavioral as opposed to insight-oriented interventions.

For clients, the relevance of ethnicity relates to the justifiable expectation that professional service will meet certain standards of quality and expertise and thus be free, for example, of racial discrimination or ethnic bias. In this context, mediators who treat all couples, regardless of their ethnic membership, *as if* they were white and Christian are likely to be seen as biased, insensitive, and possibly hurtful, whether or not this was actually intended.

On the face of it, this suggests that cultural sensitivity should become a standard part of the training of all mediators. However, although we agree, it is important to note that this goal represents a significant challenge for mediation, in at least two respects. First, the extent to which this view is widely shared is unclear. Mediators schooled in North American approaches that emphasize clarity, specificity, and order are likely to see as "wrong" the conduct of mediators schooled in Asian approaches that emphasize indirectness, nonspecificity, and loose structures (Duryea, personal communication, 1994). Further, instruction in ethnocultural sensitivity is not widely available. The need for such instruction, then, will require considerable education among mediators. Moreover, were every training program in North America to begin such instruction tomorrow, there is no widely accepted curriculum for use in that effort. The considerable effort required to assemble the material used in our review suggests that creating such a curriculum would be a major effort in its own right. The second challenge concerns the application of such a curriculum to mediation. Although our review notes a few articles in the mediation literature that address the question of ethnicity, we know of no empirical research that has examined the impact of standardized interventions across groups or the way in which interventions might be customized to fit the needs of specific groups. In short, it remains unclear how ethnoculturally sensitive mediators should use their knowledge in their efforts to provide helpful service to ethnically diverse clients. A step in the right direction would be to encourage practitioners to share their experience in this area, in journals, conferences, colloquia, and the like. Similarly, empirical research is badly needed, likely adapted from the existing literature on family therapy and psychiatry.

2. *Variations on the use of family mediation are likely to become increasingly popular.* In North America mediation was initially limited to labor-management relations. In Canada, for example, both federal and provincial ministries of labor have long maintained a roster of labor mediators. In the late 1970s, family mediation sprang up. Since then, variations on mediation have proliferated widely. Thus mediation has been and continues to be used in resolving disputes between neighbors, landlords and tenants, schoolchildren, business associates, marital partners (not interested in divorce), prisoners and prison staff, victims and offenders, abusive parents and protective agency staff, and, most recently, multiple stakeholders in public policy disputes.

This development is truly exciting, for a least four reasons. First, it implies a continuously expanding knowledge base. Thus each of the variations noted above involves its own compendium of facts, procedures, statutes, and the like. Furthermore, because these variations have all been developed recently, that compendium is likely accumulating rapidly. Second, there is no reason to believe that these various compendia will be wildly different. Rather, it is more reasonable to assume, given that human interactions are at the core of mediation, that they will all have generic elements in common as well as specific ways in which they are unique. This development implies a profession that has not existed previously: the general mediator. Akin to a general practitioner in medicine, this practitioner would have training across a range of variations, including family mediation. Thus in the future, mediation may not only be a profession at which one can earn a living on a full-time basis, but also one in which entry-level students would confront a choice: become a general mediator or specialize in one of the expanding number of variations.

Third, this speaks again but with greater urgency to the need for standardization, for example, of curricula, training, practice, ethics, accountability, certification, and the like. As it stands, mediation expertise is likely to vary widely across the variations noted above. This variation is unacceptable. It not only implies the possibility of client harm, but it undermines the credibility of mediation as a profession.

Finally, the development of the field predicts rising demand for mediation services, in terms of both the number and proportion of cases across the full range of mediation forms. On the one hand, this effect is likely to arise as a feedback variation, with client satisfaction with one form of mediation likely to incline them positively to related forms of mediation. On the other hand, such processes are likely to involve and profit from continued partnership with legal actors, especially lawyers. As the latter accept mediation as one among a family of techniques useful in conflict resolution, mutual referrals are likely to become the order of the day, all part of a promising future for family and other forms of mediation.

3. *Future research efforts will increasingly distinguish between pragmatic and basic research, and increasingly stress the importance of integration.* Research in family mediation can be conceived from two different perspectives. One perspective sees such research as essentially pragmatic in nature. It attempts to address research questions such as: Are we doing things right? What do we need to do to produce better outcomes? The alternate perspective sees such research as fundamental in nature. It attends to such research questions as: What is mediation? What do mediators do with clients? What sorts of actions on the part of the mediator have what sorts of effects with what sorts of client couples?

To date, these two perspectives have yielded two different and separate bodies of work, to the point of relying on different journals for their expression. In our view, such separateness is self-defeating. Both have something important to contribute to family mediation practice, but can only do so once the bases of mutual dialogue have been established. Previously, this establishment was unlikely, because researchers did not practice and practitioners were seldom involved in research. However, just as interdisciplinary training is likely to yield a new breed of practitioner, the same is true of second and later generations of practitioner, with training in both practice and research. Indeed, as applied to the previous distinction between general and specialized subgroups of mediators, one group, as part of its training, may be oriented toward basic research and the other group may similarly be oriented toward pragmatic research. Such evolutionary developments over the next decade speak not only to the professionalization of mediation, but also to the dynamic character of the field, dynamism that can only benefit all involved, practitioners and clients alike.

Index

Accreditation, family mediation, 443
Adults, divorce and, 50-58, 74-79
Age:
    at marriage, divorce and, 21-22
    of child, divorce and, 62-63
Agreement rate, research in family
        mediation, 312-413
Asians, family therapy and, 334-344
Assessment:
    case example 1, therapeutic family
        mediation, 174-178
    case example 2, therapeutic family
        mediation, 181-183
    process of, therapeutic family
        mediation, 153-157
Authority, child protection mediation,
        387-389
Autonomy, child protection mediation,
        398-400

Blacks, family therapy and, 314-315,
        316-318, 319-320, 320-322, 323,
        324-325

Caribbean blacks, family therapy and,
        316, 318-319, 320, 322-323,
        323-324, 325
Case selection, family mediation, 447
Characteristics, of couple, divorce and,
        21-23, 31-32
Child, divorce and, 22, 58-73, 79-89, 92-93
Child abuse, and child protection
        mediation, 399
Child custody, 227-301
    agreement, shared parenting, 286-288
    analysis, shared parenting, 241-243
    bias favoring, shared parenting, 265
    clinical practice, *vs.* sole custody
        parenting, shared parenting,
        296-298
    comparative analysis, shared
        parenting, satisfied *vs.*
        dissatisfied, 284-291
    coparental relationship, shared
        parenting, 249-250, 288-290
    divorce and, 34-37
    durability, shared parenting, 255-256
    family mediation, 227-301, 450-456

global evaluation, shared parenting,
    259-261
initiation of, shared parenting,
    285-286
legal custody, shared, with maternal
    physical custody, 231-233
legal policy, *vs.* sole custody
    parenting, shared parenting,
    292-296
logistics, shared parenting, 251-253
marital separation, shared parenting,
    285
maternal physical custody, with
    shared legal custody, 231-233
methodology, shared parenting,
    237-240
overview, 229-231
parental adjustment, shared
    parenting, 245-247
parent-child relations and, shared
    parenting, 250-251
parenting plan, shared parenting,
    266-267
policy/practice, *vs.* sole custody
    parenting, shared parenting,
    292-298
presumption, absence of, shared
    parenting, 265-266
research, shared parenting, 262-264
residence, primary, shared parenting,
    258-259
results, shared parenting, 243-259
satisfaction of shared parenting,
    253-254
satisfaction of shared parenting *vs.*
    sole custody parenting, 291
sex, *vs.* sole custody parenting,
    shared parenting, 290-291
shared parenting, 229-276, 277-279,
    279-281, 281-291
shared parenting *vs.* sole custody
    parenting, 292
sociodemographics, shared
    parenting, 284-285
socioeconomic status, shared
    parenting, 258
sociolegal policy, shared parenting,
    264-269
sole custody parenting, 283-284

support, shared parenting, 254-255,
    269
theory, shared parenting, 233-236, 261
trial period, shared parenting, 267-269
typological variation, shared
    parenting, 256-258
with maternal physical custody,
    shared parenting, 231-233
Child protection, 378-380, 400-401
    authority in mediation, 387-389
    autonomy, 398-400
    child abuse negotiable, 399
    choice, and autonomy, 398-400
    conflict management strategies,
        391-394
    fairness, and safety, 395-398
    information, providing, 390-391
    mandate, 387-389
    mediation, 377-404
    mediation defined, 382-384
    mediator, role of, 387-394
    neutrality, 395-398
    parents, helping make reasonable
        requests, 391
    parties in, 381-382
    safety, 395-398
    self-determination, 398-400
    social control, 398
    value dilemmas in practice, 394-400
    voluntary choice, 399-400
Child support, divorce and, 33-34
Choice:
    child protection mediation, 398-400
    voluntary, 399-400
Client:
    access, family mediation, 447-448
    identity, ethnicity, family therapy
        and, 364
    satisfaction, research in family
        mediation, 413-414
    therapeutic family mediation, 149
Clinical practice, 145-226
Clinical style, ethnicity and, 361-362
Cohesion, marital, divorce and, 18-19
Comediation, family mediation, 446
Concepts, therapeutic family mediation,
    149-153
Conflict management strategies, child
    protection mediation, 391-394

Consequences, of divorce, 15-16, 20,
    58-61, 80-83
Contested proceedings, divorce and, 31
Contraindications, therapeutic family
    mediation, 172-173
Coparental relations, research in family
    mediation, 415-416
Cost, research in family mediation,
    416-417
Couple characteristics, divorce and,
    21-23, 31-32
Crossgenerational conflict, ethnicity
    and, 359
Crosstraining, family mediation, 445
Culture-specific issues, ethnicity and,
    362-363
Curricula, family mediation, 445
Custody, child, 227-301
    divorce and, 34-37

Demographic trends, family mediation,
    450-451
Dimensions of divorce, 90-98
Direct effects, divorce and, 63-67
Divorce, 41-48, 84-85, 85-87, 89-103,
    103-109
    adult partners, 50-58, 74-79
    age at marriage, 21-22
    age of child, 62-63
    child and, 22, 58-73, 79-89, 92-93
    child custody, 34-37
    child development and, 438-440
    child support, 33-34
    cohesion, marital, 18-19
    consequences, 15-16, 20, 58-61, 80-83
    contested proceedings, 31
    couple characteristics, 21-23, 31-32
    decision to divorce, 18-20
    dimensions of, 90-98
    direct effects, 63-67
    duration, 32
    ecological context, 15
    ethnicity, 23, 92
    external problems, 59, 80
    fairness, 100-101
    family court, 29-41
    family development, 14-15
    family mediation, 41-48, 435-442

family process mechanisms, 61, 83-
    89
financial consequences, 54-58
frequency of, 16-17
gender of child, 61-62
gender role, 60, 81-82
grounds for, 31
indirect effects, 67-69
institutional context, 95-97
intellectual functioning, 59, 81
interactional consequences, 52-53
internal problems, 59, 80-81
interpersonal context, 94-95
litigation, 29-41
marital interaction pattern, 90-91
marital problems, 18
marital relations, 23-29, 37-41
marital separation, 20-29
marital status, 22, 97-98
matrimonial property, 32-33
mental health services, use of, 60-61,
    82-83
neutrality, 101-103
outcome, 32
parent-child relationships, 63-70
parenting, 93-94
patterns of relating, 15
personal feelings, 19
phases of, 17-41
practitioner misconduct, 99
prosocial skills, 60, 82
psychoeducational role, 98-99
psychological consequences, 51-52
remarriage, 74-77, 87-89
residential mobility, 22
safety, 99-100
severity of divorce, 83-84
short-term consequences, 49-73
social class, 21, 70-73, 91-92
social consequences, 53-54
sociocultural variation, 15
spousal support, 33
theoretical conceptualization, 14-16
timing effects, 69-70
violence, 91

Ecological context, of divorce, 15
Empowerment:

need for, therapeutic family
   mediation, feminist-informed
   model, 213-214
techniques, therapeutic family
   mediation, feminist-informed
   model, 214-216
therapeutic family mediation,
   feminist-informed model, 210-216
Ethical standards, family mediation, 443
Ethnic groups, four, profiles of, 313-352
Ethnicity, 306-376
   Asians, 334-344
   assessment, 353, 355-357
   blacks, 314-322, 323, 324-325
   Caribbean blacks, 316, 318-319, 320,
     322-324, 325
   client identity, 364
   clinical issues, 357-364
   clinical style, 361-362
   core dimensions, 309-313
   crossgenerational conflict, 359
   culture-specific issues, 362-363
   divorce and, 23, 92
   family, definition of, 310-311, 316-319,
     327-329, 337-339, 347
   Hispanics, 325-334
   husband-wife relations, 320-323,
     331-332, 340-341, 348-350
   intergenerational conflict, 358-359
   intermarriage, 353t, 357-358
   Jewish individuals, 344-352
   life cycle, 311-312, 319-320, 329-330,
     339-340, 347-348
   marital relations, 312
   modal social class, 310, 314-316,
     326-327, 335-337, 345-347
   overview, 306-309, 352-364
   parent-child relations, 312-313,
     323-324, 332, 341-342, 350-351
   relevance to practice, 352-355
   religious observance, 359-360
   social class, 361
   spousal relations, 360
   treatment, perspectives on, 313,
     324-325, 333-334, 343-344, 351-
     352
Extended family, therapeutic family
   mediation, 161-163
External problems, divorce and, 59, 80

Extrasystemic processes, therapeutic
   family mediation, 157-164

Fairness:
   child protection mediation, 395-398
   divorce, 100-101
Family, definition of, ethnicity and,
     310-311, 316-319, 327-329, 337-339,
     347
Family development, divorce and, 14-15
Family mediation, 11-48, 41-48, 84-87,
     89-103, 98-103, 103-109, 435-442,
     448-449
   accreditation, 443
   adult partners in divorce, 50-58
   age at marriage, 21-22
   age of child at divorce, 62-63
   case selection, 447
   child and, 22, 58-73, 79-89, 92-93
   child custody, 34-37, 227-301, 450-456
   child development, 438-440
   child support, 33-34
   client access, 447-448
   cohesion, marital, 18-19
   comediation, 446
   consequences of, 15-16, 20, 58-61,
     80-83
   contested proceedings, 31
   couple characteristics, 21-23, 31-32
   cross-training, 445
   curricula, 445
   decision to divorce, 18-20
   demographic trends, 450-451
   dimensions of, 90-98
   direct effects, 63-67
   divorce, 440-442
   duration, 32
   ecological context, 15
   ethical standards, 443
   ethnicity and, 23, 92, 306-376
   ethnocultural sensitivity, 456-458
   external problems, 59, 80
   fairness, 100-101
   family court, 29-41
   family development, 14-15
   family process mechanisms, 61, 83-89
   feminist-informed model, 202-206
   financial consequences, 54-58

frequency of, 16-17
gender of child, 61-62
gender roles, 60, 81-82
grounds for, 31
indirect effects, 67-69
institutional context, 95-97
intellectual functioning, 59, 81
interactional consequences, 52-53
internal problems, 59, 80-81
interpersonal context, 94-95
knowledge base, 11-48, 49-109
liability, professional, 444
litigation, 29-41
long-term consequences, 73-89
marital interaction pattern, 90-91
marital problems, 18
marital relations, 23-29, 37-41
marital separation, 20-29
marital status, 22, 97-98
matrimonial property, 32-33
mediation practice, 442-449
mental health services, use of, 60-61,
    82-83
multidisciplinary approach, 444-445
multidoor centers, 449
neutrality, 101-103
new developments, 456-460
outcome of, 32
overview, 11-14
parent-child relationships, 63-70
parenting and, 93-94
patterns of relating, 15
personal feelings, 19
phases of, 17-41
practice, 11-48, 49-109
practitioner misconduct, 99
professional status, 442-443
prosocial skills, 60, 82
psychoeducational role, 98-99
psychological consequences, 51-52
rate of, 435-437
remarriage, 74-77, 87-89
research in, 405-432
residential mobility, 22
safety, 99-100
service flexibility, 447
severity of divorce, 83-84
shared parenting, 452-456
short-term consequences, 49-73

social class, 21, 70-73, 91-92
social consequences, 53-54
sociocultural variation, 15
special cases, 448-449
spousal support, 33
stability of remarriage, 77-79
statutory reform, 437-438
team approach, 445-446
theoretical conceptualization, 14-16
therapeutic, 147-201
timing effects, 69-70
training programs, 443-444
violence, 91
Family process mechanisms, divorce
    and, 61, 83-89
Feminist critique, therapeutic family
    mediation, 204-206
Feminist-informed family mediation,
    202-206, 206-221
    empowerment, 210-216
    neutrality, 208-210
    overview, 202-204, 221-222
    violence, 217-221
Financial consequences, divorce, 54-58
Follow-up:
    case example 1, therapeutic family
        mediation, 180
    case example 2, therapeutic family
        mediation, 186
    research in family mediation, 417-
        418
    therapeutic family mediation, 168-
        169
Frequency of divorce, 16-17

Gender:
    child, divorce and, 61-62
    differences, research in family
        mediation, 414-415
    role, divorce and, 60, 81-82
Goals, therapeutic family mediation,
    169-171
Grounds, for divorce, 31

Hispanics, 325-334
Husband-wife relations, ethnicity and,
    320-323, 331-332, 340-341, 348-350

Indications for therapeutic family mediation, 172-173
Indirect effects, divorce and, 67-69
Individual session, case example 3, therapeutic family mediation, 192-195
Information, providing, child protection mediation, 390-391
Institutional context, divorce, 95-97
Intellectual functioning, divorce and, 59, 81
Interactional consequences, divorce, 52-53
Intergenerational conflict, ethnicity and, 358-359
Intermarriage, ethnicity and, 353, 357-358
Internal problems, divorce and, 59, 80-81
Interpersonal context, divorce, 94-95
Intervention, process of, therapeutic family mediation, 153-164
Interviews:
    individual, case example 1, therapeutic family mediation, 174-176
    joint, case example 1, therapeutic family mediation, 176-178

Jewish population, 344-352
Joint session, case example 3, therapeutic family mediation, 188-191

Knowledge base, family mediation, divorce, 11-48, 84-85, 85-87, 89-103, 98-103, 103-109
    academic functioning, 59, 81
    adults, 50-58, 74-79
    age at marriage, 21-22
    age of child, 62-63
    child and, 22, 58-73, 79-89, 92-93
    child custody, 34-37
    child support, 33-34
    cohesion, marital, 18-19
    consequences, 20, 58-61, 80-83
    consequences over time, 15-16
    contested proceedings, 31

coparental relationship, 52-53
couple characteristics, 21-23, 31-32
decision to divorce, 18-20
dimensions of, 90-98
direct effects, 63-67
duration, 32
ecological context, 15
equity, 100-101
ethnicity, 23, 92
external problems, 59, 80
fairness, 100-101
family development, 14-15
family process mechanisms, 61, 83-89
financial consequences, 54-58
frequency of, 16-17
gender of child, 61-62
gender role, 60, 81-82
grounds for, 31
heterosexual behavior, 60, 81-82
indirect effects, 67-69
institutional context, 95-97
intellectual functioning, 59, 81
interactional consequences, (coparental relationship), 52-53
internal problems, 59, 80-81
interpersonal context, 94-95
litigation, 29-41
marital interaction pattern, 90-91
marital problems, 18
marital relations, 23-29, 37-41
marital separation, 20-29
marital status, 22, 97-98
matrimonial property, 32-33
mental health services, use of, 60-61, 82-83
neutrality, 101-103
outcome, 32
parent-child relationships, 63-70
parenting, 93-94
patterns of relating, 15
personal feelings, 19
phases of, 17-41, 49-73, 73-89
practitioner misconduct, 99
prosocial skills, 60, 82
psychoeducational role, 98-99
psychological consequences, 51-52
remarriage, 74-77, 87-89
residential mobility, 22
safety, 99-100

security, 99-100
severity of divorce, 83-84
social class, 21, 70-73, 91-92
social consequences, 53-54
sociocultural variation, 15
spousal support, 33
stability of remarriage, 77-79
theoretical conceptualization, 14-16
timing effects, 69-70
violence, 91

Lawyers, therapeutic family mediation,
    160
Legal custody, shared, with maternal
    physical custody, 231-233
Liability, professional, family mediation,
    444
Life cycle, ethnicity and, 311-312,
    319-320, 329-330, 339-340, 347-
    348
Long-term consequences, phases of
    divorce, 73-89

Mandate, for child protection mediation,
    387-389
Marital cohesion, divorce and, 18-19
Marital interaction pattern, divorce,
    90-91
Marital problems, divorce and, 18
Marital relations:
    divorce and, 23-29, 37-41
    ethnicity and, 312
Marital status, divorce and, 22, 97-98
Maternal physical custody, with shared
    legal custody, 231-233
Matrimonial property, divorce and, 32-33
Mediation:
    child protection, 377-404
    child protection defined, 382-384
    practice overview, 442-449
    therapeutic family mediation, 166-
    168
Mental health services, use of, divorce,
    60-61, 82-83
Multidisciplinary approach, family
    mediation, 444-445
Multidoor centers, family mediation, 449

Negotiation:
    case example 1, therapeutic family
        mediation, 179-180
    case example 2, therapeutic family
        mediation, 185-186
    principles, therapeutic family
        mediation, 165-166
    process, therapeutic family
        mediation, 164-168
Neutrality:
    child protection mediation, 395-398
    divorce, 101-103
    therapeutic family mediation,
        feminist-informed model, 208-
        210

Outcome:
    of divorce, 32
    studies, research in family
        mediation, 412-418
Overview, family mediation, 11-14

Parent-child relations:
    divorce and, 63-70
    ethnicity and, 312-313, 323-324, 332,
        341-342, 350-351
Parenting, divorce and, 93-94
Parents, helping make reasonable
    requests, child protection
    mediation, 391
Partner, new, therapeutic family
    mediation, 160-161
Patterns of relating, divorce and, 15
Personal feelings, divorce and, 19
Phases of divorce, 17-41
    decision to divorce, 18-20
    family court, 29-41
    litigation, 29-41
    long-term consequences and, 73-89
    marital separation, 20-29
    short-term consequences, 49-73
Policymakers, research in family
    mediation, 423-425
Practitioner misconduct, divorce, 99
Predictors, of mediated agreement,
    research in family mediation,
    418-419

Premediation:
    case example 1, therapeutic family
        mediation, 178
    case example 2, therapeutic family
        mediation, 183-184
    process of, therapeutic family
        mediation, 157
Proceedings, contested, divorce and, 31
Process studies, research in family
    mediation, 406-412
Professional status, family mediation,
    442-443
Prosocial skills, divorce and, 60, 82
Psychoeducational role, divorce, 98-99
Psychological consequences, divorce,
    51-52

Relevance to practice, ethnicity and,
    352-355
Religious observance, ethnicity and,
    359-360
Remarriage:
    divorce, 87-89
    divorce and, 74-77
    stability, 77-79
Researchers, in family mediation,
    422-423
Research in family mediation, 405-432,
    406-419
    agreement rate, 312-413
    client satisfaction, 413-414
    coparental relations, 415-416
    cost, 416-417
    follow-up studies, 417-418
    gender differences, 414-415
    outcome studies, 412-418
    policymakers, 423-425
    practice, 425-426
    predictors, of mediated agreement,
        418-419
    process studies, 406-412
    researchers, 422-423
Residential mobility, divorce and, 22
Resources, of family, therapeutic family
    mediation, 163-164
Responsibilities, in therapeutic family
    mediation, 169-171
Role, child protection mediator, 387-394

Safety:
    child protection mediation, 395-398
    divorce, 99-100
Self-determination, child protection
    mediation, 398-400
Service flexibility, family mediation, 447
Sessions overview, case example 2,
    therapeutic family mediation,
    181-186
Severity of divorce, 83-84
Shared legal custody, with maternal
    physical custody, 231-233
Shared parenting, 229-276, 279-281,
    281-291
    agreement, 286-288
    analysis, 241-243
    and sole custody, 277-301
    bias favoring, 265
    child and, 247-249
    clinical practice, *vs.* sole custody
        parenting, 296-298
    coparental relationship, 288-290
    coparental relationships, 249-250
    durability, 255-256
    family mediation, 452-456
    global evaluation, 259-261
    initiation of, 285-286
    legal policy, *vs.* sole custody
        parenting, 292-296
    logistics, 251-253
    marital separation, 285
    methodology, 237-240
    overview, 261-269, 277-279
    parental adjustment, 245-247
    parent-child relations, 250-251
    parenting plan, 266-267
    policy/practice, *vs.* sole custody
        parenting, 292-298
    presumption, absence of, 265-266
    research, 262-264
    residence, primary, 258-259
    results of, 243-259
    satisfaction, 253-254
    sex, *vs.* sole custody parenting,
        290-291
    sociodemographics, 284-285
    socioeconomic status, 258
    sociolegal policy, 264-269
    support, 254-255, 269

theory, 233-236, 261
trial period, 267-269
typological variation, 256-258
Social class:
    divorce and, 21, 70-73, 91-92
    ethnicity and, 310, 314-316, 326-327,
        335-337, 345-347, 361
Social consequences, divorce, 53-54
Social control, child protection
    mediation, 398
Sociocultural variation, divorce and, 15
Sole custody parenting, 283-284
Sole custody parenting vs. shared
    parenting, 290, 291, 298
    clinical practice, 296-298
    discussion, 292
    legal policy, 292-296
    policy/practice, 292-298
    satisfaction, 291
    sex, 290-291
Spousal relations, ethnicity and, 360
Spousal support, divorce and, 33
Stability:
    divorce, remarriage, 77-79
    remarriage, 77-79
Statutory reform, family mediation,
    437-438
Support, child, divorce and, 33-34
Systemic processes, in therapeutic
    family mediation, 157-164

Team approach, family mediation,
    445-446
Theoretical conceptualization, divorce
    and, 14-16
Therapeutic family mediation, 172, 173,
    174-175, 186-195
    assessment, 153-157, 174-178, 181-183
    clients, 149
    contraindications, 172-173
    empowerment, 210-216, 213-214,
        214-216

extended family, 161-163
extrasystemic processes, 157-164
feminist model, 202-206
follow-up, 168-169, 180, 186
general concepts, 149-153
goals, 169-171
indications, 172-173
individual interviews, 174-176
individual session, 192-195
intervention, process of, 153-164
joint interviews, 176-178
joint session, 188-191
lawyers, 160
mediation practices, 166-168
negotiation, 164-168, 179-180, 185-
    186
neutrality, 208-210
overview, 180-181, 186, 202-204,
    221-222
partner, new, 160-161
premediation, 178, 183-184
premediation process, 157
resources, of family, 163-164
responsibilities, 169-171
sessions overview, 174-181, 181-
    186
systemic processes, 157-164
therapist, 161
violence, 217-221
Therapist, in therapeutic family
    mediation, 161
Timing effects, divorce and, 69-70
Training programs, family mediation,
    443-444

Value dilemmas, child protection
    mediation, 394-400
Violence:
    divorce, 91
    therapeutic family mediation,
        feminist-informed model, 217-
        221

About the Authors

Howard H. Irving, PhD, is a Professor in the Faculty of Social Work and is cross-appointed to the Faculty of Law, University of Toronto. He is Codirector of the Combined Law and Social Work Degree Program. Dr. Irving is a past president of Family Mediation Canada and was a board member of the American Association of Family and Conciliation Courts. He is the author of several articles and books on family mediation and has taught mediation courses in Canada, the United States, Israel, and Hong Kong. He is in active mediation practice in Toronto and has been the principal investigator in several research projects.

Michael Benjamin, PhD, is a family and educational sociologist and is currently Research Coordinator of the Student-Environment Study Group at the University of Guelph, Guelph, Ontario. His areas of interest include family mediation and higher education, about which he has published widely, including (with Howard Irving) *Family Mediation: Theory and Practice of Dispute Resolution* (Carswell, 1987). Other areas in which he has published include family therapy, family violence, and prostitution.